Move Over Darling

Christine Stovell

W F HOWES LTD

This large print edition published in 2012 by
W F Howes Ltd
Unit 4, Rearsby Business Park, Gaddesby Lane,
Rearsby, Leicester LE7 4YH

1 3 5 7 9 10 8 6 4 2

First published in the United Kingdom in 2012
by Choc Lit Limited

A CIP catalogue record for this book is available
from the British Library

ISBN 978 1 47121 652 7

Typeset by Palimpsest Book Production Limited,
Falkirk, Stirlingshire
Printed and bound in Great Britain
by MPG Books Ltd, Bodmin, Cornwall

For my indomitable mum, Doris, with love.

CHAPTER 1

Doris Day was singing in the background, telling Coralie Casey that whatever would be would be. Coralie disagreed. Doris was a goddess – but she was wrong about fate. The future *was* yours to see. Furthermore, you could look at it, decide you didn't like it very much and do something about it.

She dragged her thoughts back to the present before they had a chance to head off like a wayward dog and poke around for something nasty festering in the corners of her mind. Instead of waiting to be dealt another bad hand she'd reshuffled the cards and laid out her own destiny. She'd swapped suburban streets for country lanes and the nine-to-five for the steady rise of Sweet Cleans, her range of natural cleaning products for body and home. It wasn't completely true to say she'd moved on, but she had, at least, moved over.

Beyond the window of her workshop the late January snow spiralled in the air like down, cushioning the gentle green slopes in soft white. In seven swiftly passing months Coralie had seen the west Wales landscape in many moods and was learning to love them all. Even the rain, which seemed to fall in epic quantities in Penmorfa, was eventually followed by pale candyfloss clouds and bright blue skies.

She stopped for a moment to gaze at the delicate beauty of her garden under its white veil. A winter wonderland. Doris Day started telling her it was magic, but Coralie knew it was all down to hard work. By taking a huge gamble and some tough decisions she'd made her own dream come true. Or was making progress towards it. Who needed a crystal ball to see that things were looking good?

And her former colleagues thought *she* was the crazy one when *they* were still holed up in their offices! As for job satisfaction? She gave a small smile of contentment. Naturally, in the early days at the management consultancy, she had really believed in what she was doing. Every night, she would turn out the light feeling good because she'd nursed another dying business back to health. Rooting out clogged-up departments, weak processes and bloated boards saved an awful lot of money. But, that was before . . . Rock! Oh poor Rock! He must be desperate for food!

When she'd woken up early, unable to wait any longer to try out the idea for a new soap recipe which had popped into her head just as she was drifting off to sleep, she'd only intended to allow herself an hour before seeing to him. How could it be almost nine o'clock already? How selfish of her to lose track of time so completely when he

2

relied on her for regular meals! Throwing on her coat, she flew quickly up the garden path as fast as its dusting of powdery snow would allow and grabbed the box off the kitchen worktop.

'Ro-ock! Rock, Rock, Rock, Ro-ock!' Back out in the garden Coralie gave the plastic box of dried cat food a hearty shake, but there was no sign of the fluffy black stray who'd adopted her shortly after she'd moved in. Although she would never have admitted it to anyone else, it had taken some time to get used to her new home. Thanks to a weight of unfinished jobs, the tiny cottage had initially felt a bit unloved. Its selling point had been the workshop – and the low price, of course. The holiday let next door might have put some buyers off too, but, touch wood, all the visitors she'd encountered had been very well-behaved.

The relative isolation of the pair of cottages, which she'd found so attractive when she'd viewed them, could also exclude them from the village's warm embrace. They were accessed by a long, narrow road trailing off from what passed in Penmorfa for a main thoroughfare. By day, it was merely The Lane That Time Forgot; perfect for a bygone age when a pony and trap might have trotted merrily down to the village and back, but less suited to modern requirements and any car without a 'thin' button.

However, once the light – and her initial excitement – had faded, there had been times when the trees seemed to scratch at the sky, the dark sockets of potholes appeared to be lying in wait for the unwary traveller and the night air felt still and expectant. Having Rock squeezing through the hedgerow and bounding towards her whenever she appeared made her feel welcome. She paused to listen out for his little chirrup of greeting. Where was he? Perhaps he was in hiding from one of the farm cats who regularly tried to bully him? Poor Rock, you only had to look into his worried gold eyes to see how pathetic he was.

'Ro-ock!' She tried again, jumping to add a bit of extra impetus to her cat-food maraca.

'Hey! Little Red Riding Hood! I take it this is yours.'

The box of dried food went flying from her grasp as Coralie came close to finding out how it would feel to jump out of her skin. The Big Bad Wolf was tall, dark and stubbled, with a voice that could lead a nun astray. His eyes glinted like blue diamonds that cut right through her as he held Rock up from the other side of the fence. He was also, Coralie couldn't help but notice, wearing a black waffle bathrobe, which gaped open to reveal just the right amount of dark hair over smooth skin. Alys had recently given the cottage a makeover, hoping, she said, to appeal to the boutique hotel set, so if this holidaymaker was typical of the new breed, life was about to get interesting.

'Where did you find him?' she asked, wondering

why she was feeling so self-conscious when *he* was the one standing there half-naked.

'On my head,' he said, tucking Rock into the crook of his arm. 'He took advantage of me whilst I was sleeping.'

That would account for why Rock was looking so pleased with himself. 'He's very insecure,' she explained. 'Sometimes he just needs the comfort of being close to someone. The first time he did it to me I dreamt I was in a sauna wearing a Davy Crockett hat. I woke up with Rock's tail in my mouth and his little legs dangling down either side of my head.'

The Big Bad Wolf's mouth was set in a straight line above a granite jaw and the blue eyes regarded her with weary irritation. 'Would you like to take your cat or not?' he asked impatiently, 'because I'm freezing my balls off here.'

'Try not to drop anything until I get close to the fence, then,' Coralie advised, wondering if she should feel offended by a total stranger discussing his testicles with her. Good Sense Of Humour distinctly lacking, even if he was very good-looking. Pity. Safely back in her own home, he probably wouldn't seem that good-looking, either. One downside of Penmorfa was that a surplus of crusty old farmers made it easy to get overheated about any man lacking an abundance of nostril or ear hairs. On the other hand, standing in a frozen garden in just a dressing gown was likely to make it harder to see the funny side of things.

Either way he was a fleeting visitor, not her concern, unlike Rock, who was beginning to get restless.

'Don't worry, Rock, darling, I'm coming to get you,' she said soothingly, just in case the nervous little cat thought the impatience was directed at him.

Except getting close to the fence was slightly harder than she'd anticipated. Gardening hadn't been her highest priority since moving in; the first job was to set the workshop up and get the business running smoothly and the winter had proved far too wet and cold to entice her out to tidy up the borders. The hawthorn bushes the previous owners had planted had been beautiful with their lacy white blossom when she'd moved in, but now they were armed and dangerous with prickles. In one sense that made her feel safe, on the other she didn't especially want to snag her lovely red vintage coat. Picking her way delicately through to a gap in the clearing, Coralie reached the fence, leaned across and lifted her arms to take Rock from the man the other side before his voice went up several octaves.

'There, there!' she cooed, as much to reassure herself as the nervous stray. For all his claims to the contrary, the brief touch of the man's hands against hers as he started to transfer his unwelcome hostage over to her suggested there was plenty of hot blood in him.

'Got him?'

'Yep!' she said, as she lost her footing on a patch of ice.

The silence of the normally peaceful and tranquil garden was rudely broken by a cocktail of sound comprising some fine old-fashioned expletives, yowling and hissing and a few whimpers of fear. Once it had subsided and Coralie could bear to look, Rock was nowhere in sight, but at least there were no track marks down her neighbour's chest to show where he'd been.

'Oh, I'm so sorry! Are you all right?'

'I should have looked around for something more substantial to put on my feet than open-toe hotel slippers, that's all.' He winced.

Spa slippers, too. Coralie was impressed; she wouldn't have guessed that there was any market at all for corporate businessmen looking to chill on the remote Welsh coast, but Alys had obviously done her research. Perhaps she should have done something about blocking the cat-flap, though? Still, the stylish make-over had evidently attracted at least one weary executive to her holiday cottage. Except the man on the other side of the fence was looking more chilly than chilled.

He'd gone quite pale, but she couldn't tell if his adrenalin was priming him for fight or flight. Either way it wasn't going to do wonders for his sense of humour. If he did keel over there was no way she would be able to catch him, assuming she could even pole-vault over the fence in time.

'Just stay right where you are and I'll be fine,'

he said, reading her mind and scowling at her. 'Now, if you'll excuse me, I'm going in before I catch pneumonia.'

'Don't exaggerate,' she said, hoping a bit of levity might help. 'I'm sure a fine big man like you can handle a bit of cold.'

As his dark eyebrows rose, she noticed, at the same time, that in all the excitement his bathrobe had come completely undone making her wonder exactly what was on the other side of the fence from her. She felt the deep blush, despite the freezing air, and was mortified when a flicker of amusement danced across his eyes and the corners of his mouth lifted briefly. It was some small comfort that at least he didn't have lockjaw.

'Have pity,' he said, cracking a smile at last. 'It's still four in the morning according to my body clock. And if that's not cruel enough, various parts of me are in danger of getting frostbite out here,' he added, as if she hadn't noticed. 'So you won't mind if I go in to warm up.'

Coralie stared doubtfully at him, 'Are you quite sure you're okay? You know where I am. Don't hesitate to ask if you need help.'

He drew his bathrobe round him and gave a short bark of laughter. 'Thank you, but don't worry, I've got a cell phone.'

Now was probably not the time to tell him that anything higher tech than a yoghurt pot on a string was wasted in Penmorfa. Instead, she made an attempt at a bright and cheerful smile so their encounter would end on a pleasant note and before he wrote anything like 'peaceful cottage, shame about next door's cat' on TripAdvisor. 'Right, well I'll let you get on,' she said. 'Bye then! Oh and enjoy your holiday! You couldn't have picked a lovelier part of the world to visit.'

He turned hastily and made the sound of someone stubbing a toe. Coralie decided not to look over the fence to see if she was correct. She hung around just in case her limited first-aid skills were required until she heard his back door slam, when she deemed it safe enough to go back inside her own home. Rock was stretched out in front of the wood burner looking at one with the world, but Coralie knew she wouldn't be able to relax. Everyone had accused her of running away to live in a fairy tale; now it was complete with its very own Beast.

Gethin limped inside, trying to decide which of his feet to attend to first. *Tawelfan* was the name of the holiday cottage, Alys Bowen had told him when she'd handed him the key. *Quiet place.* Well, it wasn't especially peaceful so far. One split toe was now bleeding over the kitchen's tiled floor whilst over on the other foot his little toe had turned purple and was looking sulky.

When he'd woken up in a strange bed and discovered his even stranger new headgear, his original intention had simply been to get to the back door and forcibly eject his furry intruder. The guest robe and towelling slippers had been conveniently to hand so saved him the bother of getting dressed just to see off his unexpected guest. But then the commotion had started up in next-door's yard and he'd caught sight of the back of his neighbour's head. Her copper hair was coiled in a quaint up-do that bounced as she bobbed up and down the other side of the fence, her breath cloudy in the cold air.

The cat, in his arms, started wriggling in response to her bellowing, so putting two and two together, it didn't seem exactly gallant to give it a gentle boot or the opportunity to nip back inside behind his back, when he could easily hand it straight over. Besides, he was curious to get a better look at the *front* of his neighbour's head.

Well, the cat, presumably, had escaped unharmed but *he'd* certainly suffered for his curiosity. The new guest slippers had been trashed, but it was only good manners to avoid staining the new white grouting pink as well. A rummage in the kitchen cupboards unearthed a first-aid kit containing a giant roll of crepe bandage and a box of Gruffalo plasters. Fortunately, his essential supplies did run to aspirin and a bottle of Jack Daniels. Since he was sure he'd read something about aspirin thinning the blood, he poured himself a medicinal measure of JD instead. What the heck, his body clock was screwed anyway.

Lovely part of the world to visit, indeed! Alys had asked him if *hiraeth* had brought him back.

The Welsh word described a deep longing for home; a silent call which could only be answered by the waves and the rocks and the mountains. No, not *hiraeth* so much as a last-ditch attempt from beyond the grave to control his behaviour. So if anything had called to him when he'd crested the hill in his hired car and caught his first glimpse of the cluster of limewashed cottages below him, bound by the pewter ribbon of the sea, he'd quickly turned a deaf ear.

Resting his foot on a kitchen chair, he sipped his drink and stared at the Gruffalo and the mouse looking at each other on his toe. Like the girl peering cautiously over the fence at him, her tawny eyes widening in shock, and her Cupid's bow lips rounding in alarm. And suddenly all the anger and frustration of being dragged back to the place he thought he'd left for good diverted itself into something far more surprising; his shoulders started to shake and he threw his head back in a great shout of laughter.

A clean getaway, he reminded himself. No complications and certainly no local girls. Hell, if he'd let his father tell him what to do, he'd still be up to his knees in mud and cow muck and coming home every evening to the bitter face of the girl from the nearest farm slowly realising he'd only married her for her land. All that weight of expectation on a young couple; everyone in the village relying on them to work the land, fill the schools and keep the shops open. No pressure there then.

So the local girls were strictly off-limits, he reminded himself, even if his cute next-door neighbour came round and offered to kiss every single part of him better.

More to the point, he'd promised Ruby that wild horses wouldn't stop him making sure that everything would be in place for the show – including him. Whilst he had every confidence in her abilities, it wasn't fair to leave the kid holding the fort all by herself. Especially not with Laura Schiffman, Pamala Gray's chillingly efficient senior director, breathing down her neck.

'Let Pamala down and it won't just be your father's cottage no one's touching,' Laura had warned. Pamala Gray was not the kind of art dealer anyone messed around, especially in a tightening market. Every exhibition in each of her three galleries had to repay its outlay. If he was a less successful artist, he'd be concerned, but his gold-plated sales record insulated him from any such fears. Not that he'd take advantage of his position; he'd play the game for Ruby's sake so when the time came for her to strike out on her own, she'd be able to cash in from his patronage.

He hobbled upstairs, holding up his big toe stiffly so as not to mark the pristine beige carpet, and picked his phone up from the side of the bed, wondering if was too early to give Ruby a quick call just to reassure her. Great. No signal. Leaning out of the window to see if the reception was any better, he caught the sound of someone singing 'Just Blew In From The Windy City' in the kitchen below. Somehow it didn't come as a surprise when he cracked his head ducking back in.

CHAPTER 2

A little later, gazing round at the winter sun lighting up the whitewashed walls and gilding the oak A-framed rafters of her shop, Coralie felt restored by the sight of her neatly stacked shelves. *Sweet Cleans, Dream Body* for beauty and skincare on one side, *Sweet Cleans, Dream Home* for household and utility on the other. It was a comfort to see the battalions of gleaming bottles and tightly packed jars and imagine them all primed and ready to bring a little shine to so many neglected places. She shrugged off her red coat, smoothed out her pleated skirt with its fifties' geometric print and switched on her music. 'Secret Love' filled the air and Coralie quickly forwarded it to something that didn't make her think of anything messy, like half-naked strangers in the garden.

When Alys tapped at the door, she was glad of the diversion. Alys, who, with her husband, Huw, ran the Penmorfa Garden Centre, had inadvertently helped her to make up her mind when Coralie was still weighing up the pros and cons of moving to the area. Coralie had been exploring, following the winding road up and across the hill to where emerald fields sloped down to a turquoise sea, when she'd first come across the garden centre. It had been a gloriously hot day and noticing that there were signs for a café and something called the Craft Courtyard, she called in for a cool drink and the chance to nose around.

The converted stable buildings, clustering round the garden centre's pretty Victorian cobbled courtyard, housed an eclectic variety of both crafts and craftspeople and seemed to be attracting a healthy flow of visitors. With hindsight, she'd probably let her heart rule her head when she'd noticed there were units to rent. The Craft Courtyard in winter was a much quieter affair, but the attraction of such a lovely setting and an instant 'family' of friendly faces so close to her prospective new home had been too strong to resist.

Coralie waved Alys in. Even in her garden uniform of old jeans and black polo-neck, covered today with a black pea-coat, Alys looked stylish and chic, a bit like Helen Mirren, with her silver bob and slim figure. Alys had a lot of oomph, too. Considering her daughter, Kitty, was quietly causing havoc, she was also managing to stay very calm.

'I don't suppose Kitty's said anything to you about the baby yet,' said Alys. 'Not that I'm asking you to break any confidences.'

'No, and I know,' Coralie told her.

'I just wish she'd open up to me,' Alys sighed.

'How's Huw taking it?'

Alys fingered a bar of soap from the *Dream Body* range. 'He's having a late mid-life crisis. It doesn't suit him to think that his little girl is all grown up; he hasn't got the faintest idea what's going on under those loose tops she's wearing. He still thinks of *her* as a baby so he certainly doesn't think she's capable of being a mother.' She stroked her hands across the label on the wrapper. 'Mind you, I sometimes wonder what's going on inside his head these days. I could stand in front of him stark naked and I swear Huw wouldn't notice.'

Stark naked reminded her of her new neighbour again, so Coralie was relieved when Alys closed her eyes to raise the soap to her face and inhale the vanilla scent. It gave her a chance to rearrange her expression before Alys read the guilt there. She'd rather not have to own up to disfiguring one of her holiday tenants. 'Ah, but that's because you're secure with each other,' she said. 'Huw's just comfortable with you.'

Surely you couldn't keep feeling the way she had when her neighbour had appeared over the fence? Excitement like that every day couldn't be good for you, could it? And yet something in Alys's expression as she replaced the soap and stood up suggested that comfortable wasn't all it was cracked up to be.

Outside in the courtyard, Willow, who sold silver jewellery to the sounds of dolphin calls and rainforest music from her little shop, had arrived after everyone else as usual, but appeared to be having trouble with her door. Coralie and Alys watched as she drifted in to Rhys, the chair maker, as big and solid as one of his products.

'Oh, hello,' said Alys. 'Seems like Rhys's number has come up.'

Coralie did a double take; privately she thought that Willow, with her very faded pre-Raphaelite beauty, was well-named since she did an awful lot of drooping.

'I hope she doesn't frighten him away before the Valentine's raffle,' Alys said, folding her arms. 'Rhys has promised to donate some hand-carved plant labels. We had a weaver here once – lovely man he was, beautiful work – but Willow would keep pestering him. I think he was all for the free massages she offered to start with. Quite happy to have his pressure points relieved and that, but once she cornered him with her Tarot cards, telling him they were meant for each other, it all got a bit heavy for him. Last I heard he'd changed his name and was working up at B&Q near Llandudno.'

'Surely not?' Coralie blinked.

'Well, I might have misheard the bit about B&Q, but it was something like that,' said Alys, her laugh sounding very like Kitty's. 'But Willow is very fond of men who are good with their hands. Blacksmiths, potters, sculptors, gardeners,' she continued, sounding more serious. 'Treats them all as if they're superheroes. She forgets they're just ordinary men and like ordinary men they'll take what they're offered and then they move on.'

The throaty gurgle of an engine alerted them to Huw, oblivious to them watching, trundling past on a quad bike with Edith, his wire-haired Jack Russell looking full of her own self-importance, perched at the back. Alys watched him disappear, her expression hard to read. Gardeners, she'd said. Not Huw? He was certainly good-looking in a rumpled, lived-in way, but why would anyone who had Alys waiting for him need to play away from home? Just as she was starting to feel quite glum, she noticed Alys smiling again. 'I'll tell you what, though,' she said admiringly, 'Willow will certainly bite off more than she can chew if she has a go at this one.'

Coralie took one look over Alys's shoulder and quickly turned the sign on the door to 'Closed'.

'Oh, you've met your new neighbour, have you?' said Alys, raising an eyebrow. 'I knew he had something of a reputation, but I didn't think it was that bad!'

The closed sign didn't seem to be putting him off; he continued to bear down on them, although his progress did seem to be hampered by a barely perceptible limp.

'It's all right, Gethin,' said Alys, switching the door sign over again and beckoning him in. 'You don't have to press your face against the glass, there are plenty of warm rolls in the oven.'

She looked rather pleased with her selective misquote from *Pillow Talk*. Coralie had lent her the DVD of the film in which Doris Day was cast as an independent interior designer forced to share a temporary telephone line with a philandering composer. As Alys stepped back, Coralie took a look at the man standing in her shop and decided that some of his pillow talk was probably quite lively, too. The late morning sun slanting through the windows caught the intense, blue-black of his hair, the twinkle of his dark eyes, a glint of white teeth as he smiled. No wonder he had a reputation. Going round looking like that, he only had himself to blame.

'Little Red Riding Hood, it's you again!' He laughed, shaking his head in disbelief at her. 'Just keep your distance, will you?'

Coralie was starting to feel that simply being on the same planet as Gethin Lewis was too close. Seven months of immersing herself in the practicalities of Sweet Cleans meant she had almost blotted out the messy memories of undertaking gladiatorial combat in some very risky arenas on behalf of corporate emperors. All the whisking, heating and blending of simple, chemical-free ingredients was highly therapeutic; every batch of marigold and lavender foot balm or Squeaky Clean window cleaner gave her a sense of achievement and of brighter days ahead.

In some small way, the products she created were soothing the weary and banishing the dreary.

Maiming the man next door on first meeting felt like a retrograde step. Towering over her now, his broad shoulders blocking out the light from the door, he looked like a dark deed in her pure, pristine world. Shame she couldn't just give him a quick squirt of something and pretend he hadn't happened.

'Have I missed something?' asked Alys, looking from one to the other.

'Apart from a suspected broken toe and hypothermia?' responded Gethin mildly, picking up a bottle of Glow Surround, Coralie's all-purpose kitchen cleaner from the *Dream Home* range. 'I nearly cracked my skull open on the window too, thanks to your singing.'

'My voice isn't *that* bad,' said Coralie, feeling slightly miffed.

'Nothing wrong with it at all,' he agreed, pleasantly. 'You just took me by surprise when I was trying to pick up a phone signal. Although, if I was being picky, I'd say maybe stay away from the Doris Day numbers.'

For Alys's sake, she was prepared to keep the peace and tone the singing down for a week or so. She was even prepared to compensate him for his injuries. She pointed to the bottle he was holding. 'Please accept that, then, by way of an apology. It's very good on hard surfaces.'

'Oh, you *have* been getting to know each other,' said Alys, sounding impressed. 'Looks as if I can skip the introductions.'

'I'm Gethin Lewis,' he said, smiling and offering her his hand.

'And this is Coralie Casey,' said Alys for her, which was good because something had got her tongue.

'Coralie?' he said in a voice like brown sugar on a Welsh cake. 'That's unusual.'

The blue eyes turned on her speculatively. 'It suits you,' he nodded, 'especially with your colouring.'

'Gethin's a successful artist,' Alys explained, whilst Coralie stood dumbstruck, wondering if he would have felt so free to comment about the old Coralie in her sober black suits. 'He came from Penmorfa originally.'

'So, are you back here on holiday?' asked Coralie, recovering her powers of speech.

'Holidays are where you go to have fun, so I'm afraid that rules Penmorfa out for me,' he said, looking reflective.

'It depends on your idea of fun,' said Coralie. Personally she got a lot of satisfaction from trying out ideas for new products, but he looked the sort who might have very different expectations about soapsuds and body lotions. 'What about all the gorgeous coastal path walks? Surely you'll want to remind yourself of all those glorious views?'

The corner of his mouth just lifted. 'I appreciate the suggestion, but I'm very familiar with the local beauties.'

Beside her, Alys turned away to stifle a cough

21

that sounded very much like a muffled laugh. Coralie narrowed her eyes at him. So why was he here? Decorative as he was, she hoped he wasn't back for a prolonged period. She could just about handle the idea of having him as a neighbour for a couple of weeks, but now she'd got used to it, she liked the seclusion of her cottage. She relished being able to pop out to her workshop at the bottom of her garden whenever she liked and mix up an experimental batch of something when the idea struck. A neighbour who was a permanent fixture complaining about noise and smells would certainly cramp her style. Especially someone who wasn't fond of Doris Day and little black cats.

Successful artist, Alys said. Coralie was beginning to think that anyone who could hold a paint brush in west Wales regarded themselves as a successful artist. Just as anyone who could string a sentence together was writing a novel or a collection of poetry. She thought she could be forgiven for not identifying Gethin Lewis as one of them since he'd managed to steer clear of the usual accessories like a ponytail or a loud, hairy jumper. Although a silver hooped earring – the perennial favourite with a certain type of west Wales artistic man, generally old enough to know better – would have rather suited him, giving those dark good looks a distinctly piratical edge.

'So,' she said, trying not to dwell on the dark good looks bit, 'do you exhibit your work anywhere?'

Most would-be artists in the area had a sign outside pointing at a shed marked 'Gallery'.

'New York,' he said, with a gleam in his deep blue eyes.

'Ah,' said Coralie. At least he wouldn't be distracting her with any more half-naked appearances across the fence for very long. 'I expect your girlfriend's missing you.'

His dark eyebrows rose, making Coralie wish she'd thought more carefully before opening her mouth, but with looks like that he had to belong to someone. Despite the battered leather jacket, which gave his appearance a touch of louche edginess, he was quite different from most local artists; especially the ones who looked as if they dressed from a fancy-dress box. Carefully dishevelled hair, designer stubble, expensive jeans, black tee shirt under charcoal jumper; that understated style suggested he didn't need any gimmicks to attract attention.

'The only woman anxious to see me is the art dealer who's about to show my work, but she'll just have to learn to be patient,' he said, amiably. He returned his attention to the bottle in his hand. 'Sweet Cleans. Some kind of hobby?'

Coralie ground her teeth. Cath Kidston must have heard that one a few times, too. 'Like painting you mean?' she said, and heard him laugh. 'I'm providing a complete range of natural, eco-friendly cleaning and beauty products because there's a growing demand for them.'

'From people who can afford to pay through the

nose for bleach in a fancy bottle, you mean,' he said, returning it to the shelf. 'Good luck with finding many of those round here.'

'Gethin!' Alys chided gently before Coralie could protest about his quick dismissal of her environmentally sensitive ingredients. 'A lot's changed in recent years. You should go up to Abersaith and take a walk along the high street if you want to see what I'm talking about; there are individual shops selling handmade stationery, exclusive knitwear, coffee shops with a choice of pastel-coloured macaroons . . .'

He shook his head. 'I've seen it all before, Alys. And been back enough times to watch all the false dawns; too many of those businesses are here and gone before you blink. They seem a good idea when the sun's shining and the few holidaymakers that bother with this part of the world are about, but most of them don't survive the winter.'

'Not this time,' Alys said firmly. 'A permanent change is happening, thanks to people like Coralie who are deliberately choosing to live and work in the area.'

'Ah, I wondered why I couldn't place you,' he said, studying her face again. 'Not a local girl then?'

Coralie could imagine what he was thinking. Anyone born in Penmorfa had probably heard enough from incomers 'finding themselves' or making fresh starts to wonder if it was worth advertising the place as a centre for reincarnation. The 'muck and fluff' image of west Wales that suggested

24

it was largely populated by farmers and hippies was hard to shake off. Even her well-meaning friends had accused her off running off to Penmorfa to live in a fantasy. All the amateur psychologists amongst them had nodded sagely at her fledgling business and made knowing comments about wiping away the past. Nevertheless, she wasn't about to let *him* get away with writing her off as some kind of fantasist.

'I didn't come here on a whim,' she told him. 'When I accepted voluntary redundancy it occurred to me that with an internet connection, I had the freedom and opportunity to start my own business in a place that had always attracted me.' Even if her parents had thought she was in the throes of a nervous breakdown.

'I tested the demand for my products by taking a stall at a couple of summer fairs to see how they'd be received, and when I'd sold out by lunch-time, I realised I was on to something. I haven't looked back since. The Craft Courtyard's the ideal complement to my online business and how many people get these kind of views from their work place?' She gestured at the window. 'It certainly beats climbing the corporate ladder.'

'Hmm,' he replied, darkly. 'I'm not sure the poor sod who has to get up at four in the morning to milk cows, before he goes to his other job because he's at his wit's end wondering how to pay his fuel bills, would agree.'

'Oh, Gethin!' Alys wailed, throwing her hands up

in despair. 'Don't be such a misery! Are you deliberately trying to frighten Coralie back to the city?'

He rubbed a hand across his stubble and managed a rueful smile. 'Don't take any notice of me, Coralie. I'm sure you'll prove me wrong with Sweet Cleans, but nothing in your shop's going to help me clean up the mess my father left behind. Besides, I prefer the countryside from a distance. Call me a bad Welsh boy, but that green, green grass of home business doesn't do it for me. If I ever get the urge to look at grass, a run through Central Park suits me fine.'

Coralie didn't need an invitation to call him a bad boy; it was etched all over him. Opinionated with it, too. But soon he'd be back on a plane and back to New York where he belonged. 'I escaped to the country and you escaped from the country,' she said out loud, earning herself another penetrating glance from those deep blue eyes.

'Exactly,' he said, before turning to Alys. 'So if times have changed, why is it still so hard to get decent mobile phone coverage? As if trying to find a builder to come out and give me some quotes for work on the old cottage isn't going to be enough of a challenge.'

'Oh, that's easily remedied,' said Alys. 'Come over to the farmhouse with me and I'll get you the number for our builders and you can use the landline, but don't forget about the Pembrokeshire promise.'

'Eh?' said Coralie.

'Promise we'll do it tomorrow. Unless there's something better to do,' said Gethin, shaking his head. 'Since my phone's refusing to play, I suppose it's too much to expect that there's an internet café in the village now, is there?'

'You can get twenty-minute slots on the two PCs in the library, provided you've got a ticket and you're prepared to take turns with Wilfie, our nearly famous local poet who's trying to find a publisher, and Edna Harris, who's looking for a man on "My Single Friend",' Alys told him.

'Or, if you promise to be nice to Rock, you could come in and try my router,' Coralie heard herself say, wondering how she'd managed to make it sound like a sinvitation. Two faces turned to her in surprise. 'What?' she said. 'I was only trying to help.' Trying to help mattered to her these days. Besides, the sooner Gethin Lewis finished whatever he'd come to do, the sooner she could get on with her nice, neat life.

'Excellent idea,' said Alys beaming, but Gethin looked doubtful.

'I appreciate the offer,' he said, taking a step backwards, 'but you nearly finished me off just looking over the fence.'

'Actually that was Rock,' she felt compelled to point out, 'and it was an accident.'

'Sure it was,' he agreed, 'and thanks, but with the hours my body wants to keep at the moment, it'll be less trouble for both of us if I can find an alternative.'

27

'I'll get that number then,' sighed Alys, going out of the door.

'And safer,' he added with a smile, before following.

Coralie felt her face fall and was glad no one could see. He wasn't wrong about that.

CHAPTER 3

That evening, at the farmhouse, Alys tucked her white-blonde hair behind her ears and decided that she'd had enough of sitting at the kitchen table listening to the clock ticking her life away. Left to Huw, who'd started the business with an acre of land adjoining the Lewis farm, the garden centre would have remained little more than an expensive hobby. He'd been persuaded, when the chance came, to expand the acreage, but it had been up to Alys to come up with diverse ways to make it pay. She was pleased with how the Craft Courtyard was taking off and even the investment in the holiday cottage was beginning to look as if it would pay dividends. But instead of Huw and Kitty supporting her, as she had hoped, she was starting to feel as if she had left them both behind along the way.

She eyed them now; Penmorfa ought to be the perfect spot to create a family-run series of businesses and she had hoped that Huw and Kitty would share her vision. But far from engaging in a lively debate about it over dinner, both her husband and daughter were doing an excellent job of pretending not to have lost their appetite, each of them mesmerised by their chicken casserole as if it contained the secret of the universe. When had she become less interesting than a dead chicken?

'Well, isn't this nice?' she said, brightly. 'All of us sitting down together again – just like old times.'

There was a clattering of cutlery as both Kitty and Huw stopped eating to cast suspicious looks at her, as if daring her to go on. Which one should she start on first? Kitty had been difficult and moody since she'd come home so something was bothering her. Apart from the obvious. Alys eyed her over a glass of supermarket Cabernet Sauvignon which Kitty had turned down, claiming to have a headache. 'So, Kitty, what's the latest on the job front then? Heard anything from that agency yet?'

Kitty picked up her fork and poked at her food as if the answer was hiding under a dumpling. When she failed to find inspiration there she addressed her thoughts to something else with a soft centre – her father.

'I thought I'd take a bit of time out, so I don't make the mistake of rushing into anything.'

Huw smiled and nodded and withdrew into his own thoughts again, mechanically lifting food to his mouth. In the summer months he enjoyed giving talks to the tourists at the garden centre, but during the winter no one in Penmorfa needed a lecture on 'Vegetables for Beginners', which tended to make him feel a bit redundant. In the environs of the nursery, Huw could coax just about any plant to life, but at home he was a bit like a bulb that had withered away and shrunk underground. Alys thought the time for him to emerge from the hard soil to bloom and thrive again was long overdue.

'But you've already been here a month, Kitty,' she said, willing her husband to join in. 'It's lovely for your dad and me to have you here, but it's not going to do wonders for your career, is it?'

Alys was beginning to run out of patience. Huw was becoming so introverted that at this rate he wasn't even going to notice that Kitty was having a baby until she went into labour. Since her daughter had gone to live in Cardiff in September, she guessed that they only had until June or July to get their heads round the idea. She looked from one to the other and waited to see if Kitty would finally give in and admit that she wasn't planning to return to work any time soon.

'I'm getting a bit of work experience with Coralie,' Kitty said, making big sad eyes at her father.

'Uh-huh. And how are you going to support yourself on that?' *Not to mention the baby*, she was sorely tempted to add. Kitty, as Alys bet to herself she would, managed to squeeze out a few tears. 'Are you saying I'm not welcome? Most parents would be glad to have their daughter home. Wouldn't they, Dad?'

'What?' said Huw.

31

'It's called tough love,' said Alys, trying not to lose her rag. 'You're twenty-two years old and you haven't stuck at anything yet. You can't be an adolescent forever. At some point you're going to have to decide what you want to do with your life.'

'Fine,' said Kitty, pushing her plate away as she had done when she was a toddler. 'If you don't want me here, I'll move into the holiday cottage out of your way.'

Alys shook her head, 'I'm sorry, Kitty, but that's not possible. I've just let it out to a paying customer. We've got to pull together and bring in the money where we can.'

Huw brightened up. 'Oh, fair play to you, *cariad*. Where did you find a holidaymaker at this time of year?'

'I didn't,' Alys said. 'He found us, but he's not exactly a holidaymaker. It's Gethin Lewis. He was planning to stay at Gwyn's old place, but there's been a burst pipe and it's uninhabitable so I said he could rent the cottage whilst he sorts out what needs to be done.'

'I suppose he's come back to get shot of the place, has he?' said Huw, stabbing a mushroom. 'I mean, if Gethin Lewis could barely be bothered to come near the village whilst his father was alive, he's not going to hang on to the cottage now his father's gone, is he?'

'It wasn't as simple as that, you know. He must have had his reasons. Look how busy he's been for a start; crucial exhibitions, interviews.' She sought in vain for Huw's face against the glare of the pendant light. 'Gwyn was a hard man. He liked everyone to dance to his tune. Maybe Gethin needed to put himself first at some point.'

'Selfish,' said Huw. 'Like too many people today, putting their own pleasure first.'

'Not so selfish,' Alys said, sharply. 'He did the right thing by his father when it counted. He couldn't have found a better nursing home for Gwyn, the finest in Pembrokeshire. Anything he needed, Gethin saw that he had it.'

'Anything except his time!' Huw observed crossly. 'He could have helped put his father's cottage right sooner.'

'Do you really think so?' she asked. 'Can you imagine Gwyn welcoming a raft of renovations? Do you think he would have agreed to a travertine-tiled bathroom? Or a Shaker-style kitchen? You know how careful he was. He would have seen any attempt to modernise the cottage as a complete waste of money. Lord knows he only accepted help from Gethin when he was too feeble to refuse.'

And he drove a hard bargain. Goodness knows she and Huw had had to pay the full price when they bought the old farmhouse from him, together with the swathe of land that hadn't been sold for grazing. Huw had been a bit reluctant to take on such a big financial commitment, but Alys could see the advantages of living on site rather than to-ing and fro-ing from their previous home on the other side of the village. Lately, though, she had started to wonder if she would have taken the same decision again had she appreciated quite how much stress it would bring.

'Besides,' she said, reaching across to collect plates since everyone seemed to have stopped eating, 'it's in our interest to keep Gethin Lewis sweet. Don't forget that the track to the old cottage goes right past this house. You don't know who he might sell it to. Or what they might do with it. Now, if you've all had enough, I'm off to the *Merched y Wawr.*'

'Daughters of the Dawn,' sighed Kitty, 'Don't you just love the way they try to make the WI sound exciting here? Like a bunch of loose women.'

Alys shot a quick glance at Huw, but he was too busy staring at the space where his plate had been. 'I'm glad you're so interested, Kitty,' she said. 'You're coming with me.'

With too much jetlag keeping him awake and not enough Jack Daniels to help him sleep, Gethin put on his jacket and boots, ignored his throbbing toes and followed the narrow lane up through the snow-covered banks to where it joined a wider road. Instead of turning right towards the village, he took the left-hand fork across the land which had once been part of his father's estate, past Penmorfa Garden Centre.

The old farmhouse where he was born had been given a considerable makeover by Alys and Huw. What he'd privately dubbed the Amityville Horror now looked cosy and welcoming against the frozen fields. The cottage his father had retired to five years earlier, built at a later date for one of the more fortunate farm hands, lay hidden away up a steep unmade track that disappeared to the side of the main property.

In the fifteen years since winning first prize in a national art competition, as a nineteen-year-old, the course of his life had changed dramatically, but inside the cottage time might have stood still. His father had clung on to the farm for another couple of years after his mother's death, but gave it up in disgust when Gethin sold the work that had made him an overnight name. Contempt at the apparent ease with which Gethin had made his fortune also made him spurn financial help for as long as he was strong enough to do so.

On the hideous mottled-brown tiled fire surround in his father's old sitting room a porcelain shepherdess his mother had cherished, because it was a rare gift from his father, was still flirting with the porcelain shepherd a family photograph away. If she was anything like his temporary next-door neighbour, the china lovers were best kept apart. The woman had as good as broken his toe just looking at him. Those vintage clothes were a menace too, turning his thoughts too dangerously towards black satin and the siren sigh of seamed silk stockings.

Gethin shook his head and concentrated on the black-and-white photograph in the centre of the mantelpiece. There he was, a skinny little kid with glasses, leaning into his mother, his back to her stomach, her arms crossed over his chest to protect him. His father, just apart from them, one hand on his hip, one on his wooden staff, looking at the camera as if it would cost him money to smile.

All the helplessness of that small boy, his inability to protect his mother against his father's dark mood swings, brought a bitter taste to his mouth. Why the hell had the old hypocrite kept the picture on display when his family meant so little to him? And the old man expected him to perpetuate the misery by bringing up his own children here! If his mother had still been alive it might have been different. How she would have loved seeing grand-children running about the place!

He almost left the pale shepherdess where she'd stood for Lord knows how many years, but then he took pity on the lovers who had been apart for so long and placed her next to the young shepherd. Let them enjoy some time together whilst they could, before the house clearance guys turned up and separated them for good.

Closing the front door behind him, he took a deep breath of fresh air, noting that, yes, it really was warmer outside. Ready for sleep at last, he made his way back down the hill, the beam of the torch Alys had thoughtfully left for her guests picking out diamante clusters of snow. In his opinion, the holiday cottage's hotel-style make-over had wiped it of all personality, but it was clean, warm and the double bed was comfortable. All he had to remember was the sloping ceiling above it.

A shaft of yellow light shining into the lane from his neighbour's bedroom window reminded him that he wasn't quite alone. The village's isolated position created the worst of all worlds; long-term residents with a deeply ingrained way of doing business and all kinds of eccentric outsiders desperately seeking some rural nirvana. Wind farms, wind-chimes, woolly jumpers and crazy cat ladies – who needed it?

Before he could get to his front door, there was movement at his neighbour's bedroom window and there she was, dressed for bed, in something sleeveless and mint-green that flared from her shoulders, billowing to somewhere just below her bottom. It was also, Gethin noticed, as she bent forward and came up with her cat, very sheer. He froze, wary of doing anything that might alert her to his presence and give her completely the wrong idea. 'Samba Artist's Sordid Secret' was exactly the kind of story the British red tops would relish and whilst the New York press barely acknowledged the UK's existence, he didn't feel like putting his theory to the test.

Nevertheless he couldn't quite drag his eyes away as his neighbour kissed the cat's head and did a little twirl with it before putting it down again. With her curls loosened and touched with flame by the light behind her, she looked like a wayward angel, and when she finally reached up and drew the curtains, Gethin didn't know whether he was disappointed or relieved. Except that this wasn't Heaven, he remembered, this was Penmorfa.

'It's out of the question. The chairman of the Local Business Association has always drawn the Penmorfa Valentine's charity raffle,' insisted Delyth Morgan, clearly unable to support anything that would deprive her creepy husband, Hefin, of his moment of glory. The couple ran The Foundered Ship, and were responsible for more evil Sunday roasts of shrivelled meat and overcooked vegetables swimming in grey gloop than Kitty could bear to imagine.

Staring at the grandfather clock in the Vicar's front room, Kitty longed for an end to her evening with the *Merched y Wawr*, especially since her numb backside was making her regret her choice of a straight-back chair in the corner of the room. Her knitted tunic fell in soft folds that hid the swell of her stomach, but for all the notice anyone was taking of her, she might just as well have stretched on the sofa, sporting a 'Baby on Board' slogan tee shirt. Except that she would have been stuck between Delyth and Mair, the double act of doom. There were many good women in the room, all trying to do their best for each other, she thought, but not Delyth and Mair, who were only interested in themselves. They had been trying to stamp their collective authority on the meeting all evening, but it was Alys, Kitty noticed, who drew most of their scowls.

'But we're talking about an internationally acclaimed artist,' Alys said, looking shocked. 'Wouldn't it be marvellous publicity for the village if he could do it instead?'

'We're talking about Gethin Lewis,' said Mair, folding her skinny arms. 'I had to give him more than one smack when he started Sunday school. I'll never forget the time he tried to bite me when I prised him away from his mother. She was always too soft on him. As soon as she'd gone I made sure he was sorry. He soon got the message, I can tell you. He didn't dare play me up after that.'

And they were surprised that so few young people stayed in Penmorfa, thought Kitty, wondering wildly if she would ever have a social life again. Her rented room in a shared house in the student heartland of Cardiff had been minging, but there was always someone to have a laugh with. Her job in Events and Leisure Management had been fun whilst it lasted and her social life had been brilliant. And all that gone, thanks to being stupidly lazy about contraception.

'Quite right, too,' Delyth was saying, looking faintly amphibious in her leaf-green fleece. 'It may be marvellous publicity, as you put it, Alys, but for whom? What's he done for us? He can hardly even bring himself to acknowledge his roots. This village made Gethin Lewis what he is today and

all he's done in [   ]
in our faces.'

'Don't you thin[k   ]
giving the older w[   ]
rim of her readir[   ]
demands of his c[   ]
him, he'd be only ~~too happy to help.~~

'We can manage without help from the likes of Gethin Lewis, especially when he's shown the whole world exactly what he thinks of us!' Mair insisted, tucking a handkerchief into the elasticated waist of her flora dirndl skirt. 'When you've lived in Penmorfa as long as we have, you'll understand these things. Gethin Lewis thinks he's far too good for us. He couldn't wait to get away and I'm surprised he's got the nerve to show his face again now.'

Now they were getting to the real issue, thought Kitty; Alys could never win in their eyes because she hadn't been born in the village. Most people in the room had moved with the times, but Delyth and Mair still expected everyone to defer to their decades of experience about the way things were done.

'It's Penmorfa I'm thinking of,' said Alys, getting cross.

The Duo of Doom exchanged a look to suggest that Alys was no judge of character. 'Well, he's certainly got you on his side.' Delyth puffed her cheeks and looked even more like a disapproving frog. 'He always was a little devil with the girls.

Perhaps it's just his pretty face you're finding difficult to resist, Alys?'

Now you've done it, thought Kitty, longing for
her mother to explode. Her parents had their ups
and downs like any couple, but they never faltered
in their support of each other. If Alys, with her
drive and energy, was like a restless wave, her
father was the constant rock absorbing the pound-
ings, forever enduring. Looking at it from the
outside, there might have been an element of
predictability about the arrangement, but there
was a permanence about her parents' relationship
that made Kitty feel rather wistful. It was difficult
to imagine being in a partnership of some thirty
years when, in her experience, most blokes found
it hard to stick around for thirty days. She waited
for the fireworks, but Alys just shook her head at
the paperwork on her lap and settled back in her
chair, her mouth set in a tense line. Even her
mother, it seemed, found it difficult to tell Delyth
and Mair where to get off.

In the frosty silence all Kitty could hear was a
mint rattling against someone's false teeth until a log
cracked in the wood burner and made everyone
jump. Just then the sitting-room door opened. The
Vicar, who'd already been delayed because she'd
had to run her husband to the station when his
car refused to start, only to be called to the phone
on her return, finally surfaced.

'So sorry, ladies,' she said. With her chic dark
hair and lovely high cheekbones she was, Kitty

41

was surprised to see, a bit of a babe. For a woman who had five churches to look after, she was remarkably serene, too. 'That was the Bishop.' She smiled. 'I'm afraid there may be a slight problem with the Valentine's dance.' She settled herself between Mair and Delyth, dividing the Red Sea of Remonstration nicely, Kitty observed.

'But first, I don't suppose many of have you have undergone Criminal Record Bureau checks, have you?'

'I don't know what you're implying, Vicar,' huffed Delyth, her chest beneath the green fleece swelling with indignation.

The Vicar gently patted her arm and looked round the room, searching in vain for raised hands. 'Oh, dear. That's what I thought.'

'What difference would it make if we had?' asked Alys, leaning forward.

The Vicar gave a ladylike sigh. 'Well, because the mother-and-toddler group use the church hall twice a week, it's raised what the Bishop is calling "legitimate concerns" about the safety of the toddlers.'

'Meaning?' said Alys.

The Vicar spread her pale hands in a gesture of helplessness. 'Meaning that unless all of you have CRB checks, it's simply not reasonable for us to guarantee the safety of any toddlers you may come into contact with. The Church has to ensure that any organisation undertaking regulated activities within the hall has made the necessary checks and registrations. '

'But most of them are our grandchildren!' a plaintive voice from the other side of the room cried.

'I'm afraid that doesn't give you any legal rights in this case,' the Vicar said, shaking her head. 'We must be seen to be putting the necessary safeguards in place not just to protect and promote the welfare of children, but also to enhance public confidence. I'm very sorry to be the bearer of bad news, but it simply won't be possible for the Church to allow you to use the hall until this issue is addressed.'

'Yet another example of Health and Safety gone mad!' protested Alys, accompanied by mutinous murmurs.

'Alas, it's more than bureaucratic zeal,' said the Vicar as heads turned her way. 'I'm sorry to report that there's an additional concern. A recent inspection of the building has revealed that it falls seriously short of modern standards. The heating's inadequate, the loos are beyond antique and there's no disabled access. Unless the means are found to carry out the necessary work, it will have to be closed anyway. The Bishop did point out that when Abersaith was in a similar predicament, their historic market hall was saved when funding was secured to match the sum raised when everyone agreed to buy community shares.'

'Our church hall's not exactly an historic landmark.' Alys sighed, gathering up her paperwork. 'And there's still the immediate problem of the

Valentine's dance. Doesn't the Bishop realise how not being able to use the church hall will affect Penmorfa? Unless he reconsiders the matter, there's simply nowhere else to go.'

'Actually, Mam,' said Kitty, anxious to go home and congratulating herself on coming up with a brilliant idea that would mean Delyth and Mair having to be grateful to her mother. 'What about our Summerhouse Café? It's just about big enough. Is there any reason we couldn't hold the do there?'

CHAPTER 4

'Thanks for helping me this morning,' said Coralie. 'I'm pleased with how this *Dream Home* range is selling, even in the current climate.'

'Beats me how you came up with the idea for all this,' Kitty said, unpacking a bottle of Squeaky Clean window spray.

'It's all thanks to my fairy great-godmother,' Coralie explained, taking a box cutter to the next parcel. 'My grandmother was evacuated to a family near here. Unlike so many children, her story had a happy ending. She grew very close to her Welsh family and returned for years for holidays after she'd had my mum. Aunty Elinor, as she called her, had been in service here; she got my gran to practise her handwriting by dictating all her cleaning secrets to her.'

'Hmm, maybe something life-changing like that will happen to me,' mused Kitty, standing back to admire her handiwork.

Something life-changing *was* happening to her, Coralie nearly pointed out, except that would slow Kitty down even more and at the rate she was working they'd be there all day. Kitty had returned to Penmorfa at Christmas, apparently after a temporary work contract had ended in Cardiff. That was one reason she'd given for coming back. She still wasn't talking about the other, the little baby bump she was trying to hide. Everyone was playing along with Kitty for now, pretending nothing had changed. Not that Coralie had a problem with that approach; most people had something they didn't particularly want to talk about. And whilst Kitty wasn't going to be able to keep her secret to herself indefinitely, it would be a relief for all concerned if she turned to her mother first.

'I don't really know what I want to do,' Kitty went on, pulling at her crinkle tunic top where it was trying to hug her stomach. She was still at the stage where most people wouldn't have noticed her condition, but most people hadn't had Alys pacing their room, tearing her hair out over her daughter's determination to remain close-lipped.

Coralie took over with the unpacking, unobtrusively speeding things up whilst Kitty wandered over to the *Dream Body* sample bottles and helped herself to a dollop of hand cream.

'I keep hoping something will come to me, see. I worked in the garden centre last summer, but I get terrible hay fever and it ruined my nails,' Kitty said, flexing her fingers. 'Perhaps Gethin Lewis will spot me whilst he's here and ask me to be his next muse?'

Coralie bent over the box. She'd woken up far too early, full of the usual four-in-the-morning worries, and then found herself wondering about her neighbour. Her grandmother's notes recommended tucking a piece of muslin sprinkled with lavender oil into a pillow case to combat sleeplessness. Although Coralie lay back and tried very hard to conjure up lavender fields, she couldn't quite dismiss thoughts of alternative cures involving the man next door, possibly reclining just the other side of the wall.

'Is his work any good?' she couldn't resist asking, whilst Kitty blatantly unscrewed one of the non-samples and waved it under her nose.

'Oh, that smells lush!' Kitty eyed her over the bottle. 'I can't believe you're asking that! You must have heard of *Last Samba before Sunset*.'

'That's not him, is it?' Coralie was shocked. Posters and cards of the elegant yet deeply sexy portrayal of a couple dancing on the beach in late light, oblivious to the disapproving stares of two frumps crouched behind a windbreak and a pair of old farmers assessing them like horse flesh, adorned living room walls and student bedsits everywhere. The male figure was in shadow, his back turned, so that the attention centred on the sensual beauty of the woman with her arms outstretched moving towards him. It was an iconic image and to think, its creator had been practically naked in her back garden!

Kitty grinned and nodded. 'Watch, there'll be a

run on any magazine with a free lipstick in the express supermarket, now he's back. Even if they do offload all the rubbish colours on us here. Got to be worth a try, though. I wouldn't mind letting him have a good look at my finer points.'

The weak sunshine filtering in through the stable door, which was open whilst they went to and fro with boxes, was temporarily blocked as a shaggy-haired, good-looking blond guy leaned in at them. 'Talking about me again, Kitty?' he said, raising the shovel he'd been using to clear the paths like a trident.

'In your dreams, Adam,' Kitty sniffed, turning away to get on with the stacking.

Adam grinned, showing a chipped front tooth which, together with a slightly crooked nose, only added to his rakish charm. Coralie shook her head, puzzled by Kitty's sudden froideur. It was hard to find anything to dislike about Adam, even when he didn't turn up for work at the garden centre because he was down at the bay trying to catch a wave. She could see why Alys always forgave him.

'How are my two favourite girls, then?' he went on. 'Coralie, did I ever tell you how much I love redheads?'

'He's also quite partial to blondes, brunettes, girls with straightened hair, spiky hair, short hair, long hair, and he isn't averse to a touch of silver either,' said Kitty with a touch of vehemence that made Coralie blink.

'Cheers, Kitty,' said Adam, with a flash of his

emerald eyes. 'I thought you might be pleased to see me for once, especially as your dad and I are running around like blue-arsed flies thanks to your bright idea for the Summerhouse Café.'

'Oh, have you found someone to take it on?' asked Coralie, still wondering why the air was crackling between Kitty and Adam. Surely it was a good thing if the place was being reopened? The Polish couple who'd been running the café and who'd seemed so determined to make a go of life in Penmorfa had taken off shortly after she'd moved in, but then austerity Britain had been quite a different place to the one where they'd started their optimistic new life. Alys, she knew, worried about the loss of winter trade, but had been forced, for lack of staff, to leave it closed.

Coralie listened whilst Kitty gave her a potted history of events at the *Merched y Wawr*. 'So, the Summerhouse Café's just a stop-gap, whilst the Vicar discusses permanent provision of a community space with the Charity Commission,' Kitty concluded. 'She says that if they go down the route of restoring the existing church hall there are several funding pots we can try.'

'Cheaper to build a brand new hall,' said Adam, raising his eyebrows.

'Except there's no money for a new build!' Kitty told him, as if he was stupid. 'By saving an existing building we get points for sustainability, like they did at Abersaith.'

'Penmorfa always loses out to Abersaith,' mused

Adam. 'It's because nothing ever happens here. It's a pity Wilfie isn't better known. If he was as famous a poet as Dylan Thomas, we could claim that he wrote his best poems in the church hall and ask for funding to preserve it for the nation.'

'But,' said Coralie, who was still getting used to the idea, 'you do have a phenomenally well-known artist. Surely that has to offer some possibilities?'

Kitty and Adam exchanged glances, back on common ground.

'He's a bit controversial, see,' said Kitty. 'There are some people who hate that painting. They say he's poking fun at rural life, making us all look like yokels. Delyth and Mair will never forgive him – they say it's them behind the windbreak!'

'There's that, of course,' Adam agreed, 'then there's the fact that the smooth bastard's shagged half our women. I daresay he'll have a crack at a few more whilst he's home.' He cast a sour look at Kitty.

'Oh, you're not afraid of a bit of competition, are you?' laughed Kitty. 'Don't worry about it, Adam. I mean what sort of woman would give in to a fabulously wealthy, drop-dead-gorgeous hunk when she could have a young stud of a garden-labouring surf-bum?'

'At least I've got a job,' he shot back. 'You're still a lazy cow who runs home to mam and dad every time the money runs out. One day you're going to have to grow up.'

Sooner than he thought, Coralie predicted,

taking a step back and getting ready to protect her stock. All that was thrown, though, was another bitter look from Adam before he nodded a curt goodbye and took off.

'Really,' Kitty tutted, her face a picture of innocence as she turned back to the shelves, 'some people can be so touchy.'

By mid-afternoon the Courtyard was deserted and a cold front had closed in. A couple of cars had rolled across the tarmac of the car park earlier, spilling out the hardier variety of holidaymaker, those who didn't mind a spot of wind and weather. But most of them had been in search of shelter and some respite from the bone-chilling temperature which refused to lift despite the deceptive sunshine. Coralie didn't need to tell Kitty twice that she might as well find something more useful to do than hanging around in an empty shop.

Eventually, even Coralie decided that rather than standing there doing nothing she would go home and see what she could do to increase internet sales instead. Willow, with her pale face and cascade of dyed red hair, was looking woefully out of one panelled window like a latter day Lady of Shalott, although Coralie suspected that she was keeping her eyes peeled for Rhys rather than paying customers. She gave her a little wave as she crossed the courtyard and received a wan smile in return.

Most of them don't survive the winter. Gethin Lewis's stark conclusion about the new start-ups in the area nipped like the cold air. What *would* she do if she'd mistaken that tingle of excitement that had changed her life when she'd opened the dusty journal and started to read her grandmother's neat script? Coralie used to be able to claim that one thing she did understand was business, but how could she say that when it had all gone so spectacularly wrong?

She stopped to take some deep, steadying breaths, the raw air stinging her nostrils and making her eyes water. Across the car park the sight of Betty, her Atlantis-blue Rascal van, standing alone in a thin layer of almost untouched snow, gave her a focus and helped draw her back to the present. Poor Betty, not half as prestigious as her previous car, a luxury Audi that made light of the many business miles she used to drive, but ideal for trundling her boxes from the workshop to the Craft Courtyard and back.

Coralie jumped in and switched on the engine, the cold vinyl seat making her teeth chatter as she waited for the windscreen to defrost. Given the rather basic heating, this could sometimes be a lengthy process. Eventually a big enough gap appeared for the long wooden shed of the garden centre shop to come into view. Alys was probably poring over catalogues inside, planning for the future. Gardeners had a wonderful ability to see the potential in the most barren, unpromising ground, thought Coralie, releasing the hand brake. It wasn't a bad philosophy, although some days she looked at her own life and wondered if she would ever see green shoots again.

Realising that she was clenching the steering wheel so hard that her fingers were numb, she relaxed her shoulders and found something to listen to. Comfort music. Something to chase away all the dark thoughts before she got home and had to try to drum up new outlets for Sweet Cleans. The bass notes started and Coralie nodded. 'Move Over Darling', Doris's 1964 hit about irresistible temptation, one of her favourites. Perfect, although the line about waving her conscience goodbye almost set her off again.

A bone-jarring jolt, as one of the potholes in the road still waiting to be filled after the previous year's snow made its presence felt, brought her back down to earth. Coralie slipped down a gear and managed to coax the van over what felt like the foot-slopes of Snowdon. However, the operation appeared to have cost a front bulb which flickered weakly. Whilst Betty's compact size and manoeuvrability meant she could squeeze past tractors without too much difficulty, some caution was needed to ease her along the pock-marks and craters of the narrow lane leading up to her cottage. To negotiate those, what was ideally required was a big, solid car with a powerful engine. Like the one steaming far too fast towards her.

Uncertain condition, thought Gethin, pressing his shoulders against the supple leather of the heated driver's seat as he set off down the lane. The legal term, apparently, for the clause his father had inserted in his Will in an attempt to control him from beyond the grave.

'The meaning's clear enough,' his solicitor had told him, once the Will had rumbled through the due legal processes. 'You'll only have the benefit of your father's house if you reside there personally for the next five years. But no court in the land will enforce that condition because it's impossible to apply.'

'What about a challenge from the other potential beneficiary?' Gethin had asked, wondering how quickly he could get shot of the place.

'Litigation, litigation, litigation. It's a costly old business challenging a Will. And once the wheels are set in motion they can be very hard to stop. Especially when the costs are coming from the claimant's own pockets.'

Perhaps, somewhere, his father had sensed he'd found a loophole because he'd certainly left something behind; an unsaleable cottage and no builder to sort it out. A scramble, it seemed, for soon-to-dry-up funding streams meant that anyone who was any good was heavily involved in regeneration work up at Abersaith.

'Any progress with the other business? The "Art in Your Home" stuff?' he asked. Just to add to the fun, and his legal costs, the company responsible for all the posters of his famous painting had recently gone into liquidation owing him money, another victim of improved digital printing technologies crowding the art market.

'You know there's a strict order for creditors: tax authorities, banks . . . These things take time, but we're doing all we can to pursue your royalty payments.'

Was no one in a hurry these days? At least he'd found a builder who could spare him half-an-hour to give him a quote, albeit with a few caveats about his very busy schedule.

Gethin put his foot down. Might as well give the smart, hired Land Rover a run for his money; that's what potholes were for, wasn't it? He was just beginning to enjoy himself when he caught sight of a single light coming towards him in the dusk and hit the brakes. Almost instantly, he realised that the single light didn't belong to a motorbike, but a van whose offside light was winking so feebly that he hadn't spotted it at first. Swerving into the hedge, he winced as he heard the hawthorn branches scratching at the pristine paintwork and pulled up just a nanoparticle short of disaster.

He opened the door and heard music. Not the angels playing their harps, luckily, but bloody Doris Day telling him how much she yearned to be kissed.

'Move over, darling!' he snarled to his temporary neighbour, Coralie, when she wound down the window. 'That's what you should have done, instead of wrapping yourself up in your bloody music!'

'You were the one hogging the road!' she said, looking taken aback. 'And going far too fast!'

'I managed to see you in time and stopped,' he went on. 'If I'd been some old farmer in a tractor, you might not have been so lucky. If you'd have checked your vehicle before setting off, you'd have noticed that offside light's on the blink. Your windscreen's iced up, too.'

'The heating's dodgy,' she mumbled.

Gethin shook his head. 'It's not the only dodgy thing, is it? This has got to be one of the ugliest vans I've ever seen.'

'Oh, don't start on Betty, too!' she said, sounding so vexed that he peered into see who else was in there.

'Betty Blue, because of her colour,' she offered with a weak smile.

'Well, I'm glad you think it's funny,' he said, seething. 'I just hope my builder appreciates the joke when I tell him why I'm late. Let's get moving, shall we?'

She didn't seem especially keen on the idea, then he worked out why. 'Oh, I get it!' he said, leaning over her again. 'Women drivers can't reverse, can they? Well, don't you worry your pretty little head, I'll do the gentlemanly thing.'

He stomped back to the Land Rover and reversed it back, hard. The butt-ugly van showed no signs of following, but then he saw the driver's door open and a pair of Wellingtons drop beneath it. Shortly after, Coralie stood up in them and, with the door still open, applied her shoulder to the frame.

'Why didn't you tell me you were stuck?' he asked, running back and noticing for the first time that she'd steered into a pile of slushy snow at the side of the lane to avoid him. The Land Rover would have slid out of it comfortably, but Coralie's heap of rubbish needed some coercion.

'Get in,' he said roughly. 'Now put it in second gear – you do know which one that is, do you? Then, when I say, let the clutch out very slowly.'

Marching round to the back of the van, hoping that she really did know where second gear was and didn't find reverse instead, he hefted his shoulder against the bodywork and with a bit of brute force, the van was free. Coralie gave him a wobbly thumbs-up sign which did little to improve his mood, especially when he returned to the Land Rover and realised that it was only possible for her to get home if he reversed all the way back to the pair of cottages.

And now he was running late for the builder, too. 'Sodding mobiles!' he muttered seeing the 'service unavailable' message, having got out of the car in the vain hope of picking up a signal. Willing the guy he was supposed to be meeting to hang on at his father's house until he got there, he decided to save the lecture he was going to give his neighbour about the state of her van for another time. 'You can come in and use the landline, if it helps,' she offered, quietly. 'You might stand a better chance of getting through.'

He glared at his useless phone in frustration.

'I've only got a mobile number for the builder I'm supposed to be meeting. If he's up at the cottage there's no signal there. Besides, he's never in a hurry to answer his voicemail.' What a backwards place this was!

He shoved the phone back in his pocket. 'Thanks anyway,' he said, remembering his manners and looking at his neighbour for the first time since she'd got out of the car. 'Coralie?' he said, shocked at the sight of her. 'What's wrong?'

CHAPTER 5

Even in the fading light, he could see how pale she was, her lips drained of colour. And shaking; he could hear her keys jangling in her hand. Either she felt the cold far more than him, or he'd frightened the life out of her. He mentally replayed their near miss in the lane and all he could hear was his hectoring tone, a soundtrack of constant criticism: her music, her car, her driving. No wonder she was scared. He'd behaved like an utter bully; cruel and overbearing when she was in no position to fight back. Hell! He was no better than his father. Yet another unwelcome legacy.

'Are your house keys on that bunch?' he asked, self-disgust making his voice gruff. She nodded and his stomach lurched at the distress in her eyes.

'I think we should get you inside, that's all,' he said, more gently, 'before you're frozen solid.'

A gentle bump beside them, as her cat jumped down from wherever it had been hiding, seemed to reassure her.

'Hello, Rock,' she sighed, as the little animal rubbed itself against her Wellingtons.

'Your key, Coralie?' he reminded her. She offered it to him and he felt the cold brush of her fingers before she bent to scoop the cat up in her arms. It seemed only natural to place a guiding arm round her shoulders to usher her inside and he tried to ignore his inner voice observing what a good fit she was. None of that leaning-over problem he had with very small women, or stretching up to accommodate tall ones.

'It used to feel very cold here,' she explained, turning and catching his bemused expression as he looked around at the cosy room with its eclectic blend of junkshop finds and vintage fabrics. 'The oranges and red just warm everything up.'

'They do that all right,' he agreed, comparing it to the stream-lined minimalism of his New York apartment, somewhat necessitated by its compact size admittedly, and wondering how any man could put up with all the girlie clutter. 'But standing there won't stop you shivering.'

When Rock jumped out of her arms and strutted over to the wood burner, Gethin helped her shrug off her coat. Her feminine, floral scent and her hair in its forties' style rolls put him in mind of old-fashioned glamour and movie stars like Rita Hayworth and made him curious about whether or not she had a leading man. Then a glance at her pinched face reminded him that rather than worrying about who was or wasn't sweeping her off her feet, he ought, at least, get her to sit down.

'Shouldn't you try to catch up with your builder?' she reminded him, before perching on the edge of the oversized red sofa.

'Another time.' He shrugged. The least he could do after bawling her out was to make sure she wasn't in a state of shock before abandoning her. 'Let's get you sorted out first. This is my fault for forcing you off the road. I'm sorry if I was hard on you.'

'No.' She shook her head and hunched over her folded arms. 'You were right. I should have made sure my windscreen was completely clear before setting off. It's just that it's such a short drive from the garden centre to here. I often walk it, especially when I'm not carrying stock. I thought I could get away with it. But if anyone *had* been walking along the lane, I probably wouldn't have seen them. I could have killed someone.' Her face looked even more pallid against the blaze of colourful cushions behind her.

'But you didn't,' he said firmly. 'We both made mistakes, but there's no harm done. You're just shaken, that's all.' Mainly by his brutish behaviour, he thought, with another wave of self-disgust. 'Got any brandy here?'

'There might be a bottle at the back of the cabinet.' She waved in the direction of a dark oak thirties' sideboard. 'Help yourself.'

'I meant for you,' he said, smiling in spite of everything. 'But now that you've mentioned it . . .'

The embers in the wood burner were turning

61

silvery. He added another log from the basket beside it, patting Rock, who he'd had to disturb in the process, by way of an apology, then turned his attention to the cupboard.

'Babycham?' He threw her a look of disbelief over the Deco-patterned door.

'What?' She frowned. 'I like the Bambi glasses.'

'Well, I don't.' He shuddered. Glasses with faces? That was definitely a girlie touch too far. Tia Maria it was then, although the last time he'd drunk the syrupy liqueur was probably for a bet. He poured a couple of measures and accidentally took the seat next to her on the sofa, instead of the armchair as he'd intended.

'You really do like everything to be pre-loved,' he teased, handing her one of the Schooner sherry glasses just like the ones his gran used to own.

'Not everything,' she said, eyeing him warily as he sat back next to her. 'Some things have gone through too many hands even for me.'

Man, thought Gethin, scratching his head. The grapevine had been busy, even if the phones didn't work. Kiss the wrong girl in Penmorfa and you were branded as a philandering Lothario for the rest of your days. The gossips would try to carve him up whatever he said. Instead of after-shave, maybe he ought to sprinkle himself with a little salt and pepper before venturing out in future?

He thought of his last visit, the previous March; a bright spring day at the modern crematorium twelve miles away. Daffodils nodding and the few villagers who had made the funeral service shaking their heads that Gwyn Lewis's only son had buggered off immediately after the ceremony. Even though they'd been more than happy to drink themselves sober again at his expense on the money he'd left behind the bar in The Foundered Ship, for the wake. Just as well his hectic schedule had kept him so busy since then or he might have been tempted to remind one or two of them about that.

'The vintage look just suggested itself when I did my first craft fair,' Coralie continued, reclaiming his attention. 'It works well with the products and it's popular with customers, too. They like the association with old-fashioned values and the nod to more innocent times.'

Old-fashioned values were overrated in Gethin's opinion. Despite Alys's claims to the contrary, he was willing to bet that if you scratched at whatever visitor-friendly face Penmorfa tried to put on the same long-held petty resentments would still be festering underneath. Fair play to Coralie for believing she could tap into the tourist market, but he didn't want a bottle of over-priced bubble bath, and all his memories of the place were unhappy. He couldn't think of a single thing that would draw him back to the village.

'Besides, we throw too much away,' she said, furrowing her brow. 'Sometimes it's good to save what other people might have rejected or discarded.'

Was she speaking from experience? Had someone broken her heart and put *her* on the scrap-heap? He glanced at her and thought about what she'd said to him in her shop; if she'd escaped to Penmorfa, she must have left something pretty bad behind. Not that he had any intention of asking her what it was, because that would be dumb.

'Like Rock?' he suggested, before she got too serious.

'I suppose so,' she agreed, nodding.

'And butt-ugly vans and Bambi glasses.'

'Hey!' She shot him a look. 'You were doing really well for a while there.'

He was pleased to see some colour returning to her cheeks; that had to be a good sign.

'All right,' she admitted. 'So I might have developed a bit of taste for kitsch, too. When I was a little girl, my grandparents had a glass-fronted cabinet in their front room which was filled with all kinds of treasures: blown-glass animals, dolls in national costume, souvenirs from their holidays. I longed to open it and handle the contents, but I was never allowed. Perhaps I'm making up for it now? What started as a marketing strategy is at risk of becoming a serious eBay habit.'

A small smile lifted the sad set of her mouth. Then she raised her hand to a disobedient curl that had uncoiled and was brushing her cheek. The soft swell of her breasts beneath her black angora cardigan caught him off guard and made him catch his breath. She wasn't a little girl anymore. She turned to him and he found himself meeting her questioning tawny gaze.

He was dimly aware of the hiss of the wood burner and Rock purring to himself, but they were being drowned out by the sudden thudding of his heart. Her eyes held his and the room grew still. Gethin swallowed and dropped his gaze to her mouth. A voice inside his head ordered him to back away before things started getting messy. Even the sofa creaked a warning as he shifted his weight to get comfortable. Jesus! He really had become a monster, he decided, leaning back quickly and reaching for his glass of Tia Maria. The poor woman was in shock and here he was thinking about making a move on her!

'"Less is more" can be good, too,' he advised before draining his glass. 'Possessions only make life complicated.' So did families and one house too many. And women. He stood up to leave, but she got up at the same time and he nearly walked into her. And there was her mouth again, all soft and enticing. Keep it simple, stupid, he reminded himself and wished her good night.

Pausing on her doorstep to allow the cold air to dissipate some of the heat he'd built up, he reflected that little had he known, as a small boy, that he'd have reason to be grateful to Mair for drumming the Welsh alphabet into him. When Coralie had looked at him with eyes he could have drowned in, it was only by reciting the letters very

65

slowly in his head that stopped him confirming everything all the gossips had ever said about him.

When Coralie closed her front door behind her the next morning, she was dressed for the cold and prepared with a can of lubricant to ease the screws of the casing that housed Betty's broken headlight. She was unprepared, however, for the flat tyre that was also waiting for her. Terrific. She cast a longing look at the drawn curtains of the house next door, before quickly dismissing the thought.

Gethin Lewis probably wouldn't appreciate a summons at this hour. Besides, she could tell from the way he'd shot off at the earliest opportunity that he wasn't the kind of guy who'd welcomed having to come to her rescue. He struck her as someone who was far too self-contained to think about help at all, either giving or receiving it. She, on the other hand, was compelled to rescue stray cats, glasses with faces, forgotten recipes, and any amount of unwanted and discarded flotsam and jetsam because she needed to. Because, after everything that had happened, she liked to feel that she was still capable of saving something.

Opening the back of the van, she dug out tools and some old carpet to kneel on whilst she found a jacking point for the wheel. A stiff wheel nut almost had her weeping with frustration before she composed herself, flexed her aching fingers and freed it. Leaning panting against the wheel arch, she hoped fleetingly that Gethin Lewis would look out of his window and take pity on her. After an hour, she had finally changed a tyre, a headlight bulb and a set of clothes and was sitting in the driver's seat waiting for everything to warm up when Gethin came down his front path and waved to her.

'Need a hand with that front bulb?' he asked, when she opened the window.

'Yes,' said Coralie, inwardly sighing at what the last hour would have done to his expensive jeans. 'Tell me if it's working, will you, please?'

'But –'

'Humour me,' she insisted.

His eyebrows rose as she winked both lights at him.

'And slow down in these lanes, if you're taking your new toy out,' she advised before reversing out, 'you're not in New York now.'

The smile on her face died when the post van flagged her down at the other end of the lane. Along with the junk mail was an envelope which she knew contained more unwelcome post. Another month, another visiting order, but familiarity didn't make the routine any easier. Coralie checked the mirrors and drove away carefully. However difficult it was for her, it was so much worse for him. Ned needed her.

Hurrying past the Summerhouse Café on her way to her shop unit a few minutes later, Coralie stopped short at the sight of Kitty inside and went in to see what she was up to.

'I was thinking about how to cheer this place up for the Valentine's *Twmpath*,' Kitty said, taking a tentative stab at an enormous cobweb with a broom. 'It's lost something since Marika and Jerzy left. Jerzy mainly,' she added with a grin.

'Well, yes he *was* a good reason to drop in at the café,' Coralie had to agree, fondly remembering Jerzy, with his soulful dark eyes, floppy hair and ready smile. She pulled her Fair Isle jumper down over the waistband of her wide-leg forties' trousers and considered the matter. 'But I'm guessing for this place to keep itself it needs more than good-looking staff. How about using it for informal wedding receptions? The setting would be great for photos.'

'It would have to be a small one,' Kitty said, undoing a packet of Love Hearts. 'There's the fire certificate to consider; we're likely to be close to the maximum number for the *twmpath*.' She sighed and held out the sweets.

'"Marry Me",' laughed Coralie. 'No offence, Kitty, but you're not my type.'

'So who is?' Kitty said, slyly. 'Who are you hiding from us then? Who do you go sneaking off to meet? Anyone special?'

Guessing that she'd been the subject of some speculation, Coralie pulled a face and crunched on her Love Heart. Alys had once done some fishing on the subject of lost loves. If only it was that simple. On balance it was better to let everyone assume that she was broken-hearted than having to explain about the broken lives. 'I wish,' she said at last. 'I just about keep up with my family. My previous job took me all over the country. I used to help other companies run their businesses more efficiently. I was never in one place long enough to meet anyone and now I'm too busy.'

Kitty narrowed her eyes at her; they both knew it was all a bit glib and rehearsed. '"Will you?"' she mused, reading out the motto on the next Love Heart.

Looks as if she already had, thought Coralie, watching the way her hand fluttered lightly over her stomach.

Adam sidled in, rubbing his hands. 'Getting excited about the *twmpath* then, girls?'

Wearing a perma-tan and a red twill Superdry lumberjack shirt over scruffy jeans, his bleached-blond hair casually tousled, he clearly fancied himself as a right little Jack-the-Lad. She glanced at Kitty to see if she was sneering and was taken aback by her wistful expression.

'What is a *twmpath*, anyway?' she asked, still looking at Kitty and wondering what was going on.

'It's Welsh for hump,' said Adam evilly. 'As in hillock,' he added as Coralie blinked at him in alarm. 'It's a reference to where the musicians sat when they were playing for dancers on the village green. Now it's just the term for a Welsh barn dance.'

'It's just the kind of thing that gives Wales a bad name,' said Kitty, visibly pulling herself together and glaring at Adam to make it plain that included him, too.

'So you won't be going then?' Adam asked, coolly.

Coralie watched as Kitty held his gaze then straightened her top before turning away. 'Only in so far as that I'm helping Mam,' she said, her bangles tinkling as she picked up her broom again.

'You mean you're getting paid by your parents to do bugger all as usual?' he taunted.

Kitty swiped at the floor and when she looked up again her face was flushed with annoyance. 'Well, I certainly won't be going for the dancing, especially not with you clumping on everyone's toes in your gardening boots.'

'You know, I liked you better before you went away,' Adam said softly, going up behind her, 'when we could still have a laugh and a joke.'

'You can't be a clown all your life,' Kitty muttered. 'Some of us have moved on.'

Coralie heard Adam swear under his breath and felt a bit sorry for him. His assessment didn't seem too wide of the mark. Kitty had moved to Cardiff in September, a few months after Coralie arrived in Penmorfa. Her experience in the city had apparently made her feel that in terms of sophistication, she had left Adam behind. Getting herself pregnant there had probably made her a bit prickly, too.

'Now Coralie,' Adam went on, turning his back on Kitty, 'isn't the kind of girl to look down her nose at us like that. She's got some manners.'

'Oh no, you leave me out of this,' said Coralie, backing towards the door. 'Three in this row would make it crowded.'

'Who's rowing?' said Adam. 'You're not too proud to be seen with me, are you, Coralie? You'll dance with me, won't you?'

Coralie waited for Kitty to rescue her; she'd happily agreed to donate a basketful of her products for the raffle, but was less enthusiastic about putting herself on show, too.

'You should go.' Kitty shrugged, pushing her long dark hair away from her face and lifting her chin. 'You won't have to worry about getting stuck with Adam all evening. Everyone gets to dance with everyone else. Plenty of variety, just what Adam likes. It's another of those quaint Welsh customs everyone has to try once.'

'A bit like me.' Adam grinned.

'You'll be single forever at this rate,' Kitty told her, making Coralie feel she was seventeen years older rather than seven. 'You can't keep shutting yourself away. We've seen enough incomers who want to escape to the country and then don't like the reality. Besides, you know how pleased Mam would be to see you there. She needs a bit of cheering up.'

Coralie gave a shrug of resignation. The last thing she wanted was for the people who had accepted

71

her into their community thinking she was too proud to join in. As for Alys? She could think of many reasons for a certain amount of tension in the Bowen home, one of which was right in front of her. Or rather, right in front of Kitty. Going to the *twmpath* wasn't going to ease that particular difficulty.

CHAPTER 6

In the garden centre, a few days later when the bitter weather had given way to a milder spell, Alys moved over to water another display and brushed some soil from a label. Their plant of the month was Hebe, chosen for its range of varieties and because it was such an accommodating shrub happy to grow in a patio pot or in open borders. She particularly liked the stunning pink foliage of 'Heartbreaker' although the name was a painful reminder that, like frost under hedges, some cold spots took longer to thaw.

'Alys?'

A tentative hand touched her shoulder, sending a jet of water from the hosepipe in her hand arcing over the raised bed. A small stream, bubbling down the concrete path, revealed how long she'd been standing there.

'You were in another world,' said Gethin, scrutinising her. 'Are you all right?'

'Gethin!' she said, putting her private sadness away and pasting on a smile as she went to turn the tap off, 'any luck with finding a builder yet?'

He shook his head. 'They must all be millionaires round here, no one seems to want to quote.'

Alys wondered if there was more to it than that. Penmorfa hadn't exactly rushed to kill the fatted calf for this prodigal son, although his reappearance in the village had certainly attracted attention. With those looks he was impossible to miss. She watched as he put his hands in the pockets of his old leather jacket and shifted his glance to where the spangled frosty fields tumbled down to the cliffs and ivory foam fringed the turquoise waves.

'There's no rush with the holiday cottage, you know that,' she said. 'You can stay for as long as you need.'

He shook his head. 'If I don't get back to New York for my next exhibition soon my reputation will be in shreds.'

Alys opened her mouth and he grinned.

'Yeah, I know – home from home.'

She reached out and touched his arm. 'It's not really like that, Gethin. Believe me. Most people are very proud of what you've achieved and anyone else isn't worth bothering about. Look at how you've made a name for yourself in the big wide world. Next thing you know everyone'll be clamouring for a permanent exhibition here to celebrate your achievements.'

'Achievements!' he said, shaking his head. 'I don't think so, Alys. As far as Penmorfa's concerned, people are still waiting for me to get my come-uppance for daring to believe there *was* a bigger world for me than the family farm.'

'Life moves on, even in Penmorfa, Gethin. Attitudes change.'

He laughed as he reached past her to pull up a weed that was interloping in one of the pots.

'No, really,' said Alys. 'There are all kinds of initiatives springing up in the village: Neighbourhood Watch—'

'That's not new,' said Gethin.

Alys pressed on. 'Keep Penmorfa Tidy, Welsh classes, the Quilting Group—'

'Stitch and bitch,' muttered Gethin, shaking his head.

Alys glared at him. 'And following the success of last year's Valentine's *Twmpath*, there's even a demand for dance classes.'

Gethin grimaced. 'Nice try, Alys, but you're not tempting me to move back.'

She flicked a toe at the hosepipe curled up at her feet, in frustration, dodging a tongue of water as it spurted out at her. She couldn't let Gethin leave without at least trying to get him on board.

The Church's surprising decision to hand the church hall over to a management committee for use as a community resource was a poisoned chalice, even the Vicar agreed. On first sight, it was great news that the everyday use of the hall was in the hands of the people who mattered, the people of Penmorfa. Looked at closer, though, and there were onerous duties, not just for financial

75

responsibilities, but requirements to get the building up to scratch, and then to keep it in an acceptable state of repair.

'I'm not asking you to move back, Gethin, but I do need your help.'

His eyes narrowed. 'With what?'

'Don't look like that.' She laughed. 'It's just a small favour. At the moment, we don't even have a suitable building for all these community activities to take place, but there are a number of grants we can apply for if we renovate the church hall. In the meantime, we're hoping to secure a short-term loan of say, about thirty thousand pounds.'

'A bridging loan? Won't that be too expensive?'

'Not if we get it from ACORN, a charity offering financial support to rural communities. And it would enable us to kick-start the rebuilding work until the grants come through. We're looking at total costs in the region of about one hundred and fifty thousand, but we'll need some willing volunteers and a lot of fund-raising events to pay for it. We're making a start with this year's Valentine's dance and all I need you to do is to come along and draw the raffle.'

She saw the shutters come down and his lips start to form the refusal. She took a deep breath. 'Please. We've a huge task ahead of us for a small village and right now we can't even agree on the membership of the Hall Management Committee.'

'Let me guess who's causing all the problems.'

'Well, Mair's made it plain that she expects to take the Chair, whereas other people have hinted they'd like to see someone with, shall we say, a more forward-looking approach.'

'Someone like you, you mean?'

Alys nodded. 'Obviously, if you have to return to the States before the raffle, we'll work round it. I'm sure Delyth will be only too happy for Hefin to step in, but it's not much to ask and a community hall on the doorstep would serve such an important role in reducing isolation. Think of what it would mean to those vulnerable, frail and elderly people who would otherwise be stuck in their homes.'

People like his mother, she didn't need to spell out. Gethin had moved away but had yet to make his name when Katrin became ill. Unkind voices sometimes linked the two events, even though Gethin had visited as often as his father would allow. Poor Katrin, overruled by her husband even during her final illness; she'd been so grateful for the respite of the occasional coffee morning, despite the painful chill of the draughty church hall which was so hard for her gaunt frame to bear.

'It's a win-win, isn't it?' she continued softly. 'You can prove to the doubters that you're not such a bad guy after all, and the publicity will help draw attention to our cause.'

She watched as he gave a wry smile and held up his hands in resignation. 'Yeah, all right, Alys, next thing you'll be telling me I can walk on water, too. I'll draw the raffle for you.'

'Good.' She nodded. 'And I'll get Huw to chase up the builders for you. He ought to be able to find someone who wants to do the job.'

Her reassuring smile faded as Gethin gave a short laugh before thanking her and walking away. Yes, Huw ought to be able to help, but the question was, would he? She touched her hand to the deep pink leaves of 'Heartbreaker'. These days she was no longer sure.

Another advantage of moving to Penmorfa, thought Coralie, as she sat watching the sea after work, was that she'd saved a fortune on gym membership. The beach was a short walk away, a steep descent past the ever-changing hedgerows of the country lanes on the way down, and a challenging push uphill all the way back. If she'd ever toyed with the idea of getting a bike, the sight of even the fittest cyclists having to dismount had quickly put her off.

As for running? There were two very good reasons why she'd never been much of a runner and they were sitting right in front of her; until someone invented the sports bra that would control the bounce, fast walking was a far more comfortable activity. Her waist and hips, though, were noticeably slimmer than in her consultancy days when the sober black suits had been good for hiding the inches that had crept on during the long working weeks and too much snacking on the run.

Noticing feathery grey clouds gathering and staunching the red seep of the setting sun, Coralie lowered herself stiffly off the rock and set off across the beach for home and warmth. Reaching the top of the stone steps, she saw a figure, barely more than a silhouette in the fading light, waiting by the old lime kiln. Walking briskly to the footpath, she was startled as something she quickly recognised as a wire-haired Jack Russell shot out in front of her and gave a bad-tempered growl.

'Edith, you monster,' she muttered knowing better than to risk a finger or two petting the grumpy, pompous little dog.

'Edith!' shouted Huw. 'Come back this minute! Sorry, *bach*, I didn't see you down there. I was just watching one of the dolphins. See there!'

A black coil rose up and disappeared again under the slatey sea and they turned to each other in childlike satisfaction.

'I've been watching them since I was a little boy,' Huw said, grinning. 'And I still feel that same sense of wonder every time I'm privileged enough to see one. '

'Me, too,' agreed Coralie. 'The day I don't, I'll know it'll be time to move on.'

Huw glanced at her. 'You're not thinking of leaving us just yet, are you, lovely?'

'Oh no,' she said, crossing her fingers in her pocket and hoping it was true, 'I'm very happy here. It feels like home.'

'Pity more young people don't think that round here,' he said sadly. 'But what can we offer them? The youngsters don't have anywhere to meet up or to build a sense of belonging and when they grow up they can't find jobs or houses so they have to move away. Take us, we've got young Kitty home at the moment. She'll want to make her own way in the world, but she's got an uphill struggle from what I can see.'

How much could Huw see? Was he really as unobservant as Alys seemed to think? Coralie wondered. They both turned at the sound of footsteps and Coralie sighed inwardly at choosing rush hour in Penmorfa Cove for her quiet break.

'And here's another one who had to leave the place where he grew up to make his way in the world,' he told her, sounding not altogether pleased about it. He turned to the younger man whilst Edith yapped round his feet. 'So, Gethin, you don't get sights like this in the Big Apple, do you?'

'No, not quite the same,' Gethin agreed, his gaze travelling lazily over Coralie. Probably making sure he wasn't about to come to any harm, she thought, still feeling a bit embarrassed at how close she'd already come, on two occasions now, to mutilating the man who'd created *Last Samba before Sunset*. Although, from what she'd read, it looked as if one or two art critics might be cheering if she'd managed to prevent him picking up a brush.

'How's it going up at Gwyn's cottage?' Huw asked gruffly. 'I understand you're looking for a

80

builder. There's not that much needs doing to it, surely? Or you'd have known about it sooner, wouldn't you?'

There was the briefest of pauses before Gethin replied. 'I can see how someone might be fooled by the outside of the cottage,' he said slowly. 'But the real damage occurred after I'd moved my father out, during that cold snap when he started to go really downhill. It's pretty much uninhabitable at the moment.'

'*Duw, duw!*' said Huw.

'Good God, indeed. It doesn't quite capture it, but it's close enough,' Gethin agreed. 'It's a waste to have the place standing empty like that when it could be a great family home.'

'Yes, that's what this place needs,' Huw said, sounding much more cheerful. 'Young couples, children. A bit of life in the community. You'll need someone reliable to do the work. I'll put the word out. See who we can find.'

'I'd appreciate it,' said Gethin, his stomach rumbling loudly.

'No, not you, Edith,' Huw went on, dragging her off Gethin's jeans. 'We know there's plenty of life in you!'

Gethin was looking quite frisky too, Coralie couldn't help notice.

'Well,' said Huw, 'Alys and I were planning a meal at The Cabin up at Abersaith this evening, but Alys isn't feeling too good.'

'Oh that's a shame,' said Coralie, genuinely

81

concerned, but scenting an opportunity to escape. 'It must have been sudden. She seemed fine when I spoke to her earlier. Would a visitor cheer her up?'

'I think she's got a bit of women's trouble,' Huw said, neatly halting further lines of enquiry. 'Anyway, the hotel restaurant – wonderful food they do there now, Gethin. You wouldn't recognise the place.'

Even in the half-light Coralie could see he wasn't convinced, but then he was used to New York and schlepping down to Buddakan or a trendy bistro in Manhattan's meatpacking district or some other hip and happening joint, she thought, running out of *Sex and the City* hotspots. Welsh cuisine probably wasn't sexy enough for him now, but once you got over the sight of laver bread and cockles, all that iodine was supposed to do wonders for your love life. On the other hand, Gethin Lewis didn't look like a man who needed any chemical crutch to boost his libido.

'It would be a terrible shame to waste the table,' Huw went on slyly. 'Why don't you two take it? You haven't been there, have you, Coralie?'

Coralie knew she could lie, but she was out of practice and Huw had caught her off guard. Anyway, Gethin wouldn't want to go so she didn't have to worry.

'Excellent idea, Huw,' said Gethin, making her blink. 'We'll do that.'

'Eight o'clock suit you?' said Huw. 'I mean, it's eight o'clock we booked for.'

What else could she do? 'Eight o'clock,' she repeated, neatly trapped.

'Right you are then,' said Huw. 'Enjoy! Edith!'

He strode off into the gloom with Edith scampering along beside him. Coralie made sure he was out of earshot before she turned to Gethin, who stopped her with a smile before she could speak.

'Do you get the impression Huw's desperate to make sure there's a family living next door to him?' He grinned. 'Seems as if he's not averse to trying anything to stop me selling the land for development or something like a caravan site. Even a spot of matchmaking.'

Coralie was glad that, pulled up, the collar of her tweed jacket hid at least part of her face. 'Oh dear,' she said, squirming. 'He's not very subtle, is he? We'll just have to make up some excuse, won't we?'

'No.' Gethin rubbed his jaw. 'Think of Huw's feelings. He genuinely believes he's doing everyone a favour. He'll be racing back to the farmhouse now, drumming his fingers whilst someone at The Cabin trots off to find an appointments book they never need, because, hey, when was the last time there was a rush for tables at any restaurant round here? Think of how foolish he'll feel if he thinks we've seen through him.'

Coralie stared at him with new respect. Some of the stories circulating in Penmorfa suggested that Gethin Lewis's sole concerns were for himself. She silently wondered if she'd fallen into the trap of believing the gossips.

'You're right.' She nodded. 'I think poor Huw feels a bit like a spare part during the winter, anyway. He's been a bit grumpy since Potato Day.'

She heard Gethin choke back a laugh.

'He set up an all-day workshop on all things potato after reading up about successful winter events at other nurseries,' she went on, unable to hide her own amusement. 'It was a terrible failure. Hardly anyone turned up apart from our poet, Wilfie, who wrote a Potat-Ode to celebrate the occasion.'

'Only in Penmorfa,' said Gethin who was shaking his head at the thought of it. Even in the fading light, she could see the big smile on his face when he stopped and stared at her. 'I'm grateful to you, Coralie, thanks for saying you'll come to dinner with me.'

Coralie smiled down at her boots and started to think that, possibly, she could get through an evening with Gethin Lewis without too much trouble after all. She could even feel the faint stirrings of her appetite returning. Then he ruined it by speaking again.

'Just as well you reminded me how prickly Huw can be. I've got to keep on the right side of him because he's my last hope of getting a builder. And the sooner I get a builder, the sooner I can decide what to do about the cottage. Maybe then I'll finally be able to put Penmorfa behind me.'

CHAPTER 7

'Why not keep the cottage as a holiday home?' Coralie asked once the waiter had taken their order. Far from being as humble as its name suggested, The Cabin was a rather splendid pastel-coloured Georgian building up at Abersaith. Once a run-down bed and breakfast, new life had been breathed into it by its current owners: a woman who had been a runner-up on a TV cookery programme and her husband, a former professional rugby player.

The revamped hotel, described on its website as cool, chic and classy, was another sign of a rising tide of gentrification creeping across the once-forlorn town. To Coralie's surprise they were far from being the only diners; maybe Huw was right to anticipate a stampede of food tourists?

'Holiday? I don't have time for holidays,' Gethin said, topping up her glass. Coralie reminded herself that just because she was feeling nervous didn't mean necking a strong Shiraz in double-quick time was a good idea. She had offered to drive, not least because it would have given her some control over the evening, but Gethin had raised an eyebrow and told her he liked a more comfortable ride. She assumed it was a reference to her van rather than some frank over-sharing.

'I've got my hands full at the moment trying to be in two countries at once. I can't see it ever being any kind of home for me,' he said, the look in his deep blue eyes growing wintry. 'With all the trouble the old place is causing, it might have been easier if I'd just let it fall down.'

Coralie thought about it. Maybe all his memories and sentiment were invested elsewhere? 'Alys told me their farmhouse used to belong to your family.'

He shrugged and she felt a pang of recognition and involuntarily leaned a little closer; that show of indifference hid a few raw spots.

'That's right,' he said. 'My parents ran it as a dairy farm, but milking a hundred grumpy, smelly, enormous animals all determined to kick you to kingdom come was never my idea of fun. Good luck to Alys and Huw, they're welcome to it.'

'So you're really going to cut every tie with the place where you grew up?' Coralie twisted a corner of her neatly pressed napkin. Was it possible for anyone to walk away from their past? Hadn't she tried to do just that? But, for every step she took forward, someone was always ready to remind her of what she'd left behind.

'Look at everything you've sacrificed,' her mother regularly lamented. 'That salary!'

So where once she justified spending far too much on clothes for work on the pretext they were

86

investment pieces, she now scoured eBay and charity shops for bargains. Hardly a sacrifice.

'. . . Your old friends.' Another of her mother's favourite woes, forgetting that a day spent pulling a boardroom of directors back from a lemming-like surge towards organisational destruction hadn't always left her feeling very sociable.

'. . . Status.'

Coralie closed her eyes; she'd never felt comfortable with that slightly deferential attitude on the first day of work at a failing company.

'You know you could go back to your old job at the drop of a hat.'

When she came to her senses and gave up playing at a new career being the subtext here. Her parents still hoped she would go back to 'normal', as if stress, burnout and dreading going to work was a good thing. But her moral compass had shifted irreversibly and her former values of what was right and what was wrong belonged to someone else.

She looked up again and found Gethin studying her face. 'It's easier to go when they don't want you to stay,' he said, quietly. 'Over here, I get slated because my paintings are popular. In New York, they respect me for it.'

Coralie hoped a sympathetic nod would do. All that studied eroticism seemed a bit overworked and obvious to her; an easy way for lazy buyers to create a certain ambience or chosen because the colours matched the decor. Personally, she much preferred rootling through junk shop boxes for old frames or discarded prints to create something original for her walls. Even so, just because Gethin Lewis's work was popular didn't mean he lacked talent or wasn't a master in his *oeuvre*.

'People can say what they like about what I do because I'm doing it on my own terms,' he continued, folding his arms and looking altogether too dark and brooding to be contained by the ordered constraints and austere lines of the modern dining room. 'No one gives a damn about who you've been or where you've come from in a big city. They're all too busy getting on with their own lives.'

There was a pause whilst the waiter arrived with their first courses. The more she thought about it, the sadder it seemed that Penmorfa was missing the chance to celebrate one of its own by allowing another country to take all the plaudits. And for all his show of indifference, surely Gethin must secretly wonder how long he would have to wait for recognition in his birthplace? Wasn't a living, successful artist at least as valid as a dead poet? There was Alys trying to drum up enthusiasm to raise funds for a community space when, it seemed to Coralie, there was a fundamental breach between the village and Gethin crying out to be healed. Perhaps the money would roll in more quickly if the villagers learned to love their most famous son? The first mouthful of grilled goat's cheese with honeyed fig was a rallying call to her jaded appetite, perking her up enough to put forward a suggestion.

'Perhaps people in Penmorfa don't feel they have a stake in your success? Maybe the perception is that it's something happening in a glitzy art world that's nothing to do with them?'

'There's nothing I can do about small-mindedness,' Gethin muttered at a spoonful of spicy seafood chowder.

'Ah, but maybe if you were minded to give something back to Penmorfa the villagers would feel more inclined to share your achievements?'

'To hell with that.' He stopped to scrutinise her. 'Like what?'

'What do you think?' she asked, sitting back. 'Something more substantial than a set of mugs with a Samba print on them, obviously. I was thinking about a painting, of course. Something to hang in the new church hall, perhaps?'

'Coralie?' he said, setting down his spoon. 'Have you even seen one of my paintings? I'm not sure that the good people of this parish would regard my work and the church hall as a good match!'

It was true, from what she'd Googled, there didn't seem to be an article on Gethin Lewis that didn't include the word 'sexy'. Although the term was liberally applied to the artist as well as his work.

'Couldn't you just paint a landscape?'

'Something that captures an authentic Welsh identity, I suppose?' His dark eyes looked

89

thunderous then, to her relief, he laughed. 'Huh! The hard truth is that pretty ladies sell. The bleak imagery of moody skies, desolate hills and the realities of farming the land don't.'

As his eyes held hers, she saw the sparkle return to them. Her fork trembled a little under such close examination and a trickle of honeyed syrup went straight down her cleavage.

It took every shred of Gethin's self-control to make a pretence of studying his food when he would rather have leaned back and enjoyed the show, thanks to that accidental spill. Really, Coralie Casey was the kind of woman calories were made for; that dewy peaches-and-cream complexion, glossy cherry lips, the succulence of her body beneath that orange, silky dress. A cornucopia of curves, you could say, except it was probably better not to think about horns of plenty. Especially when he was having enough problems keeping his mind off fantasies about a warm finger, preferably his, dipping into that soft, inviting cleavage.

He'd been acutely aware of her from the moment the evening had started. Even when she'd turned to close her front door, he'd noticed how the light from her hall, spilling out into the lane, briefly illuminated her bright, piled-up hair, and an orange ribbon that clashed with her red coat. An alluring flame flickering in the dark, except he was old and wise enough to know not to play with fire. Of course, there was no harm in just looking.

Judging that he'd given her enough time to regain her composure, but returning his eyes to her face rather than looking for glistening traces of honey, he found her watching him thoughtfully.

'We should be doing more to celebrate what's unique about the village,' she told him. 'How can we build the community when we don't even have a functioning community hall?'

Yeah, good luck with that, Gethin thought, paying more attention to her low, slightly breathy voice, with its Home Counties accent, than what she was saying. No matter how hard she tried, that pattern of speech would always mark her as an outsider in Penmorfa. One, he was willing to bet, who'd arrived in the village with a pre-conceived idea of the countryside almost entirely informed by magazines. Funny how there was never any mention of the stink of slurry on the fields in those glossy pages, or the sound of farm machinery working long into the June nights. Nothing about the kids getting trashed on Saturday night or the ones who hanged themselves because there was no hope for the future. Some idyll.

'Coralie, I'm sorry, but you're mistaking me for someone who cares about what happens in Penmorfa. I stopped feeling any attachment to the place many years ago.'

She dropped her gaze in apparent disappointment, but the arrival of the waiter turning up to fuss around clearing away their plates forced her to smile and make suitable noises about their starters. He didn't blame her for trying; she was still in the honeymoon stage of her new life in the country. Perhaps all that enthusiasm would rub off on him, too? He was certainly in need of it; his productivity had slowed, although that wasn't necessarily a bad thing. No point in flooding the market. But he was occasionally aware of something else stilling his hand.

It wasn't that he was intimidated every time he set a blank canvas on his easel. Nor did he feel a sense of trepidation whenever he picked up a brush. The problem – one that he would have shaken his head in disbelief at back on the farm – was that everything had fallen in his lap so easily. All the hurt and hunger that had once fuelled and inspired him simply didn't exist anymore; somewhere along the line his grand passion had become nothing more than a pleasant pastime. Getting the work together for his forthcoming show had almost been a chore. What he needed was some reinvigoration, something to shake up his ideas.

'Maybe I should paint you?' he suggested and watched her head jerk up in surprise. 'How would you like to be the star of the village hall?'

'Paint Alys then,' she replied without missing a beat. 'She's the Chair of the new Hall Management Committee. And she's gorgeous.'

'And married,' he added, as his dish of Welsh Black beef arrived.

'Excuse me, but I thought we were discussing a

painting, not an elopement,' she said, looking up from her fish and breaking into a smile.

'Some husbands don't appreciate another man looking at their wives that closely,' he explained. Some girlfriends weren't too thrilled about that kind of intensity either, he could have added. Whatever his girlfriends said at the beginning about giving him space to work, none of them were quite so understanding when it came to him being holed up in his studio with a beautiful woman.

'Well, how do you know I don't have a significant other?'

'Rock doesn't count,' he told her, grinning to himself when her pursed lips confirmed his guess. 'And no man in his right mind would put up with so much Doris Day,' he added, laughing at her scowl.

'Mm, I don't know what goes on in your studio and I don't want to know either,' she said, quickly. 'So you can forget about trying to gauge the size of my nose or deciding what colours to mix to match my teeth whilst we're here and concentrate on your meal.'

He shrugged and picked up his fork, but now the idea had taken root, he couldn't stop thinking about how he might portray her. For the first time in longer than he cared to remember, he itched to pick up his brush.

Paint them and forget them had become his mantra. Not one that he ever said out loud about the paintings or the women, admittedly. The intimacy of painting the beautiful women he met was a kind of exorcism; by the time he'd noted every freckle and mole, the hollow at the base of a throat, the bone structure beneath the skin, the infatuation was over. And every time he managed not to get involved, it stopped him turning into his father, who'd treated his mother more like part of the furniture with every passing year.

In the Summerhouse Café on the morning of the *twmpath*, Kitty looked up as Coralie came in.

'Wow! It looks amazing in here!' Coralie said, sounding genuinely impressed.

Kitty was pleased with herself for creating such a transformation with such basic accessories. Perhaps she ought to play fairy godmother to Coralie too, since today she was wearing what appeared to be a pair of men's twill trousers with a striped cotton shirt and a pair of braces that strained either side of her ample chest. Whilst Coralie was beautiful enough to carry it off, it was the kind of look that women admired and men didn't get.

Her dad had insisted that Gethin was renovating his father's cottage to make it family-friendly, but her mam had said counting on Coralie persuading Gethin not to sell the place to the highest bidder was a bit much to expect from one date. For all Huw's scheming, Coralie didn't look like a woman celebrating her engagement. Neither was she wearing the dazed, satiated expression of someone who'd just enjoyed a few nights of vigorous horizontal romping. Kitty straightened a gingham table cloth. She might have been a bit envious of Coralie if she had.

Kitty, who had now given up any hopes of being whisked off her feet by a handsome stranger – and at the rate she was putting on weight he'd have to be quite a powerful stranger – was a bit disappointed for Coralie who had clearly missed the boat. Drawing the raffle at this evening's Valentine's dance was Gethin's last duty before flying back to America. Whilst Kitty admired Coralie's entrepreneurial spirit, she couldn't help feeling that, at pushing thirty, Coralie was wasting valuable time burying herself in the country, especially if she wanted to stand any chance of meeting someone who wasn't already in a relationship.

She eyed Coralie's outfit doubtfully. Perhaps she should offer to lend her one of her denim miniskirts for the evening? Although there probably wasn't enough stretch in any of her lacy tops.

'I thought I was meant to be giving you a hand,' said Coralie, 'but it looks as if you've done everything. Has all the cleaning been done? Do you want me to check the loos?'

Such a waste, Kitty thought regretfully, Coralie was kind too, always ready to roll up her sleeves and pitch in wherever help was required. No wonder everyone liked her. 'If you could just give me a hand with the bunting, that would be great.'

She might have imagined the briefest of glances at her stomach before Coralie quietly took over any work that required use of a stepladder.

'Oh, it looks very romantic,' Coralie said when they'd finished festooning the room with cheery bunting and strings of fairy lights. She nodded at the tables now dressed in their checked tablecloths and the flowers that Kitty had arranged in old French jam jars wrapped in raffia. 'Have you done anything like this before?'

'I worked for the Leisure and Events Manager in my last job,' Kitty told her. 'Being back here makes me realise how much I miss the challenges. Pity it was only a short-term contract. I was only the admin assistant, mind, although I did get to try the sample menus before some of the dinners. It's amazing what you can pick up about organising large groups of people just by keeping your eyes open.

'It's a bit like being a nanny,' she went on. 'I was a bit intimidated by all the important business people at first and then my manager told me to imagine them as children. After that it was easy. So long as everyone was sat at the correct table with the correct menu in front of them and the vegetarians didn't get tofu too often, everyone was happy. Well, most of the time.' She grinned.

'Morning ladies,' Adam said, breezing in, his strong arms wrapped round a stack of chairs. 'I gather the Boy Wonder's going to grace us with his presence tonight. Good of him to condescend to join us.'

Kitty shook her head. 'You've lived here so long, Adam, you're even sounding like one of the gossips.'

'Whatever,' Adam said, setting down the chairs. 'He did all right for himself though, didn't he? Made a shed-load of money painting beautiful girls. Can't be a bad way of earning a living, can it? Maybe I should have a go?'

'I think it takes some talent to be as successful as Gethin Lewis,' Kitty said, setting the silver bangles on her wrists jingling as she folded her arms. 'Still, given your penchant for drifting, I suppose you could always become a professional surfer.'

'He always did have an eye for the ladies, didn't he?' Adam went on, ignoring her. 'I mean look at the girl in that *Samba* picture – she was a bit of a babe, wasn't she? I wonder where she is now?'

'Not in Penmorfa, that's for sure,' Kitty said, thinking of the life she'd left behind in Cardiff.

'Well, just watch yourself, ladies, if he offers to paint either of you. You never know what it might lead to, eh, Coralie? Coralie?'

But somewhere during the discussion, Coralie had quietly left the room.

CHAPTER 8

Gethin got fed up of listening to fiddle music on the night air and reached for his leather jacket. It sounded as if some people were having fun, but it must have been some latent masochistic streak that had made him agree to join them. Why else had he allowed Alys to cajole him into drawing the winner of the Valentine's raffle?

Alys was one of the few villagers he had time for, he thought, standing in the crowded Summerhouse Café, as she gave him a wave and made her way through the throng towards him. Not least because she was one of the handful of people who'd bothered to make the long journey to the crematorium for his father's service.

Talking to her earlier, when he'd called in to discuss timings for the evening, in the kitchen of the farmhouse where he'd grown up, he'd felt unexpectedly moved by how different the atmosphere in the old place was now. As soon as he walked in he'd felt a homely warmth that just hadn't been there when he was a child. All the little details his mother never had time to add, like a pretty collection of blue-and-white china, the jug of early daffodils on the windowsill, and hand-made gingham curtains, transformed the room into the beating heart of the home. Some of his old anger returned too, when he saw a new red Aga and thought about his mother struggling with the temperamental old range that had once coughed in the alcove. All his success had come too late to save her.

He kissed Alys's cheek and felt the tension fizzling from her, as if she were guarding her secret self with an invisible electric wire.

'Anything wrong?' he asked.

'Red tape again!' Alys shook her head. 'The Gambling Act this time – we can only sell tickets here at the event, so we don't fall foul of it. I'm beginning to wonder if we'll make *any* money for the church hall.'

'Well, never mind, I've brought this, if it helps,' he said. He'd been surprised to find the unsigned pastel sketch of the farmhouse, one of many he'd painted whilst still living at home, framed and hanging in his father's cottage. A cheap box of twenty-four crayons, a can of fixative and a sketchbook had enabled him to work fast, making the most of every valuable break from farm work, teaching him about colour and composition. This little sketch probably wasn't quite what Coralie had hoped for, but it ought to help shift a few more raffle tickets.

'Oh,' Alys said, looking both touched and

saddened, 'that's beautiful. Are you sure you want to part with it?'

'I doubt very much that my father kept it for sentimental reasons so I have no reason to, either.'

Alys gave a small frown, but maybe it was because she had caught sight of her daughter. Kitty, pretty as a picture in a sweet little frock that did something low and tight around her breasts, was doing a pretty good job of selling tickets. The cocky guy from the garden centre was certainly interested in something; he'd draped his arm round her shoulder and was twisting a lock of her hair round his finger. In contrast to Alys, who was thinner these days than he remembered, Kitty was positively blooming. In Manhattan she'd be regarded as outsize, but she was proof that you didn't have to be rake-thin to be beautiful.

'Well, if you're quite sure, then thank you. I'll put it on the table with the other donations but I'm going to make it our star prize,' said Alys. 'Now, why don't you go and help yourself to a drink?'

Gethin decided that was a very good idea; a couple of beers would also stop him wondering where his next-door neighbour was. So would a distance of three thousand miles; that would certainly help to put her out of his mind. Then he spotted her. Her sherry-coloured curls swinging in a fifties-style ponytail secured with an orange silk bow that matched the peaches printed on her crazy yellow cocktail frock. Despite his best intentions to keep away, it cheered him up just to look at her.

Kitty, leaving her admirer casting longing looks at her, swept over with her raffle tickets to Coralie, who had her arms full with a hamper of Sweet Cleans products. The sight of the two women provoked a palpable surge in male hormones all around him, but he was quicker off the mark.

'Here, let me,' he told Coralie, taking the hamper. 'And Kitty, I'm coming back for some raffle tickets.'

He carried it to the prize table where Alys received it gratefully and Coralie gave him a 'your work is done now' look. But he was just beginning to enjoy himself.

'If anyone asks you to dance, you're taken.' He laughed. 'I'm coming back the minute I've bought my raffle tickets.'

'Think of the danger,' she reminded him, when he returned. 'I have no co-ordination and your feet will be sorry. You'd be a lot safer dancing with someone who knows the steps. Ffion's looking for a partner.' She pointed to a young woman, with hair bleached and straightened to within an inch of its life, standing awkwardly by the bar.

'Maybe,' he said, stepping close enough to catch the floral scent of Coralie's distinctive perfume. 'But I remember her when she used to follow me along the beach with a nappy full of wet sand hanging round her knees and now she's heading this way!'

'I think she's outgrown the nappy,' said Coralie still hell-bent on getting away from him.

Was he losing his touch? He took both of her hands in his and looked deep into her eyes. 'Yes, but has she forgiven me for dating her sister? You're the only one who can help me, Coralie, everyone else's memories are way too long and I don't know who's going to accuse me of what next!'

She sucked in her bottom lip as if trying to frame a tactful refusal, so he could have cheered when the caller shouted out for everyone to take their partner for the next dance. 'Don't worry, I'll take care of you,' he said close to her ear, grinning as she threw him a suspicious look. 'And, no, I don't say that to all the girls.' Well, only the pretty ones.

Maybe she'd been a bit quick to congratulate herself for staying out of trouble, thought Coralie. For all his cheeky comments, Adam hadn't been so hard to handle. After a couple of dances which revealed them to be entirely out of step with each other, she'd excused herself in order to collect her contribution to the raffle prizes and watched him head towards an over-excited cluster of teenage girls like a little boy in a sweet shop. Gethin Lewis, as her body urgently reminded her, seeing the challenge in his animated blue eyes, was all man.

Having trodden all over Adam's toes, she also found herself a bit reluctant to let Gethin partner her for another reason. The woman in a backless wisp of a red dress, all long legs and flicky dark hair dancing towards her partner in his most famous painting, was depicted with the passion and tenderness of a lover's eye. What might he read into her own limited dancing skills measured against that?

She looked around for someone else to take her place, but Kitty, in a breathtaking about-turn, had withdrawn her claws and agreed to partner Adam. Willow, looking like a cut-price Florence Welch in a purple tie-dye maxi dress that clashed with her hair, was swaying provocatively in front of an embarrassed-looking Rhys and Alys had finally persuaded Huw to take to the floor.

'Farmers' Fancy – *Ffansi Fermwyr!*' instructed the caller and, before she could do anything about it, they were off.

Gethin took her hand and placed the other round her waist, his fingers warm and firm through the thin fabric of her dress. Bad idea, she thought, as her skin tingled and every atom in her body whispered, 'Yes!'

'You owe me this one!' he told her in his low, lilting voice, bending close to make himself heard over the music before spinning her away.

'Oh?' Concentrate, she instructed her legs, as she raised her head and met his eyes.

'That authentic Welsh landscape,' his palm

scorched against hers, 'you asked me to donate for the good of the village?'

'Yes?' Just one dance, her brain was ordering, despite every cell in her being getting interested and calling out for more.

'It's over there on the prize table,' he murmured as he circled round her. 'You might win it, if your number comes up.'

They turned to face one another before linking hands again.

'So,' he said, watching her face closely. 'Do you feel lucky?'

The mischievous look in his eyes sent a jolt through her that was so shocking she missed a step and was forced to think about what her feet were doing until she'd recovered herself. He'd been standing beside her when she'd bought her raffle tickets; but surely he couldn't fix the result?

'Right hand turn!' the caller shouted, compelling her to focus on what her body was doing rather than his beside her, moving in beautiful synchronicity.

'Left hand turn!'

Kitty was smiling up at Adam, looking genuinely relaxed for once.

'Both hands turn!'

Alys and Huw were dancing self-consciously, like two people who'd forgotten the steps they'd once known so well.

'And do-si-dos!'

Poor Rhys was trapped.

'And swing!'

Coralie's head was spinning even before the rest of her joined in. Gethin Lewis had listened to her. Maybe the little unsigned picture wasn't exactly what she had in mind to engage the village in its famous son's success, but she'd asked him to give something back to Penmorfa and he had. And now he was hinting it could be hers if she wanted it. What did that mean? A little voice was whispering that such a small, apparently insignificant, picture would make a wonderful souvenir of Penmorfa if she was ever forced to leave, but she made herself ignore it. A sketch of the farmhouse, a significant landmark in the village, and, however humble, a Gethin Lewis original, deserved to stay where it could, she hoped, be admired and appreciated.

It occurred to her that whilst the picture might be staying, the artist was about to leave, which was probably just as well given how her feelings had changed in a few weeks. From actively resenting having someone next door, she couldn't help but check her appearance in the hall mirror if she heard movement in the adjoining property, just in case he happened to be leaving at the same time. She'd grown accustomed to her own thoughts and company, but now she came home disappointed on the days when her path hadn't crossed with Gethin's or if they hadn't swapped a few neighbourly words.

Coralie was afraid of losing her grip, and not

just because of the rising temperature. She hoped Gethin was holding on tight because staying cool in the heat of that smouldering glance was quite a challenge. Her hands felt as if they'd been greased as she clung on to him. The tempo of the music gathered pace, becoming more frenzied and creating a contagious sense of wild exhilaration. Reverberating in the background, like the high note of a plucked string, was the matter of the raffle draw, as she wondered whether to be flattered or worried by what Gethin might do. She was beginning to see just how seductive that kind of attention could be. Gethin, it struck her, as he shot her another burning glance, was quite like his art, really: decorative, sexy and probably found in lots of bedrooms.

'Now make your final promenade and prepare to take a new partner,' the caller instructed. 'Gentlemen you may kiss your girl farewell!'

Out of breath and laughing, Coralie forgot herself and leaned into Gethin, resting her hand on his chest as she lifted her face to his dark gaze. Something about them getting sweaty and breathless together fooled her brain into thinking that something far more intimate had taken place. Just as she was about to stand on tiptoes and stretch up to him, she became aware of people watching and quickly pulled away so that his lips missed her mouth and brushed her cheek instead. He raised an eyebrow to show that he knew she'd just chickened out, making her grateful for the heat in the room that hid her embarrassment.

But, along the line, another couple did seem to have forgotten that they were in a public place. The man who was supposed to be her new partner had taken the caller's final instruction to extremes. From the way Adam's mouth was locked against Kitty's he seemed to be anticipating not a temporary split but a lengthy separation. More of a French Fancy than a farmer's fancy, thought Coralie.

'Looks as if you're with me again,' said Gethin. But just as she decided that dancing with Gethin was a burden she could bear, Alys tapped him on the shoulder.

'Sorry to break in,' she said, 'but I think this would be a good time to draw the raffle.'

Coralie took it as a sign that it was also a good time for her to head home.

'Don't even think about going anywhere,' said Gethin, winking. 'We're only just getting started.'

'And now a special prize . . .' Gethin glanced at the prize table. From the lower-value prizes, the bottles of wine and spirits had been picked first, the craft prizes had gone in dribs and drabs and a delighted Wilfie had won a voucher for a massage from Willow. Just his pastel sketch, which Alys had kept aside as the star prize, to go.

Scanning the room, he saw Coralie clutching a blue ticket. He smiled. Here was his chance to ensure that his painting went to someone who appreciated it. 'John Singer Sargent meets Jack Vettriano' a critic had once said of his recent work: flattering, sexed-up portraits of Manhattan's most beautiful and wealthy. Not in a good way.

'But first a few words,' he said. 'I'm sure everyone would like to join me in thanking Alys and Huw for hosting this evening and I know the funds raised tonight will be going to a very worthwhile cause.' Community hall fund, Alys had confirmed. Well, good luck with that. 'With that in mind, I would like to present this,' he held the picture aloft, 'to Alys as a gesture of thanks for all her hard work.'

Alys looked at him questioningly but there were tears in her eyes as she accepted the work, almost too choked to speak. As she reached up to kiss him, he could see Delyth and Mair exchanging sour looks.

'And to tell you about this evening's top prize.'

Mair was glaring at him, which he took as a sign that no love was lost there. Well, never mind, the feeling was entirely mutual. For as long as he could remember, Mair had done her utmost to make his life miserable. As a very small boy, he'd once sunk his teeth into her arm, retaliating in the only way he could for all the times she'd laid into him with a ruler behind his mother's back for reasons he was too young to understand. Although sticking her – or someone very like her – together with someone who looked a lot like Delyth behind the windbreak in *Samba* probably hadn't helped the situation. The look she had given him when he'd walked into the room suggested that given half a chance and a metal ruler, she'd probably like to have another go at him. Except they both knew that now he had the means to fight back.

'Many years ago, as a keen amateur artist, I won the prize of a short art course. This, as you know, gave me the opportunity to turn my hobby into a profession.' He saw Delyth curl her lip at Mair. 'That profession has taken me far away from Penmorfa, and maybe one or two of you think that I've forgotten where I come from, so tonight I'd like to say a small thank you in the best way I can.'

The room grew quiet and he could feel everyone waiting.

'I'd like to make a contribution to the renovation of a hall for the village by donating one of my works for auction, with all the proceeds going to the community hall fund.'

There were low murmurs from some quarters of the room and he paused to see if anyone was bold enough to put up a protest, but Coralie, bless her, was beaming at him and had just clapped her hands together when he resumed his speech.

'This will be a new piece, especially created for the sale. My reputation, as some of you will know, rests on a painting inspired by . . .' he lingered whilst Mair gave him a furious stare, 'an image I set on the beautiful cove at Penmorfa, so it's

Penmorfa I'd like to pay tribute to now by taking, as the subject of my painting, the winner of the Valentine's raffle.'

There were more murmurs as people in the room cast nervous glances at each other.

'And that winner is . . .' He picked out a blue ticket and pretended to read it. 'Number eleven!'

Mair screwed up her ticket. He saw Coralie suck her peach-stained lip and felt like sucking it for her, although he'd definitely get another rulering from Mair if he did. He watched the emotions flicker across Coralie's face as she studied her ticket and seemed to be on the point of shoving it back in her bag. Then Rhys, the chair maker, looked over her shoulder at it and cheered, starting a ripple of applause that gradually got louder as everyone showed their approval. As the noise started to die down, smiling faces started to turn to Coralie expectantly, except for the corner of the room where Kitty and the guy from the garden centre – Adam? – were having a discussion that was becoming increasingly heated.

'So,' roared the guy, standing up and sending his chair flying, 'when did you think *would* be the right time to tell me what you've been up to!'

Alys quickly signalled for the music to start again, grabbing her husband to lead the next dance only, as Huw gave an exaggerated shake of his hips as he got up to join her, a jolt of pain creased his face and then he was clutching his back in agony. With all eyes on Huw – insisting that he didn't need medical help – and Alys enlisting the help of a couple of burly bystanders to get him over to the farmhouse, he just caught sight of Coralie sidling towards the coat lobby and pushed through the crowd after her.

CHAPTER 9

'Not so fast,' said a familiar voice behind her, just as Coralie thought she was safely outside. 'I'm coming with you.'

She looked up at the bright constellations and congratulated herself for not being the type to be easily dazzled. 'No,' she said. 'You stay here and find someone else to paint.'

He gave a short laugh and stayed by her side anyway. 'Have you any idea how much women pay me to immortalise them on canvas?'

'I pay men for things that are useful to me. Like fixing my septic tank or re-pointing my chimney,' she insisted. 'Look, I don't know what kind of game you're playing, but whatever issues you've got with this village, it's not fair to involve me.' She started to walk down the lane, picking her way carefully because it was slippery and her shoes didn't feel as clever as when she had first put them on. He muttered something under his breath, then took hold of her arm, steering her away from a frozen pothole.

'You asked me to be a little more philanthropic and I've obliged,' he pointed out, still keeping her close. 'I thought you'd be pleased to help with the fund-raising effort.'

She shook her head, trying to make sense of the swirling, contradictory thoughts that were so confusing. Part of her was beguiled by how far Penmorfa's very own bad boy was prepared to put himself out for her, but the suspicious part questioned his motives. 'You cheated!' she accused, still relying on his support to stop her sliding on the thin ice. 'I don't know how or why you did it, but that prize belongs to the person who won it!'

Even in the dark, she knew he was smiling. 'I just know what the paying public wants, that's all. A portrait of Mair or Delyth won't get you more than a tin shack for the village. Don't worry about it,' he said, patting her arm. 'It's just a raffle prize.'

But it wasn't just any old raffle prize, was it? Only one of Gethin Lewis's models had ever managed to remain anonymous. Despite intense speculation, no one had discovered the identity of the girl in *Last Samba*, but she couldn't afford to take that risk. Being in the spotlight was something she'd much rather avoid.

'You know,' he went on, 'I don't usually have this trouble persuading someone to sit for me.'

She could believe it. That voice would make a lot of women do far more than just sit for him. A sudden shiver ran through her body at the thought.

'You're not scared of letting me paint your portrait, are you?' he said, softly.

'I'm cold,' she said, which was a lot better than

admitting she was shivering because she was out in the dark with the tall, dark, dangerous wolf who could gobble her up at any moment.

He unlinked his arm from hers and wrapped it firmly round her waist instead. 'Better? I believe in making my potential models comfortable,' he explained when she shot a surprised look at him. 'I'm considerate, unlike some artists who bend their sitters into difficult positions and expect them to stay there for hours. My demands are entirely reasonable.'

For a moment, her libido got interested in his demands. What would it be like to listen to the soft caress of his voice as he told her how he wanted her? To have those midnight-blue eyes roam over every inch of her body? To be passive, helpless, whilst he did whatever he pleased? Just then a barn owl skimmed past them towards the silver fields, looking for small prey to seize. Coralie was reminded that if she didn't take care, she'd be in the grip of something difficult to escape, too.

'I promise you'll be in good hands. I like to spend time with my model and get to know her, so I present a true picture.'

Just what she was afraid of. To become, once again, the object of pity, or curiosity, or even worse, blame – why risk putting herself through all that again? It was a good thing they were nearly back at the cottages where the window in her front door was casting a welcome square of light across the lane.

'And how long does it take you to get to know your model?' she asked, thinking, with some regret, of all the things she wasn't going to let him do.

'Six sittings; six sessions over six days.'

Six, six, six. The devil's number. Which was only to be expected, since he was doing his best to tempt her. Go away, she told him silently. Was this how it would be for the rest of her life? Being crippled by guilt? Living in an emotional void, a bystander whilst Kitty had her baby, Alys and Huw celebrated their lives together and green shoots marked the passing seasons in the garden centre.

'It's not too late to go back to the dance and tell Alys there's been a mistake,' she said. They were outside her front door now and the light was just glancing off his cheekbones and the curve of his lips as he caressed her with the lovely lilt of his voice, which still betrayed his Welsh roots however hard he'd tried to escape them. It crossed her mind that she must have been a teenager the last time she'd stood on a doorstep whilst someone tried to tell her about all the good things he could do for her if only she would let him.

'Finding the right winner doesn't mean you'll necessarily end up with Delyth or Mair. Find someone who'll be pleased with the prize. Even in Penmorfa there are beautiful women who'll fall over themselves to lie on your couch. What's the problem?'

He laughed quietly and stretched one arm across the doorway before bending his head to hers. 'The problem,' he said, softly, 'is that I don't want any of those other women. I want you.'

The roar of the sea from the other side of the headland made her feel reckless. No one was guaranteed a happy ever after, but what was wrong with a happy for now? Tomorrow she'd be standing there alone, watching the jet stream of every plane that disappeared over the wide blue bay. Thinking about it crossing the ocean to where the long beaches and coves were sliced open by another waterway. Dipping down towards a city of glass towers shimmering into the air, buildings humming with thousands of people sleeping, eating, making love, laughing. And one of them would be Gethin Lewis, getting on with his life.

'Someone's going to find out that you deliberately called out the wrong number,' she whispered, her gaze dropping to his mouth, naked and sexy against the black shadow of incipient stubble, filling her with thoughts of what it would it would be like to taste the tang of salt spray on his lips whilst the dark waves crashed on the night beach.

'But I didn't,' he murmured, reaching into his pocket. He took out the square of folded blue paper and pressed it into her palm.

'Number eleven. Just like yours.'

Coralie exhaled slowly. There it was; temptation in the palm of her hand. She stared down at the ticket, letting her imagination run riot for a few seconds, daring her to claim the prize that was rightfully hers.

But that would be a terrible idea.

'There's one detail you've overlooked,' she said, ducking underneath his arm and putting her key in the lock. 'You'll be leaving soon, to return to America, and I'm staying in Penmorfa. We'll never be in the same place again.'

She stepped away from him and from thoughts of what might have been, crossing the threshold to reality and her brightly lit hall. Then she turned to face him for the last time. 'Since it's clearly impossible for me to collect my prize, would it be too much to ask you to donate a different painting? Please don't let your memories of the village get in the way of doing something good for the place. It may even help you come to terms with the past?'

His soft laughter made a mockery of her stiff little speech. How uptight did that sound? And who was she to give him advice?

'Coralie,' he said, straightening up and shaking his head at her. 'You make it sound as if I've got spare paintings lying around. All my available work is tied up in the current exhibition, and I can assure you that there's no shortage of interest. You'll just have to come to my studio in New York.'

'Very funny,' she said, dryly. 'I have a business to run, in case you hadn't noticed.'

'A week away won't make any difference.' He shrugged.

'Oh?' Coralie folded her arms. 'Because it's only a hobby, I suppose?'

'An interest in art,' he said, quietly, 'was not exactly something my father encouraged. I'm not belittling your work; in fact, by doing my bit for Penmorfa, I'm helping your business, too. The air fare and board are included in the prize, so if you really want to do something for the village, you'll do as I say. No portrait means no painting. Think about it.'

The next day Kitty woke up to a sky that was as blue as she felt and a crisp cold morning that was almost as brittle. The winter sunshine beamed onto the floral duvet warming the exact spot below which her baby somersaulted in its secret, watery world. At the beginning she'd almost convinced herself that nothing was happening; so what if her periods had stopped – she was busy at work, wasn't she? And if her breasts were tender, that was because her period was due, wasn't it? And with all that to worry about, well, no wonder she was off her food. Yes, it had been so easy to carry on as normal; even her body seemed to be colluding, her young, tight stomach muscles hugging the baby close. The neat bump and heavier breasts could, with careful clothing, be explained away as a bit of a weight gain.

But beneath it all the baby had bloomed from a blob with a heartbeat on an ultrasound scan, to someone who rolled and kicked inside her, making her back ache and her lungs feel cramped as it pushed for more space. And now she was scared:

118

scared of giving birth, scared of the responsibility and scared of having to face the future on her own. Realising that her tears had soaked the pillow, Kitty levered herself up and groped around for a tissue. She gave her nose a good no-nonsense blow and went over to the window where, she noticed, the birds were having a fit of spring fever outside. The birds were right, of course; it was far too beautiful a morning to be moping around – especially when her days of freedom were numbered – so she had a quick shower and wrapped up to go down to Penmorfa Cove.

The inlet was enclosed by steep shale cliffs and accessed by narrow stone steps which deterred most couples lugging toddlers in buggies or grannies on scooters. Kitty was aware of her extra burden and felt as if she'd aged several decades as she picked her way down. In summer, especially on the rare hot days, the fine sandy beach could be bustling with holidaymakers, although most of them didn't arrive until late morning and had cleared off again by early evening, pretty much guaranteeing you could always find some time to yourself there.

Except that this morning she wasn't alone. She watched the solitary surfer in his winter wetsuit snake along the silver barrel of a wave before spilling into a crest of foam and considered slipping away before he noticed he had company. But, as Adam righted himself, he spotted her on the shore and started wading towards her, creamy water lapping at his thighs.

'Hi, Mummy,' he said, his tone matching the icy chill from his body.

She winced, but found herself huddling a bit closer anyway, longing for a glimpse of the old, easy-going Adam. 'Look, I don't want to talk about it. All right?'

'You should have thought about that last night, before you let me kiss you,' he said, casting off his Neoprene gloves and striding towards his rucksack which was tucked into a rocky niche. 'Did you think you could fool me like everyone else?' He pulled at the collar of his wetsuit and reached round for the ripcord, tugging at it impatiently.

'You'll tear that if you're not careful,' she said, taking over so that she could watch his toned, tanned back appear as she released him. 'I just—' She took a deep breath because her throat was so tight it was difficult to get the words out. 'I just needed a bit of time to get my head round it. Once I start telling people they'll all be wanting to knit bootees, or buy little outfits, or they'll be asking me if I know what I'm having and if I've thought of any names. I'm just not ready to deal with all that. I can't believe that this,' she waved her hand at her stomach, 'is a real person waiting to happen.'

'And what about the daddy?' He turned to her at last, his green eyes glittering in a sudden shaft of sunlight. 'Is *he* ready to deal with it?'

She took a deep breath. 'I . . . The thing is . . .'

She shook her head at the damp sand whilst he unpeeled himself from the wet rubber. 'We're not together.'

'That's not what I asked,' he snapped. 'He does know, doesn't he?'

Kitty folded her arms across herself. 'Yes,' she said, cringing, 'he knows, but he's not exactly the settling down type. Now can we just talk about something else?'

'Sure,' he said, draping a towel across his shoulders and rounding on her. 'Let's talk about what a busy time you've had in Cardiff. You know, there was a time last year when I thought that you and me might have something going for us. The way you followed me round the garden centre, pretending to be interested in what I was doing.'

'I was interested!' Kitty protested, turning her back as his hands moved to his trunks. 'I was weighing up my mind wondering if I should stay here and help Mam and Dad with the business or if I should strike out on my own. I needed to find out more about what happened here and if it was for me.'

'Yeah, well it's quite apparent you found the big city a touch more exciting.' He buckled up his jeans and pulled on his hoodie, before pushing his fingers through his sun-bleached hair. She followed him as he bent to pick up a pebble, throwing it viciously into the soaring spray.

'Yes I did, in fact,' she said, feeling the anger rise. 'I worked in a great office, and I learned new skills and I had a great social life. And I met a wide range of interesting and exciting people who had more to talk about than the neighbours' business and whether or not the weather was right for planting.'

'Well, you don't need to worry about the weather when you're planting indoors, do you?' he said, with a soft laugh. 'You didn't waste any time replacing me with Mr Casual Fling, did you? Was it because you were in such a hurry that you forgot all about contraception?'

Kitty spun away from him, stomping through the wet sand that made the going tough. Sheer anger took her up the first steps, even though she was finding it hard to catch her breath, but somehow she misplaced her foot and found herself falling heavily.

'Oh, fuck!' She groaned, waiting to see what was hurting most. And then she thought of something worse and braced herself for the sweating and nausea and the abdominal cramps to begin. Staring up into the wide azure sky she watched a seagull's lonely flight as it soared away from her and listened to the roar of the waves before they crashed against the cliffs. Cradling her stomach, she wondered if that was the closest she would get to holding the shadow child waiting in the wings. The baby seemed to feel her anxiety and reassured her with a lazy stretch, as if waking from sleep, little limbs pushing against her stomach. It wasn't going anywhere, the baby, she thought, with an unexpected twinge of relief, which made her laugh.

'What are you grinning at, you fuckwit?' said Adam, his face like a worried sun appearing in the sky above her.

'The baby's all right, Adam!' She reached up as he knelt down to her and wrapped her arms around his neck. 'I didn't think I cared, but I do!'

'Of course you do, you silly mare.' He smiled gently at her, making her feel that everything might work out after all. On impulse she nuzzled in and kissed his neck only to feel him stiffen and pull away. 'Come on,' he said, sounding strained. 'Let's make sure you're in one piece and get you home.'

Maybe he did care about her? Perhaps a glimpse of what could have happened had shaken him, too? He helped her up the stone steps with more tenderness than she'd have thought possible, so she made the most of it, holding tight to him for as long as she could.

'So, are you going to tell Alys now?' he asked as he turned her hand to inspect a graze on her palm.

Looking down at his fingernails, broken by all the outdoor work he did, she got distracted by the thought of how nice it would be to see them every day, before she realised he was waiting for an answer. 'Not just yet, eh?' she murmured. 'I can't stand the thought of all the fuss.'

'Up to you.' He shrugged. 'But don't leave it too long or it'll be too late.'

The track leading towards the garden centre lay before them. 'Your surfboard,' she reminded him. 'Go on, I'll be fine now.'

Adam stopped and took hold of her hands again. That had to be a good sign. 'You need a friend,' he said, with a small smile that revealed his chipped front tooth and made her feel all warm inside. 'I'm here for you, if you need me.'

Kitty nodded and tried not to cry. Friend. That would have to do.

CHAPTER 10

In the workshop a few weeks later, Coralie pressed a button and Doris started singing 'Bewitched, Bothered and Bewildered'. Bittersweet remembrances soared around her, making Coralie tut-tut at some of the more ludicrous lyrics. She had no intention of worshipping any man's trousers, she told herself, quickly dismissing a fleeting mental glimpse of Gethin's dark denims hugging thighs that were lean and hard and pressed firmly against hers. She had far more self-control and her pressing concerns ought not to be about a man she was never going to meet again.

For a moment the tantalising possibility of being Gethin Lewis's latest muse floated up in front of her, before she dismissed it. The prize had been a PR stunt, something to do away with that residual ill-will that dogged him in his home village. With distance, she hoped that he would realise that he could make an equally grand gesture by simply presenting them with a work that didn't involve anyone from Penmorfa. Especially not her.

'Do we have to listen to this?' asked Kitty, tossing her head in a way that made Coralie fret about future customers unravelling long dark hairs from the mixture she was stirring.

'It's happy music,' said Coralie, pointing her wooden spoon in a warning gesture to silence her. 'Doris Day is wise and good, so leave her alone.'

Kitty frowned and picked at a loose thread on her top. 'Wasn't she a bit of a goer?'

Coralie huffed but managed to hold her tongue. Kitty had been tetchy and miserable since the Valentine's *Twmpath*. Coralie couldn't decide if it was Adam's kiss or the subsequent spat that was getting to her most, but Adam's happy-go-lucky attitude was bound to have made Kitty even more aware of the responsibilities she couldn't escape.

The loose thread dealt with, Kitty was now apparently all set for work. 'So what are we on today, then?'

'Goats' milk and ylang-ylang – very good for dry skin.'

'Do you drink it or bathe in it?' Kitty said, peering into the pan.

'Neither,' said Coralie, nudging her out of the way and making a mental note to dig out a spare scarf from the growing collection she used to tuck up hair whilst working. Today hers was silk with a jaunty nautical design of which she was particularly fond. 'It's soap. It'll need to cure for about a month and then it'll be ready to go.'

'Oh, I'm disappointed now.' Kitty took the hint and moved back to settle herself in the armchair by the stove. 'I was hoping it was some sort of essential nutrient. I'm that hungry. What have you got out here that I can eat?'

'Well, you can make us a pot of tea if you'd like and if you're very good I'll tell you where the cakes are hidden.'

'Nah!' said Kitty, pulling off her biker boots and wiggling her feet in their striped socks at the wood burner. 'I can't be arsed.'

Lowering the heat under the saucepan, Coralie watched Kitty getting comfortable and wondered if she'd come to work or talk. Sweet Cleans was ticking over at a rate she could cope with in her workshop, she had a roof over her head and she could pay the bills. However, she was gradually realising that drawing anything like a salary was some way off. Taking her little cottage industry to the next level would mean more than just sharing her recipes. Making it worthwhile would take her away from the very aspects of the business she relished and perilously close to the world of commercial cut and thrust she'd left behind.

'Unless one of us is arsed,' Coralie pointed out, 'there won't be anything to sell so I suggest *we* get on with some work then.'

'Oh look, here comes Mam,' observed Kitty, staying put. 'Probably needs cheering up. What with Dad's back playing up and him not being too thrilled with her getting so involved with this Hall Management Committee thing. You could cut the air with a knife at home lately.'

127

Who'd have believed it, thought Coralie wiping her hands and opening the door.

'Busy?' said Alys, giving Kitty a bit of Beady Eye Factor.

'Depends,' said Kitty, stretching contentedly.

'I've just had some good news,' Alys said, wringing her hands and waving away Coralie's offer of a seat. 'I've just had a call from ACORN, a charity that helps rural communities in need. They've approved our plans!'

'Fair play, Mam,' said Kitty, not sounding especially interested. 'What does that mean then?'

'It means we're eligible for a sizeable loan from them which means we can get on with the work until the bulk of the money from the grant is approved,' said Alys, still looking, to Coralie, very tense.

'The revamp of the church hall, you mean?' she chipped in, applauding Alys's dedication. Coralie was more than happy to support any fundraising efforts that didn't involve her, although she always found that she was particularly busy whenever Alys mentioned anything about her joining the *Merched y Wawr*.

'So, how will you pay back the loan?' she asked. Perhaps there was a similar pot of gold for rural businesses, too?

'It seems that hall management committees are generally very conscientious about repayments,' Alys replied, her uneasy body language belying her nonchalant tone. 'Once the grant money arrives it won't be a problem – we can pay it back then. Thanks to Gethin, we have a painting to sell which will guarantee that even if the grant takes time to go through the system we won't default on the bridging loan.'

'Oh, that's great!' Coralie was delighted that her faith in Gethin to do the right thing hadn't been misplaced, even if a very small part of her lamented the lost opportunity for further contact with him. 'What's the painting like?'

Everyone listened to the gas hob hissing until Doris Day moved on to 'High Hopes' and Alys cleared her throat. 'Well, we know what its subject is, don't we?' she said, giving Coralie a worried look. 'I understand that Gethin's so keen to do this to support the village's cause that he's even prepared to pay to fly you out there. I must say that's one in the eye to everyone here who's ever written him off as a totally selfish man. And given how busy he is with his current exhibition, it's very good of him to spare us his time.'

'Oh, no!' Coralie banged her wooden spoon against the pan as two eager faces turned to her. 'You must see that it's totally impractical for me. I can't just drop everything here.' Gethin Lewis might have made her feel as if she could fly again, but that didn't mean she was having her portrait painted for anyone.

'We'd take care of Sweet Cleans for you,' Alys insisted.

'And keep an eye on Rock,' Kitty joined in.

'Penmorfa's whole future depends on you!'

Now that *was* being melodramatic, thought Coralie, opening her mouth to protest. 'Wait,' she said. 'Why can't we just redraw the prize? I don't see why it has to be my portrait when the painting's being sold anyway. It could have been anybody in that room that night. '

'Not really,' said Kitty, getting up and prowling round the soap mixture. Coralie shushed her away. Was this the moment when Kitty had to admit why it couldn't have been her, why jumping on a plane would have been out of the question? She stared at her pan rather than at Kitty, afraid of doing anything which might make the younger woman think twice about her confession.

'I don't know if I should tell you this. I kind of promised to keep it to myself,' Kitty said, eventually.

Too late, already, thought Coralie. But she was sure Kitty would feel so much better once she'd unburdened herself about the pregnancy.

'The thing is, the other half of your strip of tickets was never included with the rest of the draw that night. Gethin asked me to give them to him. He told me he'd been thinking about something you'd said to him about giving everyone a stake in his work, so when I saw he'd donated a painting to the raffle, I just assumed . . .'

'He must really want to paint you,' Alys finished.

'Or something,' Kitty mumbled, before breaking into giggles and setting Alys off, too. 'Oh come on, Coralie!' said Kitty. 'Don't look so disapproving. He is lush and he's obviously dead keen on you. Don't tell me you're not tempted. I so would if it was me he'd invited to lie on his couch!'

'It's not you, though, is it?' Coralie protested, a sudden constriction of her throat making it quite hard to speak. Not that Alys and Kitty were listening. They were too busy cackling and leaning on each other for support, all differences between them apparently forgotten, leaving Coralie feeling even more isolated.

'Sorry, Coralie,' said Alys, straightening up and wiping her eyes, 'we're just jealous that we didn't get a free holiday in America and the devoted attention of a red-hot man. You'd need to sell an awful lot of soap to buy that much excitement.'

'What makes you think I want that?' said Coralie, stung. 'I came to Penmorfa to live quietly and to do something creative and fulfilling. It's not about how much I earn, but that I'm enjoying what I do. That's all the excitement I need.'

'And we respect that, of course.' Alys nodded, pulling a straight face, even though the amusement still danced in her eyes. 'You've settled seamlessly into the village. Everyone admires the way you've joined in and made a real effort to be part of the community. No one's ever had a bad word to say against you – even Delyth and Mair think you're a quiet, hard-working girl. Thirty thousand pounds is a lot to repay through cake sales and coffee mornings alone, but thanks to you we can be relaxed about the loan. I promise you that we won't let the business suffer whilst you're away.'

'Thank you, but that won't be necessary,' Coralie said, slowly lifting her eyes to face Alys. 'Aren't you forgetting that I'm not a bowl of fruit or a flower arrangement? You can't just push me around for this painting as if I were some inanimate object. You might be happy for me to drop everything, but what if you'd been in my shoes? Would you be quite so keen to jet off to the other side of the world if it meant leaving everything in the garden centre to Huw and Kitty?' She shook her head. 'I'm very sorry, Alys, but I can't help.'

Gethin was sitting in his favourite diner trying to convince himself he was pleased to be back. Today, New Yorkers were wrapped up to beat a wind chill factor so cold that, anywhere else in the world, it would have cleared the streets of its citizens. The lovely brunette passing the window clearly didn't have far to go; she was bare-headed, her glossy hair just bouncing gently on her shoulders as she walked. As if sensing his interest, she turned her face towards him. Beautiful grey eyes under perfectly groomed brows met his. Her rosy lips parted in a flawless smile and then she winked and sashayed away.

Normally that would have been enough to remind him how he loved this city.

'Only takes one dumb animal,' reminded his apprentice, nodding at the woman's fur-clad back.

'Good morning, Ruby Arnold!' he said loudly, making her wince. 'Good of you to drop in. Caffeine kicked in at last?'

Ruby mumbled something inaudible before returning to her pancakes. Gethin shook his head. So the kid partied hard, but some internal switch flipped to 'on' as soon as they were working. 'Is that the thanks I get for making sure you were registered for the Brave New Artists' Prize?'

'You did what?' Her head jerked up. 'I wasn't going to bother. You know, with the fee and all.'

'All taken care of.'

He caught a glimpse of the part of her she kept hidden, the softer, vulnerable Ruby, before the guard went up again.

'Thanks, but you should have saved your money. They won't pick a nobody like me.'

'Speculate to accumulate, Rubes,' he said, fondly. 'If you can't even be bothered to enter then you definitely won't make the cut.' He'd never imagined himself permitting anyone to share his studio – God knows, plenty of people had tried to flatter their way in – but dogged little Ruby had chipped away at his stone heart. He'd been quietly impressed with her raw talent, but it was the wounded look in her eyes that had really got to him.

Once upon a time . . . well, those early days had gone. And, if anything, the lean times had made him more determined to prove himself. He'd had his lucky break and Ruby had more than repaid hers, proving herself an able assistant with an almost intuitive knack of giving him what he needed before he realised he needed it and always putting her hand up to a mistake. No nasty surprises with Ruby; she was a quick learner.

'Hey, Mr Jones? Can I get you a refill?'

Gethin put his cup down, 'I'm good for coffee, thanks, Max,' he said to the manager. 'Come on, Rubes, I think we've let Pamala wait long enough.'

The art dealer's exacting standards were well-known. Some people survived the ordeal of working with Pamala Gray and came out the other side with enhanced reputations; others slunk away wounded, barely able to exhibit again.

'You might have shaved,' Ruby reproached him, looking up at his jaw as he got to his feet. 'You ought to at least try to keep up the good impression, for my sake if not for yours. I might need her when I win that big prize.'

Gethin laughed. 'So now you're not just in the competition, you're going to win it. I like your thinking. Listen, if Pamala Gray gets close enough to inspect my stubble, she's close enough not to care,' he said, running his hand across his chin. 'We're fine-tuning my exhibition, not going on a date. Besides,' he added with a grin, 'she's the one chasing me.' More people than ever were clamouring for his flattering portrayals of sophisticated couples and strong, beautiful women. If one or two of the stuffier art critics lifted their eyebrows at the mention of his name, what did he care? Everything was going his way, so why was he feeling so miserable?

'Here, I'll take that for you.' The manager leant over and took his tray. 'You have a nice day now, Mr Jones.'

Gethin flung his bags across his shoulder and turned up his collar, before gently shoving Ruby into the cold.

'Shouldn't he know your name by now?' Ruby tugged a beanie over her peroxide crop and fumbled in the pockets of her faux-leather jacket for gloves. Gethin handed her the lightest of the bags.

'Jones as in Tom – Max's little joke when he found out I was from Wales.'

'Whatever.' Ruby shrugged. 'But talking of the old home town, what's happening about that portrait you asked me to fit into the schedule?'

'Bad idea,' he said, shouting above the noise of a truck which had pulled up beside them, its brakes hissing noisily. 'The only way I can do it would be if we were both in the same place and the model's still refusing to come out here.'

'New York's an awfully long way to travel for a sitting,' Ruby bellowed back. 'Did you take that into consideration?'

'Jetlag,' he mumbled. Snowflakes were falling between the tall buildings and settling on Ruby's hat; he brushed them off and pulled her out of the way of an oncoming umbrella. It wouldn't do for his assistant to lose an eye now.

'Is she pretty?'

That was the other thing about Ruby; she had

a really big mouth. 'I just want to paint her and help the old place along the way,' he said, hoping to shut her up.

'Sure you do,' she said, not hiding her smile very well. 'So why don't you just give her a call and ask nicely?'

Rock didn't rush to greet Coralie when she walked up her front path; perhaps he'd heard about her refusal to co-operate and was giving her the cold shoulder, too? The black windows of the next-door cottage were as lifeless as her workshop after all the laughter had died away and it was obvious to everyone that Coralie was going to stand her ground. Kitty had threaded her arm through her mother's, leading her away without a backwards glance, as if Coralie no longer existed.

The front door was cold against her shoulder as Coralie let herself in and flopped down on her sofa without taking off her coat. She switched on a lamp which did nothing to lift her gloom and only seemed to deepen the shadows in the room. True friends would surely accept her decision, she thought, chewing her lip. Wasn't all the emotional pressure a bit unfair? She replayed the moment when Alys's white bob folded briefly across her face as she stared at the floor and how, when she looked up again, her eyes had been unusually bright.

'I really thought I could pull this off,' Alys stated quietly. 'Prove to that dreadful Delyth and Mair that Penmorfa needn't be stuck in the past, that we *can* change and grow together. But without your help, Coralie, I can see it all slipping away.'

They thought she wouldn't help, when the truth was she *couldn't* help. It was arduous enough keeping up with her regular visits to Ned along with everything else, but she knew how much they meant to him. What would the consequences be if he thought she'd abandoned him like everyone else? But if she went to New York for a week, how could she also fit in a visit to him and get all her work done?

Coralie wilted back on the sofa and only noticed she was crying when she saw teardrops falling onto her tightly clasped hands. She wiped her nose, wishing that like her fingers still scented from the essential oils she'd been working with, she, too, could come up smelling of roses. Somewhere next to the sofa was a box of tissues, and as she groped around for them, Rock slunk out with a tiny brown mouse still struggling in his jaws.

Coralie had found out during the first of the cold weather that mice were an inescapable fact of country living, albeit one that no one boasted about. Since she was surrounded by fields, there had seemed little point in catching and releasing them only to have them re-home themselves in her loft at the earliest opportunity. Having Rock about the place acted, she hoped, as a deterrent, but she wasn't about to condone torture and murder, especially when it was going on right under her feet. Grabbing Rock in a surprise attack, she got ready to catch his victim before it shot off and hid somewhere so she wouldn't be able to find it again.

The tiny creature was frozen in fear. Coralie snatched at it, hissing at Rock to keep away and fending him off with her foot. The fluffy black cat she'd come to love looked more like the spitting, feral stray who'd vigorously defended himself against her attempts to clean him up when she'd first rescued him.

'Get out!' she roared, sinking back in triumph when, after a long, baleful stare, he finally sloped out of the room. She knelt there for a moment taking slow deep breaths, before daring to look at the fluttering, fragile, flicker of life in her palms. Slowly, slowly, she uncupped her hands and took a peep at the pitiful thing inside them. To her huge relief the little body was unmarked; really, it was quite lovely when you looked at it closely: the glossy brown-grey pelt, the delicate paws and bright, beady eyes. Satisfied that the little mouse was safe, Coralie smiled to herself and savoured what felt like a hard-won achievement. She'd done it! Just one, tiny heartbeat of a life – but she'd saved it!

Lifting herself up on her knees, she was looking round the room, pondering her next move when a sudden sense of unease stilled her. Opening her hands again, she felt the small body shudder and the light leave the bright eyes as the mouse gave its last breath. No! Please no! She'd only been trying to help. Utterly wretched, she sank back and let the tears flow freely. No matter where she went or how fast she ran, there was always someone she couldn't escape from, the one person she couldn't shake off. If she could only save just one thing, maybe, just maybe, she could learn to live with herself.

CHAPTER 11

Pamala Gray had finished with Gethin by lunchtime and had passed him on to Laura Schiffman, her Senior Director. Laura wanted to catch one of the temporary exhibitions in town by a Lithuanian-born artist who did something clever with string, so Gethin found himself sitting in a museum restaurant, a temple to glass and light where, on first sight, only beautiful worshippers were admitted. Laura was talking, but her earnest, monotone delivery soon sent his attention wandering. After the rough edges, sullen faces and frustrations of Penmorfa, he'd been relieved to get back to New York, yet now the good manners and smooth service made him yearn for something that made life a little less predictable.

Even his meal was flawless: four halves of hard-boiled egg arranged on a slate, looking very much like one of the art exhibits. Each half was a thing of beauty; a glassy set white, a perfect creamy swirl rising from the dip where the yolk would have been and a glistening, miniature spring of caviar bubbling from each delicate peak like black lava. He thought of The Cabin and the generous Welsh

Black beef filling the plate and his stomach rumbled in a disappointed lament at how very empty it would be, even if he drank all of the endless refills of iced water.

'. . . and of course we're hoping to attract interest from all those collectors hoping to add to their ego-seums,' said Laura, arranging her spoon by the side of an artistically wonky bowl.

'What?' he said, looking at her worthy and almost untouched lentil soup and thinking of Coralie, sighing with satisfaction as she rounded off her chocolate pudding with more chocolates and a double espresso.

'You know,' she said, waving perfectly manicured hands, 'the new status symbol for the super-rich. Instead of leaving their art collections in storage for lack of space, or donating their collections to public museums where they might not be put on permanent display, they're buying up bus garages and underground bunkers so they can show the world what great taste they've got.'

Or not. Leaving the restaurant behind, they started their tour. Gethin began to notice collections which ought never to have gone on display but for the patrons who'd donated them insisting they be viewed in their entirety. The results said more about conspicuous consumption than love of art or good taste. Oh, there were always lots of big egos about.

Making an offer to Penmorfa that he thought Coralie couldn't refuse – wasn't that just him

141

flaunting his great big ego? Or something? Perhaps that's what Coralie thought, too, since she'd turned out not to be the pushover suggested by her soft-heartedness. The only reason he could see for her to reject his offer was that she'd seen him for the conceited prick he'd become. What other reason would she have for not playing nicely when her refusal risked hurting Penmorfa?

'Now, this is a wonderful example of what Fuller meant when she talked about lines as being points in motions,' Laura murmured, looking at the string exhibits with great reverence. Everyone else in the gallery seemed equally enthralled. Gethin noted that whilst they represented many different ethnic backgrounds, all were linked by a particular kind of well-bred, well-educated upbringing and a certain self-conscious cool. He felt a great wave of nostalgia for Delyth and Mair and had to pull himself together.

Laura hadn't noticed his lack of response. 'One day, your work could be rubbing shoulders, so to speak, with a Quinn, an Ofili or a Koons,' she whispered, pressing a pale fingertip to the space between her clear grey eyes as if trying to erase any imminent frown-lines.

Now why didn't that make him jump for joy?

'Pamala takes the long view, she's not there for the shock of the new,' Laura went on, smiling to show white, even-spaced teeth. 'She really takes care of her artists. What she sees in you is tremen-dous ability along with huge imagination and a touch of edginess. She has great expectations for your exhibition.'

Gethin stared past her at the courtyard below with an artificial tree, an amoebic blob of a sculpture, a square pond and some paving slabs and found himself thinking about the crashing exhilaration of the waves breaking on the cliffs at Penmorfa; their wild, untameable energy. How come he kept getting the feeling that he'd left something important behind? As if he was living in a monochrome world and waiting, like the wisteria arbour in the Shakespeare Garden that he had passed through that morning, for a change of temperatures to bring him some colour and life.

Laura was wearing a clever grey jumper that managed to be both flattering and tasteful; something the aesthetic part of his brain appreciated. Yet all he could think of was Coralie: the copper curls, eyes flecked with gold, a peachy-soft mouth and all the glow of whatever colour combination of crazy clothes had taken her fancy that morning. How would he set about capturing all her changing kaleidoscopic character and setting it on canvas?

Forget about Coralie, he told himself. Be smart and keep following the money. Like this guy who was literally pulling the wool over the critics' eyes with string, he thought, shaking his head at another meaningless installation. Except trying to be smart wasn't making him happy, so perhaps it was time to do something crazy?

'Laura,' he said, surprising them both. 'Would you excuse me? I have to make a phone call.'

In the lobby he paced the floor whilst a phone on the other side of the Atlantic rang itself off the wall. Just as he was about to give up, he heard her soft Home Counties voice say hello.

'What do you want me to do?' he asked, rubbing his hands over his jaw. 'Beg?'

Kitty waited until Adam had got most of the way round the greenhouse he was cleaning, then set up at one of the long tables. His eyebrows rose, but at least he didn't object to her company. Good start.

'I'm getting ahead with some early sowing,' she announced, separating the plastic seed trays. 'You never know what Mam's going to come up with next.'

Kitty had always looked up to Alys and admired her for her energetic, no-nonsense approach to life, but part of her wished that her mother would simply admit that she was backing a lost cause. 'Why she's putting herself out to rebuild the church hall for the benefit of people like Delyth and Mair, who're always looking down their noses sneering at everything she says, beats me. I don't know why they always have to take a pop at her.'

'Well, she looks half her age,' said Adam, 'and she moves with the times. But she shouldn't let those two get to her. Everyone else appreciates her hard work.'

Kitty sighed. Had Coralie been willing to play along with Gethin, her mother might not have had to have worked quite so hard, but Alys, undeterred, had carried on seizing funding opportunities with as much tenacity as Edith grappling Huw's socks.

'I'd just wish she'd save some of that energy for home, where it's needed. Dad's already being treated for high blood pressure – I found his tablets in the bathroom cabinet.'

'Then at least you know he's doing something about it,' Adam pointed out. 'Besides, it's not fair to blame Alys when she's trying to do something positive. Your dad might have other worries.'

Kitty refused to meet his eyes. All she knew was that with the usual work of the garden centre to be carried out and concerns about finding anyone suitable to run the Summerhouse Café when it reopened in the spring, it was little wonder that her father was becoming increasingly withdrawn.

'I know Mam was delighted that so many people turned up for the St David's Day event last week,' she said, on a more conciliatory note – after all, Adam had gone out of his way to help set up the garden centre when Alys had decided to turn one of their regular garden events into something much grander – 'but I never want to hear the Abersaith Male Voice Choir or smell another Welsh cake ever again.'

Battling another wave of nausea just thinking about the pervasive scent of warm cakes that seemed to suck out all the oxygen in the marquee where she'd been stationed, Kitty swallowed hard and turned her attention to Adam. Chucking-up was not the way to convince him that whilst her body might have been taken over her mind was still very much her own.

'I'd have lugged that compost in for you,' he said, tutting at her.

'I don't recall you being so worried last year.' She smiled, determined to remind him of those long, hot summer days.

'Sleeping all right?' he asked, stretching up and showing an inch of tanned, toned stomach.

Perhaps he was about to volunteer to help tire her out? She pretended to fiddle about with the first cell tray.

'Only my mate, Flat Sam – the guy with the dreads I surf with – he was telling me that when his sister was at your stage of the game, you know, when the mother and baby are sharing limited space, she found it much easier to sleep on her left side. Keeps all the blood flowing to your extremities, apparently.'

Kitty resisted the urge to tell him it was not the blood flow to *her* extremities she was interested in. 'Uh-huh,' she said, resigning herself to firming compost rather than Adam.

'Some gentle activity's good, too.' He nodded at her. 'But if you're going to be standing there, make sure you squeeze your toes from time to time. You don't want to faint, do you?'

No, thought Kitty, she wanted to scream. All this

fussing was precisely why she'd tried to keep the pregnancy to herself. Although she'd called a truce with the baby, she still wasn't ready to let it dominate her. She scowled at her cell tray and the packets of seeds, feeling that it was rapidly becoming her lot to be the bringer of new life. At one time she'd hoped Adam would worship her, but she hadn't foreseen him casting her as a fertility goddess.

'Have you made a birth plan yet?' he asked, a splash of water across his cheek giving him a look of shiny-faced enthusiasm.

'Pain free,' she snapped. 'With lots of drugs.' She looked up, grateful for a change of subject as Alys ambled in with the cordless house phone and beckoned at her.

'Someone for you. Sheena Milsom?'

Oh God, she hoped it wasn't an ante-natal appointment. Kitty took the phone and held it to her chest, waiting for her mother to leave, but Alys picked up the seeds instead. 'Greyhound,' she noted. 'A good do-er. Oh, yes, Sheena's the editor of *West Life Journal*,' she added, pressing a seed into the compost. 'She wants to talk to you about your *twmpath* photos – the ones of the Summerhouse Café all dressed up for the evening that I posted on the garden centre website.'

Kitty went over to the open doorway away from her mother and Adam who, she noted, had fallen into easy conversation whilst Alys picked up a spare cloth and wiped off a smear Adam had missed.

147

'It's very *Country Living*,' the editor told her, after a brief preamble. 'It's just what we're looking for, just right for the bride on a budget – all those flowers in jam jars and homemade bunting. So we'd really like to use the photo, for a fee, of course.'

She mentioned a sum and Kitty's sharp intake of breath drew concerned looks from Adam and her mother. Kitty waved her free hand to show that she was ok, although she was very tempted to stand over one of Adam's window-washing puddles and pretend her waters had broken just to see what he would do.

'Who was the stylist?' asked the editor, making her frown. 'Did you bring in anyone special?'

'Oh, that was me,' said Kitty. By now Adam and her mother had stopped talking and were shamelessly eavesdropping.

'Fantastic!'

Kitty glowed at the praise. At last there was someone in the world wanting to talk about the person she was rather than the one she was creating!

'Well I must say you're very talented. What's the name of your business, so I can include it in the article?'

Kitty did some rapid thinking. 'Flair on a Shoestring,' she announced confidently. 'And I'll give you my email address too.'

'Wonderful!' the editor trilled. 'Thank you! I do hope it creates lots of interest for you.'

'Who or what is Flair on a Shoestring?' said Alys, grinning at her as she took back the phone.

Kitty couldn't help but laugh. 'The idea just came to me! I wanted to convince that editor that I knew what I was talking about. Then it occurred to me that this is something I could actually do. I'm not flustered by all the preparations for big events and I reckon I've proved that I can make an ordinary room fit for a party. Put the two together and what have you got? My new styling business: weddings, birthday parties and celebrations. A-list styling on a Z-list budget.'

Adam threw his cloth into the bucket at his feet and laughed. 'Brilliant! You won't even have to get off your backside. I mean, who's going to want anything like that around here?'

Kitty felt the flush of annoyance. 'I'm serious, Adam. Everyone's worried about spending cuts and the loss of public sector jobs. They'll be plenty of potential customers in Cardiff looking for ways to cut the cost of big celebrations.' At least her mother, perching on one of the benches, had sat down to look at her thoughtfully.

'Do you know, I think you might be on to something, Kitty. And it's a business you could grow from home. Even when you were a very little girl, you had very firm ideas about your birthday parties,' she observed, looking, thought Kitty, a bit misty-eyed. 'What do you think you'd need to start up?'

'Well, the money the *West Life Journal*'s going to

pay me for the photo will buy me a few mismatched plates and some trinkets,' she volunteered, thinking aloud.

'Half your gran's stuff is still in the loft,' Alys said, leaning forward. 'We brought it with us when we moved and I never did get round to sorting it out. You should have a look at that, too.'

For the first time in months, Kitty began to feel some control over her life. She would start small, do plenty of research, accumulate some stock, maybe try an ad in the local paper. It was a really great idea and would show Adam that she wasn't going to slob around waiting for her parents to bail her out. She glanced over, hoping to catch a look of approval, just in time to see him pick up his bucket and trudge past her with his mouth set in a grim line. The baby joined in with a little kick of protest. Too bad, thought Kitty; her life-changing moment had arrived and nothing was going to stop her.

Penmorfa, thought Coralie, spotting the small gathering in the glasshouse, had been a safe haven, at least until Gethin Lewis showed up, but unless she wanted a very lonely life, there were risks she would have to take. It seemed to her, on her last visit, that Ned was dealing better with his situation. She was less afraid of what he might do. It would be a relief to send the occasional letter and maybe it would help her own compulsion to turn up in person every month.

Sullen clouds threatened rain and a stiff wind shook the life out of some of the display plants. As she quickened her pace, Adam came storming out of the glasshouse, looking as if he'd like to shake someone too and she just managed to jump out of the way as he flung a bucket of dirty water over one of the raised beds.

She was already feeling jittery about what she was facing, but no one could say that she hadn't done her bit to save Penmorfa from going the way of so many small villages dying for lack of resources. Alys, sitting on one of the benches, looked up and scowled as she came in. It wasn't quite the reaction she was hoping for. Looking at her expression, Coralie felt quite sorry for Kitty. If she'd been on the receiving end of that a few times no wonder she'd been a bit hesitant about telling her mother she was pregnant.

'I thought we were friends,' Alys said, wagging a finger at her. 'You've been living here for the best part of a year now. We thought you were one of us.'

'I am.' Coralie blinked, feeling some of the wind leave her sails. 'That's why I need to talk to you.'

Kitty stopped pretending to fiddle around with a seed tray and scuttled over to sit next to her mother. Leaning back, she forgot to hide her stomach and Coralie could see that although the exceptionally cold weather meant that outside only a few buds were swelling, Kitty didn't seem to have been affected.

Now two pairs of eyes blazed at her.

'Does the Hall Management Committee still have access to the ACORN loan?' she asked, quietly.

Alys folded her arms, and Kitty laid a protective hand on them.

'I've been thinking it over and I can't not help, can I? Not when this is the only way to pay off the loan quickly. So, I've told Gethin that if you can take care of Rock and Sweet Cleans for me, I'll sit for a portrait.'

Alys rushed over and gave her a hug, then Kitty joined in, too.

'Oh, thank you,' said Alys, pinching her cheek. 'That's brilliant, I'm so glad you've agreed to help the village. Just think of all the people who'll benefit from this, all the coffee mornings, cake sales and classes that can be restarted – you won't regret it.'

No, thought Coralie, crossing her fingers. But they might.

CHAPTER 12

'Welcome to New York, Coralie,' said Gethin, looking pleased with himself as he bent his head to kiss her lightly on the cheek. 'I knew I could count on you to do the right thing.'

'For Penmorfa,' Coralie added, still trying to catch her breath. Hardly surprising then that her head was spinning. And if her legs felt unsteady, she told herself, it was nothing to do with the rough touch of his stubble setting her skin tingling, nor was it the low, delicious murmur of his voice as he said her name. Gethin's cramped diary had meant squeezing the sittings in during the week leading up to his new exhibition. Alys might have been delighted with the speed of events, but it had meant a frantic three weeks for Coralie, who'd scrambled to leave the business in a state that someone else could manage whilst she was away.

'That's understood,' he murmured, with a smile. 'Why else would you come all this way?'

'You didn't leave me much choice,' she pointed out. 'Not if I wanted to carry on living in the village.'

'Shape up or ship out.' He laughed softly. 'Why do you think I left the place?'

Stay calm, she ordered herself, taking a deep breath. She had to keep a sense of purpose about this trip. All she had to do was sit in a studio, what was the worst that could happen?

Her sudden urge to flee became more urgent when she noticed what was going on over Gethin's shoulder. Some half-a-dozen students – all attractive women, Coralie noted – a stunning naked female model and Gethin's spiky assistant, Ruby, were all looking at her. The collective message seemed to be to wish her back to the other side of the Atlantic. It wasn't a great starting point, but what really bothered Coralie was the naked model.

'Didn't anyone mention that you'd signed up to being painted in your birthday suit?' teased Gethin, following her glance.

'That "Calendar Girls" stuff is a fund-raising cliché,' she replied, her nonchalant tone rather ruined by the blush she could feel creeping across her face.

'It certainly is if the *Merched y Wawr* are involved. You'd want more than a few strategically placed buns to hide that lot,' he grinned. 'Let me finish up here and we'll compare notes on what we're going to do for this painting. Naked doesn't have to be clichéd, you know.'

Coralie's stomach growled at him. At least one part of her still had some sense left. She took a

154

seat, trying to be inconspicuous whilst the lesson proceeded.

'I love this here. The way you've captured the curve of the hip is really beautiful,' Gethin was saying, sweeping his hands across one easel in a gesture that seemed to have the entire class holding their breath. 'Good work.'

At this praise, his student, a brunette wearing large silver hoop earrings and a small camisole top, despite the frigid temperature outside, ran the tip of her tongue over her wet lips, as if they were indulging in a spot of foreplay rather than discussing a picture. Bewitched, bothered, and bewildered, thought Coralie, although it was difficult not to be moved by a man who did such wonderful things for a dark pair of jeans and had a voice that could make the electoral register sound like *Under Milk Wood*.

'Hey, lady! New York ain't a postcard. You gotta do it, not look at it,' the taxi driver had advised earlier as they arrived outside the historic art school. It was true that she *had* spent the entire journey gasping at the cityscape unfolding before her. Privately, she'd been convinced that there were few surprises in a city she thought she knew from so many films and television series, but the screen images were no preparation for the real thing.

Penmorfa was beautiful, but this was breathtaking in a way that she just hadn't anticipated. The early spring sunshine gilded ten thousand windows of the modern skyscrapers, turning the glass to pale gold mosaics against a clear blue sky. Byzantine arches on the older buildings soared upwards to where the dark tracery of balconies, pinnacles and water towers stretched out into the distance. Yellow cabs buzzed through the streets and lights blazed in all kinds of bars and restaurants.

Yet all that exhilaration and energy couldn't quite stop her feeling of nervous excitement whenever she thought about the reality of coming face-to-face with Gethin again. It wasn't just the sight of the art school, with its imposing stone façade and splendidly ornate window arches, that had made her so reluctant to leave the cab.

Gethin had offered her the choice of meeting him during his morning class or later, for lunch. Coralie reasoned that seeing him at work would give her an idea of what it was she was letting herself in for. She hoped he wasn't arrogant enough to believe she'd only turned up so early because she was impatient to see him, as it clearly wasn't true. She glanced up now to prove to herself that that really was the case and to demonstrate her interest in the lesson, but found her gaze straying to the teacher. Except that Gethin had beaten her to it and was studying her with amused interest.

Now she remembered that she wasn't the only one with an agenda. What was he up to? Mentally mixing colours to match her skin tone? She could feel her cheeks beginning to burn again as the reality of being under such close scrutiny started to kick in. Then his face broke into a smile that made her heart skip with pleasure before she ordered it to calm down and behave.

'Okay everyone, that's it for today,' he said, clapping his hands and ignoring the disappointed groans. 'Ruby will take over and answer any questions whilst you pack up. Same time next week.'

He picked up his leather jacket and strode towards her. Her stomach rumbled another loud warning and he laughed. 'Come on, there's a diner on the corner of the block.'

Where hopefully the coffee was served in the bucket-sized cups she'd need to clear her head so she could talk sensibly to Gethin. A stack of fluffy pancakes and a lake of syrup wouldn't hurt either; imagine how her depleted blood sugars and flagging metabolism would thank her for it.

Behind his back, Ruby, her head on one side and her startled white crop giving her the look of a small, fierce budgie, had been making Angry Bird faces at her since she'd met her in reception. She seemed to think that one of her duties was to defend Gethin from all-comers and had taken Coralie's bag with a very suspicious look. Coralie ignored her. Anyway, she hadn't come all this way to be liked, but to help seal the deal for Penmorfa's Hall Management Committee, Alys in particular. If anyone had a right to be worried it was Alys. Securing a large loan was one thing, making the repayments quite another. What would Alys do if anything went wrong?

Coralie's mouth went dry just thinking about the prospect. As a businesswoman it was in Alys's interest to rebuild the community; how else could the garden centre expand and grow without local people to work and shop there? But Coralie sensed there was more to it than that, that somewhere Alys had a personal investment in this project. Coralie comforted herself with the thought that all she had to do was make sure that Alys ended up with a painting. She could do that, couldn't she? It wasn't as if she'd been asked to bungee jump off the Empire State Building. Hey, the model today had managed to stand there stark naked without being the slightest bit self-conscious. Then she glanced at Gethin, who gave her a wolfish grin and she remembered that she didn't have to take her clothes off to feel exposed.

Gethin couldn't wait to get Coralie in his studio. Just looking at her closing her eyes whilst she sucked the last of the syrup off her spoon made him feel good to be alive.

'Oh, that's better!' she said, offering him a quick, grateful smile across the table. 'Looking at all those hot dog and pretzel vendors on the streets this morning from the taxi must have made me really hungry. I was starting to feel quite light-headed.'

Must have been something in the air affecting him too, thought Gethin. Why else would he have struggled to stay grounded when Coralie appeared in the doorway of his class, turning all the monochrome to colour with her dishevelled chestnut hair and short, flared turquoise jacket?

'How was the hotel?' he asked. 'Did you get any sleep?'

'I wondered if they were expecting any princesses when I saw the size of that room and that huge bed.' She smiled, shooting him a mischievous glance that made him have all kinds of thought about the huge bed. 'Are you sure you're not about to be landed with a right royal bill?'

Gethin frowned, but only because Max, the manager, was finding every excuse in the book to hang round their table. 'Call it a small thank you for agreeing to bunk at Ruby's place for the rest of the week. Are you all right with that?'

Coralie played with her empty cup. 'It was very hospitable of her to have me to stay whilst her roommate's out of town, and besides, you've been more than generous.'

Max, leaning over the table making a show of collecting plates, turned his head so Coralie couldn't see and winked at him.

'More coffee, ma'am?' he asked, returning seconds later with a refill and placing a neatly wrapped package on the table in front of her. 'Chocolate muffin, ma'am. On the house, from the best diner in town. Just so's you'll come back and see us again,' the older man added, looking dazed when Coralie rewarded him with a smile that lit the room. What did he have to do to make her beam at him like that?

'I'll get the bill,' she said, reaching for her purse.

'You making a profit on that business yet?' he asked. 'Because unless you can look me in the eye and tell me you've got money to burn, I'm getting this.'

She opened her mouth to protest and then shrugged.

'Better,' he told her. 'Don't struggle, just give in.'

She threw him a startled look and he had to agree he could have phrased it more subtly. On the other hand, wasn't that exactly what he was thinking? It was all he could do not to reach out for her as she ducked under his arm when he opened the door for her. He couldn't quite believe she'd crossed an ocean to see him, come all the way from Penmorfa. He'd have to be made of stone not to have wanted to pull her to him and kiss her. Steady, boy, he reminded himself, just because she was standing there didn't mean she'd come to see him and certainly not of her own free will. Given half a chance, she'd be off like a shot.

Nevertheless he couldn't help noticing the glow of her cheeks still pink from the crowded diner, where the red vinyl bench seats never had a chance to grow cold. Nor could he miss that small contented sigh as she lifted her face to the fresh air in a way that made him smile and gave him a nice warm feeling.

'Eating is not a problem in this city, but there aren't too many of the true diners like that left,' he said, trying not to think too much about the nice warm feeling. 'Not those comfortable, lived-in kind of places where the food's good, the service is fast and every table's set with Frank's Hot Sauce and Aunt Jemima's. Not in Manhattan. They've torn most of them down and put up fake ones instead. They look the same, but all the heart and soul's been knocked out of them.'

He pointed to a restaurant on the corner. 'Think that's a genuine Italian restaurant? All the Italians have made their money and moved on, so it's somebody else's turn. They're all run by Mexicans now. All is not what it seems here.'

'If that's true, why do you love it here so much?' Coralie asked.

Realising he was in danger of leaving her behind if he walked at his usual pace he slowed down to give her a chance to keep up.

'Why not stay in Penmorfa if you're looking for something down-to-earth and authentic?'

'What? So everyone can tell me how easy I've got it, playing with paints instead of fighting a losing battle running a farm? That's never going to happen.'

Penmorfa had to be really important to her because why else would she fly all this way? All *he* cared about was having an excuse to study her in detail. He allowed himself a good look at her, appreciating the way her rolled bronze curls gleamed and bounced as she tripped along beside him, the concerned compassion creasing her brow.

Wait a minute! He followed her line of vision and spotted one of the city's 'Adopt me' dogs, a skinny little hound in its distinctive orange vest, looking up gratefully at its elderly carer.

'Fosterers slip those on the dogs that need a home before walking them,' he explained, as Coralie cooed over what looked to him like an overgrown bony rat showing off with an extra spring in its spindly legs as it passed them. 'It tells potential adopters that the dog's available.'

'Poor little fellow,' she said, looking stricken.

It was almost worth offering the dumb mutt a home so that her eyes would follow him with the same interest.

'I hope there's a happy ending for him,' she went on, still watching the dog sadly. 'He's very cute.'

'But not your type,' he told her, rolling his eyes. 'You can't take him back on the plane with you. The world is full of dumb creatures, Coralie, not all of them have happy endings.'

And not every home was loving.

'You said you'd escaped to the country,' he mentioned, giving in to his curiosity about what she'd left behind. 'But you never said why. What did you escape from?'

'Why does anyone choose to live in the country?' She smiled, a little too brightly. 'For a better quality of life, of course.'

Bullshit. There was a bust-up behind her, he'd bet on it. 'Having your portrait painted can be very therapeutic,' he told her. Next time Ruby

162

wisecracked about his interest in Coralie, he could confidently reply that she was barking up the wrong tree. The last thing he needed was someone crying on his shoulder over some clown who didn't appreciate her.

One of many advantages of being single was that he didn't have to bother himself with anyone else's concerns, like who did the floral arrangements for that elegant wedding at the Plaza Athénée, or whose fortieth birthday went from wake to baby shower when, at the eleventh hour, she'd found a straight man and got pregnant. Hell, if he'd wanted to listen to emotional problems, he'd have become a hairdresser. At least he could tell his clients to shut their mouths.

'Coming face-to-face with yourself like that shows you all kinds of stuff about yourself.'

A shadow flickered across her face and some of her liveliness and energy abandoned her. Definitely a broken heart. No wonder she went around half the time looking so haunted, but he could take her mind off that.

'Don't worry about it.' He smiled, offering her his arm. 'It's going to be fun. First sitting tomorrow. Early.'

Coralie woke up in a tiny apartment in downtown Manhattan the next day, after a short night of not so much drifting as diving into sleep only to paddle around in the shallows from around three in the morning when her body started telling her it was time to get up. The springs of the sofa bed twanged as she wrenched herself upright, but the room remained disconcertingly black and silent.

She pushed up her eye-mask and winced as the light came flooding in. Ruby was mouthing something at her. Coralie pulled out her earplugs; there was no cure for New York City noise, especially when the apartment was situated on a busy street, but two wodges of pink foam did a lot to absorb it.

'You want coffee?' Ruby repeated.

'Yes, please!' Coralie said, with what she hoped was a grateful, thank-you-for-thinking-of-me smile.

'Get to it then.' Ruby cocked her head towards the tiny windowless kitchenette crammed into an alcove leading off the living room with a hint of sadistic pleasure. 'Gethin doesn't like to be kept waiting. Especially when he's being so generous.'

If he was that generous why couldn't he just put his hand in his pocket and buy Penmorfa a new community hall, thought Coralie, ignoring the distrust with which she was being regarded. She straightened up after digging out her wash bag from her suitcase stashed under the sofa and found Ruby raising her pierced eyebrows at her bargain stripy-cotton gents' pyjamas.

'You know, Gethin never has to ask a woman twice to sit for him, so I'm just wondering what your game is?'

Bunching her fingers into her towel, Coralie chose not to say something she might regret and

164

marched over to Ruby's narrow bathroom. It couldn't have been more of a contrast to her hotel suite, where the vast bathroom was equipped with a gigantic white bath and a silver fountain of a shower. No free samples of bathroom goodies for her to compare with Sweet Cleans products, either. She frowned, temporarily distracted by thoughts that the packaging she'd picked for her range looked somewhat rustic and naïve compared to the sleek toiletries that had been on offer at the hotel. That was something to think about later. For now she had to deal with Ruby.

Coralie was pretty sure she hadn't been doing anything antisocial in her sleep because she was certain she hadn't been asleep for long enough. Maybe the reality of being lumbered with a complete stranger in such proximity was starting to hit home. Recharged by her shower, Coralie had just resolved to try to be extra nice to her hostess when she heard a voice outside the door.

'Hey, I hope you didn't help yourself to any of the hotel's towels. Some of them come with hitch-hikers,' Ruby shouted. 'There are no bedbugs in my life and I'd like it to stay that way.'

Strangely enough, there hadn't been any mention in the hotel literature of the bedbugs that had invaded so many of the city's biggest names. It wasn't, apparently, something Manhattanites liked to boast about. Little wonder then that the hotel air, a notice on the wall explained, had been infused with calming, restorative aromas to revive the weary traveller. Pity she couldn't have chucked some of that into her suitcase.

'So why did you take the risk?' Barging past in a cloud of steam, Coralie dragged on her clothes, shook out her curls and did some quick sums. 'Listen, I appreciate you putting me up, but it's obviously not convenient for me to stay so I'll look for somewhere else.'

'No can do. If you're modelling for Gethin, I want to know where you are.' Ruby scowled. 'Gethin's a great artist. He's got a big exhibition coming up and he doesn't need to chase round Manhattan looking for you. He's really put himself out to fit this portrait into his schedule, you know, and it's my job to see that you jump when he tells you to.'

'No problem,' said Coralie, reaching for her short turquoise jacket. 'Believe me, I want to get this over with as much as you do.'

Ruby stuck a piece of gum in her mouth and chewed on it thoughtfully. 'So why *did* you come all this way if you didn't want your picture painted? Did you think you could get a bit closer to the artist?'

'I'm doing this,' said Coralie, with as much patience as she could muster given that her body was telling her it didn't know which way was up, 'for the sake of the village I love.'

'Playing hard to get, eh?' Ruby nodded. 'Smart tactic. Just don't kid yourself it'll work.'

CHAPTER 13

The Foundered Ship was in full swing. Or it was if you stared at the vicious swirls of the greasy red carpet for too long, thought Kitty. Dark panelled walls and fake beams were enough to give you cabin fever if there were more than five people in the saloon, and a stingy little fire burnt the leg off anyone sitting right next to it, leaving everyone else freezing. According to the calendar it was almost spring, but in Penmorfa the icy winds still gusting across the west Wales coast were keeping tourists away from the Craft Courtyard.

As bored as she was feeling, the novelty of trying out Coralie's products having completely worn off, it was easy to act casually when Adam had put his head round the door of Sweet Cleans to propose knocking off for a quiet lunchtime drink. The Foundered Ship had all the pizzazz of a weak shandy, but the atmosphere was marginally warmer there than at home. With her mother embracing the whole community hall fundraising thing almost to the point of obsession she'd initially felt a bit sorry for her father. Now, she was proud of what her mother had achieved and thought she deserved better than her father's curmudgeonly comments whenever she left the house to attend a committee meeting.

Hefin, behind the bar, looked meaningfully across to the corner where Kitty was trying to hide and winked lasciviously at Adam who was getting the drinks. 'Some pork scratchings for the lady?' he suggested. What a charmer, thought Kitty, shaking her head as Adam turned and raised his eyebrows at her.

Adam hitched his shirt up to dig his wallet out of his back pocket and Kitty stared sorrowfully at his backside and thought how lovely and taut it was, what with all the gardening and surfing. Not that she would be seeing it any time soon. She managed a smile as Adam came towards her and placed a diet cola on the beer mat in front of her. Something, she supposed, that had been put there so that the punters didn't have to chip their glasses off the sticky table. 'Cheers,' said Adam, raising his glass of Brains Dark beer. 'Your very good health and—'

'Yeah, thanks,' she said quickly, conscious that Hefin, leaning over the counter, was making no attempt to hide his shameless eavesdropping. She turned her attention back to Adam, giving him another smile so he wouldn't think she was being grouchy. She'd had time to nip into the loo and had managed to make a passable stab at looking glamorous without seeming to have tried too hard. Just the two coats of mascara, foundation, blusher and a slick of pink lip gloss.

Adam was fussing round, asking if she was warm enough and if her chair was comfortable. 'You know, that diet cola stuff has a lot of rubbish in it, artificial sweeteners and all that. I don't think you should be drinking it anymore. Let me get you some fruit juice instead. You ought to be thinking about the—'

'I am!' she hissed, nodding at Hefin who was still hanging on their every word. 'Flip, I've barely drunk anything but water for months now.'

'I think you've been cheating on that diet,' Hefin called over. 'Looks to me like you've put on a few pounds.'

Kitty was about to tell him what he could go do with himself, but she knew that part of her anger was sheer disappointment that there was no chance of Adam even making a token gesture to get her into bed. She was heartily sick of being treated like a pregnant Mother Teresa. The door creaked open, and Wilfie shuffled in, both hands deep in his trouser pockets, jangling his change. He wasn't a pretty sight, but Kitty was delighted to see him because whilst he was droning on about real ale to Hefin, she could concentrate on trying to show Adam she was still a woman.

'Will you let me have a feel?' Adam asked, his eyes shining.

Not perhaps the most romantic approach she'd ever had but a good sign nevertheless. 'What, in front of all these people?' She laughed, looking round the almost empty saloon.

'Well you don't have to take anything off, do you?' Adam smiled.

'Depends what you're trying to feel.' She giggled.

'You know.' He eyed her stomach. 'I just want to feel the baby kicking. That would be wicked.'

Kitty looked round in alarm, but one of the beer pumps running dry was causing a diversion over at the bar.

'Can we not talk about this here?' she begged.

'Sorry,' he said, with a sheepish smile that revealed his chipped front tooth. 'You're the first girl I've felt I could ask. Couldn't exactly go up to any of my mates' wives or girlfriends and put my hands on their stomachs, could I?'

'Why not? You're not usually afraid to cop a feel, are you?' The hurt flared up in his eyes and her pithy comment felt plain mean.

'Yeah, thanks, Kitty. Nice to know how little you think of me, like I'm some kind of low-life.' He put down his glass and started to move away, but she managed to get a hand across the table in time.

'Please don't go,' she said quickly. 'I was out of order.' She took a deep breath and wished she could explain just how depressing it was that she only had his attention because he was interested in the baby, not because he'd changed his mind about her. She stared down at his hand beneath hers, waiting for her vision to stop swimming with tears.

'Hey,' he said, touching his other hand to her

chin and lifting it so he could look at her. 'What's all this?'

'Hormones,' she whispered, because she knew that's what he'd want to hear.

'Got to be.' He pressed his knuckles very gently into her cheek. 'You're not usually so sensitive about calling me names.'

'Yeah, well. You're not usually so sensitive when I do. You are allowed to say stuff back, you know. I'm still the same person I was last summer.'

He dragged his green gaze away from her and when he turned back his expression was bleak. They both knew it wasn't true. Kitty did a quick check – Hefin and Wilfie were still farting around trying to restore the flow of Old Blue Tongue, or whatever the guest beer happened to be, so she sidled closer to Adam and grabbed hold of his free hand.

'There,' she said, placing his palm over her stomach just in time to catch the ripple of limbs moving inside.

'Whoa!' said Adam, his delight infectious, making them both break into giggles.

'What's going on over there?' Hefin called over sharply. 'We don't want any petting in this pub, thank you.' Another flaccid, frothy sound from the recalcitrant pump spared Kitty having to tell him that chance would be a fine thing. Even so, Adam moved away again, putting some distance between them and ruining their moment of intimacy.

'You're not serious about this Flair on a Shoestring

171

stuff, are you?' he asked, looking worried. 'I mean, it's not just a question of arranging a few bits and pieces, is it? You've got to lift boxes and climb ladders, too.'

Anyone would think he was the one carrying the baby, she thought mutinously. 'So? Look, I'm not going to take any risks, am I? I can't afford to put myself out of business before I've got started.'

'I wasn't thinking about the business.' He glared at her.

'It's a good job that I am then,' she said, glaring back. 'How do you think I'm going to provide for – what you're thinking about – if I don't start planning for the future? I can't live on thin air. Besides, you're the one who's always accusing me of sitting around on my backside, sponging off Mam and Dad. I thought you'd be pleased for me!'

Adam looked beaten. 'What about the father?' he asked, flatly. 'Whatever you think about him, he's involved. Surely he ought to face up to his financial responsibilities?'

'Ha!' she said, nastily. 'He wouldn't know what a responsibility was if it hit him in the face. Trust me, Adam, it's better that I do this on my own.'

'Sitting comfortably?' Ruby asked over Gethin's shoulder.

Coralie harrumphed at her and concentrated on the morning sun rosily reflected in the tall buildings she could see from Gethin's rented Upper

West Side studio. Having overcome her initial nerves, she wondered what she'd been so worried about. So long as she sat there and did as she was told, no one really took any notice of her. No wonder portraiture was peopled by so many serious subjects; Whistler's mother, probably bored out of her mind, Ophelia turning blue in a cold bath unnoticed by Millais, Lucien Freud's benefits supervisor, not exactly having a laugh a minute. Kitty said Gethin was known as a fast worker. Coralie hoped she was right.

Leaning back a little, Coralie could just see a roof garden in miniature below, with tall grasses and shrubs and a palette of flowers from white through to pale pink. Whilst she was looking, a doll-sized woman appeared, apparently in her dressing gown, and arranged herself on a cushioned lounger. She looked far more comfortable than Coralie, who was sitting on a rag-covered stool. Especially since the stool was balanced on a plank placed across two crates.

'Eyes to me,' Gethin ordered. 'Or you'll fall over.'

'I thought you said you didn't expect your sitters to assume difficult positions,' she grumbled.

'What's difficult about sitting down?' If he was hoping to sound innocent, he'd blown it with a flash of those wicked blue eyes. 'You're the right height for the light, that's all. Just do as you're told and it'll all be over with before you know it.'

At least Ruby appreciated the joke, grinning and shaking her head as she handed him a new brush.

If doing what she was told meant the painting would be finished quickly, then fine. So, if Gethin wanted her to look at him then, dammit, she'd do just that. It wasn't so hard to do. He was wearing old jeans that had seen much better days, but hugged his hips attractively, and a loose-fitting shirt that had once been navy blue. If she knew more about paint colours she might have been able to name some of those decorating it, but she was more interested in the fact that a couple of the top buttons were undone. When he leaned forward her lofty position afforded her the odd tantalising glimpse of his chest, which was entertaining even if it did remind her of their first meeting.

'I do hope Rock's all right,' she said out loud. He'd been a bit cool with her since the mouse incident and she hadn't really had time to make it up to him.

'Hudson?' said Ruby, wringing out a rag at the surgical-looking steel sink. 'Didn't you know he left the building with Elvis?'

'This Rock was reborn as an alley cat.' Gethin stood back and frowned at her when she moaned in protest. 'Coralie, he's almost feral. He foraged for himself before you came along, and he's smart enough to know a soft touch when he sees one.'

'He was in a very sorry state when he first started hanging around,' she remonstrated. 'His eyes were runny, he wasn't keeping himself clean and he was practically starving.'

Gethin shook his head. 'And now you think you've got him eating out of your hand – except he knows it's the other way round.'

Good teeth too, thought Coralie, sighing as he gave her a wry smile before returning to his work. Kitty had joked that the real reason Gethin had left Penmorfa was because he'd run out of women. 'Likes his freedom too much, see. Plenty of farmers round here, desperate for a wife, but not Gethin Lewis. Well, not one of his own, anyway.'

It was true that the iron bedstead with its crumpled sheets standing at one end of the studio looked as if it had seen plenty of action, although with no blinds at the long windows it was very public, even this high up. Gethin, seeing her giving it a wild look, like a frightened horse, when they'd first entered the long, stripped-back room, had raised his eyebrows at her. 'Relax,' he'd told her. 'It's a prop. Now go behind the screen and take your top off. Ruby will make sure you're decent. Oh, and I'd like you to wear your hair down, please.'

So much for all that stuff about the erotic tension between artist and model, the voyeur-painter with his sexualised gaze reducing his sitter to an object of lust. Anything less erotic than her hard perch was hard to imagine and, for all the tension when he studied her, she was beginning to wonder if he'd even noticed she was a woman.

Also, whilst he was undeniably decorative, Gethin wasn't stopping her bottom from going to sleep. She shifted a buttock and the plank wobbled.

'To me!' Gethin growled. So much for all the fun he'd suggested it might be. Outside, the sunlight had turned pale lemon, but the studio remained cool. The white walls and white-tiled splashback behind the sink were made more clinical by the metal tables which looked as if they'd originally been intended for use in an operating theatre. Even though they were laid out with brushes and paints rather than forceps and retractors, the effect was equally daunting; both sets of tools could open you up in strange and unexpected ways.

She caught his eye and he smiled at her lazily and almost sent her flying.

'You look as if you're on a throne,' he explained. 'Penmorfa's Queen of Clean.'

Why did he make it sound as if she was repressed? Ruby guffawed.

'What's wrong with that?' Coralie complained. 'It keeps a lot of local suppliers busy. I source wax from a beekeeper near Cardigan, lavender flower heads from a grower on the Pembrokeshire borders and herbs from the garden centre.'

'Everything you ever needed right on your doorstep, then?' he said, dabbing at the canvas.

Coralie bit her lip. Why did it sound so unadventurous when he said it? It wasn't as if she hadn't taken any risks; doing her accounts often made her pulse race. And she had plans – just looking at some of the window displays in the huge department stores on 5th Avenue had given her fresh ideas for the business. Having her own doorstep was a good thing; most of her single friends were still renting, but because she'd been prepared to move to an undiscovered area, she'd been able to stretch to buying. And what a beautiful area it was too, with a breathtaking coastline and stupendous view from the cliffs of dramatic churning surf. Of course she was happy!

It was just occasionally, when one of her friends announced her engagement or if she received another excited call about a new baby, that the evenings in Penmorfa seemed especially quiet. And once in a while, when she scattered confetti over another happy couple, she felt a lump in her throat and wondered if there was a man out there who could love her for who she was. There was always Wilfie, she supposed, if she needed some male company, although thinking it over, she didn't need male company *that* much.

Gethin came out from behind his easel. His ruffled dark hair made her thoughts stray to wondering how it would feel to push her fingers through it. What would it be like, she tried to imagine as he lifted his chin and ran his hand across his stubbled jaw, to feel the hard, rough touch of his skin against hers? Now, if she was more like Kitty, she wouldn't be wasting time thinking about it, she'd be grabbing some excitement whilst she could. Coralie came to and found him glowering at her with passionate intensity. Had the sight of her, wobbling on a stool, with her bra straps pulled down beneath some orange sheet thing Ruby had wrapped round her, pushed him over the edge?

'Your shoulders are drooping and you're fidgeting around all over the place,' he complained, throwing his brush down. 'No wonder I can't get this right. Okay, everyone, we'll have to leave it there.'

'Not going so well, eh?' said Ruby, once Gethin had sent Coralie off to explore the stores, because he couldn't stand the frustration of looking at her and not being able to paint her any longer. 'Why's that?'

Gethin scratched his head to see if it would stimulate his brain into coming up with an answer he liked better. 'Post success stress?'

Ruby laughed. 'That's a new name for it.'

He pointed to the brushes in the sink, indicating that she should get on with it. 'I'm serious. Everything's ready for the exhibition, but there'll be the usual merry-go-round with the press to deal with afterwards.'

'The press come with the joy of being the people's painter,' Ruby said above the noise of the running tap. 'Remember that when you get your next print royalties.'

Make that 'if', he nearly admitted. According to his solicitor, the administrators who'd taken over the firm that had handled all the reprints were still doing their best to avoid settling up with him.

'Of course,' he acknowledged airily, 'but it makes it hard to concentrate on a new work.'

'Something's hard,' Ruby muttered.

Gethin strolled over, leaned against the sink so he could glare at her more easily and folded his arms. 'I beg your pardon?'

'Making a decision,' she said, shaking out a wet brush so that it sprayed over his shoulder. 'You see, I've spent many hours watching you in this studio. You flirt, charm, pay compliments so the sitter relaxes, but all the time, you're watching and working. A brush stroke here, a retouch of colour there – you're fast, perceptive, you flatter them with a sheen of glamour so they'll tell their friends, who'll want the same. But this time,' she looked at him with an amused grin, 'you don't even know where to begin.'

'Don't be ridiculous!' He snorted. 'I'll just have to study her more closely.'

He turned his back on Ruby whose penetrating gaze had all the innocence of an Exocet. Yep, that's what he'd do. The more opportunities he had to study his subject, the better her portrait would be. And once he'd painted out his current obsession, he could get back to his normal, untroubled life and stop thinking crazy thoughts about Coralie Casey.

CHAPTER 14

'This sitting's cancelled,' he told Coralie when she turned up at the studio the next morning, ignoring Ruby who was smirking at him knowingly.

'We'll run out of time if we don't get on with it,' said Coralie, not looking best pleased.

'Not all guys can perform on demand,' Ruby butted in, shrugging her shoulders and rolling her gum round her cheeks.

He fixed her with a death-ray glare. 'If you'd just let me explain,' he went on, 'I'm cancelling the sitting because we're going out for the day instead. It's just as valid a way of building up a picture of you as studying you in my studio.'

Better, in fact, he thought, ignoring Coralie's doubtful expression, because he wouldn't have Ruby psychoanalysing him or sniggering at him behind his back.

Battery Park was one of his favourite places. As much as he enjoyed the hustle and bustle of the city, he liked the breezy walk along the waterfront, enjoying all the contrasts like the juxtaposition between the upscale condos and the monuments to the past. Once upon a time important visitors arriving by sea were heralded by enormous jets of water pumped into the sky by fireboats from Pier A. If, like him, those crews could see Coralie's hair making such a vibrant splash of colour against the shimmering blues of the Hudson River, the big sky and the glass towers of New Jersey glinting on the opposite bank, he was sure they'd be out there again today, queuing up to pay tribute.

He'd taken her to the National September 11 Memorial first; the water, like so many tears, cascading down into the pools where the Twin Towers once stood. So many lost and fractured lives. In a palpably sad and sombre atmosphere, they'd stood to pay their respects before moving on. Now, drawn by the bright sunshine on another freezing cold day, they joined the couples strolling along the Esplanade, the joggers and dog-walkers proof that ordinary life and simple pleasures could and should resume after tragedy.

He turned to her, hoping to see her big smile widening with pleasure and was taken aback by her glum expression.

'Oughtn't we be getting back to the studio now?' she asked, an anxious frown creasing her brow. 'Six sittings, you said. This is my third day here – how are we going to fit them all in?'

'You know, your haste to get away from me is a little indecent,' he told her, slightly miffed that he wasn't making half the impression on her as she was on him. 'Especially since you kept me waiting so long in the first place.'

'Why draw this thing out any longer than is necessary?' She shrugged, with another frown. 'Shouldn't you get it out of the way so that you can concentrate on your exhibition?'

'The more I concentrate on you,' he reminded her, 'the quicker we'll be done. Just relax, will you, or you'll risk missing what's so fantastic about this city. Take a look at that, for example.' He pointed to the waterfront.

'Oh! It *is* beautiful,' she said, and he could see some of the tension leave her shoulders. 'It's a vast stretch of water, so much bigger than I expected! And it's wonderful to smell sea air again!'

She pushed her hair back as the spring breeze lifted it in a ripple of copper waves.

Nope, he thought, trying to frame the image to keep in his mind's eye, he definitely wouldn't have been able to catch that joyous expression in his studio. The idea of simply walking round with her was a stroke of genius, except that everywhere they went would always be indelibly stained by the memory of her, which didn't seem quite so clever. He was willing to bet there was nothing in the Sweet Cleans range strong enough to wipe away anything like that.

'Anyone would think you'd been away from it for weeks,' he told her. 'You're not feeling that cooped up already, are you?'

A pair of cute girls in running vests jogged

towards them, but he was too busy watching Coralie, waiting for her to wrinkle her nose, or tilt her head on one side whilst she thought about it. All the funny little expressions he was learning about.

'This city's amazing, but I wouldn't want to move away from the sea,' she said, with a quick, shy smile that made him catch his breath. 'Not now I can walk to the beach every day.'

And he wouldn't go back to Penmorfa, not once he'd discharged his duties there. He'd made his mind up about that a long time ago, only now when he thought about it, it made him feel depressed. He shot a quick glance at Coralie just to prove to himself that it was nothing to do with her and saw that she was rapt at the sight of a Chihuahua dressed in a pink frock and sitting in a buggy being pushed by an elderly Japanese woman. Another dumb mutt had beaten him to her affection.

Not that he was looking for her affection, he reminded himself. She wasn't even his type, he thought, taking a quick mental note of the way her eyes crinkled with amusement. His preference was for women who knew how to play the game. Who wouldn't bug him in the morning, or nag him for an engagement ring. Coralie was just a lovely, uncomplicated woman trying to live the good life in the countryside – although once she woke up to the reality, she'd find, like all the rest of the incomers in search of the dream, that you couldn't spin gold out of straw. It still peeved him that she didn't even seem to notice he was there.

Still, it wasn't all bad if he experienced the odd frisson. In the studio it would add something extra to the painting and Ruby would have to eat her words and praise his dedication to his work. But something was upside-down when he was starting to take account of what Ruby thought, he frowned to himself. Who was the master and who was the pupil here? Besides, he had the rest of his life to think about work, but less than a week to think about Coralie. It was plain good manners to see that she got the most out of her visit.

She suddenly grabbed his arm. 'Look!' she said, as if he'd never noticed it before, 'the Statue of Liberty! And I was so determined not to be impressed,' she said, darting in front of another jogger for a better look. 'I've seen it so many times on screen – but it just takes your breath away, doesn't it?'

'You think it would survive as such an enduring symbol if you could pin it down so easily?' he asked, trying to ignore the voice that was asking him if he wasn't trying to do just that with the real live woman in front of him. 'Everyone thinks they know New York from the movies, but you have to be here to know how it really feels.'

'No wonder so many immigrants have been so inspired by the sight!' She leaned out across the rails, trying to get a better view of Ellis Island, where the ships bringing new arrivals had once docked.

'Nearly twelve million people have passed through the gates there,' he told her. 'Some of them probably came from Penmorfa. When the railways came in the nineteenth century, it put the old cargo ships that used to dock at Abersaith out of business. The industries that served them declined, meaning hard times for the surrounding villages, too. The next wave of ships to dock at Abersaith came to carry Welsh emigrants away to New York. The architect Frank Lloyd Wright's family was amongst those who made the long Atlantic crossing.'

Leaving the life blood of the little towns to drain away ever since, as men like him turned their backs on the old ways. 'You've got to ask yourself why they all left,' he added, more for his own benefit.

'Looking at this, they must have believed they really were on the brink of a brave new world.' Coralie turned to face him so that the vivid seascape glistened behind her.

'Yep,' he said, drawing her back from the rail to sit on one of the benches. 'Once they were off that boat, they could be whoever they liked.'

'Is that what you did?' she asked. 'Left the boy behind in Penmorfa and became a famous artist here?'

'Coralie,' he said, 'I came by plane. It's not quite the same.'

'But you've made your name here,' she insisted. 'I can see how anyone could fall for all this, but surely there must be part of you that still belongs in Penmorfa?'

He took a long, hard look at her and shook his head. 'Not one little bit. Not now. Not ever.'

Coralie was deeply concerned about how little there was to show for what felt like hours spent sitting on a stool, wrapped in an orange sheet.

'Will there be any value in a blank canvas if I persuade you to sign it?' she asked, chewing her lip. After a second and then a third session during which Gethin freely distributed his scowls between her, the canvas and Ruby, whose mission seemed to be to wind Gethin up, the portrait had barely progressed. With only two full days of her trip left to go, she wondered if they could hoodwink the art world into believing it was a bold step in a new direction.

Even Ruby's pierced eyebrows raised when he called yet another halt to the sitting and proposed a further sightseeing tour instead. 'It's too good a day to miss the view,' he'd insisted, when she'd been half-hearted about seeing the Empire State Building. 'And look, there's not even too much of a queue.'

Coralie followed him in to the marble-lined entrance lobby with its towering relief image of the skyscraper superimposed on a map of New York State. All that glitz only made her suspicious that it was designed to soften the blow that the view probably wasn't all it was cracked up to be.

'All this trailing round the tourist traps,' she said,

looking up at him. 'You're not trying to tell me something, are you? You haven't changed your mind about donating a painting to Penmorfa, have you?'

'Indulge me, Coralie.' He shook his head as he handed her her ticket. 'Pander to my artistic ego. If I have a yearning to show you the view, that's what we'll do.'

A small observation deck right up in the sky couldn't possibly offer many places to hide. If he thought he could wriggle out of answering her question, she decided, smiling to herself as they piled into one of the first set of elevators, he'd have no choice but to hear her out once they were up there.

'We can go outside on the 86th floor observation deck, but I wanted you to see this first,' he said, leading her over to more elevators.

The highest observation deck was closed in, wasn't it? That was good; he couldn't even pretend that the wind was carrying her words away.

'All the way up to the tippy-top!' the operator announced, shutting the doors behind them.

The only problem was that standing beside Gethin, as the old-fashioned lift cage climbed steadily to the 102nd floor, she was beginning to lose sight of her goal. It was getting harder and harder to keep her feet firmly on the ground. Gethin had spent an awful lot of time with her; was it only because he was serious about his work? And when he grinned down at her like that, exuding excitement and danger, was it simply because he needed to get a better look at her? The Empire State Building's Art Deco spire was once intended as a mooring mast for airships, but if she wasn't very careful, she'd also be floating on air. The operator pulled open the doors and Gethin led her outside to the observatory.

'The view here's even more spectacular and it's less crowded. Three hundred and sixty degrees of the Big Apple.'

Coralie sucked in her breath, all her preconceived ideas about hype blown away by the reality of seeing the city spread out before her.

'Now tell me you're not impressed,' he said, triumphantly. 'You think you've got views in Penmorfa, but they're nothing like this.'

'You may have a point,' she admitted, giving in. The Chrysler spire looked fabulous glittering against the Manhattan skyline and the backdrop of the East River. And from here, she thought, turning and looking down, she could see how the distinctively shaped Flatiron building got its name, too.

'There's the Great Lady again,' said Gethin, leaning over her shoulder and pointing to the Statue of Liberty rising from New York Bay. 'I bet you're glad you let me take you all the way now.'

Kitty would have said they hadn't even got off first base. It was a difficult thought to ignore, especially when he was close like that. A young American woman, her rich brown hair tied up in a ponytail, waiting by the elevator with a couple who could have been her parents, caught her eye and smiled.

'Hey, you guys look happy,' she said, pointing at Coralie's camera. 'Want me to take a picture of you, before we go?'

Judging that it was less embarrassing to simply submit rather than explain, Coralie handed her camera over. The worst that could happen was that she might have been suckered by a camera snatcher, but since it was an entirely average piece of kit, this seemed unlikely.

Vertigo, she decided when Gethin pulled her nearer, forcing her to meet his twinkling blue eyes. That must be why her stomach had given a little lurch.

'Aw! That's great!' cooed their new pony-tailed fan. 'You guys make such a cute couple!'

'That's very kind of you,' Gethin told her as she handed the camera back. 'Now we'll always have something to remind us of today, won't we, sweetheart?'

She gave him a look and he grinned back at her, deep blue eyes full of mischief. Definitely vertigo, she told herself. What else would explain that giddy feeling when he leaned close to her? Or the tingle of excitement when he rested his fingers lightly on her shoulder? In case of a sudden fit of light-headedness, she decided it was wise to hang on to him whilst he pointed out all the famous landmarks. There was Brooklyn

Bridge, 800 acres of Central Park, iconic buildings like the New York Times everywhere she looked and beyond, in the distance, Connecticut, New Jersey, Pennsylvania and Massachusetts. All the places which had just been names to her but which she'd forever associate with one day in New York when she felt as if she was on top of the world.

A lick of black glass nagged at the corner of her vision for attention. Kitty's voice told her to ignore it and concentrate on the good feelings, but curiosity got the better of her. Leaning forward for a better look, she recognised it as the hotel where she had spent her first night in the city and she came back down to earth. Playing the tourist was all very well, but imagine what would have happened at the consultancy if she'd allowed herself to be so distracted from the task in hand? What would Alys do if she returned to Penmorfa empty-handed?

Gethin frowned at her. 'Something bugging you, Coralie? Why can't you just relax and enjoy me showing you round?'

'I guess I'm just not very good at relaxing,' she said, trying to smile.

'Then I'm going to have to find a way to make you.' He sighed. 'These sittings are going nowhere. For a start you're going to have to trust me.'

He took her arm as she raised it in protest, moving her along as a tall, pale-skinned Russian couple, exotic in their expensive designer sunglasses, came up to look out of the window beside them. 'Stop trying to control everything, Coralie. Not everything's neat and tidy or sweet and clean, but that's what makes it exciting. Why don't you let go and see what happens?'

He reached over and took both of her hands in his, rubbing his thumbs over her short, neatly manicured nails. 'What are you scared of?'

'Nothing.' Coralie took her hands back. 'I just want to do my best for Penmorfa, that's all,' she said, stubbornly.

'But that's not why you're afraid,' he said, leading her towards the elevator. 'Do you want to be like the kid on the beach who watches everyone else have fun? Put it behind you, whatever it is. Sometimes you've just got to accept that you can't build sandcastles without getting your hands dirty.'

'Going down,' the operator announced as the elevator doors opened.

A bit like me, thought Coralie, feeling her spirits sinking along with her stock. Producing a range of cleaning products didn't mean that everything about her was necessarily snow white.

'Look, we'll give it another shot tomorrow morning,' he said, as they stopped again at the 86th floor. 'Then I'll have to put in an appearance at the gallery, before the reception for the new show.'

Coralie nodded, determined not to let her bruised ego spoil the opportunity to experience that amazing view of the city from the open-air observatory. Raw air rushing towards them and people jostling for the best views made conversation difficult, giving her a few moments for reflection whilst she waited. For all her protests, she had started to feel quite intrigued about her portrait. Surely, you'd need to be made of granite not to be a bit curious about what that deep-blue gaze would reveal? Except she'd been secretly hoping that the person he could see was more like the glamorous, free-spirited dancer in *Samba* than a prim, buttoned-up nobody, afraid of getting creases in her skirt.

By the time they were back in the street again, she'd managed to rally her flagging spirits. With his show about to open, Gethin really didn't need a temperamental model on his hands, too – or any excuse to call off the final sitting.

'I'm really looking forward to the reception, even though it will be my last night here,' she admitted, dredging up a smile. 'It's coming round quickly, isn't it?'

Too quickly. In a very short space of time, she'd got used to being by his side, enjoying the quiet thrill of listening to that wonderful voice, feeling the pride he took in the city he adored. Seeing his new works would be a real privilege – assuming she felt relaxed enough about the painting's progress to enjoy it.

'You're booked for tomorrow evening, too,' he said, rather formally.

'Yes, I suppose we'll need another sitting,' she agreed with relief. Six, he'd told her at the beginning. She hoped that he could produce a finished work in fewer. Penmorfa's future depended on it.

CHAPTER 15

In Penmorfa, Alys, returning from another committee meeting, was just about to open the back door when she caught sight of movement in the kitchen and stopped, feeling terribly sad. The man she could see through the kitchen window, as she stood on the outside looking in, was still her own dear Huw – strong and solid, with warm, brown eyes and silver hair curling into the nape of his neck. But Huw, the man she had loved for all her adult life, no longer pulled her to him.

Their move to the farmhouse, with a bigger mortgage, all the legal costs, and the strain of the recession, had taken its toll on Huw's health and sent his blood pressure soaring. As the one who'd pressed for them to make the change, Alys felt it was her responsibility to do whatever she could to ease their financial burden. But although she was optimistic about the future of the garden centre, especially now Kitty had come up with such an innovative idea to add to their family businesses, it all seemed a bit futile if she'd lost Huw along the way.

She had tried to be understanding when, increasingly, he'd been unable or unwilling to make love, but sometimes she despaired of ever hearing the rise and fall of his breathing beside her in bed again, or of feeling the fortress of his arms wrapping round her.

'Just leave it, will you?' was all he would say when she'd begged him to talk about the problem. But the most hurtful moment had been when he'd taken himself off to the spare room the previous summer, when Alys's hot flushes were keeping them both awake, and just when she was feeling especially insecure. It had been a painful and difficult time. A dark chasm had opened before them, yet somehow they had both, separately, looked over the precipice and had decided to step back from the edge. But even their most casual moments of intimacy were still forced and unnatural.

Nevertheless, Huw smiled as she padded into the room in her socks, having kicked off her boots at the door. 'Your fingers are cold,' he told her, catching her hand just briefly, before turning to pour her a glass of wine. 'Go and sit by the stove and warm up. Kitty's turned in for an early night so we didn't wait for you to eat.'

'Is she unwell?' Alys worried.

Huw pulled a face. 'She's just tired, you know, thinking about this wedding styling scheme of hers. I've saved you some lasagne.'

When Huw placed it before her, she chewed a forkful and forced herself to swallow.

195

'The meeting went on a bit, didn't it?' he said, wiping his hands on the red check tea towel.

'Mair took a bit of convincing before she signed the paperwork. She still can't believe that Gethin's work is worth good money. She's obsessed with how we're going to make the repayments on the loan. What she refuses to see is that it's little more than a paper exercise with the sum we're about to raise from the sale of the painting.

'And then I stayed on to talk to the Vicar. I think she's finding looking after five churches a bit of a struggle. It doesn't help that her husband's academic research has taken him away from home so much lately, of course. I know she misses him when he's not there. Oh, and we've confirmed the date for the official handover of Gethin's painting and the date for the charity auction.'

'Alys, you don't need to account for every minute,' he said lightly.

He ran some hot water and began scraping at the empty lasagne dish. Alys gritted her teeth as the noise went through her and fought the urge to tell him just to leave it to soak. How many more times would she have to remind him that he'd waste less water dumping everything in the dishwasher? Thirty years of marriage and he still made a ritual out of hand washing dishes at the sink. She stopped pushing pasta round her plate and put her fork down.

'Finished?'

She watched his back as he worked at the sink,

196

wiping her plate and rinsing it under the tap. More waste. 'Oh, for goodness sake!' she begged, 'why don't you stop doing that and sit down with me?' He dried his hands again, screwing up the tea towel and leaving it in a damp heap beside the sink. Alys resisted the urge to march over, shake it out and hang it neatly on the stove. Or maybe it was Huw who needed a good shake. Finally, he lowered himself into the Windsor chair at the other side of the long pine table. One of the cats jumped into his lap and Alys watched as his strong fingers burrowed into the soft fur behind its ear as Edith looked on jealously.

'All right, let's talk.'

Alys waited, suddenly nervous.

'When are you going to get round to telling me that our daughter's expecting our first grandchild?'

Alys breathed again. This was not the conversation she would have chosen to have, but it was one they needed to have. Soon she would have to face up to Huw and talk to him about the other problem on her mind. Delyth and Mair might only be stabbing in the dark, but some of their comments were keeping her awake at night. For now, this was a more immediate issue. One thing at a time.

'I haven't discussed it with you, Huw, because so far Kitty hasn't even been able to tell me.' She laid her hand on the table, hoping that he would take it. 'I wanted to give her the opportunity to discuss it with us in her own time. We have to let her come to terms with the changes she's facing in her own way, Huw. She's always worked her problems out by herself, ever since she was a little girl. I'd rather give her some space here, where I can keep an eye on her, than press her and have her take flight. Just try to be patient . . .'

'Don't you think, Alys,' he said, standing up suddenly and sending the cat flying, 'that my patience has been tried enough?'

Alys heard the cut of his breath as he sat in the back lobby and changed his slippers for gardening boots. Edith scampered after him. There was a rasp as he zipped up a fleece, the rustle of waxed cotton as an outdoor coat was shrugged on, then the slamming of the door.

Gethin glanced down at Coralie, who was subdued, at his side. When he'd taken her by surprise that morning and invited her out for an evening date, he'd been secretly hoping for a warmer response, but instead she'd been rather fretful about the lack of progress on the portrait. He had to admit to some mild feelings of concern himself. Great apes had produced superior artwork to his clumsy daubs. Nothing he applied to the canvas came close to capturing Coralie. How tough could it be when those colours and curves just invited themselves to be traced in sensuous strokes?

'So now you've got it so bad you can't even be in the same room as her when you paint,' Ruby had commented that morning, when she'd found him alone in the studio staring impotently at his failed portrait. But Ruby talked a load of rubbish; all he needed was to get a proper look at Coralie. Some talent would help, too.

'I'm taking her to the opera. I think it'll help to catch her off-guard, when she's not so aware of being watched. I can always finish the work later.'

'You're going to have to. There's a lot of setting up to do before the reception. It'll take both of us to keep Pamala Gray happy,' she'd scolded, shaking her head. 'Opera? You said those Puccini arias all sound the same.'

'It's Bizet,' he informed her, trying to gain the upper hand. 'Carmen, acclaimed for the brilliancy of its melody and harmony.'

'"Love is a rebellious bird"', said Ruby, mysteriously, adding in response to his raised eyebrows, 'It's a line from one of the show's big numbers.'

'All right, you proved you know more about opera than me,' he admitted. 'I just want to show her the Met.'

'Just the Met?'

Ruby was always ready to speak her mind, but Coralie was probably too kind to wonder out loud if his skills really were as limited as some critics had suggested. He realised how much her good opinion mattered to him and he was fast running out of time to earn it.

'Now, that's what the tourist guides would recommend you do for a romantic date,' he pointed out as they skirted the corner of Central

Park and saw the lines of horse-drawn carriages waiting to take couples on a tour.

She looked at him warily, but at least it was nice to see her face rather than her cold shoulder.

'And it'll part you with your cash pretty smartish,' he added as an aside, before they turned into West 63rd Street, the constant pulse of yellow cabs just slowing for the lights at Columbus. 'But I think a ride in the park is overrated,' he felt her stiffen beside him, 'compared to this.'

Coralie slowed to a halt and her hand flew up to her mouth as the Lincoln Center and the white façade of the Metropolitan Opera House, with its five distinctive arched windows lit up, appeared in front of them. Gethin wasn't a great believer in guardian angels, but he offered up some silent thanks to his, just in case. If his artistic powers had deserted him, his observant eye served him well. He'd run an inquisitive eye over Coralie's music and film collection, the evening he'd nearly run *her* into a ditch in Penmorfa. One film in particular had attracted his attention because it wasn't anything to do with Doris Day.

'Thank you,' she said, stopping him as they reached the top of the steps before crossing the plaza. 'This is very special. I know this is going to sound silly, but I've always wanted to do this ever since I saw that film, *Moonstruck*. One of my favourite scenes is when Cher, as Loretta Castorini, and Nicolas Cage, as Ronny Cammareri, all dressed up in their evening clothes, are searching the crowds for each other in vain, then catch that first sight of each other by the fountain here.'

'What a coincidence.' He grinned. 'Shame it wasn't a premiere or the season's opener, or we could have done the whole black tie thing.' He thought of her in a strapless evening gown and a waterfall necklace of diamonds and pearls warm in her cleavage.

'That would have been fun, but I'm glad I didn't wear my ball gown tonight, I might have felt a little overdressed,' Coralie admitted, looking at the people swarming towards the doors and the predominantly smart but casual vibe.

Gethin rather wished she had. Somehow it made him think about undressing her; peeling back that cashmere wrap would be a start so that he could see what it was that was silky and sleeveless and floated from her shoulders and swung just above her knees. As it was her distinctive perfume was giving him ideas about nuzzling her neck and burying his face in the feminine, floral scent of her.

'What is that perfume you're wearing?' he asked, lightly, glad that she was too busy soaking up the sights to pay too much attention to his question.

She gave him a quick, wry smile, 'Je Reviens.'

Yep, he ought to be able to see the funny side of that, too. She wouldn't be returning, would she? A couple of days and she'd be out of his life for good. No complications. Just the way he liked it. Since they were just by the fountain, radiant with

201

white light and sparkling in the middle of the plaza, he stopped and stepped back to look at her.

'Coralie, you look beautiful. Thank you for coming with me tonight.' Then he took one of her hands and kissed it. 'How's that, Loretta?' He winked, and felt ridiculously pleased that he'd mugged up on the film when she raised her eyebrows and gave him a delighted smile. The next thing he knew he'd wrapped a hand round her waist, pulling her towards him so he could feel the sweet warmth of her body close against his.

In the maelstrom of voices and footsteps surrounding them, there was a moment of stillness as her smile faded and her soft tawny eyes held his.

'So,' she said, slipping out of his arms, 'are we going inside or is this as far as we get?'

He wanted to tell her he'd like to go much further, only the show was about to begin and her eager glance towards the arched windows showed him how keen she was not to miss it. If the only way he could get her to look at him for any length of time was in the studio, he was certainly losing his touch.

Coralie shuffled forward with the surge of people squeezing through the door behind a silver-haired Japanese man, who was keeping a protective hold of his petite, beautiful wife. At least she could pretend that her burning face was due to the crush of bodies all around her. She must have imagined that seductive message in Gethin's dark eyes.

What would a man like him see in her anyway? She'd overheard one or two cruel comments, back in the days of the management consultancy, from men who'd stereotyped her because of her job and the serious dress code that went with it. And Gethin had already decided that her idea of a good night was the ten o'clock news and a mug of Horlicks, making sure, of course that she'd removed her makeup and brushed her teeth first. The really depressing thing was that he was right.

Once inside the opera house, the sight of the huge Chagall murals each side of a stunning star-burst crystal chandelier made it impossible for her to dwell on wistful thoughts about Gethin Lewis. Instead, she quietly enjoyed the feel of his hand on the small of her back as he gently guided her through the crowds, up the curving white marble staircase carpeted in plush red, to the front row balcony. As she sat there, feeling the strong, comforting pressure of his arm against hers, under the golden glow of the auditorium's gilded ceiling, she made up her mind to forget about the disastrous sittings, to forget about Penmorfa and the church hall fund and simply enjoy every moment of the evening.

'It's about to begin,' Gethin said, leaning closer and pointing at the elaborate crystal chandeliers gracefully rising upwards to open the view of the stage. The excited murmurs and last-minute coughs from the audience reached a crescendo then abruptly died away. Fizzing with pleasurable anticipation, Coralie smiled up at Gethin, who surprised her by reaching across and laying his warm hand over hers. Before she could decide what to do about it, the curtains opened to reveal two figures under an intensely vivid gash of crimson. And as the dancers moved across the stage in a thrilling and tempestuous *pas de deux*, anticipating the love affair between Carmen and Don José, she simply sat back and surrendered herself to the whole experience.

'Oh, that was amazing!' she said, fighting to be heard above the sustained applause which split the dramatic silence at the end of the performance. 'What a production! So professional and such wonderful voices. Mind you, the story's depressing. Poor Don José, he paid a heavy price for falling in love with the wrong girl, didn't he?'

'Yep, they should have listened to Doris. Their lips certainly shouldn't have touched!' He laughed. 'Now, would you like a drink, since you didn't have one in the interval? We can get one here?'

Back to reality. She'd been too busy people-watching, laughing and chatting with Gethin and simply absorbing the atmosphere of the occasion to want to leave her seat during the intermission, but the evening was rapidly drawing to a close. She shook her head, gaining herself some time to squash down the sudden lump in her throat that was making it hard to talk.

'No, you're right.' He reached for her hand as

they stood up to squeeze along the row of seats. 'We'll go somewhere quieter.' He started to edge his way forward. 'Isn't that what always happens in opera?' he asked, over his shoulder, as they waited for a gap. 'They were two people from different sides of the tracks. They were never going to settle down in a cottage with roses round the door and have babies together.'

He could have been speaking about them, thought Coralie, a sudden sense of anti-climax making her feel glum. 'Just because you can see it coming doesn't mean you have to like it,' she mumbled.

He stood back to allow her to thread her way into the queue of people squeezing towards the stairs and fell into step behind her. Imagine if she'd fallen for Gethin Lewis, she thought, trying to ignore the warmth of his body against hers as he ushered her through the throng.

Two people from different sides of the ocean. What chance could there be for them when the place of her dreams was the place of his night-mares? Move over darling? Not a hope; of course it would never work.

'Thank you for tonight, Gethin,' she said, making a determined attempt to compose herself once they were outside. 'I'll always remember it.'

'And so will I, Coralie.' He smiled. 'You may be a lousy model but your face was a picture there. You lived every moment of that story, didn't you?'

Not the opera, she wanted to tell him, the

evening. To put all her problems to one side for a few hours and to sit there, daring to dream that the attractive man holding her hand was someone who cared for her, had given her a glimpse of how life could be. She closed her eyes before the shimmer of tears she could feel welling up were caught by the sparkle of the strings of white lights in the trees and betrayed her.

'Hey.' He lifted her chin. 'I was joking about the model bit. It's not you. It's me.' His hand was warm against her cheek and it took all she had not to lean into him when she was so aware of how very lonely her life had become.

'Coralie?'

The lilt of his accent almost made her knees buckle. She swallowed hard and opened her eyes to find his dark gaze on hers, full of yearning. In her head, she could hear Doris Day singing out a warning, telling her that their lips shouldn't touch, but Coralie ignored her. Who cared about the rest of the world? Who cared about tomorrow? Then her arms went up and she lifted her face to meet his lips as his mouth came down on hers. All that mattered was the heat of his hands through the silk of her dress and his hot, hard body pressing against hers.

Oh, the relief of giving into what every fibre of her being had been crying out to do was all the sweeter for the agony of waiting. This was Gethin. Gethin Lewis, who'd branded himself on her imagination ever since that first unforgettable glimpse of him on the other side of her fence. She pressed her hands to the hard planes of his face, breathing in his citrus cologne blended with the warm, clean male smell of him, the rough brush of his stubble against her fingertips confirming he was real. Just for a fraction of a second, she almost laughed at the novelty of what she was doing – kissing *Gethin Lewis*, the man she'd almost maimed in her garden – but then his mouth moved against hers, demanding her attention, sweeping her away on a raft of delicious sensations and dark promise of what might come.

'Coralie?'

She pulled away reluctantly. That he'd even been capable of breaking off in the middle of a kiss to her was a bit depressing. Maybe she wasn't getting it right. Just the way his tongue teased her lips made her gasp with pleasurable anticipation and set her skin tingling. If she'd been having half the effect on him, he wouldn't have been able to come up for air. But then he thought she was prim and proper, neat and tidy. She'd have to try harder to banish any lingering impressions he might have had about her preferring a cup of tea to making love.

'We're becoming a sideshow here,' he said, gently, when she looked up to meet his eyes. 'Would you like to go somewhere a bit less public?'

Still wrapped in his arms, she peered round him. Yup, they were still in the Lincoln Center, weren't they? No wonder people were grinning at them or walking away shaking their heads. She buried her face in his chest before looking up at him and nodding.

'My place?'

'Yes,' she said, looking him in the eye and leaving him in no doubt that her intention was not to do the dishes or push the Hoover round.

CHAPTER 16

Gethin managed to rustle up a taxi with impressive speed, but a couple of blocks might just as well have been a trip to the moon, so giant a leap was it for Coralie and her stretched nerves. Before she managed to take control of her breathing, she was also worried that it would take a life-support pack for her to climb the grey marble steps up to his third-floor apartment.

Inside, he drew her close. 'Are you quite sure about this, Coralie?' he murmured, stroking the soft nape of her neck.

From somewhere unbidden, the dark memories welled up – the life lost, the lives wasted. Then something wonderful happened; as unexpectedly as they had appeared, the doubts faded and the worried voices fell silence. She felt as if she belonged in his arms.

'What do you think?' she asked softly, smiling up at him. Then he kissed her, his lips moving gently and slowly with hers, and the heat began to build. She closed her eyes, shivering with the thrilling sensation of his skin grazing hers as he bent his head to kiss her throat.

Her hands moved to unbutton the rest of his shirt. Somehow it was mostly undone and hanging loose anyway. Of course, that didn't mean that he didn't still consider that she was the one who was buttoned-up. Maybe there was a chance he'd think she was removing his shirt because it was crumpled and she wanted to iron it? She decided on the direct approach and reached for his belt buckle. His sharp intake of breath indicated that she'd hit the spot, but before she'd managed to congratulate herself, his hand slid under her dress and she forgot what she was thinking.

'That's a yes,' she gasped a few minutes later, lying on his bed, just in case he was in any doubt, 'I'm sure.'

Straightening up, she pushed his shirt off his shoulders and enjoyed getting acquainted with the sight of his lean, hard body that she'd only previously glimpsed. She made him lie down and traced the fine dark hairs across his chest, then followed to where they formed a dark line from his flat stomach downwards. Retracing the path her fingers had taken with her lips, she teased him with fluttery kisses and delicate nips, whilst her hands restrained him.

'I'm a patient man,' he said huskily, breaking free and rolling her on to her back, 'but I have my limits and you're pushing them.'

His mouth moved to her throat. 'I've waited a long time for this . . .'

His breath was warm against her skin as he moved slowly down her body.

'You have?' She shuddered as the relentless progress of his tongue set off wavelets of pleasure rippling across her body.

'Uh-huh.' He propped himself up to look at her. 'Ever since the moment I saw you doing your Little Red Riding Hood act out in the garden at Penmorfa.'

Her only answer was a soft, involuntary moan, because his lips, following his fingers to explore her inner thigh, were doing something strange to her breathing pattern. She lifted her head at the same time as him and found herself looking into his deep, dark, midnight gaze. The Big Bad Wolf, all lean, hard and hungry, a slow smile playing across his face.

Gethin propped himself up on his elbow so that he could get his fill of Coralie in the morning light: silky dark lashes, the pale, smooth skin of her back, her chestnut curls contrasting with the white pillow. It was a room that he'd always thought of as tranquil, the sliding shoji doors dividing it from the living room maximising the light and enhancing the apartment's understated opulence. But now he was feeling anything but tranquil.

Flashbacks of the night before fast forwarded through his brain: his hand on Coralie's thigh, the slipperiness of silk sliding under his impatient fingers, her soft mouth hot against his. The soundtrack, too: whispers turning into moans, her breath in short, urgent gasps by his ear and then nothing but sweet, mindless oblivion.

Coralie stirred in her sleep and turned towards him, her amber eyes trusting as her lashes fluttered and she glimpsed the first sight of him. When she reached up and traced his jaw with her fingers, he dropped his head to kiss her shoulder before anything in his expression betrayed his confusion. His body felt wonderful, as if it had only just experienced what it really was to make love, but his brain was telling him to wrap up everything quickly. His brain had a point. Any minute now, Pamala Gray would be setting her terrier, Laura Schiffman, on him, reminding him that he was meeting her at the gallery at lunchtime to go over the final details for the evening reception yet again. Although, why they couldn't just get on with it without him, he didn't know. The paintings could practically sell themselves.

In which case . . .

'Hey, you,' Coralie murmured, winding her hands round his neck. He pulled her towards him, feeling his pulse leap at the sweet morning smell of her. God, how he longed to plunge into all that luscious heat and softness! Somehow, he managed to find enough willpower to hold back. He knew enough about her to realise that this wasn't her usual style; there was a shyness about her which made a refreshing change from some of the women who commissioned him to paint them and acted as if they'd bought his body along with his talent.

Coralie's reticence made her more of a challenge, too; made him eager to discover the part of her she was withholding. Time had to be marching on, but he couldn't bear the thought of losing what might be the last opportunity to feel her soft curves against his body.

'Thank you for last night,' he murmured, running his fingertip across her lips. 'It was very special. You're lovely – do you know that?'

But when he stole a glance at her to see if her thoughts reflected his, he was alarmed to see her eyes brimming with tears. Oh, not now; he didn't have time for a scene.

'I'm not,' she whispered, her pupils contracting as the cold daylight glanced across her pale face. 'There's something I need to tell you.'

Uh-oh! The on-off boyfriend was back on the scene, perhaps, and now she was recriminating herself for giving in to temptation? He didn't know whether to be relieved at the lucky escape from more emotional involvement than he could cope with or insulted that she'd used him.

'Whatever it is,' he said carefully, 'it shouldn't affect what's taken place between us. There's nothing you need feel guilty about.'

'You sound like my mum,' she said with a weak smile. 'She's always accusing me of punishing myself for something that wasn't my fault.'

'Well, you should listen to your mother. I wish I could still listen to mine, but it's too late now.' Where had that come from? This really wasn't the moment to air his family's misfortunes. Especially when he had such a full day ahead of him. But something about the woman lying next to him seem to fit so well, as if she were part of him, and it was making him drop his guard. He lifted his head just enough to catch a glance of his bedside clock. Ten-thirty already and he was supposed to be at the gallery by one o'clock. Heck, where was the morning going?

And then he felt Coralie's body quiver and saw the tears starting to spill down her face.

'Come on, *cariad*,' he said, holding out his arms and gathering her up. 'Nothing's that bad.'

He lay still, rubbing her back until she cried herself out. Could he take the day off? Tell Pamala he was sick? Something was making his head swim and confusing his thinking. One thing at a time. First he'd try to find out what was causing Coralie so much distress. Probably best just to let her get it off her chest.

'So, tell me about it,' he said gently.

After a deep breath, he heard her gather herself ready to speak.

'Before I moved to Penmorfa, I used to work for a management consultancy, in the Process Improvement Unit – that means axing jobs to you and me. It's easy to make struggling firms more efficient; you either get them to run better computer systems or lose staff. Most of the time you can pat yourself on the back and tell yourself that the human sacrifices are worth it. Another company is saved and people's jobs are secure – until the next round at least.'

'Quite a responsibility,' he observed, sympathetic but at the same time willing her to get to the point.

She nodded and went on. 'Only this time, the company I was sent to was close to home. My boss assured me everything would be fine. Except that I knew one of the employees through a mutual acquaintance, a guy called Ned Wallace. Ned was a nice enough guy, a bit of a lad, liked all the trappings, you know? Designer suits, go-faster car – all bought on credit, it transpired later. He never believed for one moment that he was expendable, but the management level there was far too top-heavy so it was the obvious place to cut. Ned, of course, was then faced with the reality of not being able to finance his extravagant lifestyle. That was the moment when all the careful calculations I'd made in the seclusion of a tidy office became a messy, uncontrollable reality.'

She paused to collect herself again. 'On the surface Ned took it quite well. Joked about how he was going to blow the redundancy money on the holiday of a lifetime, but no one realised that he was far from being all right.'

'So?' He stroked her shoulder. 'You can't make everything better, Coralie. Sounds like the guy was a loser, carrying that amount of debt. You might even have done him a favour.'

She cleared her throat so that she could carry on. Fresh tears started sliding down her cheeks on to the pillow. 'No. He lost everything he had, but he wasn't the only victim. He was distressed about how his fiancée would take the news that he'd lost his job. So, he drove round aimlessly, screwing up the courage to go home, and he completely failed to notice a pedestrian crossing. He didn't see a young trainee teacher, Hayley Butterfield, returning to her flat from the convenience store across the road.'

'Oh, no.' He stared at the ceiling feeling helpless.

'Hayley was killed instantly, although Ned Wallace didn't know that because he just kept driving. Somehow, he convinced himself if he didn't stop, it hadn't really happened, so he just kept going until he got home. It took three days before his conscience got the better of him. Even then he only handed himself in because he realised he'd been found out. He'd had his car repaired, you see, the day after the accident. He guessed, correctly as it transpired, that the mechanic would see the appeal for information and put two and two together.'

She paused to swipe at her tears. 'Three days, imagine that. And a young woman lying dead and her family's lives in ruin because of what I'd done.'

'No.' He sat up and drew her to him. 'You can't blame yourself for that. It was him, the driver, who killed that girl, not you.' He looked at her pinched face. 'Oh, Coralie. That's the burden you've been carrying all this time? The reason you took yourself off to the middle of nowhere? So you could hide away from it all?'

She took a deep, shuddering breath. If he could

have stayed there with her, he would have, but that would mean letting too many people down. The gallery assistants, Ruby, everyone who was working so hard to make this day a success for him. So he tried to make it better as far as he could. He took her face gently in his hands and made her look at him. 'Listen, Coralie, you have to forgive yourself or it'll ruin your life, too.'

'But it wasn't just Hayley's family who suffered that day. My decision cost Ned Wallace dearly, his family disowned him, his fiancée called off their wedding. He was left with no one.'

'Some people would call that retribution.'

'Not me, I—'

'Forget about it, Coralie,' he said, letting her go. 'You've lived with this for long enough. It's time to move on.'

He couldn't help stealing another glance at his clock. And she saw him. He groaned inwardly; the fact that he'd been smiling and trying to sound friendly and reassuring didn't make him feel any less of a bastard for not giving her every bit of his attention.

'Coralie, I'm sorry—'

'No, really, it's fine.' The vulnerability in her eyes, when she stared at him as if trying to convince herself she'd been mistaken, could have broken his heart. Really, she didn't know how much better it was this way.

'I really shouldn't be going on at you when you've got so much to do.' She turned on her side before swinging her legs to the edge of the bed. Her shoulders drooped as she paused, very briefly, and he began to register how much she was hurting. He longed to pull her back to him and cradle her against his chest. Except he was so afraid that eventually he'd only end up hurting her more.

'Perhaps you'd call a cab for me?'

'Hey, look – let's both shower and have breakfast then we could go together, if you like?'

Jesus, he was gabbling, but with that vulnerable expression she was wearing he was afraid that he'd fill a gap by saying something stupid, like ordering her to tear up her ticket and asking her to stay with him. He wished he could make everything all right for her.

'I don't think that's a good idea, do you, not when you've got such a busy day ahead and the reception this evening.'

The reception! Maybe that would be his chance to put things right?

'You are coming tonight, aren't you?' he asked desperately. 'Only, I'd like you to see the new work before you go.'

Go. He looked past her, at the black metal fire escapes snaking down the yellow brick apartment blocks opposite and tried not to think about how much he'd miss her. Otherwise, he'd start wondering why he'd utterly failed to paint her portrait, and why all that heat and intimacy had only left an increasing craving for her. Not looking at her made

it easier for him to inject the right note of cheer-
fulness into his voice. The mistake he made was
glancing at her and seeing how the lovely soft
morning smile had vanished from her face to be
replaced by something shadowed and hidden. He
almost relented and reached out for her.

'Just one thing,' she said quietly.

He held his breath.

'The portrait . . .'

'I'll scrap the whole idea, if you like,' he said,
lifting his hands. 'You were never very happy with
the whole idea, were you?' he pointed out, trying
to sound like a reasonable man rather than a guilty
one. 'So, it's not fair to put you through that kind
of ordeal when it's not really working for either of
us. I'll sort something out for the charity auction.
I won't let Penmorfa down.'

'Well,' she stood up, giving him a tight little
smile, before gathering up her clothes, 'you're all
heart.'

At the sound of the shower he flopped back on
the bed and let out a long breath.

There had been no other choice, he thought, after
the taxi had driven her away. Penmorfa was
renowned for its outstanding natural beauty, but
however lovely Coralie was, it didn't mean he
wanted to spend the rest of his life there. It was
better that he forgot about her. Every time he
thought about the place where he grew up it
reminded him that according to precedent, Lewis

men weren't good to their women. Hadn't his father shamelessly taken all the love his mother gave him and worn it down in the cold and mud and the long, hard hours at the farm? He thought he'd escaped his destiny by leaving Penmorfa behind; the last thing he'd expected was that it would follow him.

Now Coralie's absence was all around him. He couldn't face Ruby's sarcasm, either, so he tapped out a text telling her he'd meet her at the gallery and set off. Outside, he crossed a grating and the ozone smell of the subway rose up beneath him, the accompanying hot air feeling uncomfortably like a forewarning that there'd be hell to pay for behaving so badly. Crossing the roadway into the Park, he was so busy trying to convince himself that all he'd done was neatly sidestep a difficult obstacle that he was almost hit by an oncoming roller-blader.

Having dodged past the cyclists and joggers, he hoped that looking at the scenery would make him feel more at peace. The cherry trees were still waiting to come into blossom, but the last of the daffodils, that always reminded him of home, now turned their heads away in another rebuke.

Even the birds seemed less than harmonious: sharp-beaked starlings, so much more aggressive looking than their European counterparts, made a thuggish crew, strutting in their shiny green-and-black, two-tone plumage. A huge pigeon, clumping along like a dinosaur walking the plains, watched stupidly as a cluster of sparrows stole the scraps of bread from under its feet. Somehow Gethin couldn't help but identify with it; he was pretty sure that he had just allowed something to be snatched away from under his nose, too.

CHAPTER 17

Forty-five minutes, thought Coralie, feeling dazed. Not even a full hour to get out of Gethin's apartment. She'd once seen a programme about low-temperature surgery. A reduced need for food and air was supposed to keep the patient comfortably numb and preserve the vital organs. Maybe the frozen feeling around her heart would prove to be similarly protective?

So much tidier this way, she tried to tell herself, as the taxi dropped her outside Ruby's apartment block. *Surgically* clean. No hanging around like a persistent stain. Why pretend it could be any other way? It wasn't as if they had a future together, but if all Gethin Lewis had been after was a one-night stand, he could have saved her a lot of time and effort by dropping the pretence that it was all about art.

Letting her forehead rest lightly against Ruby's aquamarine door as she inserted the key, she stared down at the oily-green linoleum lining the communal spaces. Except that no one had forced her into his bed; she'd gone to him gladly. Ruby's Uncle Sam poster pointed at her accusingly as she opened the door. Deep down, hadn't she always accepted that part of his attraction was that there *was* no future for them? Maybe she'd even tried out her confession for precisely that reason? So that she could say some of those troubling words out loud *because* there was nothing to lose?

Coralie closed her eyes and exhaled slowly.

'You okay?'

Since her good luck fairy had clearly taken the day off, it wasn't surprising that her wish to be alone so that she could bury her head in a pillow and cry her eyes out hadn't been granted, either.

Ruby, dressed to go out in tight leather trousers and a short, white tee shirt, stopped checking her hair in her hand mirror to give Coralie the full benefit of her bright, beady-eyed gaze.

'I'm still trying to decide,' Coralie said, taking off her evening shoes and sitting on the sofa bed next to her. There was no point at all in rushing into the bathroom to change when it was obvious to them both that she was still wearing the clothes she'd gone out in. 'It's been a night of seduction, conflict and tragic resolution.'

'That *Carmen*, it's a hell of an opera,' said Ruby, padding out to the kitchenette and returning with two cans of Coke. 'What about you and Gethin?'

Coralie choked out a laugh and pressed the cold can to her cheek. The shock stopped the laughter spilling into tears. 'He's giving up on the portrait and donating a painting to the charity auction instead.'

Ruby chewed her gum, thoughtfully. 'He's not finishing the work?'

Got it in one, Coralie agreed silently. Finishing work clearly wasn't Gethin's strong point. 'He's got the exhibition to think about now. That'll keep him busy.'

'He's always busy,' Ruby said cheerfully, stretching her legs and admiring the black nail varnish on her toes. 'There are a lot of beautiful women to paint in Manhattan.'

Boy, did that make her feel good. Coralie plucked at her dress whilst her blurred vision cleared. Since she had company she'd have to wait until she was in the shower to cry her eyes out now.

'And by the time he's finished painting them, he's sick of the sight of them,' Ruby added, strapping up her studded gladiator sandals, before picking up her jacket. 'Don't look like that,' she said laughing at Coralie's disapproving expression. 'It may be an intense relationship for a short time, but it's only paint. It's not love or death. He's not inviting anyone into his studio promising them a big white dress, two kids on the porch and a happy ever after.' She seemed to be about to leave but stopped and cocked her head on one side. 'So he's really not going any further with your portrait, eh? That's different.'

Inside the smart Chelsea gallery that evening, Coralie was surprised to find Ruby had been looking out for her.

'I can always say you had a headache or something,' she suggested.

Coralie shook her head and swallowed hard. She almost preferred the rude Ruby incarnation to the one suddenly taking pity on her; perhaps clearing up after Gethin outside the studio as well as inside was one of her regular duties? She was brazening out the evening in her favourite peach-printed cocktail dress and kitten heels. All she had to do, she thought, whipping out her compact mirror, was to retouch her painted-on coral smile. Gethin might have drawn a line under their relationship, but she was determined to make her exit in style.

Her courage nearly deserted her when she looked around the stark room and saw what everyone was wearing. Any colour within the range grey to black seemed to be the dress code for the evening, she noticed, wondering how many variations of grey there were and feeling like a fruit display in her brightly coloured dress. If Lady Gaga was going to put in an appearance, as Ruby had suggested, she would certainly liven the place up.

Ruby grabbed a drink from a passing waiter and handed it to Coralie. 'Get this down you quick,' she advised, watching her with a trace of pity. 'I'll see what's happened to Gethin.'

Coralie decided it would be better to soak up the paintings, rather than draining her glass. Even if her relationship, if it could be called that, with Gethin was a non-starter she hoped that his work would leave a lasting impression. Would his style have altered much since the surreal glamour of *Last Samba before Sunset*? And which of the pictures, she pondered, would he send to Penmorfa's Hall Management Committee?

But, as she moved round the room, it occurred to her that she would probably have felt more comfortable back in a boardroom discussing figures than taking a view on the kind of figures before her now. Where were all the abstract paintings when you needed them? With every beautifully depicted curve of back, buttock and breast Coralie yearned for a landscape drawing to break up all the flesh.

'Oh, look! A brown painting,' she overheard a well-dressed elderly lady confide to her young male companion. 'I'm looking for a brown painting to go in the new apartment.'

Coralie examined the brown painting and noticed a pattern emerging through the umber, cinnamon and walnut tones. It was a bit like looking through a wooden blind, because the artist *was* looking through a wooden blind at . . .

'Oh my!' exclaimed the elderly lady, spotting it too. 'Am I looking at someone's *ass*?'

Having wondered if it was fair to form a true impression of Gethin as an artist from the ubiquitous reproductions of his most famous painting, it seemed to her that the works on display were quite lazy, as if Gethin had taken the easy route and returned to the same old theme. No wonder he'd found her difficult to paint. Plenty of people seemed to like them though, since the gallery was becoming increasingly full. And with the buzz of so many fans clamouring to talk to him, Coralie judged she had all evening to frame a tactful opinion.

She was just beginning to relax when a row of fashionably thin women parted like corn waving in the breeze, only the force parting them was Gethin strolling towards her.

'Coralie! Thank God, you're here!' He took hold of her arm and started to steer her away. 'I was worried you wouldn't come. Can we talk?'

'Don't wander off, Gethin, you're wanted,' said a glacial-looking, Grace Kelly look-alike, grabbing his elbow.

Again, thought Coralie, feeling somewhat mollified when he shook his arm free and stood his ground.

'Laura, this is Coralie Casey, my guest from Wales. Coralie, Laura Schiffman, Pamala Gray's Senior Director.'

'How lovely to meet you,' Laura chimed, scanning her face, presumably against a mental check list of the great and good on the guest list, then turned back to Gethin. 'Pamala would like to speak to you. Now. You will excuse him won't you, Coralie?'

That rather suggested she wasn't on the VIP list.

'Let me walk you round instead,' Laura insisted, erring on the diplomatic side, just in case. She dragged Coralie away, whilst Gethin, his mouth set in a tense line, marched off the other way. Two attractive gay men waved to him as he passed.

'Show of hands,' she heard one of them say, as a young woman walked in wearing a black gown that revealed most of her ample assets. 'Do we think those are for real?'

'Gethin's spontaneity is unsurpassed,' said Laura, pointing at a turgid-looking painting of a bored couple. 'Everything he turns his gaze towards transcends the ordinary.' She kept rubbing the back of her hand where a rough, red patch of skin was blooming angrily. 'Must have exhausted everything in Duane Reade trying to fix this one,' she said, seeing that Coralie had noticed it.

Coralie fished in her bag and found a small pot of her Happy Hands cream. 'Try this,' she said, offering it to her, 'it's very gentle, mainly beeswax and almond oil, but it's very soothing.'

The other woman looked doubtful. 'I don't think . . .'

'I make them myself,' Coralie added, meaning to reassure her but seemingly causing further alarm. Laura smiled bravely and rubbed the tiniest amount on her sore hand. No doubt it would be washed off as soon as she could get to the ladies'.

When Gethin reappeared, he was engulfed by well-wishers. Although he caught her eye several times, he never quite seemed to be able to extricate himself for long enough to talk to her. In a way, it made it easier for her to remain detached. What was there to talk about now? Apart from the charity auction? Her only worry, judging from the number of people at the reception, was that the exhibition might be so successful that all the paintings would sell.

Ruby appeared, flushed with heat and excitement, but her face dropped when she saw that Coralie was on her own.

'I'll text Gethin from the airport tomorrow. Don't disturb him now, he's still busy,' said Coralie, staring at his back whilst the next potential candidate to commission a portrait flicked her long hair at him.

Ruby looked so tearful when she opened her arms to give Coralie a stiff hug and wish her well that it almost set her off, too. She was pushing through the crowd when Gethin grabbed her arm.

'Just hang on, will you? My driver will take you home.'

'What, all the way to Penmorfa? He must have quite a car.'

Gethin's brow creased and he swore softly under his breath. 'Look, I know I've messed up really badly,' he said, following her towards the door. 'I've never been unable to paint a woman before. I was scared I was losing my touch.'

'Your touch is fine,' she assured him. 'But your bedside manner leaves a lot to be desired.'

'I'm sorry.' He bent his head and seemed to be struggling for words. 'Please wait. When I've finished here, we'll find a place to talk.'

'About what?' she said, feeling her chest tighten. 'This is as good as it gets. You live here and I live in Penmorfa. There'll never be a place for us.'

He let out a long sigh and stared at the ceiling and when he looked at her again, the blue-black eyes were wretched.

'What?' She caught her breath.

'Try not to think too badly of me when you look back on this.'

'Why would I do that?' Coralie gave a short laugh and was surprised to feel her anger slipping away. How could she remain angry when he'd turned the key and given her a glimpse of what life could be like without the fear and guilt?

Smiling, she reached up to hold him for one last time. 'I've finished looking back. From now on, I'm only moving forward.'

She closed her eyes as his warm, rough jaw touched her cheek and kissed him goodbye. No looking back, she reminded herself. And kept walking.

Someone was making a heck of a racket in his head, thought Gethin, coming to on the sofa where he'd cosied up with a bottle of Jack Daniels the previous evening.

'Open the fricking door!' someone was bellowing. Ruby; he'd recognise her dulcet tones anywhere, but how had she got inside his head? He levered himself up and then wished he hadn't, especially when the hammering went on. A door chain rattled, more distant, but still loud enough to set his teeth on edge. Then another voice, a deep juicy drawl, added to the cacophony.

'Hey, lady! Keep the noise down, will ya?'

Gethin groaned; the apartment opposite belonged to a now-reclusive actress who'd been a huge Hollywood star in the eighties. Whilst the actress had withdrawn from public life, she and her minder regularly starred in his. Generally it was via a billet-doux from his landlord, accusing him of some imaginary infringement of his tenancy agreement. Occasionally, like today, the minder would put in an unwelcome cameo appearance and invite him or his guests to remain silent on the landing, or tiptoe on their way out down the stairs. When the time came to move on, Gethin was going to buy himself a vuvuzela and play them a farewell salute so they'd always remember him.

'Butt out of this, buddy,' Ruby snarled, 'before I give you something to complain about!'

'Oh yeah? That's really funny! Come on then, surprise me.'

Okay, that was enough. Ruby could talk the talk but the guy across the corridor was built like a truck and the medical bills would be enormous. For the guy. Gethin got up, opened the door and pulled his bristling assistant in before she got carried away and started swinging punches.

'How dumb are you?' she roared at him, making him wince.

'Not so dumb that I pick a fight with a guy three times my size.' He grinned.

'Oh, that's right,' she sneered, trying and failing

to push her face in his, 'I forgot. You like to humiliate them into submission, don't you?'

'Eh?' The Jack Daniels wasn't helping him here. He edged his way back to the sofa and lay back and looked at the ceiling as if it could give him a few clues as to why Ruby was so mad.

'You moron!' Ruby threw off her khaki jacket and sat down heavily beside him, cruelly bouncing the springs. The tee shirt she was wearing proclaimed her to be very, very happy. The one that said she was very, very mad was probably in the wash. 'You know, snubbing Pamala Gray in her own gallery was a terrible idea.'

Gethin would have shaken his head only it hurt too much. He had done that, hadn't he? But when the art dealer had clicked her fingers at him to get his attention, as if he was one of the waiters, just as he was beginning to realise that Coralie had walked out of his life for good, he was damned if he could switch off and obediently come to heel.

'But, hey, I guess when you're a big shot, you can afford to behave badly once in while.'

Gethin breathed out. 'I'll send flowers.'

'Good luck with that,' Ruby snorted. 'So what are you going to do about Coralie?'

'What did you *want* me to do?' He wrenched himself up. 'Propose to her?' Self-disgust was making him tetchy.

She shook her head, and the white spikes of her hair quivered. He had some sympathy with them. 'You dragged the poor woman all this way on some flimsy pretext about painting her portrait and you didn't even manage that?'

'It wasn't working,' he said flatly. 'She wouldn't relax; what kind of portrait will it make?'

Ruby sneered at him. 'Hey, you're the one with all the talent; don't blame the sitter. Or maybe you were so busy trying to get her to relax, that you lost sight of the fact you were supposed to be *painting* her.'

Gethin shuffled under her intense scrutiny, trying to get physically if not emotionally comfortable. 'I tried the usual tourist stuff.'

'Yeah, sex and the city – but not the official tour, right?'

'I liked you before you turned into my mother,' he grumbled.

'Your mother would be ashamed of you!' Ruby said, her voice shaking. 'If you'd used your eyes last night you'd have seen how brave Coralie was being and taken pity on her. What the fuck were you thinking of? Couldn't you see how much she was hurting? Or maybe you were *too* busy thinking about the f—'

'Careful!' he warned.

'Well,' she remonstrated, 'anyone could tell she wasn't like those other women, the ones who *hope* you're going to screw them when they commission a portrait.'

'Don't.' His head was hurting too much to listen to this stuff.

'Or what?' Ruby shook her head. 'You've been

233

running away from getting involved all the time I've known you. Anyone would think you're afraid of making a commitment. Then someone comes all this way to be with you and you let her slip through your hands.'

'The only thing I know I've got in common with her is Penmorfa and we can't even agree about that! Nothing flourishes there except gossip and that includes Sweet Cleans. I've seen more incomers fail at their idealistic attempts to start a new life in the country than you've had hot dinners. I'm right about that business, you wait and see.'

'Gee,' she said sarcastically, 'that'll keep you warm at night. What's wrong with you? You're not getting any younger, you know. You'll end up a lonely old man.'

Like his father. Gethin narrowed his eyes at her. 'When you've quite finished chewing my ear, there's a hot shower waiting for me.'

Ruby sniffed at him. 'Yeah, and you could do with it, too. You'd better freshen up because it's gonna be a long day.'

Gethin raised his eyebrows. Pamala Gray, he supposed. And a large slice of humble pie.

Ruby looked at him beadily. 'Have you seen what the critics are saying about your show?'

CHAPTER 18

In her parents' house in Surrey, where she had broken her journey for a few days, Coralie smiled as her mother returned to the living room with a box of chocolates. 'I must say, darling, it's been lovely having you back,' Susan Casey said, sitting next to her.

Coralie leaned back against the deep cream-and-gold cushions. It was a comfortable room: soft neutrals with touches of gold and pale pink, tasteful landscapes on the wall and Carol Klein's *Life in a Cottage Garden* bookmarked on the glass coffee table. She ought to at least try to relax. A quick phone call to Alys should have taken care of her immediate concerns and staved off some close questioning. And yet . . . No, it wouldn't do to dwell on what wasn't to be. Coralie made a conscious effort to make the most of her brief respite. She watched her mother affectionately, noting that she'd added a few copper lowlights to her regular colour as a nod to what was once flame-red hair.

'It's been very quiet since you've been gone,' Susan said, laying one hand lightly on Coralie's knee.

'I'm not dead,' said Coralie, the sudden almost-tears spilling into a splutter of laughter. 'And I'm only a drive away.'

'A *long* drive,' her mother said reproachfully. 'Your dad finds the motorways tiring now. We're neither of us getting any younger.'

'Mum, you're fifty-four and regularly attend Pilates classes!' Coralie frowned at her. 'You're hardly a candidate for Dial-a-Ride. Besides, you and Dad are perfectly capable of tracking down obscure graveyards, so you're not exactly housebound.'

'You make us sound like a couple of body-snatchers,' her mother grumbled. 'It makes a good day out, that's all. It's far more meaningful to see a moss-covered headstone than simply looking online.'

Tracing their ancestry was a hobby her parents embraced with equal enthusiasm, although, thankfully, they were less inclined to regale her with blow-by-blow accounts of their discoveries these days.

'Well, *I* think we have more time to talk now. We can speak to each other at any time of the day,' Coralie said, hoping to avert the Too Far Away conversation or the inevitable discussion about the family tree. With so many of her cousins adding twigs to it, her mother was growing more concerned about the future of their own branch.

'I suppose so,' sighed her mother. 'And we can text each other. Well, we could if you had a signal. At least we can send emails.'

'You're pleased with that new iPad, then?' Coralie laughed, seeing her mother's glance stray to her latest toy sitting next to Carol Klein on the coffee table in front of them. 'See? There's really no need for anyone to be out of touch. Everyone knows where everyone is these days.'

'If you two are going to sit there nattering, you won't mind if I go and watch the football in the kitchen, will you?' her father said, winking at her as he rose from the armchair.

'So tell me, is Gethin Lewis as sexy in real life as he looks in his photos?' asked her mother, as soon as he'd left the room. Coralie's heart, which was supposed to be convalescing, leapt into her throat, and she had to pretend to think about it so as not to leak any clues her mother might spot.

'He's certainly what they'd call "lush" up our way,' she agreed, concentrating on the box of chocolates her mother had just opened. 'But there's an unbelievably gorgeous queue of New York women who think so, too. Hmm, is this tiramisu?'

'Coralie, *this* is your way, this is where you're from, remember?' Her mother frowned, poring over the illustrated guide to the contents.

As if she could forget! Even the drive back from the airport had raised ghosts. Sitting in the back seat, she was glad that her parents had been chatting about nothing in particular when they passed the Old Mill. Taking the project there had seemed such an attractive option; a young company, lovely

237

offices in a beautiful riverside setting and located close to home so that she'd have more time to catch up with her friends. At the time she'd congratulated herself on a lucky break, but how she wished she'd turned it down.

'Fund-raising exercise, you said. I suppose you were the best person to talk to him in New York given your managerial skills,' said Susan, abandoning progeny for posterity in the apparent hope of distinguishing the family history by any means.

Coralie shifted uneasily. She hadn't exactly lied about why she was going to New York, she'd just been sketchy about the precise details, knowing what a fuss her mother would make about her daughter being painted by a famous artist. But now there would be no portrait anyway, so it didn't matter.

'It must have been good to think on your feet again. Don't you miss using your brain?'

'Don't worry about my brain, Mum, it's fine.' It was just her heart that wasn't doing too well. 'I've been thinking it over and I'm seriously thinking about outsourcing some lines to a contract manufacturer, so I can expand the business. I know it's early days, but it looks as if the demand's there, so I ought to think about how best to keep pace with it.'

'Bugger!' Susan raised a hand to one cheek. 'That was toffee not coffee. I'll have to watch my crowns. Look, wasn't the whole point of this exercise for you to do something less stressful? I mean, you've got a perfectly good career waiting for you here, if you're bored. Oh, Coralie,' she went on with a sigh that was only slightly muffled by the toffee, 'please don't tell me you're still wasting your time on that dreadful man! It just makes me feel so angry. I feel as if we're all paying for what he did. When I think of you, burying yourself away in the back of beyond . . .'

Her pained expression was replaced by a look of concentration as she steered the toffee past her crowns. Coralie quickly picked up the iPad to take advantage of the lull. 'This is brilliant,' she enthused, 'the images are so sharp and clear!'

'Aren't they just?' Her mother leaned in, enveloping her with the warm, woody scent of Estée Lauder's Knowing. 'Oh! Why don't you show me something from Gethin Lewis's exhibition?'

Coralie could think of many reasons why, nevertheless a small, masochistic part of her wanted to remind herself of everything she'd walked away from. 'Hmm, okay.' She tapped in a search, 'Pamala Gray Gallery . . . Chicago . . . Paris . . . ah, here we are . . . New York.'

'Very swish! *Did* Lady Gaga turn up?'

'If she did, it was after I'd gone,' Coralie replied, clicking on the list of current exhibitions. 'That's strange, it's not listed. I wonder why?' She quickly keyed in another search, which produced a flurry of reviews, and clicked on the *New York Times*.

⋆ ⋆ ⋆

In New York Gethin was engaging in his new favourite pastime of sprawling on the sofa. He hit the remote control and watched the TV adverts; each and every one of them a warning of the possible woe betiding any American omitting to take out insurance. Here's granny lying on the floor with no one to hear her cries, here's the charred remains of your house, here's your sick pet. Health? Man, that was another minefield! Don't buy the cheap tablets or your cholesterol will kill you, your asthma will choke you, your heart will fail. In comparison, a little thing like his exhibition bombing didn't seem so bad.

'Derivative,' had been one of the observations. 'More originality in a painting-by-numbers kit.' From the same critics who not so long ago had been declaring his work to be 'dynamic, well-composed with an agreeable tension'. Who did these people think they were? Yet, deep down, he couldn't help feeling he'd been found out. By sticking to the tried-and-tested formula he'd painted himself into a dead end. If he'd reached the point when he could barely be bothered to pick up a brush, why should anyone else care?

In Penmorfa, the morning air was still cool as Kitty, panting with the effort, hefted another box into Alys's capacious Berlingo. Letting it go with some relief, she was just gathering strength to push it into a better position when someone asked her what she thought she was doing. She steadied herself with a deep breath before turning round. Adam's arms were folded across his broad chest and there was concern in his sea-green eyes. Kitty gave an inward sigh. He looked better in an old tee shirt, tatty jeans and boots than most men did when they were dressed up; no wonder so many female visitors to the garden centre were always finding reasons to get him to carry stuff to their car.

'I've taken a stall at a wedding fair at Llandrindod Wells,' she told him, resting on the boot for a second to let her swimming head settle. 'I'd like to spread the word about my low-cost wedding styling solutions to a few more brides-to-be and show them the kind of themes I can offer.'

'Jesus, Kitty, that's nearly a hundred miles away! Does Alys know what you're up to?'

'Mam's doing Hall Management Committee stuff again today and I can't be bothered to chase after Dad. He's a miserable so-and-so lately, always moaning about his back but never doing anything about it. I don't know how Mam puts up with him.' She stood up and closed the tailgate with some effort.

'Kitty!' He stood in front of her and rested his fingertips on her shoulders, ensuring he had her attention. 'You really shouldn't be doing that journey on your own. Not at this stage of the game. You know what that road's like through the mountains. What happens if something goes wrong?'

'I'll call the AA.' She shrugged, looking away.

He shook her shoulders gently. 'You know I wasn't talking about the sodding car!'

Kitty reached up and placed her hands on top of his. 'Don't try to stop me,' she said softly. 'Can't you see, I have to get used to coping on my own? I have to learn to be a grown-up now for this one's sake,' she added, nodding at her stomach. 'There are all kinds of reasons why I could skip this fair today. It would be so much easier to find an excuse and not go, but where's that going to get me? Yes, I am nervous about the drive and I'm worried that the fair will be a complete waste of time and money, but I'll never know what I can do until I try.'

Adam pulled her closer and rested his chin lightly on her head. 'Let me come with you. I just want to see you get there and back in one piece.'

For a few moments she let herself enjoy the comfort of being in his strong arms, being held against his chest and breathing in the warm, masculine scent of him, then she wriggled out his grasp and put on a brave smile. 'Thank you, but it won't help me in the long run. Besides,' she grinned up at him, 'you've got work to do. Mam's sloped off, Dad's nowhere to be found. Someone's got to keep this place going.'

Adam gave her a resigned smile, showing his chipped front tooth. Funny how all the scuffs and imperfections in his face only gave it more character. 'Okay, but just let me give the car a quick once over before you set off.'

She stood back and watched whilst he refilled the washer bottles and checked the oil. 'The tyres look all right for now too, although I think the front two will need replacing before long. How's the spare?'

'Adam!' She pushed him away gently. 'At this rate, the fair'll be over before I get there!'

She eased herself into the driver's seat and wound down the window. 'Don't look so worried!' She blew him a kiss then set off, watching him in the rear window until he was out of sight, trying not to think about how much more she would enjoy the day if he was at her side.

Gethin dragged a hand across his face as the weatherman came on with a warning about falling temperatures. Perhaps if he'd been less preoccupied thinking about Coralie, he might have felt the winds of change blowing across his reception, the cluster of critics gathering like storm clouds to rain on his parade. The reviews had been so toxic that the gallery might just as well have been at the centre of an exclusion zone it was so empty.

Pamala Gray, minimising the risk from fall-out, had taken the unprecedented step of closing the exhibition, bringing in a newly trendy Dutch artist specialising in avant-garde sculptures as a hurried replacement. Gethin had always brushed aside any suggestions that in New York, at least, the world of art and fashion was inextricably linked. Easy to do when everyone was scrambling for a piece of him, but what else would explain why he'd fallen so dramatically out of favour when all he'd done was to produce more of the same?

And what would Coralie say? Not that she could think much worse of him. He couldn't believe how much he missed her; his world, which was already black and white without her, had now faded to a depressing shade of grey.

Wasn't this exactly why it had been such a bad idea to get involved with a girl from Penmorfa? Now he couldn't even walk round New York without looking for her. The city streets were full of people but seemed empty without her, and every famous landmark and tourist postcard only served to taunt him about what he'd lost. He missed her mad clothes, the coils of chestnut hair, her laughter and, even though she'd only been there for one night, he sure as hell missed the sweet warmth of her in his bed.

Yep, it was payback time all round. The sting in the tail for thinking he could get away with taking what he wanted and giving the bare minimum in return was the unpleasant discovery that for all his efforts to escape his fate, he was no better than the man he least wanted to become. Utterly defeated, he buried his head in his hands, wondering what he could possibly do that wouldn't have Coralie thinking he was a desperate man, just trying to impress her because he'd fallen on hard times. And then a voice on the TV broke through to him.

'Prices for Gethin Lewis peaked last year,' some clever dick so-called art consultant was telling the camera as news of his humiliation reached the screen. 'So anyone thinking of buying his work as an investment would be wise to place their money elsewhere. It's not that the big money buyers aren't there – pre-sales estimates for a series of landscapes by Lewis's compatriot, Sheri William, were smashed by collectors. Of course, Lewis remains very popular with the public, reprints of his most famous painting *Last Samba before Sunset* are said to have made him a fortune, but the selective buyer is now looking elsewhere.'

'Oh, man!' What was any painting of his worth to the people of Penmorfa now? Any dealer or collector watching the press releases and seeing that his exhibition had been closed prematurely would be worried that he had lost impact in the art world and be nervous about his work. Mair and Delyth had always wanted to wipe the floor with him, and a floor sander would probably be all they could afford out of the auction proceeds to reinstate their precious community centre. But was it too late for him to do something about it?

A lane closure on the motorway meant that Coralie's journey home took far longer than she'd anticipated when she set off from her parents hoping to get back in the light. By the time she reached the narrow lane that curled down to Penmorfa, the village was in darkness and she was shaking with fatigue. Not that there were any guarantees that she would sleep. Not only was she was apprehensive about how Sweet Cleans had fared in her absence, although she was sure Kitty would have done her best, but now there was Alys to face, too.

As she persuaded Betty up the hill through the other side of the village, a shadowy canopy of branches loomed over the dark lanes. The road dwindled to a thin strip, slowly unravelling in the car's headlights. But, outside the farmhouse, the beams picked up something worrying, a shape in Alys's Berlingo, as if someone was slumped over the steering wheel. She pulled up beside it and wrenched open the driver's door.

'Kitty!'

'I'm fine.' Even in the artificial light Kitty's face was very pale as she lifted her head and pushed her hair back. 'It's been a long day, that's all.'

'I hope you're doing a better job of convincing yourself than you are me!' Coralie muttered fiercely as she crouched down beside her. 'What's happened?'

Kitty explained that she'd been driving back through the Cambrian mountains after a wedding fair, when she had to pull over for a pee. She'd been compelled to stop twice more on the way home, once at a public loo and once to use the facilities in a supermarket, and had been alarmed to find a trace of blood as she wiped herself. Her back was hurting, too.

'Don't worry, everything's going to be all right. Stay calm, and I'll get help.' Coralie put her arm around her in comfort.

'No, don't go!' Kitty said, looking scared. 'Oh, frigging hell, I'm tired, Coralie. I'll probably feel better in a minute. I've just got to take this as a warning, a sign to take it easy for the next few days and let everything settle down.'

They both looked up at the sound of footsteps coming towards them. Kitty's bottom lip started to tremble and a tear ran down her cheek.

'I think the baby's coming, Mam,' she said, reaching out towards her.

Coralie shuffled out of the way so that Alys could get closer.

'What baby's that then, love? This one here?' Alys asked gently, rubbing Kitty's hard tummy. 'The one you haven't been telling us about?' She turned anxiously to Coralie before touching her lips to her daughter's forehead.

'Now try to relax as best you can whilst we get you inside. It's probably a false alarm and it'll settle down once you've rested. After all, you're not due yet, are you?'

CHAPTER 19

Rock's rapturous welcome and mewling cries broke the silence of the lonely lane and went some way to making up for the emptiness of the adjoining holiday cottage. Once Alys had appeared Coralie had made a tactful withdrawal, leaving mother and daughter to handle their new situation in their own way. Crouching to stroke Rock, Coralie felt unexpectedly weepy and was grateful that he was ready to overlook being deprived of first his mouse and then her company. Whereas some cats would be a bit stand-offish after being deserted for a week, Rock was far too needy to play games, greeting her as if she'd returned after years of absence.

Picking Rock up, since getting to her front door with a small cat threading through her legs was hampering progress, she allowed herself one brief glance at the neighbouring windows just to confirm that there was really no one at home.

'Just you and me then, Rock.'

She opened the door which led straight into her living room and all the warm colours and vintage fabrics she had chosen to please herself. Instead of cheering her up, the bright colours jarred and her clever charity shop nostalgic nods to domestic bliss looked shabby and second-hand. What was wrong? This was her home, the place she'd come to find her own slice of the Good Life. Why did she suddenly feel like chucking everything in a skip and starting again? Why, instead of feeling peaceful, did her home feel empty and quiet? She pressed a few buttons and music flooded the room; Doris started singing 'Lullaby on Broadway' and Coralie stomped over and switched her off. From now on she was going to listen to Tinie Tempah or Plan B. Anything but Doris.

Kitty let everything go in a frightened rush of tears. Alys led her inside, holding her close and letting her sob out her fears. 'There, there, it's all going to be fine. I must say, I thought my grand-child was in danger of going off to school before you let on,' she said, trying to keep her own emotions in check.

'I just thought everyone would think I was stupid. I mean me – getting pregnant! I couldn't believe it myself at first. I mean, we did use contra-ception . . . most of the time.'

'After you'd had a little practice run without first, I suppose,' Alys said, giving her a squeeze. 'I hope you've given him hell.' She felt her daughter stiffen as she tried to hold back more tears and knew there was worse to come. 'You haven't told him? Or he doesn't want to know?'

'Both,' Kitty mumbled into Alys's tee shirt. 'I didn't tell him because he wouldn't want to know.'

Alys couldn't help the sigh that escaped.

'Oh, Mam,' said Kitty pulling herself up with difficulty. 'I'm not completely stupid. I have been doing all the other things right; not drinking, being careful with my diet. I've been seeing Nurse Williams regularly, too.'

'I know,' said Alys. 'She told me she was looking after you.'

'Isn't that illegal or something?' Kitty frowned.

'So sue us,' said Alys. 'Someone needed to keep an eye on you.'

Kitty opened her mouth to reply, but her retort was stifled by the spasm of pain that made her double up.

'Breathe through it,' said Alys. 'There's a good girl.' She waited until the contraction had passed and Kitty managed a weak smile. 'I think we'll ring the hospital just to be on the safe side, but I'm sure there's no need to panic; it's often tricky to tell what's happening with first babies. Then I'll wake your dad up so he comes, too. Just in case he has to drive.'

'Mam? Whilst you fetch Dad, I just need to make a quick phone call.'

Gethin dragged himself into the bathroom and stood under the cold shower to wash away the last of his hangover. The cold jets of water, like acupuncture needles in his skull, were supposed to take his mind off the pain, but did nothing for his guilty conscience. When he looked in the mirror, the same dumb prick stared back at him; the one who'd taken advantage of a good-natured woman who'd trailed all the way out to America for the sake of others. He should have given her the attention she deserved when she needed it, and should have addressed her fears instead of brushing them aside, but he'd behaved just like his father, who'd never listened to his mother. Whenever his mother had tried to express her concerns for the farm, her father had rubbished them and made her look small. As for all that selfless devotion to him? Had his father respected it? Had he, hell! All he'd done was take her love and trample all over it.

Maybe it would be better for Coralie if he did keep away, but there was something he could still do to prove he wasn't all bad. Gethin picked up the old jeans and shirt he wore when he was working. He'd promised that there would be a painting for the handover ceremony at the end of April when everyone in Penmorfa would have an opportunity to see the work. And if he wanted to avoid letting everyone down, there'd be an awful lot of midnight oil to burn if he was to meet the deadline. He squared his shoulders and rubbed his hands together, eager for the challenge. A Lewis man by name, but no longer, if he could help it, in nature.

★   ★   ★

The first faint blush of dawn was illuminating the sky when Kitty and her parents arrived at the hospital. By the time the midwife had finished her initial checks, a pale sun cast a lemon light over the white walls. At first Kitty clutched at the daylight, grateful that she wasn't hemmed in by inky-black squares of night. But, as her contractions racked up in strength and frequency, even the sight of clouds scudding across the blue began to annoy her and she jumped every time the door opened.

'It's all right,' said Alys, who was looking much happier now that the midwife had reassured her that the baby was doing well. 'Your dad's waiting outside until it's all over.'

'I wish I bloody could,' Kitty said, as the screw of pain in her back tightened again.

'Try to relax,' said Alys, smoothing the hair from her brow. 'I know it's easier said than done, but believe me, fighting it won't help.'

Her mother was clearly too old to remember that this was seriously painful.

'Fuuuck!'

'Nice greeting!' she heard someone say as the contraction subsided. Good, she thought, resting back on the pillow, now it can begin.

'Adam?'

Kitty grinned at the surprise in her mother's voice.

'Oh good,' said the midwife following him into the room, 'your partner's arrived!'

'Birthing partner!' Adam added quickly. 'A spare one at that since she's already got her mum here.'

'Shame,' muttered the midwife, looking disappointed. 'Lovely looking man like you. I'm not sure you should be here, in that case.'

'Don't you dare go!' Kitty bellowed, finding some strength.

The midwife thought about it. 'Hmm, well, Mum seems to want you here . . .'

'Yes, I sodding do!' roared Kitty, feeling like a huge monster baby herself.

'Well, since we're not busy . . .'

Kitty saw Adam twinkle at the nurse, then quickly wiped the smile off his face when Alys gave him her hard stare. Was it something genetic that made him flirt with every woman he met?

'You got round to telling your mum at last then,' he said, bending down to drop a kiss on Kitty's forehead, as she reached for the gas and air. 'I offered to be here just in case,' he explained, pulling up a seat next to Alys. 'Although, I never seriously thought she'd take me up on it,' he added, grinning back at Kitty.

'I'm just going to check to see how she's progressing,' said the midwife.

'Do you want to swap places?' Kitty heard her mother offer. 'You're very close to the business end.' She was glad that Alys refrained from making any further comment; Adam was looking quite self-conscious enough. Then, as the next contraction broke over her, Kitty reached out and grabbed his hand as if someone had just thrown her a lifeline.

'I want to push!' she yelled. She was sorry for swearing at the midwife when she suggested she might not be quite ready, but it was very fucking annoying, to say the least, to be advised to stop, and highly satisfying when she finally got the green light. Kitty gave everything she had into one almighty push and nearly as much to a second. By the time she'd got to what felt like the tenth or possibly the twentieth, her initial enthusiasm was beginning to wane.

'I can't do this anymore,' she wailed.

'You got to!' said Adam, sounding horrified.

'I want to go home now!'

'Don't be silly,' said Alys, suddenly not sounding so reassuringly like mummy. 'Working yourself into a tantrum isn't going to help any of us.'

She heard a small muffled sob and sensed someone quietening her mother. Then Adam was there, holding her face, making her look into his eyes.

'Come on now, sweetheart,' he said gently. 'Just keep calm and think of how close you are to seeing your beautiful baby. Stick with it, girl.'

'You're doing really well,' said the midwife. 'I can see baby's head now. Baby's got lovely blonde hair.'

Hair? For a split second, she forgot the pain. A real baby with real hair! And then she sensed something like the first ripples of a distant tsunami heading her way and braced herself for it to break.

254

Kitty grunted and the grunt turned into a roar of pain and triumph. Suddenly everyone in the room was crying.

'You beauty!' said Adam, wiping away the tears to kiss her and then Alys. Alys managed to stop him kissing the midwife, who was just wiping the baby ready to pass to Kitty.

'Well done, Mummy,' said the midwife, handing him over. 'Here's your beautiful son.'

Kitty took her eyes off her baby just long enough to smile at Adam. 'What do you think of him, Daddy?'

'So that's what all the bickering between Kitty and Adam was about!' said Coralie the next afternoon when Alys called into the shop with the news.

'"My only love sprung from my only hate",' quoted Alys, sending Coralie's thoughts off in a direction she didn't especially want them to follow.

'I could see the sparks flying between them last summer, but I was a bit slow on the uptake,' Alys continued, looking thoughtful. 'No wonder some of the flower beds were looking a bit neglected.'

'But why didn't Kitty tell Adam about the baby sooner?'

'I think she assumed he wouldn't be able to handle it; with good reason, I guess. He's never going to be an easy dog to keep on the porch.' Alys perched on the stool next to the counter. 'This way at least she knew he'd be there for the birth of his son.'

'I wished I'd seen his face, I bet it was a picture.' Coralie smiled, thinking how unfair it was that she was about to spoil Alys's happy mood.

'Well, fair play to him, he didn't faint, not even when he realised what Kitty was saying. He looked over the moon, actually.' Alys sighed and shook her head when her eyes met Coralie's. Adam settling down? However lovely it seemed, they both knew it was unlikely to happen.

'Have they chosen a name yet?'

A shadow flitted across Alys's face. 'I think she feels she wants to get to know him first. I'm worried that she's spent so long denying this baby's existence that she's finding it particularly hard to accept he's here. I'm thinking about putting her and the baby in the holiday cottage. Would you mind? Adam's still sharing a place with his brother, but I thought it would be a way to encourage the three of them to get to know each other without me and Huw cramping their style. Who knows if Adam will stick around for the long haul, but let's give them all the best possible chance. I think Kitty's got enough to cope with just getting her head around being a mum.'

Whilst it would be nice to have company again, Coralie wasn't convinced that a screaming baby would make up for Gethin's absence. 'Well, Kitty can always give me a shout if she needs anything. Though I can't say I'm an expert on babies.'

Nor was she ever likely to be, she thought, feeling glum.

Alys gave her a sharp look, 'I must say, you're looking very sleek. Something to do with New York?'

Coralie acknowledged the compliment with a smile. Alys didn't look entirely convinced by the silky black shirt teamed with black jersey boot-cut trousers. Since she'd brought them back with her though, it seemed a waste not to wear the clothes she'd been storing at her parents. Especially when she'd spent so much on them in the first place. Her hot brush had been amongst her things too, so she'd straightened out the kinks and swept her hair back in a simple pony tail rather than fiddling around with scarves.

'Well, it did make me think twice about where I want to go with Sweet Cleans. I'm thinking about redesigning the brand, maybe going for something a bit more sophisticated. When I approached Tessa at The Cabin at Abersaith about my range, she thought it looked a bit amateurish. Different styling might make it a better fit.'

'The Cabin *is* a very upmarket hotel,' Alys said frowning, 'though there's a high chance that someone like Keira or Sienna or one of those other actresses will discover you, if Tessa agrees to stock you.'

Coralie hesitated. When an email had arrived from the Pamala Gray Gallery her hopes had been raised then dashed. Her dejection was somewhat mollified when she read on. Laura Schiffman, who'd done such a good job of fielding Gethin on the night of the disastrous reception, had written to send warm thanks for the sample of Happy Hands which had apparently soothed her eczema like no other cream.

So impressed was she by its efficacy that she'd even ordered a dozen more to give to her stressed-out colleagues and friends. The interest had caused Coralie to wonder yet again if she could muddle on with Sweet Cleans on her own, or if it was time to think big. She decided against sharing her thoughts with Alys, putting off the discussion that would certainly cause the older woman additional worry.

'But are you sure that's the direction you want to follow?' Alys went on. 'Most people are trying to save money. I mean, we're even pushing plants for austerity Britain now. Some of our customers are uneasy about buying roses which have racked up air-miles, so there's been a real resurgence of interest in grow-your-own cut flowers like dahlias, roses and gladioli.'

The sound of R&B blasting from a white van crunching down the road beside the garden centre from the old cottage made them both look up.

'I haven't seen any of those for a while,' said Alys. 'They can't have very much left to do.'

'I suppose it will go on the market, will it?' Coralie asked casually.

Alys, who'd picked up a pot of Happy Hands, removed her glasses to give her a close inspection, making Coralie feel she'd rather revealed her less-than-happy hand. If there was any chance of running into Gethin she wanted to be prepared.

'It doesn't look like the same place now, that's all I can tell you,' Alys replied. 'Mind you, it should never have been allowed to get so run-down. Nothing to do with Gethin, by the way,' she added, reading Coralie's expression. 'He did his best for Gwyn, even though the old boy could be so stubborn and difficult.'

Maybe it was a family trait. Coralie pretended to tidy her greetings card display, something she'd taken on trial because she felt sorry for the artist. If Alys couldn't see her face, maybe they'd stay on safer ground.

Coralie blew out a long breath and, omitting the details, explained that Gethin was planning to substitute the portrait with one of his existing works.

'Oh, that's all right!' Alys laughed. 'I'm sorry that it was a wasted exercise for you, although –' she shot Coralie a quick smile – 'I hope you *did* manage to enjoy yourself. And I daresay there'll be a few comments about lowering the tone, but the point is that an original work by Gethin Lewis, however, erm, racy, will sell for an awful lot of money! Besides, there's nothing the rest of the Hall Management Committee can do but grumble. ACORN have already approved the loan.'

Coralie folded her arms. According to what she'd read online, the reason Gethin's work had sold for such extravagant sums was mainly due to investors hoping to make money from another *Last Samba before Sunset*. Everyone loved a winner, but how would they feel about an artist whose work had so dramatically fallen out of favour?

CHAPTER 20

Gethin's shoulders were burning, but at least his stomach had stopped complaining. His back ached from standing for so long and his throbbing brain was warning him that he was going to have one hell of a tension headache when this was all over. But still it wasn't fucking right. He swiped at the canvas again, frustrated that his hands just couldn't translate what was in his head, repeatedly reverting to the cynically sensual crowd-pleasing oeuvre that had swollen his bank account and left him emotionally bankrupt.

He'd painted through sunset, oblivious to the glass windows turning to gold in the late light. The neon signs above the bars and clubs winked unnoticed by him as the last commuters hurried home and the first pleasure-seekers arrived in search of something to take their cares away. He'd been painting too urgently to think about food. As for drink? He'd had such a bad taste in his mouth for so long he wondered if there was anything that could ever wash it away, although his imagination was telling him he could smell coffee.

'She's worth it, you know.' Ruby, a cardboard cup in each hand, kicked the door shut behind her and looked round for a flat surface that had escaped the worst of the paint.

'Hi, Rubes, what are you doing here? Haven't you got work to do? There's a big exhibition ahead, you know.'

She shook her head. 'I still can't believe I was shortlisted! "Brave New Artists: Rising Stars". And one of them's me! Oh, man!' She slid down the wall and sat cross-legged on the floor, as if the weight of everything that had happened in such a short space of time was too much for her.

'It's great news, Rubes.' He passed her a coffee and then sat down beside her to rest his aching shoulders. 'I want to see you get the prize for the best painting, too.'

'I feel bad,' she said, plucking at the silver dog tag round her neck. 'It should have been you getting all the attention.'

'Oh, I'm not short of attention.' He patted her knee. 'And I couldn't be happier for you. So the judges approved of the digital image then? That's terrific.'

'Yes, now I have to submit the physical painting for judging. '

Ruby gave him a rueful smile and he shoved gently against her shoulder. 'You should get out of here now then, before someone spots you hanging around with a loser. I'm finished here, you know that.'

She pulled a face. 'I owe you. You were the one who took me on when I had nowhere to go. I would have had to leave school if you hadn't paid my fees and found me somewhere to live.'

He rose stiffly to his feet. 'I was shrewd enough to spot talent, that's all.' He shrugged. 'Besides, none of the other applicants ticked the boxes about being able to lift five gallons of paint or work off ladders. For a tiny girl, you punch way above your weight.'

'People should be more loyal,' she said, getting up and shoving her hands in her pockets. She stared moodily out of the black windows at her reflection. 'This isn't about fashion, it's about an artist creating something fresh and original.'

Gethin raised his brows at her. 'So tell me, when did I last do that? The fact is, Rubes, I've been playing the system for too long, rote-producing stuff with no heart and soul. I've been found out.'

She lifted her eyes to him, meeting his in the glass. They both knew it was true. 'So take your chance and make the most of it. Don't go down the same route as me.'

'At least you'll always have *Last Samba before Sunset*,' she said, trying to cheer him up. 'That'll keep you off the streets.'

Yeah, maybe, but what did that painting mean to him now? The royalties from shelves full of *Samba* merchandise – the prints, coasters, mugs and mouse mats – had enabled him to set up in New York. They'd also helped to keep the old man in comfort in an expensive private nursing home where he could be certain that the well-trained staff could cope kindly with the frailties of his failing mind and body. For where was the good in making a dying man suffer for past hurts he struggled to remember?

And even if the administrators for his art publishers paid up, as he was assured they would shortly, sales had to be reaching saturation point. He'd even watched a documentary programme about supposedly lost tribes, where one of the elders was wearing a *Samba* tee shirt with his loin cloth in a startling ancient world meets modern combo. Yup, *Samba* had been so huge he'd almost choked on it. No wonder he'd lost his appetite for producing new work when all the public was looking for was more of the same. Getting that hunger back made him feel nervous and excited all at once; a bit like falling in love.

'Go on, Rubes, it's late,' he told her, eager to get on. 'Your girlfriend'll be waiting for you.'

'Yeah.' She grinned. 'It's good to have her back. Not having her around when Coralie was there made me appreciate her more.'

'That's the way it goes,' he agreed. 'You don't know what you've got until it's gone.'

She shuffled up to him and, uncaring of the paint on his shirt, wrapped her arms stiffly around him. From someone who'd been so badly used by her mother's partner it was a huge deal. Ruby had come a long way from the scarred, scared, borderline dropout she'd been when he'd first noticed her potential.

'When are you leaving,' she muttered into his chest.

'The unveiling ceremony's next week and I'm running out of time. So hop it.' He dropped a kiss on her fluffy blonde head and she stepped away.

'Oh man!' she said, looking at the canvas for the first time. 'You've really done it now.'

'Promise me you'll bring your children up at Penmorfa.'

His father's final words. This from the man who'd been so quick to banish him from the place. And Gethin had been happy enough to agree if it meant the old man had one fewer burden on his conscience when he closed his eyes for the last time. The voice was suddenly so clear in his head that Gethin could almost imagine his father was up at the cottage waiting.

The hired Mondeo he was driving past the garden centre and up the rutted track towards his father's cottage wasn't nearly as luxurious as the Land Rover he'd used last time, or as much fun. But it would stop any rumblings about him flashing his cash and he hoped any villagers catching sight of him the day before he was due to hand over his painting would approve of his frugal choice and feel more generously disposed towards him.

Behind him the green tracery of the overlapping trees gradually closed a veil over the little village and it was easy to forget it was there. But for the intrusive arrival of PVC windows and the occasional plastic door squatting brutishly in the once-humble terraced houses, nothing much ever seemed to change. Penmorfa was everything he'd been glad to leave and yet – maybe he had a touch of *hiraeth*? – he was almost glad to see the place again.

He could, of course, have stayed in the States, but it was time to make decisions about his father's cottage. It was as good a place as any to let the fuss about his latest exhibition blow over, which, he was confident, it would. And Coralie? Maybe this was his chance to show that he was willing to do all he could to make amends.

'What's that you're driving there, boy?' he could imagine his father saying, leaning out of the window of his ancient Land Rover. 'Some sort of girl's car, is it?'

For a moment he was reminded of the old man's cutting sense of humour, sharpened and honed by a quick and clever mind. Mam, bless her, hadn't been the brightest tool in the box, lovely as she was, and hadn't always kept up with Gwyn's voracious reading and lively curiosity. No wonder the old man had lost his rag at times, hemmed in by his land, his cattle, and with no outlet for that keen mind – and yet he'd been eager for his own son to perpetuate the misery.

'Don't think you've won,' he muttered out loud, 'this is only temporary. The whole idea of me staying here is preposterous.'

His father's aspirations for him had always been narrow: the farm or nothing. Qualifications were a waste of time; university a waste of money. 'Watch me, boy, and you'll learn everything you need to know.'

So he'd watched his parents struggling to earn a living wage, seen them buckle under concerns about BSE, Foot and Mouth disease, the withdrawal of subsidies and the rising cost of feed and fuel. What he'd learned was that he'd be better off following his passion, pursuing his artistic ambitions, instead. His father had accused him of treachery, of walking away from the fight to rejuvenate the industry and keep the local community alive. And, later, even of being the cause of his mother's early death.

The old man had never given in and admitted that he might have been right to leave. Not even after the sale of the old farmhouse, when the monies, as he'd later found out once his father had been too ill to refuse help, had barely been enough to keep him once outstanding debts had been paid. Well, it was too late to resurrect the family farm, but maybe he could do his bit for the community?

A sickly farmyard odour that he always associated with his father wafted into the car. Gethin waited to hear his dry snicker behind him and glanced up into the mirror. His harshest critics would have agreed with his father's assessment: that he'd overreached his ambition and should have stayed on the farm. But they hadn't seen anything yet. This time, he'd thrown out all the artifice and pretension and returned to first principles to paint what really moved him. At long last he could look himself in the eye and know that the work he was about to unveil came straight from the heart.

The thin smile he'd found, against the odds, was replaced by sheer amazement when he reached the cottage and wondered if he was at the right place. The practical brown-framed replacement windows his father had been forced to install when the originals had gone beyond repair, had been swapped for something far more sympathetic to the character of the building. The ugly rendering had been painted a sunny cream, the front door given a heritage paint makeover in a powdery seaside blue and a new slate roof sat snugly against the weather.

Inside, the mephitic stink of mildew mixed with plague pit had been ousted by the smell of fresh paint and new carpets. Plastered walls and new ceilings gave the rooms a clean, modern feel. Cream units and oak worktops gave the kitchen what the magazines would have described as a classic country feel, though not one that his father would ever have recognised, and the ghastly avocado bathroom – a so-called improvement installed in the seventies which his father insisted was 'good enough for me, boy; it'll get me clean, won't it?'– had been replaced with a modern white suite and a power shower. All he was missing, he thought, as it suddenly occurred to him, was some furniture. At least he'd had the sense to stop off at what he thought of as Penmorfa's shoddy goods store, where you were nearly beaten back by the smell of cheap plastic before you'd got through the door, to buy a sleeping bag and some basics.

He trudged back to the car just in time to be snarled at by a wire-haired Jack Russell as it leapt off the back of a quad bike before heading off on important business in the undergrowth. Huw Bowen, his hair sticking up from the breeze in an 'owner most like dog' moment, looked just as gruff.

'Alys saw you go past. She was worried that you might be hungry so she sent you up some lunch.' Regarding him suspiciously, Huw handed him a thin cotton bag that was heavy with a couple of foil-wrapped packages and a flask. His expression suggested that the gesture was nothing to do with him and he sincerely hoped that Alys had laced it with laxatives.

'Alys is a thoughtful woman,' he said. 'You're a very lucky man, Huw.'

Huw flushed, as if he'd hit a nerve, and glared at him. 'Just don't let her down, will you? She's worked hard trying to persuade her committee that you're genuinely trying to help the village, which is no easy task considering how many people still think that *Samba* painting was a bit of a piss-take. Mair's been going around telling everyone you're about to present them with another painting of a scantily-clad floozy on the beach and turn Penmorfa into the laughingstock of Wales again.'

Gethin shook his head. Nothing had changed. And he was trying to help these people? He took a deep breath. Not these people. One person: himself.

The clouds, which were almost as dark as Huw's face, let loose an April shower that threatened to soak them in seconds. Gethin beckoned to the cottage and Huw and Edith hurried after him.

'Tell Alys not to worry,' he shouted above the sound of the rain echoing in the bare hall. 'It's an entirely new work, that hasn't been created for an exhibition or gallery. I hope it will have resonance for everyone who comes into contact with it.'

Huw nodded, not looking completely convinced. 'So, everything all right here?'

'As far as I can tell the builders you recommended did a good job. Trying to oversee it at a distance, I was afraid I would come in to wet plaster and wires dangling out the ceiling, but they were as good as their word. I'm grateful to you, Huw.'

Huw's expression softened and he relaxed enough for Edith to leap out of his arms and skedaddle upstairs to take herself off on a tour.

'But you've got no furniture!' Huw said, slightly out of breath from chasing after her, as he returned with Edith squirming in his arms. 'You can't stay here, boy. Where are you going to sleep? Young

Kitty's in the holiday cottage – and that's another story, I can tell you. There's The Cabin at Abersaith, though it's pricey, mind you, although I daresay if anyone can afford it, you can.'

Gethin waved his hand, slightly too close to Edith who tried to take a couple of fingers off in passing.

'Thanks, I'll be all right here.'

Huw positively beamed. 'Getting a feel of the old place again, eh, boy? That's the spirit! I wouldn't want to be away from it for a moment longer than I had to be if it was mine, either. Maybe you'll decide to return to the village, after all, then no one will be able to say that you think you're too good for us.'

Gethin refrained from saying anything to darken his mood again. He still couldn't make up his mind where he stood with Huw, but that was true of so many people in the village. And one woman in particular. 'And in the meantime,' he said instead, 'your good wife has packed more food than I can possibly eat. Would you care to share some lunch?' He opened one parcel and handed a chicken salad sandwich in good, thick granary bread over to the older man who, with Edith slavering in his arms, took a huge appreciative bite.

Good, thought Gethin. If Alys had laced the food with laxatives, he wouldn't be the only one suffering.

'Pinky-winky,' announced Alys, looking over her reading glasses as the glass doors of the garden centre shop slid open. Coralie, who had wandered into the revamped former shed for company, wondered if she'd been spending too much time with her grandson.

'The names they come up with now!' she went on, with a smile, coming out from behind the counter.

'What, Kitty and Adam?' New parents some-times got a bit carried away, but the new baby would have to grow up tough if he got lumbered with that.

'Oh no, he's definitely James, after Adam's late father.' A shadow flitted briefly across Alys's face. 'I'm relieved one of them came to a decision, and since Adam's only got his brother and sister now it seemed a lovely gesture. Do you know I had visions of that poor child starting school still being called The Baby if it was left to Kitty. No, it's one of our catalogue range of new plants. Lovely orna-mental hydrangea, though.'

Coralie hoped that Alys, who could get very passionate about plant trends, wasn't going to nag her about the dominant trend in her own garden, which was mainly to let it look after itself.

'Bird Poo Remover.'

Coralie looked up.

'I must order some,' Alys reminded herself. 'Everyone'll be wanting to clean up their garden furniture soon. Have you seen how much mess the house martins have made over Willow's unit? She's having to dash for it every time she crosses the threshold. Wilfie got stuck in there with her for ages recently. Came out looking quite dishevelled. Still, nothing you can do about it once they've established their nests, of course.'

Willow and Wilfie? Coralie shook her head; she still couldn't quite believe the evidence of her own eyes.

'Poor man,' Alys went on. Although as far as Coralie could tell, whatever was going on in Willow's unit was doing Wilfie the world of good. Even his beard looked clean and tidy these days.

'Imagine how much it must have hurt Gethin to be described as an indifferent painter who'd got away with pulling the wool over everyone's eyes for far too long? It just goes to prove how little those New York critics know,' Alys continued, as she slowly paced one side of the shop, checking her stock. 'I'm confident that none of this nonsense about the current exhibition closing hurriedly will make a blind bit of difference over here. The publicity might even help. I daresay even Delyth and Mair will be on his side, now that the Big Apple's spat out one of Penmorfa's own. They all love a loser round here.'

'He certainly doesn't need to face any more criticism,' Coralie had to agree. 'Getting that from the city he loves must have come as a terrible shock.'

'Anyway, we'll make sure we put on a good show of strength at the presentation ceremony and give him the reception he deserves,' Alys called over. 'Have you managed to catch up with him yet?'

In fact, when Coralie heard he was back in the village, she *had* decided that she ought to talk to him sooner rather than later, just to dissipate some of the potential awkwardness between them. But somehow she hadn't screwed up enough courage to do it. She looked down at her feet.

'No? Well, never mind – here he comes now!'

CHAPTER 21

Oh no! Coralie's stomach lurched. He was just as gorgeous as she remembered. So much for telling herself that when she saw him it would be like digging out an old picture of a pop idol she'd once had a crush on. Part of her hoped to discover that her libido had tricked her into falling for someone who, in hindsight, she might be embarrassed by.

She remembered vividly her shame as a teenager after she'd got carried away at a Christmas party for the staff of the local supermarket where she worked on Saturdays. Snogging the manager of the meat counter, who'd looked almost attractive under fairy lights after a glass of Lambrusco, seemed like a particularly poor idea when he turned up at her house and offered her mum free sausages hoping to ingratiate himself with her.

But seeing Gethin again, all she could do was congratulate herself on her impeccable taste. Even in the height of summer it was never scorching in Penmorfa, due to its proximity to the sea, but today it was pleasantly warm and it was great to see Gethin without his leather jacket. She could admire his fine forearms, with their dusting of dark hair, and the curve of strong biceps disappearing under his short-sleeved black tee shirt. His thick dark hair was unruly, his jaw was set off by at a least a day's worth of stubble – though she'd have to run her fingers across it to be sure – and his dark eyes looked just as sexy in broad daylight as they did across a pillow. In fact, he looked as if he'd just rolled out of bed.

'Who died?' he said, looking from her to Alys and frowning. Coralie winced.

'Oh, we are all in black, aren't we?' Alys beamed.

It was true that Alys and Gethin were both wearing black tee shirts and jeans, and both wearing them very well in their own ways, but Coralie had resurrected another of her management consultancy outfits.

'Coralie looks well, doesn't she?' Alys nodded at the black silk vest top and straight linen skirt.

'What happened to all the colour?' Gethin asked, his scowl deepening.

'It's lovely to see you again too, Gethin,' Coralie said, miffed. 'I told you in New York, if you remember, that I was going to start looking forward. The retro clothes didn't feel right anymore.'

'So you've shrugged them off, along with the past, have you?' he growled.

Coralie went over to pick up a packet of seeds that had fallen off one of the shelves as an excuse to hide her face. Giant Red carrot seeds, renowned for their size and vigour. Gethin looked big and vigorous too, although the carrots, she hoped, were less prickly.

'Goodness me,' said Alys, 'someone got out of bed the wrong side this morning. I hope you'll be in a better mood this evening at the presentation ceremony. Come here and give me a kiss, you great brute!'

'The things I do for you, Alys,' he said, shaking his head. A smile spread across his face at last, lighting up the dark corner where they were standing as he held her, then kissed her on both cheeks.

'And don't forget Coralie,' Alys reminded him. 'She was the one who went all the way out to America to get you on board.'

'As if.'

Even that brief contact was enough to make her want to burst into tears because every pulse in her body was beating a little 'touch me' tattoo at having him so close.

'I apologise, but I'm still trying to figure out where everything is up at the cottage. Like hot water,' he added, running a hand across his stubble. 'I was so travel weary when I set the timer switch that I punched in the wrong programme.'

That explained why he looked as if he'd slept in his clothes then. And that mildly musky, wildly attractive masculine scent of him.

'Not quite what you needed after a long journey, you must be worn out,' Alys agreed. 'And although Huw and I don't usually hire out our bath, I'm prepared to make an exception if you'd like your back scrubbed. Unless Coralie wants to do it . . .'

Coralie glared at her.

'Don't look so worried,' Gethin said, with the ghost of a smile. He took the seeds from her and slotted them back into place. 'I reckon a cold shower will do me good.'

'Well,' Alys said, clearly choking back a laugh, 'it looks as if we've got a really good crowd coming this evening. I'm so looking forward to seeing what you've got to offer us. Which reminds me, I need to check how many chairs we've got. Coralie, can you mind the counter for me?'

'I came back to try to make amends,' Gethin said.

'How?' Coralie wandered away and leaned back against the counter. He followed and stood in front of her, longing to touch her but afraid. The brief flare of heat of her body as he'd leaned in to greet her was the only warmth he'd felt. It wasn't just her bright clothes that had cooled.

'You made it obvious the way you felt about Penmorfa and, by extension, me, in New York. That's one bridge burning.'

'I can start by fixing it for Alys,' he said, trying not to lose hope.

'Really? I hope so because Delyth and Mair will have a field day laying all the blame at her feet if anything goes wrong.' She shook her head and he longed for just one recalcitrant curl to escape from the sleek chignon that made her seem so frosty and remote.

Gethin folded his arms. He'd given up caring about what a few small-minded people with nothing else on their minds thought of him years ago. It seemed to have escaped her notice that there was only one person he was trying to impress. 'Not in front of me, they won't,' he told her, aching for her to drop her guard. 'Don't look like that,' he said reproachfully. 'I'm not going anywhere until I've smoothed everything over here.'

'So you can lie low until all the fuss about your latest exhibition dies down over there, I suppose,' she said, tightly.

'I'm not lying low or running away from anything, Coralie. There are far more pleasant places where I could cool my heels if I wanted to. I'm running to something. I came back because of you. And I don't have any plans for the immediate future that don't include you.'

He waited for her to say something, but the silence was only broken by the sound of Edith dancing around outside the glass doors, barking her head off and trying to see off anyone thinking about going into the shop. Good work, Edith.

'Think about it. I could introduce you to some great contacts in New York,' he pointed out and got the faintest of smiles in return.

'You already did,' she said, surprising him. 'I gave Laura Schiffman a sample of my Happy Hands cream. Not only did she like it, but she bought more of it for her girlfriends, one of whom, it turns out, was rather well-connected.'

'Go on,' he said, smiling back.

'She's a buyer with one of the big cosmetic houses, though our discussions are only at a very early stage.' She shrugged. 'The thing is I've been searching for growth opportunities for the business. Involvement with a large organisation would provide marketing and research and develop opportunities I could only dream of, but I do have some concerns for Sweet Cleans.'

He nodded. 'You think it could threaten Sweet Cleans' natural, wholesome image?'

A shadow crossed her face and she bit her lip. 'No, it's back to lifestyle choices; whether to stay small in the country, or get involved with big business.' She looked at him steadily. 'Right now, I'm happy with the life I've got here.'

Gethin pushed his fingers through his hair. 'Those kinds of opportunities don't come round every day and you must know the risk you're taking if you stay here.'

'I've done my sums,' she told him, firmly.

'Yes, you're the accountant,' he said. 'But you don't know how hard it is to live here.'

'I know it didn't suit you,' she began, when he rolled his eyes. 'But there are compensations: it's a close-knit community, there's almost no crime, everyone talks—'

'Oh, they do that all right,' he shot back.

'How can you say that? How long is it since you

actually lived here? Those are outdated prejudices. You think you have moved on since you left Penmorfa, but Penmorfa's changed, too.'

'Not as far as I can tell.' He grimaced.

'You haven't exactly given yourself a chance to find out, have you?' Coralie tugged fretfully at the hem of the depressing black vest. 'Anyway, surely it's easier to ignore a bit of ignorant tittle-tattle than having the New York press trash your exhibition?'

Gethin grimaced. 'Critics are entitled to their opinion. I'll get over that, but I can't live in this goldfish bowl.'

'Well, that's that then,' she said, except that made it sound as if they might have had a future, when, unless he acted fast, they didn't even have a relationship.

What if Gethin's work *had* plummeted in value? Later, in the Summerhouse Café which had once more been pressed into service for the evening, Coralie wiped her damp palms together and hoped that the ordinary buyers, the ones who knew what they liked and didn't care about critical opinion, were still out there. A good Gethin Lewis would surely still sell well? As for the artist himself? Feeling tears prick her eyes, she took a deep steadying breath and concentrated on practical matters. Coralie could feel her heart pounding as she waited to see Gethin's painting at last. At first she'd been afraid that no one would turn up to the presentation ceremony, but Alys and the Hall Management Committee had, it seemed, been quietly drumming up interest. Kitty, and a couple of young mums hoping to resume the mother-and-toddler group again, appeared pushing buggies; the woman with the jet black hair who ran flower arranging classes took a chair at the end of a row next to her husband; and some elderly residents shuffled to the front row. All the people who would benefit when the refurbished hall reopened.

The thudding in Coralie's chest moved up a gear when a local TV reporter and camera crew started setting up. If the piece was aired, news of the charity auction would reach a far wider audience than the notice on the Hall Management Committee's website. It might even ignite some competitive bidding on the day. On the other hand, if anything went wrong, there was every chance that Delyth would make sure her grandson would post the footage on YouTube so that they could enjoy the sight of Alys's humiliation over and over again.

Whatever had happened between them, Gethin had come through for the village where he grew up. Not only had he fulfilled his promise, but he'd even cared enough to arrive in person to unveil the work. For that alone, he deserved her support. She glanced up at him at last, sitting next to Alys on the raised platform, and realised with a pang how tired and drawn he was. Everyone fell silent as he stood up abruptly to make some last-minute checks, scrutinising the lighting and adjusting the level of the easel. Alys's hand fluttered to her chest and she reached for a glass of water to wet her lips. Gethin, reseating himself next to her, gave her a small nod and Alys stood up to speak. Coralie pressed her lips together, willing herself to stay calm for a few agonising seconds more. Despite everything that was left unsaid between them, she was proud of Gethin and the very small part she had played in delivering the project. And even if she detested everything she saw when the covers came off the painting, she'd be the first one cheering and singing its praise.

Gethin felt everyone's attention turning to him, as Alys concluded her short speech, but he was only aware of one face. Coralie looked amazing in a tasteful, slim-fitting taupe dress and a swept-back hairdo that made her look serious, sophisticated and even more like a stranger to him. The dress depressed the hell out of him and he longed for her to loosen her copper waves and become the woman he knew. Just when he thought he'd caught hold of her, she'd slipped out of reach again.

'I hope you can all see properly,' he said, sounding more confident than he felt. 'I have to admit that things have changed since the night when I rashly offered to donate a painting to help raise funds for this village. I was, perhaps, guilty of believing my own myth, of thinking I was better than I was.

Sometimes we all need a reality check to see where we've gone wrong.'

There was some nervous laughter in the room.

'So,' he went on, 'I promised the Hall Management Committee a painting that would have resonance for everyone who looked at it, yet at the same time, I wanted to stay true to myself. Well, this is it . . .'

There was yet more nervous laughter from the audience and some shuffling from the seats beside him where the Hall Management Committee were assembled. He took a long look round the room and reached for the cloth covering the canvas.

Alys could see how anxiously Coralie was watching Gethin, although he almost seemed to be avoiding looking in her direction. Maybe, like her, he missed the old Coralie and all her vintage glad rags. This new, cool Coralie, looking very chic in a Roland Mouret rip-off, was a bit of a stranger. Alys was deeply indebted to her for going so far to get Gethin on board, but whether it had put some of her inner ghosts to rest was hard to tell. She looked from Coralie to Gethin and frowned; a palpable tension in the room had put paid to the festive atmosphere as everyone grew quiet. And then Gethin pulled away the white sheet covering the canvas.

There were shocked gasps and splutters of outrage, but when Alys dared look she saw a portrait that was so infused with raw emotions, it almost hurt. If anyone had any doubts about Gethin's artistic ability, that he had somehow stretched remarkably little talent a very long way – which Alys didn't believe for one moment – *Girl in a Coral Dress*, as he had entitled it, was proof of how gifted he was.

'I thought you promised me I was going to see something a bit saucy?' she heard one of the parish council members complaining to his wife, a woman with fiercely dyed black hair who was responsible for some of the more inspired flower arrangements in Penmorfa's tiny church.

'And this so-called work of art is the thanks we get,' said Delyth, folding her arms, 'from the boy who owes everything he is today to this village.'

The one consolation was that Delyth had earned herself a reproachful look from the Vicar, who was staring at her with great sadness.

'Mrs Bowen,' said a reporter she recognised from the county newspaper, frantically opening a notebook. The young woman had to raise her voice to be heard in the rising noise. 'You're Chair of the Hall Management Committee. Had you seen the new Gethin Lewis before today?'

'Given that the object of this painting was to raise funds for a project in Penmorfa, some of us were anticipating a work more reflective of village life,' another reporter was shouting, waving a recorder at her. 'Can you explain to everyone what the link is?'

'The link,' sneered Mair, puffing up, 'is that

Gethin Lewis has just unveiled another of his mistresses.'

'Not that she looks very happy about it,' Delyth agreed. 'But then I suppose she had to wait until Alys decided she'd finished with him.'

'Oh, for goodness sake!' Alys protested. 'Don't be so ridiculous!'

'Ridiculous, is it?' said Mair.

'Shut your big fat gob!' Kitty shouted, practically in tears as she pushed through the crowd to stand by Alys's side. Jamie, in his buggy, started bawling. Poor thing, Alys registered miserably. 'My mother has worked harder for this village than the rest of you put together. How dare you tell such filthy lies about her!'

Alys felt sick as Delyth and Mair exchanged glances.

'I expect you've been too busy producing father-less children to know about your mother's weakness for younger men,' Mair said, smugly.

'You complete bitch!' howled Kitty. 'Take that back!'

'Ask your mother why that nice couple who used to run the Summerhouse Café left so suddenly then. Ask her about young Jerzy,' Delyth purred.

'You seem to know what's going on ladies,' said a reporter, eagerly. 'Perhaps you know who the woman is in Gethin Lewis's portrait?'

'Another floozy,' Mair said, airily. 'Just like the one in that *Samba* nonsense.'

Alys's legs were shaking, but the words she was

so desperate to find were eluding her. Then everyone took a step back. The Vicar calmly stilled the troubled gaggle with a wave of her pale hands.

'I think you're both letting your imaginations get away with you,' she rebuked Delyth and Mair gently. 'Your view of the artist as some sort of debaucher of women is quite mistaken. I can assure you that the model for *Samba* was categorically *not* involved with the artist.'

'Charitable as ever, dear Vicar,' Mair said, talking to the Vicar as if she were a newborn lamb with no knowledge of the world beyond a spring field.

'No, not charitable,' the Vicar insisted, firm but completely untroubled. She looked round the crowd making sure she had everyone's full attention. 'I know for a fact that the model for *Last Samba before Sunset* did not have sexual relations of any description with the artist.' She paused to give a modest smile. 'I know, because I *was* the model!'

Trembling with relief, Alys turned round smiling and grateful for the Vicar's intervention, but the smile froze on her face as she caught sight of Kitty staring at her in disgust.

'Kitty,' she said quickly, as her daughter started pushing everyone out of the way. Everywhere was in chaos. No one was worried about Gethin's painting anymore; all the cameras were trained on the Vicar, who was batting questions away with a promise of a full interview in due course. After a split second's hesitation she decided to leave them to it and chased after her daughter.

'Wait, Kitty,' she said, catching up with her and clasping hold of her arm. 'It's not what you think!'

'Isn't it?' Kitty tore her arm away furiously. 'You tell me what it is then. Did you or did you not have a relationship with Jerzy?'

Alys shook her head, trying to find the right words.

'How could you, Mam? You meant everything to me; you were the person I most looked up to in the whole world, the one I thought would keep me safe. No wonder poor Dad doesn't want to have anything to do with you. Just don't ever talk to me again, okay?' Kitty pushed her away, crying. 'You make me feel sick!'

CHAPTER 22

Coralie took advantage of the tumult around her to take a few moments more to assimilate her feelings. So long as she never let her hair down ever again, there was a good chance no one would associate her with the pale-faced woman with her cascade of copper curls staring so trustingly from the painting. She lifted her gaze from her nude patent court shoes to take another quick squint at the portrait.

Maybe it wasn't such a disaster; Gethin had summed her up in colour and emotion rather than a precise physical resemblance. Anyway, no one had come rushing up thrusting a mic under her nose yet. In fact, since someone had stuck their head out of the mob clustering round the Vicar shouting that the model in *Samba* had been uncovered, the members of the press had all been too busy trying to submit their stories to notice her.

And by the time he's finished painting them, he's sick of the sight of them. Isn't that what Ruby had told her? *It may be an intense relationship for a short time, but it's only paint.* Was that a bad thing? She considered how she felt about that night. How her body had tingled and ached, as if, for once in a long, long time, she was truly alive and her pulse rate took off just remembering.

That intense relationship had resulted in a portrait that was neither chivalrous nor exploitative. It was tender but not sentimental. If she hadn't known better she would have said that it revealed some pretty naked feelings for the sitter. She tried to steal a glance at the man who'd made her feel reborn, but he'd been engulfed in the crowd. Then someone tapped her lightly on the shoulder.

'Hello, Coralie,' he said. 'You missed our last meeting so I thought I'd come to see you for a change. It looks like I picked a good time.'

'Selfish as ever!' Gethin heard Delyth declare as he pushed past them in pursuit of Coralie, who he'd lost sight of whilst he'd been surrounded by the baying crowd, screaming questions at him. 'Turning the village into a peepshow once again! You always have to bring sex into it, don't you? I suppose the beauty of this landscape isn't good enough for you!'

'Poor Alys,' said Mair loudly. 'If only she'd listened to us in the first place. However will the poor woman cope with such a very public humiliation? All that effort spent grooming the artist only to be traded in for a younger model!'

'Hypocritical old bat,' Gethin snarled to himself. He gritted his teeth and walked on, knowing that

290

anything he said to defend Alys would be wilfully misinterpreted. Besides, anyone who knew Alys would never believe their lies. Instead, he concentrated on what he was going to say to Coralie. One minute more, he thought, walking towards her front door, and she'd be back in his arms and everything would be fine again. His heart was pounding and his mouth was dry and every second apart from all the softness and heat of her made each footstep feel like a mile. All he needed was to be close to the woman who'd been driving him crazy ever since she'd set her cat on him.

He was looking round, waiting for Rock to leap out from behind a bush somewhere, doing his 'feel sorry for me' act, when Coralie opened the door. They stared at each other for a moment. From the look on her face he needed Rock to hurry up and appear to teach him a few tricks about winning her over.

'Oh, Gethin,' she said at last, her sad face pale and haunted. 'I'm so sorry but this isn't a good time.'

Gethin scratched his head; this wasn't the way it was supposed to be. One of his art teachers had once told him that he needed to face his feelings when emotions were running high rather than slamming the door on them. All right, it hadn't been easy to admit what he felt for the woman in front of him, but he'd ripped open his chest and poured his heart all over that canvas for her.

'Hey, Coralie,' someone called from within, 'tell

whoever that is we're busy here. You've kept me waiting long enough.'

'Please tell me that's your brother,' he said, feeling sick. But Coralie just shook her head.

'I need to talk to you,' she said, dropping her voice, 'but this isn't the right time.'

'Why not? Don't you want me to meet your friend in there? Come on, why not invite me in so we can all have a nice chat?'

'It's Ned Wallace, Gethin, and he's very vulnerable right now.'

What about me? He was about to say before he realised what she was telling him. 'The guy who killed that girl? You felt so bad about him, you got involved with him? Coralie, let me tell you that rescuing stray cats is one thing, but you just crossed the line, baby. We're done now.'

'Gethin!' She reached out to try to stop him, but if he stayed there any longer he was afraid that he might cry, so he shook her off and walked away.

Alys, crouched on a stool out of sight in the kitchenette, closed her eyes and waited until the hubbub of voices in the café subsided and all the reporters had hurried off in search of phone signals. Then, when she could be certain of escaping curious glances, she made her way home.

Gethin's portrait of Coralie was far removed from the decadent sensuality of his usual oeuvre; it was a weighty, sober reflection of a man who was either very clever or very much in love. But

292

what did this radical new direction mean for the charity auction? Would the collectors who were still interested in his previous paintings want to buy something so untried, so raw?

But worse than her worries about what money might be raised for the village she loved, was the fear of what this spelled for her family. With Delyth and Mair spreading their poison, was there anyone left who would believe her side of the story? Hers wasn't such a very big crime, but even if she got the chance to explain, would her daughter, fragile, flooded with hormones and struggling with a new baby, understand? Now she was afraid of what else she might lose.

There was no sign of Huw when she got in but, since he frequently took himself off to read, Alys saw no point in disturbing him. She took the stairs quietly, avoiding the squeakier treads and only felt able to relax once she'd closed her bedroom door.

She wiped off her makeup carefully, clinging to the comfort of an old routine, put away the purple silk dress bought for the occasion in a spirit of such optimism and, sinking gratefully on to her bed, thanked her lucky stars that she could escape Huw's scrutiny, at least until morning. Given Kitty's very real preoccupation when she'd first arrived back home, it had been easy enough to fob her off with the excuse that Huw had moved to a spare room because he was having trouble sleeping. Now, instead of feeling embarrassed by their separate beds, she was relieved.

Pulling up the covers, she closed her eyes, even though sleep seemed unlikely. Then the door opened and Huw appeared, lit by the landing light, his warm brown eyes creased into a smile.

'Alys,' he chided gently. 'Fancy keeping me in suspense! Aren't you going to tell me how it went?'

'I didn't think you were that interested,' she mumbled through a fake yawn.

'This place doesn't run itself, you know,' he said, perching on the edge of the bed. 'Someone's had to do the paperwork whilst you've been gallivanting at these meetings.'

When he reached across and smoothed a lock of hair off from her face, she was unable to stop the guilty tear that slid down her face.

'Oh, Huw,' she said, sitting up and reaching for him.

'Don't you want to tell me all about it?' he asked, gently.

'Do you want to tell me about it?' Coralie forced herself to put away her own pain to do what she could for the young man sitting across the room from her. Ned Wallace, driving without due care and attention, had been found guilty of killing an innocent pedestrian, but she felt responsible for the blood on his hands.

'Give me a moment, will you?' he said, closing his eyes.

Was this some kind of karmic justice that he'd

picked this moment to turn up on her doorstep? Just when she was beginning to think that being happy again was a real possibility? She brushed aside her thoughts; the least she owed Ned after everything he'd endured was her time.

'Regaining my freedom was a big high – but now it's beginning to sink in that I'll never get my old life back.'

Coralie watched him with a heavy heart. If only she'd listened to her inner voice, none of this would have happened. She'd gradually become aware of a sense of unease about her career at the consultancy. The content hadn't changed, so she realised something had shifted within herself. Work that had once appealed to her strong sense of order began to feel unjust and she started to wonder if some companies were simply hiring her as a face-saving means to cover ruthless cuts.

If only she'd resigned, she might have prevented all the misery for countless unseen victims instead of swelling corporation coffers. If only she hadn't struck Ned Wallace from the payroll, Hayley Butterfield might be a qualified teacher, enjoying her pupils, her friends and her family. But if she could save Ned, convince him that he had a future worth living for, then perhaps she could help salve her own conscience?

'So, *Girl in a Coral Dress*, how does it feel to have all eyes on you?' he asked, softly. 'I wonder if there's any money in it for me if I go to the papers with some juicy snippets about the model?'

Rock ducked out of his way as Ned reached out and tried to stroke him.

'If you need money,' Coralie said, hoping her voice didn't betray her sudden alarm, 'I'm sure I can help.'

He smiled and she was conscious once again of what a pleasant face he had, something that had struck her when they were first introduced, although the soft brown hair with its natural high-lights was much shorter now. There were shadows, too, under the grey eyes.

'Oh, Coralie,' he said, softly, 'what do you take me for, a blackmailer?' He shook his head. 'You gave me hope. You stood by me when everyone walked away.'

Coralie looked away, sparing him further humili-ation as he lifted his hand to his eyes to rub fiercely at the tears welling there. Horribly aware that his old self would have been mortified by the thin shirt, stiff supermarket jeans and fake Timberlands he was wearing, she let pity overcome her reserva-tions and resolved to do whatever she could to support him on the long road ahead.

'You gave me some dignity, made me feel different to the rest of them,' he continued.

'Well, you were different. It's not like you were a murderer or an armed robber . . .'

'Or a nonce?' he said. 'I just killed a young woman, right?'

'You didn't set out to harm anyone,' she replied, at a loss again, knowing that she was unable to make it better. 'But you've served your sentence now.'

He nodded. 'It takes a bit of getting used to, being out,' he said, looking calmer. 'It's the choice, you see. In there, once you've answered all the questions, filled in all the forms, handed over your property to be bagged and tagged, part of you doesn't exist anymore. Right now, I'm not even capable of choosing my own toiletries.'

She felt another wave of pity for him. 'If I'd have known you were about to be released, I could have met you.'

He leaned towards her. 'If you hadn't missed your last visit, you would have known, but it looks as if you've had other stuff on your mind.'

Unable to stop herself, she shrunk further back in her chair. He noticed, and buried his face in his hands before returning his gaze to her, pupils like black pin-pricks in his pale face. Rock yowled and jumped up on her lap.

'I haven't come to make trouble, Coralie. I think I've got a job lined up in a hotel kitchen in North Wales, but you were sort of on the way. In so far that anywhere's on the way when you haven't got a car. I only want to get my head down somewhere safe for the night – this sofa's fine – and a lift to the station tomorrow and then I'll be out of your hair for good.' He gave a short laugh, 'I don't think there's much of a future in this relationship, do you?'

Her throat constricted and her chest felt tight,

squeezing her lungs and making her heart pound in protest. It wasn't just their relationship that was about to end. Not once the word got out that he was there. But everyone else had turned their backs on Ned Wallace; she owed it to him to make amends.

What the fuck? In the old cottage's bare bathroom the next morning, no amount of cold water splashed over Gethin's shivering body could turn Coralie's words into anything that made sense. Thinking that he might have overreacted, he'd returned to her house much later the previous evening, for what? To prove to himself that he'd been mistaken? That Coralie wasn't really inside with another man? But the welcoming hall light that usually spilled through the glass door panel across the front path had been extinguished, whilst the living-room lamps still shone brightly behind the closed curtains. The longer he'd stood in the dark lane with his imagination driving him insane, the worse he felt.

Now, hurriedly drying himself on the beach towel he'd purchased in his whirlwind shopping spree along the journey, he dragged on some clothes and rolled up his sleeping bag, along with all those romantic notions he'd been nursing. Huh! To think that he'd rejected the idea of booking a room at The Cabin at Abersaith for the duration of his stay because he liked the thought of being closer to Coralie.

With his rosy glow to keep him warm, he'd fantasised about entertaining Coralie there. Imagined the two of them, sitting in a ring of tea lights whilst they chinked glasses and drank a toast to each other, having feasted on something clever he'd rustled up for her. Going out to watch the stars, or wind their way down to Penmorfa cove to taste each other's kisses against the backdrop of the wild sea. So much for that! Might as well book himself into a hotel in London, before catching his flight home, and enjoy the nightlife there instead.

Gethin surveyed the fragments of his dreams: two glasses, two plates, a box of candles. He thought about gathering the lot up in the fleecy blanket he had bought, too, and kicking it over the nearest cliff. Since it wouldn't help him or the environment he left everything where it was. Whoever turned up at the cottage next could have a romantic tête-à-tête instead. Closing the chalky blue door behind him for the last time, Gethin couldn't help but catch his breath at the beauty of the landscape in the early morning light.

The location of the cottage was lovely; secluded and sheltered on one side by tall trees yet with superb views to the front of swathes of green unfolding to the sea. He was almost sorry he wasn't coming back. Reaching the car he turned to look at the house once more. In the soft sunshine it looked friendly and surprisingly inviting. For the first time in his life, he considered the possibility that there might have been more to Gwyn's move than downsizing to save money. Perhaps his father had simply been striving to remain in striking distance of everything he held dear?

Another message he'd got too late, Gethin thought, driving slowly past the farmhouse and making a mental note to make contact with Alys. No matter how lovely the cottage looked, it was the last place on earth he wanted to live. Not when it meant seeing Coralie with Ned Wallace, for crying out loud. Being tender-hearted was one thing, but shacking up with the guy on his release? Well, he wasn't going to stick around to find out how her pity had somehow been twisted into some sick form of love whilst the man was in prison.

Yet, whatever noises his solicitor made about the terms of the Will being too uncertain to be enforced, neither could he sit back and think of the other beneficiary, whom he detested, living there. What a mess!

Paying for petrol in the garage where he'd stopped to fill up before the long journey, Gethin's glance strayed to the flickering images on the wall-mounted plasma screen babbling in the background. 'Penmorfa's Vicar is now in the frame!' said the reporter, struggling to keep a straight face. 'Racy Reverend, minxy Marianne Parry, is under pressure as the lid is lifted on her secret past. But attention is turning to the quiet young woman who villagers say moved here less than a year ago and about whom very little is known.

The question everyone's asking is "Who's that girl in the coral dress?"' Good luck with that, he thought, hardening his heart, because he sure as hell didn't know.

CHAPTER 23

The pale morning light crept behind the curtains and fell across the bed. It seemed a lifetime ago that Alys had sat in the kitchen longing for her husband and daughter to notice her. To feel something more than the seconds being counted away. Now, she'd certainly got their attention and it spelled the ruin of all her hopes and dreams for her family.

Huw was curled into her, one arm across her chest, his body warm and familiar. Alys listened to the rise and fall of his breathing, whilst she lay very still, trying to make the moment last, treasuring it for as long as possible. Eventually, though, Huw began to stir. She ran her fingers through his thick hair, her heart skipping a beat as he pulled away to smile at her.

'That wasn't so terrible, was it?' He grinned, looking, despite the silver hair, as boyish as when they'd made love for the very first time on a sweet, summer night.

'Huw, it was wonderful.' But simply being by his side again was wonderful, however fleetingly.

He propped himself up against the pillows to

look at her, reaching out to brush away the tears that were flowing unchecked down her cheek. 'Oh, Alys, what have I done to you? Where do I begin to tell you how sorry I am?'

'*You've* done nothing to apologise for,' she gulped.

'Oh yes, I have – I should have responded to your pain far sooner. But just when I'd got my head around going to the doctors, they replaced Doctor Thomas with that slip of a girl and I got cold feet. When I got round to seeing her about my back, she asked if everything else was all right, so I finally mentioned the problem and she changed my blood pressure tablets. If only I'd known how easy it would be.'

'You wouldn't have been on those tablets if I hadn't forced us to move.'

'You didn't force us, *cariad*, it was a joint decision, the right one for our family. You don't have to shoulder the responsibility for everything, you know. I'm only sorry you felt you had to. I was embarrassed, Alys,' he said, his soft, brown eyes revealing just how exposed and vulnerable he was feeling. 'You know what it's like here. I was sure everyone would find out what was wrong and everyone would be talking about me behind my back. So I tried to ignore it. I kept thinking that it would all get better, as if by burying my head in the sand the problem would just go away. No wonder you lost faith in me.'

'Oh, Huw.' She swallowed, her throat aching.

'I never lost faith in you. I thought it was me. I felt so old and unattractive – I didn't mind not making love, but you wouldn't come near me, wouldn't hold me . . .'

He studied her face. 'How could you have doubted your beauty when that boy from the café was so taken with you? Someone who was young and vigorous – not like me.'

'Huw,' she said, desperate for him to believe her, 'I was never unfaithful to you.'

He leaned back against the old brass bedstead Alys had inherited from her aunt, the place where they'd always been able to make up after their quarrels. Until now. 'Infidelity isn't always a physical act. I used to watch you laugh and talk to Jerzy in a way you hadn't done with me for months.'

Alys fiddled with the cream wool of the cover she'd painstakingly crocheted when they were first married. 'He was just a lost boy, Huw. Someone far from home, stuck in a relationship that was draining the life from him. You know how demanding Marika could be.'

'True,' Huw agreed amiably, 'but I don't suppose it helped her when she found him trying to seduce you in the potting shed.'

'Oh, Huw, hardly!' she protested, feeling herself blushing. 'He forgot himself and kissed me, that's all.'

'And you kissed him back, according to Marika. She wasn't very happy when she came running to me,' he added, sternly.

Alys shook her head in disbelief. 'Why didn't you say anything before, Huw?'

'Least said, soonest mended? I was afraid of losing you altogether,' he said, looking abashed. 'Thought if I pushed you too hard you might be off on a plane to Gdansk!'

'That wasn't even a remote possibility! Nothing happened,' she said, meeting his gaze. 'I realised immediately how foolishly I was behaving and stopped right there. It never went any further. I do admit to being flattered, especially . . .'

'Especially since I'd withdrawn my services,' Huw said, dryly.

A harmless crush, she'd told herself at the time. Nevertheless, she *had* found herself watching the way Jerzy moved and wondering about his touch. So when he had held her close and kissed her, she'd wallowed in the release of that sudden, sharp, illicit thrill . . . until the realisation of her own stupidity left her cold.

'Oh, Huw, what kind of support was I when you needed me? How can you possibly want me to stay?' She shook her head, swallowing tears at the sadness in his warm brown eyes. 'You know it'll be all over the village now, that I'd been having a torrid affair? Delyth and Mair will see to that. I think they've been longing to drop that bombshell when they thought it would do most damage. Kitty believes it, too.'

'Hush!' he said, moving closer. 'We've both made mistakes, Alys, but no one can hurt us unless we let them.'

Alys closed her eyes trying to stop the tears. She ran her hands across the silver hairs of his chest and breathed in the warm, male smell of him, her own dear Huw. Daring to open her eyes she found him watching her: tender, loving, filled with wanting.

'Oh, I've missed you so much,' she murmured, shivering as he pulled her close.

'I've been lonely too, love. And I know that my life's not complete without you,' he said, gently folding her to him, kissing her face and stroking her back before drawing her down to the bed.

'Huw, the curtains are still closed. They'll be wondering where we are at the garden centre.'

'If Delyth and Mair like to talk,' she heard him say as her mind went blank. 'Let's give them plenty to gossip about.'

'You shouldn't have long to wait. It's a reliable service even if the trains are few and far between,' said Coralie, letting the engine tick over whilst she waited for Ned to get out of the van. 'Are you sure you're all right for money?'

'Coralie.' He shocked her by reaching across to switch off the ignition. 'Hayley Butterfield is dead. It doesn't matter how much you try to do for everyone, it's never going to bring her back.'

She winced and took a long deep breath, but it still shuddered in her throat.

'And it's not your fault. You need to know that.' He leaned back in his chair. '*I* was the one driving

306

far too fast along a quiet shopping parade at night. I told myself I'd probably clipped my wing mirror on something. And then I looked in my rear view mirror . . . I panicked, drove home and – well, you know the rest. I still can't believe that I thought I could get on with my life.'

He shook his head. 'I pretended everything was normal. Didn't even tell my fiancée I'd been made redundant. I watched the appeals. I agreed what a bloody terrible thing it was that someone had taken away a young girl's life. I even said what a good person she must have been, carrying an organ donor card so that her death wasn't completely senseless.'

'You were distraught; you'd just lost your job, your income. None of that would have happened if I hadn't visited your offices in the first place!'

'An innocent girl didn't die because of a decision you took about company strategy,' he said, furiously. There was a pause whilst he struggled to compose himself. He took a deep breath then continued more quietly. 'I was – am – what they call a functioning alcoholic. Someone you'd never know had a drinking problem, because I'd got so good at hiding it. The first thing I did after work every night was to head for a bar. I would have been over the limit that night whether I'd lost my job or not,' he stated flatly. 'De-stressing, being sociable, networking, whatever spin you put on it, what I really liked to do was unwind with a drink.'

'So,' he went on, 'I didn't stop to report the

accident because I knew I'd be breathalysed. I ignored that poor kid lying in the road and prayed that I'd be sober before they found me. And I pleaded guilty to hide the truth because I thought I'd get a lighter sentence. But it's not that easy . . .'

Coralie covered her face with her hands, but he forced her to look at him

'It wasn't your fault; it was mine. I killed her. I'm the one who has to live with that. But if it hadn't been for your regular visits when I was at my lowest ebb, I would have found a way to finish myself off. Two lives would have been lost, two families left without hope. By talking to me, making me feel human when no one else would, you made me see a purpose to this life. I'll always be grateful for that, but I want to forget you, and forget the past. All either of us can do now for Hayley Butterfield is to carry on living the best way we can.'

Penmorfa, on her return, was eerily calm. There was no sign, as she would have predicted, that anyone had ever been at Gwyn's cottage, no answer at the farmhouse and Kitty was nowhere to be found. Needing to clear her head, she left the house and walked down to the cove. A solitary figure in the large landscape, she stood and watched the trail of an aeroplane high above. The hustle and bustle of a once-flourishing waterway was silent now except for the occasional pleasure

boat braving the shifting sands of the bar to negotiate the grey and silted-up river.

If history had taken a different course, it might
have been Penmorfa pulsating with life, but the
little village had failed to catch the tide of pros-
perity. If events had taken another course, she
might be looking forward to a brave new world in
America, expanding her business and, perhaps,
trusting herself to love again.

'So long Frank Lloyd Wright,' she said, turning
away from the sea and watching her footprints sink
in the sand as she walked away from it all and
went home to pack. As night fell, she loaded the
van and took the winding road through Penmorfa.
At the other side, she slowed down, to take a last
look in the mirror at the cluster of lights from a
scattering of houses disappearing over her shoulder.
In the wire carrier, firmly strapped in beside her,
Rock was mewling pitifully. She blamed herself for
not doing enough to get him acclimatised to it.
He'd been too ill to protest about it when he'd first
turned up on her doorstep, and had meekly put
up with the indignity. Now he was probably sitting
there anticipating a trip to the vet's and wondering
what was about to happen to him.

Poor Rock. Apart from doing everything she
could to make it as physically comfortable for him,
she couldn't do anything about making him feel
emotionally secure. It was going to be a long trip
unless . . . taking a deep breath, Coralie fumbled
around for some music. Doris's singing filled the

car, telling them whatever would be would be and Rock curled up and went to sleep.

'Depraved,' someone muttered, as Reverend Parry cleared her throat. Alys couldn't be sure but she was pretty certain that it came from Delyth or Mair, so she shot a withering look in their direction anyway.

'It makes my blood boil, Marianne,' she'd told the Vicar before the meeting, 'to see overpaid footballers obtaining injunctions preventing the press publishing any stories that could damage their lucrative sponsorship deals, whereas it's open season with you. You've been left defenceless.'

'Oh, Alys,' Marianne Parry had smiled, 'I'm not in the least bit defenceless. I do have a friend in a very high place.'

Nevertheless, since Reverend Parry was the one still being plagued by reporters, she had agreed to give an interview before the Hall Management Committee meeting commenced, hoping to stop any further press speculation. 'The Bishop's becoming a little weary of me being the story, rather than spreading the Word,' she said of her appearance all over the red-tops.

Whilst they waited for a couple of stragglers to settle, Alys tried not to look at the thickly painted wood-chip paper and a clashing floral border of the Foundered Ship's club room. It made her feel too depressed about the community hall which was still desperately needed.

The two weeks since the unveiling ceremony had been as bad as any that Alys could remember in Penmorfa. Even during the most horrendous crisis, such as when the last outbreak of Foot and Mouth had come perilously close to the village, everyone pulled together. Now all that united them was the search for a scapegoat and they hadn't even been able to agree on that. The press feeding frenzy for the Vicar's story had brought what many people were saying was the exactly the wrong kind of attention to the village and opened up old wounds about *Last Samba at Sunset*. Some people were cross with Alys, muttering that none of this would have happened if she hadn't 'got involved', as they put it, with Gethin Lewis in the first place. Others were annoyed with Gethin for presenting them with a portrait of uncertain value instead of sticking to what he did best. And where were all her hopes for Coralie and Gethin now?

At least Coralie hadn't had to hear one of the reporters remarking that it was a pity Gethin had squandered the opportunity to show off her fine assets. The only person to come up with an explanation as to why what had started as an act of generosity that was supposed to benefit the village had turned it upside down, was Willow, who insisted it was all to do with Mercury going retrograde.

Alys would have felt even worse about it all if it hadn't been for Huw, who'd been constantly by her side in the days immediately after the ceremony, fending off the press and mercilessly quelling any muttered criticism of his wife. It was Huw, too, who'd discovered that Kingston Gravell, the presenter of the popular art and antiques programme *Gravell's Gavel,* had a holiday cottage at Abersaith and had persuaded him to take a look at the painting.

'It's all about the quality of the work,' Kingston Gravell told them, in that deep, comforting voice everyone knew from their television. 'You don't have to be an expert to see that this is an outstanding portrait. The artist has captured his subject in all her vulnerable, sensitive beauty. Her lovely face is tilted towards the artist in a shared moment of intimacy, her bare shoulders, above the coral dress, lean towards him,' he'd said, smiling kindly. 'The only fly in the ointment is that experienced, high-level buyers only put their hands in their pockets for strong, consistent performers. Gethin Lewis's reputation has taken a big hit. There's a danger that the best dealers and collectors will avoid this auction, especially if there's any suspicion that the artist is using it as a tactic to get rid of something he wants to offload or feels is second-rate.'

He shook his head and, although Alys could tell he wished he could say more to reassure her, she could see from the expression in his eyes that he wasn't confident. 'I'll take some soundings and see what I can do, of course, but this is a considerable departure from Lewis's usual oeuvre and I don't need to tell you that we're now in a whole new financial climate. With so many needy causes, all charity functions struggle to reach their targets; the money's just not there.'

Sensing Alys's fears, Huw had been wonderfully reassuring, telling her that if Kingston approved of the painting, buyers would, too. Alys closed her eyes against the tears that sprang to them whenever she thought about how close she'd come to losing Huw. She was luckier than she deserved that he was still by her side. The only person who completely refused to engage with her was Kitty. Her daughter had stopped short of severing all contact but treated her with all the formality of a stranger. Alys didn't need Willow to read her stars to see that it would be a very long time before she was forgiven.

Now the room went quiet as Marianne Parry beamed her lovely smile at everyone and started to speak.

CHAPTER 24

'When I was a little girl,' Marianne began, 'I would probably have burst into tears if someone had told me I was going to be a vicar when I grew up. Our vicar was an old man, with bushy eyebrows and a beard.'

A few thin smiles broke the tension in the room.

'I dreamt of being a dancer and for many years it seemed that my dream would come true,' she explained. 'I started when I was six and took several rosettes. Then, when I was twelve, I began entering competitions. I was working hard, doing something I loved, leading what on the surface at least seemed a very glamorous life, except that I was empty inside.'

She smiled at the people gathered in the room and even Mair didn't purse her lips in disapproval. Anyone less like a floozy than their calm, elegant Vicar would be hard to imagine. 'At about the same time, I became aware that someone was trying to speak to me, but I tried not to listen. I wanted to find fulfilment in dance, not in doing God's work. God was very patient with me, even when I kept finding reasons not to listen to Him.

When I was in my early twenties even I realised that my glamorous life was leaving me overdrawn spiritually. I found time in my schedule to rent a cottage here, and when I looked into my heart, God was waiting for me!'

There were a couple of murmurs of approval, but the Vicar held up her hand and continued.

'I used to come down to the cove in the evening when it was quiet and dance, not to entertain others, but to celebrate the joy of finding my vocation. Sometimes I would see a young man there, with a sketch book. The young man and I got talking and I learned that he had ambitions of being a professional artist, but was being put under great pressure to carry on the family farm. I gave him the only advice I knew. I told him to look into his heart and trust where it led him.

'Gethin Lewis, for of course it was him, asked if he could make a few sketches of me. Later, he asked my permission to use them for a larger work. And to ask if I would mind very much if he took the liberty of adding himself to the painting as my shadowy partner to turn my little dance into a love story.

'I was very happy to agree – although I think we both might have had second thoughts had either of us known that those small sketches would take us on such an extraordinary journey – but just to set the record absolutely straight they did not lead to Gethin Lewis's bed. He was a troubled young man not yet twenty and I was already engaged to the marvellous man who was to become my dear husband.'

There was silence and then someone started to clap and soon everyone was united in their whole-hearted support for the Vicar. Alys even noticed one of the reporters dabbing at his eye, as they obediently packed up and left the meeting to continue.

Then it was Alys's turn to speak. 'I know that the work Gethin Lewis submitted was nothing like the work we were expecting or were promised. However, if we return the loan we've been granted by ACORN, we can say goodbye to our hopes of restoring the church hall and Penmorfa will wait a very long time for the community space it so badly needs. Or, we can take a calculated risk and go ahead with the charity auction . . .'

'We won't get a garden shed for that now!' someone said angrily. 'His stuff's not worth a candle!'

'It's possible that demand for his previous oeuvre may have dropped,' Alys agreed, trying not to think about the possible fallout from the closure of his New York exhibition. 'But before we rush to any conclusions and reach a decision that may jeop-ardise something that might be of benefit to us all, I think you should listen to what the leading London art critics have to say about this latest work.'

She gave silent thanks to Kingston, who'd emailed her with the news that the tide was beginning to turn back in their favour. "'Welsh artist Gethin Lewis's true potential has been released at last. This often controversial artist is in a philosophical mood with his latest work. *Girl in a Coral Dress* – a reminder, of course, of the vivid scarlet dress that draws the eye in his earlier piece – is a poignant and inspired painting which hails a new maturity and direction for Lewis and reinvigorates the market for his work.'"

'Now,' said Alys, 'I would urge everyone to remember that whatever the minority say about him, Gethin Lewis did return to his birthplace to unveil what is being heralded as an important new work and I think it's only proper that we should acknowledge a true son of Penmorfa. Let's put it to the vote.'

Kitty's eyes welled up with angry tears every time she thought about her mother. Although she was determined to keep her mind occupied, it seemed that wherever she went something was guaranteed to remind her of Delyth and Mair's smug innuendos. Even the hedgerows around Penmorfa were ripe with the heady, dirty-sexy smell of May blossom, she thought, as a few white petals rained down on her.

The hawthorn tree had a complicated mythology too – symbol of abandonment and fertility or chastity and cleansing, depending on your point of view. As a hedging plant its dense growth was thick and impenetrable and was supposed to offer a psychic shield, but nothing could expunge all thoughts of Alys and Jerzy from her mind.

She shot past the farmhouse as quickly as she could, the vibrations from the cobbled courtyard making Jamie's gurgle wobble, and found Adam filling hanging baskets in one of the glasshouses. A sunbeam was playing with his untidy blond hair, brushing the planes of his tanned cheeks with gold and lovingly gilding his muscular arms. A tray of petunias blew purple trumpet-faces at him as if he were a hero straight from a Greek myth, except of course that she knew all about his Achilles heel. As much as she wanted to believe that the smile that lit up his eyes as he saw them approaching was just for her, Kitty was sure that every woman he came across that day would get the same treatment. It was better to be realistic about these things; and if you couldn't even trust your own mother, who could you trust?

'Hey,' he said, 'who'd have believed it of Rev Marianne, eh? I hope she doesn't regret that particular confession. She's all over the papers again today.'

Typical Adam; he'd probably have a crack at her now, she thought murderously. 'Here,' she said, shaking off her backpack. 'I haven't got time to worry about that. Everything he needs is in there. I've put in plenty of nappies, there's wipes – this milk'll need to go in the fridge.'

'Kitty!' Adam rubbed her back, gently. 'Jeez! Remind me to work on those knots in your shoulders later. You're a mass of tension. Just chillax; you know I can handle whatever the little guy slings at me.'

He crouched down and made silly faces at Jamie, setting off a frenzy of little limbs waggling.

She exhaled, letting go of some of the pressure before it brought on a thundering headache. It wasn't fair to take it out on Adam, when it was her mother who was the lying cheat. 'Thanks,' she said, forcing a smile. 'If I get to do the styling for this engagement party, the money'll be really handy.'

He sighed and stood up, eyeing her doubtfully. 'I still think you're taking on too much too soon. Your body needs a chance to recover before you start dashing off all over the place.'

'Been reading the baby books again?' she teased, touched by his thoughtfulness all the same. He really could be kind. She went to brush a smudge of soil off his cheek and he caught hold of her hand and kissed her fingers. If only he knew how much she longed to spend more time with him instead of rushing off on business.

'I don't like seeing you worrying about money,' he said softly, giving her a nice, cosy, cared-for feeling. 'I mean, if you do too much,' he added, breaking away, 'your milk might dry up and then you might have trouble feeding this little fellow.'

Kitty swallowed hard, desperate not to let the tears pricking her eyes spill over, furious for allowing herself to believe that any of that tenderness was meant for her. 'Yeah and if I don't go to work, the cash'll dry up, too,' she said, snatching her hand away, 'which will have pretty much the same effect. Listen, I'm grateful to you for looking after him. Are you sure you don't mind?'

'Kitty, I'm his dad.' He frowned at her then swatted away a fly that was hovering in front of the buggy. 'Anyway, we've always got *Mamgu* at hand if we get into trouble, haven't we, eh?'

Oh, yes, good old Gran. She snorted, pursing her lips before an ugly comment tainted the sweetly-fragrant air.

'Do you want the paper?' he offered, grabbing it from the table and opening up the centre pages. 'I've caught up with the Vicar's secret past now.'

'I really don't have the time,' she said. Or the inclination, she nearly added, unable to stop herself looking. Besides a large shot of the Vicar in her younger days looking very minxy, there was a much smaller reproduction of *Girl in a Coral Dress.*

Adam noticed what she'd seen and winked. 'Loads of speculation about Coralie too, and how she might have inspired Gethin's work to take such an unexpected direction.'

A flicker of sympathy for Coralie was extinguished as she belatedly realised what her reticence on the subject of Gethin had been about. Yet another example of the destructive power of sex, she decided wearily. What really hurt was that she'd always looked up to Alys and hated her for proving to be so fallible at a time when she really needed that strength and support.

'Say bye-bye to Mummy,' Adam said, bending down to shake one of Jamie's hands at her.

I already have, Kitty decided.

Coralie found her parents sitting in the conservatory. Her mother, in a pair of animal-print reading glasses, alternated between tapping at the iPad in front of her and frowning at the results. Her father, stretched out on his leather recliner with Rock curled up in his lap, was examining the back of his eyelids. Catching sight of her, her mother gave a small cry of relief, waking Rock who dug his claws in and almost castrated her father.

'It's okay, Mum,' Coralie smiled, sitting beside her on the rattan sofa.

'I wish you'd let one of us come with you, darling,' said her mother, laying down her iPad. 'It was awful to think of you all on your own visiting the spot where that poor young woman died.'

Coralie took her hand. 'I'm sorry you were upset, Mum. But it was something I needed to do.'

She'd gone to lay a small posy of flowers beneath the memorial plaque erected by Hayley's family, inscribed with her name and the dates of her poignantly brief life. As she had stood to pay her respects a shaft of sunlight had stroked the pale petals and she had felt a sudden sense of release.

Her mother searched her face, with a shimmer of tears in her eyes. Coralie took a deep breath and forced herself to speak, trying to keep her voice from breaking. 'I'm sorry for everything I've put you and Dad through. All the worry. You were both right to question my motives when I gave up the consultancy and moved away. I wasn't really in the right frame of mind, was I?'

She took a tissue from the box her mother was offering her and wiped her eyes.

'We wanted you to be happy, that's why we were so concerned. We wanted to be sure you were doing the right thing for you and not simply taking yourself off into some self-imposed exile. What we should have been telling you, darling, is how proud we are of you.'

Coralie looked up and saw the love in her mother's expression.

'Many people would have given up under the stress you've endured, but you found a way to cope with the terrible ordeal you suffered. Some people would say that Ned Wallace didn't deserve your kindness – a life for a life – but he's the one who has to live with the results of his actions and the consequences for the rest of his life.

'Your grandmother would have been proud, too, to think that you'd built a new life for yourself in the place where she found a loving home as an evacuee. She would have been over the moon to know that you'd created a business from her old recipes.'

They paused to remember the woman who'd meant so much to both of them.

'Mum,' said Coralie, as an idea came to her. 'Can I borrow your iPad for a moment?'

She quickly found the organ donor register online and entered her details. It wouldn't bring Hayley back, but it was a small recognition of her life.

'Oh, good idea,' Susan Casey said. 'Brian? You're next.'

Coralie leaned back exhausted, but happier than she'd been in many months.

'Just looking at the calendar,' her mother said, poring over her iPad again. 'Now, when would be a good idea for us to come up and meet your new man?'

Coralie laughed. 'There's no one to meet, Mum.'

She watched as her mother clicked on a new tab and turned her portrait towards her. 'Coralie,' she said, 'you can't hide anything from me, I'm your mother. I can see the look in your eyes in this beautiful portrait and so can the artist. Now, why are you still here when there's a business and a man waiting for you in Penmorfa?'

Coralie leaned in and kissed her so that her parents couldn't read her expression. She loved them very much, but sadly, there would be no changes to make to their little branch of the family tree any time soon.

By the time Kitty got back she was wilting after a hugely busy day. The sound of laughter from the direction of the raised beds where the shrubs were displayed made her hesitate. Treading softly, she drew closer and saw Alys and Adam having a wonderful time playing with the baby. Anyone who didn't know better might take it for a lovely family scene. Except that everyone in Penmorfa knew that Alys was an adulteress and Adam couldn't be trusted to keep it in his pants. Resenting them both for making her life even harder, she was especially snappy as she marched over and snatched Jamie from Alys's arms.

'I'll take him now, thank you,' she said, ignoring the way her mother recoiled as if she'd been struck.

'Oh, no you don't.' Adam took hold of the buggy. 'I'm sure you're tired, but that's no way to speak to us, especially not your mother. A thank you wouldn't go amiss.'

'As far as I can see you've both been enjoying yourselves whilst I've been working,' she said, knowing she was being unreasonable. 'What's there to say thank you for?'

Alys put her hands on her hips. 'Now I'm the one doubting my mothering skills.' She glared at Kitty. 'Because I swear I brought you up to have some manners. You might have the courtesy to hear what else Adam has to say.'

Kitty's head was pounding and all she wanted to do was get home and sit down, if Jamie would let her. She shrugged and Alys nodded. 'You know where I am if you need me, Kitty. Nothing's changed.'

But it had, thought Kitty, as her mother walked away.

'Wait there,' said Adam, unfolding a garden chair for her before disappearing, only to returning a few minutes later with a bottle of ice cold mineral water. Kitty opened it and took a deep drink and began to feel guilty about her outburst.

Adam watched her for a while and when he spoke his voice was tight with emotion. 'I know when I'm not wanted,' he said sadly. 'I can see you've only been putting up with having me around for the little guy's sake, and I appreciate it, but I think it's time I got out of your hair now before our relationship deteriorates any further.

'I've also been doing some thinking about what you said about work. I know I'll never be the kind of high-powered bloke you'll probably end up with, but I'm going to do what I can to make things easier for you. I've managed to get some milking work in addition to working here. I really hate the thought of not seeing the little guy in the mornings, but I guess you'd prefer the extra money to having me around.'

'But what about,' she swallowed hard, 'Jamie? When will he see you?'

'I'm sure you'll come up with a practical solution,' he said, looking utterly miserable. 'You're the big ideas woman, aren't you?'

CHAPTER 25

Fat buds of shocking-pink rhododendrons were swelling in the late May sunshine, clashing gloriously with deep purple cornets of lilac blossom swaying in the fresh breeze. Coralie saw everything with a new appreciation and a sense that, like one of Alys's perennials once the brown leaves of the previous year's growth had been cleared away, she was about to bloom again.

'Whatever you did, you're looking much better for it,' Alys said, putting down the wheelbarrow she was pushing and eyeing Coralie's fifties' print skirt with the cropped summer jacket approvingly. 'I couldn't bear you in all that tailored stuff.'

The remnants of her office wardrobe were the right size, but, as she'd come to realise, they no longer fitted the person she'd become. Coralie looked down at herself with a rueful smile. 'I thought I was leaving the past behind, but now I really have.'

Before she could go any further, Willow and Wilfie scurried past, giggling, supposedly to open Willow's jewellery shop, but as soon as they were inside, the door was locked again and the blinds stayed closed.

'I think Wilfie's found true love,' Alys said as they edged away by mutual consent. 'But I do hope he doesn't start writing any sonnets about it.'

'He's found something,' Coralie snorted. 'I bet Rhys is relieved.'

'Well, not anymore he isn't, but Wilfie is,' said Alys, naughtily. 'You know, Willow's giving up her shop.'

'I did see a tall blond guy looking at Willow's unit recently. I wasn't sure if he was looking at jewellery or had come for a massage.'

Alys pulled a face. 'That's Willow's brother, Ash. He's going to keep the jewellery business going and Willow and Wilfie are taking over the café. They're planning to keep it going all year round, by supplementing the loss of income in the winter with creative writing and yoga classes.'

'Really?' Coralie felt her eyebrows lift.

'I must say, I was a bit sceptical about it, but Wilfie did hospitality and catering at college and they're both taking their food hygiene qualifications. Probably in there swotting for it now.' She winked at Coralie. 'Truly, I was surprised by Wilfie's chocolate brownies. They're lush, very moist and chewy – you should try one. I don't know if he's got a secret ingredient or a particularly deft touch.'

Their eyes met and they both giggled.

'Come here, you,' she said, pulling Coralie to her and hugging her. As she let her go she rested her hands lightly on Coralie's shoulders, her face serious. 'Gethin rang.'

Coralie closed her eyes whilst the ground steadied itself again. 'About the sale of the painting, I suppose. How are things looking for the gala auction?'

Alys looked at her in exasperation. 'I don't care if I never hear those words again! I've wasted too much time on this whole hall renovation stuff already. Displacement activity, I think they call it, trying to paper over the cracks in my own life, pretending that I was a better person than I was because I was working for the good of the community. Ha!' She shook her head. 'I only got involved because it was easier than facing up to the problems at home. I neglected Huw and was such a terrible mother that my own daughter couldn't even come to me with her problems.'

Coralie made a small noise of protest, but Alys hadn't finished. 'Don't you think it's about time you put Gethin out of his misery?'

'What about my misery? He's the one who wouldn't listen to me! The one who stormed off before I could explain,' Coralie said, her voice thick with suppressed emotion.

Alys sighed heavily. 'Coralie, that boy had a dog's life growing up, his mother was twelve years younger than his father and was always in awe of him. She was never quite strong enough to stand up to Gwyn's violent mood swings. It's no excuse, but Gwyn wasn't a well man. Gethin begged his mother to leave him but Katrin said Gwyn needed someone to look after him. And by the time he'd made his name, the money came too late to help her. She died just before the sale of *Samba*, never knew how famous it would make her son.

'Gethin's coped through the years by a combination of hiding his feelings and never standing still for long enough to let any one person get close to him. Until now.'

She caught hold of Coralie's hands and held her gaze. 'You only have to look at that portrait to know what Gethin feels about you, but if you care about him at all, you're going to have to show him.'

'So you had to drive nearly all the way to Cardiff for a feature on country weddings?' Huw shook his head at Kitty. 'It's a bit soon to be doing all that, isn't it? No wonder you've had a long day. All right, love?'

This to her mother who'd come in looking, Kitty had to admit, pretty wrung out from yet another meeting about the charity auction.

Alys hung her handbag on the back of a chair, bending to kiss Huw as she did. 'I think I've done enough to stave off the lynch mob if Gethin ever returns,' she said with a weary smile which faded when she saw Kitty's expression. She was starting to look her age, Kitty thought guiltily.

'These magazines expect a lot for their money, don't they?' Huw went on, returning to her. 'You're a new mum. Couldn't everyone have come here? To the country? That would be more authentic, wouldn't it?'

'Yes, Dad.' Kitty was too weary to disagree. 'But that's why they employed me to do the styling. To get the look without the inconvenience of actually being in the countryside. I couldn't turn them down, there's too much competition out there.'

Getting the feel of a relaxed, inexpensive wedding had been enormously hard work. The flowers, which were supposed to look as if they'd been picked from a garden, had looked weedy and dejected in the proofs, so Kitty had been forced to cheat and glam them up with some costly tall-stemmed white freesias. She still had her doubts about the rough hessian tablecloths, although that hardy perennial, the vintage fabric bunting, had wowed everyone, as usual. The tea lights in painted jam jars were very popular, too; sometimes she had to pinch herself when she thought how well she was getting paid to use such cheap, everyday props.

'I made a chicken pie before I went to the meeting,' Alys told her, washing her hands at the sink. 'Would you like to stay?'

Kitty was about to refuse, but having sat down she was too tired to stomp off again. Jamie was quiet, which meant that she could eat in peace, too. Besides, no one made pastry like her mother.

Thinking about it made her mouth water and the aroma of the cooked food filling the kitchen made her keenly aware that her stomach was empty. Her evenings weren't exactly full either. With early starts at the dairy farm, Adam had taken to making flying visits in the evening, staying only long enough to say good night to Jamie, then leaving immediately. She closed her eyes and braced herself for another long night with no one to talk to.

'There are no strings,' Alys said, pushing her white bob from her face as she bent to open the Aga. 'Just food. I won't read anything into it one way or another.'

Kitty hesitated, torn between wanting to eat and bridging the gulf between her and her mother, then Huw made them all jump by banging his fist on the table. 'I've had enough of this, young lady!' he roared, making Jamie's eyes fly open. 'You've put your mother through too much already. And that young man of yours. Now bloody well stay where you are and eat.'

Jamie's bottom lip started to quiver, but Huw picked him up and settled him in the crook of his arm, jiggling him up and down whilst he poured wine for them all and Alys dished up in silence. Kitty knew that a couple of sips of wine probably wouldn't hurt Jamie. But whether it was the wine or the melt-in-the-mouth perfection of Alys's pie, or perhaps it was simply being in the warm, relaxed atmosphere of her parents' home, she wasn't sure, but she felt the brittle carapace that had been holding her feelings in check starting to crack. Had she simply not noticed the way her parents interacted before? The way her mother's gaze softened when she looked towards her father? Or her father, catching Alys's fingers after they'd finished eating, rubbing his thumb across the back of her hand? They made being a couple look natural and easy, not like the way she was with Adam which felt like walking on broken glass.

'There are no guarantees with love,' her father said, reading her mind. 'You can't hold some of it back, like a deposit, so you can get your money back if something goes wrong. You have to give yourself wholeheartedly, whatever the cost.'

Still in Huw's arm, Jamie's fingers opened like anemones at the sound of the voice rumbling beneath him. Huw extended a red, rough fore-finger and Kitty swallowed a lump in her throat as her son gripped it and went back to sleep.

'Whatever you think you've heard from the gossips,' he went on, 'you've punished your mother enough. You made your mind up without letting her have her say and she's just accepted whatever you've dished out. You've got everyone running round in circles after you. Adam's working all hours, your mother's babysitting as well as trying to run the garden centre. And, despite all the thanks she's got, she's still fighting for this village and looking for funding so that the place has got a community facility everyone can use.'

'But, Dad,' she had to say it. 'How can you just pretend nothing's happened? How can you trust—'

He held up his hand to stop her. 'Because only your mother and I know what really goes on behind closed doors. You talk about trust, Kitty. Where was the trust when you came running home pregnant? Wasn't not confiding in your mother a form of betrayal? And what about Adam? Where was your trust in him to do the right thing?'

He shook his head sadly. 'Love isn't easy, but you can't keep holding back if you want to give it a chance. Just like any of those plants out there, you have to cherish it when it's delicate, nourish it to give it strength and show it some sunshine so it can blossom.'

Across the table from her, Alys was quietly sobbing. Kitty went over to her and held her very tight, breathing in the musky floral scent of Shalimar that Alys loved.

In her old bedroom the next morning, Kitty sat on the edge of her single bed, staring out of the window, pondering on what to do about Adam. Edith, looking full of her own self-importance, trotted off down the garden, followed shortly afterwards by Alys and Huw, holding Jamie in his arms. Lime clouds of *Alchemilla mollis* foamed at their feet as her parents, side by side, ambled down the path. Snippets of laughter and conversation drifted up in the morning air along with the scent of orange-blossom.

Kitty drew back from the window, conscious of not wanting to intrude on what seemed an intimate moment. No one looking at her parents now would see any outward sign of all the recent tension in their relationship. With hindsight, the separate bedrooms nonsense had been an obvious clue, but no one apart from her would have known about that.

What really worried her was how she'd failed to spot the signs; if the foundations of a relationship that she had always thought of as so constant and enduring, had been quietly slipping away under her nose, what hope was there for her and Adam? How would she know if she could trust him? She couldn't imagine him deliberately hurting her, but his naturally gregarious and sociable personality meant he didn't even have to go out of his way to attract female attention. Was she strong enough to let him be the man he was without letting jealousy and resentment come between them?

'If this is the right thing for me to do,' she said out loud. 'Please let there be a sign.'

Kitty scanned the sky searching – for what? The clouds to part? A giant thumbs up perhaps? She looked again at the garden where, as her parents walked further away, her mother brushed past a crimson camellia, the shattered blossom spilling bloodied petals over the lawn behind them. Kitty's hand fluttered to her chest and she shook her head. Was that it? That something so perfect could disintegrate at a touch? Was that her sign?

But when she dared to look again, her father was holding tight to both Alys and Jamie and her parents were staring into each other faces, looking at each other as if they hadn't seen one another for thirty years. Well, maybe they hadn't.

Leaving them to their private moment, Kitty turned away from the window, smiling a watery smile to herself and swallowing the lump in her throat. If, after all those years together, her parents could still look at each other with a love and tenderness that moved her to tears, maybe she and Adam could figure it out. When she got in she would ring him.

Gethin still couldn't work out where he'd gone so wrong with Coralie, except that some people said that his father had never worked out his feelings for his mother, either, until she wasn't there anymore. But at least he'd done the right thing by Ruby. Plenty of people were talking about her on this bright June day; everyone had an opinion. The white marble interior of the impressive stone-vaulted entrance hall of the New York Public Library had probably hosted a few remarkable occasions in its time, but today's event was something special. The photographers were everywhere, setting the marble gleaming with spangles of white light from their flashes.

Where earlier in the day the tap of every heel had rung out across the empty space, all the sharp sounds were now absorbed by the gathering crowd who, in turn, sent out new ripples of conversation and laughter. Gethin's aching heart swelled with pride as Ruby, looking amazing in black silk crêpe de Chine Vera Wang pants and black stretch tee posed for the cameras. The judges of the Brave New Artists' Prize for rising stars had picked a worthy winner.

To the right of her, Ruby's vast, prize-winning painting, the first of her dramatic interpretations of how the Pre-Raphaelite vision might look transferred to modern-day New York, was creating quite a buzz. Her reworking of Edward Burne-Jones's *The Golden Stairs*, featuring eighteen of her lesbian and gay friends who now filled the stone staircase behind her, had been inspired. Ruby had painstakingly caught the mood of the original work whilst adding her own character and spark. Looking round the room, everyone, from her models – some carrying musical instruments, all dressed in dove grey, and all desperately trying to keep straight faces – to the art enthusiasts applauding wildly in the hall, sensed that something big was happening.

Gethin was delighted by all the goodwill and support for his protégée. Satisfied that Ruby's career was off to a flying start, he caught her eye, gave her a quick thumbs up and left her to it. Although the stirrings of excitement about *Girl in a Coral Dress* were beginning to reach New York, the fallout from his previous exhibition was too fresh, so he'd deliberately kept a low profile. Even so it didn't stop someone stopping him as he tried to push through the crowd to leave.

'Hey, buddy, you're not that Welsh guy, are you?'

'No,' said Gethin walking on.

'So you're not the "Green Green Grass of Home" dude, then?'

Hell, thought Gethin, gritting his teeth and carrying on. He knew he had one or two grey hairs, but if someone really had confused him with the septuagenarian singer, it was time he got a decent night's sleep.

He stomped down the steps of the library, acknowledging the stone lions guarding the building. Patience and Fortitude, they'd been nicknamed, for the qualities New Yorkers would need to possess to get through The Great Depression. Right now, he didn't feel too cheerful and he'd pretty much run out of patience and fortitude. That probably meant he wasn't much of a New Yorker.

Deciding that a walk across the city would reconnect him, his black mood wasn't helped by a ticket tout pushing a leaflet under his nose inviting him to take a sightseeing tour. Now he didn't even look as if he belonged here. The trouble was, he thought, dropping his head and picking up his pace, he wasn't sure where he belonged anymore. The Big Apple had blown a big fat raspberry at him and, although he sometimes imagined he did hear the call of the Welsh mountains and valleys, he guessed that his longing was for the lush curves and dips of one woman who drew him back there.

'Will ya do us all a favour and call her,' Ruby had said to him only that morning, after she'd apparently spoken to him for ten minutes without him hearing a word.

At this rate he'd have to get the glove puppets out to explain to Ruby, since she insisted on being deliberately obtuse, that he and Coralie were finished. Part of him still clung on to the hope that New York might be the very place she might turn up, especially if she was exploring new options for Sweet Cleans.

'I'm sorry, I can't help you,' Laura Schiffman had said, shaking her head when he'd pressed her for information about her friend in the cosmetic industry. 'But when you do see Coralie next, I'd love you to get hold of some of her Rose Works body lotion, for me,' she'd added, brightening up.

How he longed to phone Coralie and tell her, just so he could hear her voice and imagine her smile. Sometimes he even started to dial the number so he could listen to her answerphone message, but he never pressed 'call' for fear of making the ache worse.

If anything, his thinking was muddier by the time he got to his apartment, where the mailman was trying to negotiate his satchel-cart past a doggie-do. Gethin knew how he felt. 'How you doing today? Your wife on the mend now?' he called out.

'Not so bad. Something she ate apparently. I guess that means I'm excused cooking duties now. These are for you. Two letters *and* a parcel.'

CHAPTER 26

Gethin took the steps two at time and, once inside, poured himself some iced water before opening his mail. The first envelope looked like something his solicitor might send him. Formal confirmation that the royalties owed to him were coming at last? But by the time he'd finished reading it through, he'd had to take another long drink of iced water. He needed it to cool down. A thirty-day notice to quit? How was this even frigging possible? He stared at the shoji screen room divider for a full minute because it took him that long to believe what he'd just read.

Somehow his landlord was trying to suggest that in contravention of his tenancy agreement, he was using the apartment as a second home. That his main residence was in Penmorfa, west Wales. His only proof, which would be a joke if it wasn't so frigging serious, appeared to be an article in the *New York Times*, quoting an art critic suggesting the reason his work had become so lacklustre was because of the time he was devoting to renovating his desirable country residence!

Well, that was pure garbage and he could dispute

it – probably, although he resented the time and money he would waste chasing round. However, it wasn't so easy to defend himself against the second, and more concrete claim, that one of his guests made violent threats to another occupant of the building and created a public nuisance.

'Oh, Rubes.' He rubbed his jaw. She'd certainly given him a wake-up call that day. Unfortunately she'd woken half the building, too – the complaining half.

He picked up the next letter, still chewing over his predicament. Unless he took action fast, in thirty days he could be homeless. That was the reality. Out on the streets with the crazy dude who occasionally showed up on the corner of his block, rocking and swearing. Not a great place to be in New York, especially when it snowed. Jesus! Those guys had always seemed so other, nothing to do with his life, but now he was discovering just how quickly the ground beneath your feet could turn to sand. Next time he saw the crazy dude, he'd slip him more than a couple of singles, just so he'd remember him in future. In a couple of weeks they could be new best friends.

He tore open the second envelope. Might as well get all the bad news out of the way at once. A photograph dropped out, landing face down on the floor. It looked as if the landlord had set a private investigator on him, too. Photographic evidence of his 'desirable country residence', perhaps? Why would anyone bother to get photographs printed these days, unless there was something they particularly wanted to rub your face in?

He turned the print over and his breath caught at the sight.

Apart from someone who valued what other people disdained. Who didn't mind that some of her things were pre-loved. Who wanted to scoop up all the unwanted animals. Maybe she'd feel sorry for him if he lost his apartment – except she'd probably decide that the crazy dude was in greater need. There she was smiling self-consciously beside him, he with his arm round her waist, at the top of the Empire State, and he couldn't help smiling back even though the sight of her filled him with longing.

His fingers were trembling as he took out the letter inside. When he'd read it all the way through he felt like hell for not giving her the chance to explain the situation to him. Ned Wallace had turned to her because he had nowhere else to go and because of the kind-hearted person she was, she'd been unable to turn him away.

You told me once that having a portrait painted could be therapeutic, she'd written, *but coming face to face with myself in your beautiful painting just made me more aware of how bad I felt inside. I'm so sorry for hurting you.*

Why was she apologising when he was the one who was afraid of getting tangled up with messy emotions? Perhaps if he'd given her more time that morning in his apartment instead of letting her go, he might have spared them both a lot of heartache.

Ned Wallace had been imprisoned, but it was Coralie who'd been locked up. Blaming herself for what she saw as her part in a young girl's death. Putting her own life on hold out of a sense of duty to put right all the wrongs. Well, as far as he was concerned, Ned Wallace should still be rotting in prison. And yet it was because the murdering, drunken, deceitful bastard had been released that Coralie had been set free.

The parcel contained a box – Pandora's he hoped, after all the bad and sad news. He fingered it, trying to guess its contents, afraid that the expectations he was beginning to feel were about to be crushed. Opening it at last, he drew back the tissue paper and light gleamed on a glass dome. He lifted it in front of his face, shook it gently and watched silvery flakes of fake snow shimmer round the Empire State. Not quite a crystal ball, but he didn't need to look into the future to see that things were looking up.

He turned the key and the tinny notes tinkled out. Not 'New York, New York', like nearly every snow-globe he'd ever come across, but 'Que Sera Sera'. Doris Day was trying to tell him the future wasn't his to see, but she was wrong. He may have been blind but he wasn't stupid. And he knew exactly what was coming next.

★   ★   ★

Kitty was trying to do as her father had suggested and put her whole self in. Earlier in the day she'd prepared a chilli, put some beers in the fridge and put on the dark floral hitch-skirt dress that she knew was one of Adam's favourites.

'I thought you might like to bath Jamie,' she suggested, trying not to mind that he barely flicked a glance at her before rolling up his sleeves and filling up the baby bath. Leaning against the door frame, she admired the deft way Adam managed to wash Jamie's hair without the usual trauma. Must be those strong arms making the baby feel secure, because the minute she attempted the manoeuvre it was a toss-up to see which of them ended up with a wobbly bottom lip first. Seeing how much father and son were enjoying the experience, she felt guilty for ever thinking she could keep them apart.

When Jamie was dry and sweet-smelling again and they were back downstairs, she passed Adam a beer and he sat back on one of the dining chairs, watching her on the sofa slowly unbutton the front of her dress to give Jamie his evening feed.

'You make a beautiful mummy,' he said, with a husky break in his voice.

'You don't make such a bad daddy.' It was true, she realised, smiling at how awkward and unsure of himself he looked. Just because he was never going to make great partner material, didn't mean he wasn't capable of being a brilliant dad. No one could criticise the way he doted on Jamie. Having a baby with the shaggy-haired, sexy beach-bum who struggled to turn up for work at the garden centre when the surf was right, hadn't exactly been at the forefront of her mind when she had first seen him stripped to the waist riding a quad bike on a baking hot day in late July.

Nope, the only thing she'd been thinking about from that first moment was sex. Fortunately, she soon found out, after a couple of days trailing round after him pretending to learn how to prune the spring-flowering shrubs and helping him spread nets over the soft fruits bushes before the birds stripped them, that he was a like-minded spirit. The pair of them had become quite adept at spreading and stripping activities as July rolled into August; most of them outside, working up a sweat in the steamy summer fields. Kitty let her gaze drop to the curve of his biceps beneath the rolled-up sleeves and shivered at the memory. It was when the passion had turned into something deeper and her emotions got in the way that she had started to panic.

Adam set the bottle down on the table beside him, wiped his lips and sat down next to her. Her breath slowed as he put one arm round her shoulders and leaned closer to stroke Jamie's cheek. She watched as his finger moved slowly from the baby and gently traced the blue veins of her breast, as if she was not just beautiful but desirable, too. She looked back at him and the frost that seemed to have been surrounding her heart melted.

Don't hold back, that's what her dad had said.

'You don't have to say anything back,' she said whilst she still felt brave. 'But I think I love you.'

Think? That didn't sound very whole-hearted, did it? What about the way her heart lifted at the thought of him and everything seemed better, brighter, safer because he was there?

'What I mean is, I do, love you, that is.'

'What you mean,' said Adam, grinning, 'is that you've only just realised.'

Kitty scowled at him. Later she'd have words with her father. So much for putting your whole self in; all she had done was dug a bloody great hole for herself and now Adam was laughing down at her.

'Must be quite tough for a Cardiff career girl and thrusting entrepreneur to discover she's fallen for a lowly labouring gardener,' he breathed into her hair.

'Oh, don't sound so bloody pleased with yourself,' she said, trying to keep her voice down so as not to wake Jamie. 'I forgot you get women falling for you so often you must be sick of hearing it.'

'Yeah, it's hard being me.' He sighed, making her squirm with embarrassment. 'Especially when the only girl for me is the one woman who's been holding back.'

'Anyone I know?' she muttered, doing her best to control her rising excitement.

He swallowed. 'I was beginning to lose hope. Kept telling myself that I was punching above my weight to think a woman as clever and talented as you would be interested in someone who works with their hands, like me.'

'I like what you do with your hands,' she couldn't resist telling him.

'And that's one of the many reasons why I love you.'

He leaned over and kissed her then and she grabbed hold of his hair and pulled him even closer, almost forgetting Jamie, who grunted in his sleep. Adam lifted him out of her arms and gently laid him in the carrycot beside the sofa. When he turned back, his face was serious.

'There's just one thing,' he said, looking completely defenceless. 'If you want to be with me, let's do it properly. Take my name. Marry me, Kitty.'

She swallowed hard and closed her eyes whilst she found the strength to reply. 'You're not just asking because of him. Because of Jamie? I don't want you to ever look back and say I trapped you into a proposal.'

'Kitty,' he said, taking her face gently in his palms, 'I love *you* and I don't mind how many times I have to tell you, I'll keep saying it until you believe me. I love you with all my heart and nothing would make me happier than the honour of becoming your husband. So, what do you say?'

On the last Saturday of June, Coralie looked around her at the sunlit fields of Penmorfa rolling down to a sparkling sea beneath a perfect Pembrokeshire blue sky and hoped that the outlook would seem as bright at the end of the day. There had been a difficult moment, that morning, during the erection of the marquee for the day's gala auction, when a strong sea breeze almost sabotaged the event before it began. Thankfully, the forecast was for the wind to ease during the afternoon, staying just bracing enough to keep everyone awake rather than tearing their hats off or turning the marquee, where Adam was directing people to their seats, into a Zeppelin.

'At least if it was raining,' said Kitty joining her with Jamie flat-out in his buggy, snoozing peacefully under a parasol, 'the VIPs could see how badly we need a community hall. If they think it's like this all the time, they might think we can manage without it and only make stingy bids.'

'I'm sure they won't,' said Coralie, thinking how pretty Kitty looked in a white, floaty top that contrasted with her dark hair. Everyone had really dressed up for the occasion, all the bright colours making it a truly gala occasion. 'It's going to be fine, you'll see. Hold still a minute.' She leaned across and gently rubbed at an unblended blob of concealer where Kitty had tried to hide faint shadows under her eyes from all the broken nights. But there was no hiding Kitty's new-found happiness. Or the diamond-and-sapphire cluster on her finger that caught the light to become a rainbow of shimmering shooting stars as Kitty lifted her hand.

'Getting used to that yet?' She laughed.

'Isn't it lush?' Kitty grinned, flexing her fingers to admire all the twinkling gems. 'That's babies for you! They change everything. They can even make someone like Adam behave like good husband material. He's only proposed to me because he can't bear to be parted from this little fellow. Do you know I even drew up a list of reasons for and against marrying him: two columns, "yes" and "no"?'

Coralie shook her head, not fooled in the slightest by Kitty's feeble effort to play her excitement down. 'Rubbish, Kitty. The only one who couldn't see how besotted Adam was with you was *you!*'

For all her and Alys's fears that Adam wouldn't be good with commitment, he'd surprised everyone. Although maybe that was being unfair to him. When she thought about it, he'd only ever teased and flirted with other women right under Kitty's nose and with the sole purpose of making her jealous. His behaviour, when Kitty wasn't around, had always been entirely chivalrous.

'I wish I'd trusted him sooner,' Kitty admitted, her voice shaking a little. 'I never thought someone as sexy as Adam would pick me. I was so afraid of being hurt that I was mean to everyone.'

'Now you're being mean to yourself,' Coralie said gently, rubbing her shoulder. 'He's a good man, a great dad and this is the start of your bright future together.'

'And what about you?' Kitty asked, eyeing her from a strand of hair that had blown across her face. 'Isn't it about time you stopped being hard on yourself and grabbed hold of your bright future?'

Coralie's throat tightened. She'd written, laying her feelings bare to Gethin, asking him to come. Now it was up to him. 'I'm taking it one day at a time,' she said, reaching up to massage the back of her neck, 'so let's see what we can do to make this a good one for Alys.'

'Yes, let's.' A protest from the buggy set Kitty jiggling it frantically. 'I'm that nervous for Mam. She's worked so hard for this. You know she's got that black guy off that art and antiques programme to be the auctioneer?'

'*Gravell's Gavel*? It's great, isn't it? I love Kingston Gravell! He comes across as such a nice man. How on earth did Alys manage that?'

'It was due to Dad actually,' Kitty said, proudly. 'What's more Kingston Gravell liked the location here so much that he phoned to say he's bringing a TV crew with him in case they can use some footage from today in their show!'

Coralie gulped and reminded herself that the cameras would not be pointing at her, but at a portrait of her. One that had attracted remarkably little interest in the subject, fortunately, since it was a little more sober than all the razzmatazz of *Samba* and the sensational outing of the Vicar. Nevertheless, she was thankful that she no longer carried the burden of Hayley Butterfield's death like a shameful secret or she would have felt sickened by the thought of so much publicity.

'You've done masses, too,' she added. 'Look at all these people you've managed to get here.'

'I spent hours sending out invitations, but it was worth it.' Kitty nodded. 'And I'm glad I added one day's free styling from Flair on a Shoestring to the list of lots. Think of all the free publicity I'm going to get now!'

Coralie only hoped that it would be good publicity. The market was nervous about *Girl in a Coral Dress* because it was such a radical departure from anything Gethin had produced before. Putting a brave face on it, Alys and the Hall Management Committee had determined to raise what funds they could by extending the auction to include five lots in addition to the final lot, when the portrait would be auctioned. And whilst donations had been generous, it would still be dreadful, not to mention embarrassing, if a spa day at The Cabin at Abersaith went for more money than her portrait.

'Oh look,' she said, temporarily distracted. 'There's Derek Brockway – the weatherman!'

'He's a keen walker so I thought he'd be interested in the location.' Kitty nodded. 'I'm hoping

Jamie Owen, the broadcaster, will be able to make it, too.' Her eyes widened at the sight of a clean-cut couple walking hand-in-hand and she grabbed Coralie's arm. 'That's not—'

Coralie nodded. 'Willow and Wilfie. Yes! They've bought just about everything in the Sweet Cleans range since they started seeing each other.'

In a light linen jacket over a white shirt and almost clean jeans, Wilfie, who had shaved off his beard, had gone from Bill Oddie to Ben Fogle in a dramatic transformation. Willow too, had ditched the extreme henna, an overkill of kohl and a fug of patchouli oil and looked ten years younger for it. They were followed by a stream of people making their way along the path. Behind them in the car park a minibus roared to a halt and a group of jovial-looking men spilled out, grabbing their jackets.

'Oh lord, the Abersaith Male Voice Choir again,' said Kitty as they surged towards them. 'Tell 'em you've got a partner or they'll stop and chat you up all afternoon and we'll never get on with the auction.'

It wasn't a tactic that seemed to work, since none of the choir was put off by Kitty having Jamie, who was fast asleep in his buggy and missed all the attention his mother was attracting, although Adam, Coralie noticed, glared at one or two of the younger members as they entered the marquee.

'Oh, look over there,' Kitty said, pointing to a cluster of figures, just as Coralie's knees went weak as she spotted the familiar figure, too. 'Isn't that Gethin?'

CHAPTER 27

Gethin was delighted to have arrived in Penmorfa with sufficient time to spare so as not to have to use the short cut across the field to the garden centre, especially as it was full of cows. Paint hadn't impressed, pheromones had failed, but Eau de Farmyard definitely wouldn't clear the air between him and Coralie. Priming Huw to make bids up to the value of the ACORN loan on his behalf – the financial wrangles with the poster company administrators happily resolved – meant he had managed to get in one set of good books and ensured there'd be at least one taker for *Girl in a Coral Dress*. If he didn't have the real thing, he'd always have the painting to remind him.

And, he thought, scanning the people in an array of finery, like the two women in front of him following the chipped-stone path towards the marquee, he wasn't even the last to arrive. At the sound of footsteps crunching behind them, one of the women in front of him glanced over her shoulder, but the half-smile turned stone-cold when she saw who it was.

354

'I'm surprised you've got the nerve to show your face round here,' said Delyth.

The lime green feathers quivering on her head looked like a parrot had just used it as a launch pad. If that was a fascinator, it wasn't working for him.

'Lovely to see you, too.' Gethin smiled.

'Come to ruin another occasion?' said Mair, from beneath a large purple ostrich feather.

Gethin overtook and blocked their path. 'I'm here to see that plenty of money's raised for a good cause, but if you ladies came looking for a scrap, let's do it now, so as not to spoil everyone's fun. Now just *what* is your problem?'

'Don't pretend you don't know!' Delyth's shiny satin green chest swelled massively. 'I lost my daughter because of you. I never had the pleasure of seeing her married.'

'Delyth,' said Gethin, calmly, 'unless you know differently, the last I heard, Cerys was alive and well in New Zealand with three kids and a rugged sheep shearer in tow.'

'Oh!' Delyth said, dramatically, clutching hold of Mair. 'But she wouldn't have looked at that man if you hadn't spurned her! If you'd done the right thing by her, she would still be here and I wouldn't be a lonely woman.'

Gethin sighed. 'I'm sure your son and his family at Abersaith will be sorry to hear you seem to have forgotten them. Cerys wasn't running away from me; she was running away from you! That poor girl was the only kid in the village who couldn't do a damn thing without you poking your nose in. You didn't even let her join the rest of us on the beach in the evenings.'

'She was a good girl. I wanted her to stay that way!'

'I wish it had been as exciting as you seem to think. We'd listen to some music, sharing a tin of beer between us, if we were lucky. I think someone might have got hold of a spliff once, except we were all too afraid to inhale in case we became drug-crazed lunatics. Oh, and there might have been the odd outbreak of low-level snogging.'

'My Cerys was too good for any of that,' Delyth said, defiantly.

'If you hadn't set such strict rules for her, she might not have been so hell-bent on tasting forbidden fruit. She was a lovely girl, Delyth, but she was a menace, always trying to seduce one of the lads.'

'You and your filthy mouth!' said Delyth. 'She never went out after dark.'

'I hate to shock you, Delyth, but making love without the lights out is possible. She must have been in her element when you encouraged her to watch the sheep-shearing competition. All those macho Kiwi guys, flexing their muscles in public. Lucky for her, it was love at first sight when Shane set eyes on her, wasn't it? He was a smashing bloke, if you'd care to find out, but you never gave them a chance. So, if you didn't see Cerys get married, that was your choice. She's still out there, Delyth, and so are the rest of your grandchildren. Isn't it about time you got to know them – before it's too late?'

'You're a fine one to talk about it being too late,' sneered Mair. 'Did you think about the burden you placed on your poor parents, swanning off with your new art college friends? Far too good for the rest of us, you thought you were. All that extra work for your mother – you sent her to an early grave.'

'I don't think anyone sends anyone else to an early grave, Mair. My mother had breast cancer, but she ignored all the warning signs because she didn't want, as she put it, to be mutilated. She was afraid of my father's reaction. Afraid of being rejected.' He had to swallow hard to keep his voice calm. 'If anyone had a hand in her death it was you, Mair, because you never forgave my father for marrying her and not you, and even after they were married, you couldn't leave him alone, could you?'

Mair's hand flew to her mouth.

'Don't deny it, because I saw you with him once. I may only have been a child but I knew what was happening.'

'He should have married me. But what could I offer? She was a farmer's only daughter with land and I had nothing but myself.'

That part sounded like his father, anyway. Careful with money from the start.

'He paid for his decision in the end. Your father was a clever man, frustrated by the limitations of his life. We could have achieved great things together, but instead he was stuck here doing a job he hated. And, of course, once you came along, there was no escape.'

'And you've been trying to get rid of me ever since.' Gethin glowered at her. 'Well, here's the really good news, Mair. No amount of your poison's going to shift me, because I'm back for oh, let's say at least five years . . .'

Mair's face was a sight to behold as she registered what he was telling her. 'That's right.' He nodded. 'We both know the terms of my father's Will, don't we? And, maybe, if you'd been a bit more subtle about conducting your affair with him, I might have felt inclined to just give up my interest in the cottage and hand it all over to you. Unluckily for you, though, I've decided I like it here, so don't go choosing new curtains for the place, will you? You might have been my father's mistress, but you'll never be mistress of his house.'

'And that, ladies,' said the Vicar, who'd been standing behind them and had heard it all, 'means that from now on I shall expect no stone throwing or mud flinging from either of you.'

Part of Gethin almost felt sorry for the two old women as, looking ashen and subdued, they retreated towards the marquee. The long shadows of the past still stained the present no matter what you tried to do to wipe it away. Then Marianne Parry laid her hand gently on his arm.

'Gethin, I visited your father at the end of his life. He was very frail by then, as you know, both in mind and body, but in his lucid moments, he was full of remorse about your mother's death.'

'He never said that to me,' Gethin said, shaking his head.

'I think he was too ashamed. He was a very troubled soul, scarred by the deprivations of his own upbringing, unable to express his feelings, who didn't realise quite how much he'd lost until it was too late. That's why he was so desperate for you to stay here, to raise children here, so that your mother's spirit would live on in some small way. I know that will never make up for his behaviour when she was alive, but I hope that makes it a little more understandable.'

He could see her kind face through his blurred vision and felt the gentle squeeze of her hand. 'Now,' she added, 'shall we raise money for a good cause?'

Inside the marquee, Alys sipped appreciatively at her Welsh sparkling Brut, supplied on such generous terms by the Glyndwr vineyard. Kingston Gravell's chocolaty tones had sweet-talked his audience and got them waving their programmes wildly; some, Alys suspected, purely for the benefit of his twinkling smile and warm gaze. But now things were getting serious. All around her handkerchiefs were being surreptitiously dabbed at moist eyes as the Abersaith Male Voice Choir concluded their set with 'The Ash Grove'.

Alys hoped that the references in the lyrics to kind faces and childhood friends would tug at some heartstrings and make the audience more receptive than a few of them had appeared when they'd taken their seats. Eyebrows had been raised at the presence of some dignitaries, like the Bishop and their Assembly Member, who, people were muttering, were only there to bask in the reflected glory. Many of those gathered had made conspicuous efforts to dress up for the television cameras with some very fixed hair-dos and a couple of dazzling home dye jobs on display, although Delyth and Mair had made predictably barbed comments about what they regarded as an unnecessary intrusion into village life.

One couple who seemed to have shed an awful lot of hair between them were Willow and Wilfie. Alys did a double take seeing them sitting in the front row. It almost looked as if a makeover programme had visited the Craft Courtyard with everyone so shiny and scrubbed up. Huw, at her side, she thought smiling to herself, had escaped, though, and looked as delightfully crumpled as ever. He reached for her hand, sensing her sudden nerves, and gave it a reassuring squeeze as Kingston Gravell took the podium once more.

She flashed a grateful smile at Huw then led the applause. Kingston's enthusiasm for *Girl in a Coral*

Dress had gone a long way towards a change of heart about Gethin's work in Penmorfa, as well as some kind comments and real appreciation for what she'd achieved, too.

Kingston's beguiling manner was winning everyone over, but this was the real test. Looking round to see how his warm-up patter was being received by the audience, she caught sight of the man Kingston had pointed out to her as the art critic and newspaper columnist Jay Jewell, his arms folded and face impassive. A passing cloud sent a shadow slanting across the rows of seats and a cool breeze rippled the lining of the marquee. Alys twisted her hands together, anxious that nothing would spoil the big moment.

'Relax,' Huw said softly to her, instantly making her feel better.

The sun came out again, making the white interior glow and there was a hushed silence as Kingston paused theatrically. 'So now,' he said quietly, 'I'm going to open the bidding . . .'

'Six thousand pounds!' roared Huw, making everyone jump. Alys turned her head slowly and blinked at him. They barely had six thousand pennies. What the hell was he doing?

In the back row, Gethin released the breath he'd been holding as the gavel came down; *Girl in a Coral Dress* had just changed his life.

'Sold!' Kingston Gravell announced, smiling. One hundred and seventy-four thousand pounds.

The marquee flaps opened and the sea mist swirled in, hanging in the air like smoke over a battlefield as a stampede of reporters charged off in search of phone signals. Gethin sat in shock whilst the Bishop and an Assembly Member argued loudly over a cab and the minibus driver made a fruitless search for the Abersaith Male Voice Choir who'd been swift to decamp to the Foundered Ship. In the cacophony of squeals and yelling, tears and congratulations, he dimly heard a couple of soft explosions.

One night with Coralie and his life had turned into a scene from the Apocalypse. Heck, he should have been forewarned the minute she looked over the fence at him.

Coralie stood in the middle of a little group, holding a champagne flute in each hand. Alys and Huw stood on one side of her, Adam, holding Jamie, and Kitty were on the other. Together they formed a small semi-circle to shield Gethin, who was slumped forward in his chair, his head in his hands.

'Well go on, girl,' said Adam, giving her a nudge. 'Don't take all day about it.'

'Gethin?'

He lifted his head slowly, his eyes taking the long route up as they first rested on Coralie's red peep-toe shoes before lingering on her bare legs and travelling over the pale green crêpe de Chine tea dress with its scattering of roses. By the time the dark midnight eyes arrived at hers, she was blushing.

'You can put the glasses down, Coralie,' he said, with that rich Welsh lilt that had her legs turning to jelly, 'the bubbles are going to my head just drinking in the sight of you.'

'Smooth talking,' Adam said admiringly. 'No wonder you've got yourself such a reputation.'

'Just take the glasses, will you, Adam?' Gethin growled at him.

Since Adam already had his hands full, Kitty took the glasses and put them out of the way.

Gethin stood up and came towards her, never taking his eyes off her. 'I've been waiting to do this for so long,' he said, his voice breaking as he reached to stroke her cheek. Then he bent his head and brushed her lips so gently that it was all she could do not to grab at his shirt and pull him towards her.

'Well, get on with it, man,' Adam said impatiently. 'You two have got some time to make up!'

Gethin flashed them a big grin, his teeth white against the dark stubble, then planted his lips firmly on hers to a spontaneous round of applause and cheering.

A flash of light made them all turn round and everyone glared at the photographer.

'Excuse me,' the photographer said, carrying on regardless. 'You're the girl in the coral dress, aren't you? What's your name?'

'It's Doris bloody Day,' Huw snarled at him. 'Now piss off!'

'Huw!' Alys laughed.

'Well,' said Huw looking sheepish.

'Oh, Gethin!' said Alys, clearly unable to contain herself any longer. 'What a result! What recognition of your talent! One hundred and seventy-four thousand pounds. Thank you! Now we can create a community hall to do Penmorfa proud!' The delight turned to bemusement as she turned back to her husband. 'But Huw, what did you think you were doing? I thought *we* were going to have to sell everything to pay for Coralie's portrait for a while there.'

'Yes, what were you doing, Huw?' Coralie asked, still trying not to burst with happiness because Gethin's arm was wrapped firmly round her waist. She was so close she could feel the rumble of protest as he started to speak.

'Huw . . .' he warned.

'Coralie, *bach*,' Huw insisted. 'Let's just say that one way or another, your young man was determined to win the girl in the coral dress, even though someone else won her portrait. Now get yourselves a glass each will you, so we can drink a toast. Now then,' he continued, resting his gaze on everyone in turn, 'here's to love and happiness and the *Girl in a Coral Dress*!'

'I'm sure that's more than one toast, Dad,' laughed Kitty.

'I don't think you can have too many celebrations,

can you?' said Gethin, turning to Coralie and smiling down at her in a way that made her glad he was holding her up. 'So, I'd like to propose a toast too, if you'll hear me out.'

He cleared his throat and looked almost shy as he started to speak. 'It's no secret that I couldn't wait to leave Penmorfa. I thought I was escaping a place with a particular mind-set, a cold, unforgiving location.' He looked around at them, as if to acknowledge his misapprehension. 'It's taken me fifteen years, since I won the art competition that showed me a different future and thousands of miles, to realise that it's not about where you are, but the people you're with.

'I'd like to say thank you to you, Alys, for understanding and for always taking me as you found me, not how others said I was. To you, Huw, I'm indebted to you for persuading some builders to transform Dad's cottage and helping me to see the place in a new light. And to you, Kitty and Adam, for so clearly demonstrating that life and love will always endure even in the smallest of villages. Together you've shown me the heart of Penmorfa and how a loving, caring family will always keep it beating. Here's to you!'

He raised his glass, but Alys interjected. 'I think you're crediting the wrong people with changing the direction of your life, aren't you?' she said softly. 'Don't leave it too late to tell her.'

'Ah,' he said, 'I was just getting to that. I think Coralie deserves my special thanks.'

'Well, it looks as if we're going to be doing much more toasting, this evening,' said Huw. 'Come on, everyone back to the farmhouse!'

Coralie would have liked some time alone with Gethin. She started to follow, but Gethin's grip tightened on her waist as he held her back.

'We've got other plans, Huw, if you don't mind.'

'Right you are, boy!' Huw said cheerfully, over his shoulder. Then he spotted an unopened bottle of sparkling wine and hurried back with it. 'Take this the pair of you; you'll get a terrible thirst on you with all that catching up.'

What was once Gethin's father's run-down cottage now felt cosy and welcoming with some simple furnishings and subtle lighting, but Coralie suspected Gethin hadn't taken her there just to admire the transformation. The planes of his face looked sharper; he'd lost a little weight, too.

'Forgive me, will you?' he said, drawing a ragged breath.

'Hush,' she said, pressing her fingers to his lips. 'There's nothing to forgive.'

'I was afraid of getting involved, of turning into someone like my father, but every time I tried to walk away from you I became more like him.'

Coralie put her arms round him and held him closer.

'I couldn't stop thinking about you,' he said, stroking her hair. 'You brightening up my life class the moment you walked in the room. You in

Battery Park adding all the colour to the day. You 102 floors up in the sky. Your face at the opera. I don't know where we go from here, Coralie. All I know is that I don't want to let you go.'

'There's an awful lot we don't know about each other,' she said, pulling away again.

'I'd know the scent of your skin blindfolded,' he said. 'That's good enough for me.'

'That's just sex,' she teased, looking into his dark eyes. Her hair had started to come undone and she felt him gently release the clip that was holding it in position and let it tumble round her face.

'There are worse starting points.' He placed his fingers under her chin, coaxing her to look at him. 'Look at that portrait and tell me that I don't know you.'

'Ah, that's just paint.' She smiled.

'Paint's all I've got to show you how I feel,' he murmured.

'Paint them and forget them, Ruby said.'

'Yeah, she also told me never to let you out of my sight again, when she said goodbye to me at JFK. She wants to see us both there next time. If there is a next time . . .'

'I don't care where we go,' she said quietly. 'So long as we're together. We'll work something out.'

'What is there to work out?' he asked, sending her heart soaring. 'I know the tilt of your head when you look at the sea, I know that dewy-eyed look when you see some dumb animal, I know how lovely you look first thing in the morning.'

He dropped his gaze to her lips. 'And I know how to make you cry out my name.'

A small sob escaped her throat and he pulled her to him and kissed her, his firm mouth on hers, his body hard against her.

'Coralie.' He laughed, touching his forehead to hers. 'Just come upstairs to my bed will you?'

He sat her on the big iron-framed bed and told her to keep her eyes closed for a minute. She could hear him fumbling with matches, cursing every so often, and wanted to laugh. But when she was allowed to look, he'd lit a circle of tea lights all round them. A little world, outside the real world. He stretched out beside her and just looked at her until she thought she'd go crazy with longing if he didn't put his hands on her.

'I still can't believe you're here,' she said, searching the depths of his sexy dark eyes. 'I'm so pleased you made it to the auction. I didn't know if you would, when I wrote to you. And I haven't even thanked you for coming,' she added, still aching for him to touch her.

'I haven't yet,' he said, with a husky catch in his voice that made her shiver with longing, 'and you will.'

'I'll start now then, shall I?' she whispered, kneeling up so she could untie her wrap dress.

'That's a good trick.' He whistled softly as the silky material slipped off her shoulders. 'It's probably just as well I didn't know about it earlier.'

Coralie was going to say something clever, but

his hand cupped her breast, and his thumb stroked her nipple through the thin satin. With his free hand he reached round and unclasped her bra. 'That's a good trick, too!' was all she could gasp before losing herself in a quest to see what else they could do together.

Much later, when the tea lights had burned down twice and the chill had long worn off what was left of the sparkling wine, Coralie sat up and looked at Gethin stretched out beside her and told herself how happy she was. He had a body she could never get tired of seeing, a perfectly assembled combination of lean, hard, rough and smooth. And he knew exactly what to do with it, which was very lucky for her, too.

He scooted over and wrapped his arm across her hips and rested his head in her lap. She slid her fingers through his hair, thinking how much she'd missed him, how she would miss him again and how wrong it would be to get too used to having him around.

He jerked his head up, caught her expression and pulled himself up to sit beside her. 'Spill it, Coralie. Come on, no secrets now. Not after what we've shared. Tell me what's wrong.'

She shook her head, feeling awkward. 'Where do we go from here? That's all I was wondering.'

'Hey,' he said softly. 'If you don't know how I feel about you by now, I don't know what else to do.'

She twisted the sheet. It was stupidly insecure to ask for any more than that.

He smiled down at her, pulling her close and dropping a kiss on her hair. 'We're going to catch up on all the things we've missed, everything we didn't say and do, and we're going to be doing plenty more of this. It'll be perfect.'

'Yes, it will, won't it?' she agreed, wishing she could be certain. Something still bothered her. But when he stroked her shoulder and nibbled her neck and pulled her down beside him, she couldn't remember what the problem was.

CHAPTER 28

'Can you believe it's only six months since you went out to New York?' Alys asked, smacking her lips and pouting into the mirror. Coralie, standing behind her, tried to dodge the golden October sunlight slanting in through the bedroom window whilst she squinted into Alys's beautiful old-fashioned dressing table mirror attempting to pin up her hair.

'Bleurgh!' said Alys, applying her lipstick, 'I am *so* not used to wearing all this makeup. I feel like a clown! And next week you're off *again*.'

'Alys, you look even more gorgeous than ever. Adam's mates will all be falling in love with you.' Coralie grinned, winking at her.

'Get that clip in your hair, before I do something slow and messy with it that would ruin Kitty's wedding day,' Alys warned.

Coralie, leaning over her shoulder, laughed. 'But, it's not fair! As chief bridesmaid, isn't one of *my* duties to get off with one of the groomsmen? They'll never notice me with you around. Any chance that Adam might have gone to school with Jared Leto?'

'Jared? No.' Alys picked up one of her pink, pearl-drop earrings. 'He left a couple of years before Adam started.'

'And now Wilfie's taken, too!'

They exchanged looks of disbelief in the mirror, still unable to believe how well Wilfie had scrubbed up.

'Anyway,' Alys said, turning her head slowly from side-to-side in a last-minute inspection. 'You don't need Jared or Wilfie. Not now you've got Gethin.'

Whether anyone would ever 'get' Gethin, as Alys put it, remained a moot point, but it had been a very happy, if busy summer, she thought, straightening up before she was on the receiving end of a liberal spray of Shalimar.

'I do think it's strange though,' Alys said wistfully, 'that the events that reconnected Gethin with his Welsh roots seem to have taken you in the opposite direction.'

One day at a time, Coralie reminded herself. 'I'm so happy to see Gethin so fired up about his work again. I love the stuff he's doing now.' He'd begun working *en plein air*, painting outside to catch the light across the sea in Penmorfa Bay or making brief, lightning sketches of the faces of the people who lived and worked in the small, rural community.

'Yes, but you've done well for yourself, too. Selling your Happy Hands and Rose Works recipes to a major cosmetic house is quite a coup in these difficult times.'

'*If* I do.' Coralie tied the sash of her turquoise taffeta dress, feeling very relieved that Kitty hadn't let the little bridesmaids have their way. Purple was so not her colour. 'I'm still not sure that's what I want to do. That's partly why we're going to New York next week. Gethin's gallery have changed their tune and want to reopen talks with him, and we'll catch up with his former assistant's new exhibition, too.'

'And have some time for each other, I hope,' said Alys.

Coralie looked at herself and frowned. For all Kitty's claims that the strapless bodice of her bridesmaid dress was self-supporting, she was still convinced that unless she was very careful she could easily end up looking like the novelty act at a seedy club.

'Are you decent, ladies?'

As she ever could be, thought Coralie, chewing her lip and looking doubtfully at her reflection.

Huw, pretending to cover his eyes, walked into the bedroom. More used to seeing him in a rather antique pair of moleskin trousers topped with a corduroy jacket of the same vintage, Coralie thought he looked incredibly distinguished with his well-cut silver hair against the black of his morning suit.

'Oh, look at you!' Alys jumped to her feet to brush some imaginary fluff off his shoulders. 'Don't you look handsome?'

Huw grinned and pulled his wife in to kiss her,

despite Alys's squawks about her makeup. 'Where's the bride-to-be then? Not in here?'

'We're just going up to her room now, to help her into her dress.' Alys beamed. 'Is she getting impatient then?'

Huw scratched his head. 'Well, I don't know. I can't find her.'

'Oh, Lord!' Alys plonked herself down on the stool again. 'She'll break that boy's heart if she backs out now. I do hope she hasn't got cold feet.'

'Nope! I wore my wellies.' Kitty laughed, padding in, her feet in thick socks. 'You didn't really think I'd jilt Adam, did you? It was just that I was looking at my bouquet and it struck me that one thing was missing, so I dashed down to the garden centre for a sprig of myrtle to tie in for good luck. And when I checked the table decorations in the marquee, one string of fake pearls on the top table had given way, but the beads looked so pretty spilling across the linen tablecloth that I didn't bother to clear them up.'

'Kitty!' screeched Alys. 'Never mind all that! What about you? I know you're thrilled to be back in your old jeans, but wearing them with one of Adam's hoodies and your hair in rollers is not a great bridal look. Have you seen what the time is?'

Come on, Kitty, thought Gethin, beginning to feel nervous. To think he'd been worried that with all his secret preparations he'd be the one most likely to be late to the wedding. Everyone in the congregation was starting to lean out of their seats, wondering if they'd shelled out on all those Egyptian cotton sheets and towel bales in vain. Adam, poor sod, stood squarely at the front of the church, staring firmly ahead. He felt for him. It was hard enough for the guy anyway, with no parents to support him, although the best man, his older brother, was taking good care of him.

Whilst the organ swelled to cover the audible murmurs, Gethin reacquainted himself with the room. Penmorfa's tiny chapel was unchanged; its simple interior unadorned except for the lectern and altar cloths which were lovingly embroidered with a design of wheat and fish. As a little boy he'd thought the fishes particularly exuberant, as if, with the village being so close to the sea, someone hadn't been able to resist making them look as if they could smell the salt air and were just about to dive for freedom. He just hoped Kitty hadn't done the same.

Just then he heard heels clipping behind him and the processional music began as Alys, looking ravishing in an Edwardian-style suit in a dusky pink silk, hurried down the aisle to take her place. Alys wouldn't make a bad mother-in-law, he thought, looking at her appreciatively as she gave Adam's brother a quick thumbs up before sliding into the pew. Like one of her own garden centre prize blooms, she just got better-looking every year. Was that a tear he noticed shimmering on her cheek beneath her glorious wide-brimmed hat? Overflowing emotions, probably, on this momentous day. Joy, of course, and now that her daughter had turned up at last, more than a little relief.

Gethin turned and got a quick glimpse of Huw looking dashing in his morning suit. How hard, he wondered, had Kitty worked to persuade her father to dress up for the occasion? Not very, he guessed. 'But, Dad,' he could hear her saying, with a catch in her voice. 'Please. For me.' He could imagine the look that went with it too; any resistance from Huw would have been futile.

The bride looked beautiful but the star of the show for him was the chief bridesmaid, a girl with sherry-coloured curls and rosebud lips, who was smiling at him with tears in her lovely, tawny eyes. Gethin felt his smile grow wide and his heart beat faster, although this was probably not the moment to pull her onto his lap.

Kitty, apparently reading his mind, stopped to throw him a suspicious look beneath her veil. He was grateful to one of the little bridesmaids for recovering the situation with a swift prod to her silk-covered back. Coralie, regaining her composure, gathered them all up and shepherded the whole party towards the altar. He didn't blame Kitty for a certain amount of mistrust. He'd been doing some thinking, keeping his plans close to his chest, and the only part he'd managed to figure was that everything hinged on Coralie. It was anyone's guess what happened after that.

As Kitty reached the altar, her astonished gasp showed that Adam had been keeping a surprise of his own. He turned, grinning broadly, to reveal a real shiner of a black eye, leading Kitty to throw all protocol out of the window by fussing and cooing all over him.

The Vicar, in her own imitable style, calmly restored order, welcoming the congregation and revealing that the groom's black eye was nothing more sinister than the result of an early-morning surfing session to burn off some pre-wedding nerves. 'So now,' she continued, 'on this day when Kitty and Adam prepare to launch, well, maybe not a surfboard, but a new boat, shall we say, in which to sail through life and learn the ropes together, let us begin . . .'

Letting the words of the solemnisation of matrimony flow over him, Gethin took a deep breath and looked round the room whilst he tried to refocus. Somehow the pews had managed to accommodate what felt like the whole of Penmorfa, but it was a bit of a squeeze. Kitty's Cardiff friends and Adam's surfing mates were already eyeing each other up. Some of the couples amongst them sat hand in hand, reliving their own special day; others were thoughtfully anticipating their own. And that had to be Adam's older sister, the physiotherapist, since she looked so much like her brother. He remembered Adam joking she was the brains department of the family.

All at once, the fidgeting and shuffling in the congregation seemed to stop.

In the sudden quiet the Vicar's calm voice rang out clear and true above what seemed to be a collective holding of breath. You couldn't help it, he thought, the power and poetry of the words just grabbed you, whether you believed in them or not. All that dreadful day of judgement stuff and secrets of all hearts being disclosed was guaranteed to make you feel guilty about something. But at least Coralie, smiling reassuringly at one of the little bridesmaids, had shed her secret worries about what might be in store for her when the final trumpet sounded. Unable to take his eyes off her, he leaned forward to catch a glimpse of her face in profile and had to take a deep breath when she looked over her shoulder, caught his eye and gave him a dazzling smile.

'And now,' said the Vicar, gently, 'I am required to ask anyone present who knows a reason why these persons may not lawfully marry to declare it now.'

As the newly declared husband and wife joyfully headed up the aisle to warm smiles all round, Coralie gathered up the little bridesmaids and took the best man's arm. Keeping her eyes firmly ahead until the group emerged, blinking, into the bright October sunshine; she didn't dare look at Gethin's face in case she forgot what she was supposed to be doing. The smallest bridesmaid, who was already getting twitchy, was bound to scoot off whilst she was distracted. Kitty and Adam couldn't have wished for a more perfect beginning to their married life; the ceremony had been beautiful and she didn't want anything to spoil the photos now.

Kitty was fussing over Adam's black eye again and taking every opportunity to smother him with kisses. You'd have to be very cynical indeed, she decided, to question the chance of them finding lasting happiness. Despite Kitty's slight wobble before the ceremony when she'd had a good cry on Alys's shoulder because everything was so perfect, and the attack of nerves that had given Adam such a shiner, you only had to look at the pair of them, ducking under a shower of rose petals and coming up all smiles, to see how right they looked together.

Whilst the photographer was getting them in position, Coralie shaded her eyes from the sun's brilliant gaze, unable to stop herself looking round. The little church was set on top of a hill, against the backdrop of the rolling fields and the sparkling sea, with the scattering of houses that made up the small settlement of Penmorfa roughly following the winding road. She couldn't help scanning the half-circle of fluttering, brightly coloured silks, confections of hats and smoothly tailored suits for one tall, dark figure in particular.

'Come in closer, lovely,' someone said to her, as they shuffled up for the next group picture. 'We don't bite. Well, not all of us anyway.' One of Adam's surf mates with laughing eyes and a lazy smile reached out his hand and pulled her towards him. 'Here,' he said, winking at her. 'You'll be safe next to me.'

'I think she'll be safer with me!' said a disapproving voice behind her. Coralie's fickle new friend, giving her a regretful smile, spotted one of Kitty's very pretty Cardiff girlfriends and made a rapid decision to abandon her for a damsel in a perilously plunging frock.

Coralie looked up and found herself staring straight into a dark blue gaze, like a midnight sea.

'Move over, darling,' said Gethin, slipping in next to her.

Kitty stole a look at Adam as he sat down on her parent's big brass bed beside her and her breath caught, because he was looking so sexy. She liked the way he looked at work, rough, ready, looking like a bad boy in his sweaty tee shirt and torn jeans, but this was a new, exciting Adam, a cool, sophisticated stranger in a crisp white shirt that was crying out to be unbuttoned.

'Want me to take him for a while?' he offered, reaching over her to stroke Jamie's head. Now he was making her feel weak at the knees because he was so sweet, too. He really was lush, her new husband. And he was all hers; the love in his eyes when they made their vows had reassured her of that.

'You're all right.' She smiled. 'He's just about asleep now. Once he's off I'll pop him in the travel cot and Mam'll take over.' Suddenly the idea seemed too terrifying to contemplate and she found herself choking back the tears.

'Oh love, what is it?' Adam wrapped his arms round her.

'Do you think he'll be all right?'

'He'll be fine, sweetheart. We're only leaving him for one night.'

It had taken her so long to feel like a proper mother, but now that it had happened, Kitty felt ashamed of how detached she'd felt about this poor, innocent scrap in her arms. She gulped back the tears, hoping that Jamie hadn't been aware of her initial coldness towards him and vowing to make it up to him for the rest of her life.

'We can take him with us, if you'd prefer,' said Adam, scanning her face with concerned eyes. 'We're a proper family now, after all. I'm sure they won't mind at the hotel.'

They *were* a proper family. And with the warm wishes from their friends and the good example of Alys and Huw to follow, Kitty knew that they had laid the foundations of the strongest of futures together. Everything had been perfect, but one of her favourite moments had been at the reception, after all the speeches. Alys had risen to recite Gillian Clarke's beautiful wedding poem, *Er Gwell, Er Gwaeth*, For Better, For Worse, and Huw had watched her with such tenderness and pride that the tears had started raining down again.

Kitty took another look at her husband and had to agree that they probably wouldn't bat an eyelid about accommodating a small baby in The Cabin's honeymoon suite. But she would. Jamie was snoring gently, his angelic lips puffing in his sleep, with only the slightest break in the rhythm as the cool cot sheet touched his back when she laid him down.

'I think our son will be safe and happy with his grandparents, don't you?' She smiled at Adam, who was standing over the cot beside her. 'Right now I just want to be a proper wife.' She moved into him, breathing him in and closing her eyes as his fingers traced the nape of her neck and downwards across her bare shoulders.

'Don't stop,' she murmured.

'We have to,' he told her, nuzzling her neck. 'We're neglecting our guests.'

'They think I'm changing into my evening outfit. No one will miss us for five minutes.'

'Five minutes!' Adam laughed. 'There'll be a time for fast and furious, but not tonight.'

'I suppose it would be more romantic to wait,' she agreed, sneakily stroking the gratifying bulge in his trousers in case she could change his mind. 'It is our wedding night.'

'Not just our wedding night.' He smiled, his eyes dark with desire. 'It's the first night of the rest of our lives together.'

Together. That sounded good. Kitty reached up and pulled him to her, kissing him hard, relieved, happy and looking forward to the future.

* * *

Coralie smiled at Alys, clinging to Huw as Rick Astley sang 'Never Gonna Give You Up' as they passed. Alys, looking radiantly happy, gave her a little wave over Huw's shoulder as Gethin led her away from the dance floor.

'Come on, Coralie, we've done our duty,' he said, folding back one of the flaps so they could escape from the heaving marquee, 'now it's our time.'

CHAPTER 29

'Where are you taking me?' Coralie asked, since the evening air was cool across her bare shoulders.

Gethin didn't answer, but stopped to wrap the frivolous white marabou shrug that went with her bridesmaid dress round her. Her shoulders felt less exposed but a sudden irrational fear that time was running out for her and Gethin still left her feeling chilly. She had the strongest feeling that life was about to change. She could feel the shift in Gethin. He was trying hard not to show it, but she knew him well enough now to know that he was hiding something.

Summer had been special, full of memories to treasure and take out in the cold of winter. Two people, from opposite sides of the Atlantic, who had made something precious together. So if, after their holiday together in New York, it was her fate to return alone then she would accept it, even though it would break her heart in pieces. If this was his goodbye to Penmorfa, she thought, realising that he was leading her towards the sandy cove, she wouldn't spoil the moment for him.

'Here, let me go first.' He sounded nervous, but his grip was warm and secure as ever as he took her hand and guided her down the stone steps. The black waves broke below them, whispering across the sand and the salt air touched her lips in a ghostly kiss. Then Gethin smiled up at her and hoisted her into his arms to carry her over the rocks to the flat sand. She took off her ballet pumps so they could walk along the beach together, and slipped her hand into his.

'Oh, what a pity,' she said, spotting a small driftwood fire ahead of them, being tended by a couple of teenagers. 'I was hoping we'd have the place to ourselves.'

Whilst it wasn't unusual, even on the coldest evenings, to see small groups of young people gathered together for the sake of having somewhere warm to sit and talk, it was nevertheless disappointing. She would have liked to gather up close to Gethin. *Cwtching* the Welsh called it, cuddling and protecting all in one, a *cwtch* being a private space in a room or in two people's hearts.

'Why? What did you have in mind?' he asked, squeezing her hand and settling her fears a bit more. There were just two boys sitting by the fire this evening. To her surprise, instead of passing them by, Gethin stopped and handed each of the boys a hefty tip and they scooted off, making appreciative noises about their windfall.

'Why, Mr Lewis? Have you planned this?' she

exclaimed, smiling up at him and slipping a finger between the buttons of his shirt.

'I want to talk to you,' he said, removing her hand. 'But if you carry on like that I'll forget what I wanted to say. Sit down, will you?'

He straightened out the blanket where the teenagers had been sprawling and patted the space beside him. But when she leaned into him she could feel the tension in his shoulders. Should she be worrying, after all? The moon touched the oily black waves with silver, but, even feeling the warmth of Gethin's body against hers, she started to fret again that there was no bright lining but only dark clouds ahead for them.

'Gethin?'

She saw him shake his head. 'Heck, Coralie, you've got me lost for words. And have done from the moment you set your cat on me.'

'I did not set Rock on you!' she protested. 'It was your fault for letting go of him. And you weren't lost for words for very long! You weren't very happy,' she added, trying not to laugh when she thought about the look of disbelief on his face as he stood half-naked in the next-door garden.

'All right then,' he admitted, 'I was just lost.'

'You!' This time she did laugh. 'You were one of the most self-contained, opinionated men I'd ever met! You predicted Sweet Cleans wouldn't last the winter, remember?'

'I might have been wrong about that.' He

shrugged. 'Is that why you didn't try to rescue me? Stray cats, Bambi glasses, forgotten frocks and broken lives . . . why not me?'

The low lilt of his lovely voice was getting to her. 'You didn't need rescuing,' she said, feeling her throat constrict.

'Oh, I did,' he said pushing his hands through his hair. 'I needed saving from myself. If you hadn't come along, I would have ended up a sad, lonely, old man, just like my father.'

Coralie started to dare to hope that maybe it would be all right after all. 'So what did you want to say to me?' she said, softly.

He heaved a sigh. 'Do you mind about *Girl in a Coral Dress*?'

Not quite what she was expecting. Coralie straightened up. 'Of *course* not! It's wonderful news. It's lovely to see you getting the recognition you deserve from your own country.'

Kingston Gravell had done them more than one favour when he'd persuaded his good friend Jay Jewell, the art critic, to come to the gala auction. As an avid collector too, he'd not only bought the painting for such a satisfactory sum, but he had also generously offered it on a three-year loan to the National Museum, meaning *Girl in a Coral Dress* had been added to the collection of works by modern Welsh artists.

'Good,' he said carefully. 'I know I told you that paint was all I had to show you how I feel . . .'

Coralie slid her arm around him. 'It's fine,

honestly. You don't have to explain. I know how much you care.'

He exhaled deeply. 'Why is this so difficult?' He shook his head before reaching into a basket on the corner of the blanket and flicking a switch.

Not their last samba? She panicked as he pulled her to her feet. Then Doris Day started singing 'Secret Love' and Gethin drew her close to him. He smelled of sea air and firewood and his thighs were warm and hard against hers as they swayed under the starlit sky. Fireworks from the reception, still going on high on the hill above them, erupted over their head in a glittering shower. She looked up and held his gaze, wanting to stay like that forever, knowing it was impossible.

'Hey,' he touched his hand to her cheek, 'why the tears?'

'I escaped to the country, you escaped from the country, isn't that what you're going to tell me? That we're never going to be happy in the same place. Doris was right, our lips should *never* have touched. We should have stuck with our first impressions.'

She heard him laugh. 'Coralie, I hate to be the one to tell you this, but Doris Day gets it wrong sometimes. Everyone's moved over; Alys has got her family back, Kitty and Adam are together where they should be. That just leaves you and me.'

He folded her in and she grabbed hold of him,

feeling the lean, hard strength of him and never wanting to let him go.

'I was so afraid of hurting you,' he said into her hair. 'I didn't want to make a commitment, didn't want to mess you up the way my father did my mother. And then, when I thought I'd never see you again . . .' He shook his head and his body was tense against hers. 'Coralie, we can live in the country, we can live in the city, we can live on the moon for all I care, just don't leave me.'

'I can't,' she whispered, swallowing her tears. 'I don't know what the future holds, but I only want to move forward with you.'

All the tension left his body as his mouth came down on hers, making her shudder with pleasure and her pulse race. She slid her fingers inside his shirt and heard him catch his breath. This was going to be hell on the bridesmaid frock, thought Coralie, as he pulled her towards the blanket, but when was she ever going to wear a turquoise taffeta strapless number again, anyway?

Before they could get any further though, there was bellowing from the top of the stone steps. Coralie looked up to find Kitty and Adam waving madly at them, then something came flying towards her in the dark.

'I need to ask you something, Coralie,' said Gethin, after a short pause whilst they waited for Kitty and Adam to disappear, the sound of the couple's laughter carrying down to them. 'The whole future of Penmorfa depends on you.'

Great. Alys had said something very like that to her once and life hadn't been the same since. 'Go on,' she said, unhappily.

'Coralie,' said Gethin, holding the remnants of Kitty's bouquet. 'Would you believe me if I told you that I love you?'

She looked at him, his anxious expression, his shirt hanging out and his hair untidy, the pathetic flowers shedding petals in his hand, and suddenly he didn't seem so self-contained anymore, but a real, warm, loving man. A man she would cherish forever.

'Yes,' she replied, smiling up at him. 'Yes, Gethin. I believe you. And I love you.'

She laughed as he dropped the bouquet and punched the air, before quickly pulling her into her arms to silence her with a kiss, but just when she was starting to think about *cwtching* up together again, he broke away to look at her.

'Coralie, you didn't go to Tiffany's when you were in New York, did you?'

She shook her head, puzzled. 'No,' she said, 'but I do know they don't serve breakfast.'

'You're correct,' he said, smiling as he lifted his hands and gently cradled her face. 'That's settled then, I'll take you there next week; what they do have is a pretty good selection of rings.'

ÜBUNGSGRAMMATIK

Deutsch als Fremdsprache

Axel Hering
Magdalena Matussek
Michaela Perlmann-Balme

Hueber Verlag

Quellenverzeichnis

Seite 21:   Foto: MHV-Archiv (Jens Funke)
Seite 53:   Foto: PhotoDisc (Ryan McVay), Getty Images, Hamburg
Seite 59:   Zeichnung: Ludwig Richter, Verlag Rogner & Bernhard, Hamburg
Seite 63/79:   Foto: MHV-Archiv (Dieter Reichler)
Seite 91:   Fotos oben: (Ken Usami), unten: (Kim Steele) PhotoDisc, Getty Images, Hamburg;
                 Mitte: Gerd Pfeiffer, München
Seite 135/137:   Fotos: MHV-Archiv (Werner Bönzli/Jens Funke)
Seite 145:   Foto: Gerd Pfeiffer, München
Seite 159:   Fotos: Süddeutscher Verlag, Bilderdienst, DIZ München

7.   6.   5. | Die letzten Ziffern
2012   11   10   09   08 | bezeichnen Zahl und Jahr des Druckes.
Alle Drucke dieser Auflage können, da unverändert,
nebeneinander benutzt werden.
1. Auflage
© 2002 Hueber Verlag, 85737 Ismaning, Deutschland
Verlagsredaktion: Dörte Weers, Thomas Stark, Hueber Verlag, Ismaning
Umschlaggestaltung: Marlene Kern, München
Zeichnungen: Martin Guhl, Cartoon-Caricature-Center, München
Layout: Thomas Schack, Ismaning
Druck und Bindung: Druckerei C.H.Beck, Nördlingen
Printed in Germany
ISBN 978-3-19-001657-0

INHALT

A   Anhang

Die *em*-Übungsgrammatik richtet sich an Lernende der oberen Grundstufe und der Mittelstufe. Sie eignet sich mit dem integrierten Lösungsschlüssel als Selbstlernmaterial und bildet die ideale Ergänzung für Lernende, die mit dem Lehrwerk *em* arbeiten. Das Buch ist aber auch lehrwerkunabhängig einsetzbar.

Die *em*-Übungsgrammatik vermittelt einen Überblick über die frequenten Phänomene der deutschen Grammatik. Sprechüblichkeit der modernen Gegenwartssprache steht im Vordergrund. Zweifelsfälle und Ausnahmen werden ausgeblendet. Dadurch bleibt der Umfang überschaubar.

Diese Grammatik erschließt sich nicht nur Grammatik-Profis. Die Kenntnis der Grammatik-Termini ist nicht notwendig. Auch wer nicht sicher ist, was z.B. ein Temporaladverb oder ein Konzessivsatz ist, findet sich mit Hilfe von Inhaltsübersicht und Register rasch zurecht. Das Inhaltsverzeichnis führt nicht nur die üblichen Begriffe wie z.B. Verb, Nomen etc. auf, sondern erklärt diese gleichzeitig mit einem Beispiel. Diese zweiteiligen Titel bilden auch die Kopfzeile der jeweiligen Doppelseite. So werden das Durchblättern und Auffinden leicht gemacht.

Jedes Kapitel ist als Doppelseite aufgebaut: Auf der linken „Darstellungsseite" sind die Strukturen und Regeln des jeweiligen Phänomens zusammengefasst – immer von den Hauptschwierigkeiten und -fehlerquellen der Lernenden ausgehend. Gegenüber auf der rechten Seite stehen die Übungen. Diese Gegenüberstellung von Regel und Übung vermeidet mühsames Blättern und bietet ein hohes Maß an Übersichtlichkeit. Darüber hinaus bringt dieser Aufbau eine Aufteilung des Stoffs in gleichmäßige Lernportionen mit sich. Auf jeder Doppelseite wird nur so viel Stoff präsentiert, wie die Lernenden in einer Unterrichts- bzw. Lernsequenz aufnehmen und verarbeiten können.

Die Darstellungsseite gliedert sich in die Abschnitte Funktion – Formen – Alternativen. Ausgangspunkt ist damit der funktionale Aspekt der grammatischen Strukturen. Das garantiert Praxisnähe: Wann bzw. wofür eine bestimmte Struktur verwendet wird, ist dem Lernenden sofort einleuchtend. Die Darstellung der Formen erfolgt in übersichtlichen Tabellen und Rastern. Die „Alternativen" rücken Variationsmöglichkeiten in den Blick und ermöglichen damit den gezielten Ausbau der Ausdrucksdrucksfähigkeit.

Die Übungen sind nach Schwierigkeitsgrad gestaffelt:
 -Übungen sprechen Lernende am Ende der Grundstufe und am Anfang der Mittelstufe an (*em*-Brückenkurs),
 -Übungen setzen Mittelstufenkenntnisse voraus (*em*-Hauptkurs),
 -Übungen eignen sich für Lernende, die das Niveau der Zentralen Mittelstufenprüfung erreichen wollen (*em*-Abschlusskurs).
Geübt wird vornehmlich an authentischen Texten. Häufig handelt es sich um Zeitungsartikel oder Dialoge mit kommunikativer Situierung. Thematisch orientiert sich die Auswahl der Übungen an den Vorgaben des *Zertifikats Deutsch* und der *Zentralen Mittelstufenprüfung*.

Autoren und Verlag

GENUS

der Mond – das Wasser – die Sonne

1 **Funktion**

der Mond
la lune
měsíc

das Wasser
l'eau
voda

die Sonne
le soleil
slunce

In vielen Sprachen werden die Nomen nach dem Genus unterschieden. In der deutschen Sprache gibt es das maskuline *(der Mond)*, das neutrale *(das Wasser)* und das feminine *(die Sonne)* Genus.

2 **Formen**

Bei vielen Nomen kann man das Genus leider nicht sehen. Deshalb lernen Sie die Nomen am besten immer zusammen mit dem Artikel. Bei einigen Nomen kann man das Genus aber erkennen.

ⓐ Das Genus richtet sich nach dem biologischen Geschlecht:

der Mann, der Student, der Professor	maskulin
die Frau, die Studentin*, die Professorin*	feminin

aber: *das Mädchen, das Fräulein, das Kind, die Person*
* Bei Berufen hat das feminine Wort in der Regel die Endung *-in*.

ⓑ Das Genus kann man an der Nachsilbe erkennen:

-er	*der Fehler*		
	aber: *das Fenster, die Leiter*		maskulin
-ling	*der Schmetterling*		
-chen	*das Häuschen*	Diminutive	neutral
-lein	*das Bächlein*		
-t	*die Fahrt*		feminin
-e*	*die Reise*		
-ung	*die Zeitung*		
-heit/-keit	*die Freiheit, die Fröhlichkeit*		
-schaft	*die Mannschaft*		
-ei	*die Bäckerei*		

* aber: *der Junge* etc. *n*-Deklination 📖 **s. Seite 16**. Wortbildung 📖 **s. Seite 20**

ⓒ Das Genus kann man an der Bedeutung erkennen:

der Morgen, der Montag, der Januar,	Tageszeiten, Wochentage,	maskulin
der Frühling, ... aber: *die Nacht*	Monate, Jahreszeiten	
der Norden, der Süden, der Osten	Himmelsrichtungen	
der Wind, der Regen, ... aber: *die Wolke*	Wetter	
der Wein, der Schnaps, ... aber: *das Bier*	alkoholische Getränke	
der BMW, der Mercedes, der VW	Automarken	
das Blau, das Weiß	Farbnamen	neutral
die Yamaha, die Harley-Davidson	Motorradmarken	feminin

1 Mann oder Frau? – der oder die?

a) *der* Sohn	e) .... Tochter	i) .... Schülerin
b) .... Tante	f) .... Onkel	j) .... Cousin
c) .... Bäcker	g) .... Nichte	k) .... Kundin
d) .... Politiker	h) .... Ministerin	l) .... Schwester

2 Maskulin, neutral oder feminin? – Unterstreichen Sie die Nachsilbe und ergänzen Sie den Artikel.

a) *die* Kind<u>heit</u>	h) .... Fernseher	o) .... Möglichkeit
b) .... Freundschaft	i) .... Liebe	p) .... Schmetterling
c) .... Schüler	j) .... Schrift	q) .... Hähnchen
d) .... Freiheit	k) .... Wäscherei	r) .... Computer
e) .... Sicht	l) .... Frühling	s) .... Lösung
f) .... Gruppe	m) .... Formulierung	t) .... Krankheit
g) .... Schalter	n) .... Brötchen	u) .... Bücherei

3 Wetter, Jahreszeit, Farbe oder ...? – Ergänzen Sie den Artikel.

a) *der* Regen	g) .... Schneeweiß	m) .... Nacht
b) .... Dienstag	h) .... Sturm	n) .... Wein
c) .... Bier	i) .... Mittag	o) .... Audi
d) .... Wolke	j) .... Schnee	p) .... Samstag
e) .... Königsblau	k) .... Yamaha	q) .... Osten
f) .... Westen	l) .... Winter	r) .... Peugeot

4 Maskulin? Neutral? Feminin? – Sortieren Sie die Nomen.

Abend I Abendrot I Blümchen I Champagner I Fahrt I Fiat Punto I Frechheit I Freitag I Hilfe I Hühnchen I Kawasaki I Leistung I Leser I Mädchen I Mai I März I Nebel I Norden I Opel I Schönheit I Schwierigkeit I Spätsommer I Vorlesung I Wirklichkeit

der	das	die
Abend		

1

PLURAL

die Tage – die Bücher – die Rosen

1 Funktion

> *Sag mal, hat die Freundin von Udo immer noch eine Katze?*

> *Ich glaube, sie hat jetzt sogar sechs Katzen.*

2 Formen

-e	der Tag	die Tage	die meisten maskulinen und neutralen Nomen
	das Ereignis	die Ereignisse	Konsonantenverdoppelung
¨e	der Bart	die Bärte	maskuline Nomen: oft mit Umlaut
	die Kuh	die Kühe	feminine Nomen: immer mit Umlaut

-en/	die Frau	die Frauen	die meisten femininen Nomen
-n	die Universität	die Universitäten	viele Fremdwörter
	die Freundin	die Freundinnen	Konsonantenverdoppelung
	der Student	die Studenten	alle maskulinen Nomen der *n*-Deklination
	der Russe	die Russen	s. Seite 16
	der Staat	die Staaten	einige weitere maskuline Nomen

-	der Fehler	die Fehler	maskuline und neutrale Nomen auf
	das Zeichen	die Zeichen	-er, -en, -el, -chen, -lein, -sel
¨	der Apfel	die Äpfel	mit Umlaut nur maskuline Nomen

-er	das Lied	die Lieder	neutrale Nomen
	der Geist	die Geister	einige maskuline Nomen
¨er	das Buch	die Bücher	immer mit Umlaut
	der Mann	die Männer	

-s	das Foto	die Fotos	Nomen, die auf -a, -i, -o enden
	der Opa	die Opas	aber: *das Thema/die Themen – die Firma/die Firmen*
	der Lkw	die Lkws	Abkürzungen
	das Team	die Teams	Fremdwörter aus dem Englischen und Französischen

ÜBUNGEN

1 **Wie heißt der Plural? Umlaut oder kein Umlaut? – Sortieren Sie die Nomen.**

der Arzt I das Blatt I der Baum I der Beruf I das Buch I der Computer I das Ergebnis I das Fach I das Heft I das Jahr I der Kalender I der Kugelschreiber I der Ordner I der Stuhl I der Zettel

-e	¨e	-	¨er
	Ärzte		*Blätter*

2 –en/-n, –s oder –nen? – Ergänzen Sie die Pluralendungen.

a) die Bibliothek/ *en*   f) die Fotokopie/.........   k) der Buchstabe/.........
b) das Kino/ *s*   g) die Vorlesung/.........   l) die Universität/.........
c) das Thema/.........   h) der Name/.........   m) das Dia/.........
d) der Radiergummi/......... i) die Studentin/.........   n) die Dozentin/.........
e) die Professorin/......... j) die CD/.........   o) die Übung/.........

3 Prüfungsstress – Ergänzen Sie die Nomen im Plural.

Liebe Lisa,

wie geht es Dir? Hier an der Uni ist zur Zeit viel los, denn in den

(a) Prüfungen (Prüfung) muss man viel wissen, und dafür müssen wir lernen.

Nur um Max mache ich mir langsam (b) .... (Sorge).

In drei (c) .... (Woche) hat er Examen, und eigentlich sollte er dafür

etwas tun. Stattdessen sitzt er ständig in (d) .... (Café) und plaudert

dort mit anderen (e) .... (Student). Und nachmittags trifft er sich

mit seinen (f) .... (Freundin). Die (g) .... (Abend)

verbringt er damit, dass er für seine Wohngemeinschaft kocht. Und nachts tanzt er in

allen (h) .... (Disco) der Stadt. Das kann doch nicht gut gehen! Ruf

ihn mal an, vielleicht hört er ja auf Dich. Dir alles Liebe und bis bald!

Deine Elisabeth

4 Ein Dia-Abend – Ergänzen Sie den Text.

der Berg I das Bild I das Dia I der Freund I der Gast I der Markt I der Sonnenschirm I der Strand I die Stunde I ~~die Urlaubsreise~~ I

Hallo, Petra! Ich hab dir ja schon erzählt, dass unsere letzten beiden (a) *Urlaubsreisen* wirklich toll waren – und gestern Abend haben wir uns mit unserem neuen Projektor die (b) .... angesehen – einfach fantastisch! Wir haben auch einige (c) .... eingeladen. Und ich muss sagen, Uli hat wirklich prima foto-grafiert! Zuerst die (d) .... mit den schönen Obst- und Gemüseständen, dann das Meer und die (e) .... mit den bunten (f) ....
.... Am Schluss gab es dann noch die (g) .... aus der Schweiz: Die hohen (h) .... dort sind immer wieder toll! Die ganze Vorführung hat drei (i) .... gedauert! Und stell dir vor, unsere (j) .... haben sich überhaupt nicht gelangweilt!

KASUS

Die Kinder schenken ihrem Vater einen Computer.

1 Funktion

a bei Verben

Da im Deutschen die Satzglieder auf unterschiedlichen Positionen stehen können, dienen die Kasus zur Unterscheidung der Ergänzungen.

	Alex	*schenkt*	*seiner Freundin*	*einen Fotoapparat.*
Kasus	Wer? Nominativ-Ergänzung	Verb	Wem? Dativ-Ergänzung	Was? Akkusativ-Ergänzung

	Seiner Freundin	*gefällt*	*das Geschenk.*
Kasus	Wem? Dativ-Ergänzung	Verb	Was? Nominativ-Ergänzung

Verbergänzungen 📖 **s. Seite 88**

b bei Präpositionen

		Präposition	+ Kasus	
Eva denkt oft		*an*	*ihren letzten Urlaub.*	Akkusativ
Das ist ein Geschenk		*zu*	*ihrem Geburtstag.*	Dativ
Er schenkt ihn ihr		*statt*	*eines CD-Players.*	Genitiv

Präpositionen 📖 **s. Seite 64-73**, Verben mit Präpositionen 📖 **s. Seite 90**, Genitiv 📖 **s. Seite 14**

2 Formen

Im Deutschen erkennt man den Kasus hauptsächlich durch das Kasus-Signal am Artikelwort oder Adjektiv.

	maskulin	neutral	feminin	Plural
Nominativ	*der Tag*	*das Jahr*	*die Woche*	*die Tage/Jahre/Wochen*
Akkusativ	*den Tag*	*das Jahr*	*die Woche*	*die Tage/Jahre/Wochen*
Dativ	*dem Tag*	*dem Jahr*	*der Woche*	*den Tagen/Jahren/Wochen*
Genitiv	*des Tages*	*des Jahres*	*der Woche*	*der Tage/Jahre/Wochen*

Die Nomen enden im Dativ Plural auf *-n (Tagen, Jahren, Wochen)*. Ausnahme: Wenn der Plural auf *-s* endet *(mit den Autos)*.

n-Deklination 📖 **s. Seite 16/17**, Adjektivdeklination 📖 **s. Seite 30-35**, Satzstrukturen 📖 **s. Seite 132-135**

1 **Ein Wundermittel – Bestimmen Sie den Kasus.**

a) <u>Diese revolutionäre Creme</u> hilft <u>jedem Menschen</u>.
     Nominativ   *Dativ*

b) <u>Sonnenlicht, Umwelteinflüsse und Rauchen</u> schaden <u>der Haut</u>.

c) <u>Die meisten</u> kennen <u>das Problem</u>, dass <u>die Haut</u> frühzeitig altert.

d) Mit <u>diesem neuen Produkt</u> kann <u>man</u> <u>den Alterungsprozess</u> umkehren.

e) Bei <u>regelmäßiger Anwendung</u> sieht <u>die Haut</u> <u>einer 50-jährigen Frau</u> gleich viel jünger aus.

2 **Auf dem Markt – Ergänzen Sie im Akkusativ.**

1 Euro I 1 Flasche I 1 Kilo I 1 Tag I ~~1 Zentner~~

a) Huch, ist das schwer. Wie viel wiegt denn dieser Kartoffelsack? – *Einen Zentner.*
b) Was kostet die Petersilie? – Genau ....
c) Schau mal, da gibt es frische Milch.
Sollen wir uns .... mitnehmen?
d) Wenn Sie frische Eier wollen, müssen Sie noch ....
warten. Unser Bauer liefert erst morgen.
e) Geben Sie mir bitte .... von den neuen Kartoffeln.

3 **Er macht jetzt eine gute Figur! – Ergänzen Sie im Dativ.**

Ich habe (a) *meinem Mann* (mein Mann) stundenlang zugeredet, bei (b) ....
.... (das Fitness-Programm) mitzumachen. Er treibt ja
selbst nicht so gerne Sport, und am liebsten sieht er (c) .... (der
Sportler, Pl.) im Fernsehen zu. Aber auf (d) .... (das Foto, Pl.)
vom letzten Urlaub sieht man ganz deutlich, dass er zu viel wiegt. Mit so (e) ....
.... (eine Figur) hätte ich mich bestimmt nicht in ihn verliebt. Es hat eine
Zeit lang gedauert, bis er (f) .... (mein
Vorschlag) zugestimmt hat. Ein Argument hat ihn schließlich überzeugt: Wenn du Sport
treibst, gefällst du sicher allen (g) .... (meine
Freundin, Pl.) viel besser!

4 **Geburtstage – Formulieren Sie Sätze.**

	Nominativ	Dativ	Akkusativ
a) backen	Frau Sommer	mein Vater	Kuchen (m)
b) schenken	mein Bruder und ich	meine Schwester	CD-Player (m)
c) kochen	meine Schwester	ihre Freunde (Pl.)	Menü (n)
d) schenken	mein Vater	seine Nachbarinnen (Pl.)	Blumen (Pl.)
e) pflücken	Leo	seine Freundin	Blumenstrauß (m)

a) *Frau Sommer backt meinem Vater einen Kuchen.*

1

GENITIV

die Rechte des Bürgers

1 Funktion

a bei Nomen

Das Nomen im Genitiv (Genitivattribut) gibt den Besitzer an:

		Nomen	+ Genitiv
Wessen Haus ist das?	*Das ist*	*das Ferienhaus*	*eines Freundes.*

In der Umgangssprache wird oft *von* + Dativ verwendet:
Das ist das Ferienhaus von einem Freund.

b bei Präpositionen

Einige wenige Präpositionen brauchen eine Ergänzung im Genitiv 📖 **s. Seite 64-73**:

	Präposition	+ Genitiv
Wir fahren	*trotz*	*des schlechten Wetters.*

2 Formen

a Deklination

maskulin	neutral	feminin	Plural	
des Monats	*des Jahres*	*der Woche*	*der Monate/Jahre/Wochen*	normale Deklination
des Menschen			*der Menschen*	*n*-Deklination

n-Deklination 📖 **s. Seite 16**

b maskuline und neutrale Nomen der normalen Deklination

-s	*Vaters, Fahrers*	mehrsilbige Nomen
-es	*Tages, Jahres*	oft bei einsilbigen Nomen*
	Prozesses, Reflexes	Nomen, die auf *-s, -ss, -ß, - tsch, -x, -z, -tz* enden
	Zeugnisses, Ergebnisses	Nomen auf *-nis*: Verdoppelung des *s*

* aber: *des Chefs, des Films*

c Eigennamen

Norberts Fahrrad *Agnes' Sonnenbrille*	vorangestellte Eigennamen im Genitiv

d *von* + Dativ

das Fahrrad von Norbert *die Sonnenbrille von Agnes* *das Ferienhaus von meinem Freund*	häufig in der gesprochenen Sprache
der Import von Zitronen *der Anbau von Wein*	Nomen ohne Artikel

1 **So eine Unordnung – Ergänzen Sie den Text.**

a) Das ist doch die Hose von Herbert! – Du hast recht, das ist *Herberts Hose*.

b) Sag mal, sind das nicht die Socken von Hugo? – Nein, das sind doch nicht
....

c) Tom lässt aber auch alles liegen! Hier sind seine Bücher. – Nein, das sind ganz sicher
nicht ....

d) Anna ist wirklich unmöglich. Schau mal, ihr nasses Handtuch liegt mitten im
Wohnzimmer. – Na, hör mal, das ist doch nicht ....
...., das ist deins!

2 **Ein Mann wird 50 – Ergänzen Sie die Endung und das Nomen im Genitiv.**

⟨ der Bauch I der Diätplan I die ~~Geburtstagsfeier~~ I die Gesundheit I die Glatze I die Zeit

Hallo, Silke,
stell dir vor, gestern hab ich zufällig Fritz getroffen. Du weißt ja, während (a) sein*er Geburtstagsfeier* bekam er plötzlich eine Krise. Luise hat mir erzählt, dass er jetzt dichtes schwarzes Haar statt (b) sein...............
.... haben wollte. Und anstelle (c) sein............... dicken
.... sollten starke Muskeln treten. Auch wegen
(d) d............ .... wollte er nun regelmäßig Sport treiben.
Offenbar hat er dann auch Diät gemacht und mithilfe (e) ein...............
.... 10 Kilo abgenommen. Innerhalb (f) kurz...............
.... hat er sich so verändert, dass ich ihn gestern fast
nicht wiedererkannt hätte. Also mir hat Fritz früher viel besser gefallen.
So, das war das Wichtigste.
Liebe Grüße *Gabi*

3 **Alte Fotos – Formulieren Sie Sätze mit dem Genitiv.**

a) Das ist die Mutter von meinem Freund.
Das ist die Mutter meines Freundes.

b) Ach schau mal, das ist die Katze von Frau Sturm.

c) Und der Typ da, das ist der Sohn von unserem Lateinlehrer.

d) Wie nett! Das ist ja Kathi, als sie ganz jung war! Sie war schon immer die beste Freundin
von meinem Bruder.

4 **Fachliteratur richtig lesen – Ergänzen Sie den Artikel und das Nomen im Genitiv.**

Es dürfte schwer sein, heute noch ein Thema zu finden, in dem die Fülle (a) *der*
Fachliteratur (die Fachliteratur) nicht die Aufnahmefähigkeit (b) ....
.... (der Einzelne) weit übersteigt. Deshalb hat das frühzeitige Training
(c) .... (das Lesen) eine wesentliche Bedeutung. Wichtig ist, dass
man eine klare Definition (d) .... (die Erkenntnis-
ziele) im Kopf hat. Erst dann hat das Durchsehen (e) .... (die Texte)
einen Sinn.

N-DEKLINATION

Kennen Sie den Namen des neuen Kollegen?

1 Funktion

Alle maskulinen Nomen, die auf *-e* enden (*der Franzose, der Löwe*), und einige andere maskuline Nomen, die ein Lebewesen (*der Mensch, der Herr*) bezeichnen, werden nach der *n*-Deklination dekliniert.

2 Formen

	Singular	Plural
Nominativ	*der Kunde*	*die Kunden*
Akkusativ	*den Kunden*	*die Kunden*
Dativ	*dem Kunden*	*den Kunden*
Genitiv	*des Kunden*	*der Kunden*

Dieser Deklination folgen:

a alle maskulinen Nomen, die auf *-e* enden:

der Junge, der Kollege, der Kunde, der Neffe, der Zeuge ...	Personen
der Chinese, der Franzose, der Grieche, der Pole, der Russe ...	Nationalitäten*
der Affe, der Hase, der Löwe, der Rabe ...	Tiere

* aber: *der Deutsche/ein Deutscher* s. Adjektivdeklination 📖 **Seite 30-35**

Ein zusätzliches *-s* im Genitiv Singular haben:

der Buchstabe, des Buchstabens	*der Glaube, des Glaubens*
der Friede(n), des Friedens	*der Name, des Namens*
der Gedanke, des Gedankens	*der Wille, des Willens*

b einige andere maskuline Nomen:

der Bär, der Bauer, der Herr (den Herrn, dem Herrn, des Herrn, Plural: die Herren), der Mensch, der Nachbar ...

c alle maskulinen Nomen aus dem Lateinischen und Griechischen mit den Endungen:

-and/-ant	*der Doktorand, der Demonstrant, der Elefant ...*
-ent	*der Präsident, der Student, der Referent ...*
-ist	*der Idealist, der Journalist, der Terrorist ...*
-oge	*der Biologe, der Pädagoge, der Psychologe ...*
-at	*der Bürokrat, der Demokrat, der Diplomat ...*
andere	*der Architekt, der Philosoph, der Ökonom, der Fotograf ...*

Außerdem gibt es ein neutrales Nomen: *das Herz, das Herz, dem Herzen, des Herzens* – Plural: *die Herzen*

1 n-Deklination oder normale Deklination? – Sortieren Sie die Nomen mit Artikel.

Assistent I Bauer I Chef I Direktor I Experte I Familie I Herz I Hund I Informatiker I
Ingenieur I Katze I Löwe I Mathematiker I Nachbar I Name I Produzent I Professor I Russe I
Tourist

n-Deklination	normale Deklination
der Assistent	

2 Ein Interview – Ergänzen Sie die Nomen.

Bürokrat I Gedanke I Jurist I Kommilitone I Paragraf I Student I Wille

Ein Berliner in Ägypten

(a) Juristen, die Karriere machen wollen, gehen gewöhnlich nicht nach
Kairo. Warum sind Sie nach Ägypten gegangen?
Ich fand mein Studium am Anfang unglaublich langweilig: nichts als
(b) .... Da bin ich aus Neugier mal mit einem
(c) .... in eine Vorlesung über islamisches Recht
gegangen, und wir waren begeistert.
Und wie sind Sie auf den (d) .... **gekommen, in Kairo
weiterzustudieren?**
Zum einen habe ich einen Horror davor, mal einer dieser ganz normalen
(e) .... zu werden, zum anderen wollte ich einfach
was erleben.
Können Sie das auch anderen (f) .... **empfehlen?**
Ja, unbedingt. Und ich habe den festen (g) .... , im nächsten Jahr in Kairo mein Referendariat zu machen.

3 Zurück aus dem Urlaub – Formulieren Sie Antworten.
a) Frau Sommer, schön, dass Sie wieder da sind. Ihr Kollege möchte Sie dringend sprechen.
(gleich anrufen) *Gut, ich werde den Kollegen gleich anrufen.*
b) Dann wollte der Lieferant wissen, wie viele Tische und Stühle wir für das Sommerfest
brauchen. (telefonieren mit) *In Ordnung, ...*
c) Und der Fotograf möchte wissen, wann er die Fotos vorbeibringen soll. (sprechen mit)
Gut, ...
d) Herr Schäfer aus der Buchhaltung bittet um Rückruf. (sofort anrufen) *O.k., ...*
e) Und dann kommt der Praktikant heute zum ersten Mal. (gleich einarbeiten) *Na gut, ...*
f) Unser Kunde aus Japan hat sich übrigens schon zweimal über die verspätete Lieferung
beschwert. (sich in Verbindung setzen mit) *Auch das noch! Gut, ...*

ADJEKTIV/PARTIZIP ALS NOMEN

der Unbekannte - ein Unbekannter

1 Funktion

Nomen aus Adjektiven und Partizipien bezeichnen Personen und Abstrakta.

Nomen	Adjektiv/Partizip	
ein Unbekannter	*ein unbekannter Mann*	Person
der große Unbekannte	*der große unbekannte Mann*	
die schöne Rothaarige	*die schöne rothaarige Frau*	
nichts Neues	*keine neuen Informationen*	Abstrakta

2 Formen

ⓐ maskuline und feminine Nomen: Bezeichnung von Personen

Nomen – maskulin	Nomen – feminin		
der Bekannte – ein Bekannter	*die/eine Bekannte*	*bekannt*	Adjektiv
der Arbeitslose – ein Arbeitsloser	*die/eine Arbeitslose*	*arbeitslos*	
der Farbige – ein Farbiger	*die/eine Farbige*	*farbig*	
der Gesunde – ein Gesunder	*die/eine Gesunde*	*gesund*	
der Kranke – ein Kranker	*die/eine Kranke*	*krank*	
der Reisende – ein Reisender	*die/eine Reisende*	*reisend*	Partizip I:
der Anwesende – ein Anwesender	*die/eine Anwesende*	*anwesend*	Infinitiv + *d*
			Partizip II:
der Vorgesetzte – ein Vorgesetzter	*die/eine Vorgesetzte*	*vorgesetzt*	*(ge-)....-t*
der Betrunkene – ein Betrunkener	*die/eine Betrunkene*	*betrunken*	*(ge-)....-n*

aber: *der Junge, ein Junge* ist ein Nomen der *n*-Deklination 📖 **s. Seite 16**

ⓑ neutrale Nomen: Bezeichnung von Abstrakta

das Gute	*alles Gute*	*etwas Gutes*	*gut*
das Wahre		*wenig Wahres*	*wahr*
das Schöne		*viel Schönes*	*schön*
das Neue		*nichts Neues*	*neu*

Adjektive, die als Nomen verwendet werden, werden nach den Regeln der Adjektivdeklination dekliniert, 📖 **s. Seite 30-35.**

ÜBUNGEN

1 Wie heißen die Nomen?

Adjektiv/Partizip	maskulin *der*	maskulin *ein*	feminin *die/eine*	Plural *die/-*
a) fremd	*Fremde*	*Fremder*	*Fremde*	*Fremden/ Fremde*
b) deutsch				

Adjektiv/Partizip	maskulin *der*	maskulin *ein*	feminin *die/eine*	Plural *die/-*
c) verwandt				
d) angestellt				
e) abgeordnet				
f) verliebt				

2 Was sind das für Leute? – Ergänzen Sie das passende Nomen.

a) Jemand, der arbeitslos ist, ist *ein Arbeitsloser*.
b) Jemand, der angestellt ist, ist ....
c) Jemand, der reist, ist ....
d) Jemand, der betrunken ist, ist ....
e) Jemand, der abwesend ist, ist ....
f) Alle, die anwesend sind, sind ....

3 Gegenteile – Wie heißen die Nomen? Achten Sie auf die Artikel.

arm I ~~bekannt~~ I falsch I gesund I schuldig I schwarz I tot I uninteressant

a) ein Fremder und ein *Bekannter*
b) der Unschuldige und der ....
c) alle Reichen und alle ....
d) ein Kranker und ein ....
e) ein Weißer und ein ....
f) der Lebende und der ....
g) etwas Interessantes und nichts ....
h) viel Richtiges und wenig ....

4 Mentales Training – Ergänzen Sie das passende Nomen.

angenehm I ~~erfreulich~~ I folgend	schwierig I unterbewusst	besser I neu I wichtig
Kein Mensch entdeckt am frühen Morgen in seinem Gesicht nur (a) *Erfreuliches*! Wenn Ihnen Ihr Gesicht frühmorgens nicht gefällt, können Sie (b) .... tun: Machen Sie Ihre Augen für einen Moment zu und denken Sie an etwas (c) .... !	Wenn es Probleme gibt und Sie wirklich etwas (d) .... vor sich haben, sagen Sie sich dreimal am Tag: Ja, ich kann es! Solche Sätze wirken auf das (e)... .	Das ist nichts (f) .... , trotzdem sagen wir es noch einmal: Wenn Sie etwas (g) .... nicht vergessen wollen, schreiben Sie es auf! Es gibt nichts (h) .... , um sich etwas zu merken!

WORTBILDUNG

der Herzschlag – das Erlebnis

1 Zusammensetzung

Zwei oder mehr Wörter bilden einen neuen Ausdruck. Das letzte Nomen bestimmt Genus und Numerus.

die Sonne + *der Schein*	= *der Sonnenschein*	Nomen	+ Nomen
der Mond + *der Schein*	= *der Mondschein*		
kurz + *die Meldung*	= *die Kurzmeldung*	Adjektiv	+ Nomen
warten + *das Zimmer*	= *das Wartezimmer*	Verb	+ Nomen
neben + *die Kosten* (Pl.)	= *die Nebenkosten*	Präposition	+ Nomen

Fugenzeichen

kennzeichnen die Verbindungsstelle zwischen den Teilen bestimmter zusammengesetzter Nomen. Feste Regeln für die Verwendung gibt es nicht. Sie tauchen immer auf bei:

Wirtschaftsmacht	... den Nachsilben *-ung, -heit, -keit, -schaft, -tum, -ling, -ion,- ität*
Arbeitsmarkt	... vom Verb abgeleiteten Nomen, die auf *-t* enden
Ankunftszeit	aber: *Arbeitgeber, Arbeitnehmer*
Verhaltensforscher	... nominalisierten Infinitiven

Die Fugenzeichen *-n* bzw. *-er* lassen sich aus der Pluralendung erklären:
z.B. *die Gruppenreisen, der Kundendienst, die Büchersendung, der Bilderrahmen*

2 Nominalisierung

Aus einem Verb oder Adjektiv wird ein Nomen:

das Gefühl (fühlen)	aus dem Verb	Vorsilbe *Ge-*
das Essen (essen)		Infinitiv
der Flug (fliegen)		Wortstamm
die Nähe (nah)	aus dem Adjektiv	

3 Ableitung

Bildung von Nomen aus anderen Wortarten durch Nachsilben

Nachsilbe	*der*	Nachsilbe	*das*	Nachsilbe	*die*
-er	*Sender*	-nis	*Erlebnis*	-e, -ei	*Liebe, Bäckerei*
-ling	*Lehrling*		*(die Kenntnis)*	-t	*Fahrt*
-ismus	*Kapitalismus*	-sal	*Schicksal*	-heit	*Kindheit*
-ist	*Kapitalist*	-sel	*Rätsel*	-keit	*Ähnlichkeit*
-us	*Zyklus*	-tum	*Wachstum*	-schaft	*Leidenschaft*
			(der Reichtum)	-ung	*Prüfung*
		-ment	*Parlament*	-anz/-enz	*Toleranz, Tendenz*
		-ar/-är	*Vokabular,*	-ie	*Harmonie*
			Militär	-ik/-atik	*Lyrik, Problematik*
			(aber: der Sekre-	-ion/-tion	*Region, Organisation*
			tär, Millionär)	-ität	*Souveränität*

Feminin-Endung *-in* bei Personen-, Berufs- und Funktionsbezeichnungen:

maskulin	Plural	feminin	Plural
Emigrant	*Emigranten*	*Emigrantin*	*Emigrantinnen*

1 Bilden Sie feminine Formen, a–f im Singular, g–n im Plural.

a) der Archäologe
die Archäologin
b) der Autor
c) der Fabrikant
d) der Hörer

e) der Historiker
f) der Kommissar
g) der Leser
h) der Physiker
i) der Politiker

j) der Spezialist
k) der Student
l) der Zuschauer
m) der Redakteur
n) der Chef

2 Bilden Sie zusammengesetzte Nomen. Setzen Sie den passenden Artikel dazu. Jeweils eine Zusammensetzung ist nicht möglich.

a) das Geld – das Geschäft, das Institut, der Automat, der Mann, der Schein, die Anlage
das Geldgeschäft, ...
b) die Kunst – das Werk, das Buch, der Grund, der Händler, die Ausstellung, die Galerie
c) die Schule – der Abend, das Ballett, das Haus, der Ski, der Grund, hoch, grün
d) groß – der Markt, die Familie, die Liebe, die Macht, die Mutter, die Stadt
e) der Laden – der Baum, das Buch, die Blumen, die Schreibwaren, die Spielwaren
f) die Zeit – frei, hoch, die Reise, der Punkt, der Tisch, das Mahl, die Schule

3 Wie heißen diese Internationalismen?

die   Aggress-, Emo-, Evolu-, Informa-, Kommunika-, Na-, Varia-,
         Identi-, Kapazi-, Solidari-,
         Demokrat-, Diplomat-, Droger-, Philosoph-, Soziolog-, Theolog-

das   Argu-, Doku-, Instru-, Testa-,
         Invent-, Gloss-,

der   Ego-, Fasch-, Kapital-, Katholiz-, Kommun-, Protestant-

die Aggression, die ...

4 Fugen-s oder keins? Ergänzen Sie, wo nötig.

Wetten im Internet

Jana Gutmann, 30, ist eine junge (a) Geschäft͜frau aus Hamburg. Früher hat sie (b) Kommunikation.......wissenschaft und (c) Betrieb.......wirtschaft studiert und nebenher ihr Geld als (d) Foto.......modell verdient. Heute hat sie ihr eigenes Internet-Wettbüro. Allerdings kein normales Wettbüro mit langweiligen (e) Sport.......wetten, sondern eines mit hohem (f) Unterhaltung.......wert.

Bekommt die (g) Leben.......gefährtin des neuen James-Bond-Darstellers ein Kind? Wer ist im Moment die (h) Liebling.......freundin des englischen Prinzen William? Hat der amerikanische Präsident (i) Beziehung.......-probleme? „Alles, was diskutiert wird, ist eine Wette wert", sagt Jana. Die Höhe des Gewinns ist von der (j) Teilnehmer.......zahl abhängig. Bezahlt wird per (k) Bank.......einzug oder per (l) Kredit.......karte. Jeweils am (m) Monat.......ende und am (n) Jahr.......ende wird ein Sieger ermittelt.

BESTIMMTER ARTIKEL

der Brief – dieses Buch – jede Zeitung

1 Funktion

Im Unterschied z.B. zu den slawischen Sprachen verwendet man im Deutschen Artikelwörter. Sie zeigen das Genus, den Numerus und den Kasus des folgenden Nomens an.

ⓐ Der bestimmte Artikel ...

... signalisiert, dass die Person oder Sache im Text vorher schon einmal explizit erwähnt wurde oder implizit enthalten ist. Oder sie ist aus der Alltagswelt bekannt:

Das war ein tolles Hotel! Die Zimmer waren sehr gemütlich.	Kontext
Hallo, wie war's in der Arbeit?	Alltagswelt

... signalisiert, dass es sich um etwas handelt, das nur einmal existiert:

der Bodensee, der Rhein, die Alpen, die Sonne	Seen, Flüsse, Gebirge, Gestirne, Gebäude
die Mongolei, die Schweiz, die Türkei, der Irak	wenige Ländernamen
Das war der schönste Tag meines Lebens!	Superlativ
der 22. Oktober, am Freitag, das zweite Bier	Datum, Ordinalzahl

... signalisiert, dass ein Exemplar stellvertretend für die ganze Art steht:

Die Seerose ist eine Wasserpflanze.	Generalisierung

ⓑ Der Demonstrativartikel kennzeichnet das folgende Nomen als besonders auffällig:

Sag mal, siehst du diesen/den gut aussehenden Mann da hinten?	Anstelle von *dieser* kann auch der bestimmte Artikel benutzt werden.
In jenen Tagen waren sie glücklich.	signalisiert Ferne; heute etwas veraltet
Ich kenne hier jede Straße.	signalisiert: jedes einzelne Exemplar nur im Singular

ⓒ Der bestimmte Artikel als Pronomen:

Wo ist die Zeitung? – Die liegt da drüben. / Ich kenne hier jeden.

2 Formen

ⓐ Artikelwörter und Pronomen*

	maskulin	neutral	feminin	Plural
Nominativ	*der*	*das*	*die*	*die*
Akkusativ	*den*	*das*	*die*	*die*
Dativ	*dem*	*dem*	*der*	*den*
Genitiv	*des (*dessen)*	*des (*dessen)*	*der (*deren)*	*der (*deren)*

Genauso: *dieser – jener – jeder* (Plural: *alle*)

ⓑ Präpositionen und bestimmter Artikel

an, bei, in, von, zu	+ *dem*	*am, beim, im, vom, zum*
zu	+ *der*	*zur*
an, in	+ *das*	*ans, ins*

1 Kontaktanzeige – Ergänzen Sie den Text.

‹ am I ans I ~~den~~ I den I den I der I der I des I die I im I im

Sommer in München

Radeln, schwimmen und dann ein Picknick an (a) *den* Osterseen machen, barfuß durch (b) ....
Englischen Garten laufen, frühstücken in (c) .... Lenbachgalerie, lange spazieren gehen,
(d) .... schönsten Sonnenuntergang (e) .... Sommers (f) .... Starnberger
See beobachten, wenn's regnet, in (g) .... gemütliche Sauna (h) .... Zentrum gehen
und (i) .... August vielleicht ein paar Tage (j) .... Mittelmeer fahren. (k) ....
netteste Typ Münchens sucht eine Partnerin mit Geist und Lebensfreude zwischen 45 und 50.

2 Hätten Sie's gewusst? – Ergänzen Sie den bestimmten Artikel.
a) Wofür steht bei*m* Videorekorder *die* Taste mit .... doppelten Dreiecken, die nach links
zeigen?
☐ A) Pause ☐ B) schneller Vorlauf ☐ C) Wiedergabe ☐ D) schneller Rücklauf
b) Wer hat .... Telefon erfunden?
☐ A) Graham Bell ☐ B) Philipp Reis ☐ C) Thomas Edison ☐ D) Werner von Siemens
c) Wie hieß .... Forschungsschiff von Charles Darwin?
☐ A) Dolphin ☐ B) Calypso ☐ C) Beagle ☐ D) Dove
d) Welches ist .... intelligenteste Haustier?
☐ A) Hund ☐ B) Schwein ☐ C) Katze ☐ D) Kuh
e) Auf welchen Tieren überquerte Hannibal .... Alpen?
☐ A) Pferden ☐ B) Elefanten ☐ C) Eseln ☐ D) Kamelen
f) Wann ist .... „Tag .... Arbeit"?
☐ A) 17. Juni ☐ B) 1. Mai ☐ C) 3. Oktober ☐ D) 1. November

Lösung: a) D; b) B; c) C; d) B; e) B; f) B

3 Warum wurde in Übung 1 und Übung 2 der bestimmte
Artikel verwendet? Bestimmen Sie die Regel.

4 Ergänzen Sie den bestimmten Artikel.

Elefant spaziert durch Karlsruhe

Karlsruhe (dpa) Ein Elefant hat mitten in Karlsruhe für Aufregung gesorgt. Wie
(a) *die* Polizei (b) a........ Freitag mitteilte, glaubte sie zuerst an einen Scherz, als
Anrufer (c) a........ Donnerstag von einem Elefanten (d) in .... Stadt berichteten.
(e) .... alarmierten Polizisten trauten ihren Augen kaum, als sie (f) ....
Rüsseltier an (g) .... belebtesten Hauptverkehrsstraße sahen. (h) ....
Elefant verspeiste gerade Gras und einen jungen Baum. Erst herbeigerufene
Mitarbeiter (i) .... Zirkus Busch konnten dann (j) .... dickhäutigen
Ausreißer dazu bewegen, nach Hause zurückzukehren.

UNBESTIMMTER ARTIKEL

ein König – ein Schloss – eine Fee

1 Funktion

Der unbestimmte Artikel signalisiert, dass etwas folgt, das noch nicht näher identifiziert ist.

Es war einmal eine Fee, die in einem Wald in der Nähe eines Schlosses wohnte. Die Fee hatte eine Kugel aus Glas. Mithilfe der Kugel konnte sie wahrsagen.	häufig beim ersten Auftreten im Text; beim nächsten Auftreten im Text mit dem bestimmten Artikel weitergeführt 📖 **s. Seite 22**
Der/Ein Elefant ist ein Rüsseltier. Elefanten sind Rüsseltiere.	in Definitionen bei dem Nomen, das die übergeordnete Klasse bezeichnet
Hast du eigentlich einen eigenen Computer? – Noch nicht, aber ich kauf mir bald einen.	als Pronomen

2 Formen

ⓐ unbestimmter Artikel

	maskulin	neutral	feminin	Plural
Nominativ	*ein*	*ein*	*eine*	-
Akkusativ	*einen*	*ein*	*eine*	-
Dativ	*einem*	*einem*	*einer*	-
Genitiv	*eines*	*eines*	*einer*	-* / *von* + Dativ

* Nur mit Adjektiv: *Snowboard-Fahren ist eher ein Hobby junger Leute.*

ⓑ Negativ- und Possessivartikel

	maskulin	neutral	feminin	Plural
Nominativ	*kein*	*kein*	*keine*	*keine*
Akkusativ	*keinen*	*kein*	*keine*	*keine*
Dativ	*keinem*	*keinem*	*keiner*	*keinen*
Genitiv	*keines*	*keines*	*keiner*	*keiner*

Genauso: Possessivartikel *mein, dein* usw. 📖 **s. Seite 28**

ⓒ Pronomen

Nur die Formen in den blauen Kästen werden anders dekliniert:

	maskulin	neutral	feminin	Plural
Nominativ	*einer*	*ein(e)s*	*eine*	*welche*
Akkusativ	*einen*	*ein(e)s*	*eine*	*welche*
Dativ	*einem*	*einem*	*einer*	*welchen*
Genitiv	*eines*	*eines*	*einer*	*welcher*

Genauso: Negativ- und Possessivpronomen

3 Varianten

Standardsprache	Umgangssprache
Das ist wirklich ein cooler Typ!	*Das ist wirklich 'n cooler Typ!*
Hast du einen Freund?	*Hast du 'nen Freund?*
Ich bin bei einer Tante eingeladen.	*Ich bin bei 'ner Tante eingeladen.*

1 **Wissen Sie's? – Definieren Sie die Begriffe.**

a) Was ist eine Fee?   Mann aus dem Mittelalter mit Pferd
b) Was ist ein Zwerg?   übernatürliche Wesen ohne Körper
c) Was ist eine Hexe?   Frau mit magischen Kräften
d) Was sind Geister?   gefährliches Tier, das Feuer spuckt
e) Was ist ein Ritter?   sehr kleiner Mann mit Bart und Zipfelmütze
f) Was ist ein Drache?   hässliche, alte Frau, die zaubern kann und meistens böse ist

a) *Eine Fee ist eine Frau mit magischen Kräften.*

2 **Was ist denn das? – Formulieren Sie Sätze mit dem Genitiv Singular und dem Plural mit von + Dativ.**

a) der Rat/Freund   d) der Ton/Flöte
    Das ist der Rat eines Freundes.   e) der Gesang/Vogel
    Das ist der Rat von Freunden.   f) das Schreien/Möwe
b) der Geruch/Zitrone   g) der Schatten/Wolke
c) der Duft/Rose

3 **Ein fantastischer Koch – Ergänzen Sie den unbestimmten Artikel und die Pronomen.**

a) Also, Erna, ich brauche zuerst *ein* scharfes Messer. Hast du denn überhaupt *eins*? Ach hier, danke!
b) Und sag mal, gibt es in dieser Küche eigentlich .... Holzbretter? Dann reich mir doch bitte mal .... !
c) Erna, ... Bratpfanne kann ich auch nirgends finden! Hast du k........................?
d) Sag mal, hast du überhaupt .... Zwiebeln und .... Karotten eingekauft?
e) So, und jetzt brauche ich noch .... Topf mit Wasser. Ich glaube, da drüben steht .... Danke sehr, meine Liebe.
f) Ach, könntest du mir bitte mal .... große Schüssel bringen?
g) Danke! Ich habe vorhin .... Flasche Weißwein in den Kühlschrank gestellt. Schenk mir doch bitte .... Glas ein! Und nimm dir selber auch ....
h) .... wunderbares Essen! Erna, jetzt brauchen wir bloß noch .... Kerze auf dem Tisch. Na, wie schmeckt das? Ich bin doch .... fantastischer Koch!

4 **Lesen Sie den Text jetzt in der umgangssprachlichen Variante laut vor.**

a) Also, Erna, ich brauch zuerst 'n scharfes Messer.

5 **Fehlerkorrektur – Ergänzen Sie die fehlenden Artikel (bestimmte 📖 s. Seite 22 und unbestimmte) an der richtigen Stelle.**

Meine Freundin Christine hat *ein* Baby bekommen. Deshalb muss ich noch schnell in Geschäft, um Geschenk zu kaufen. Hast du vielleicht Idee, was ich Christine für Baby schenken könnte? Baby ist Junge, kleines Auto wäre ganz gut. Aber dafür ist Junge jetzt noch ein bisschen zu klein. Vielleicht Mütze für nächsten Winter. Mal sehen, Geschenk darf auch nicht zu teuer sein. Auf jeden Fall kaufe ich Buch mit Jogaübungen für Christine.

NULLARTIKEL

Brot und Spiele

Der Nullartikel steht ...

Schau, da fliegt ein Vogel. *Schau, da fliegen Vögel.*	... als Plural des unbestimmten Artikels 📖 **s. Seite 24**
Rom ist die Hauptstadt von Italien. *Asien ist der größte Kontinent der Erde.*	... vor Namen der meisten Länder, Kontinente und Städte
Lisa, das ist Uwe. *Sei leise, Onkel Fritz schläft!*	... vor Eigennamen
Auf Wiedersehen, Frau Dr. Semmler.	... vor Anreden und Titeln
Lance ist Amerikaner.	... vor Nationalitäten
Tanja wird Sängerin. *Max arbeitet jetzt als Profi-Boxer.*	... vor Berufen
Möchten Sie Kaffee oder Tee?	... vor Stoffen
Der Stuhl hier ist aus Holz.	... vor Materialien
Wir brauchen noch Mineralwasser.	... vor unbestimmten Mengen
„Freiheit, Gleichheit, Brüderlichkeit" war *die Parole der Französischen Revolution.*	... vor Abstrakta
Ingeborg hat wirklich Mut. *Max machte vor Freude einen Luftsprung.*	... vor Eigenschaften und Gefühlen
bei Wind und Regen, mit Mühe *ein Zimmer ohne Dusche, zu Abend essen*	... vor Nomen in genereller Bedeutung, besonders nach *mit, ohne, zu*
Bitte ein Glas Orangensaft. *Ich hätte gern ein Kilo Zwiebeln.*	... vor Nomen nach Maß-, Gewichts- und Mengenangaben
Tom kommt nächsten Montag.	... vor Zeitangaben ohne Präposition
Hilfe leisten, Atem holen, Frieden schließen *in Frage stellen, in Gefahr sein, in Gang setzen*	... vor Nomen-Verb-Verbindungen

Wenn das Nomen z.B. durch ein Adjektiv oder einen Relativsatz erweitert ist, muss ein Artikel stehen:

das südliche Afrika *Ach, da kommen ja der alte Tom und die verrückte Tante Frieda.* *Wo ist der Tee, den du gestern gekauft hast?*	bestimmter Artikel
Puh, das ist ja ein scheußlicher Kaffee!	unbestimmter Artikel

ÜBUNGEN

1 **Warum Nullartikel? – Kreuzen Sie an.**

Besser schlafen

Es sind vor allem die verschiedenen Ereignisse eines Tages, die das Gedanken-Karussell im Kopfkissen *in Gang setzen*. Obwohl man müde ist, klappt es mit dem Einschlafen nicht. Aber auch *Kaffee, Alkohol* und *Nikotin* können Einschlaf-störungen verursachen. Gut für das Einschlafen sind *Einschlafrituale*: „So wie *Kindern*, die nur mithilfe von *Gute-Nacht-Geschichten* einschlafen können, hilft auch *Erwachsenen* eine gewisse Einschlaf-Routine", meint *Professor Hartmann.*

	Plural	Stoff	Eigen-name	generelle Bedeutung	Nomen-Verb-Verbindungen
in Gang setzen					✕
Kaffee, Alkohol, Nikotin					
Einschlafstörungen					
Einschlafrituale					
Kindern					
Hilfe					
Gute-Nacht-Geschichten					
Erwachsenen					
Professor Hartmann					

2 Neue Produkte für die Küche – Ergänzen Sie den Nullartikel, den bestimmten Artikel oder den unbestimmten Artikel.

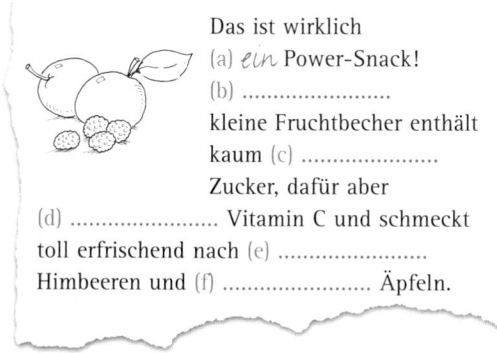

Das ist wirklich (a) *ein* Power-Snack! (b) .... kleine Fruchtbecher enthält kaum (c) .... Zucker, dafür aber (d) .... Vitamin C und schmeckt toll erfrischend nach (e) .... Himbeeren und (f) .... Äpfeln.

Sie mögen (g) .... Zitronen, Sie wollen aber (h) .... Säure nicht? Dann ist für Sie (i) .... Zitronenöl mit (j) .... Vitamin E genau das Richtige für (k) .... Salatsoßen und (l) .... Marinaden. Übrigens: (m) .... Zitronenöl stammt aus (n) .... Sizilien.

3 Ein Brief aus Italien – Ergänzen Sie den bestimmten Artikel, den unbestimmten Artikel oder den Nullartikel. Manchmal gibt es zwei Möglichkeiten.

Liebe (a) ..../........ Katharina,
wie geht es Dir? Stell Dir vor, ich bin in (b) ..../........ Florenz und mache seit vier Tagen (c) .... Sprachkurs. (d) .... Kurs ist immer (e) a...................... Vormittag, danach mache ich meine Hausaufgaben mit zwei anderen Studentinnen in (f) .... kleinen „ristorante" neben (g) .... Schule.
Nachmittags schauen wir uns meistens zu dritt (h)...................... Stadt an – und hier gibt es wirklich viel zu sehen! In (i) .... „Uffizien" waren wir schon – das ist (j) .... schönste Gemäldesammlung, die ich kenne. Und es gibt noch so viel anderes zu besichtigen! Meistens endet unsere Tour in (k)...................... Café oder in (l) .... Park.
Ich wohne bei (m) .... italienischen Familie, und abends esse ich meistens dort. Später treffe ich mich dann noch mit einigen anderen Studenten in (n)...................... Diskothek oder in (o) .... Bar und trinke ein paar Gläser (p) .... Wein.
So, und genau dorthin gehe ich jetzt auch, denn ich habe mich mit (q) .... Eva und (r)...................... Frederico verabredet. (s)...................... Frederico ist (t) .... Spanier und arbeitet als (u) .... Software-Spezialist bei (v) .... Computerfirma.
Hast Du (w) .... Lust, mich hier zu besuchen? Schreib mir doch mal!
Alles Liebe,
Deine (x)...................... Sandra

POSSESSIVARTIKEL

mein Schlüssel

1 Funktion

Der Possessivartikel und das Possessivpronomen signalisieren „Besitz" oder „Zusammengehörigkeit".

So, ich hab jetzt meinen *Autoschlüssel, und da sind* meine *Handschuhe. Ich suche jetzt nur noch* meine *Brille.*	Possessivartikel
Ist das eigentlich Ihr Auto? – Ja, das ist meins.	Possessivpronomen

2 Formen

a Possessivartikel

	maskulin	neutral	feminin	Plural
ich	*mein*	*mein*	*meine*	*meine*
du	*dein*	*dein*	*deine*	*deine*
er	*sein*	*sein*	*seine*	*seine*
es	*sein*	*sein*	*seine*	*seine*
sie	*ihr*	*ihr*	*ihre*	*ihre*
wir	*unser*	*unser*	*uns(e)re*	*uns(e)re*
ihr	*euer*	*euer*	*eure*	*eure*
sie/Sie	*ihr/Ihr*	*ihr/Ihr*	*ihre/Ihre*	*ihre/Ihre*

Deklination

	maskulin	neutral	feminin	Plural
Nominativ	*mein*	*mein*	*meine*	*meine*
Akkusativ	*meinen*	*mein*	*meine*	*meine*
Dativ	*meinem*	*meinem*	*meiner*	*meinen*
Genitiv	*meines*	*meines*	*meiner*	*meiner*

Genauso: *dein, deinen, deinem, deines; sein, seinen, seinem ...*

Akkusativ

Wo wohnt eigentlich Tom? – Keine Sorge, ich habe seine Adresse.

3. Person maskulin

feminin

Dativ

Diesen Ring will ich Julia zu ihrem Geburtstag schenken.

3. Person maskulin
feminin

b Possessivpronomen

Nur die Pronomen in den blau markierten Kästen werden anders dekliniert:

	maskulin	neutral	feminin	Plural
Nominativ	*meiner*	*mein(e)s*	*meine*	*meine*
Akkusativ	*meinen*	*mein(e)s*	*meine*	*meine*
Dativ	*meinem*	*meinem*	*meiner*	*meinen*
Genitiv	*meines*	*meines*	*meiner*	*meiner*

1 **Kurz vor dem Abflug – Ergänzen Sie die Possessivartikel.**
- Frau Haller, wo ist eigentlich (a) *mein* Pass?
- Tut mir leid, ich weiß nicht, wo Sie (b) .... Pass haben.
- Ich fliege nachher doch nach Zürich.
  Wissen Sie vielleicht, wo ich (c) .... Ticket hingelegt habe?
- Nein, aber schauen Sie doch mal in (d) .... Büro nach.
  Es könnte auf (e) .... Schreibtisch liegen.
- Ach, natürlich! Danke sehr!
- So, jetzt rufe ich Ihnen aber gleich ein Taxi! (f) .... Flugzeug geht
  nämlich in einer Stunde!

2 **Auf Prominentenjagd in Hollywood – Formulieren Sie Antworten mit dem Possessivartikel.**
a) Wohnt hier Silvester Stallone? (die Villa) – Ja, das ist *seine Villa*.
b) Und mit diesem Auto fährt Richard Gere herum? (der Wagen) – Genau, das ist
   .... , aber er fährt nicht gerne Auto.
c) Das ist doch die Straße, die nach Frank Sinatra benannt wurde? (die Straße) – Ja, man
   könnte sagen, dass das .... ist.
d) Und in diesem Fitness-Studio kommt wirklich Jane Fonda öfter vorbei? (das Fitness-
   Studio) – Ja, denn das ist .... eigenes ....

3 **Stars privat – Ergänzen Sie die Possessivartikel.**

KIM BASINGER, US-Schauspielerin, ist privat nicht so mutig wie in (a) *ihren* Filmen. „Ich habe immer noch Angst vor (b) .... öffentlichen Auftritten", sagte die Schauspielerin jetzt. Schon in (c) .... Schulzeit habe (d) .... Mutter die Lehrer um Verständnis für Kims Schüchternheit gebeten. Heute ist Basinger aber der Meinung, es sei besser, sich (e) .... Ängsten zu stellen.

RICHARD GERE, US-Schauspieler, hat (f) .... (g) .... Filmkarriere unter anderem mangelnden Selbstbewusst- sein zu verdanken. „(h) .... Meinung von mir selbst war früher nicht sehr hoch", sagte der 50 Jahre alte Frauenschwarm. Aus ähnlichen Gründen seien die meisten (i) .... Kollegen Schauspieler geworden, meinte Gere.

4 **Nach einer Party – Ergänzen Sie das Possessivpronomen.**
a) Tom, sind das deine Schuhe? – Ja, das sind *meine*.
b) Und diese Jacke hier. Ist die auch von dir? – Nein, das ist nicht .... , ich
   glaube, die ist von Steven.
c) Sind das auch seine Zigaretten? – Zeig mal her! Ja, das sind ....
d) Und dieses Brillenetui hier gehört doch Liz? – Genau, das ist ....
e) Und dieser Ring ist sicher von Julia. – Ja, das muss .... sein.

2

ADJEKTIVDEKLINATION *TYP 1*

der rote Stein

1   Funktion

Da im Deutschen die Satzglieder auf unterschiedlichen Positionen stehen können, dienen die Kasus-Signale 📖 **s. Seite 12** zur Unterscheidung der Ergänzungen.
Das Kasus-Signal ist ...

... entweder am Artikelwort (Adjektivdeklination Typ 1):	*Den alten Film sehe ich immer wieder gern.*
... oder am Adjektiv (Adjektivdeklination Typ 2 📖 **s. Seite 32**):	*Im Gloria läuft heute nur ein alter Film.*

2   Formen

Wenn das Kasus-Signal am Artikelwort ist, bekommt das Adjektiv die Endung *-en*, nur in der markierten „Pistolenform" die Endung *-e*.

	maskulin			neutral			feminin			Plural		
NOM	*der*	*rote*	*Stein*	*das*	*helle*	*Licht*	*die*	*klare*	*Luft*	*die*	*runden*	*Formen*
AKK	*den*	*roten*	*Stein*	*das*	*helle*	*Licht*	*die*	*klare*	*Luft*	*die*	*runden*	*Formen*
DAT	*dem*	*roten*	*Stein*	*dem*	*hellen*	*Licht*	*der*	*klaren*	*Luft*	*den*	*runden*	*Formen*
GEN	*des*	*roten*	*Steines*	*des*	*hellen*	*Lichtes*	*der*	*klaren*	*Luft*	*der*	*runden*	*Formen*

Genauso nach den Artikelwörtern *dieser, jener, jeder, welcher, mancher, alle*.

Wenn ein Nomen mehrere Adjektive hat, werden alle Adjektive gleich dekliniert: *die roten, gelben und braunen Blätter.*

Besondere Adjektive:

hoch	*der*	*hohe*	*Turm*	
dunkel	*eine*	*dunkle*	*Straße*	Adjektive auf *-el* und *-er*
teuer	*meine*	*teure*	*Uhr*	aber: *bitter, finster: eine bittere Medizin*
prima	*eine*	*prima*	*Idee*	Adjektive auf *-a* werden nicht dekliniert
Münchner	*das*	*Münchner*	*Bier*	Adjektive von Städtenamen und einigen
Wiener	*der*	*Wiener*	*Walzer*	Ländernamen enden auf *-er*, werden groß-
Schweizer		*Schweizer*	*Käse*	geschrieben und nicht dekliniert

---

ÜBUNGEN

1   Herbst – Unterstreichen Sie die Kasus-Signale und ergänzen Sie die Adjektivendungen im Nominativ.

maskulin
a) dieser blaue Himmel
b) der bunt...... Wald
c) jener alt...... Baum

neutral
d) das herrlich...... Wetter
e) dieses einmalig...... Blau
f) jedes einzeln...... Blatt

feminin
g) die klar...... Luft
h) die einzig...... Wolke
i) diese prima...... Idee

2 Ein Picknick im Grünen – Unterstreichen Sie die Kasus-Signale und ergänzen Sie die Adjektivendungen.

Akkusativ

a) über den
ganz*en* See

b) für das geplant......
Picknick

c) ohne die kleinst......
Pause

Dativ

d) zu dem alt......
Waldarbeiter

e) mit diesem klein......
Boot

f) in der golden......
Abendsonne

Genitiv

g) während des ganz......
Tages

h) trotz des gut......
Wetters

i) wegen der beginnend......
Dunkelheit

3 Natur pur – Unterstreichen Sie die Kasus-Signale und ergänzen Sie die Adjektivendungen im Plural.

a) durch die herbst-
lich*en* Wälder

b) für alle hungrig......
Tiere

c) um die hölzern......
Bänke

d) zwischen den dunkl......
Bäumen

e) unter diesen hoh......
Tannen

f) mit den grün......
Zweigen

g) unterhalb der hoh...... Berge

h) jenseits der verschneit......
Alpen

i) während der kürzer
werdend...... Tage

4 Haushaltstipps – Ergänzen Sie die Adjektive.

KÜHLSCHRANK: Wenn Ihr Kühlschrank nur die halb (a) *volle* (voll)
Flasche Wein von gestern Abend und den (b) ....
(restlich) (c) .... (Schweiz) Käse enthält, verbraucht
er mehr Energie als in (d) .... (gefüllt) Zustand.
Füllen Sie ihn also auf: Mit dem (e) .... (grün) Salat
zum Beispiel, den (f) .... (Wiener) Würstchen oder
auch der gerade (g) .... (gekauft) Flasche Wein.

GESCHIRRSPÜLMASCHINE: Auf dem (h) ....
(gespült) Geschirr sind die (i) .... (traurig) Reste der
Tomatensoße vom (j) .... (gestrig) Abendessen noch
zu sehen? Dann war die Maschine wohl zu voll! Räumen Sie Ihre Spül-
maschine beim (k) .... (nächst) Mal so ein, dass das
Wasser überall hinkommt, und reinigen Sie regelmäßig alle Siebe und
Filter.

WASCHMASCHINE: Stopfen Sie nicht die (l) ....
(ganz) Schmutzwäsche der (m) .... (letzt) Wochen
mit Gewalt in die (n) .... (arm), (o) ....
(alt) Maschine, sonst wird der Motor zu stark belastet. Und waschen
Sie die (p) .... (dunkel) T-Shirts getrennt von den
(q) .... (weiß) Hemden.

ADJEKTIVDEKLINATION *TYP 2*

roter Stein – helles Licht – klare Luft

Formen

Wenn es keinen Artikel (Nullartikel) gibt oder das Artikelwort kein Kasus-Signal hat *(ein, kein, mein usw.)*, bekommt das Adjektiv das Kasus-Signal.
Ausnahme: Genitiv maskulin und neutral: *-en*. Hier hat das Nomen das Kasus-Signal.

	maskulin	neutral	feminin	Plural
NOM	*roter* Stein	*helles* Licht	*klare* Luft	*runde* Formen
AKK	*roten* Stein	*helles* Licht	*klare* Luft	*runde* Formen
DAT	*rotem* Stein	*hellem* Licht	*klarer* Luft	*runden* Formen
GEN	*roten* Steines	*hellen* Lichtes	*klarer* Luft	*runder* Formen

Genauso: nach Kardinalzahlen, z.B. *mit drei grünen Smaragden, anstelle zehn roter Edelsteine.*

Wenn ein Nomen mehrere Adjektive hat, werden alle Adjektive gleich dekliniert: *in klarer, frischer Luft.*

ÜBUNGEN

1 **Welche Artikelwörter haben kein Kasus-Signal, welche haben eins? – Kreuzen Sie an.**

	ohne	mit		ohne	mit		ohne	mit
ein	☒	☐	seinen	☐	☐	unser	☐	☐
einen	☐	☐	sein	☐	☐	unsere	☐	☐
kein	☐	☐	mein	☐	☐	dein	☐	☐
keine	☐	☐	deinem	☐	☐	meinen	☐	☐
Ihr	☐	☐	Ihre	☐	☐	Ihren	☐	☐

2 **Sommer – Ergänzen Sie die Adjektivendungen im Nominativ.**

maskulin	neutral	feminin	Plural
a) ein weit*er* Weg	e) unser verrostet...... Rad	i) leis...... Musik	m) hoh...... Tannen
b) rot...... Wein	f) dein alt...... Radio	j) gesalzen...... Butter	n) süß...... Trauben
c) französisch...... Käse	g) dunkl...... Brot	k) würzig...... Wurst	o) lachend...... Kinder
d) stark...... Kaffee	h) ein scharf...... Messer	l) frisch...... Milch	p) groß...... Bäume

3   Aktivurlaub – Ergänzen Sie die Adjektive.

Akkusativ

Sie wollen mal richtig raus aus dem Alltag? Sie mögen (a) *gutes* (gut) Essen und (b) ....
(exzellent) Wein, lieben (c) .... (klassisch) Musik und wünschen sich nebenbei auch
noch (d) .... (sportlich) Aktivitäten? Dann buchen Sie für ein (e) ....
(lang) Wochenende ein (f) .... (komfortabel) Doppel- oder Einzelzimmer
in unserem Hotel! Sie werden hier (g) .... (unvergesslich) Tage verbringen!

Dativ

Bei (h) .... (frisch) Neuschnee können Sie auf allen Pisten Ski fahren oder in
(i) .... (klar) Bergluft einmalige Wanderungen machen. Danach geht's in den Fitness-
Raum: Mit (j) .... (gezielt) Muskeltraining gegen den Speck! Nach dem Sport in die
Sauna und danach in (k) .... (eiskalt) Wasser schwimmen: Da vergessen Sie den
Alltag bestimmt! Übrigens: Unsere Skikurse finden alle in (l) .... (klein) Gruppen statt.

Genitiv

Sie werden sich innerhalb (m) .... (kürzest) Zeit wie neu geboren fühlen!
Auf der Basis (n) .... (individuell) Beratung wird Ihr ganz persönliches
Fitness-Programm zusammengestellt: Anstelle (o) .... (untrainiert) Muskeln
und (p) .... (trüb) Gedanken werden bald Waschbrettbauch und Optimismus
ihr Leben bestimmen.

4   Deine blauen Augen sind phänomenal! – Ergänzen Sie die Adjektivendungen.

(a) Blauäugig*e* Männer haben offenbar (b) besser...... Chancen beim Flirten – auf jeden
Fall bei (c) englisch...... Frauen. Denn nach einer kürzlich veröffentlichten Studie von
(d) britisch...... Psychologen der Universität Manchester ist dort fast jede zweite Frau von
(e) blau...... Augen fasziniert. (f) Verschieden...... Testmänner mussten sich für die Studie
(g) farbig...... Kontaktlinsen einsetzen und wurden so fotografiert. Die Testfrauen mussten
anhand der Fotos dann (h) folgend...... Fragen beantworten und auf einer Skala bewerten:
Ist das ein (i) sympathisch...... Mann? Ist das ein (j) attraktiv...... Mann? Ist das ein
(k) intelligent...... Mann? Dabei wussten sie nicht, dass es bei der Befragung um die
Augen ging. Das Ergebnis:
(l) Braunäugig...... Männer wirken nur auf 21 Prozent der Frauen attraktiv, 33 Prozent
bevorzugen (m) grün...... Augen. Bei Männern mit (n) blau...... Augen wurden 46 Prozent
der befragten Frauen schwach. Darüber hinaus haben (o) blauäugig...... Männer einen
weiteren Vorteil: „Findet man jemanden wegen (p) schön...... Augen attraktiv, spricht man
ihm auch (q) höher...... Intelligenz zu", hat Studienleiter Geoffrey Beattle herausgefunden.

5   Computer und Co. – Formulieren Sie Sätze.

a) ein I leistungsfähig I Computer I sein I heutzutage I billig
    Ein leistungsfähiger Computer ist heutzutage billig.
b) ein I gut I und I augenschonend I Bildschirm I dürfen I nicht I flimmern
c) ein I professionell I Drucker I müssen I hoch I Farbqualität I bieten
d) zwei I klein I Aktiv-Boxen I sein I auch I im I Kaufpreis I enthalten
e) an das I Telefon I können I ein I modern I Faxgerät I angeschlossen werden

ADJEKTIVDEKLINATION *TYP 3*

ein roter Stein in einem hellen Licht

Die Adjektivdeklination Typ 3 ist eine Mischung aus den Deklinationen Typ 1 und Typ 2.
Der unbestimmte Artikel, der negative Artikel und die Possessivartikel haben manchmal ...
... ein Kasus-Signal ⟼ Adjektivdeklination Typ 1 (helle Kästen) **s. Seite 30,**
... kein Kasus-Signal ⟼ Adjektivdeklination Typ 2 (blaue Kästen) **s. Seite 32.**

	maskulin			neutral			feminin			Plural		
NOM	ein	roter	Stein	ein	helles	Licht	eine	klare	Luft	–	runde	Formen
AKK	einen	roten	Stein	ein	helles	Licht	eine	klare	Luft	–	runde	Formen
DAT	einem	roten	Stein	einem	hellen	Licht	einer	klaren	Luft	–	runden	Formen
GEN	eines	roten	Steines	eines	hellen	Lichtes	einer	klaren	Luft	–	runder	Formen

	maskulin			neutral			feminin			Plural		
NOM	kein	roter	Stein	kein	helles	Licht	keine	klare	Luft	keine	runden	Formen
AKK	keinen	roten	Stein	kein	helles	Licht	keine	klare	Luft	keine	runden	Formen
DAT	keinem	roten	Stein	keinem	hellen	Licht	keiner	klaren	Luft	keinen	runden	Formen
GEN	keines	roten	Steines	keines	hellen	Lichtes	keiner	klaren	Luft	keiner	runden	Formen

Genauso *mein roter Stein*, ... (alle Possessivartikel)

ÜBUNGEN

__1__ Welche Artikelwörter haben ein Kasus-Signal, welche haben keins? – Kreuzen Sie an.

	mit	ohne
einen	✗	
ein		
keinem		
kein		
deinen		
dein		
keine		

	mit	ohne
einem		
meine		
mein		
seiner		
sein		
unseres		
unser		

	mit	ohne
euren		
euer		
eurer		
ihr		
Ihrem		
Ihr		
ihren		

__2__ Unterstreichen Sie die Kasus-Signale in Übung 1.

__3__ Studenten ziehen um – Ergänzen Sie die Adjektivendungen.

maskulin

a) so ein schön*er* Schreibtisch

b) einen ganz...... Tag

c) mit einem gemietet...... Lkw

d) statt eines privat...... Wagens

neutral

e) ein modern...... Telefon

f) ohne sein alt...... Regal

g) aber mit meinem wunderbar...... Bett

h) trotz unseres eng...... Treppenhauses

feminin

i) eine ziemlich hässlich...... Lampe

j) eine gebraucht...... Geschirrspülmaschine

k) neben meiner neu...... Mikrowelle

l) unterhalb deiner alt...... Küchenuhr

maskulin	neutral	feminin

maskulin
m) weiter...... Pläne
n) keine antik...... Stühle

neutral
o) zusätzlich...... Probleme
p) seine ganz...... Bücher

feminin
q) viel...... Fragen
r) unsere nächst......
   Wochenenden

__4__ **Eine neue Wohnung – Ergänzen Sie die Adjektive.**

Tobias hat endlich eine (a) *neue* (neu) und Gott sei Dank nicht sehr (b) ....
(teuer) Wohnung gefunden. Sie hat eine (c) .... (hell) Küche, eine
(d) .... (sonnig) Terrasse, ein (e) .... (klein) Wohnzimmer,
einen (f) .... (dunkel) Flur, und im Badezimmer steht eine
(g) .... (wunderschön), (h) .... (altmodisch) Badewanne.
Tobias sucht jetzt noch einen (i) .... (gebraucht) Fernseher und einen
(j) .... (gemütlich) Sessel. Und dafür hat er auch schon eine
(k) .... (wichtig) Verabredung. Er will heute Nachmittag mit seiner
Freundin Vera in die Stadt gehen und die Sachen kaufen, die noch fehlen. Aber das ist
gar nicht so einfach: Denn ein (l) .... (schön) und (m) ....
(gemütlich) Sessel ist ziemlich teuer, und Vera will eigentlich keinen (n) ....
(gebraucht) Fernseher. Sie möchte lieber ein (o) .... (modern) Gerät mit
einem (p) .... (groß) Bildschirm. Das ist aber für Tobias viel zu teuer,
deshalb kauft er erst einmal gar nichts. Er fährt mit seinem (q) .... (rostig)
Fahrrad nach Hause und setzt sich dort an seinen (r) .... (alt) Computer.
Dazu trinkt er ein (s) .... (München) Weißbier.

__5__ **Im Internetcafé – Ergänzen Sie die Adjektivendungen.**

Im Internetcafé

Alle Leute sind hier allein, denn jeder Gast kommuniziert über seinen (a) eigen*en*
Bildschirm gerade mit dem Rest der (b) groß....... (c) weit....... Welt. 5 Euro kostet
jede Stunde, die man am Computer verbringt. An allen (d) verfügbar.......
Computern kann man online die (e) neuest....... Zeitungen lesen, mit (f) ander.......
Leuten „chatten" oder sich zu Hause in (g) angenehm....... Erinnerung bringen.
Jonathan zum Beispiel muss gerade eine (h) schwierig....... Frage beantworten, die
ihm sein (i) alt....... Freund Pit in Kanada stellt. Pit hat schon allen (j) gemeinsam.......
Freunden in Kanada erzählt, dass Deutschland ein (k) schön....... Land ist. Aber
besonders interessiert ihn, wie die (l) hübsch....... Studentin heißt, von der Jonathan
das (m) letzt....... Mal erzählt hat. Jonathan hat schon zwei (n) klein....... Bier getrunken, und jedes (o) weiter....... Bier vermehrt seine Tippfehler beim Plaudern mit Pit.
Aber das macht nichts, denn bei diesem (p) elektronisch....... Brief kommt es nicht
so sehr auf (q) genau....... Rechtschreibung an.
Und Tanja schreibt gerade an ihren (r) neu....... Freund in Berlin. Eine E-Mail für
Verliebte – in diesem Fall ist natürlich jedes (s) einzeln....... Wort wichtig.

__6__ **Unterstreichen Sie in Übung 5 alle Artikelwörter, die vor einem Adjektiv stehen
und ein Kasus-Signal haben.**

ARTIKEL ODER ADJEKTIV?

alle netten Kollegen – mehrere unklare Antworten

1   Funktion

Um die Adjektivdeklination richtig zu machen, muss man wissen, ob das Wort vor dem Adjektiv ein Artikelwort oder selber ein Adjektiv ist. Das ist besonders bei Wörtern schwierig, die Mengenangaben bezeichnen.

2   Formen

Artikel	Adjektive		Nomen	
alle	*geltenden*		*Regeln*	Artikelwörter mit
keine	*neuen*		*Projekte*	Kasus-Signal ⟼
manche	*schönen*		*Stunden*	Adjektivdeklination
solche	*weitreichenden*		*Pläne*	Typ 1
	einige	*weitere*	*Fragen*	immer mit Nullartikel
	etliche	*interessante*	*Aspekte*	⟼ Adjektiv-
	*mehrere**	*unklare*	*Antworten*	deklination Typ 2
die	*viele***	*neue*	*Informationen*	mit Nullartikel ⟼
	vielen	*neuen*	*Informationen*	Adjektivdeklination Typ 2,
	*wenige***	*gut informierte*	*Personen*	mit bestimmtem Artikel
die	*wenigen*	*gut informierten*	*Personen*	⟼ Adjektivdeklination Typ 1

Genauso wie *viele* und *wenige: andere, folgende, verschiedene, zahlreiche.*

 * *mehrere = einige* nicht verwechseln mit *mehr. mehr* ist der Komparativ von *viel* und wird nicht dekliniert: *mehr gutes Geld.* So auch *weniger: weniger schlechte Luft*

** Im Singular: *viel neues Wissen, wenig freier Raum*

Pronomen

Wie viele Freunde hast du eigentlich eingeladen? – Alle.	*alle, einige, keine*,
Haben Sie alle Fragen beantwortet? – Nein, nur einige.	*manche, solche*
Gibt es noch Brötchen? – Nein, es gibt keine *mehr.*	können auch als Pronomen
Das sind aber schöne Stifte! Solche *möchte ich auch haben.*	verwendet werden.

 * 📖 **s. Seite 24** (unbestimmter Artikel)

ÜBUNGEN

1   Benimmregeln fürs Büro – Unterstreichen Sie die Artikelwörter und die unbestimmten Zahladjektive. Ergänzen Sie die Adjektivendungen.

TELEFON
Führen Sie keine (a) privat*en* Gespräche vom Firmenapparat aus,
besonders dann nicht, wenn Sie zahlreiche auswärts (b) wohnend...... Freunde
und Bekannte haben. In etlichen (c) modern...... Firmen gilt jedoch ein pragmatischer
Umgang mit diesem Thema, wenn nicht allzu viel (d) wertvoll...... Arbeitszeit geopfert wird
und sich die Kosten im Rahmen halten.

DUZEN

Wenn Sie neu in einer Firma anfangen, werden Sie natürlich nicht alle (e) älter...... Kollegen duzen. Aber für die zahlreichen (f) jugendlich...... Freunde des „Du" sind bessere Zeiten in Sicht: Es gibt mehrere (g) eindeutig...... Hinweise darauf, dass der Trend dahin geht, sich beim Vornamen zu nennen – selbst in etlichen (h) konservativ...... Branchen.

FÜSSE

Die Füße bleiben unter dem Tisch, denn der Chef mag keine (i) entspannt...... Mitarbeiter. Auch wenn Sie glauben, alle (j) cool...... Leute müssten die Füße auf den Tisch legen: Das ist nicht so, und manche (k) wichtig...... Geschäftspartner reagieren auf diese bequeme Haltung ausgesprochen allergisch.

2 **So geht's nicht weiter! – Formulieren Sie Sätze mit dem Akkusativ.**

Wir fordern ...
a) weniger unbezahlt Überstunden
   ... weniger unbezahlte Überstunden!
b) mehr frei Zeit
c) mehr bezahlt Urlaub
d) nur wenig künstlich Licht im Büro
e) viel frisch Luft
f) mehr grün Pflanzen

3 **Betriebsversammlung – Formulieren Sie Sätze.**

a) Auf der Betriebsversammlung sieht man heute auch ‖ zahlreich ‖ unbekannt ‖ Gesichter
   Auf der Betriebsversammlung sieht man heute auch zahlreiche unbekannte Gesichter.
b) Es gibt nur noch ‖ wenig ‖ frei ‖ Plätze
c) Der Personalchef hat ‖ viel ‖ neu ‖ Informationen
d) Er äußert sich tatsächlich zu ‖ all ‖ gestellt ‖ Fragen
e) Es gibt allerdings auch ‖ etlich ‖ gut hörbar ‖ Zwischenrufe
f) Ein junger Mitarbeiter macht ‖ einig ‖ kritisch ‖ Bemerkungen
g) Der Personalchef beantwortet plötzlich ‖ kein ‖ weiter ‖ Fragen ‖ mehr

4 **Alltägliches – Ergänzen Sie die Artikelwörter, Adjektive und Pronomen.**

einiges ‖ mehr ‖ mehrere (2x) ‖ solche ‖ viel (2̶x̶) ‖ viele ‖ wenig (2x) ‖ wenige

a) Terry hat heute leider nicht *viel* Zeit.
b) Andy verdient nur 800 Euro pro Monat. Das ist ziemlich ....
c) Ich bin heute so müde! Ich habe eigentlich nur .... Lust, ins Kino zu gehen.
d) Ich kenne nur .... Leute, die so viel essen können wie Hugo.
e) Karin hat wirklich zu .... Arbeit. Sie braucht .... Zeit für sich.
f) In dem Bereich ist sie Expertin. Da weiß sie ....
g) Ich habe zum Geburtstag gleich .... CDs von Mozart bekommen!
h) Das sind aber schöne Gläser! .... hätte ich auch gern.
i) So .... Brote hast du gemacht? Wer soll denn die alle essen?
j) Wo warst du denn gestern? Ich habe .... Male versucht, dich anzurufen!

3

KOMPARATIV UND SUPERLATIV

jung – jünger – am jüngsten

__1__ Funktion: Vergleich

Moritz ist 10 Jahre alt.	*Julia ist erst 5.*	*Alex ist erst 8 Monate alt.*
Er ist noch jung.	*Sie ist jünger als Moritz.*	*Er ist am jüngsten.*

__2__ Formen

a beim Verb

				Grundform	nicht dekliniert
Alex ist		*dick.*	.	Grundform	nicht dekliniert
Fritz ist		*dick*	*er.*	Komparativ	
Karl ist	*am*	*dick*	*st*	*en.*	Superlativ

b beim Nomen

					Grundform	Adjektivdeklination	📖 **s. Seite 30-35**
ein		*dick*	*er*	*Mann*	Grundform	Adjektivdeklination	📖 **s. Seite 30-35**
ein		*dick*	*er*	*er*	*Mann*	Komparativ	
der		*dick*	*st*	*e*	*Mann*	Superlativ	Superlativ nur mit bestimmtem Artikel

c unregelmäßige Formen

alt	*älter*	*ältest-*	*a* ⟹ *ä*	bei vielen einsilbigen
groß	*größer*	*größt-*	*o* ⟹ *ö*	Adjektiven
jung	*jünger*	*jüngst-*	*u* ⟹ *ü*	
frisch	*frischer*	*frischest-*	nach -*s*, -*d*, -*sch*, -*ss*, -*ß*, -*t*, -*tz*, -*x*, -*z*: -*est*-	
intelligent	*intelligenter*	*intelligentest-*	Ausnahme: *größt-*	
dunkel	*dunkler*	*dunkelst-*	-*e*- fällt im Komparativ weg	
teuer	*teurer*	*teuerst-*		
hoch	*höher*	*höchst-*		
nah	*näher*	*nächst-*		
viel	*mehr*	*meist-*	*mehr/weniger* stehen vor artikellosen Nomen	
gut	*besser*	*best-*	und werden nicht dekliniert: *Mehr Unfälle,*	
gern	*lieber*	*liebst-*	*aber weniger Tote!*	

d *wie* oder *als*?

Ist New York so groß wie Hongkong?	Grundform + *wie*
Nein, New York ist doch nicht so groß wie Hongkong.	
New York hat aber mehr Einwohner als Hongkong.	Komparativ + *als*
Hongkong hat weniger Einwohner als New York.	

e Relativer Superlativ

Die schönsten Häuser Frankreichs. Max wohnt in einem davon.
Max wohnt in einem *der schönsten Häuser Frankreichs.*
= Genitiv Plural

1 Ergänzen Sie die Tabelle.

a)	arm	*ärmer*	*am ärmsten*
b)	hart		
c)		mehr	
d)	breit		
e)	stark		
f)			am besten
g)	teuer		
h)			am liebsten
i)	klug		
j)	schwach		

2 Unübertrefflich – Ergänzen Sie das passende Adjektiv im Superlativ.

giftig | hoch | lang | ~~schnell~~ | schwierig

a) Der Gepard ist das *schnellste* Säugetier der Welt.
b) Der Mount Everest ist der .... Berg der Welt.
c) Der Nil ist der .... Fluss der Welt.
d) Die Kobra ist die .... Schlange der Welt.
e) Deutsch ist sicher nicht die .... Sprache der Welt.

3 Vergleichen Sie! – Formulieren Sie Sätze mit dem Komparativ und als bzw. mit *nicht so ... wie.*

a) Zu Hause gibt Herbert nicht so viel Geld aus wie im Urlaub.
   Zu Hause gibt Herbert weniger Geld aus als im Urlaub.
b) Im Urlaub schmeckt ihm der Wein besser als zu Hause.
   Zu Hause schmeckt ihm der Wein nicht so gut wie im Urlaub.
c) Im Urlaub schläft Herbert nicht so schlecht wie zu Hause. (gut)
d) Zu Hause steht er früher auf als im Urlaub. (spät)
e) Im Urlaub ist er nicht so müde wie zu Hause. (aktiv)
f) Im Urlaub ist es sowieso spannender als zu Hause. (langweilig)

4 Keine Übertreibungen – Ergänzen Sie den Superlativ und formulieren Sie dann Sätze mit dem relativen Superlativ.

a) Claudia Schiffer ist die *schönste* Frau Europas. (schön)
   Das stimmt nun wirklich nicht! – *Na gut, aber sie ist eine der schönsten Frauen Europas.*
b) Der Mops ist der .... Hund der Welt. (hässlich)
   Jetzt übertreibst du aber! – *O.k., aber ...*
c) Rothenburg ist die .... Stadt in Deutschland. (hübsch)
   So ein Unsinn! – *Na ja, aber ...*
d) In München gibt es das .... technische Museum Europas. (gut)
   Das stimmt einfach nicht. – *Na gut, aber ...*
e) Harald ist wirklich der .... Mensch der Welt! (nett)
   Finde ich nicht. – *Gut, aber ...*

GRADUIERUNG DURCH ADVERBIEN

sehr schön

1 Funktion

Verstärkung oder Abschwächung der Bedeutung eines Adjektivs.

Lernt Paul eigentlich viel für sein Examen?	*Also ich finde, dass er*	*zu* *sehr* *ziemlich*	*viel (-)* *viel (++)* *viel (+)* *viel*	*lernt.*

2 Formen

a Adverbien und Adjektive

Verstärkung	Verstärkung einer Negation	Abschwächung	über dem Normalmaß
*außerordentlich **hübsch***	*Der Film war gar/ überhaupt nicht gut. – Er hat mir gar/überhaupt nicht gefallen.*	*einigermaßen **frisch***	*zu **dick***
*ausgesprochen **schön***		*ganz** **nett***	*viel zu **dick***
*besonders **schlecht***		*halbwegs **pünktlich***	*allzu **dünn***
ganz **leer***		*recht **schnell***	
*sehr **schnell***		*relativ **groß***	
*überaus **sparsam***		*vergleichsweise **klein***	
*ungewöhnlich **laut***		*ziemlich **teuer***	

* betont   ** unbetont

b Wortbildung

Diese Zusammensetzungen werden vor allem in der Werbe-, Umgangs- und Jugendsprache verwendet. Sie können aber nicht mit jedem Adjektiv kombiniert werden *(ein ~~stockschöner~~ Garten)*:

hochaktuell	*tiefblau*	*affenstark*	*riesengroß*
extrabreit	*superschnell*	*bildschön*	*stockfinster*
vollklimatisiert	*topmodern*	*nagelneu*	*todtraurig*

ÜBUNGEN

1 Ein vergleichsweise netter Abend – Verstärkung oder Abschwächung? Kreuzen Sie an.

	Ver- stärkung	Ab- schwächung
a) Na, das war ja ein ausgesprochen schlechter Film.	X	
b) Was? Also ich fand den Film recht gut.		
c) „Gut" sagst du? Also, die Schauspieler haben vielleicht ganz nett gespielt,		
d) aber die Handlung war doch einigermaßen uninteressant.		
e) Und den Schluss fand ich überhaupt nicht logisch.		
f) Was? Ich fand, der Schluss war besonders spannend.		
g) Dafür habe ich auf den engen Sitzen ganz steife Beine bekommen.		

2 Ein überaus schöner Mann! – Ergänzen Sie die passenden Adverbien.

Verstärkung ++	Abschwächung +	
■ Also, Kurt hat ja eine (a) *ausgesprochen* lange Nase.	■ Na ja, sie ist zwar (b) .... lang, aber trotzdem schön.	~~ausge-sprochen~~ relativ
■ Und er hat auch (c) .... große Ohren.	■ Ja, die sind schon (d) .... groß, aber man sieht sie ja kaum.	ungewöhnlich ziemlich
■ Einen (e) .... dicken Bauch hat er übrigens auch.	■ Hm. Dick würde ich nicht sagen. Er ist einfach (f) .... stark.	recht sehr
■ Und dann noch diese (g) .... kurzen Beine. Er sieht wirklich wie eine kleine Kugel aus.	■ Das ist nicht wahr! Seine Beine sind vielleicht (h) .... kurz, aber mir gefällt der Mann.	besonders vergleichs-weise

3 Kino – Ergänzen Sie die Sätze mit zu und dem passenden Adjektiv.

■ Das Abendessen war wirklich sehr gut! Ich kann mich kaum noch bewegen. Ich habe wieder mal viel (a) *zu viel* gegessen.

■ Jetzt werde bloß nicht müde! Unser Film fängt gleich an. Ich will auf keinen Fall (b) .... kommen.

■ Ach, das letzte Mal waren wir doch auch schon viel (c) .... im Kino und mussten noch ewig warten.

■ Aber heute sind wir schon spät dran! Sag mal, warum fährst du eigentlich nur 30? Hier darf man 60 fahren! Du fährst viel (d) ....

■ Immer mit der Ruhe! Wir kommen schon noch rechtzeitig. Die Werbung hat das letzte Mal fast eine Stunde gedauert. Das ist einfach (e) ....

■ Ach, ich glaube, du schläfst während des Films wieder ein. Du bist einfach viel (f) .... , um ins Kino zu gehen.

4 Extragut! – Ergänzen Sie die passenden Vorsilben.

⟨ extra I hoch (2x) I stock I super I tod I top I voll

a) Unsere Bratwürste sind *extra*lang und schmecken ....gut.

b) Diese ....moderne Küchenmaschine funktioniert natürlich ....auto-matisch.

c) Gerade wenn Sie sich ....müde fühlen, wirkt unser Kräutertee Wunder! Trinken Sie zwei Tassen und Sie sind wieder ....fit.

d) An manchen Tagen kann man kaum noch gehen und man ist ....steif. Mit unserer ....wirksamen Pflanzencreme werden Sie schnell wieder beweglich.

ZAHLWÖRTER

eins, zwei, drei – erstens, zweitens, drittens

1 Funktion

Ich glaube, sie hat fünf *Katzen.*	*Wie viel? Wie viele?*	Mengenangabe
Die Veranstaltung beginnt am 5.7. *um* 16 *Uhr.*	*Wann?*	Zeitangabe
Das ist erst mein zweites *Bier.*	*Das wievielte?*	Position in einer Reihe

2 Formen

a Kardinalzahlen

1	*Ich muss unbedingt zur Bank. Ich hab nur noch* einen *Euro in der Tasche, und im Geldbeutel ist auch nur noch* einer.	Deklination wie unbestimmter Artikel/ Pronomen 📖 **s. Seite 24**
	Ich habe jetzt einen *Monat Urlaub.*	beim Sprechen betont
	Eins *und* eins *ist zwei.* Aber: *Ein mal eins ist eins.*	beim Zählen und Rechnen: *eins*
2–999.999	*Sie hat* zwölf *Enkel,* drei *Jungen und* neun *Mädchen.*	nicht dekliniert
1.000.000 1.000.000.000	*eine* Million, *zwei* Millionen ... *eine* Milliarde, *zwei* Milliarden ...	feminine Nomen
	Könnten Sie mir bitten diesen Hunderter *wechseln?*	maskuline Nomen
	Das ist ein Film aus den Fünfzigern. *(aus den 50er Jahren)* *Die Zuschauer kamen zu* Hunderten. *(mehreren Hundert)* Zehntausende *demonstrierten gegen den Krieg. (mehrere Zehntausend)*	Plural

b Ordinalzahlen

1.	*der/die/das*	erste	**Datum (dekliniert*):**	
2.		zweite	*Der Kurs beginnt am Montag, den* zwölften neunten. *(12.9.)*	
3.		dritte		
4.		vierte	*Heute ist der* fünfundzwanzigste sechste. *(25.6.)*	
...		...	*Er hat am* vierten zweiten *Geburtstag. (4.2.)*	
7.		siebte	**Reihenfolge:**	
8.		achte	*Wir fahren nicht in Urlaub, denn zu Hause ist es* erstens *ruhiger und* zweitens *billiger.*	
...		...		
20.		zwanzigste	*Beim Radrennen wurde er* Zweiter. (dekliniert*)	
...		...	**Herrschernamen (dekliniert*):**	
100.		hundertste	*Karl V. – Karl der* Fünfte	
101.		hunderterste	*Friedrich II. – Friedrich der* Zweite	
102.		hundertzweite	**Personenzahl:**	
...		...	*Wir kommen* zu zweit. *Im letzten Kurs waren wir nur* zu dritt.	

* Adjektivdeklination 📖 **s. Seite 30-35**

__1__ **Wann fahren die Züge wohin? – Lesen Sie den Fahrplan laut vor.**

a) 8.32 Uhr – Rom
b) 11.11 Uhr – Prag
c) 12.58 Uhr – Paris
d) 16.14 Uhr – Brüssel
e) 18.06 Uhr – Barcelona
f) 00.53 Uhr – Warschau

um acht Uhr zweiunddreißig
nach Rom

__2__ **Daten und Termine – Lesen Sie den Text laut vor.**
a) Den Wievielten haben wir heute? – Moment mal, gestern war Montag, der 23., dann haben wir heute Dienstag, den 24.
b) In diesem Monat bekommen wir unser Gehalt erst am 31., denn es gibt Probleme in der Buchhaltung.
c) Unser Geschäft ist vom 14.8. bis zum 1.9. geschlossen. Ab 4.9. sind wir wieder für Sie da.
d) In diesem Jahr dauern die Herbstferien vom 30.10. bis zum 3.11.

__3__ **Sommerferien – Ergänzen Sie die Zahlen in der richtigen Form.**
a) Gott sei Dank, in *einer* (1) Woche beginnen die Ferien.
b) Sigls fahren dieses Jahr wieder mit ihren Söhnen in den Urlaub. – Mit allen? – Nein, ... (1) will nicht, er will lieber mit seiner Freundin wegfahren.
c) Was ist denn das für Musik? – Ich glaube, das ist ein Hit aus den .... (80er).
d) Im letzten Sommer waren wir in Finnland. Da gab es .... (1 000, Plural) von Mücken.
e) Können Sie mir bitte diesen .... (50er) wechseln? Am besten in zwei .... (20er) und einen .... (10er).

__4__ **Klatsch und Tratsch – Ergänzen Sie die Ordinalzahlen in der richtigen Form.**
a) Stell dir vor, er heiratet jetzt schon zum *dritten* (3.) Mal. Ich kenne ja nur seine .... (1.) Frau, und die ist eigentlich sehr nett. Seine .... (2.) Frau soll eine ziemliche Hexe gewesen sein.
b) Doris hat aber auch wirklich Pech. Das ist jetzt ihr .... (4.) Auto, und gestern ist ihr jemand reingefahren. Beim .... (3.) Auto war nach kurzer Zeit der Motor kaputt, das .... (2.) hat ihr Freund ruiniert, und ihr .... (1.) Wagen war sehr bald durchgerostet.
c) Ich hab ihm das schon zum .... (100.) Mal gesagt, aber es nützt nichts. Er lässt seine Sachen überall liegen.
d) Silvia ist von ihrem neuen Nachbarn total begeistert: .... (1.) sieht er prima aus, ... (2.) hat er viel Humor, und dann kann er auch noch sehr gut kochen.
e) Petra hat jetzt einen neuen Freund, aber mit ihrem alten versteht sie sich auch noch sehr gut. Sie fahren im Sommer sogar zu .... (3) in den Urlaub.

3

PARTIZIP ALS ADJEKTIV

die kochende Suppe – die gekochte Suppe

_1_ Funktion

der Zug, der durch einen Tunnel fährt *Der Zug fährt durch einen Tunnel.*	transformiert eine verbale Struktur (Satz) in eine
der durch einen Tunnel fahrende Zug	nominale Struktur (Adjektiv + Nomen)

Längere Partizipialattribute werden im Deutschen nur in der Schriftsprache gebraucht – und auch da ausschließlich in Texten mit gehobenem Sprachniveau, z.B. in juristischen oder wissenschaftlichen Texten. Meist ist die verbale Struktur stilistisch besser.
Verbalstil/Nominalstil 📖 **s. Seite 182**

_2_ Formen

Partizip I		Infinitiv	d	Adjektivendung	
das		*parken*	*d*	*e*	*Auto*

Partizip II	(ge)	Stamm	t	Adjektivendung	
das	*ge*	*park*	*t*	*e*	*Auto*
der		*verkauf*	*t*	*e*	*Wagen*

unregelmäßige Partizipien 📖 **s. Seite 184**

Partizip als Adjektiv		Die Handlung ...	verbale Struktur
die gerade eintreffende Sendung	Partizip I	... dauert an (Aktiv)	*Die Sendung trifft gerade ein.*
die täglich einzunehmenden Tabletten	zu + Partizip I (Gerundiv)	... muss/kann realisiert werden (Passiv)	*die Tabletten, die täglich eingenommen werden müssen/können*
die gestern eingetroffene Sendung	Partizip II	... ist abgeschlossen (Aktiv)	*die Sendung, die gestern eingetroffen ist*
der gefasste Dieb		(Passiv)	*Der Dieb wurde gefasst.*

Kein Partizip II als Adjektiv haben *sein* und *haben* und Verben ohne Akkusativergänzung mit *haben* im Perfekt, z.B. *arbeiten, leben, schlafen, sitzen, stehen, antworten, danken, drohen, gefallen, nützen, schaden.*

ÜBUNGEN

_1_ Das Happi-Kochstudio empfiehlt – Markieren Sie im folgenden Text die Partizipien I und die Partizipien II.

Für dieses Rezept benötigen Sie folgende Zutaten:
2 Liter kochendes Wasser, 3 gewürfelte Kartoffeln, 3 geschälte Karotten, einen Bund gehackte Petersilie, ein frisch geschlachtetes Huhn, unsere nicht spritzende Margarine, 4 getrocknete Lorbeerblätter, 1 klein geschnittene Peperoni, eine ungespritzte Zitrone – und natürlich unsere bewährten aromatisierenden Zusätze.

Welches Partizip passt? Manchmal sind auch beide Lösungen möglich.

Nomen	Verb	Partizip I	Partizip II
a) die Nachfrage	steigen	*die steigende Nachfrage*	*die gestiegene Nachfrage*
b) das Angebot	sinken		
c) die Zahl der offenen Stellen	zunehmen		
d) die Kosten	reduzieren		
e) Rechnungen	bezahlen		
f) die wirtschaftliche Lage	sich verbessern		

Ein feiner Urlaub – Entscheiden Sie: Partizip I oder Partizip II.

a) Hinter der Rezeption sitzt ein *unrasierter* Portier! (nicht rasieren)
b) Die billigsten Zimmer haben nicht einmal *fließendes* Wasser! (fließen)
c) Frisch .... Brot gibt es nur einmal pro Woche! (backen)
d) Ein ständig .... Paar im Nachbarzimmer! (streiten)
e) .... Hunde vor dem Balkon! (bellen)
f) Die Zimmer haben schlecht .... Türen! (schließen)
g) Kein ordentlich .... Bad! (putzen)
h) Unter dem Bett eine .... Maus! (vertrocknen)

Ein Autounfall – Formulieren Sie die Relativsätze als Partizipien.

a) drei Autofahrer, die verletzt sind
   drei verletzte Autofahrer
b) auf der Straße, die verschneit ist
c) die Passagiere, die aus dem Wrack befreit werden müssen
d) mit einem Airbag, der nicht funktioniert
e) mit Bremsen, die quietschen
f) der Krankenwagen, der sofort alarmiert wurde
g) die Unfallgefahr, die nicht unterschätzt werden darf

Ein neuer Sportwagen – Ergänzen Sie das Partizip.

Auf der letzten Frankfurter Automobilausstellung
wurde ein neu (a) *entwickelter* (entwickeln)
offener Sportwagen präsentiert.
Vor der (b) ....
(versammeln) Fachpresse wies der
Vorsitzende des Konzerns auf die
technischen Innovationen des Prototyps hin.
An erster Stelle nannte er das aus Aluminium (c) .... (herstellen), in
Sekundenschnelle (d) .... (geöffnet werden können) Dach.
Den Antrieb übernehmen drei synchron (e) .... (arbeiten), per Computer
(f) .... (steuern) Elektromotoren. Ein Sicherheitssystem erlaubt das
Öffnen und Schließen nur bei (g) .... (laufen) Motor und
(h) .... (stehen) Fahrzeug. Dem Beifall (i) ....
(klatschen) Publikum versprach der Vorsitzende einen knapp (j) ....
(kalkulieren) Preis.

WORTBILDUNG

schriftlich – praktisch – unfähig

1 Funktion und Formen

a Ableitung – Bildung von Adjektiven aus Nomen und Verben durch Nachsilbe

Nachsilbe	Beispiel	Nachsilbe	Beispiel
-lich	*täglich, monatlich**	-abel	*praktikabel*
	schriftlich	-ant	*elegant*
	menschlich	-ent	*intelligent*
-isch	*fachmännisch*	-ibel	*sensibel*
	griechisch, lateinisch	-ell, -iell	*manuell, potenziell*
-bar	*spürbar*	-iv	*aggressiv*
-ig	*witzig*	-ös	*nervös*

* Temporaladjektive 📖 **s. Seite 62**

b Zusammensetzung – zwei oder mehr Wörter bilden ein neues Adjektiv

hell + grau ⟶ *hellgrau*	Adjektiv + Adjektiv
lernen + willig ⟶ *lernwillig*	Verb + Adjektiv
die Leistung + fähig ⟶ *leistungsfähig*	Nomen + Adjektiv
der Alkohol + frei ⟶ *alkoholfrei*	

c Negation – Bedeutungsänderung durch Vor- oder Nachsilbe

Vorsilbe	Beispiel	Vor-/Nachsilbe	Beispiel
a-	*atypisch*	ir-	*irreal*
de-/des-/dis-	*desillusioniert*	miss-	*missverständlich*
il-	*illegitim*	non-	*nonverbal*
in-	*instabil*	un-	*unfähig*
		-los	*hilflos*

d Verstärkung – Bedeutungsänderung durch Zusammensetzung

	Beispiel
hoch	*hochaktuell*

📖 **s. Seite 40** (Graduierung)

2 Alternativen

Das Problem ist lösbar.	*lässt sich lösen*	*kann gelöst werden*
Der Schaden ist reparabel.	*lässt sich reparieren*	*kann repariert werden*
inkompetent	*nicht kompetent*	
ungebildet	*nicht gebildet*	

📖 **s. Seite 116** (Passiv-Ersatzformen)

1 Ordnen Sie Ausdrücke mit gleicher Bedeutung zu.

desillusioniert	a) bewegt sich sehr viel
uninformiert	b) hat keine Illusionen mehr
hochinteressant	c) lässt sich leicht machen
hyperaktiv	d) der Schaden lässt sich nicht beheben
irreparabel	e) weiß nicht Bescheid
praktikabel	f) sehr wissenswert

2 Analyse – Ordnen Sie die Adjektive aus den Texten.

Negation		-lich	
Verstärkung	*himmelhoch,*	-isch	
-ig		andere	

Wildwest. Natur ohne Grenzen – himmelhoch und abgrundtief. Der neue Tour-Set-Führer „Colorado" beschreibt ein Mekka für aktive Urlauber. Toller Freizeitspaß zwischen Gipfeln und Canyons. Der Führer ist kostenfrei erhältlich.

Revue. Ob rasant, feurig, traurig oder witzig – das Deutsche Theater in München wartet mit musikalischen Spitzenproduktionen auf. Unsere Leser kommen in den Genuss von supergünstigen Karten.

Flair. Unternehmen Sie einen Streifzug durch nächtliche Schlossgärten, erleben Sie den Charme königlicher Architektur in den romantischen Potsdamer Schlössern. Unvergessliche Stunden erwarten Sie.

3 Was bedeuten diese Wörter?
a) alkoholfrei, gebührenfrei
   ohne Alkohol, ...
b) anpassungsfähig, lernfähig
c) humorvoll, liebevoll
d) verantwortungslos, bargeldlos
e) preiswert, überlegenswert
f) funktionsbereit, hilfsbereit
g) erfolgreich, zahlreich

4 Wein – Formulieren Sie mit –bar.
a) Der neue Müller-Thurgau lässt sich wirklich gut trinken.
   Er ist wirklich gut trinkbar.
b) Der 98er Riesling kann leider nicht mehr geliefert werden.
c) Diesen Jahrgang kann man nicht mehr bezahlen.
d) Der Markenname auf dem Etikett lässt sich schwer lesen.
e) Eine Lieferung frei Haus lässt sich nicht durchführen.
f) Unser Lieferproblem kann gelöst werden.

5 Wie heißt das Gegenteil? – Bilden Sie die Negation mit Vorsilben.
a) befristet
   unbefristet
b) kritisch
c) berechtigt
d) formell
e) höflich
f) kompetent
g) übersichtlich
h) unterbrochen
i) ordentlich
j) rational
k) relevant
l) verbindlich
m) verständlich
n) vernünftig

PERSONALPRONOMEN

er und sie – der und die

1   Funktion

Mein alter Freund Werner **hat gerade angerufen.** *Er* **hat jetzt einen neuen Job.**	unbetonte Weiterführung im Text
Stell dir vor, *der* **hat jetzt einen neuen Job.**	betonte Weiterführung im Text

Die betonten Pronomen werden hauptsächlich in Alltagsdialogen verwendet.

2   Formen
ⓐ unbetonte Pronomen

			maskulin	neutral	feminin			
Nominativ	*ich*	*du*	*er*	*es*	*sie*	*wir*	*ihr*	*sie*
Akkusativ	*mich*	*dich*	*ihn*	*es*	*sie*	*uns*	*euch*	*sie*
Dativ	*mir*	*dir*	*ihm*	*ihm*	*ihr*	*uns*	*euch*	*ihnen*

Rechtschreibung: Die formelle Anrede *Sie, Ihnen* wird großgeschrieben.

ⓑ betonte Pronomen

			maskulin	neutral	feminin			
Nominativ			*der*	*das*	*die*			*die*
Akkusativ			*den*	*das*	*die*			*die*
Dativ			*dem*	*dem*	*der*			*denen*

Die betonten Pronomen gibt es nur in der 3. Person Singular und Plural.

3   Satzstrukturen
ⓐ unbetonte Pronomen

Der Chef braucht sein Handy. *Ich habe* *es ihm* *gerade gebracht.*	Das Personalpronomen im Akkusativ steht vor dem Pronomen im Dativ.
Wir haben *ihm einen/diesen/den/ keinen/welche gekauft.*	Alle anderen Pronomen stehen nach dem Pronomen im Dativ.

ⓑ betonte Pronomen

Das *haben wir ihm gerade gebracht.* *Den* *habe ich ihm gekauft.*	Die betonten Pronomen stehen meistens auf Position 1.

ÜBUNGEN

1   Leserbrief an Dr. Sommer – Ergänzen Sie die unbetonten Pronomen.

Schüchtern!

(a) *ich* weiß nicht mehr, was (b) .... machen soll. In meiner Schule gibt es einen süßen Jungen, der (c) .... wirklich gefällt. Gestern hat (d) .... (e) .... gefragt, ob (f) .... mit (g) .... auf das Sommerfest am nächsten Samstag gehen will. (h) ....

4

habe mich nicht getraut, „ja" zu sagen, obwohl (i) .... schon Lust gehabt hätte. Immer wenn (j) .... (k) .... in der Pause oder nach der Schule sehe, dann werde (l) .... rot, und mein Kopf ist absolut leer.

(m) .... habe schon mit meinen Freundinnen darüber gesprochen. (n) .... sagen, dass (o) .... mal was mit (p) .... unternehmen soll, aber dazu fehlt (q) .... der Mut. Können Sie (r) .... bitte einen Rat geben? Was soll (s) .... machen?

Jana (14)

2   Teenager unter sich – Ergänzen Sie die betonten Pronomen.

■ Schau mal, siehst du da hinten den Typen mit den blonden Haaren? (a) *Den* finde ich richtig cool!

■ Stimmt. (b) .... find ich auch süß. Aber der große, der da am Tisch gegenüber sitzt, (c) .... gefällt mir noch besser. Kennst du (d) .... zufällig?

■ Welchen meinst du denn? (e) .... mit der Sonnenbrille oder (f) .... daneben?

■ (g) .... Großen mit der Brille. Aber schau jetzt nicht rüber, (h) .... merken sonst, dass wir über sie reden.

■ O.k. Ach, da kommt ja Ulrike! Na, (i) .... sieht ja wieder mal schrecklich aus!

■ Und das Kleid, das (j) .... anhat. (k) .... hat ja eine scheußliche Farbe. Dein Blonder geht übrigens gerade rüber zu Ulrike! Was (l) .... wohl vorhat?

■ So was! Jetzt tanzt (m) .... auch noch mit (n) ....

■ Und was macht mein Typ mit der Brille? Wo ist (o) .... denn hingegangen? Siehst du (p) .... irgendwo?

■ Nee, (q) .... kann ich nirgends entdecken.

■ Na ja, so interessant ist (r) .... auch gar nicht gewesen.

3   Vater hat einen Computer – Formulieren Sie Antworten mit den unbetonten Pronomen im Akkusativ und Dativ.

a) Max, gibst du mir mal das Kabel her? – Moment, *ich gebe es dir gleich.*

b) Und bring mir doch bitte auch gleich den Stecker mit. – Gut, ...

c) Julia, erklärst du mir mal, wie diese Programme funktionieren? – Klar, ...

d) Und zeig mir bitte auch noch, wie man ins Internet kommt. – O.k., ...

e) Ach, Max, erklärst du mir mal die Funktion dieser Tasten? – Moment, ...

4   Vater repariert etwas – Ergänzen Sie mir und die betonten Pronomen.

a) Julia, ich brauche den Schraubenzieher. Bringst du *mir den* mal!

b) Wo ist eigentlich das Werkzeug? Max, suchst du .... bitte?

c) Max, neben dir liegen die Schrauben. Gibst du .... mal?

d) Ach, Max, den Hammer brauche ich noch. Reichst du .... bitte her?

e) Und die Luftpumpe ist in der Garage. Kannst du .... auch gleich bringen?

f) Kinder, das geht nicht ohne Bohrer! Holt .... doch aus dem Keller.

5   Antworten Sie jetzt mit dir und den unbetonten Pronomen.

a) *Ich hab gerade keine Zeit! Max soll ihn dir bringen!*

ES

Na, wie geht's?

Funktion und Formen

a als Pronomen – *es* ist obligatorisch

	es ersetzt ...
Dieses Mineralwasser schmeckt prima. Es hat auch nicht so viel Kohlensäure.	... ein Nomen im Nominativ
Vera hat es* in dem neuen Getränkemarkt besorgt.	... ein Nomen im Akkusativ
Meine Kolleginnen sind topfit, ich bin es* leider nicht.	... ein Adjektiv oder Partizip
Manchmal gehe ich nach der Arbeit zum Joggen, aber ich muss sagen, ich tue es* nicht sehr gern.	... einen Satzteil oder einen ganzen Satz

* Hier kann *es* nicht auf Position 1 stehen.

b als unpersönliches Subjekt oder Objekt – *es* ist obligatorisch

es regnet, es schneit, es donnert, es blitzt, es ist kalt	Wetter	*es =* Subjekt
Es ist 10 Uhr. Es ist noch früh. Es wird bald Mitternacht.	Zeit	
Es geht mir gut. Es tut mir weh. Es juckt mich am Bein.	persönliches Befinden	
Es schmeckt mir gut. Es gefällt mir nicht. Es duftet hier nach Flieder.	Sinneseindrücke	
es klopft, es klingelt, es läutet, es pfeift, es raschelt	Geräusche	
es gibt, es handelt sich um, es geht um, es kommt an auf, es hängt ab von	Thema	
Er hat es eilig. Er hat es weit gebracht. Sie nimmt es leicht. Er hatte es schwer. Sie meint es ernst.	feste Wendungen	*es =* Objekt

c als Repräsentant für einen Nebensatz oder Infinitivsatz – *es* ist nicht obligatorisch*

Es ist wunderbar, dass du heute Abend kochst. *Es tut mir leid, dass du nicht kommen kannst.*	*dass*-Satz
Es ist normal, auch im Urlaub mal an den Job zu denken. *Ich liebe es, in meiner Hängematte zu liegen.*	Infinitivsatz
Es ist noch unsicher, ob er morgen kommen kann. *Es ist noch noch nicht klar, wen er mitbringt.*	indirekter Fragesatz

* Wenn der Nebensatz oder Infinitivsatz vorangestellt ist, fällt *es* weg oder wird ersetzt durch *das*: *Dass du heute Abend kochst, (das) ist wunderbar.*

d Betonung des Subjekts – *es* ist nicht obligatorisch*

Es haben sich einige Probleme ergeben. *Es werden heute weniger Briefe geschrieben als früher.*	*es* auf Position 1

* *Einige Probleme haben sich ergeben.*

e gesprochene Sprache

Na, wie geht's? *Mir schmeckt's prima.*	*es* kann zu *'s* verkürzt werden

1 Welt der Bücher – Formulieren Sie Sätze.

a) In diesem Buch | gehen um | einen kleinen Jungen
   In diesem Buch geht es um einen kleinen Jungen.
b) Diesen Harry-Potter-Band | geben | leider gerade nicht
c) bei diesem Roman | ankommen auf | den Schluss
d) abhängen von | Vermarktung, wie gut sich ein Buch verkauft
e) bei diesem Atlas | sich handeln um | einen Sprachatlas

2 Menschen wie Silvia – Formulieren Sie die Sätze um. Beginnen Sie mit dem unterstrichenen Satzteil.

a) Es gibt viele <u>Menschen wie Silvia</u>.
   Menschen wie Silvia gibt es viele.
b) Es regnet <u>seit drei Tagen</u> ununterbrochen, und es geht <u>ihr</u> wirklich schlecht.
c) Es summt <u>in ihrem Kopf</u> wie in einem Bienenkorb.
d) Es ist auch schon <u>spät</u>, sie muss jetzt ins Bett.
e) Es gefällt <u>ihr</u> auch nicht, dass Rudolf sich nicht meldet.

3 Nur Fliegen ist schöner – Sind folgende Sätze richtig oder falsch? Kreuzen Sie an.

	richtig	falsch
a) Billige Flüge gibt leider nicht mehr.		×
b) Sich am Flughafen zu orientieren kann schwierig sein.		
c) Bei diesem Surfbrett handelt sich um Sperrgepäck.		
d) Ob die Maschine pünktlich startet, ist nicht sicher.		
e) Wenn neblig ist, kann die Maschine nicht landen.		
f) Wo ist denn mein Ticket? – Also ich habe nicht.		
g) Dich wiederzusehen ist wunderschön!		

4 Korrigieren Sie die falschen Sätze aus Übung 3.

a) *Billige Flüge gibt es leider nicht mehr.*

5 Tipps zum Abschalten – Markieren Sie, an welcher Stelle im Text es fehlt.

Sie haben im Job weit gebracht, und deshalb haben Sie auch den ganzen Tag sehr   ~~es~~ es
eilig. Umso wichtiger ist, nach der Arbeit abschalten zu können. Denn nur so erholt   es
sich ihr Nervensystem – und Sie brauchen ja am nächsten Tag wieder in Bestform,   es
denn Sie wollen in Ihrem Job ja noch weit bringen. Leider gibt bei uns keinen Knopf   es es
zum Ausschalten wie bei einer Maschine. Ihnen kann körperlich gut gehen, aber wenn   es
Streit mit der Kollegin gegeben hat, ist klar, dass Sie nicht einfach abschalten können.   es
Finden Sie heraus, wie Sie persönlich am besten entspannen können. Manche Leute
mögen, in der Hängematte zu träumen. Andere nehmen ein Bad mit Prickel-Kugeln,   es
dann sprudelt in der Badewanne überall – und für manche gibt nur eins: eine   es 's
Viertelstunde mit geschlossenen Augen ausruhen.

DAS

Das sind meine Freunde.

1 Funktion

Was ist denn das da? – Das hier ist ein Wetterfrosch.	*das* verweist auf einen Gegenstand und wird häufig mit *da* und *hier/dort* kombiniert.
Zu welcher Tageszeit das Meer am saubersten ist, das haben jetzt britische Forscher untersucht.	*das* verweist auf etwas, das vorher schon im Text stand.
Wer hat denn gerade angerufen? – Das war unser Nachbar. *Das schneit heute vielleicht.* *Sie meint das wirklich ernst.*	*das* wird häufig statt *es* in Gesprächen gebraucht, um etwas besonders zu betonen oder hervorzuheben.*

* In folgenden Fällen kann *es* nicht durch *das* ersetzt werden: *es geht gut/schlecht, es gibt, es handelt sich um, es eilig haben, es weit bringen, es leicht nehmen, es schwer haben.* *es* 📖 **s. Seite 50.**

2 Formen

Nominativ	*Das sind alle meine Freundinnen.*
Akkusativ	*Das meint sie wirklich ernst.* *Sie meint das wirklich ernst.*

das steht meistens auf Position 1.
Die Verbform richtet sich nach dem Subjekt des Satzes: *Schau dir mal dieses Foto an: Das sind wir und das seid ihr.*

betont: Die wichtige Information steht vor dem Pronomen.	unbetont: Die wichtige Information kommt noch.
Mal laut Musik zu hören, das ist doch normal. *Wie du das machst, das gefällt mir gut.* *Mit dem Studium in England – das meint sie ernst.*	*Es ist doch normal, mal laut Musik zu hören.* *Es gefällt mir gut, wie du das machst.* *Sie meint es ernst mit dem Studium in England.*

ÜBUNGEN

1 Schülerleben – Formulieren Sie Sätze.

a) um sieben Uhr morgens duschen – hassen
Um sieben Uhr morgens duschen – das hasse ich.
b) Vokabeln lernen – überhaupt nicht mögen
c) morgens lange schlafen – mögen
d) gemütlich frühstücken – super finden
e) die Mathearbeit morgen schreiben müssen – mir gar nicht gefallen

2 Urlaubsfotos – Formulieren Sie Sätze mit das hier und das da.

a) wir am Strand – Schmids von Zimmer 401
   Schau mal, das hier sind wir am Strand, und das da sind die Schmids von Zimmer 401.
b) du im Swimmingpool – ich im Liegestuhl
c) Peter mit seinem Mountainbike – ihr beim Volleyballspielen
d) Frau Bolte mit ihrem schrecklichen Hund – meine Freunde auf dem Segelboot
e) der nette Ober – du, als du mit ihm geflirtet hast
f) Herr Schmid, der schon ziemlich viel Bier getrunken hat – wir alle beim Sommerfest

3 Alltag – Ersetzen Sie es durch das.

a) Mich freut es, dass du noch bleiben kannst.
   Das freut mich, dass du noch bleiben kannst.
b) Mir schmeckt es wirklich sehr gut.
c) Mir gefällt es einfach nicht.
d) Ich finde es gut, dass du kommst.
e) Es ist doch normal, am Sonntag mal auszuschlafen.

4 Das Interview der Woche – Ergänzen Sie das oder es.

Frau Stein, Sie sind noch jung und haben (a) es schon weit gebracht: Sie sind mit 25 Jahren eine der erfolg- reichsten Schauspielerinnen in Deutschland und sicher die, die die meisten Stofftiere hat. Wozu brauchen Schauspieler Maskottchen?

Wir sind alle nicht ganz normal, wir Schauspieler. Beim Theater gibt (b) .... eine Menge Aber-glauben.

Sie beginnen sowohl privat wie beruflich einen neuen Lebens-abschnitt. Handelt (c) .... sich da um einen Zufall?

(d) .... sehe ich beruflich nicht so. Privat schon eher. Seit der Trennung von meinem Partner gibt (e) .... natürlich auch häufiger Momente, in denen (f) .... mir nicht so gut geht.

Was erwarten Sie von Ihren Freunden?

Ich brauche viel Geborgenheit und Zärtlichkeit. Ich will aber auch objektive Kritik von meinen Freunden. (g) .... brauche ich zum Leben.

Bei Männern sagt man: (h) .... gibt drei große Lieben im Leben. Bei den Frauen auch?

(i) .... werde ich ausprobie-ren, und dann sage ich Ihnen Bescheid.

Eine Kollegin hat mal über Sie gesagt: „Die Deutschen mögen solche Frauen, wie Sie eine sind: rund, dick und blond."

(j) .... ist für mich ein Zeichen von Verbitterung. Diese Kollegin hat (k) .... wahnsin-nig schwer gehabt und erlebt dann jemanden wie mich, der in kurzer Zeit nach oben kommt. (l) .... hat sie sicher nicht so gemeint.

Frau Stein, wir danken Ihnen für dieses Gespräch.

INDEFINITPRONOMEN

man – jemand/niemand – etwas/nichts

__1__ Funktion

Wenn *man* das Abitur hat, kann *man* an der Universität studieren.	alle Menschen, die Leute
Hier ist es so laut, dass *man* sein eigenes Wort nicht versteht.	Verallgemeinerung
Klopft da *jemand*? – Ich höre *niemanden*.	unbestimmte oder unbekannte Person
Irgendjemand hat mich gefragt, wo du bist.	Verstärkung
Ich hab dir *etwas/was* mitgebracht!	unbestimmte Sachen oder Sachverhalte
Wir haben *nichts* von ihm gehört.	
Wenn mir doch nur *irgendetwas* einfallen würde!	Verstärkung

__2__ Formen

Nominativ	man	(irgend)jemand	niemand	(irgend)etwas	nichts
Akkusativ	einen	(irgend)jemand(en)	niemand(en)	(irgend)etwas	nichts
Dativ	einem	(irgend)jemand(em)	niemand(em)	(irgend)etwas	nichts

Wenn ihr noch *(irgend)jemanden* aus unserem Kurs seht, sagt *ihm*, wo *er* uns morgen treffen kann.	*(irgend)jemand* wird im Text mit *er/ihn/ihm* weitergeführt
Falls du noch *irgendetwas* von der Prüfung hörst, sag *es* mir.	*(irgend)etwas* wird mit *es/das* weitergeführt

Standardsprache	Umgangssprache
Irgendjemand hat gesagt, dass du krank bist.	*Irgendwer* hat gesagt, dass du krank bist.
Dir wird schon noch irgendetwas einfallen.	*Dir wird schon noch irgendwas/was einfallen.*

ÜBUNGEN

__1__ In einer Berghütte – Ergänzen Sie etwas/was oder nichts.

■ Hey, kannst du mich nicht hören? Ich hab dich (a) *etwas / was* gefragt!

■ Was sagst du? Gibt es hier überhaupt elektrisches Licht? Es ist absolut (b) .... zu sehen.

■ Warte mal, wenn ich den Vorhang und den Fensterladen aufmache, kommt vielleicht ein bisschen Licht rein.

■ Nein, das nützt auch (c) .... Es ist immer noch stockdunkel.

■ Du hast doch im Auto sicher (d) .... , womit wir Licht machen können!

■ Ja, im Handschuhfach habe ich eine Taschenlampe, die hole ich mal.

■ Huch, hast du das auch gehört? Da bewegt sich (e) ....

■ Du bist ein Angsthase, da ist wirklich (f) ....

2 An der Hotelrezeption – Ergänzen Sie jemand und niemand.

- ■ Hallo, hallo, ist da (a) *jemand*? Wir möchten unser Zimmer bezahlen.
- ■ Ich kann (b) .... sehen. Aber du könntest unser Gepäck schon ins Auto laden.
- ■ Hier ist immer noch (c) .... gekommen. Ich gehe jetzt mal in die Küche, da ist sicher (d) ....
- ■ Und? Hast du (e) .... gefunden?
- ■ Nein, das Hotel ist wie ausgestorben. In der Küche war auch (f) ....
- ■ Also, wenn in fünf Minuten (g) .... hier ist, dann fahren wir einfach weiter, ohne zu bezahlen.
- ■ Aha, jetzt kommt (h) ....

3 Ein Montagmorgen – Ergänzen Sie man/einen/einem.

Wenn (a) *man* morgens zu spät aufwacht und wenn (b) .... nicht richtig ausgeschlafen ist, reicht es eigentlich schon. (c) .... kommt kaum aus dem Bett, dann findet (d) .... den zweiten Schuh nicht, und der Kaffee weckt (e) .... auch nicht so richtig auf. Das Auto springt nicht an, und dann verpasst (f) .... auch noch den Bus! Im Büro schaut (g) .... der Chef so komisch an, weil (h) .... nur ein kleines bisschen zu spät gekommen ist. Alter Pedant! Der Kollege erzählt (i) .... sein Wochenende in allen Einzelheiten, so ein Langweiler! In der Besprechung muss (j) .... sich dann sehr konzentrieren, um nicht einzuschlafen – wirklich eine uninteressante Präsentation! Den Kollegen ist wieder gar nichts Neues eingefallen. Schön wär's, wenn (k) .... sich zurücklehnen und ein kleines Schläfchen machen könnte. – Tja, es wird (l) .... wirklich nicht leicht gemacht!

4 Ein Telefonat – Ergänzen Sie jemand/er/ihn.

Ja, wir haben heute das Thema fertig besprochen. Aber wenn (a) *jemand* noch weitere Fragen hat, dann soll (b) .... ins Kolloquium kommen.

Gut, und wenn du noch (c) .... aus unserem Seminar triffst, grüß (d) .... von mir.

5 Prüfungsstress – Formulieren Sie unpersönlich mit man/einen.

a) In der Bibliothek ist das Buch, das ich gerade brauche, immer ausgeliehen.
   In der Bibliothek ist das Buch, das man gerade braucht, immer ausgeliehen.
b) Das kann mich wirklich wahnsinnig machen. Wie soll ich da meine Seminararbeit rechtzeitig fertig bekommen?
c) Bei der Vorlesung über Reptilien musst du unbedingt mitschreiben.
d) Denn wenn du in der Prüfung nicht weißt, was der Professor über Krokodile gesagt hat, kannst du leicht durchfallen.
e) Wenn ich doch nur wüsste, was mich in der Zukunft erwartet.

PRÄPOSITIONALPRONOMEN

Worüber? Darüber!

1   Funktion

ⓐ Repräsentant von präpositionalen Ergänzungen

Lisa, worüber ärgerst du dich denn so?	bei Sachen
Ach, ich ärgere mich über den angebrannten Kuchen.	und Sachverhalten
Also darüber würde ich mich nicht so ärgern.	

Von wem hat sie sich denn gerade verabschiedet?	bei Personen/Lebewesen/
Ich glaube, von ihrer Mutter. Wenn sie sich von ihr	Institutionen:
verabschiedet, muss sie immer weinen.	Präposition/Fragewort + Pronomen

ⓑ Repräsentant von Nebensätzen

Ich kann mich genau daran erinnern, dass du einkaufen wolltest.	*dass*-Satz
Er kann sich einfach nicht daran gewöhnen, so früh aufzustehen.	Infinitivsatz
Wir sprechen gerade darüber, was wir morgen kochen.	indirekter
Das hängt davon ab, ob Helga zu Besuch kommt oder nicht.	Fragesatz

2   Formen

ⓐ bei Sachen

| Frage | *wofür?* | *woran?* | Fragewort: |
	womit?	*worüber? ...*	*wo(r)**+ Präposition
Antwort	*dafür*	*daran*	Pronomen:
	damit	*darüber ...*	*da(r)**+ Präposition

* Das *-r-* wird eingefügt, wenn zwei Vokale aufeinandertreffen.

ⓑ bei Personen/Lebewesen/Institutionen

| Frage | *für wen?* | *an wen?* | Präposition + Fragewort |
	mit wem?	*über wen? ...*	
Antwort	*für ihn/sie*	*an ihn/sie*	Präposition + Pronomen
	mit ihm/ihr	*über ihn/sie ...*	

ÜBUNGEN

1   Unterstreichen Sie die präpositionalen Ergänzungen und formulieren Sie Fragen dazu.

Rentner gewinnt 64 Millionen Dollar

Chicago (AP) Ein 63 Jahre alter Kleinunternehmer hat in Chicago den Jackpot geknackt und 64 Millionen Dollar gewonnen. Wir haben mit Alex Snow gesprochen und ihn nach seinen Plänen gefragt. „Zuerst habe ich es nicht geglaubt, als mir meine Frau von dem Gewinn erzählt hat, aber dann habe ich mich bei dem Chef der Lottostelle erkundigt, und es hat gestimmt!" Jetzt kann sich das Ehepaar endlich den ersten Urlaub seit 43 Jahren leisten. „Wir freuen uns natürlich sehr über den Gewinn, aber jetzt müssen wir uns noch auf einen gemeinsamen Urlaubsort einigen." Weil er und seine Frau so viel Geld gar nicht ausgeben können, will er einen großen Teil an wohltätige Organisationen und an seine vier Kinder und sechs Enkel verteilen.

Mit wem haben Sie gesprochen?
Wonach haben Sie ihn gefragt?

2 Hier hört jemand schlecht! – Stellen Sie Fragen.

a) Du weißt doch, wir waren dieses Jahr mit Franz im Urlaub. Am Anfang haben wir uns ja sehr über das Hotelzimmer geärgert.

b) Wir wollten uns schon beim Hoteldirektor beschweren.

c) Aber dann haben wir uns an die Aussicht gewöhnt.

d) Und stell dir vor, Franz hat sich in seine Surflehrerin verliebt.

e) Zuerst hat er sich ja nur für die neuen Surfbretter interessiert.

f) Und dann hat er an einem Surfkurs teilgenommen.

g) Und da hat er sich dann verliebt. Jetzt denkt er nur noch an seine neue Freundin.

Wie bitte? Worüber habt ihr euch geärgert?

Was sagst du? Bei wem wolltet ihr euch beschweren?

3 Vor dem Urlaub – Ergänzen Sie die Präpositionalpronomen.

a) Ich kann mich genau *daran* erinnern, dass du die Tickets besorgen wolltest.

b) Hast du denn schon .... angefangen, deinen Koffer zu packen?

c) Nein, ich denke gerade .... nach, welche Kleider ich mitnehmen soll.

d) Sag mal, du wolltest doch .... denken, die Zeitung abzubestellen.

e) Ach, ich freu mich schon richtig .... , morgen Abend nur im T-Shirt auf einer Terrasse zu sitzen.

4 Streit in der Wohngemeinschaft – Ergänzen Sie die Verben und die präpositionale Ergänzung.

(a) *Über wen ärgerst* du dich eigentlich so? – Über Bruno!

Es (b) .... wieder mal .... , dass er nicht abwäscht, wenn er gekocht hat. Und dass er Bratkartoffeln mit Zwiebeln gemacht hat, weiß das ganze Haus, denn sogar im Treppenhaus (c) .... es .... Und dann bringt er fast jeden Abend seine Freunde mit und (d) .... bis Mitternacht Karten! Und wenn ich mich (e) .... , dass es zu laut ist, sagt er nur, ich soll mir etwas in die Ohren stecken! Könntest du nicht mal (f) .... ? Vielleicht (g) .... er ja .... !

sich ärgern über
es geht um
riechen nach
spielen mit
sich beschweren über
sprechen mit
hören auf

57

LOKALADVERBIEN (1)

da und dort

1   Funktion

Hallo, Mami, ich bin hier oben.	*wo?*	Ort
Stellt die Gartenstühle nach unten, in den Keller.	*wohin?*	Richtung
Den alten Spiegel habe ich von unten, der war noch im Keller.	*woher?*	

2   Formen

ⓐ Adverbien

Wo?	Wohin? *nach / -hin*	Woher? *von / -her*
da	*dahin*	*von da / daher*
hier	*hierhin*	*von hier*
dort	*dorthin*	*von dort / dorther*
außen*	*nach außen*	*von außen*
draußen**	*nach draußen / hinaus*	*von draußen*
oben	*nach oben / hinauf / aufwärts*	*von oben*
vorn	*nach vorn / vorwärts*	*von vorn*
links, rechts	*nach links, nach rechts*	*von links, von rechts*

* *außen/innen* = an der äußeren/inneren Seite: *Das Gebäude wurde innen und außen renoviert.*

** *draußen/drinnen* = außerhalb/innerhalb eines Raumes: *Draußen regnet es. Die Kinder sind schon drinnen.*

ⓑ Kombination von zwei Lokaladverbien

Ich bin hier oben. *Das Gartentor ist hinten links.* *Die Bierkästen stehen dort unten.*	Zur Präzisierung des Ortes (*Wo?*) kann man zwei Lokaladverbien miteinander kombinieren.

ⓒ Adjektive aus Lokaladverbien

Adverbien	Adjektive
das Stockwerk oben	*das obere Stockwerk*
die Tür vorne	*die vordere Tür*
der Baum rechts	*der rechte Baum*

ÜBUNGEN

1   Wo? – Ergänzen Sie die Lokaladverbien.

⟨ außen I da I ~~dort~~ I draußen I hier oben I oben

a) Wart ihr schon einmal in Rom? – Ja, wir waren letztes Jahr *dort*.

b) Wo wohnt bitte Frau Wagner? – .... im dritten Stock.

c) Julia, wo bist du denn? – .... auf dem Balkon.

d) Oh je, es regnet! Und die Gartenmöbel stehen immer noch ....

e) Guck dir mal unser Gartenhäuschen an! .... geht die ganze Farbe ab.

f) Bist du heute Abend zu Hause? – Ja, ich bin auf jeden Fall ....

2 Wohin? Woher? – Ergänzen Sie die Präposition und die Lokaladverbien.

a) Woher kommt denn dieser Lärm? – Ich glaube, *von oben* aus dem Kinderzimmer.

b) Das Wetter ist so schön heute! Wir sollten noch ein bisschen .... gehen.

c) Ich bleibe hier unten im Garten. – Ich nicht. Ich gehe .... und setze mich auf den Balkon.

d) Wo ist denn das Mineralwasser? – Ich hab die Kästen .... in den Keller gestellt.

e) Wie komme ich bitte zum Bahnhof? – Gehen Sie immer geradeaus und biegen Sie an der zweiten Kreuzung .... ab.

f) Woher kommt denn dieser schreckliche Gestank? – Ich glaube .... , mach doch bitte die Fenster zu!

3 Eine Idylle – Ergänzen Sie die Lokaladverbien und -adjektive.

hinten I linken I links I nach oben I nach unten I oben I oberen I rechten I rechts I ~~unten~~ I vorne

Das Bild zeigt das Leben in einer Kleinstadt. Man sieht ein Haus, in dem eine Großfamilie lebt. (a) *Unten* kommt der Vater gerade aus der Haustür, er schaut (b) .... in den Himmel. Vor ihm steht seine Frau mit einem Baby auf dem Arm. (c) .... im Bild sieht man Kinder, Vögel und einen kleinen Hund. (d) .... im Bild spielen zwei kleine Jungen, (e) .... im Bild steht ein Brunnen, an dem eine Frau Wasser holt. Im (f) .... Stockwerk schaut ein Mann aus dem Fenster (g) .... auf die Straße, dabei raucht er ganz gemütlich seine Pfeife. Ganz (h) .... sieht man ein Liebespaar, das sich küsst. (i) .... im Bild steht die Kirche mit zwei Kirchtürmen. Den (j) .... Kirchturm sieht man ganz, den (k) .... nur halb.

5

LOKALADVERBIEN (2)

hin und her

1 Funktion

hin	*Wo läufst du denn hin?*	Richtung vom Sprecher weg
her	*Wo kommst du denn her?*	Richtung zum Sprecher

2 Formen

ⓐ *hin-* und *her-* + Verb

hin-	her-
Bringst du die Kinder morgen in die Schule? – Na gut, ich bring sie hin.	*Ich kann hier nicht vom Telefon weg. Bringst du mir bitte mal den Ordner her?*
Könntest du mich bitte hinfahren?	*Wie lange seit ihr denn hergefahren?*
Gehst du auch zu Florian? – Ja, ich komme auch hin.	*Immer fahren wir zu euch. Jetzt kommt ihr mal her!*
Jetzt ist Schluss! Setzt euch hin!	*Setz dich doch mal her zu mir!*
Sie träumte so vor sich hin. *Er starrte die ganze Zeit vor sich hin.*	*Der Hund lief die ganze Zeit vor/neben/hinter mir her.*
In Verbindung mit *vor sich*: Handlung, die nicht an einen Partner adressiert ist.	In Verbindung mit *vor, hinter, neben*: zwei Bewegungen in gleicher Richtung.

ⓑ *hin-/her-* + Präposition + Verb

hin-	her-
Max trug seine Einkäufe ins Haus hinein. *Paula sah traurig zum Fenster hinaus.*	*Kommen Sie doch bitte herein!* *Gehen Sie mehr aus sich heraus, wenn Sie erfolgreich sein wollen!*
Die Katze ist den Baum hinaufgeklettert. *Er sah lange zu ihr hinüber.*	*Die Katze sprang vom Baum herunter.* *Könnten Sie mir bitte das Salz herüberreichen?*

ⓒ Neutralisierung von *hin-* und *her-*

Gesprochene Sprache			
Komm rein!		rein	hinein – herein
Ach, gehen wir doch kurz mal raus!		raus	hinaus – heraus
Ich bin hier oben im Baumhaus. Komm doch auch rauf!		rauf	hinauf – herauf
Peter! Steig sofort vom Schrank runter!		runter	hinunter – herunter
Ich schick Ihnen das Fax gleich rüber.		rüber	hinüber – herüber

5

1   **Ein Sommerabend – Ergänzen Sie** raus, rauf, rein, rüber, runter.

a) Es ist so schön warm draußen. Wollen wir uns nicht in den Garten *raus*setzen?

b) Ich glaube, wir können sogar draußen essen. Stell doch die Gartenmöbel schon mal ....

c) Bei den Nachbarn ist heute Abend ein Gartenfest. Sie haben gefragt, ob wir nicht .... kommen wollen.

d) Tom, ich glaube, wir haben keinen Wein mehr. – Doch, doch, ich geh gleich .... in den Keller und hol noch welchen ....

e) Wo ist denn bei euch die Toilette? – Oben im ersten Stock links. – Gut, dann geh ich jetzt mal kurz ....

f) So langsam wird es mir hier draußen zu kalt. Können wir uns nicht .... setzen?

2   **Kurz vor dem Gipfel – Ergänzen Sie** hin **oder** her.

■ Bernd, komm doch (a) *her* zu mir!

■ Ich würde ja gerne, aber ich trau mich nicht. Rechts und links geht es ja schließlich ziemlich tief (b) ....unter.

■ Ach, dir kann überhaupt nichts passieren. Du darfst halt nicht (c) ....schauen.

■ Nein, ich bleibe hier. Schau (d) .... , hier ist ein wunderschöner Platz. Willst du nicht zu mir (e) ....kommen? Dann können wir unser Picknick gemütlich zusammen machen.

■ Hier oben hat man aber einen besseren Ausblick! Man kann sogar bis nach Italien (f) ....übersehen. Toll! Aber gut, ich komm zu dir.

3   **Gespräch beim Abendessen – Ergänzen Sie die Verben.**

herfahren I ~~herschicken~~ I hinbringen I hinfahren I hingehen I hinlegen I hinstellen

Mutter: Unsere Waschmaschine ist jetzt schon wieder kaputt. Morgen früh will die Firma einen Mechaniker (a) *herschicken*. – Max, wenn du das Glas so schief hältst, kann ich dir nicht einschenken. (b) .... das Glas bitte .... !

Lisa: Mutti, darf ich morgen zu der Geburtstagsfeier von Florian? Bitte!!! Alle anderen aus meiner Klasse (c) .... auch ....

Mutter: Ja, gut. Ich (d) .... dich dann morgen Nachmittag .... Bloß, wie kommst du am Abend wieder zurück nach Hause?

Vater: Ich kann nach der Arbeit (e) .... und Lisa abholen. Max, lass diesen Unsinn mit dem Messer! (f) .... es sofort ....

Mutter: Stellt euch vor, als ich vorhin vom Italienischkurs nach Hause gefahren bin, (g) .... die ganze Zeit ein Polizeiauto hinter mir .... (Perfekt).

TEMPORALADVERBIEN UND -ADJEKTIVE

morgen – morgens – morgendlich

1   Funktion

Wann wollen wir denn mit unserem Sportprogramm anfangen?	*Wie wäre es mit morgen?*	Zeitpunkt
Ab wann sind Sie in München?	*Ab übermorgen.*	
Seit wann joggst du eigentlich?	*Seit gestern.*	Zeitraum
Bis wann kann ich die Bücher haben?	*Bis übermorgen.*	
Wie lange dauert dein Englischkurs?	*Das ist ein dreimonatiger Kurs.*	Zeitdauer
Wie oft gehst du zum Joggen?	*In letzter Zeit ziemlich oft.* Wenn es geht, *täglich*. Sonst immer *dienstags* und *freitags*.	Häufigkeit Wiederholung
Zuerst laufe ich eine halbe Stunde, und dann gehe ich noch fünf Minuten.		zeitliche Reihenfolge

2   Formen
ⓐ Adverbien

morgens mittags abends (...)	Nomen + -s	Tageszeiten	Wiederholung
montags mittwochs freitags (...)	Nomen + -s	Wochentage	

zuerst	*dann/danach*	*anschließend*	*schließlich/zuletzt*	zeitliche Reihenfolge

immer	*meistens**	*oft*	*öfters*	*manchmal*	*selten*	*nie*	Häufigkeit
100 %						0 %	

* *meistens* = sehr oft: Ich jogge *meistens* im Wald.
 am meisten = Superlativ von *viel*: Paul isst von uns allen *am meisten*.

ⓑ Adjektive

Er fährt täglich mit dem Rad zur Arbeit. *Die wöchentliche Arbeitszeit beträgt 38,5 Stunden.*	Adjektiv auf *-lich* mit Umlaut	Wiederholung
Sein morgendliches Frühstück besteht aus einer Zigarette und schwarzem Kaffee.	ohne Umlaut: *morgendlich, monatlich*	
Sie nimmt an einem mehrtägigen Fortbildungskurs teil.	Adjektiv auf *-ig* mit Umlaut	Dauer

ÜBUNGEN

1   **Wann? Bis wann? Seit wann? Wie oft? Wie lange? – Formulieren Sie Fragen.**
  a) Das ist eine zweistündige Vorlesung.
     Wie lange dauert die Vorlesung?
  b) Ich esse täglich in der Mensa, das Essen ist gar nicht so schlecht.
  c) Dienstags findet ein Kolloquium zur Vorlesung statt.

5

d) Seit vorgestern habe ich einen Computer.

e) Bis übermorgen muss ich eine eigene E-Mail-Adresse haben.

f) Diese Zeitschrift erscheint monatlich.

2 Lehrer-Alltag – Ergänzen Sie die Temporaladverbien und –adjektive.

abendliche | abends | morgendliche | ~~morgens~~ | täglich | wöchentliche

(a) *Morgens* muss Anna um halb sieben aufstehen, denn sie ist Lehrerin für Physik und Mathematik. Um diese Uhrzeit ist sie oft noch etwas müde, deshalb fällt das (b) .... Joggen meistens aus. Sie fährt aber (c) .... mit dem Rad in die Schule, um sich fit zu halten. Ihre (d) .... Stundenzahl beträgt 24 Stunden. Das ist ziemlich viel, findet Anna. (e) .... ist sie auch oft müde, und der (f) .... Spaziergang findet deshalb nicht immer statt.

3 Ein Sportlehrer – Ergänzen Sie meistens oder am meisten.

Wenn ich nach Hause komme, mache ich mir (a) *meistens* erst mal einen Kaffee und lese die Zeitung. Von allen Teilen interessiert mich da der Sportteil (b) .... , aber (c) .... lese ich auch die Kommentare zu den politischen Ereignissen. Nach der Zeitungslektüre mache ich (d) .... noch etwas Sport. Nach dem Abendessen gehe ich dann (e) .... noch in eine Kneipe oder manchmal auch ins Kino. Action-Filme interessieren mich (f) .... , da langweilt man sich nämlich (g) .... nicht.

4 Wie oft? Wie lange? – Ergänzen Sie das Adjektiv oder Adverb auf –lich oder –ig.

a) Diese Zeitschrift erscheint *wöchentlich*. (jede Woche)

b) Woher kann Tanja denn plötzlich so gut Italienisch? – Sie hat an einem .... (4 Wochen) Sprachkurs teilgenommen.

c) Ute verdient .... (jeden Monat) ungefähr 2000 Euro.

d) Sie hat eine .... (1 Stunde) Mittagspause.

e) Toni liest .... (jeden Tag) die „Süddeutsche Zeitung".

f) Er ist gerade auf einem .... (zwei Tage) Fortbildungsseminar.

g) Jetzt ist es kurz vor fünf. Der Zug muss gleich kommen, denn er fährt .... (jede Stunde).

5 Gestern Abend – Formulieren Sie Sätze in der richtigen Reihenfolge. Verwenden Sie die Adverbien zuerst, dann, danach, zuletzt.

a) sich umziehen und eine halbe Stunde joggen

b) ~~einen Kaffee trinken und die Zeitung lesen~~

c) die 23-Uhr-Nachrichten im Fernsehen anschauen

d) sich duschen und sich die Haare waschen

e) eine Kleinigkeit essen

Also, gestern Abend bin ich ziemlich früh nach Hause gekommen.
Zuerst habe ich einen Kaffee getrunken und die Zeitung gelesen.

LOKALE PRÄPOSITIONEN (1)

zu – bei – durch – um ...

a Präpositionen mit Dativ

ab	Der Flug geht *ab* Frankfurt. *Ab* der nächsten Ampel fahren Sie bitte immer geradeaus.	Ausgangspunkt
aus	Er nahm das Geschenk *aus* dem Schrank.	Bewegung aus einem Raum
	Sie kommt *aus* Finnland.	Herkunft generell
bei	Starnberg liegt *bei* München.	Ort in der Nähe
	Eva wohnt noch *bei* ihren Eltern.	Person
	Er arbeitet *bei* einer Werbeagentur, sie *bei* BMW.	Arbeitsplatz, Firma
gegenüber	Das Hotel liegt *gegenüber* der Post.* Das Hotel liegt der Post *gegenüber*.* Mir *gegenüber* saß ein Kollege aus Rom.*	auf der anderen Seite eines Platzes, einer Straße u.a.
nach	Sie fährt mit dem Zug *nach* Frankfurt. *nach* Süden** / Hause / oben / vorne / links ...	Richtungsangaben
von	Ich komme gerade *von* meinem Bruder. Die Flasche ist *vom* Tisch gefallen.	Herkunft aktuell
von ... aus	*Von* hier *aus* hat man eine tolle Aussicht.	Perspektive
	Alle Seminare werden *von* Berlin *aus* organisiert.	Ausgangsort eines Ereignisses
zu	Ich fahre jetzt *zu* meiner Freundin / *zur* Arbeit / *zum* Flughafen ...	Ziel

* bei Nomen Vor- oder Nachstellung, bei Pronomen nur Nachstellung
** bei Nomen mit bestimmtem Artikel *in*: *Der Zug fährt in den Süden / in das schöne*
   Frankfurt / in die Türkei.

b Präpositionen mit Akkusativ

bis	Der Zug geht nur *bis* Frankfurt. (ohne Artikel) Ich bringe dich *bis* zur Bushaltestelle. (Dativ)* Er fuhr uns *bis* vors Kino. (Akkusativ)*	Endpunkt
durch	Der Magier ging *durch* die Tür.	
entlang	Sie spazierten den Fluss *entlang*.**	Parallelität
gegen	Das Motorrad fuhr *gegen* einen Bus.	Herstellung eines Kontakts
um	Die Gäste standen *um* das Buffet (herum). Wir bauen einen Zaun *um* den Garten (herum).	Umkreisung

* Oft mit zweiter Präposition. Der Kasus richtet sich dann nach der zweiten Präposition.
** immer nachgestellt

c Präpositionen mit Genitiv

innerhalb	Das Ticket gilt nur *innerhalb* der Stadtgrenze.	Begrenzung
außerhalb	*Außerhalb* der Stadt ist die Luft viel besser.	

Im Zusammenhang mit Städte- und Ländernamen sowie in der gesprochenen Sprache wird
auch *von* + Dativ verwendet: *innerhalb von Oslo – außerhalb von Frankreich*

1 **Urlaubsfreuden I – Markieren Sie die passende Präposition. Es können auch zwei Lösungen richtig sein.**

<u>nach</u> – zu – in	a) Nach seinem Abitur ist Stefan zuerst mal ... England gefahren.
bei – mit – zu	b) Dort kann er ... Freunden wohnen.
bei – vor – außerhalb von	c) Sie haben ein Haus ... Cambridge.
Von ... ab – Von ... aus – Aus ... heraus	d) ... seinem Zimmer ... hat er eine tolle Aussicht auf einen Park.
entlang – gegenüber – durch	e) Aber Stefan liebt es, am frühen Morgen den Fluss ... zu joggen.
um – neben – innerhalb	f) Anschließend läuft er ... den ganzen Park herum.
Bis – Bis nach – Bis zu	g) ... Hause sind es zu Fuß 30 Minuten.

2 **Woher kommt Paul gerade? – Antworten Sie mit** aus **oder** von**. Es gibt manchmal zwei Möglichkeiten.**

<del>Büro</del> I Ute I London I Klinik I Kino I Skifahren I Keller I Arbeit I Gardasee I sein Chef I Wasser I Bahnhof I Joggen I oben I Domplatz I U-Bahn

Woher kommt Paul?   *Aus dem Büro.*

3 **Petra und Joachim – Ergänzen Sie** bei, zu **oder** nach**.**

Petra ist gleich nach ihrem 18. Geburtstag (a) *zu* Karl-Heinz, ihrem Freund, gezogen. Sie hat es (b) .... ihren Eltern einfach nicht mehr ausgehalten. Aber (c) .... Karl-Heinz auch nicht lange. (d) .... Hause zurück (e) .... ihren Eltern wollte sie auf gar keinen Fall, also ist sie vorübergehend (f) .... Steffi, ihrer besten Freundin, gezogen. Aber das ist auch keine Lösung. Sie hat sich deshalb entschlossen, (g) .... Paris zu gehen. Sie wird dort (h) .... einer Modefirma arbeiten und befürchtet, dass Karl-Heinz dann gleich (i) .... ihr zu Besuch kommt.
Joachim ist 24. Er wohnt noch immer (j) .... seiner Mutter. Sie hat eine 3-Zimmer-Wohnung (k) .... Starnberg. Jeden Morgen fährt er (l) .... München (m) .... Universität. Da er im Sommer (n) .... Frankreich fahren möchte, hat er für die Semesterferien einen Job (o) .... Siemens angenommen. Er muss dann jeden Morgen um sechs Uhr aufstehen, um gerade noch rechtzeitig (p) .... Arbeit zu kommen. Da ihn seine Mutter nervös macht, verbringt er die Wochenenden oft (q) .... Steffi. Aber (r) .... der wohnt im Moment so eine verrückte Petra.

4 **Urlaubsfreuden II – Ergänzen Sie die Präpositionen.**

Liebste Karin,
endlich Urlaub im sonnigen Süden – haben Tom und ich uns gedacht, als wir in Frankfurt (a) *aus dem Bus in das Flugzeug gestiegen sind. Unser Flug* (b) .... *Frankfurt war ganz in Ordnung – bis auf das Gewitter,* (c) .... *das wir geflogen sind. Aber dann ... Die erste Überraschung war das Hotel, das wir* (d) .... *Deutschland .... gebucht hatten.* (e) .... *unserem Balkon .... hat man zwar eine tolle Aussicht – aber direkt unserem Zimmer* (f) .... *ist eine Diskothek! Für den Lärm tagsüber sorgen die Baustellen, die sich* (g) .... *das Hotel gruppiert haben. Unser einziger Trost ist das Meer! Man kann kilometerweit den Strand* (h) .... *laufen. Viele Grüße von deiner tapferen Freundin Claudia*

LOKALE PRÄPOSITIONEN (2): WECHSELPRÄPOSITIONEN

in – an – auf ...

Die folgenden Präpositionen stehen mit dem Dativ, wenn sie „Ort" (Wo?) bedeuten, mit dem Akkusativ, wenn sie „Richtung" (Wohin?) bedeuten:

		Wo? + Dativ	Wohin? + Akkusativ
in	▢	*Die Zeitung ist im (in dem) Wohnzimmer.*	*Er geht ins (in das) Wohnzimmer.*
an	⊸	*Ich saß am (an dem) Klavier.*	*Ich setzte mich ans (an das) Klavier.*
auf	⊙	*Das Buch liegt auf der Kommode.*	*Sie legt das Buch auf die Kommode.*
über	⊙	*Die Lampe hängt über dem Bett.*	*Ich hänge die Lampe über das Bett.*
unter	⊖	*Der Hund liegt unter dem Tisch.*	*Der Hund legt sich unter den Tisch.*
vor	⊥	*Die Bank steht vor dem Haus.*	*Wir stellen die Bank vor das Haus.*
hinter	⌀	*Das Auto parkt hinter dem Haus.*	*Ich fahre das Auto hinter das Haus.*
neben	O|	*Er saß neben einem hübschen Mädchen.*	*Er setzte sich neben ein hübsches Mädchen.*
zwischen	|O|	*Jetzt sitzt er zwischen zwei hübschen Mädchen.*	*Dann setzte er sich zwischen zwei hübsche Mädchen.*

Umgangssprachlich auch: *überm (über dem), übers (über das), unterm, unters, vorm, vors, hinterm, hinters*

Bitte unterscheiden Sie:

nach – in	*Ich fahre nach Italien / Rom ...*	*nach* bei Länder- und Städtenamen ohne Artikel
	Ich fahre in die Türkei / Bundesrepublik Deutschland / USA ...	*in* bei Länder- und Städtenamen mit Artikel
zu – in	*Ich gehe zum Bahnhof.*	Ziel
	Ich gehe in den Bahnhof.	Gebäude

Bei *Post, Bank, Polizei, Bahnhof, Flughafen* gibt es eine spezielle Verwendung von *auf:*
Ich gehe auf die Post / Bank / Polizei / den Bahnhof / den Flughafen. (Alternative: *zu)*

5

1   Dativ oder Akkusativ? – Ergänzen Sie den Artikel.

■ Sag mal, wollen wir heute nicht in (a) d*as* neue italienische Lokal in (b) d...... Maximilianstraße gehen? Du weißt schon, hinter (c) d...... Oper.
■ Ich habe gehört, dass man in (d) d...... Lokal zwar gut, aber auch ganz schön teuer isst.
■ Gerd hat gesagt, man muss in (e) d...... Lokal gehen – und zwar soll man unbedingt das Menü von der Tageskarte nehmen, die an (f) d...... Wand hängt.
■ Ein ganzes Menü – das ist mir zu viel und liegt mir dann nur (g) i...... Magen. Ich schaue lieber in (h) d...... Karte.
■ Und Gerd sagt, auf (i) d...... Tisch stellen sie jeden Tag frische Orchideen.
■ Ein bisschen übertrieben, oder? Ich hätte lieber für das Geld was Ordentliches auf (j) d...... Teller.
■ Wollen wir uns an (k) d...... Bar oder vor (l) d...... Restaurant treffen? Wir könnten auch vorher noch in (m) d...... Maximilianstraße einen kleinen Schaufensterbummel machen.
■ Das wird mir zeitlich zu knapp. Ich stehe Punkt 8 vor (n) d...... Eingangstür. In (o) d...... Bar können wir ja nachher gehen. Wenn wir dann noch einen Pfennig in (p) d...... Tasche haben!

2   Wohin gehen/fahren Sie, wenn Sie Folgendes tun wollen? – Ergänzen Sie in, auf oder zu (zu 📖 s. Seite 64). Manchmal gibt es zwei Möglichkeiten.

⟨ der Arzt I der Bahnhof I die Bank I ~~die Drogerie~~ I die Post I das Reisebüro I das Theater

a) Wenn Sie Sonnencreme kaufen wollen, *gehen Sie zur / in die Drogerie* .
b) Wenn Sie Geld überweisen wollen, ...
c) Wenn Sie Briefmarken brauchen, ...
d) Wenn Sie eine Reise buchen wollen, ...
e) Wenn Sie gesund werden wollen, ...
f) Wenn Sie Goethes „Faust" sehen möchten, ...
g) Wenn Sie nach Nürnberg fahren möchten, ...

3   Reiselust – Ergänzen Sie die Wechselpräpositionen und Artikel bzw. Pronomen.

Ein Stadtstreicher in New York

Frankfurt – Die Stewardessen (a) *in der* Lufthansa-Maschine trauten ihren Augen nicht. (b) .... ihnen saß (c) .... Luxus-Sessel der Reihe 3 ein ärmlich gekleideter älterer Mann. „Eine Flasche Sekt bitte", verlangte der Fluggast (d) .... abgetragenen Mantel. Die Überprüfung ergab: Einem Stadtstreicher war es gelungen, sich als blinder Passagier (e) .... Flugzeug zu schmuggeln. Hubert H. kannte sich gut aus (f) .... Frankfurter Flughafen. Wenn es (g) .... Straßen und Plätzen und (h) .... Parks der Stadt zu kalt wurde, fand er (i) .... Gebäuden des Flughafens eine warme Unterkunft. Jetzt packte ihn die Reiselust. Unerkannt spazierte er (j) .... Großraum-Jet und setzte sich selbstbewusst (k) .... erste Klasse. Dort machte er es sich (l) .... eleganten Geschäftsleuten bequem. (m) .... New Yorker Kennedy Airport stellte sich heraus, dass sich (n) .... löcherigen Anzug des Obdachlosen weder ein Pass noch ein Pfennig Geld befanden. Nach sechsstündigem Aufenthalt wurde Hubert H. (o) .... seine Heimatstadt Frankfurt zurücktransportiert. Nach einer Vernehmung (p) .... dortigen Polizeistation durfte er gehen.

TEMPORALE PRÄPOSITIONEN (1): ZEITDAUER

seit – bis – während ...

ab = von ... an	*Ab heute* habe ich einen Internet-Anschluss. *Von nächster Woche an* bin ich verreist.	+ DAT	Beginn in der Gegenwart / Zukunft
seit	Ich bin *seit letzter Woche* krank.		Beginn in der Vergangen- heit und Dauer bis zur Gegenwart
von ... bis	Wir sind *vom 8.1. bis 21.1.* verreist.		Beginn und Ende
zwischen	Die Praxis ist *zwischen Weihnachten und Neujahr* geschlossen.		
bis zu	Paul bleibt noch *bis zum Ende der Woche.*		Endpunkt
bei*	*Beim Joggen* hat sie mir von ihrem neuen Job erzählt.		Gleichzeitigkeit
über	Ich fahre *übers Wochenende* weg.	+ AKK	Zeitraum
bis	*Bis nächste Woche* muss ich mich entscheiden.		
während	*Während der Woche* gehe ich nie aus.	+ GEN	
innerhalb	Ich muss *innerhalb eines Monats* antworten. Ich muss *innerhalb von einem Monat* antworten. (*von* + DAT: gesprochene Sprache)		
außerhalb	*Außerhalb der Öffnungszeiten* bin ich in dringenden Fällen zu Hause erreichbar.		

* oft mit nominalisiertem Infinitiv

Für die Angabe der Länge eines Zeitraums gebraucht man den Akkusativ ohne Präposition:
Hans und Inge waren einen Monat (lang) in Schottland.

ÜBUNGEN

1

Hans im Glück I – Markieren Sie die passenden Präpositionen.

<u>seit</u> – bis – ab	a) Hans lebt erst ... zwei Jahren in München.
während – I – über	b) Als Kind hat er fünf Jahre ... auf dem Land gelebt.
Über – Zwischen – Bis zu	c) ... seinem 19. Lebensjahr hat er in Köln gewohnt.
Außerhalb – Innerhalb – Während	d) ... der ersten vier Semester seines Studiums war er in Heidelberg.
Von ... an – Von ... bis – Bis ... zu	e) ... 1997 ... 1999 studierte er dort Philosophie.
Zwischen – Bei – Über	f) ... das Wochenende fuhr er meistens zu seiner Kölner Freundin.
Bei – Ab – Innerhalb	g) ... 1999 stand für Hans der Entschluss, nach München zu gehen, fest.
Bis zu – Innerhalb – Während	h) Hans im Glück: ... einer Woche hatte er in München eine passende Wohnung.
beim – zwischen dem – seit	i) Er hatte die Annonce ganz zufällig ... Herumblättern in der Zeitung gefunden.
bis zu – I – ab	j) Bald muss er schon wieder umziehen, denn er wird ... ein Jahr in London arbeiten.

2

Firmenalltag – Ergänzen Sie während, innerhalb oder außerhalb.

a) Entwickeln Sie bitte *innerhalb* einer Woche eine neue Werbestrategie!
b) .... der Arbeitszeit dürfen Sie nicht privat ins Internet.
c) Die Rechnung muss .... der nächsten 14 Tage bezahlt werden.
d) .... der Bürozeiten können Sie mich auf meinem Mobiltelefon erreichen.
e) Können wir das nicht .... des Essens besprechen?
f) .... von zwei Stunden musste eine Entscheidung getroffen werden.

3

ab, von ... an, von ... bis, bis zu oder zwischen? – Ergänzen Sie die richtige Präposition und – wo nötig – den Artikel.

a) *Bis zum* 23.12. ist die Praxis geöffnet, ... 27.12. .... 7.1. wenden Sie sich bitte an meinen Urlaubsvertreter.
b) .... 1. Januar des nächsten Jahres gilt die um zwei Prozentpunkte höhere Mehrwertsteuer. .... Mitte des Jahres soll auch über eine Erhöhung der Erbschaftsteuer entschieden werden.
c) Sie wollen einen Termin .... dem 21. und 24. März? Das wird leider nicht klappen, denn .... 20. .... bin ich auf einem Kongress – und zwar .... 24. März.

4

Arbeit und Freizeit – Ergänzen Sie die Präpositionen.

ab I beim I bis I bis zum I ~~übers~~ I während

■ Hast du Lust, (a) *übers* Wochenende mit zum Skifahren zu gehen?
■ Lust schon, aber ich muss (b) .... nächsten Mittwoch meine Seminararbeit fertig haben. Und mir ist (c) .... jetzt kaum etwas eingefallen. Und (d) .... Dienstagabend habe ich wieder den Kneipenjob.
■ Du wirst sehen, (e) .... Wintersport kommen einem oft die besten Ideen. Stell dir vor, mir ist neulich (f) .... eines Sauna-Gangs ein geniales Konzept für ein Psychologiereferat eingefallen.

5

Hans im Glück II – Ergänzen Sie – wo nötig – die Präpositionen und die Artikel.

Liebe Evelyn,
stell dir vor, es hat mit London geklappt! (a) *Ab* nächster Woche werde ich dort (b) .... ein Jahr bei einer Werbeagentur als „creative assistant" arbeiten. Ich musste mich (c) .... drei Tagen entscheiden. Ich hoffe, es geht (d) .... Januar .... finanziell ein wenig aufwärts mit mir. Nötig wäre es! Anstrengend wird es sicherlich: Als ich mir (e) .... einen Tag lang die Agentur angesehen habe, sind die meisten Leute zwar erst so (f) .... 10 und 11 Uhr gekommen, dann ging es aber (g) .... 9 Uhr abends rund. (h) .... Abendessen hat man mir erzählt, dass das normal ist. (i) .... wichtigen Projekten bleiben die Leute angeblich auch mal (j) .... Nacht im Büro. Im Vergleich zu München ist selbst wochentags eine Menge los in London – leider kann ich das Freizeitangebot nur (k) .... Arbeitszeit nutzen! (l) .... nächsten paar Wochen werde ich mich um meine neue Wohnung kümmern müssen, aber dann kommst du mich ja hoffentlich mal (m) .... ein verlängertes Wochenende besuchen. (n) .... dann!

Dein Hans

5

TEMPORALE PRÄPOSITIONEN (2): ZEITPUNKT

an – in – um ...

an	Sie besucht mich *am Dienstag.*	+ DAT	Tag
	Bertolt Brecht wurde *am 10.2.1898* geboren.		Datum
	Ich möchte lieber *am Vormittag* einkaufen.*		Tageszeit
	Paula besucht mich *an Ostern.*		Feiertag
aus	Dieser Tisch ist *aus dem 17. Jahrhundert.*		zeitliche Herkunft
in	Ich besuche dich *in der nächsten Woche.*		Woche
	Richard verreist *im August.*		Monat
	Im Frühling ist Mallorca am schönsten.		Jahreszeit
	In den 70ern waren viele Studenten politisch aktiv.		Jahrzehnt
	Bertolt Brecht ist *im 19. Jahrhundert* geboren.		Jahrhundert
	Aber: Er ist *1898* geboren.		
	Im nächsten Jahr fliege ich nach Australien.		Zukunft
	Ich habe ihn *in letzter Zeit* oft gesehen.		Zeitraum
nach	*Nach dem Kino* gehen wir noch essen.		
vor	Ich war *vor der Prüfung* ziemlich nervös.		
zu	*Zu dieser Zeit* war ich in London.		Zeitpunkt/Zeitraum in der Vergangenheit**
gegen	Wir kommen erst *gegen Abend.*	+ AKK	ungenaue Tageszeit
	Die Party beginnt *gegen 8.*		ungenaue Uhrzeit
	Dieses Gebäude entstand *gegen Ende des 17. Jahrhunderts.*		ungenaue Zeitangabe
um	Das Flugzeug startet *um 22.16 Uhr.*		genaue Uhrzeit
	Dieses Gebäude ist *um 1700* entstanden.		ungenaue Zeitangabe mit Jahreszahl

* aber: *in der Nacht*

** immer in Verbindung mit den Nomen *Zeit/Zeitpunkt*

ÜBUNGEN

1 **Der Mensch und die Zeit – Markieren Sie die passende Präposition.**

am – im – l	a) Eva-Maria wurde ... 28.1.1975 geboren.
l – in – innerhalb	b) Ihr Bruder Paul ist ... 1977 geboren.
Vor – Seit – Ab	c) ... einem Jahr ist Bärbel nach Hamburg gezogen.
in – l – gegen	d) Wir treffen uns so ... halb acht.
nach – um – an	e) Wir waren ... 10 vor 8 verabredet.
Im – Am – Vor	f) ... nächsten Jahr werde ich sicher nach Rom fahren.
vor – nach – in	g) Wir können erst ... der Vorlesung schwimmen gehen.
gegen – während – an	h) Ich kann dich erst ... Weihnachten besuchen.
zu – um – gegen	i) Dieses Bild wurde ... 1800 gemalt.
in – vor – innerhalb	j) Peter ist ... den letzten Wochen so still geworden.
am – im – um	k) Warst du ... Vormittag in der Stadt?
Während – Bis – Im	l) ... Herbst bin ich am liebsten in den Bergen.
an – um – in	m) Herbert kam erst spät ... der Nacht von der Reise zurück.
zu – in – bei	n) Ich hatte ... dem Zeitpunkt einfach kein Geld.
gegen – um – zu	o) Das Stück wurde ... Ende des 19. Jahrhunderts komponiert.

5

2 an oder in? um oder gegen? – Ergänzen Sie die richtige Präposition und – wo nötig – den Artikel.

an oder in		um oder gegen	
a) *am* Nachmittag	f) .... Ostern	k) *um* 19.52 Uhr.	
b) .... Nacht	g) .... Morgen	l) .... sieben (ungefähr)	
c) .... zwei Wochen	h) .... Mai	m) .... halb vier (genau)	
d) 28.2.1987	i) .... Montag	n) .... Mitte des 18. Jahr-	
e) .... Herbst	j) .... letzten Jahr	hunderts	
		o) 1900	

3 vor oder seit? – Ergänzen Sie die Präpositionen und – wo nötig – den Artikel.

- ■ Wie lange arbeiten Sie schon hier?
- ■ (a) *seit* 30 Jahren. Ich habe fast auf den Tag genau (b) .... 30 Jahren hier angefangen.
- ■ (c) .... damals hat sich sicherlich eine Menge verändert?
- ■ Natürlich. Die größte Veränderung kam (d) .... 12 Jahren – durch die Fusion.
- ■ Was ist (e) .... dieser Zeit so anders?
- ■ Nun, als unsere Firma (f) .... 12 Jahren übernommen wurde, wurden alle früheren Extras sofort gestrichen. Und (g) .... zwei Jahren gibt es regelmäßig Samstagsarbeit.

4 in oder zu? – Ergänzen Sie die Präpositionen und – wo nötig – den Artikel.

a) *In* meiner Jugendzeit träumte ich davon, in ferne Länder zu reisen. Bloß hatte ich .... Zeit überhaupt kein Geld.

b) Die industrielle Agrarproduktion ist .... letzter Zeit wieder ziemlich ins Gerede gekommen.

c) „ .... meiner Zeit hätte es ein solches Benehmen nicht gegeben!", schimpfte die alte Dame mindestens fünfmal pro Tag.

d) .... Zeit König Ludwigs I. lebten die meisten Bayern noch auf dem Land.

e) „Ich habe .... nächster Zeit leider keine einzige freie Minute für dich, mein Schatz", sagte der Firmenchef zu seiner misstrauischen Ehefrau.

5 Hans und Evelyn – Ergänzen Sie die Präpositionen und – wo nötig – den Artikel.

Lieber Hans,
über Deinen Brief aus London habe ich mich wirklich sehr gefreut. Auch bei mir hat sich (a) *in den* letzten Wochen und Monaten viel getan. (b) .... meiner Ausbildung zur Innenarchitektin habe ich (c) .... Frühling ein Praktikum bei einem Antiquitäten-händler begonnen. Es macht mir ausgesprochen Spaß, und ich lerne so „wichtige" Dinge wie z.B., ob ein französischer Tisch (d) .... frühen, mittleren oder späten 18. Jahr-hundert stammt. Oder ob ein englischer Schrank (e) .... 1900 oder schon (f) .... Mitte des 19. Jahrhunderts angefertigt wurde. Nicht nur Dein neuer Job in London ist anstren-gend: Ich muss (g) .... fünf Wochentagen (h) .... Punkt 8.30 Uhr anfangen und komme meist erst so (i) .... 8 Uhr abends nach Haus. Was deine nette Einladung nach London betrifft: (j) .... März kann ich auf gar keinen Fall weg, aber vielleicht klappt es ja (k) .... Ostern. Bis bald!
Deine Evelyn

PS: Ich weiß, Du hast (l) .... letzten Wochenende angerufen, aber (m) .... Zeitpunkt war ich bei meinen Eltern.

PRÄPOSITIONEN

wegen – trotz – für – aus ...

1   kausale Präpositionen

Warum ist das so? ⟶ Grund, Ursache

wegen	*Wegen eines Unfalls hatte die U-Bahn Verspätung.*	+ Genitiv* /
	Wegen seinem Charme konnte ich ihm nicht böse sein.	Dativ
	Ich habe das wegen dir / deinetwegen getan.	
angesichts*	*Angesichts seiner finanziellen Situation musste er auf*	+ Genitiv
	den Hauskauf verzichten.	
aufgrund*	*Aufgrund der Krise wurden zahlreiche Fabriken geschlossen.*	
infolge*	*Infolge der Sparpolitik werden die Renten gekürzt.*	
aus	*Ich habe ihm aus Mitleid geholfen.*	+ Dativ
vor	*Er zitterte vor Angst.*	

* vor allem schriftsprachlich   Kausalsätze 📖 **s. Seite 170**

2   konzessive Präpositionen

Angabe eines Grundes, der gegen eine Handlung, Beschaffenheit oder einen Zustand spricht:

trotz	*Trotz seiner Grippe ist er ins Kino gegangen.*	+ Genitiv

Konzessivsätze 📖 **s. Seite 178**

3   finale Präpositionen

Wofür / Wozu / Für wen brauchst/tust du das? ⟶ Ziel, Zweck, Addressat

für	*Ich mache das nicht für dich, sondern für meine Karriere.*	+ Akkusativ
zu	*Was brauchst du alles zum Kochen* heute Abend?*	+ Dativ

* oft mit substantiviertem Infinitiv   Finalsätze 📖 **s. Seite 174**

4   modale Präpositionen

Wie mache ich das? ⟶ Art und Weise   *Wie* ist das? ⟶ Eigenschaft, Beschaffenheit

aus	*Dieser Tisch ist aus Aluminium.*	+ DAT	Beschaffenheit
in	*Ich erkläre dir alles im Einzelnen.*		Art des Erklärens
	Meinst du das im Ernst?		und Meinens
mit	*Ich fahre mit dem Auto nach Berlin.*		Art und Weise
nach	*Nach Ansicht des Experten ist der Schaden groß.*		Eigenschaft
	Meiner Meinung nach* ist die Lage äußerst ernst.		
zu	*Zu meiner großen Freude ist Paul wieder gesund.*		Gefühlsausdruck
auf	*Wie heißt das auf Spanisch?*	+ AKK	Sprache
	Ich komme auf jeden Fall.		Art und Weise
durch	*Die Stadt wurde durch Bomben zerstört.*		Art und Weise
für	*Für so viel Arbeit wirst du so schlecht bezahlt.*		Vergleich
ohne	*Ohne Diplom bekommst du den Job nicht.*		Eigenschaft
mithilfe	*Mithilfe dieser neuen Therapie** wurde er geheilt.*	+ GEN	Art und Weise
mittels	*Er öffnete das Schloss mittels eines Drahtes.*		

* mit Possessivartikel immer nachgestellt; ** auch: *mithilfe von* + Dativ; Modalsatz

📖 **s. Seite 180**

1 **Das liebe Geld! – Ergänzen Sie die Ausdrücke in Klammern.**

a) Wegen (seine schlechten Finanzen) kann sich Paul dieses Jahr keinen teuren Urlaub leisten. Aus (dieser Grund) ist er ziemlich schlecht gelaunt. Zu (die Überraschung seiner Freunde) plant er jetzt, mit (das Fahrrad) quer durch Deutschland zu fahren.
Wegen seiner schlechten Finanzen kann sich Paul dieses Jahr keinen teuren Urlaub leisten.

b) Infolge (geringere Steuereinnahmen) droht nach (ein Bericht der Süddeutschen Zeitung) ein Haushaltsloch von vier Milliarden Euro. Aufgrund (die geplante Familienförderung) wird für das nächste Jahr noch eine weitere Finanzlücke in Höhe von fünf Milliarden Euro erwartet. Angesichts (diese Belastungen) plant die Regierung, zu (die Gegenfinanzierung) die Steuern zu erhöhen.

2 **Komische Vögel – Ergänzen Sie die Präpositionen.**
auf (2x) I aus I durch I für (2x) I in (2x) I mithilfe (2x) I nach I ohne I trotz

ÖSTERREICHER SCHRECKEN VÖGEL AB

Wien – Einen Weltrekord (a) *im* (+ dem) Abschrecken gefräßiger Vögel will ein kleiner Ort in Österreich aufstellen. (b) .... der gesamten Bevölkerung sollen in Wippenham bis Herbst Vogelscheuchen gebastelt werden. (c) .... diese Weise möchte man nicht nur die lästigen Feldräuber loswerden – und das (d) .... Gewaltanwendung. „Wir machen die Aktion auch (e) .... eine Eintragung ins Guinnessbuch der Rekorde.", so der Bürgermeister. (f) .... einiger Bedenken der Landschaftsschützer hat man die ersten 1000 Vogelscheuchen (g) .... Holz und Stoff bereits aufgestellt.

HILFLOSER VATER SCHEITERT AN MILCHFLASCHE

Braunschweig – (h) .... Panik, seine kleine Tochter könnte verhungern, hat ein Vater aus Braunschweig die Polizei alarmiert. Dem 24 Jahre alten Mann gelang es den Polizeiangaben (i) .... nicht, die Milch des Kindes zu erwärmen. (j) .... einen „Großeinsatz" der Polizei kam das schreiende Kind doch noch zu seinem Abendessen. (k) .... eines Buches (l) .... junge Väter will er künftig derartige Notrufe überflüssig machen. Doch leider ist das Buch (m) .... Schwedisch!

3 **Die Macht der Liebe – Ergänzen Sie die Präpositionen sowie die Ausdrücke in Klammern.**
~~aus~~ I in I mit I ohne I trotz I wegen I zu (2x) I vor

(a) *Aus Liebe* (Liebe) ist Karl (b) .... (das schlechte Wetter) am Wochenende zu seiner kranken Freundin Anne gefahren. (c) „ .... (der starke Schneefall) kommst du aber besser (d) .... (der Zug)", rief sie besorgt am Telefon. Er hörte leider nicht auf sie: Die Straßen waren (e) .... (ein schrecklicher Zustand): spiegelglatt und voll. (f) .... (sein großer Ärger) waren auch noch viele Sonntagsfahrer unterwegs. (g) .... (das Pausemachen) hatte er keine Nerven mehr. (h) .... (Unterbrechung) fuhr Karl, bis er an seinem Ziel war. Die junge Frau weinte (i) .... (Freude), als sie ihn sah.

MODALPARTIKELN

Das ist aber teuer!

Im gesprochenen Deutsch drücken diese zusätzlichen Wörter eine Absicht oder emotionale Färbung aus. Wie häufig diese Wörter gebraucht werden, hängt vom Sprecher ab. Man kann auch mehrere Partikeln in einem Satz kombinieren. Die meisten Partikeln haben mehrere Funktionen bzw. Bedeutungen.

Aussagesätze

eben	*Die letzte U-Bahn für heute ist vor 5 Minuten abgefahren. Dann müssen wir eben zu Fuß gehen.*	Unabänderliche Konsequenz
halt	*Warum willst du denn nicht? Ich will halt nicht.*	Resignation
einfach	*Diese Übung verstehe ich einfach nicht.* *Wenn Sie kein Bargeld dabeihaben, dann geben Sie mir einfach einen Scheck.*	Unzufriedenheit Problemlösung
eigentlich	*Eigentlich wollte er heute kommen.*	Erstaunen, Kritik
*ja**	*Das ist ja bekannt.* *Sie brauchen mich nicht mehr. Dann kann ich ja gehen.*	Bekanntes Selbstverständliches
schon	*Das wird schon gut gehen.*	Beruhigung

Aufforderungen

mal	*Würden Sie mir mal helfen?* *Gib mir doch mal den Hammer.* *Könnten Sie mir bitte mal ihren Stift leihen?*	Bitte
doch	*Setz dich doch in den Sessel.* *Das hättest du mir doch sagen können.*	Rat
*ja*** *bloß* *nur*	*Tu das ja nicht.* *Tu das bloß nicht.* *Tu das nur nicht.*	Warnung
ruhig	*Lass das Licht ruhig an, wenn du rausgehst. Es verbraucht nicht viel Strom.*	Ermunterung

Fragen

denn	*Was gibt es denn zu essen? Hast du denn keinen Hunger?* *Was macht denn eigentlich unser alter Freund Tim?*	Interesse
eigentlich	*Warst du eigentlich schon mal in der neuen Disco?*	

Ausrufe

doch	*Das ist doch nicht richtig!*	Gegensatz
*ja** *aber*	*Es hat ja geschneit. Das ist ja gar nicht teuer.* *Das ist aber teuer. Das ist aber nett.*	Überraschung
vielleicht	*Das ist vielleicht ein Service!*	Verärgerung

* unbetont ** betont

1 Empfehlungen – Formulieren Sie kleine Dialoge mit doch mal und eigentlich.
a) den Artikel in der „Frankfurter Allgemeinen Zeitung" (FAZ) lesen
   Lies doch mal den Artikel in der FAZ! – Ich lese eigentlich nicht gerne die FAZ.
b) klassische Musik hören   d) die alten Fotos anschauen
c) mit deiner Chefin sprechen e) ein bisschen mehr Sport treiben

2 Theaterbesuch – Ergänzen Sie aber, denn, ja, ruhig, vielleicht. Manchmal gibt es mehrere Möglichkeiten.

Vorher:

Was, es gibt noch Karten für die „Zauberflöte"? Das ist (a) ja super.
Was sollen die Karten (b) .... kosten? Nur 10 Euro? Das ist (c) .... wirklich preiswert. Das können wir uns (d) .... leisten, finde ich.

Nachher:

Das Stück war (e) .... langatmig. Das hätte ich mir (f) .... denken können. Wer schaut sich (g) .... heute noch Opern an? Und außerdem: Die Königin der Nacht hat (h) .... leise gesungen.

3 Beim Psychoanalytiker – Ergänzen Sie in diesem Dialog eben, einfach, doch, denn. Manchmal gibt es mehrere Möglichkeiten.

Patientin   Heute ist mir nicht nach Reden zumute. Mir fällt (a) *einfach* nichts ein, was wichtig wäre ...
Psychologin Wichtig oder unwichtig, darauf kommt es (b) .... gar nicht an.
Patientin   Ich will (c) .... nicht.
Psychologin Möchten Sie (d) .... darüber sprechen, warum Sie nicht reden möchten?
Patientin   Ich fühle mich (e) .... nicht wohl. Wollen Sie wirklich wissen, wie es mir geht? Das ist Ihnen (f) .... völlig egal.
Psychologin Warum? Sie sind (g) .... meine Patientin.

4 Alte Bekannte – Ergänzen Sie denn, eigentlich und ja. Manchmal gibt es mehrere Möglichkeiten.

■ Mensch, das ist (a) *ja* eine Überraschung. Wie kommst du (b) .... hierher?
■ Ach, ich habe in der Nähe zu tun. Das ist (c) .... wirklich ein Zufall, dich zu treffen. Wie geht es dir (d) .... so?
■ Ganz gut, danke. Sag mal, weißt du (e) .... , ob Andrea noch hier wohnt?
■ Nein, leider nicht.
■ Lebt (f) .... euer Hund noch?
■ Nein, der war (g) .... damals schon 16 Jahre alt.
■ Hast du (h) .... die Eva mal wieder gesehen?
■ Ja, die sehe ich (i) .... regelmäßig. Die arbeitet (j) .... hier in der Nähe.
■ Hat die (k) .... ihren Freund geheiratet?
■ Nein. Aber das war (l) .... klar, die haben (m) .... wirklich nicht zusammengepasst.
■ Stimmt. Ich muss leider weiter. Hier ist meine Telefonnummer. Wir könnten (n) .... mal zusammen was trinken gehen.

5

PRÄSENS

ich lerne

1 Funktion

Sag mal, wo ist denn die Monika?
Die kommt doch sonst auf jede Party.

Die ist schon seit Wochen im Krankenhaus.
Beinbruch! Aber übermorgen kommt sie raus.

„Und – was machst du gerade so?"	in diesem Moment Gegenwärtiges
Ich studiere seit drei Monaten in Berlin.	Handlungen und Zustände, die zum Zeitpunkt des Sprechens noch andauern
Ich fliege erst nächsten Donnerstag.	Zukünftiges (+ Zeitangabe)
Die Erde ist rund.	zeitlos Gültiges
Als Maria die Tür öffnet, steht Karl vor ihr. Er bittet sie um Verzeihung.	Vergangenes (um es lebendiger zu schildern)

2 Formen

a regelmäßige Verben

	sagen	antworten	reisen	sammeln
ich	sage	antworte	reise	sammle
du	sagst	antwortest	reist	sammelst
er/sie/es	sagt	antwortet	reist	sammelt
wir	sagen	antworten	reisen	sammeln
ihr	sagt	antwortet	reist	sammelt
sie/Sie	sagen	antworten	reisen	sammeln

b unregelmäßige Verben

	sehen	geben	schlafen	halten	stoßen	laufen	wissen
ich							weiß
du	siehst	gibst	schläfst	hältst	stößt	läufst	weißt
er/sie/es	sieht	gibt	schläft	hält*	stößt	läuft	weiß
	e ➞ ie	e ➞ i	a ➞ ä	a ➞ ä	o ➞ ö	au ➞ äu	i ➞ ei

* Stamm auf *-t*, aber ohne *e*-Erweiterung
Liste der unregelmäßigen Verben 📖 **s. Seite 184**

Um die Aktualität des Gegenwärtigen zu betonen, gibt es drei Möglichkeiten:

Siehst du nicht, dass ich gerade arbeite? – Er wohnt derzeit in Rom.	*gerade, derzeit, im Augenblick, im Moment* u.a.
Was hältst du von seinem Brief? – Ich bin gerade dabei, ihn zu lesen.	*dabei sein* + Infinitiv mit *zu*
Stör die Mutter jetzt nicht. Sie ist gerade am/beim Kochen.	*sein + am/beim* + nominalisierter Infinitiv (umgangssprachlich)

6

1   Vorstellungsgespräch – Fragen Sie mit seit wann + schon.

a) in München leben   c) Ingenieur sein   e) bei BMW arbeiten

b) Spanisch lernen   d) Golf spielen   f) Rallyes fahren

a) *Seit wann leben Sie schon in München?*

2   Muttersorgen – Ergänzen Sie die Verben im Präsens.

Lieber Harald,
ich (a) weiß (wissen), dass Du in Kürze nach Brasilien (b) .... (fliegen) und von
morgens bis abends (c) .... (arbeiten), aber vielleicht (d) .... (lesen) Du
ja meine Zeilen doch noch. Ich (e) .... (hoffen), Du (f) .... (nehmen) es
mir nicht übel, wenn ich Dich jetzt noch mit meinen Sorgen (g) .... (belästigen).
Ich habe entdeckt, dass mein Sohn (h) .... (stehlen). Ich (i) .... (sehen)
schon seit langem, dass er sehr viel Geld (j) .... (ausgeben). Wenn man ihn
(k) .... (fragen), von wem er es (l) .... (bekommen), dann
(m) .... (sehen) er weg und (n) .... (antworten):
„Ich (o) .... (stehlen) nicht, ich (p) .... (sammeln) nur."
Das (q) .... (brechen) mir das Herz! Was (r) .... (raten) Du mir?
Alles Liebe
Deine Angelika

6

3   Pläne für die Zukunft – Formulieren Sie Sätze im Präsens.

a) nächstes Wochenende I besuchen I mich I meine Freundin Paula • am Samstag I gehen I
wir I zum Einkaufen • in einer Woche I fahren I wir I nach Berlin • kommen I ihr I mit
Nächstes Wochenende besucht mich meine Freundin Paula. Am Samstag ...

b) im Oktober I beginnen I ich I mit meinem Studium • ich I studieren I dann I Ökonomie I
in Konstanz am Bodensee • ich I brauchen I drei Jahre I dafür • danach I machen I ich I
ein Aufbaustudium I in Harvard

c) in etwa zehn Jahren I übernehmen I ich I die Firma I meines Vaters • anschließend I
gründen I ich I eine Familie I und I bauen I ein Haus • in 20 Jahren I bekommen I ich I
die Midlife-Crisis • dann I suchen I ich I mir I eine Freundin • in 30 Jahren I sein I ich I
vielleicht I bereits I Großvater • und in 40 Jahren I aufhören I ich I zu arbeiten

4   Abgelehnt – Beantworten Sie die Fragen negativ. Verwenden Sie die angegebenen
Verben und abwechselnd ich bin gerade dabei und ich bin gerade am.

a) „Kommst du mit zum Schwimmen?" – (aufräumen)
„Nein, ich bin gerade dabei, aufzuräumen."

b) „Hast du Lust, ein Eis zu essen?" – (abnehmen)
„Nein, ich bin gerade am Abnehmen."

c) „Möchtest du eine Zigarette?" – (mir das Rauchen abgewöhnen)

d) „Hast du einen Moment Zeit für mich?" – (weggehen)

e) „Wollen wir eine Runde Tennis spielen?" – (mein Auto reparieren)

f) „Kannst du deine Frau rufen?" – (fernsehen)

g) „Hilfst du mir bei den Hausaufgaben?" – (die Küche putzen)

h) „Siehst du dir nicht die Nachrichten an?" – (Koffer packen)

PERFEKT

ich habe gesucht – ich bin gefahren

1 Funktion

„Was hast du gestern Abend gemacht?" – „Ich habe meine Eltern besucht."	Tempus für die Vergangenheit in der gesprochenen Sprache
Seitdem er weggezogen ist, sehen wir uns nur noch selten.	abgeschlossene Vorgänge in der Vergangenheit mit Gegenwartsbezug
Morgen in einer Woche habe ich die Arbeiten an diesem Projekt abgeschlossen.	für Zukünftiges (als Ersatz für das Futur II)

2 Formen

a *haben* und *sein*

haben	*Ich habe die Koffer gepackt.*	die meisten Verben
	Wir haben uns gut unterhalten.	alle reflexiven Verben
sein	*Ich bin ins Kino gegangen.*	Verben der Ortsveränderung (ohne Akkusativ): *fahren, kommen, gehen* u.a.*
	Ich bin heute erst um 12 Uhr aufgewacht.	Verben der Zustandsveränderung: *einschlafen, aufstehen, werden* u.a.
	Wir sind zu Hause geblieben.	*sein, bleiben*

* Einige Verben der Ortsveränderung – *fahren, fliegen, reiten* – können auch eine Akkusativergänzung haben. Sie bilden dann das Perfekt mit *haben*: *Ich habe immer diese Automarke gefahren.*

b Partizip II

			Partizip II		
regelmäßige Verben		*ge*	*mach*	*t*	*hat gearbeitet, hat geholt, hat gesagt ...*
	ab	*ge*	*sag*	*t*	*hat aufgemacht, hat festgestellt ...*
			verkauf	*t**	*hat erzählt, hat besucht, hat zerstört ...*
			telefoniert	*t**	*hat studiert, ist passiert ...*
unregelmäßige Verben		*ge*	*fahr*	*en*	*hat getrunken, ist gegangen ...*
	an	*ge*	*komm*	*en*	*hat weggenommen, ist mitgefahren ...*
			zerriss	*en**	*hat verglichen, ist gelungen ...*
Mischverben		*ge*	*kann*	*t*	*hat gebracht, hat genannt, hat gewusst ...*

* Die Verben mit *be-, emp-, ent-, er-, ge-, miss-, ver-, zer-* (untrennbare Verben) sowie die Verben auf *-ieren* bilden das Perfekt ohne *ge-*.

sein und *haben* und die Modalverben (*wollen, müssen, können* ...) stehen meist im Präteritum, selten im Perfekt.

trennbare und untrennbare Verben s. Seite 106-109; unregelmäßige Verben s. Seite 184

3 Satzstruktur

	POS 2: *haben/sein*		Ende: Partizip II
Ich	*habe*	*den Koffer*	*gepackt.*
Ich	*bin*	*ins Kino*	*gegangen.*

1 Bilden Sie von folgenden Verben das Partizip II und tragen Sie es ein.

schreiben I ankommen I streiten I ~~rasieren~~ I ausmachen I anbieten I bekämpfen I denken I umziehen I abstellen I versuchen I einladen I misstrauen I entdecken I schneiden I besprechen I sich entscheiden I studieren I wegbringen I empfehlen

(...)ge-...-t	(...)ge-...-en	...-t	...-en
		rasiert	

2 Gespräch mit einem Nachtwächter – Ergänzen Sie haben bzw. sein in der richtigen Form.

Herr Fachner, (a) *ist* **denn heute Nacht viel passiert?**
Nein, Gott sei Dank nicht. Ich (b) .... meine Runden gemacht, ohne dass es etwas gegeben (c) ....
Wie vielen Menschen (d) .... **Sie denn schon begegnet?**
Nach ein Uhr (e) .... ich höchstens vier oder fünf gesehen. Die meisten Lokale in unserer kleinen Stadt (f) .... ja ab Mitternacht geschlossen.
Wir (g) .... **Sie gestern tagsüber kaum erreicht. Wo** (h) .... **Sie denn so gewesen?**
Zuerst (i) .... ich mich um meinen normalen Job als Postbote gekümmert, und dann (j) .... ich nach Hause gefahren, wo ich geschlafen (k) ....
Wie (l) .... **Sie überhaupt dazu gekommen, als Nachtwächter zu arbeiten?**

Nun, der Bürgermeister (m) .... mich gefragt, und da (n) .... ich einfach zugesagt. Wir (o) .... in Mainburg immer schon einen Nachtwächter gehabt, und der alte (p) .... gestorben.
Was (q) .... **denn Ihre Frau zu ihrem neuen Job gesagt?**
Zuerst (r) .... sie ein wenig dumm geschaut, weil sich das natürlich auf unser Familienleben ausgewirkt (s) .... , aber dann (t) .... sie sich wieder beruhigt.
(u) .... **Sie auf Ihrer Runde denn schon einmal richtig Angst gehabt?**
Ja, schon. Einmal, da (v) .... einem Bauern nachts sein bissiger Hund weggelaufen. Und der (w) .... mich dann durch die Straßen gejagt. Zum Glück (x) .... aber dann die Polizei gekommen.

6

3 Gesundheitsstress – Formulieren Sie Sätze im Perfekt.
a) Der Arzt (verbieten) meinem Vater das Rauchen.
   Der Arzt hat meinem Vater das Rauchen verboten.
b) In einem Monat (überstehen) er die schlimmste Krise.
c) Der Arzt (sagen) ihm auch, dass er mehr Sport treiben muss.
d) Heute (laufen) mein Vater erstmals eine halbe Stunde. Das (umbringen) ihn fast.
e) Danach (sich hinlegen) er gleich wieder und (einschlafen).
f) Erst um 12 Uhr (aufstehen) er und (gehen) ins Bad.
g) Zum Mittagessen (bekommen) er nur Gemüse und etwas gekochten Fisch.
h) Das (gefallen) ihm überhaupt nicht, und vor lauter Ärger (explodieren) er fast!

PRÄTERITUM

er ging

1 Funktion

Es war einmal ein König. Der liebte eine Köchin ... *Der Vorschlag der Regierung, die Öko-Steuer zu erhöhen, stieß bei der Opposition auf Kritik.* *Sie kritisierte vor allem den Zeitpunkt des Vorschlags und kündigte harte Verhandlungen an.*	Tempus für die Vergangenheit in der geschriebenen Sprache (Berichte, Erzählungen, Meldungen in den Medien)
„Du hattest doch gestern so starke Kopfschmerzen. Sind sie weg?" – *„Ja, zum Glück. Die Schmerzen waren wirklich schlimm, ich konnte mich kaum noch auf den Beinen halten, und es gab im ganzen Haus keine Tablette."*	bei *haben* und *sein* häufig statt des Perfekts, bei *es gibt* und den Modalverben (*wollen, müssen ...*) fast immer statt des Perfekts

2 Formen

	regelmäßige Verben		unregel-mäßige Verben	Hilfsverben		Misch-verben	Modal-verben
	fragen	*warten*	*kommen*	*sein*	*haben*	*denken*	*können*
ich	*frag*te	*wart*ete	*kam*	*war*	*hatte*	*dachte*	*konnte*
du	*frag*test	*wart*etest	*kam*st	*warst*	*hattest*	*dachtest*	*konntest*
er/sie/es	*frag*te	*wart*ete	*kam*	*war*	*hatte*	*dachte*	*konnte*
wir	*frag*ten	*wart*eten	*kam*en	*waren*	*hatten*	*dachten*	*konnten*
ihr	*frag*tet	*wart*etet	*kam*t	*wart*	*hattet*	*dachtet*	*konntet*
sie/Sie	*frag*ten	*wart*eten	*kam*en	*waren*	*hatten*	*dachten*	*konnten*

ÜBUNGEN

1 Bilden Sie das Präteritum.

a) ich   *legte*   legen
b) du .... anfangen
c) er .... glauben
d) wir .... argumentieren
e) sie (Pl.) .... rennen
f) ihr .... haben
g) ich .... liegen
h) wir .... denken
i) sie .... sitzen

j) es .... regnen
k) ich .... nehmen
l) ihr .... sein
m) wir .... dürfen
n) er .... antworten
o) du .... wollen
p) er .... hängen
q) sie .... zerstören
r) sie (Pl.) .... bringen

2 König Johann im Glück – Formulieren Sie das folgende Märchen im Präteritum.

König Johann ist ein mächtiger König. In seinem Land leben 30 Millionen Menschen. Aber all seine Macht und sein Reichtum bringen ihm kein Glück. Er fühlt sich einsam, und die Leute an seinem Hof beginnen, sich Sorgen zu machen. Doch eines Tages rettet ihn seine Hofköchin

Fanni aus seiner Depression. Sie versucht, durch ständig neue Knödel-Rezepte die Laune des Königs zu verbessern. Jeden Abend bis spät in die Nacht studiert sie deswegen Kochbücher. Als man dem König eines Tages ihre neueste Kreation, einen Spinat-Pilz-Knödel mit 20 cm Durchmesser, bringt, weiß er, dass sein Leben wieder einen Sinn hat. Obwohl er nach dem Essen des riesigen Knödels kaum noch sitzen kann, lässt er die Hofköchin kommen. König Johann verliebt sich sofort in sie. „Meine Knödel-Königin" nennt er sie satt lächelnd. Bald darauf macht er ihr einen Heiratsantrag. Sie will zuerst nicht, da sie bereits verlobt ist, aber als man sie mit lebenslangem Reichtum lockt, stimmt sie zu.

König Johann war ein mächtiger Mann. In seinem Land ...

3 Unheimliche Begegnung – Formulieren Sie die mündliche Aussage eines Zeugen als schriftlichen Bericht. Ersetzen Sie dabei das Perfekt durch das Präteritum. Beachten Sie den Wechsel der Perspektive.

„Ich bin gerade aus dem Restaurant gekommen, da habe ich gesehen, wie ein Bagger auf den Parkplatz gefahren ist. Er hat dabei mehrere Autos beschädigt, auch mein Auto. Dann hat der Bagger endlich angehalten. Aus dem Fahrzeug ist ein junger Mann gestiegen. Als ich versucht habe, ihn festzuhalten, hat der Mann etwas von „persönlichen Problemen" erzählt. Er ist dann freiwillig stehen geblieben und hat mich gebeten, nichts davon seiner Freundin zu erzählen. Der Mann hat einen sehr verwirrten Eindruck auf mich gemacht. Ich habe dann über mein Handy die Polizei angerufen, die nach etwa 10 Minuten gekommen ist."

Der Zeuge kam gerade aus dem Restaurant, als er ...

4 Bett-Rekord – Ergänzen Sie die Verben im Präteritum.

berühren I drehen I drücken I gehen I haben I lassen I liegen I ~~sein~~ I wählen I wechseln

Belgier dreht sich 120 000 Mal im Bett um

Brüssel – Der Postangestellte Walter Franck hat sich 120 000 Mal im Bett umgedreht, um damit ins Guinnessbuch der Rekorde zu kommen. Die Bewegung (a) *war* einfach: Der Rekordkandidat (b) .... auf dem Rücken und (c) .... sich dann zur Seite, (d) .... mit der Nase die Matratze und (e) .... wieder in die ursprüngliche Position. Franck (f) .... für seine spektakuläre Aktion nicht sein eigenes Bett. Er (g) .... stattdessen eine Liege im Hinterzimmer seiner Stammkneipe aufstellen, denn dort (h) .... er das richtige Publikum für seine sportliche Höchstleistung. Alle seine Freunde (i) .... ihm die Daumen. Der Rekordversuch (j) .... an diesem Dienstag erfolgreich zu Ende.

PLUSQUAMPERFEKT

er war gegangen

1 Funktion

Nachdem Wolfgang die Wahrheit über Maria erfahren hatte, *weinte er. Er konnte es immer noch nicht glauben. Nie zuvor* war *er einer solchen Frau* begegnet. *Aber nachdem er so* behandelt worden war, *konnte er nicht länger mit ihr zusammen sein. Alles, was sie mir* erzählt hatte, *habe ich im Kopf behalten.*	Tempus der Vorzeitigkeit gegenüber dem Präteritum / Perfekt

2 Formen

Präteritum von *haben/sein* + Partizip II

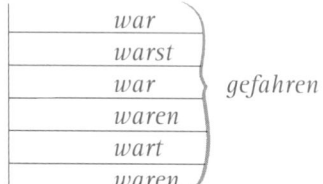

ich	hatte			war	
du	hattest			warst	
er/sie/es	hatte	*gearbeitet*		war	*gefahren*
wir	hatten			waren	
ihr	hattet			wart	
sie/Sie	hatten			waren	

Welche Verben das Plusquamperfekt mit *haben* und welche mit *sein* bilden 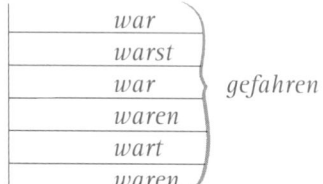 **s. Seite 78** (Perfekt), **s. Seite 110** (Passiv).

6

ÜBUNGEN

1 Gerade noch mal gut gegangen! – Unterstreichen Sie die Verben. In welchem Tempus stehen sie hier?

a) *Plusquamperfekt*

Vorhang explodiert in Waschmaschine
Köln – Damit (a) hatte die Hausfrau nicht gerechnet: Eine Nacht lang (b) hängte sie einen Duschvorhang zum Lüften vor ihre Wohnung, nachdem sie ihn mit Waschbenzin (c) gereinigt hatte. Trotzdem (d) gab es eine Explosion, als sie den Vorhang in der Maschine (e) wusch. Drei Wände (f) wurden verschoben, es (g) entstand ein Sachschaden von 20 000 Euro. „Ich (h) habe meinen Augen nicht getraut, als ich die Verwüstung (i) gesehen habe", (j) sagte die Frau. (k) Verletzt wurde niemand. Die Kriminalpolizei (l) glaubt, dass sich die explosiven Reste am Vorhang durch die Minusgrade während der Nacht nicht komplett (m) verflüchtigt hatten.

Polizei belohnt spontane Hilfe
Frankfurt – Er (n) hatte durch seine spontane Hilfe eine Frau vor einem Raubüberfall bewahrt. Dafür (o) wurde ein 52-jähriger slowenischer Busfahrer jetzt vom Polizeipräsidium mit 200 Euro belohnt. Der Mann (p) hatte Anfang November beim Heimweg von der Arbeit Geräusche und Hilferufe aus einer Einfahrt gehört. Dort (q) versuchte gerade ein Unbekannter, eine 30-jährige Frau auszurauben, die sich heftig (r) wehrte. Der Täter (s) stieß auf der Flucht mit dem Busfahrer zusammen. Dabei (t) erlitt der Slowene eine Knieverletzung. „Aber das (u) macht nichts. Hauptsache, man (v) hat den Täter gefasst!"

2 „Jurassic Parc" – Ergänzen Sie die Verben im angegebenen Tempus.

Dino-Park in Argentinien entdeckt

Buenos Aires – In Argentinien (a) (entdecken; Perf.) Wissenschaftler einen etwa 150 Millionen Jahre alten Dinosaurier-Friedhof mit versteinerten Knochen. „Von einem Dinosaurier (b) (sein; Präs.) fast das vollständige Skelett erhalten", (c) (berichten; Prät.) einer der dort tätigen Wissenschaftler. Die Nachrichtenagentur ANA (d) (schreiben; Prät.) von einem „Jurassic Parc" in Patagonien. Paläontologen (e) (hoffen; Plusq.) seit langem, eine Lücke in der Forschung schließen zu können. Argentinien (f) (sich erweisen; Präs.) immer mehr als einer der wichtigsten Fundorte der Paläontologie: Erst vor einem Jahr (g) (finden; Plusq. Passiv) die Überreste des längsten bekannten Dinosauriers. Der pflanzenfressende Riese (h) (kommen; Präs.) auf eine Länge von 48 bis 59 Metern. Bauarbeiter (i) (geben; Plusq.) entsprechende Hinweise. Im Jahr zuvor (j) (finden; Plusq.) Forscher in Patagonien bereits Überreste des vermutlich größten fleischfressenden Dinos. „An der neuen Fundstätte (k) (ausgraben; Perf. Passiv) auch Versteinerungen von Schildkröten, Flugechsen und sogar einem Säugetier", (l) (mitteilen; Prät.) der Wissenschaftler.

In Argentinien haben Wissenschaftler einen etwa 150 Millionen Jahre alten Dinosaurier-Friedhof mit versteinerten Knochen entdeckt.

3 So ein Pech! – Ergänzen Sie die Verben im Präteritum und Plusquamperfekt.

London – Den Rekord der kürzesten Ehe halten John und Margaret D. Ihr „Bund fürs Leben" (a) *dauerte* (dauern) nur 52 Minuten, nachdem sie bereits über ein Jahr (b) .... (zusammenleben). Bereits an der Hochzeitstafel (c) .... (geraten) die beiden in einen lautstarken Streit über das Ziel ihrer Flitterwochen. Nachdem der frischgebackene Ehemann die Hochzeitstorte auf die Braut (d) .... (werfen) und ohne ein Wort (e) .... (gehen), (f) .... (werden) die Ehe noch am selben Tag geschieden.

Würzburg – Nachdem er beruflich nur Fehlschläge (g) .... (erleben), (h) .... (sollen) es wenigstens einmal klappen: Dieter B. (i) .... (planen) einen Postraub. Doch auch diesmal mit bescheidenem Erfolg: Nachdem er der Post-Angestellten einen Zettel mit der Aufschrift „Dies ist ein Raubüberfall" (j) .... (hinlegen), (k) .... (erklären) ihm diese, dass sie das nichts angehe, weil sie dafür nicht zuständig sei. Entnervt (l) .... (aufgeben) Dieter B. seinen Plan wieder ....

4 Armer Anton – Formulieren Sie nachdem-Sätze im Plusquamperfekt und den Hauptsatz jeweils im Präteritum.

a) er I die Nacht zuvor I schlecht schlafen • sein I er I heute Morgen I sehr müde
   Nachdem er die Nacht zuvor schlecht geschlafen hatte, war er heute Morgen sehr müde.
b) er I einen Anruf seiner kranken Mutter I erhalten • nicht gehen können I er I ins Kino
c) sein Kollege I krank werden • übernehmen müssen I er I dessen Arbeit I auch noch
d) er I sein Auto I von der Reparatur I abholen • kaputtgehen I es I gleich wieder
e) er I die Verabredung mit seiner Freundin I vergessen • warten I sie I umsonst
f) deswegen I Streit mit ihr I geben + es • er I gehen I zu Freunden I Karten spielen

FUTUR

Es wird regnen.

1 Funktion

Futur I	*Sie wird die Prüfung bestehen.*	Zukünftiges
Futur II	*Morgen wird sie die Prüfung bestanden haben.*	in der Zukunft Abgeschlossenes

Häufig hat das Futur eine modale Funktion:

Peter wird jetzt denken, ich liebe ihn.	Sicherheit
Morgen wird er es schon wieder vergessen haben.	
Herr Meier ist heute nicht da. Er wird krank sein.	Vermutung
Joschi hat sich nicht gemeldet. Er wird das Problem alleine gelöst haben.	
Du wirst jetzt dein Zimmer aufräumen!	energische Aufforderung
In einer Stunde wirst du dein Zimmer aufgeräumt haben!	

Diese Funktion kann man durch Modalwörter verdeutlichen:

Peter wird jetzt sicher denken, ...	+ *bestimmt / sicherlich / mit Sicherheit*	Sicherheit
Er wird wohl krank sein.	+ *wohl / vermutlich / wahrscheinlich*	Vermutung

2 Satzstruktur

		POS 2: *werden*		Ende: Infinitiv
Futur I	*Er*	*wird*	*viel*	*erleben.*
		POS 2: *werden*		Ende: Infinitiv Perfekt
Futur II	*Er*	*wird*	*viel*	*erlebt haben.*

werden 📖 **s. Seite 86**

3 Alternativen

Sie besteht die Prüfung morgen.	Präsens	Zukünftiges
Morgen hat sie die Prüfung schon bestanden.	Perfekt	in der Zukunft Abgeschlossenes

Peter denkt jetzt (bestimmt), dass ...	Präsens (+ *bestimmt / sicher ...*)	Sicherheit
Morgen hat er es (bestimmt) schon wieder vergessen.	Perfekt (+ *bestimmt / sicher ...*)	
Er ist wahrscheinlich krank.	Präsens + *wohl / vermutlich / wahrscheinlich ...*	Vermutung
Er hat das Problem wohl alleine gelöst.	Perfekt + *wohl / vermutlich / wahrscheinlich ...*	
Du räumst jetzt dein Zimmer auf!	Präsens	energische Aufforderung
In einer Stunde hast du dein Zimmer aufgeräumt!	Perfekt + Zeitangabe	
Räum jetzt dein Zimmer auf!	Imperativ	

1 **Zukunft (Z), Sicherheit (S), Vermutung (V) oder energische Aufforderung (A)?**

Z	S	V	A	
✗				a) Peter wird nächsten Montag ins Krankenhaus gehen.
				b) Er wird dort wohl mindestens zwei Wochen liegen.
				c) Er wird dort bestimmt hinter jeder hübschen Krankenschwester her sein.
				d) „Nach der Operation wirst du mich sofort besuchen!", hat er gesagt.
				e) Wenn er wieder draußen ist, wird er zu seinen Eltern fahren.
				f) Die werden sich jetzt vermutlich ziemliche Sorgen um ihn machen.

2 **Fragen an den Börsenexperten – Beantworten Sie die Fragen und drücken Sie dabei Sicherheit (S) bzw. Vermutung (V) aus.**

a) Besuchen Sie morgen den Börsen-Club? (S) (Ja, …)
   Ja, ich werde mit Sicherheit morgen den Börsen-Club besuchen.
b) Geben Sie dann auch ein paar Tipps für den „Neuen Markt"? (S) (Ja, …)
c) Kommt es dieses Jahr wieder zu einer Krise? (V) (Nein, …)
d) Investieren Sie in nächster Zeit auch in Aktienfonds? (V) (Ja, …)

3 **Arme Kinder – Formulieren Sie die energischen Aufforderungen im Futur.**

a) Mach jetzt sofort deine Hausaufgaben!
   Du wirst jetzt sofort deine Hausaufgaben machen!
b) Putz dein Fahrrad!
c) Räum jetzt den Hobbyraum auf!
d) Geh sofort mit dem Hund spazieren!
e) Schaltet auf der Stelle den Fernseher aus!

4 **Das Auto der Zukunft – Formulieren Sie den Text im Futur.**

Das Auto der Zukunft verursacht kaum noch Umweltprobleme. Es hat einen Wasserstoff-
oder Elektroantrieb. Außerdem ist es leiser als die Autos von heute. Und es ist viel sicherer:
Airbags schützen die Körper der Passagiere nicht nur von vorne und seitlich, sondern auch
von oben und im Fußraum. Es gibt dann ein Radar, das die Bremse automatisch betätigt.
Das Auto der Zukunft wird kaum noch Umweltprobleme verursachen. Es …

5 **Trennungsschmerz – Formulieren Sie die Vermutungen mit Futur I bzw. II.**

Liebe Hanna!
Du hast wohl schon gedacht, ich habe Dich vergessen, weil ich mich so lange nicht gerührt habe.
Ich nehme an, Du hast von meiner Trennung von Maria bereits gehört. Wahrscheinlich ist sie
unglücklicher über unsere Trennung als ich. Aber so, wie ich sie einschätze, hat sie mich ver-
mutlich in einem Monat schon vergessen. Demnächst erzähle ich Dir mehr. Es interessiert Dich
ja vielleicht, wie das passiert ist.
Bis bald! Alex

Du wirst (wohl) schon gedacht haben, ich habe Dich vergessen, …

6

WERDEN

*ich werde berühmt – ich werde berühmt sein –
ich werde gefeiert*

1 Funktion

Hallo, Franz, du siehst aber schlecht aus. Bist du krank?

Nein, aber ich werde es bald sein. Ständig werde ich von
meinem Chef schikaniert. Ich werde von Tag zu Tag nervöser.

Vollverb	+ Adjektiv	*Die Reichen werden immer reicher.*	Vorgang ("Prozess")
	+ Nomen	*Mein Sohn studiert, er wird Arzt.*	
Hilfsverb	+ Infinitiv	*Er wird sicher bald kommen.*	Futur
		Franz wird erst morgen hier sein.	
	+ Partizip II	*Mein Auto wird heute repariert.*	Passiv
	+ Infinitiv	*Ich würde gern weniger arbeiten.*	Konjunktiv II

Futur 📖 **s. Seite 84**, Passiv 📖 **s. Seite 110**, Konjunktiv II 📖 **s. Seite 118**

2 Formen

	Präsens	Präteritum	Perfekt		Plusquamperfekt	
ich	*werde*	*wurde*	*bin*		*war*	
du	*wirst*	*wurdest*	*bist*		*warst*	
er/sie/es	*wird*	*wurde*	*ist*	*geworden/ worden*	*war*	*geworden/ worden*
wir	*werden*	*wurden*	*sind*		*waren*	
ihr	*werdet*	*wurdet*	*seid*		*wart*	
sie/Sie	*werden*	*wurden*	*sind*		*waren*	

Die Partizip-II-Formen von *werden* als Vollverb und *werden* als Hilfsverb sind unterschiedlich.
Vollverb: *Ich bin wieder gesund geworden.* (Perfekt Aktiv)
Hilfsverb: *Ich bin geheilt worden.* (Perfekt Passiv)

ÜBUNGEN

1 Vorgang (V), Futur (F), Passiv (P) oder Konjunktiv II (K)? – Bestimmen Sie die Funktion von werden.

	V	F	P	K
a) Es wird noch lange dauern, bis Michael fertig studiert hat.		X		
b) Ihr werdet am Flughafen abgeholt.				
c) Herr Becker wird erst übermorgen wieder da sein.				
d) Wir würden euch gerne zu Weihnachten einladen.				
e) Welche Mannschaft wurde beim letzten Mal Europameister?				
f) Martha ist in letzter Zeit so still geworden.				
g) Ich werde im Sommer nach Brasilien fahren.				
h) Von welcher Zeitschrift ist dieser Computer getestet worden?				

6

2 Männerrunde – Formulieren Sie den Zustand als Vorgang (werden).

a) Ist Eva immer noch so eifersüchtig?

Ja, *sie wird* immer eifersüchtig, sobald sie eine hübsche Frau in meiner Nähe sieht.

b) Diese Schauspielerin da, ist die berühmt?

Nein, noch nicht, aber vielleicht .... eines Tages berühmt.

c) Bist du Manuela wegen neulich immer noch böse?

Ja natürlich, wenn ich nur ihren Namen höre, ... böse.

d) Sag mal, was ist eigentlich mit Jens? Ich habe gehört, er ist jetzt Börsenmakler.

Nein, noch nicht, aber .... einer. Er macht gerade einen Kurs.

e) Schau mal, die neue Kellnerin, ist die nicht charmant?

Nicht besonders. .... erst charmant, wenn es um ihr Trinkgeld geht.

f) Apropos zahlen, der Laden hier ist ganz schön teuer.

Ja, ... viel teurer .... (Perfekt), seitdem der Besitzer gewechselt hat.

3 Expertengespräche – Ergänzen Sie worden oder geworden.

■ „Ich habe gehört, bei allen Druckern sind die Preise total reduziert (a) *worden*.“

■ „Stimmt, die sind jetzt richtig billig (b) .... Mein Drucker ist neulich repariert (c) .... , und das war fast so teuer wie ein Neukauf. Da bin ich ganz schön sauer (d) ....“

■ „Aber wenn die jetzt so billig sind, sind die dann nicht auch schlechter (e) .... ?“

■ „Nein, das ist dasselbe wie bei den CD-Spielern, Videorekordern und noch früher bei den Farbfernsehern. Da sind die Preise nach einiger Zeit auch rapide gesenkt (f) ....“

■ „Also, die Fernseher sind definitiv schlechter (g) .... Lauter technische Spielereien, die nach kurzer Zeit kaputtgehen! Mir ist jetzt so ein Ding angeboten (h) .... , da ist mir schon beim Lesen des Prospekts ganz schwindelig (i) .... !“

4 Fliegende Entdeckungen – Ergänzen Sie werden. Achten Sie auf das Tempus.

Ein neuer Komet

München – Ein neuer Komet ist entdeckt (a) *worden*. Bei klarem Wetter kann man „S4 Linear" mit einem guten Fernglas entdecken. Anfang August (b) .... er am „Großen Wagen" vorbeiziehen. Um Mitternacht kann er besonders gut beobachtet (c) .... Ob ein Komet zum strahlenden Star am Himmel (d) .... , hängt davon ab, wie oft ein Komet schon in Sonnennähe war. Kometen (e) .... nach ihren Entdeckern benannt. In diesem Fall handelt es sich um das Weltraum-Programm „Linear", mit dessen Teleskopen der Komet im September vergangenen Jahres entdeckt (f) ....

Fliegen, die länger leben

Washington – In den USA ist eine Genveränderung gefunden (g) .... , die Fliegen doppelt so lange leben lässt. Das Gen (h) .... eines Tages vielleicht auch das menschliche Leben verlängern, da es – ohne diese Mutation – auch beim Menschen vorhanden ist. „Nachteile sind bislang nicht entdeckt (i) .... ", kommentierte ein Genetiker vom kalifornischen Institut für Technologie die Forschungsergebnisse. Fliegen, die mit dem Gen „Indy" („I'm not dead yet" – „Ich bin noch nicht tot") behandelt (j) .... , seien am Ende ihres langen Lebens nicht inaktiver (k) .... als ganz normale Exemplare. Wer (l) .... nicht gerne doppelt so lange leben?

6

VERBERGÄNZUNGEN

Ich frage dich, du antwortest mir.

1 Funktion

Das Verb „dirigiert" den Satz. Vom Verb hängt es ab, wie viele Elemente in einem Satz obligatorisch sind und in welchem Kasus sie stehen. Man nennt solche Elemente Ergänzungen.

2 Formen

Subjekt Ergänzung NOM	Prädikat Verb	Objekt Ergänzung DAT	Objekt Ergänzung AKK	Objekt Ergänzung GEN
Der Hund	*schläft.*			
Es	*regnet.*			
Peter	*trifft*		*seine Freundin.*	
Sie	*besucht*		*eine Ausstellung.*	
Es	*gibt*		*keinen Nachtisch.*	
Er	*hat*		*einen neuen BMW.*	
Sie	*hilft*	*ihrer Mutter.*		
Tom	*gefällt*	*mir.*		
Das Kaufhaus	*liefert*	*uns*	*den Fernseher.*	
Ich	*schenke*	*ihrem Sohn*	*ein Fahrrad.*	
Man	*überführte*		*ihn*	*des Mordes.*

Die Dativ-Ergänzung gibt meist den Adressaten / das Ziel der Handlung an, die Akkusativ-Ergänzung den Gegenstand der Handlung.

	Ergänzung NOM	Verb	Ergänzung NOM: Prädikatsnominativ
sein	*Fritz*	*ist*	*ein Schäferhund.*
werden	*Bernd*	*wird*	*ein großer Pianist.*
bleiben	*Er*	*bleibt*	*ein alter Geizhals.*
heißen	*Der Berg*	*heißt*	*Kleiner Watzmann.*

	Ergänzung NOM	Verb	Ergänzung temporal/lokal/modal
sein	*Sein Geburtstag*	*ist*	*am 1. August.*
bleiben	*Ihr*	*bleibt*	*zu Hause?*
werden	*Er*	*wird*	*berühmt.*

Liste der wichtigsten Verben und ihrer Ergänzungen s. Seite 193-197,
Verben mit Präpositionen s. Seite 203-206

6

1 Prädikatsnominativ (N), Akkusativ (A), Dativ (D) oder Genitiv (G)? – Identifizieren Sie den Kasus der Ergänzungen.

N	A	D	G	
	✗			Ich sehe heute meinen Cousin zum ersten Mal.
				Warum folgt dir dieser Kerl eigentlich?
				Peter wird nie ein guter Tennisspieler.
				Du hast mir die Geschichte schon dreimal erzählt!
				Die Polizei verdächtigte meinen Nachbarn des Mordes.

2 Was passt zusammen? Nehmen Sie, wenn nötig, die Liste auf S. 193 zu Hilfe.

a) Thomas hat   mir heute nichts.
b) Es gelingt   mein Problem.
c) Leihst du   mir dein Auto?
d) Er kennt   großen Hunger.
e) Ich danke   dir für die Hilfe.

f) Er ist   ein fairer Spieler.
g) Du wirst   nett zu sein.
h) Man überführte   dir kein Wort.
i) Ich glaube   mich des Betrugs.
j) Er scheint   immer fauler.

3 Meine Freunde – Setzen Sie die Ergänzung im richtigen Kasus ein.

MICHELLE ist wie (a) ....ich........ (ich), denn auch (b) .... (sie) schmeckt alles, was (c) .... (wir Frauen) dick macht. Und: Sie sagt (d) .... (jeder) deutlich (e) .... (ihre Meinung).
SONJA ist und bleibt (f) .... (ein ewiger Problemfall). Denn (g) .... (diese Frau) misslingt alles, was sie anpackt. Trotzdem: Ich vertraue (h) .... (kein Mensch) so wie (i) .... (sie). Denn es gibt kaum (j) .... (ein Mensch), der (k) .... (andere) so gut zuhören kann.
(l) .... (Mein Freund) ERIK gehört seit zwei Jahren eine Internet-Firma. Seitdem hat er (m) .... (kein ruhiger Moment) mehr. Wegen seiner Arbeit hat er fast alle (n) .... (private Kontakte) verloren. Nur noch zu Weihnachten schreibt er (o) .... (seine alten Freunde) (p) .... (ein Gruß). Neulich bin ich (q) .... (er) zufällig auf einer Party begegnet, und er hat (r) .... (ich) erzählt, dass das Finanzamt versucht, (s) .... (er) (t) .... (der Steuerbetrug) zu überführen – wie er es im schönsten Juristen-Deutsch formuliert hat.

4 Gaunereien – Formulieren Sie Sätze.

a) ein Gaunerstück I beschäftigen I das Münchner Oberlandesgericht
 Ein Gaunerstück beschäftigt das Münchner Oberlandesgericht.
b) ein langjähriger Mitarbeiter der Spionageabwehr BND I verkaufen (Perf.) I der Dienst I von 1990 bis 1995 I dessen eigene geheime Informationen
c) als „Nachrichtenquelle" I auftreten (Prät.) I ein ehemaliger Kollege
d) der 49-Jährige I zurückbezahlen müssen I jetzt I der ergaunerte Agentenlohn
e) die Aufklärung I dauern (Prät.) I Monate • und I bedürfen (Prät.) I die Hilfe polnischer Kollegen
f) das Duo I anbieten (Plusq.) I seine Informationen I auch der polnische Geheimdienst
g) dieser I informieren (Prät.) I die Münchner Kollegen
h) so I gelingen (Prät.) I die deutschen Justizbehörden • die guten Geschäfte der beiden I ein Ende zu bereiten

VERBEN MIT PRÄPOSITIONEN

Max denkt gern an seinen Urlaub.

Viele Verben haben nicht (nur) eine Akkusativ-Ergänzung oder eine Dativ-Ergänzung, sondern (zusätzlich) eine Präpositional-Ergänzung. Es hängt von der Präposition ab, in welchem Kasus das Nomen steht.

ⓐ Verben mit Präpositionen + Akkusativ
auf, für, gegen, über, um

	auf	Akkusativ
Ich *antworte* **ihm**	*auf*	*seine letzte E-Mail.*
Die Kinder *freuen sich*	*auf*	*die großen Ferien.*

ⓑ Verben mit Präpositionen + Dativ
aus, bei, mit, nach, unter, von, vor, zu

	aus	Dativ
Dieses Haus *besteht*	*aus*	*Holz und Glas.*
Das Buch *wurde*	*aus*	*dem Englischen übersetzt.*

ⓒ Verben mit Präpositionen + Akkusativ/Dativ
an, in

	an	Akkusativ
Tom *denkt* **ständig**	*an*	*seinen nächsten Urlaub.*

	an	Dativ
Heinz *arbeitet* **seit Jahren**	*an*	*seiner Dissertation.*

ⓓ Verben mit *als* + Gleichsetzungskasus

Nominativ		*als*	Nominativ
Er	*arbeitet*	*als*	*Ingenieur beim Öko-Institut.*

	Akkusativ	*als*	Akkusativ
Man *bezeichnet*	**ihn**	*als*	*ausgezeichneten Spezialisten.*

ⓔ Manche Verben können mehrere Präpositionen (gleichzeitig) haben:

Er spricht *mit seiner Kollegin immer nur* über *das Wetter.*

Es ist erst November, aber die Kinder freuen sich *schon* auf *Weihnachten.*
Bernd freut sich *über den Brief, den er von seiner Freundin bekommen hat.*

Liste der wichtigsten Verben mit Präpositionen **s. Seite 203-206**

1 Studiengang „Interkulturelle Kommunikation" – Unterstreichen Sie die zu den Verben gehörenden Präpositionen und tragen Sie sie in die Liste ein.

In diesem Studium *geht es* hauptsächlich <u>um</u> die Kommunikation zwischen Menschen aus verschiedenen Kulturkreisen. Videoaufzeichnungen *helfen* bei der Analyse von Gesprächen und nonverbalen Signalen, und die Studenten *denken* gemeinsam über mögliche Strategien *nach*, um Kommunikationsschwierigkeiten zu vermeiden. So *gelten* die Finnen in Deutschland nur deshalb als Schweiger, weil wir sie nicht zu Wort kommen lassen. Südeuropäer *freuen sich* über körperliche Nähe und *empfinden* die Deutschen als sehr distanzierte Gesprächspartner. Und in Japan sollte man an Folgendes *denken*: Wer *sich* dort mit Geschäftspartnern zum Mittagessen *trifft*, sollte sich beim Essen nicht laut die Nase putzen, denn das *gilt* als grobe Unhöflichkeit.

um	bei	über	als	an	mit
es geht um					

2 Studenten sprechen über Deutschland – Ergänzen Sie die Präpositionen.

„(a) *An* das dauernde Händeschütteln kann ich mich einfach nicht gewöhnen", sagt Ai Kohatsu aus Japan. Und sie sehnt sich (b) da...................... , endlich einmal wieder wirklich frischen Fisch zu essen.

„Am Anfang habe ich mich (c) .... Stress, Stau und Verkehr geärgert", sagt Rafaela Rodriguez aus Ecuador. Aber inzwischen interessiert sie sich mehr (d) .... die neuen Leute, die sie kennengelernt hat.

„Deutsche gelten im technischen Bereich (e) .... Pragmatiker", sagt Jorge Gómez aus Spanien. Er wundert sich nur etwas (f) .... einige deutsche Gewohnheiten. „Hier gibt es Leute, die schon zum Mittagessen Bier trinken."

3 Einmal Urlaub machen – Ergänzen Sie – wo nötig – die Präpositionen und die Endungen.

Im letzten Frühjahr hatte Lisa sehr viel zu tun, sie musste in kurzer Zeit ein Buch (a) *aus* d*em* Russischen (b) .... Deutsche übersetzen. Als sie damit fertig war, war sie völlig erschöpft. Alle rieten ihr: Mach mal Urlaub und erhol dich (c) .... d................ Stress. Schließlich hatten sie Lisa (d) da................ überzeugt, dass sie wirklich eine Pause machen musste. Sie ging also in ein Reisebüro und informierte sich (e) .... mögliche Urlaubsziele. Zu Hause dachte sie (f) .... d................ verschiedenen Angebote nach und entschied sich (g) .... ein................ kleines Hotel in Süditalien – sie träumte schon (h) .... Sonne, Meer und Strand. Sie würde sich (i) .... frisch................ Fisch und Salat ernähren, abends würde sie Wein trinken, und vielleicht würde sie sich sogar (j) .... ein................ Italiener verlieben – wer weiß? Bei diesem Gedanken musste Lisa (k) .... sich selbst lachen, denn sie war glücklich verheiratet und hatte schon vier Enkelkinder.

91

REFLEXIVE VERBEN

Ich wasche mich. Ich wasche mir die Hände.

1 Funktion

Es gibt in der deutschen Sprache Verben, die immer reflexiv sind, und es gibt Verben, die reflexiv sein können:

reflexiv	*Gestern hat sich hier ein schwerer Unfall ereignet.*	ohne spezielle
	Ich habe mich um eine neue Stelle beworben.	Bedeutung
teil-reflexiv	*Ich habe gehört, die Müllers bauen sich ein Haus.*	„für sich selbst"
	Die beiden streiten sich ja schon wieder.	„miteinander"
	Er mag sie nicht, sie mag ihn nicht. – Sie mögen sich nicht.	„wechselseitig"*

* Manche Verben mit Präposition können eine wechselseitige Beziehung ausdrücken, ohne selbst reflexiv zu sein: *Die beiden Löwen kämpften miteinander.*

Liste der wichtigsten Verben mit Präpositionen  **s. Seite 203-206**

2 Formen

Dativ und Akkusativ unterscheiden sich nur in der 1. und 2. Person Singular:

	Akkusativ	Dativ		Akkusativ = Dativ
ich	*mich*	*mir*	*wir*	*uns*
du	*dich*	*dir*	*ihr*	*euch*
er/sie/es	*sich*		*sie*	*sich*

Normalerweise steht das Reflexivpronomen im Akkusativ:
Ich wasche mich.

Wenn es bereits eine Akkusativ-Ergänzung oder einen *dass*-Satz/Infinitivsatz in dieser Funktion gibt, steht das Reflexivpronomen im Dativ:
Ich wasche mir die Hände.
Du bildest dir wohl ein, dass dein Arbeitsplatz sicher ist?

3 Satzstrukturen

Hauptsatz	*Jens kämmt sich die Haare selten.*	nach dem konjugierten Verb
	Er kämmt sie sich eigentlich nie.	nach dem Personalpronomen
Nebensatz	*Ich glaube, dass sich Max gut amüsiert.*	nach dem Konnektor*
Infinitiv mit *zu*	*Es ist sehr mühsam, sich auf diese Prüfung vorzubereiten.*	auf Position 1

* auch möglich:
Ich glaube, dass Max sich gut amüsiert hat.  **s. auch Seite 134** (Mittelfeld)

1 Aus Erfahrung wird man klug – Steht das Reflexivpronomen im Akkusativ (A) oder Dativ (D)? Kreuzen Sie an.

A	D	
✗		a) Vor jedem Sonnenbad sollte man sich gut eincremen.
		b) Ich habe mir im Urlaub leider einen ziemlichen Sonnenbrand geholt.
		c) Erst nach einer Woche hat sich meine Haut wieder erholt.
		d) Ich lege mich seitdem kaum noch in die Sonne.
		e) Und wenn doch, dann setze ich mir immer eine Mütze auf.

2 Partyromanze – Ergänzen Sie die Reflexivpronomen bzw. –einander.

Es war auf einer dieser Medien-Partys, als (a) *sich* Karin und Jack, der stadtbekannte Frauenheld und Angeber, zum ersten Mal begegneten. Sie unterhielten (b) .... über Filme und sprachen den ganzen Abend nur (c) mit...................... . „Ich sehe (d) .... am liebsten Experimentalfilme an", äußerte (e) .... Jack bedeutungsvoll, „vor allem die aus den späten 60ern." Er war zufrieden, als er ihren bewundernden Blick sah. „Und du, was siehst du (f) .... am liebsten an?" Vor dieser Frage hatte sie (g) .... schon gefürchtet. „Ich liebe auch Experimentalfilme", log sie, „ich beschäftige (h) .... besonders mit Filmen aus den frühen 70ern." – „Du machst (i) .... wohl über mich lustig?", dachte Jack, sagte aber: „Super! Wir könnten (j) .... ja mal im „Cineasmodrom" treffen, um (k) .... welche anzuschauen." Bei diesen Worten berührten (l) .... zufällig ihre Hände, und sie verliebten (m) .... – vor allem sie (n) .... in ihn. Arme Karin!

3 Trennungsberatung – Formulieren Sie Sätze mit den angegebenen Verben und den passenden Reflexivpronomen.

a) (streiten) Sie oft mit ihrem Partner?
   Streiten Sie sich oft mit ihrem Partner?
b) (überlegen) Sie manchmal, (trennen) von ihm?
c) Aber Sie (fürchten) vor dem Alleinsein?
d) Dann (kaufen + sollten) Sie auf jeden Fall unseren Ratgeber „ex". Sie finden dort 1000 Tipps, wie Sie (gewöhnen) an ein Leben ohne „sie" oder „ihn".
e) Am besten, Sie (besorgen) das Buch noch heute, um auf das Leben von morgen (vorbereiten).

4 Erziehung zur Selbstständigkeit – Formulieren Sie Sätze im Imperativ.

a) Meine Nase läuft. (sich die Nase putzen)
   Dann putz dir doch die Nase!
b) Meine Haare sind ganz unordentlich. (sich die Haare kämmen)
c) Der Pullover ist mir viel zu warm. (sich den Pullover ausziehen)
d) Meine Hände sind ganz dreckig. (sich die Hände waschen)
e) In der Zeitung wird ein ganz billiges Fahrrad angeboten. (sich das Fahrrad kaufen)
f) Unsere Tennisschläger sind noch im Keller. (sich die Tennisschläger raufholen)

5 Formulieren Sie die Sätze aus Übung 4 mit Personalpronomen.

a) *Dann putz sie dir doch.*

MODALVERBEN (1)

Ich kann schon, darf aber nicht.

1 Funktion

a können

*Der kleine Max kann schon drei Wörter sagen.**	Fähigkeit
Man kann hier tolle Pullover kaufen.	Möglichkeit/Gelegenheit
Du kannst mein Auto nehmen / nicht nehmen.	Erlaubnis/Verbot
Könnten Sie mir bitte die Flasche reichen?	Bitte
Kann/Könnte ich Ihnen heute Abend die Stadt zeigen?	Vorschlag

* in der gesprochenen Sprache oft auch: *Der kleine Max kann schon drei Wörter.*

b dürfen

Du darfst mein Auto nehmen / nicht nehmen.	Erlaubnis/Verbot
Darf/Dürfte ich Sie um einen Gefallen bitten?	Bitte
Darf/Dürfte ich eine Frage stellen?	
Darf/Dürfte ich Ihnen heute Abend die Stadt zeigen?	Vorschlag

Bei der Funktion „Erlaubnis/Verbot" betont *dürfen* stärker als *können* ein
Hierarchieverhältnis: **Ich** bin die entscheidende Instanz, die erlaubt oder verbietet. Bei den
Funktionen „Bitte" und „Vorschlag" wirkt *dürfen* formeller.

Formen s. Tabelle **Seite 192**

2 Alternativen

Er kann diese Arbeit allein tun.	*Er ist*	*fähig, in der Lage, geeignet,*	*diese Arbeit allein zu tun.*	Fähigkeit
Sie kann mit dem neuen Job sofort beginnen.	*Sie hat die*	*Gelegenheit, Möglichkeit, Chance,*	*mit dem neuen Job sofort zu beginnen.*	Möglichkeit/ Gelegenheit
Sie kann/darf hier parken.	*Sie hat das*	*Recht, die Erlaubnis, die Genehmigung,*	*hier zu parken.*	Erlaubnis
Man darf/kann in diesem Gebäude nicht rauchen.	*Es ist*	*verboten, untersagt, nicht erlaubt,*	*hier zu rauchen.*	Verbot
Kannst/Könntest du mir beim Kochen helfen?	*Wärst du so lieb, mir beim Kochen zu helfen? Hilfst du mir beim Kochen?*			Bitte
Kann/Darf ich Ihnen noch einen Kaffee anbieten?	*Möchten Sie vielleicht noch einen Kaffee?*			Vorschlag

__1__ Kindheitserinnerungen – Ergänzen Sie dürfen im Präteritum.

Als Kind (a) *durfte* ich jeden Nachmittag spielen. Du dagegen (b) .... nur am Wochenende mit anderen Kindern zusammen sein. Am schlimmsten war es bei Karin. Sie (c) .... weder fernsehen noch ins Kino gehen. Ihr dagegen, Alex und Vivi, (d) .... bei euren Eltern alles machen. – Stimmt. Wir (e) .... alles tun, was nicht gefährlich war. Unsere Eltern erlaubten uns alles, was sie in ihrer Kindheit nicht (f) ....

__2__ Studentengespräche – Ergänzen Sie können oder dürfen. Manchmal sind auch zwei Lösungen möglich.

a) Professor Huber *kann* erst nächste Woche mit seinen Veranstaltungen beginnen.
b) Du .... nur dann einen Platz in seinem Seminar bekommen, wenn du dich rechtzeitig angemeldet hast.
c) Außerdem .... man nur teilnehmen, wenn man einen Aufnahmetest besteht.
d) Am Ende des Semesters .... du entweder eine Seminararbeit oder eine Klausur schreiben.
e) Wer erfolgreich ist, ... später an einem Fortsetzungsseminar teilnehmen.
f) Wenn du willst, ... ich dir beim Ausfüllen des Fragebogens helfen.
g) Super! Vielleicht .... wir uns morgen Mittag in der Mensa treffen?
h) Prima Idee! Aber jetzt muss ich schnell in das Hauptseminar von meinem Germanistikprofessor. Bei dem .... man keine Minute zu spät kommen!

__3__ Peterchen, das Wunderkind – Formulieren Sie Sätze mit können oder dürfen.

a) Im Alter von sechs Monaten war er schon fähig, „Mama" zu sagen.
   Im Alter von sechs Monaten konnte er schon „Mama" sagen.
b) Nach weiteren *sechs* Monaten hatten wir die Gelegenheit, die ersten Gespräche mit ihm zu führen. Du hattest in diesem Alter nur eine Fähigkeit: Schreien.
c) Mit vier Jahren bekam er die Sondergenehmigung, die Schule zu besuchen.
d) Als Peterchen fünf war, war er bereits in der Lage, sich mit euch über Aktien zu unterhalten.
e) In der Schule hatten die Lehrer kaum eine Chance, ihm etwas beizubringen.
f) Und er war so höflich. Wenn Besuch kam, fragte er sofort: Möchten Sie vielleicht ein Stück Kuchen?
g) Es war allerdings verboten, ihn zu berühren: Er biss sofort zu.

__4__ Eine Brieffreundschaft – Ergänzen Sie die Alternativen zu können und dürfen.

⟨ Recht I ~~in der Lage~~ I Möglichkeit I erlauben I verbieten I fähig I untersagen I

Liebe Erika!

Leider konnte ich Dir nicht früher antworten – ich war zeitlich einfach nicht (a) in der Lage dazu. Stell Dir vor, unser Chef hat uns (b) .... , während der Arbeit privat zu telefonieren. Ich könnte mir vorstellen, er ist dazu (c) .... , das auch zu kontrollieren. Früher hat er uns (d) .... , wenigstens ein paar private Anrufe zu machen. Ich jedenfalls finde, jeder hat das (e) .... auf ein bisschen Privatleben auch im Büro. Wenigstens habe ich noch die (f) .... , Dir vom Büro aus zu schreiben. Das lasse ich mir nicht auch noch (g) .... !

MODALVERBEN (2)

Ich muss und soll, will aber nicht.

1 Funktion

	Notwendigkeit durch ...
Der Reifen ist kaputt. Du musst einen neuen kaufen.	... äußere Umstände
Sie müssen die Gebühren bis Ende des Monats zahlen.	... Autoritäten
Ich muss mich wieder mehr um meinen Hund kümmern. *Ich müsste mal wieder meiner Tante schreiben.*	... innere Verpflichtung (abgeschwächt)
Herr Becker hat angerufen. Sie sollen zurückrufen. *Ihr sollt euer Zimmer endlich aufräumen.* *Unsere Tochter soll reich heiraten.*	Erwartung an eine andere Person/Aufforderung
Mit dem Husten sollten* Sie besser zum Arzt (gehen). *Ich sollte* mehr Sport treiben.*	Rat/Empfehlung
Hier soll ein neues Krankenhaus entstehen.	unpersönlicher Plan
Die Stadt will hier ein neues Krankenhaus bauen. *Ich will im nächsten Urlaub nach Portugal fahren.*	Plan/Absicht

* Konjunktiv II

Formen s. Tabelle 📖 **Seite 192**

2 Alternativen

Das Geld ist weg, *wir müssen sparen.*	*Es ist leider notwendig/erforderlich, dass* *wir sparen.* *Es bleibt uns nichts anderes übrig, als zu sparen.* *Wir sind gezwungen zu sparen.*	Notwendigkeit
Ich musste dem *Verletzten helfen.*	*Ich war verpflichtet, dem Verletzten zu helfen.*	
Er muss noch viel tun.	*Er hat noch viel zu tun.*	
Du musst nicht rennen.	*Du brauchst* nicht zu rennen.*	negativ einschränkend
Ich muss nur/bloß *noch 10 Minuten* *arbeiten.*	*Ich brauche* nur/bloß noch 10 Minuten zu* *arbeiten.*	
Sie sollen ihm das *Geld bis morgen* *zurückgeben.*	*Er erwartet / verlangt / fordert Sie auf, dass Sie* *ihm das Geld bis morgen zurückgeben.* *Geben Sie ihm das Geld bis morgen zurück!*	Erwartung/ Aufforderung
Du solltest öfter mal *zuhören.*	*Es ist ratsam/empfehlenswert, öfter mal* *zuzuhören.* *Es wäre besser, wenn du öfter mal* *zuhören würdest.*	Rat/ Empfehlung
Ich soll am Flughafen *abgeholt werden.*	*Es ist vorgesehen/geplant, dass ich am* *Flughafen abgeholt werde.*	unpersönlicher Plan
Er will das Haus *kaufen.*	*Er beabsichtigt / hat vor, das Haus zu kaufen.* (schwächer:) *Er möchte das Haus kaufen.*	Plan/Absicht

* *brauchen* + *zu* kann nur negativ oder einschränkend verwendet werden.

1 Notwendigkeit (N), Erwartung (E), Rat (R) oder Plan (P)? – Kreuzen Sie an.

N	E	R	P	
		X		a) Ihr solltet es mal mit Homöopathie versuchen.
				b) Wir mussten eine Woche in diesem lauten Hotel bleiben.
				c) Man will hier bis Herbst einen Kindergarten bauen.
				d) Wir sollen unsere Schulden bis Jahresende zurückzahlen.
				e) Du solltest dir diesen Film unbedingt ansehen.
				f) Wir müssen die Rechnung erst bei Lieferung bezahlen.

2 Szenen einer Ehe – Ergänzen Sie müssen und sollen. Manchmal gibt es zwei Lösungen.

■ Wir (a) *müssen* uns beeilen, das Taxi wartet.

■ Aber ich weiß doch noch gar nicht, was ich anziehen (b) .... Was meinst du? Vielleicht (c) .... ich doch besser das kurze grüne Kleid anziehen.

■ Du weißt genau, dass wir bei meinen Eltern immer pünktlich sein (d) ....

■ (e) .... du eigentlich in diesem Ton mit mir reden?

■ Um acht Uhr (f) .... wir da sein. Jetzt ist es schon fünf vor acht.

■ Hetz mich nicht, deine Mutter (g) .... sich freuen, dass ich überhaupt mitkomme!

■ Wir (h) .... jetzt los! Es (i) .... übrigens eine Überraschung zum Essen geben!

■ Oje, (j) .... das sein? Da hätten wir besser hier bei uns noch etwas gegessen.

3 Mutter ist die Beste – Ersetzen Sie müssen durch brauchen + zu und umgekehrt.

a) Der Wagen ist schon gewaschen. Ihr müsst ihn nicht mehr waschen.
   Ihr braucht ihn nicht mehr zu waschen.

b) Die Schuhe sind schon geputzt. Du brauchst sie nicht mehr zu putzen.
   Du musst sie nicht mehr putzen.

c) Die Blumen sind schon eingepflanzt. Paul muss sie nur noch gießen.

d) Die Einkaufstüten sind noch nicht ausgepackt. Ihr müsst sie nur noch auspacken.

e) Der Hund ist schon abgeholt. Eva braucht ihn bloß noch zu füttern.

f) Wir brauchen nicht essen zu gehen. Ich habe bereits gekocht.

g) Du musst den Kindern keine Geschichte vorlesen. Ich mache das schon.

4 Studenten vor der Prüfung – Bilden Sie Sätze mit sollen, müssen oder wollen.

a) Es ist besser, wenn ich mir während des Vortrags Notizen mache.
   Ich sollte mir während des Vortrags Notizen machen.

b) Man erwartet von mir, dass ich das Examen mit Bestnote mache.

c) Darum bin ich gezwungen, jeden Tag bis Mitternacht zu lernen.

d) Leider ist es notwendig, dass ich noch dreißig Bücher durchlese.

e) Mein Vater verlangt von mir, dass ich ab nächstem Jahr in seiner Firma arbeite.

f) Dann habe ich Tag für Tag zu tun, was der „alte Herr" sagt.

g) Er hat leider erst in 10 Jahren vor, sich aus der Firmenleitung zurückzuziehen.

h) Ich glaube, es wäre besser, wenn ich erst mal ein halbes Jahr verreise.

6

MODALVERBEN SUBJEKTIV (1)

Er soll der Dieb gewesen sein. Er will den Unfall gesehen haben.

_1_ Funktion

sollen:
Sebastian gibt nur wieder, was andere über Max behaupten. Er selbst ist nicht sicher, ob diese Information stimmt.

wollen:
Sebastian gibt wieder, was Max von sich selbst behauptet. Ob diese Behauptung stimmt, ist eine ganz andere Frage.

_2_ Formen

		Modalverb		Infinitiv
Gegenwart	*Jan*	*soll*	*zehn Fremdsprachen*	*beherrschen.*
	Jan	*will*	*zehn Fremdsprachen*	*beherrschen.*

		Modalverb		Infinitiv Perfekt
Vergangenheit	*Katja*	*soll*	*die Katze*	*gerettet haben.*
	Katja	*will*	*die beste Tänzerin*	*gewesen sein.*

Ob *sollen* und *wollen* subjektive oder objektive Bedeutung haben, hängt im Präsens vom Kontext ab:

Jan soll zehn Fremdsprachen beherrschen.	a) objektive Bedeutung*: Jans Eltern wollen das. b) subjektive Bedeutung: Man behauptet das über ihn.
Jan will zehn Fremdsprachen beherrschen.	a) objektive Bedeutung*: Das ist Jans Ziel. b) subjektive Bedeutung: Jan behauptet das über sich selbst.

* s. Seite 96

In der Vergangenheit sieht man den Bedeutungsunterschied bereits an der Form:
objektiv: *Max sollte zehn Fremdsprachen beherrschen.*
subjektiv: *Max soll zehn Fremdsprachen beherrscht haben.*

_3_ Alternativen

sollen	*Es heißt / Man sagt/behauptet/erzählt, dass er den Wagen gestohlen hat.* *Angeblich / Gerüchten zufolge hat er den Wagen gestohlen.*
wollen	*Er behauptet, / Er sagt von sich, / Er versichert, dass er die Frau nicht überfallen hat.*

1 Diese Müllers! – Wo behaupten andere etwas über die Müllers (1) und wo behaupten die Müllers selbst etwas über sich (2)?

	1	2
a) Die Müllers sollen sich ein Haus gekauft haben.	X	
b) Sie sollen das Haus bar bezahlt haben.		
c) Sie wollen im Lotto gewonnen haben.		
d) Herr Müller soll unsaubere Geschäfte machen.		
e) Er soll deswegen sogar schon im Gefängnis gewesen sein.		
f) Herr Müller will während dieser Zeit im Ausland gewesen sein.		

2 Der Angeber – Ergänzen Sie wollen oder sollen.
a) Hast du schon gehört? Der neue Kollege *soll* in Harvard studiert haben.
b) Er .... der Beste in seiner Klasse gewesen sein. Wenigstens behauptet er es.
c) Er .... das Studium in Rekordzeit beendet haben. So wird über ihn erzählt.
d) Man .... ihm anschließend ein Promotionsstipendium angeboten haben.
e) Er .... seine Diplomarbeit in nur drei Monaten geschrieben haben. Das erzählt er jedem.
f) Er .... seine Karriere schon ab dem zweiten Semester vorbereitet haben. So sagt man.
g) Schon jetzt .... er der Liebling vom Chef sein. Das habe ich in der Kantine gehört.
h) Er .... seinem Chef schon viele Verbesserungen vorgeschlagen haben. So ein Angeber!

3 Steuergerüchte – Formulieren Sie die Sätze mit wollen und sollen.
a) Es wird berichtet, dass die Mehrwertsteuer bald schon wieder erhöht wird.
Die Mehrwertsteuer soll bald schon wieder erhöht werden.
b) Das Nachrichtenmagazin „Fakten" behauptet, als erstes Presseorgan davon erfahren zu haben.
c) Es heißt, dass es innerhalb der Regierung noch Differenzen über den Zeitpunkt gibt.
d) Angeblich ist der Wirtschaftsminister gegen eine sofortige Erhöhung.
e) Der Finanzminister versichert, alle Alternativen geprüft zu haben.
f) Gerüchten zufolge beträgt die Erhöhung nur 1,5 Prozent.

4 Berufsrisiko! – Ersetzen Sie wollen und sollen durch Alternativen mit derselben Bedeutung.
Der weltberühmte Pilzforscher A. Helliwell soll an einem Pilz-Omelett gestorben sein (angeblich). Seit seinem sechsten Lebensjahr soll er sich für Pilze interessiert haben (Man berichtet, dass ...). In seiner Jugend soll er ein Einzelgänger gewesen sein (Es heißt, dass ...). Schon mit 18 will er Deutschlands Pilzexperte Nr. 1 gewesen sein (Er behauptete, dass ...). Auf einem internationalen Pilzkongress soll er seine spätere Frau Charlotte kennengelernt haben (Gerüchten zufolge ...). Sie will große Teile ihres Vermögens für die Rettung gefährdeter Pilzarten ausgegeben haben (Sie versichert, dass ...).

Der weltberühmte Pilzforscher A. Helliwell ist angeblich an einem Pilzomelett gestorben. ...

6

MODALVERBEN SUBJEKTIV (2)

Das muss / dürfte / könnte Hans sein.

1 Funktion

Das muss doch Hans sein. Und das kann nur Eva sein.

Du müsstest eigentlich Peter sein. Und du dürftest seine Frau sein.

Der dort drüben könnte unser Mathelehrer sein.

Auf einem Klassentreffen nach 30 Jahren sehen die meisten ganz anders aus als früher. Deshalb ist häufig nur zu vermuten, wer welcher ehemalige Mitschüler oder Lehrer ist. **Vermutungen** kann man im Deutschen mit Modalverben ausdrücken. Welches man nimmt, hängt von der Sicherheit der Vermutung ab:

100 % absolut sicher	90 % fast sicher	75 % wahrscheinlich	50 % möglich
muss *kann nur / kann nicht*	*müsste* *müsste eigentlich*	*dürfte*	*könnte*

2 Formen

		Modalverb		Infinitiv
Gegenwart	*Das*	*dürfte*	*mein Sportlehrer*	*sein.*
	Er	*muss*	*eine Menge Geld*	*verdienen.*

		Modalverb		Infinitiv Perfekt
Vergangenheit	*Das*	*dürfte*	*mein Sportlehrer*	*gewesen sein.*
	Er	*muss*	*eine Menge Geld*	*verdient haben.*

Die „objektive" oder „subjektive" Bedeutung von *müssen* hängt im Präsens vom Kontext ab:
Er muss viel Geld verdienen.
objektiv: *Er hat eine große Familie zu ernähren. Er ist gezwungen, viel Geld zu verdienen.*
subjektiv: *Er ist ein sehr erfolgreicher Fernsehstar. Ich bin sicher, dass er viel Geld verdient.*

In der Vergangenheit sieht man den Bedeutungsunterschied bereits an der Form:
objektiv: *Er musste viel Geld verdienen. / Er hat viel Geld verdienen müssen.*
subjektiv: *Er muss viel Geld verdient haben.*

3 Alternativen

100 %	*Mit Sicherheit / Bestimmt / Zweifellos hat Max diesen Witz erzählt.* *Ich bin (mir) (ganz) sicher, dass Max diesen Witz erzählt hat.*
90 %	*Ich bin (mir) fast sicher, / Es ist so gut wie sicher, dass Max diesen Witz erzählt hat.*
75 %	*Wahrscheinlich/Vermutlich hat Max diesen Witz erzählt.* *Ich vermute, / Ich nehme an, dass Max diesen Witz erzählt hat.* *Diesen Witz wird wohl Max erzählt haben.* Seite 84
50 %	*Möglicherweise/Vielleicht hat Max diesen Witz erzählt.* *Es ist denkbar, / Ich halte es für möglich, dass Max diesen Witz erzählt hat.*

1 Wie sicher ist sich Alexander: 100 %, 90 %, 75 % oder 50 %? Kreuzen Sie an.

	100%	90%	75%	50%
a) Franz muss krank sein.	✗			
b) Er könnte sich überarbeitet haben.				
c) Der neue Chef dürfte so um die 50 sein.				
d) Das kann ihr nur Manfred erzählt haben.				
e) Er müsste jetzt schon verreist sein.				

2 Auf Schlüsselsuche – Ergänzen Sie die Modalverben.

■ Jemand (a) *muss* meine Autoschlüssel weggenommen haben. Da bin ich mir absolut sicher.

■ Es gibt ja auch noch andere Möglichkeiten. Du (b) .... sie im Büro vergessen haben.

■ Das (c) .... nicht sein. Ich weiß genau, dass ich sie auf den Tisch gelegt habe.

■ Dann (d) .... sie nur wieder in einem deiner 1000 Mäntel stecken, wie das letzte Mal.

■ Wer ruft denn da schon wieder an?

■ Das (e) .... Norbert sein. Ich bin mir sicher.

■ Er soll den Ersatzschlüssel mitbringen. Er (f) .... eigentlich noch einen haben.

3 Hobbykriminologen – Formulieren Sie die Sätze mit Modalverben.

„Der Gärtner war zweifel-los der Mörder."

„Kein anderer hatte die Möglichkeit, dieses Verbrechen zu begehen."

„Das Motiv war vermutlich Geldgier."

„Vielleicht hat aber auch Eifersucht eine Rolle gespielt."

„Man nimmt an, dass auch der Chauffeur beteiligt war."

„Es ist so gut wie sicher, dass der Fall bald abgeschlossen ist."

Der Gärtner muss der Mörder gewesen sein.

4 Jugendliche am Matterhorn verunglückt – Ersetzen Sie die Modalverben durch Alternativen.

Leichtsinn und mangelhafte Vorbereitung dürften der Grund gewesen sein, warum vier Jugendliche am Matterhorn tödlich verunglückt sind (vermutlich). Diese müssen nach Ansicht der Rettungsmannschaft bei Nebel vom richtigen Weg abgekommen sein (überzeugt sein). Zu diesem Zeitpunkt dürfte es bereits dunkel gewesen sein (wahrscheinlich). Dabei könnten einige der Jugendlichen in Panik geraten sein (möglicherweise). Es kann sich bei ihnen nur um völlige Anfänger gehandelt haben (mit Sicherheit). Die Schweizer Behörden: Sie müssen aus Sparsamkeitsgründen auf einen Bergführer verzichtet haben (bestimmt).

Leichtsinn und mangelhafte Vorbereitung waren vermutlich der Grund, warum vier Jugendliche am Matterhorn tödlich verunglückt sind.

6

KENNEN – WISSEN – KÖNNEN • MÖGEN – GEFALLEN ...

Kennst du den Mann?
Gefällt dir das Haus?

Kannst du gut Japanisch?

ⓐ *kennen – wissen – können*

Na ja, „gut" ist übertrieben.
Aber ich kenne mittlerweile
viele Schriftzeichen und weiß,
wie die wichtigsten Regeln
funktionieren.

kennen (kannte/ hat gekannt)	Ich *kenne* Frau Sakurai gut. Ich *kenne* die japanische Küche.	+ AKK	Information durch eigene Erfahrung (Personen/Sachen)
wissen (weiß/wusste/ hat gewusst)	Ich *weiß,* dass die japanische Küche sehr fettarm ist.	+ Nebensatz	Information durch Kenntnisse (Tatsachen)
	Ich *weiß** den Weg / die Antwort / eine Lösung / einen guten Arzt.	+ AKK	
	Sie *weiß* alles über uns. Was *wissen* Sie über dieses Projekt?	+ über (+ AKK)	detaillierte Information
	Wussten Sie von diesem Projekt?	+ von (+ DAT)	vage Information
können (konnte/ hat ... können)	Ich *kann* fließend Japanisch.** Ich *kann* japanisch kochen. Sie *können* mich abends anrufen.	+ Infinitiv	Fähigkeit/ Möglichkeit

* Hier ist auch *kennen* möglich. **Das Verb *sprechen* fällt oft weg.

ⓑ *mögen – gefallen – schmecken – lieben – gern(e) haben – gern(e) machen / tun*

mögen (mochte/ hat gemocht)	*Magst du Hunde? – Nein, ich* mag *Hunde überhaupt nicht.*	+ AKK	Zustimmung/ Sympathie
möchte* (= Kon- junktiv II)	Ich *möchte* ein Eis.		höfliche Umschrei- bung von *ich will*
gefallen (gefällt/gefiel/ hat gefallen)	Es *gefällt* mir, wie er seine Kinder erzieht. Dieses Kleid *gefällt* mir sehr.	+ DAT	etwas/jemanden gut/ schön finden (nicht für Essen und Trinken)
schmecken	Mir *schmeckt* diese Suppe.		ein Essen oder Ge- tränk gut finden
lieben	Er *liebte* seine Frau. Aber er *liebte* auch seine Freiheit.	+ AKK	etwas/jemanden außer- gewöhnlich mögen
gern(e)/lieber/ am liebsten haben	Ich *habe* sie sehr *gern,* lieber übrigens als ihre Schwester.		= *mögen*
gern(e)/lieber/ am liebsten machen/tun	Was machst du in deiner Freizeit *am liebsten? Treibst du* gern *Sport* *oder bist du* lieber *einfach nur faul?*		eine Aktivität mögen

* nur im Präsens (im Präteritum: *ich wollte*)

1 Urlaubsbekanntschaften – Wurden in den folgenden Sätzen kennen, wissen und können richtig verwendet? Korrigieren Sie, wo nötig.

Location:	What's Related

Korrektur

Lieber Alex,

<u>kennst</u> Du noch, wer ich bin? Es ist ja schon lange her, dass wir uns in Rom getroffen haben, und ich <u>kann</u> Dich ja kaum. Deshalb <u>weiß</u> ich nicht, ob es richtig ist, Dir diese E-Mail zu schicken. Aber ich <u>weiß</u> nur wenige Männer, mit denen ich mich gleich so gut unterhalten habe. <u>Kannst</u> Du Dich noch an unser kleines Café erinnern? Ich <u>weiß</u> mich genau an den Abend erinnern, als wir uns <u>kennen</u>gelernt haben. Vielleicht <u>kennst</u> Du mir ja mal antworten.

Ciao! Maria

P.S.: Wie findest Du mein Deutsch? Leider <u>weiß</u> ich immer noch nicht so genau zwischen können, kennen und wissen zu unterscheiden.

weißt

2 Wer weiß Bescheid? – Ergänzen Sie kennen, wissen oder können.

a) *Wissen* Sie, wie man nach der Arbeit am besten abschalten .... ? Ich .... jemanden, der alles, was ihm im Kopf herumgeht, auf einen Zettel schreibt und diesen dann feierlich verbrennt. .... Sie auch einen Trick?

b) Birgit .... (Prät.) nichts von Peters Plan, ein neues Auto zu kaufen. Wenn sie .... hätte, was er vorhat, hätte sie laut protestiert. Als der Wagen dann plötzlich vor der Haustür stand, ... sie nichts mehr daran ändern.

c) Was .... Sie über Goethe? .... Sie ein Theaterstück von ihm? Haben Sie .... , dass er Beamter war? Ich habe mal jemanden .... , der den halben „Faust" auswendig .... (Prät.).

3 Nachbarschaftshilfe – Ergänzen Sie die Verben.

gefallen (3x) I gern haben (2x) I lieben (2x) I mögen (2x) I schmecken I möchte

■ Wie (a) *gefällt* dir eigentlich dein neuer Nachbar?
■ Ein süßer Typ. Ich (b) .... ihn sehr. Ich war sogar schon zum Essen bei ihm.
■ Das ging aber schnell. Und – hat es dir (c) .... ?
■ Was? Ach so, das Essen. Ja, aber was mir besonders (d) .... hat, war seine sensible Art. Ich (e) .... es .... , wenn Männer zuhören können.
■ Oje, dann hast du wieder mal den ganzen Abend geredet. Nicht jeder Mann (f) .... das.
■ Nein ich glaube, er (g) .... mich ganz .... Er hat mir übrigens erzählt, dass er geschieden ist. Seine Frau hat nach acht Jahren plötzlich gemerkt, dass sie ihn nicht mehr (h) .... Sie hat jetzt einen anderen. Und weißt du, was? Er (i) .... es, durch Antiquitätenläden zu ziehen. Besonders (j) .... ihm alte japanische Möbel. Er (k) .... mit mir am Samstag auf die Antiquitätenmesse gehen. Ist das nicht süß?

LEGEN/LIEGEN • SETZEN/SITZEN

Ich lege das Buch auf den Tisch. Das Buch liegt auf dem Tisch.

1 Funktion

„Noch vor 5 Minuten stand das Rad neben der Haustür. Ich habe es selbst dorthin gestellt."

Handlung	Resultat
Sie setzt die Katze auf den Boden.	*Die Katze sitzt auf dem Boden.*
Paul stellt die Flasche in den Schrank.	*Die Flasche steht im Schrank.*
Er legt die Zeitung auf den Tisch.	*Die Zeitung liegt auf dem Tisch.*
Ich hänge das Regal an die Wand.	*Das Regal hängt an der Wand.*
Er steckt den Schlüssel ins Schloss.	*Der Schlüssel steckt im Schloss.*

2 Formen

regelmäßige Verben mit Akkusativ			unregelmäßige Verben, kein Akkusativ		
	Präteritum	Perfekt		Präteritum	Perfekt
setzen	*setzte*	*hat gesetzt*	*sitzen*	*saß*	*hat gesessen*
stellen	*stellte*	*hat gestellt*	*stehen*	*stand*	*hat gestanden*
legen	*legte*	*hat gelegt*	*liegen*	*lag*	*hat gelegen*
hängen	*hängte*	*hat gehängt*	*hängen*	*hing*	*hat gehangen*
Wohin? – Präposition + Akkusativ			*Wo?* – Präposition + Dativ		

Das Verb *stecken* ist mit und ohne Akkusativ regelmäßig:
Eva steckte sich eine Blume ins Haar. – In Evas Haar steckte eine Blume.

ÜBUNGEN

1 Wer macht was bzw. wer ist wo? – Verbinden Sie beide Teile.

Alex liegt	auf die Gartenbank.
Karin stellt den Blumenstrauß	in großen Schwierigkeiten.
Max hängt	an der Bushaltestelle.
Veronika steckt	auf der Wiese.
Christina legt sich	auf dem Barhocker.
Jürgen setzt sich	in die Jackentasche.
Felix hängt wie eine Spinne	den Mantel in den Schrank.
Georg sitzt	ins Bett.
Karl-Heinz steckt den Brief	an der Felswand.
Erich steht	auf den Tisch.

2 Formulieren Sie die Sätze aus Übung 1 im Präteritum und Perfekt.

Alex lag auf der Wiese.
Alex hat auf der Wiese gelegen.

3 Familienalltag – Ergänzen Sie die Verben und die Artikel.

⟨ liegen (2x) I legen I stecken (2x) I sitzen (2x) I setzen (3x) I hängen (2x) I stehen I stellen

a) ■ Sag mal, wo *liegt* eigentlich meine Brille? Ich habe sie eben erst auf ....
Schreibtisch ....
■ Dann wird sie da wohl immer noch .... – Aber nein, ich sehe gerade, du
hast dir .... Brille wieder mal auf........................... , ohne es zu merken.
■ In welcher Jacke .... denn der verdammte Ausweis schon wieder?
■ Du hast ihn doch gerade selbst in .... Hosentasche ....

b) ■ Ich glaub', ich muss mich einen Moment .... Der Weg ist so steil.
■ Das kommt davon, wenn man wie du den ganzen Tag im Büro ....
■ Das stimmt nicht. In der Mittagspause .... ich mich oft auf ....
Bank im Park nebenan.
■ Na, dann .... du ja schon wieder!

c) ■ Warum hast du denn den Vogelkäfig so hoch an .... Decke .... ?
■ Der alte Platz, wo er bisher .... (Prät.), hat mir nicht mehr gefallen.
■ Ich glaube, dem Vogel ist es am liebsten, sein Käfig .... auf einem Tisch.
■ Fein, dann .... ihn doch zu dir auf .... Schreibtisch.

4 Unordnung – Formulieren Sie Fragen und Antworten mit liegen, stehen, hängen,
stecken, sitzen.

Wo ist denn die Milch? – Die steht im Regal.

5 Formulieren Sie Fragen und Antworten wie in Übung 4, aber mit legen, stellen,
hängen, stecken und setzen.

Wohin hat er die Milch getan? – Die hat er ins Regal gestellt.

TRENNBARE VERBEN

abholen – Ich hole dich ab.

1 Funktion

kommen	Durch verschiedene Vorsilben ...
ankommen – am Bahnhof	... werden neue Verben gebildet.
auskommen – mit seinem Geld	... ändert sich die Bedeutung.
aufkommen – ein Wind kommt auf	
hinkommen – an ein Ziel	

2 Formen

trennbare Vorsilben, die Vorsilbe wird betont

Vorsilbe	Beispiel	Vorsilbe	Beispiel
ab	*abholen*	*los*	*loslassen*
an	*anfangen*	*mit*	*mitteilen*
auf	*aufhören*	*nach*	*nachsprechen*
aus	*ausgehen*	*über**	*überlaufen*
bei	*beibringen*	*unter**	*untergehen*
durch*	*durchsetzen*	*um**	*umschalten*
ein	*einziehen*	*vor*	*vorhaben*
entgegen	*entgegensetzen*	*weg*	*wegwerfen*
fest	*festhalten*	*weiter*	*weiterfahren*
fort	*fortgehen*	*wider**	*widerspiegeln*
gegenüber	*gegenüberstellen*	*zu*	*zulassen*
gleich	*gleichsetzen*	*zurück*	*zurücklassen*
her	*herkommen*	*zusammen*	*zusammensetzen*
hin	*hinfahren*	*u.a.*	

* auch als untrennbare Vorsilbe, **s. Seite 108**

3 Satzstrukturen

		Hauptsatz	
	Verb Teil 1		Verb Teil 2
Ich	*stehe*	*um 6 Uhr*	*auf.*
Ich	*stand*	*um 6 Uhr*	*auf.*
Ich	*bin*	*um 6 Uhr*	*aufgestanden.*

Hauptsatz	Nebensatz / Infinitivsatz			Hauptsatz
	Konnektor		Verb	
Ich bin todmüde,	*wenn*	*ich um 6 Uhr*	*aufstehe.*	
	Wenn	*ich um 6 Uhr*	*aufstehe,*	*bin ich todmüde.*
Ich habe vor,		*um 6 Uhr*	*aufzustehen.*	

1   Hausarbeit – Streichen Sie die Verben, deren Vorsilbe nicht trennbar ist.

a) das Putzmittel besorgen
b) den Abfall rausbringen
c) das Geschirr abräumen
d) den kaputten Socken wegwerfen
e) den Schmutz zusammenkehren
f) die Altkleider aussortieren
g) die Küche aufräumen
h) die Pflanzen versorgen
i) die Regale abstauben
j) die Schubladen ausräumen
k) die verbrauchten Batterien entsorgen

2   Was kann man alles machen? – Formulieren Sie höfliche Bitten. Mehrere Lösungen sind möglich.

ab- I an- I auf- I aus- I los- I mit- I weg- I zu-

a) bei unserem Spiel
b) das Seil / die Schnur
c) das Fenster
d) das Licht im Keller
e) das Preisschild von der neuen Hose
f) den Fleck am Ärmel
g) den Videorekorder
h) die Dose

a) *Bitte mach bei unserem Spiel mit.*

3   So eine Nervensäge! – Formulieren Sie Kurzdialoge.

diese Zeitschrift mal ausleihen I diese neue CD mal anhören I dein Handy mitnehmen I damit meine Mutter mal kurz anrufen I deinen Computer einschalten I deine neuen Rollerblades mal ausprobieren

ER: *Hast du was dagegen, wenn ich mir die Zeitschrift mal ausleihe?*
SIE: *Nein, leih sie dir ruhig aus.*

4   Mutter und Tochter – Formulieren Sie Kurzdialoge.

einen warmen Pulli anziehen I Milch einkaufen I mit den Hausaufgaben weitermachen (fertig machen) I mit dem Telefonieren aufhören (anfangen) I den Mülleimer raustragen

Mutter: *Zieh bitte einen warmen Pulli an.*
Tochter: *Aber ich habe doch schon einen angezogen.*

5   Bedeutungswandel – Welche Vorsilbe passt?

einsehen – absehen – aufsehen – zusehen	a) Er sah stundenlang nicht von seinem Buch *auf*.
	b) Er sieht nicht .... , dass er einen Fehler gemacht hat.
	c) Sie kann nicht ....sehen, wann sie fertig wird.
anbringen – beibringen – vorbringen – wegbringen	d) Bring doch bitte die leeren Flaschen ....
	e) Ich würde gerne eine Bitte ....bringen.
	f) Unsere Lehrerin bringt uns täglich etwas Neues ....
abschreiben – aufschreiben – ausschreiben – umschreiben	g) Ich bin seit einiger Zeit sehr vergesslich. Ich muss mir einfach alles ....schreiben.
	h) Peter versuchte, in der Prüfung bei seinem Nachbarn ....zuschreiben.
	i) Wir werden diese Stelle sofort neu ....schreiben.

UNTRENNBARE VERBEN

schreiben – beschreiben

1 Funktion

Bedeutungs- änderung	Ich schreibe dir eine Karte. Ich beschreibe dir den Weg. Dieser Vorschlag gefällt mir. Aber meinem Freund missfällt er.	Durch verschiedene Vorsilben … … werden neue Verben gebildet … ändert sich die Bedeutung
Struktur- änderung	Ich staune. Ich staune über dein Werk. Ich bestaune dein Werk.	Mit Vorsilbe brauchen einige Verben eine Akkusativ-Ergänzung.

2 Formen

Vorsilbe unbetont und nicht vom Verb trennbar	Beispiel	Vorsilbe trennbar und untrennbar	Beispiel untrennbar	Beispiel trennbar
be- emp- ent- er- ge- miss- ver- zer-	behandeln empfinden entschließen erklären gefallen missfallen verbessern zerreißen	durch über unter um wieder wider	durchqueren übertreiben untersuchen umfahren (= um die Stadt herumfahren) wiederholen (= noch einmal sagen) widersprechen	durchsetzen überlaufen untergehen umfahren (= den Baum umstoßen) wiederholen (= zurückholen) widerspiegeln

Bei manchen Verben existiert die Version ohne Vorsilbe nicht:
gewinnen – ~~winnen~~, verlieren – ~~lieren~~ …

3 Satzstrukturen

	Verb Teil 1		Verb Teil 2	
Siegfried	besiegt	den Drachen.		untrennbar
Siegfried	hat	den Drachen	besiegt.	
Der Schatz	ging	im Rhein	unter.	trennbar
Der Schatz	ist	im Rhein	untergegangen.	

ÜBUNGEN

1 Trennbar oder nicht? Formulieren Sie Sätze.

a) wir I garantieren I zu bearbeiten I den Antrag I zügig
Wir garantieren, den Antrag zügig zu bearbeiten.
b) wir I durchführen I die Reformen I zügig
c) wir I uns freuen I dass Sie gestern I unser Angebot annehmen
d) wir I erweitern I unser Angebot I baldmöglichst
e) wir I erhöhen I die Preise I im nächsten Jahr

2 Sorgen einer Gastgeberin – Welches Verb passt in den Satz?

beantworten/antworten I begrüßen/grüßen I bekämpfen/kämpfen I bemerken/merken I
benutzen/nutzen I beraten/raten I berichten/richten I beschließen/schließen I besitzen/sitzen I
bestehen/stehen I besuchen/suchen

Hallo Anna,

endlich komme ich dazu, Deinen Brief zu *(a)* beantworten. Bei mir gibt es einiges zu

(b) ....

Am vergangenen Sonntag haben mich Max, Vanessa und Michelle mit noch drei Freunden

(c) .... So eine Überraschung! Nachdem ich alle *(d)* ....

hatte, *(e)* .... ich, dass ich nur zwei Gläser habe. Du kennst doch meine

Studentenbude. Sollten wir wirklich aus der Flasche trinken oder gemeinsam die beiden Gläser

(f) .... ? Max *(g)* .... mir, einfach zu improvisieren. Ich

(h) .... , diesen Rat anzunehmen. Denn ich *(i)* .... bereits mit einem

neuen Problem. Meine Einrichtung *(j)* .... – wie du ja weißt – nur aus Tisch,

Bett und Stuhl. Mindestens zwei von uns mussten also auf dem Boden *(k)* ....

Aber wir hatten dann doch viel Spaß.

Gerade klingelt es an der Tür. Demnächst mehr.

Gruß und Kuss, Deine Eva

3 Analyse – Unterstreichen Sie die Verben mit Vorsilben und sortieren Sie sie.

Siegfried, Königssohn aus den Niederlanden, bricht von seiner Heimatstadt
Xanten am Niederrhein auf, um sich in fernen Ländern einen Namen zu
machen. Auf der Reise gewinnt er den Schatz der Nibelungen, er erkämpft
sich eine Tarnkappe, die ihn unsichtbar machen kann, und er
ersticht einen Drachen und badet in seinem Blut.
Schließlich kommt Siegfried nach Worms, wo König
Gunther regiert. Um Gunthers Schwester Kriemhild zur
Frau zu bekommen, verspricht Siegfried dem König,
ihm zu helfen, die schöne, aber übermenschlich starke Brunhild von
Island zur Frau zu gewinnen. Gunther muss seine zukünftige Braut im Wettkampf besiegen.
Dazu wird von mehreren Männern ein riesiger Speer herbei-
geschleppt. Riesengroß ist auch der Stein, den er wegstoßen muss. Gunther verliert den Mut. Er fürchtet, dass er sich
gegen Brunhild nicht durchsetzen wird. Siegfried unterstützt
Gunther. Er zieht seine Tarnkappe an und wird dadurch für
die Zuschauer des Wettkampfes unsichtbar.

untrennbar	trennbar
	aufbrechen

4 Formulieren Sie den Text im Perfekt und die Sätze mit sein, haben, werden und Modalverben im Präteritum.

Siegfried, Königssohn aus den Niederlanden, ist von seiner Heimatstadt Xanten am
Niederrhein aufgebrochen, um sich in fernen Ländern einen Namen zu machen. Auf der Reise
hat der junge Held ...

PASSIV

wird ... informiert

1 Funktion

Der Vorstandsvorsitzende informiert die Aktionäre.
Aktiv: Wer handelt?

Die Aktionäre werden informiert.
Passiv: Was passiert?

Das Passiv wird häufig bei Beschreibungen von Arbeitsvorgängen, Produktionsverfahren, Regeln, Vorschriften und allgemeinen Aussagen benutzt.

2 Formen

a Konjugation

Präsens	ich	werde	informiert	
Präteritum	ich	wurde	informiert	
Perfekt	ich	bin	informiert	worden
Plusquamperfekt	ich	war	informiert	worden
Futur I	ich	werde	informiert	werden

b Umformung Aktiv ⟶ Passiv
Die Akkusativ-Ergänzung des Aktivsatzes wird eine Nominativ-Ergänzung:

		Akkusativ-Ergänzung	
Die Firmenleitung	*ersetzt*	*den alten Zentralcomputer.*	
Der alte Zentralcomputer	*wird*		*ersetzt.*
Nominativ-Ergänzung	werden		Partizip II

Gibt es im Passivsatz keinen Nominativ, steht *es* oder ein anderer Satzteil auf Position 1. Bei Sätzen ohne Subjekt steht das Verb in der 3. Person Singular:

Position 1	werden			Partizip II
Es	*wurde*	*lange*	*über die Projekte*	*verhandelt.*
Über die Projekte	*wurde*	*lange*		*verhandelt.*
Lange	*wurde*		*über die Projekte*	*verhandelt.*

Das logische Subjekt/Agens wird im Passivsatz normalerweise nicht genannt. Wenn man es besonders betonen will, kann man es mit einer Präposition einfügen.

Subjekt			
Der Pressesprecher	*informiert*	*die Öffentlichkeit.*	
Die Öffentlichkeit	*wurde*		*informiert.*
Die Öffentlichkeit	*wurde*	*vom Pressesprecher**	*informiert.*
Die Öffentlichkeit	*wurde*	*durch den Pressesprecher**	*informiert.*
	werden	logisches Subjekt / Agens	Partizip II

von + Dativ: Personen, Institutionen; *durch* + Akkusativ: Instrument

1   Ein sehr persönlicher Arbeitsplatz – Formulieren Sie Sätze im Passiv Präteritum.

a) alle Mitarbeiter I informieren
   Alle Mitarbeiter wurden informiert.
b) die alte Kantine I renovieren
c) die Wände I weiß streichen
d) neue Lampen I installieren
e) endlich I eine Klimaanlage I einbauen
f) die Renovierung I übrigens von den Mitarbeitern höchstpersönlich I durchführen

2   Formulieren Sie die Sätze von Übung 1 im Passiv Perfekt.

a) *Alle Mitarbeiter sind informiert worden.*

3   E-Mail aus dem Büro – Formulieren Sie den Text im Passiv.

```
Liebe Diana,
nur ganz kurz zu meinem neuen Job. Horror pur! Hier beginnt man um
7.30 Uhr mit der Arbeit, man spricht nicht über Privates und im Team
arbeitet man auch nicht. Stattdessen denken alle ständig an die
Konkurrenz. Natürlich raucht man nicht, man lacht nur selten und
feiert nie! Hilfe!
Bis bald!
Deine Tanja
```

Liebe Diana,
nur ganz kurz zu meinem neuen Job. Horror pur! Hier wird um 7.30 Uhr mit der Arbeit begonnen, ...

4   Chatten und shoppen – Formulieren Sie den Text im Passiv und nennen Sie das Agens mit von oder durch.

a) Das Internet ermöglicht ganz neue Kommunikationsformen.
   Durch das Internet werden ganz neue Kommunikationsformen ermöglicht.
b) Man plaudert und flirtet in „Chatrooms".
c) Hier sprechen dich wildfremde Leute an.
d) Ein persönliches Passwort schützt die Daten, wenn man per Internet einkauft und bezahlt.
e) Wenn man die Kreditkarten-Daten ungesichert eingibt, missbraucht vielleicht ein unberechtigter „Einkäufer" das eigene Konto.

5   Das @-Zeichen – Formulieren Sie das Passiv ins Aktiv um und das Aktiv ins Passiv.
Das @-Zeichen ist für E-Mail-Adressen ausgewählt worden, weil man dieses Zeichen in keiner Sprache dieser Welt benutzt. Man braucht das Zeichen als Trennung zwischen dem Adressaten-Namen und dem Provider-Namen. Für das @-Zeichen werden meistens die Tasten „Alt Gr" und „Q" gedrückt.
Man hat das @-Zeichen für E-Mail-Adressen ausgewählt, weil ...

6

PASSIV MIT MODALVERBEN

muss informiert werden

ⓐ Konjugation

		Modalverb		Infinitiv Präsens Passiv	
Präsens	*Die Öffentlichkeit*	*kann* *muss* *will* *darf* *soll*	*heute*	*informiert werden.*	
Präteritum	*Die Öffentlichkeit*	*konnte* *musste* *wollte* *durfte* *sollte*	*heute*	*informiert werden.*	

		haben		Infinitiv Präsens Passiv	Modalverb
Perfekt*	*Die Öffentlichkeit*	*hat*	*heute*	*informiert werden*	*können.* *müssen.* *wollen.* *dürfen.* *sollen.*

* nur selten gebraucht

ⓑ Umformung Aktiv *wollen* ⟶ Passiv *sollen:*

Aktiv	*Der Journalist will den Skandal aufdecken.*
Passiv	*Der Skandal soll aufgedeckt werden.*

Modalverben 📖 **s. Seite 94-101, 192**

6

ÜBUNGEN

1 **Haben Sie das schon gehört? – Formulieren Sie Aktivsätze mit dem Modalverb wollen.**
   a) Alle Altbauwohnungen sollen renoviert werden.
   b) Das veraltete Heizungssystem soll modernisiert werden.
   c) In jeder Wohnung sollen moderne Fenster eingebaut werden.
   d) Die alten Bäder sollen erneuert werden.
   e) Der Hinterhof soll begrünt werden.
   f) Neue Bäume sollen gepflanzt werden.
   g) Im ganzen Haus sollen die Mieten erhöht werden.

   Die Hausbesitzer ...
   a) ... *wollen alle Altbauwohnungen renovieren.*

2   Große Pläne – Formulieren Sie Passivsätze mit sollen.

Die Stadtregierung ...
a) ... will ein modernes Einkaufszentrum bauen.
   Ein modernes Einkaufszentrum soll gebaut werden.
b) ... will einen großen Kinderspielplatz anlegen.
c) ... will Frühlingsblumen pflanzen.
d) ... will im Zentrum eine Fußgängerzone einrichten.
e) ... will mehr Straßen zu Spielstraßen machen.
f) ... will einen neuen Tunnel bauen.
g) ... will mehr Straßenlampen aufstellen.

3   Stress im Büro – Formulieren Sie Passivsätze im Präteritum mit können.
a) Das Programm war abgestürzt, und keiner konnte den Computer neu starten.
   Das Programm war abgestürzt, und der Computer konnte nicht neu gestartet werden.
b) Niemand wusste, wie man das neue Faxgerät richtig bedient.
c) Keiner hatte Zeit, den Termin mit dem Unternehmensberater vorzubereiten.
d) Der Kopierer war auch kaputt, deshalb konnte man die Unterlagen nicht kopieren.
e) Die Leitung war dauernd besetzt, deshalb konnte keiner den Reparaturservice benachrichtigen.
f) Die Besprechung mit dem Abteilungsleiter konnte man auch nicht planen.
g) Und dann gab es noch das Problem mit der Portomaschine, weshalb man die Post nicht rechtzeitig verschicken konnte.

4   Kriminelle Pläne – Formulieren Sie Passivsätze mit dem Modalverb müssen.
a) Die Bank Tag und Nacht beobachten!
   Die Bank muss Tag und Nacht beobachtet werden.
b) Einen genauen Plan machen!
c) Ein Fluchtauto organisieren!
d) Die Nummernschilder unbedingt austauschen!
e) Ein Bankkonto für Schwarzgeld eröffnen!
f) Pässe und Flugtickets besorgen!
g) Den Boss laufend informieren!

6

5   Der Kaufhauserpresser Dagobert – Formulieren Sie Passivsätze.
a) Der Kaufhausbesitzer sollte das Geld in einer Plastiktüte auf einer Baustelle deponieren.
   Das Geld sollte in einer Plastiktüte auf einer Baustelle deponiert werden.
b) Erfahrene Beamte sollten den Ort beobachten.
c) Sie konnten die Geldübergabe aber nicht verhindern.
d) Denn der Sprechfunk im Polizeiwagen war kaputt (kein Passiv möglich), und man konnte ihn nicht mehr rechtzeitig reparieren.
e) Laut Polizeisprecher muss man den Erpresser nun anhand alter Fotos identifizieren.
f) Die Zeugen konnten den Mann allerdings nicht erkennen.
g) Die Polizei will den Kaufhauserpresser Dagobert aber ganz sicher beim nächsten Mal fassen.

ZUSTANDSPASSIV

Die Tür ist geöffnet.

<u>1</u>   Funktion

 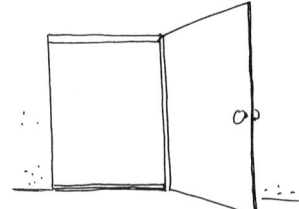 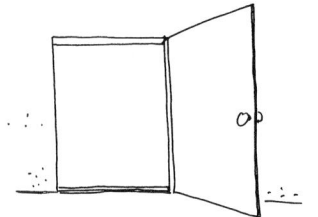

Etwas passiert.
Die Tür wird geöffnet.

Etwas ist passiert.
Die Tür wurde geöffnet.
Die Tür ist geöffnet worden.

Es gibt einen neuen Zustand.
Die Tür ist geöffnet.

<u>2</u>   Formen

		konj. Verb		Partizip II	
Präsens	*Das Geschäft*	*ist*	*jetzt*	*geöffnet.*	
Präteritum	*Das Geschäft*	*war*	*gestern*	*geöffnet.*	
Futur	*Das Geschäft*	*wird*	*auch morgen*	*geöffnet*	*sein.*

ÜBUNGEN

<u>1</u>   **Der Weg einer E-Mail – Unterstreichen Sie alle Passivformen.**

Das Mail-Programm <u>wird</u> vom Sender – also von Ihnen – <u>gestartet</u>. Man muss aber nicht online gehen, um die Mail zu schreiben. Ist der elektronische Brief geschrieben, werden die fertigen Nachrichten gespeichert. Erst durch die Verbindung zum Internet und einen Klick auf „senden" kann der elektronische Brief losgeschickt werden.

Vom Postausgang Ihres Providers werden die Mails dann zum Posteingang des Mail-Empfängers gesendet. Der Empfänger wird über neue E-Mails nur dann benachrichtigt, wenn eine Verbindung zum Internet besteht. Viele Programme sind so eingerichtet, dass der Posteingang in bestimmten Intervallen überprüft wird. Neue E-Mails können dann automatisch abgerufen werden.

<u>2</u>   **Tragen Sie die Passivformen aus Übung 1 in das Schema ein und ordnen Sie zu.**

	Passiv	Passiv + Modalverb	Zustands-passiv
wird gestartet	✗		

3 Alles schon erledigt – Formulieren Sie Sätze im Zustandspassiv mit schon/bereits.

a) Würdest du mir bitte mal das Modem auspacken?	*Das Modem ist schon ausgepackt.*
b) Und können wir jetzt das Gerät an den Computer anschließen?	
c) Ach, und jetzt schalte doch mal den Strom ein!	
d) Leg doch mal die CD ein und starte sie.	
e) Sag mal, kannst du eigentlich auch die Software installieren?	
f) So, und jetzt können wir den Internet-Zugang herstellen.	
g) Und jetzt gebe ich mal mein Passwort ein.	

4 Wie geht es zu Hause? – Formulieren Sie Antworten im Zustandspassiv.

a) Hast du den Kuchen für Tante Heidi schon gebacken?	*Ja, der Kuchen ist gebacken.*
b) Und die Blumen habt ihr auch gegossen?	*Natürlich, ...*
c) Hat eigentlich jemand die Wäsche aufgehängt?	*Selbstverständlich, ...*
d) Und wenn du Zeit hast, könntest du vielleicht die Steckdose in meinem Zimmer reparieren.	*Stell dir vor, ...*
e) Wenn noch jemand das Faxgerät einschalten könnte, das wäre prima!	*Schon erledigt, ...*
f) Und die Rechnungen hast du sicher auch schon bezahlt.	*Tut mir leid, ...* (+ noch nicht)

5 Ein netter Mann! – Formulieren Sie Sätze im Zustandspassiv Präteritum.

Hallo, Jana, ... ja, wirklich schade, dass du gestern Abend nicht da warst. Ja, es war ein wunderschönes Fest, und heute Morgen dachte ich, jetzt muss ich erst mal alles aufräumen. Aber du kennst ja Peter! Alles war schon fertig:

a) Gläser abräumen *Die Gläser waren schon abgeräumt.*
b) Geschirr abwaschen ....
c) Aschenbecher (Pl.) ausleeren ....
d) Zimmer lüften ....
e) Frühstückstisch decken ....
f) Kaffee kochen ....
g) Orangensaft einschenken ....

6

PASSIV-ERSATZFORMEN

Die Reparatur ist machbar.

1 Funktion

Ersatzformen	Passiv
Die Reparatur ist machbar.	*Die Reparatur kann gemacht werden.*
Die Reparatur lässt sich machen.	
Die Reparatur ist zu machen.	
Das ist eine noch zu lösende Aufgabe.	*Das ist eine Aufgabe, die noch gelöst werden muss.*

Die Ersatzformen werden oft anstelle des Passivs verwendet, um eine Häufung von Passiv-konstruktionen zu vermeiden. Die Ersatzformen haben zwar eine passive Bedeutung, aber das Verb steht im Aktiv.

2 Formen

Ersatzformen		Passiv mit Modalverb
ist bezahlbar	*sein + Adjektiv auf*	*kann bezahlt werden*
ist unverkäuflich	*-bar oder -lich*	*kann nicht verkauft werden*
lässt sich machen	*sich lassen + Infinitiv*	*kann gemacht werden*
ist abzuholen	*sein + zu + Infinitiv*	*kann/muss/soll abgeholt werden*
ist nicht zu verkaufen		*kann/muss/soll/darf nicht verkauft werden*
der zu lernende Stoff	*zu + Partizip I +*	*der Stoff, der gelernt werden kann/muss/soll*
ein durchzuführendes Experiment	Adjektivdeklination (Gerundiv)	*ein Experiment, das durchgeführt werden muss/soll/kann*

Adjektive auf *-bar* oder *-lich*, Bedeutungsunterschied:

*lös*lich	*Salz ist in Wasser löslich.*	in Flüssigkeit
*lös*bar	*Die Aufgabe ist lösbar.*	durch Nachdenken
*leser*lich	*Er hat eine leserliche Schrift.*	Man kann die Handschrift gut lesen.
*les*bar	*Der Roman ist gut lesbar.*	Der Roman ist in verständlicher Sprache geschrieben.

ÜBUNGEN

1 Was ist das? – Bilden Sie Adjektive mit -bar.
a) Wasser, das getrunken werden kann, ist *trinkbares Wasser.*
b) Früchte, die gegessen werden können, sind ....
c) Stoff, der sich leicht waschen lässt, ist ....
d) Preise, die nicht zu bezahlen sind, sind ....
e) Eine Idee, die gebraucht werden kann, ist eine ....
f) Eine Farbe, die nicht zu definieren ist, ist eine ....

2 Was ist das? – Bilden Sie Adjektive mit -lich.
a) Eine Schrift, die nicht gelesen werden kann, ist eine *unleserliche Schrift.*
b) Material, das leicht zu zerbrechen ist, ist ....
c) Ein Produkt, das sich nicht verkaufen lässt, ist ein ....

d) Ein Text, der gut verstanden werden kann, ist ein ....
e) Ein Fehler, der nicht zu verzeihen ist, ist ein ....
f) Leichtsinn, der nicht verantwortet werden kann, ist ....

3 Laufen ist gesund – Formulieren Sie Sätze mit sein + zu + Infinitiv.
a) Ein Profi erklärt, worauf beim Laufen geachtet werden muss.
   Ein Profi erklärt, worauf beim Laufen zu achten ist.
b) Die Schuhe sollen zur Stabilisierung des Fußes fest geschnürt werden.
c) Die Muskulatur sollte vor jedem Lauf aufgewärmt werden.
d) Bei Verletzungen muss der Fuß mindestens sechs Wochen lang ruhig gestellt werden.
e) Der Fuß muss bei Schmerzen entlastet werden.

4 Wissenschaftliches Arbeiten – Formulieren Sie die Sätze mit dem Gerundiv.
a) Ein Text, der noch korrigiert werden muss, ist ein *noch zu korrigierender Text.*
b) Ein Ergebnis, das noch veröffentlicht werden muss, ist ein ...
c) Ein Thema, das noch weiter zu bearbeiten ist, ist ein ...
d) Ein Formular, das ausgefüllt werden muss, ist ein ...
e) Eine Prüfung, die abgelegt werden muss, ist eine ...
f) Ein Prüfungstermin, der nicht zu verschieben ist, ist ein ...
g) Ein Vorschlag, der ernst genommen werden muss, ist ein ...

5 Unterstreichen Sie die Modalverben und den Infinitiv Passiv.

Tipps und Tricks für den Joballtag nach dem Urlaub

Hören Sie zuerst den Anrufbeantworter ab, denn dort warten die wichtigsten Nachrichten. Danach sollten die E-Mails gelesen werden, denn sie können direkt beantwortet und dann gelöscht werden. Die Post kann in drei Stapel sortiert werden: Stapel eins für Sachen, die sofort erledigt werden müssen. Stapel zwei für Projekte, die auch später bearbeitet werden können. Stapel drei für Informationen, die Sie irgendwann einmal studieren können. Alles andere sollte gleich weggeworfen werden. Und so kann auch die Urlaubslaune in den Alltag gerettet werden: Gehen Sie die ersten Tage ruhig und entspannt an.

6 Formulieren Sie den Text neu. Ersetzen Sie das Passiv durch sein + zu + Infinitiv, bei dem Modalverb können benutzen Sie sich lassen + Infinitiv.
Hören Sie zuerst den Anrufbeantworter ab, denn dort warten die wichtigsten Nachrichten. Danach sind die E-Mails zu lesen, ...

7 Computer & Co – Formulieren Sie Sätze mit sich lassen + Infinitiv.
a) Alle Texte sind einfach zu bearbeiten.
   Alle Texte lassen sich einfach bearbeiten.
b) Ein neues Grafikprogramm kann mühelos installiert werden.
c) Die Soundkarte des Computers kann ersetzt werden.
d) Allerdings sind einige Anfangsprobleme unvermeidlich.
e) Die meisten Schwierigkeiten sind aber schnell zu überwinden.

KONJUNKTIV II (1): GEGENWART

würde – wäre – hätte

<u>1</u>   Funktion

> *Ich wäre gern reich und schön.*
> *Ich hätte gern einen Sportwagen.*
> *Ich wäre gern auf Hawaii.*
> *Ich hätte gern einen Filmstar*
> *als Mann.*

<u>2</u>   Formen

ⓐ ohne Hilfsverb *würde*

Die Form des Konjunktivs II wird vom Präteritum abgeleitet:

	Präteritum	Konjunktiv II
a – ä	*kam*	*käme*
o – ö*	*konnte*	*könnte*
u – ü	*wusste*	*wüsste*

* Ausnahmen sind *wollte* und *sollte*.

Bei den regelmäßigen Verben ist der Konjunktiv II mit dem Indikativ Präteritum identisch. Deshalb verwendet man ihn nur bei den Hilfs- und Modalverben sowie einigen unregelmäßigen Verben: *käme, fände, wüsste, schliefe, bliebe* u.a.

	Hilfsverben		Modalverben		unregelmäßige Verben	regelmäßige Verben
	sein	*haben*	*müssen*	*sollen*	*gehen*	*zählen*
ich	*wäre*	*hätte*	*müsste*	*sollte*	*ginge*	*zählte*
du	*wär(e)st*	*hättest*	*müsstest*	*solltest*	*gingest*	*zähltest*
er/sie/es	*wäre*	*hätte*	*müsste*	*sollte*	*ginge*	*zählte*
wir	*wären*	*hätten*	*müssten*	*sollten*	*gingen*	*zählten*
ihr	*wär(e)t*	*hättet*	*müsstet*	*solltet*	*ginget*	*zähltet*
sie/Sie	*wären*	*hätten*	*müssten*	*sollten*	*gingen*	*zählten*

ⓑ mit Hilfsverb *würde*

Bei den meisten Verben wird der Konjunktiv II in der Gegenwart mit *würde* + Infinitiv gebildet:

ich	*würde*	
du	*würdest*	*gehen*
er/sie/es	*würde*	

wir	*würden*	
ihr	*würdet*	*gehen*
sie/Sie	*würden*	

Passiv		*würde*		Partizip II	
	Das Haus	*würde*	*schneller*	*gebaut,*	*wenn mehr Bauarbeiter da wären.*

Würden Sie bitte das Fenster öffnen? – Konjunktiv II in der Aufforderung s. Seite 140

1 Bilden Sie zuerst das Präteritum und dann den Konjunktiv II.

a) kommen ich *kam* ich *käme*
b) wissen er .... er ....
c) haben sie (Pl.) .... sie (Pl.) ....
d) sein wir .... wir ....
e) bleiben ich .... ich ....
f) können ihr .... ihr ....
g) finden du .... du ....
h) repariert werden er .... er ....
i) sollen er .... er ....
j) halten ich .... ich ....
k) sein ihr .... ihr ....
l) wollen sie (Pl.) .... sie (Pl.) ....
m) dürfen er .... er ....
n) gefangen werden sie (Pl.) .... sie (Pl.) ....
o) gehen es .... es ....

2 Arme Monika – Formulieren Sie Sätze im Konjunktiv II.

a) Sie ist erst 12. (17 sein)
   Aber sie wäre gern schon 17.
b) Sie hat ein Zimmer zusammen mit ihrer Schwester. (allein)
c) Sie sieht durchschnittlich aus. (bildhübsch sein)
d) Sie darf noch kein Make-up tragen. (sich schminken)
e) Sie hat nur ein altes Fahrrad. (Mofa)
f) Sie fährt mit ihren Eltern in den Urlaub. (Freundinnen)
g) Sie sitzt in der Schule neben Max. (Hans-Peter)

6

3 Zeitprobleme – Formulieren Sie Sätze im Konjunktiv II.

a) Es ist schon halb vier. (Taxi / längst da sein müssen)
   Das Taxi müsste längst da sein.
b) Es ist schon Viertel nach zwölf. (wir / jetzt Mittagspause machen können)
c) Es wird schon dunkel. (ich / gerne nach Hause fahren)
d) Es ist schon zehn Uhr nachts. (ich / gerne wissen / wo Peter bleibt)
e) Es ist schon fast Mitternacht. (du / schon seit zwei Stunden schlafen müssen)
f) Es ist erst sechs Uhr früh. (ich / gern noch im Bett bleiben)
g) Es sind jetzt leider keine Ferien. (sonst / ihr / ausschlafen dürfen)

4 Besserwisser – Formulieren Sie Ratschläge im Konjunktiv II mit würde + Infinitiv.

a) Hans isst viel zu wenig.
   An seiner Stelle würde ich mehr / nicht so wenig essen.
b) Ellen schläft zu wenig.
c) Karl-Heinz trinkt zu viel.
d) Die beiden Kollegen fehlen in der Arbeit oft aus gesundheitlichen Gründen.
e) Meine Eltern kümmern sich nur ganz selten um den alten Onkel.
f) Meine Tochter schickt ihre Kinder viel zu spät ins Bett.

KONJUNKTIV II (2): VERGANGENHEIT

hätte getan – wäre gefahren

1 Funktion

Fast wäre ein Unfall passiert. *Ich hätte diese Arbeit längst erledigen sollen.*	irreale Aussagen in der Vergangenheit

2 Formen

a Den drei Vergangenheitsformen im Indikativ steht im Konjunktiv II nur eine Vergangenheitsform gegenüber:

Indikativ	Konjunktiv II	Indikativ	Konjunktiv II
ich arbeitete		*ich fuhr*	
ich habe gearbeitet		*ich bin gefahren*	
ich hatte gearbeitet	*ich hätte gearbeitet*	*ich war gefahren*	*ich wäre gefahren*

b Der Konjunktiv II der Vergangenheit wird mit *haben/sein* und Partizip II gebildet:

	Konjunktiv II von *haben*	+ Partizip II		Konjunktiv II von *sein*	+ Partizip II
ich	*hätte*			*wäre*	
du	*hättest*			*wär(e)st*	
er/sie/es	*hätte*	*geschrieben*		*wäre*	*geblieben*
wir	*hätten*			*wären*	
ihr	*hättet*			*wär(e)t*	
sie/Sie	*hätten*			*wären*	

		Konjunktiv II von *sein*		Partizip II	*worden*
Passiv	*Ich*	*wäre*	*gerne*	*informiert*	*worden.*

c Modalverben bilden den Konjunktiv II der Vergangenheit mit *haben* und doppeltem Infinitiv:

	Konjunktiv II von *haben*	Infinitiv Vollverb	Infinitiv Modalverb
ich	*hätte*		*müssen*
du	*hättest*		*können*
er/sie/es	*hätte*	*gehen*	*dürfen*
wir	*hätten*		*sollen*
ihr	*hättet*		*wollen*
sie/Sie	*hätten*		*können*

1 Bilden Sie den Konjunktiv II der Vergangenheit.

a) ich sang
ich hätte gesungen
b) sie lief
c) wir dachten
d) wir haben gedacht
e) es wurde gebaut

f) du warst
g) du bist gewesen
h) ihr durftet fernsehen
i) wir wurden verletzt
j) er wuchs
k) sie boten an

l) es ist passiert
m) sie waren gestiegen
n) sie hatte
o) sie hat gehabt
p) sie hatte gehabt
q) ich musste lesen

2 Urlaubsstress – Formulieren Sie Sätze mit fast im Konjunktiv II der Vergangenheit.

a) War das Reisebüro nicht schon geschlossen?
Nein, aber fast wäre es schon geschlossen gewesen.
b) Habt ihr das Flugzeug verpasst?
c) Habt ihr bei dem Unwetter überhaupt landen können?
d) Musstet ihr wieder stundenlang auf das Flugzeug warten?
e) Bist du am Strand bestohlen worden?
f) Ist deine Frau im Urwald wieder von Moskitos gestochen worden?

3 Schlechte Stimmung – Formulieren Sie Sätze im Konjunktiv II der Vergangenheit.

a) Sie I diese Arbeit I unbedingt bis heute I erledigen müssen
Sie hätten diese Arbeit unbedingt bis heute erledigen müssen!
b) der neue Kollege I diesen Fall I schon am Mittwoch I bearbeiten sollen
c) meine Assistentin I Ihnen I alle nötigen Informationen I geben können
d) Sie I vor unseren Geschäftspartnern I nicht darüber I reden dürfen
e) Ihre Mitarbeiter I mehr auf die Details I achten müssen
f) man I jemand anderen I für diesen Job I nehmen sollen

4 Die Lieblingstante – Ergänzen Sie den Konjunktiv II der Vergangenheit.

Liebe Tante Clarissa,
als ich neulich in Berlin war, (a) *hätte* ich Dich gern besucht (besuchen), weil Du ja meine
Lieblingstante bist, aber leider hatte ich Deine Adresse nicht dabei. Weißt Du noch, wie Du mir geholfen
hast, als ich damals die Spielschulden hatte? Was (b) .... ich damals ohne Dich ....
(tun)! Ich (c) .... mich damals gern bei Dir persönlich .... (bedanken), aber Du
weißt ja, wie viel Stress ich immer habe. Ich (d) .... jedenfalls gern .... (wissen),
wie es Dir geht. Vielleicht gibt es ja jetzt wieder eine Möglichkeit, mehr Kontakt miteinander zu haben,
denn ich habe wieder ein kleines Problem. Stell Dir vor, fast (e) .... ich neulich ins Gefängnis
.... (kommen), weil die Banken völlig illusorische Vorstellungen über die finanziellen
Möglichkeiten eines jungen Geschäftsmannes haben. Vielleicht (f) .... es besser ....
(sein), ich (g) .... ins Ausland .... (gehen), aber mit welchem Geld? Dabei
(h) .... mir nur 25.000 Euro .... (fehlen), um diese Hyänen zufriedenzustellen!
Vielleicht (i) .... Du Lust (haben; Gegenwart), Deinem Lieblingsneffen einen kleinen Kredit
zu geben?
Ich melde mich bald persönlich!
Dein Alex

6

KONJUNKTIV II (3): BEDINGUNGEN

Was wäre, wenn ...

<u>1</u>　Funktion

Realer Plan: Indikativ　　　　Irrealer Plan, Wunschtraum: Konjunktiv II

<u>2</u>　Satzstrukturen

Weil die Sachverhalte nicht der Realität entsprechen, müssen aus negativen Sätzen positive werden und umgekehrt:

Realität	Wunsch
Ich bin noch nicht 18. Deshalb darf ich noch nicht Motorrad fahren.	*Wenn ich schon 18 wäre, dürfte ich Motorrad fahren.*
Ich bin arbeitslos. Deswegen habe ich Schulden.	*Wenn ich nicht arbeitslos wäre, dann hätte ich keine Schulden.*

a Gegenwart

Wenn	*ich den Job*	*bekommen würde,*	*(dann) hätte ich mehr Geld.*
Würde	*ich den Job*	*bekommen,*	*(dann) hätte ich mehr Geld.*
Wenn	*ich den Job*	*bekommen könnte,*	*(dann) könnte ich mir mehr leisten.*

b Vergangenheit

Wenn	*ich den Job*	*bekommen hätte,*	*(dann) hätte ich mehr Geld gehabt.*
Hätte	*ich den Job*	*bekommen,*	*(dann) hätte ich mehr Geld gehabt.*
Hätte	*ich den Job*	*bekommen können,*	*(dann) hätte ich mir mehr leisten können.*

<u>3</u>　Alternativen

Konjunktiv II	Adverb
Wenn mich mein Chef nicht in ein längeres Gespräch verwickelt hätte, wäre ich pünktlich gewesen.	*Mein Chef hat mich in ein längeres Gespräch verwickelt. Sonst wäre ich pünktlich gewesen.* Oder: *Deshalb war ich nicht pünktlich.*

1 Schön wär's! – Verbinden Sie beide Satzhälften zu irrealen Bedingungssätzen.

a) Es wäre schön, ... wenn wir zuerst essen gingen?
b) Sie hätten die Wohnung bekommen, ... wenn er einen Stadtplan hätte.
c) Es wäre mir lieber, ... wenn Sie sich früher gemeldet hätten.
d) Wäre es Ihnen angenehmer, ... wenn es nicht so viel geregnet hätte.
e) Der Urlaub wäre besser gewesen, ... wenn du bald wiederkommen würdest.
f) Er würde den Weg auch dann nicht finden, ... wenn Sie morgen kommen könnten.

2 Menschen und Tiere – Formulieren Sie irreale Bedingungssätze mit wenn.

a) Ein sechsjähriges Mädchen in New York hat einen jungen
   Alligator gefunden. Deshalb ist er nicht verhungert.
   Wenn das sechsjährige Mädchen den jungen Alligator nicht
   gefunden hätte, (dann) wäre er verhungert.
b) Ein Dieb hat in eine fremde Handtasche gegriffen. Dabei
   wurde er von einer Tarantel gebissen.
c) Kakerlaken haben einen „sechsten Sinn". Deshalb können sie
   so frühzeitig jeden Menschen erkennen.
d) Die Finnin Karoliina S. ist eines Morgens neben einer Kobra
   aufgewacht. Seitdem muss sie zu einem Psychotherapeuten
   gehen.
e) Der Gewehrschrank stand offen. Ein Jagdhund hat mit dem
   Gewehr gespielt und dabei sein Herrchen erschossen.

3 Szenen einer Ehe – Formulieren Sie Bedingungssätze mit wenn im Konjunktiv II.

■ du I nicht so faul I sein, • haben I wir I jetzt auch ein Haus
  Wenn du nicht so faul wärst, hätten wir jetzt auch ein Haus.
■ du I weniger Geld I ausgegeben haben, • dann I wir I mehr I haben sparen können
■ was heißt hier, • ich I weniger I ausgegeben haben (?)
■ das heißt zum Beispiel, • du I weniger oft I zu diesem italienischen Masseur I gegangen
  sein
■ ich I einen Körper I wie du I haben, • ich I mich schämen
■ ich I so oft I meinen Körper I denken an I wie du, • dann I wir I uns nicht einmal I ein
  Puppenhaus I leisten können

4 Meine Freunde – Formulieren Sie Bedingungssätze mit wenn im Konjunktiv II.

a) Anna liebt ihren Mann immer noch. Sonst hätte sie ihn längst fortgejagt.
   Wenn Anna ihren Mann nicht immer noch lieben würde, hätte sie ihn längst fortgejagt.
b) Ernst hat überhaupt keinen Geschmack. Sonst hätte er diesen Sakko nicht gekauft.
c) Maria ist sehr gutmütig. Sonst wäre sie längst explodiert.
d) Fritz hat kein Geld. Sonst hätte er sich längst ein neues Auto gekauft.
e) Ulrich ist momentan sehr beschäftigt. Sonst würde er sich sicher bei mir melden.

KONJUNKTIV II (4): WÜNSCHE, IRREALE FOLGEN

Wäre ich doch bloß ...
zu ... , als dass

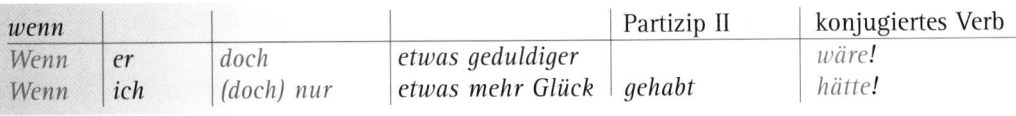

1 Funktion

a Wünsche

Wenn der Typ doch endlich verschwinden würde!

b irreale Folgen

Das Buch ist zu langweilig, als dass man wach bleiben könnte.

2 Satzstrukturen

a Wünsche

wenn				Partizip II	konjugiertes Verb
Wenn	*er*	*doch*	*etwas geduldiger*		*wäre!*
Wenn	*ich*	*(doch) nur*	*etwas mehr Glück*	*gehabt*	*hätte!*

konjugiertes Verb				Partizip II
Wären	*die Kinder*	*bloß*	*etwas leiser!*	
Hätte	*ich ihm*	*(doch) bloß*	*nicht das Auto*	*gegeben!*

b irreale Folgen

Hauptsatz			Nebensatz		
			Konnektor		Verb
Der Wein ist	*zu*	*sauer,*	*als dass*	*man ihn noch*	*trinken könnte.*
Die Formel war	*zu*	*komplex,*	*als dass*	*ich sie in 5 Minuten*	*hätte* erklären können.*

* Bei Modalverben steht *hätte* vor den beiden Infinitiven.

3 Alternativen

	zu + um... zu + Infinitiv
Das Problem ist zu komplex, als dass man es beim Mittagessen besprechen könnte.	*Das Problem* ist *zu komplex, um es beim Mittagessen zu besprechen.**
	Das Problem ist *so komplex, dass man es beim Mittagessen nicht besprechen kann.*
	so... dass (Indikativ)

* Das Modalverb entfällt hier.

ÜBUNGEN

1 Wünsche, nichts als Wünsche – Ergänzen Sie wenn, doch und das Verb im Konjunktiv II.

a) Wenn ich *doch* meine Freundin öfter *sehen würde* ! (sehen)

b) .... er .... einen besseren Job .... ! (bekommen)

c) .... das Fernsehprogramm nicht immer so langweilig .... ! (sein)

6

d) .... der Wagen etwas schneller .... !
(fahren)

e) .... wir .... etwas mehr Glück im Lotto .... ! (haben)

f) .... das Wetter nicht so schlecht .... ! (sein)

2 **Elternsorgen** – Formulieren Sie Wunschsätze mit wenn. Verwenden Sie abwechselnd bloß und nur.

a) Unser Alex ist leider ziemlich schlecht in der Schule.
   Wenn unser Alex bloß nicht so schlecht in der Schule wäre!

b) Er hat im Moment lauter andere Dinge im Kopf.

c) Seine Freunde haben so einen schlechten Einfluss auf ihn.

d) Außerdem läuft er jeden Tag mit dieser Petra herum.

e) Seitdem macht er nicht einmal das Notwendigste. (+ *wenigstens* statt *nicht einmal*)

f) Bei jedem Gespräch über das Thema reagiert er total kindisch.

g) Er sieht die halbe Nacht fern.

h) Vermutlich schafft er dieses Schuljahr nicht.

i) Er versucht es nicht einmal.

j) Er ist eben nicht so fleißig wie sein Vater in dem Alter.

3 **30 Jahre später** – Formulieren Sie die Sätze aus Übung 2 in der Vergangenheit und ohne wenn. Verwenden Sie abwechselnd doch bloß und doch nur.

a) *Wäre ich doch bloß nicht so schlecht in der Schule gewesen!*

4 **Menschen und ihre Schwächen** – Formulieren Sie Sätze mit den Alternativen von zu ... als dass.

a) Peter ist zu ungeschickt, als dass er die Lampe montieren könnte.
   Peter ist zu ungeschickt, um die Lampe zu montieren.
   Peter ist so ungeschickt, dass er die Lampe nicht montieren kann.

b) Charlotte ist zu vergesslich, als dass sie dieses Projekt durchführen könnte.

c) Herr Meier war zu unzuverlässig, als dass er diesen Job hätte übernehmen können.

d) Eva ist zu kaputt, als dass sie noch in die Disco gehen könnte.

e) Sibylle war zu verärgert über Karl, als dass sie mit ihm noch länger hätte zusammenleben wollen.

f) Frau Schneider ist zu geizig, als dass sie sich einen neuen Wintermantel kaufen würde.

5 **Urlaubserinnerungen** – Formulieren Sie Sätze mit zu ... als dass.

a) Das Essen war sehr fett. Ich konnte es gar nicht vertragen.
   Das Essen war zu fett, als dass ich es hätte vertragen können.

b) Die Discos waren schrecklich laut. Ich konnte überhaupt nicht schlafen.

c) Das Meer dort ist sehr warm. Es erfrischt einen gar nicht.

d) Die Zimmer waren ausgesprochen klein. Man konnte sich gar nicht setzen.

e) Die Leute dort sind total unfreundlich. Ich möchte sie nicht wiedersehen.

f) Die Hitze war sehr groß. Ich habe mich nicht erholt.

g) Aber der Barkeeper war süß. Ich konnte ihm nicht widerstehen.

KONJUNKTIV II (5): VERGLEICHE

als ob – als

1 Funktion

„Du siehst aus, *als ob* du gerade ein Gespenst gesehen hättest."

2 Satzstrukturen

ⓐ Hauptsatz, Hauptsatz

Hauptsatz	Hauptsatz				
	Konnektor	konj. Verb		Infinitiv / P II	
Du rennst,	*als*	*würde*	*dich die Polizei*	*verfolgen*[1].	
Er isst / aß,	*als*	*hätte*	*er eine Woche nichts*	*bekommen*[2].	

ⓑ Hauptsatz, Nebensatz

Hauptsatz	Nebensatz				
	Konnektor			Infinitiv / P II	konj. Verb
Du rennst,	*als ob**	*dich die Polizei*		*verfolgen*	*würde*[1].
Er isst / aß,	*als ob**	*er eine Woche nichts*		*bekommen*	*hätte*[2].

[1] Gegenwart; [2] Vergangenheit
* statt *als ob* umgangssprachlich auch *als wenn*

ⓒ Verwendung
Irreale Vergleichssätze stehen oft nach Verben des persönlichen Befindens und der Wahrnehmung:

Ich fühle mich, *Es geht mir schlecht,* *Mir ist zumute,*	*als ob ich einen Stein verschluckt hätte.* *als hätte ich einen Stein verschluckt.*
Es scheint (mir), *Ich habe den Eindruck,* *Er sieht aus,*	*als ob er wieder gesund wäre.* *als wäre er wieder gesund.*
Die Musik klingt, *Die Musik hört sich an,* *Die Musik wirkt auf mich,*	*als ob jemand einer Katze auf den Schwanz getreten wäre.* *als wäre jemand einer Katze auf den Schwanz getreten.*

3 Alternativen

als ob + Verb	*wie* + Nomen
Er benahm sich, als ob er verrückt wäre.	*Er benahm sich wie ein Verrückter.*

1 **Menschen und Tiere im Stress – Formulieren Sie Sätze mit als ob.**

a) Das Mädchen rief so laut, (ich / schwerhörig / sein)
Das Mädchen rief so laut, als ob ich schwerhörig wäre.
b) Die Katze schrie, (sie / große Schmerzen / haben)
c) Karl war wütend. Er sah aus, (er / gleich / explodieren)
d) Der Autofahrer beschimpfte mich so, (ich / seinen Wagen / kaputt gemacht haben)
e) Der Hund bellte, (ich / ein Einbrecher / sein)
f) Eva weinte so, (sie / nie wieder / aufhören)

2 **Formulieren Sie dieselben Sätze mit als.**

a) *Das Mädchen rief so laut, als wäre ich schwerhörig.*

3 **Komische Leute! – Formulieren Sie irreale Vergleichssätze.**

a) Herr Petersen hat erst seit kurzem den Führerschein. (als ob)
Aber er fährt so schnell, *als ob er schon lange / seit langem den Führerschein hätte.*
b) Er hat nicht den sichersten Wagen der Welt. (als ob)
Aber er fährt so riskant, ...
c) Außerdem sieht er nicht gerade hervorragend. (als)
Aber er tut so, ...

d) Frau Martens hat kein unangenehmes Erlebnis gehabt. (als)
Aber sie macht den Eindruck, ...
e) Sie ist in Wirklichkeit nicht einsam. (als ob)
Aber sie macht den Eindruck, ...
f) Sie ist ziemlich reich. (als)
Aber sie sieht aus, ...

g) Egon und Eva-Maria sind keine engen Freunde mehr. (als ob)
Aber Egon benimmt sich so, ...
h) Er hat ihren Brief bekommen. (als ob)
Aber Egon tut so, ...
i) Er weiß, es hat keinen Sinn mehr, sich mit ihr zu treffen. (als)
Aber er tut so, ...

4 **Schöne Firma! – Formulieren Sie Sätze mit als anstelle von wie.**

a) Der neue Chef behandelt mich wie einen totalen Anfänger.
Der neue Chef behandelt mich, als wäre ich ein totaler Anfänger.
b) Jeden Morgen beschimpft er mich wie einen kleinen Schuljungen.
c) Seine Sekretärin benimmt sich wie die Königin von England.
d) Meine Kollegen reden über mich wie über einen Idioten.
e) Selbst der Hund des Pförtners behandelt mich wie Luft.
f) Die Dame am Empfang sieht mich wie einen Fremden an.
g) Die neue Praktikantin spricht mit mir wie meine Vorgesetzte.

INDIREKTE REDE

Der Politiker meinte, die Steuern seien zu hoch.

1 Funktion

Wiedergabe von Aussagen anderer Personen

2 Formen

gesprochene Sprache	*Der Minister meinte, er hat keine Möglichkeit, die Steuern zu senken.*	meistens Indikativ
geschriebene Sprache	*Der Minister meinte, er habe keine Möglichkeit, die Steuern zu senken.*	Konjunktiv I nur in der 3. Person Singular
	Max sagt, du seist zu Hause.	*sein*: Konjunktiv I in allen Formen
	Eva meint, ich solle zum Arzt gehen.	Modalverben: Konjunktiv I in der 1. und 3. Person Singular
	Die Oppositionsparteien betonten, sie hätten ein besseres Steuerkonzept.	sonst: Konjunktiv II

ⓐ Gegenwart

	„normale" Verben			haben	sein	Modalverben
ich	*käme*	*würde*		*hätte*	*sei*	*könne*
du	*käm(e)st*	*würdest*		*hättest*	*sei(e)st*	*könntest*
er/sie/es	*komme*	*würde*	*kommen*	*habe*	*sei*	*könne*
wir	*kämen*	*würden*		*hätten*	*seien*	*könnten*
ihr	*käm(e)t*	*würdet*		*hättet*	*sei(e)t*	*könntet*
sie/Sie	*kämen*	*würden*		*hätten*	*seien*	*könnten*

Die blau gedruckten Formen sind Konjunktiv I, die anderen Konjunktiv II.

ⓑ Vergangenheit

Nur ein Tempus. Es repräsentiert die drei Vergangenheitstempora der direkten Rede:

er	*habe*	geholfen
sie	*hätten*	

er	*sei*	gelaufen
sie	*seien*	

ⓒ Perspektivenwechsel

Der Minister (gestern in Köln):	„Ich	bin	heute	hierhergekommen, ..."
Der Minister sagte,	er	sei	gestern	nach Köln gekommen, ...

ⓓ Fragesätze s. auch Seite 142:

	„*Warum haben Sie das Buch veröffentlicht?*"	Joseph L.: „ ..."
Auf die Frage,	*warum er das Buch veröffentlicht habe,*	antwortete Joseph L., ...

3 Satzstrukturen

Hauptsatz	*Er ist der Meinung, man müsse dieses Gesetz noch ändern.*
Nebensatz mit *dass*	*Er ist der Meinung, dass man dieses Gesetz noch ändern müsse.*

1 Markieren Sie in den Zeitungsartikeln die indirekte Rede.

> **Nach Operation Glatze statt Wuschelkopf**
>
> **Aveiro** – Ein Schönheitszentrum im nordportugiesischen Aveiro muss einen Patienten entschädigen, der nach einer Haarwurzelbehandlung eine Glatze bekommen hat. Ziel der Behandlung <u>sei</u> die Einsetzung künstlichen Haars <u>gewesen</u>, berichtete das portugiesische Magazin *Espresso*. Statt wallendes Haar zu tragen, sei der Mann nun aber völlig kahl. Ein Gericht in Aveiro habe die Schönheitsklinik dazu verurteilt, dem Kläger die 3300 Euro zurückzuzahlen. Außerdem müsse sie ihn für sein „seelisches Leiden" mit weiteren 3000 Euro entschädigen. Man hätte den Mann vorher über die möglichen Folgen informieren müssen, begründete das Gericht sein Urteil.
>
> **Die Braut sagt „Nein"**
>
> **Prag** – Schock vor dem Traualtar: Mit einem entschiedenen „Nein" antwortete eine junge Braut in Tschechien auf die alles entscheidende Frage des Pfarrers. Die Zeremonie sei daraufhin abgebrochen worden, das Bankett habe jedoch stattgefunden, berichteten Zeitungen in der tschechischen Hauptstadt. „Es herrschte eine Stimmung wie auf einer Beerdigung", kommentierte der Bräutigam. Für das überraschende Scheitern wählte er einen originellen Vergleich: Es sei, als ob man Billard spiele, und die Kugel rolle wider Erwarten nicht ins Loch. Nach ihren Gründen habe er seine Ex-Braut nicht gefragt: „Das übersteigt sowieso mein Verständnis", meinte er.

2 **Eine Buchvorstellung – Ergänzen Sie die Verben im Konjunktiv I bzw. Konjunktiv II.**
In seiner Rede zur Präsentation des jüngsten Gedichtbands von Skandal-Autor Joseph L. sagte der bekannte Literaturkritiker Alfred Maria W., es (a) *gebe* (geben) kaum einen Autor der Gegenwart, den er so spannend (b) .... (finden) wie Joseph L. Selbst beim wiederholten Lesen von „Anton" (c) .... (haben) er den Eindruck, dass Literatur auch heutzutage noch provozieren (d) .... (kann). Was damit genau gemeint (e) .... (sein), (f) .... (wollen) er zum jetzigen Zeitpunkt noch nicht verraten. Viele Leute (g) .... (haben) Angst vor der Lektüre eines solchen „literarischen Pamphlets", fuhr der Kritiker fort. Aber diese Leute (h) .... (müssen) sich fragen, ob sie in Wirklichkeit nicht Angst vor sich selbst (i) .... (haben). Auf die Frage, ob er und das Publikum in den Genuss einer Lesung (j) .... (kommen), antwortete der anwesende Erfolgsautor gewohnt provokant, er (k) .... (wissen) es nicht.

3 **Rede und (k)eine Antwort – Verwandeln Sie die direkte in die indirekte Rede.**
a) Der Reporter stellte dem Parteivorsitzenden die Frage: „Wie beurteilen Sie die Chancen Ihrer Partei bei der kommenden Wahl?" Der Vorsitzende antwortete: „Ich bin, wie immer, optimistisch."
   Der Reporter stellte dem Parteivorsitzenden die Frage, wie er die Chancen seiner Partei beurteile. Der Vorsitzende antwortete, er sei, wie immer, optimistisch.
b) Der Richter fragte den Zeugen: „Können Sie sich noch genau an den Unfall erinnern?" Der Zeuge erwiderte: „Ich habe noch jedes Detail in Erinnerung."
c) Der Journalist wollte von der Schauspielerin wissen: „Wie alt sind Sie?" Die Schauspielerin antwortete: „Das geht Sie gar nichts an."
d) In der Krisensitzung betonte der Vorstandsvorsitzende: „Wir müssen wegen der schlechten Auftragslage harte Maßnahmen ergreifen." Sein Assistent fügte hinzu: „Die Großaktionäre werden schon ungeduldig."

NOMEN-VERB-VERBINDUNGEN

Kritik üben

_1   Funktion

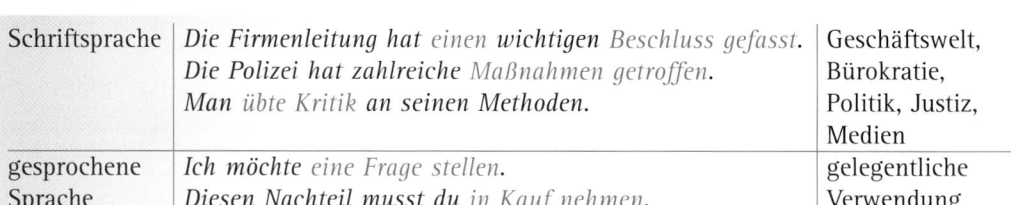

Und – für welches Modell hat sich Herr Dr. Meiser entschieden?

Tut mir leid, aber er hatte einfach noch keine Zeit, *eine Entscheidung* **zu** *treffen*.

Mit Nomen-Verb-Verbindungen wird der Sprache ein „offizieller Charakter" verliehen.

| Schriftsprache | *Die Firmenleitung hat einen wichtigen Beschluss gefasst.*
 Die Polizei hat zahlreiche Maßnahmen getroffen.
 Man übte Kritik an seinen Methoden. | Geschäftswelt, Bürokratie, Politik, Justiz, Medien |
| gesprochene Sprache | *Ich möchte eine Frage stellen.*
 Diesen Nachteil musst du in Kauf nehmen. | gelegentliche Verwendung |

Liste mit Nomen-Verb-Verbindungen s. Seite 198

_2   Formen

Präposition	Artikel	Nomen	Funktionsverb	„einfaches" Verb
	–	*Kritik*	*üben*	*kritisieren*
	den	*Vorzug*	*geben*	*vorziehen*
	eine	*Entscheidung*	*treffen*	*(sich) entscheiden*
in		*Erwägung*	*ziehen*	*erwägen*
im		*Sterben*	*liegen*	*sterben*

Manchmal kann man kein „einfaches" Verb bilden:
Das Gesetz tritt am 1.1. nächsten Jahres in Kraft. – gültig werden

Bedeutungsgruppen von Verben in Nomen-Verb-Verbindungen:

| aktivisch | *Er zieht diese Theorie in Zweifel.*
 Man stellt mir ein Auto zur Verfügung. | *bringen, führen, geben, machen, stellen, ziehen u.a.* |
| passivisch | *Mir steht ein Auto zur Verfügung.* | *finden, kommen, stehen u.a.* |

ÜBUNGEN

_1   Kampfhundverbot – Markieren Sie die Nomen-Verb-Verbindungen.

Kampfhundverbot: Ja oder nein?
Meinungen zum Thema

6

Klaus O., Journalist: „Immer mehr Menschen <u>vertreten die Ansicht</u>, man sollte Abschied nehmen von der Vorstellung, dass man ein Tier haben kann, das andere Menschen in Gefahr bringt. Die Politik sollte endlich die passenden Maßnahmen ergreifen."

Sigmund M., Psychologe: „Ich bin zu der Auffassung gelangt, dass ein Verbot auf überzeugte Kampfhundbesitzer keinen großen Eindruck machen würde. Darüber muss man sich im Klaren sein. Eher sollte man ‚Wiederholungstäter' unter psychologische Beobachtung stellen."

Jan R., Kampfhundbesitzer: „Also ich finde ein Verbot total übertrieben. Nach den Unfällen müssen wir Kampfhundbesitzer sicherlich ein paar Einschränkungen in Kauf nehmen. Und man muss natürlich auch die Frage stellen, wer überhaupt qualifiziert ist, solche Tiere zu besitzen."

2 **Nachrichten aus aller Welt – Ersetzen Sie die unterstrichenen Verben durch die angegebenen Nomen-Verb-Verbindungen.**

a) **Brasilien** – Tausende brasilianische Landarbeiter <u>streiken</u>, um gegen die Politik ihrer Regierung zu protestieren. (in Streik treten)

b) **Seoul** – Vertreter der ASEAN-Staaten <u>haben</u> <u>beschlossen</u>, die Zusammenarbeit ihrer Länder zu vertiefen. (den Beschluss fassen)

c) **Washington** – Noch ist völlig unklar, ob <u>sich</u> die EU und die USA in allen strittigen Punkten <u>einigen</u> werden. (einen Kompromiss erzielen)

d) **London** – Die Umweltminister der EU diskutieren derzeit über die Frage, ab wann die verschärften Umweltvorschriften <u>gelten</u> sollen. (in Kraft treten)

e) **Moskau** – Die russische Regierung <u>bereitet</u> die Bergung eines abgestürzten Flugzeugs im Kaukasus <u>vor</u>. (Vorbereitungen treffen zu) Experten <u>bezweifeln</u> den Erfolg dieses Plans. (in Zweifel ziehen)

Tausende brasilianischer Landarbeiter sind in Streik getreten, um ...

3 **Klaus B., Hausbesitzer und Wichtigtuer – Übersetzen Sie seinen Brief in „normales" Deutsch.**

sich äußern I bestrafen I (die Interessen) berücksichtigen I erlauben I fotografieren I hören I mitteilen I ~~ansprechen~~ I sich unterhalten I verdächtigen I vorwerfen

Sehr geehrte Frau Sperling,
ich muss ein Thema <u>zur Sprache bringen</u>, das mir sehr unangenehm ist. Mir ist <u>zu Ohren gekommen</u>, dass Sie ihre Wohnung seit einiger Zeit untervermieten. Ich muss Sie davon <u>in Kenntnis setzen</u>, dass ich Ihnen dazu nie <u>die Erlaubnis gegeben habe</u>, und möchte Sie bitten, zu diesem Punkt unverzüglich <u>Stellung zu nehmen</u>. Außerdem <u>stehen Sie im Verdacht</u>, dass Sie auf ihrem Balkon Marihuana anpflanzen. So etwas <u>steht unter Strafe</u>! Ein Nachbar hat <u>ein Foto</u> von ihrer letzten Ernte <u>gemacht</u>. Außerdem wird gegen Sie <u>der Vorwurf erhoben</u>, dass Sie nach 22 Uhr noch laute Musik hören und keinerlei <u>Rücksicht</u> auf die übrigen Hausbewohner <u>nehmen</u>. Wir sollten über alle Punkte so schnell wie möglich <u>ein</u> ernsthaftes <u>Gespräch führen</u>.

Hochachtungsvoll
Klaus B.

sehr geehrte Frau Sperling,
ich muss ein Thema ansprechen, ...

HAUPTSATZ

Das Ticket habe ich schon besorgt.

1 Funktion

Die Satzglieder des Hauptsatzes – außer dem Verb – können an verschiedenen Stellen positioniert werden. Das ermöglicht eine Variation des Satzbaus. Texte werden durch diese Variation abwechslungsreich und lesen sich flüssig.

2 Satzstruktur

Position 1	Position 2 konj. Verb	Mittelfeld			Ende
Wir Subjekt (NOM)	*nehmen*	*den Flug.* AKK-Ergänzung			
Das Ticket AKK-Ergänzung	*habe*	*ich* Subjekt (NOM)	*mir*	*schon*	*besorgt.* Partizip II
Weil ich wenig Zeit habe, Nebensatz	*fliege*	*ich* Subjekt (NOM)	*schon*	*heute Abend*	*ab.* Vorsilbe
Bis zum Abflug Angabe	*müssen*	*wir* Subjekt (NOM)	*noch*	*einiges*	*erledigen.* Infinitiv

Position 2 Satzende	Nur das Verb hat im Hauptsatz eine feste Position: die Position 2. Dort steht der zweite Teil des Verbs und bildet mit dem ersten Teil eine Klammer.
Position 1	Andere Satzteile (Ergänzungen im Akkusativ oder Dativ, eine Angabe oder ein Nebensatz) können das Subjekt von Position 1 verdrängen. Steht das Subjekt nicht auf Position 1, dann rückt es auf Position 3.
Position 3, 4 usw.	Mittelfeld 📖 **s. Seite 134**

Position 0	Position 1	Position 2	Position 3, 4 ...
Und	*wir*	*fragen*	*uns, was als Nächstes kommt.*
Aber	*sicher*	*wisst*	*ihr eine Antwort.*
Denn	*ihr*	*habt*	*euch alles gut überlegt.*
Oder	*ihr*	*habt*	*etwas darüber gelesen.*

Position 0	Die Konnektoren *aber, denn, und, oder, sondern* stehen vor dem eigentlichen Satzanfang auf Position 0; 📖 **s. Seite 146**

ÜBUNGEN

1 Zugunglück – Analysieren Sie die Positionen 0, 1 und 2 in diesem Text.

Lange haben wir in der Redaktion über diesen Kommentar diskutiert. Denn Journalisten sind ja glücklicherweise nicht ganz abgestumpft. Und so fragen wir uns in so einer Situation natürlich auch, ob man bei einer solchen Tragödie überhaupt etwas sagen soll. Aber es kann doch nützlich sein, sich ein paar Zahlen klarzumachen. Es dauert im Durchschnitt ziemlich genau vier Tage, bis der Verkehr auf unseren Straßen genauso viele Tote gefordert hat, wie in dem Zug gestorben sind. Denn Tag für Tag lassen 25 Menschen im Straßenverkehr ihr Leben. In unserem Land muss nur eine Stunde vergehen, und sechzig Menschen werden verletzt.

Position 0	Position 1	Position 2
–	*Lange*	*haben*
Denn	*Journalisten*	*sind*

2   **Mobilität – Korrigieren Sie die Fehler in der Satzstruktur.**
   a) Täglich Menschen sterben im Straßenverkehr.
      Täglich sterben Menschen im Straßenverkehr.
   b) Die Statistik sagt: In jeder Stunde es gibt in Deutschland sechzig Verletzte.
   c) Das der Preis für unsere Mobilität ist.
   d) Bei einem Zug hundertprozentige Sicherheit ist nicht möglich.
   e) In einem Auto mit Airbags wir haben auch keine totale Sicherheit.
   f) Neue Technik nicht automatisch ein besseres Leben garantiert.
   g) Denn bringt der Fortschritt auch viele Gefahren.
   h) Aber denken wir meistens nicht an diese Folgen.
   i) Und wollen wir auch nichts davon hören.

3   **S-Bahn-Probleme – Setzen Sie die unterstrichenen Satzglieder auf Position 1.**
   a) Ich wollte <u>gestern</u> einen Ausflug machen.
      Gestern wollte ich einen Ausflug machen.
   b) Ich wollte mit der S-Bahn fahren, <u>weil mein Fahrrad kaputt ist</u>.
   c) Ich stand <u>gegen zwei Uhr nachmittags</u> am Bahnsteig.
   d) Ich wartete <u>über vierzig Minuten</u> auf die S-Bahn.
   e) Ich wurde <u>nach einer halben Stunde</u> langsam sauer.
   f) Ich war fast eingeschlafen, <u>als die S-Bahn endlich kam</u>.
   g) Ich finde <u>eine so lange Wartezeit</u> unzumutbar.

4   **Der vergessene Mantel – Verbessern Sie diesen Brief, indem Sie andere Satzteile auf Position 1 stellen oder zwei oder mehrere Sätze verbinden.**

```
An das
Fundbüro der Deutschen Bahn

Sehr geehrte Damen und Herren,
ich habe gestern im Zug meinen Mantel vergessen. Ich habe ihn in dem
ICE um 17.33 Uhr von München nach Frankfurt liegen lassen. Ich möchte
Sie fragen, ob jemand den Mantel bei Ihnen abgegeben hat. Der Mantel
ist grün. Er ist aus Wolle. Ein roter Schal steckte in der Tasche des
Mantels. Bitte schicken Sie mir den Mantel, wenn das möglich ist. Bitte
lassen Sie mir eine Nachricht zukommen, wenn ich den Mantel selber
abholen soll. Ich übernehme selbstverständlich die Kosten für das Porto.
Herzlichen Dank im Voraus.

Mit freundlichen Grüßen
Ihre Elisabeth Goodman
```

Sehr geehrte Damen und Herren,
gestern habe ich im Zug meinen Mantel vergessen.

MITTELFELD DES SATZES

... heute wegen des schönen Wetters unbedingt ins Freibad ...

1 Subjekt und Objekt im Mittelfeld

POS 1	POS 2		Mittelfeld		Ende
1 *Henry*	*leiht*	*seinem Freund*	*manchmal*	*sein Lieblingsauto.*	
2 *Manchmal*	*leiht*	*Henry*	*seinem Freund*	*sein Lieblingsauto.*	
3 *Henry*	*leiht*	*ihm*	*manchmal*	*sein Lieblingsauto.*	
4 *Er*	*leiht*	*es*	*ihm*	*manchmal.*	
5 *Gestern*	*hat*	*er*	*es*	*ihm*	*geliehen.*
6 *Ihm*	*würde*	*er*	*auch sein schönstes Buch*		*leihen.*
7 *Seinen Teddy*	*wird*	*Henry*	*ihm*	*aber nie*	*leihen.*
8 *Er*	*hat*	*ihm*	*einen*		*geschenkt.*

Mittelfeld	Alle Satzteile außer dem Verb (Position 2 und Ende) sind im Hauptsatz in ihrer Position variabel. Sie können entweder auf Position 1 oder im Mittelfeld stehen.
Subjekt	steht entweder auf Position 1 (Beispiel 1, 3, 4, 8) oder direkt nach dem Verb (Beispiel 2).
Pronomen	• stehen vor Nomen (kurz vor lang) (Beispiel 3). • stehen direkt nach dem Verb (Beispiel 3, 4, 5, 6, 8) bzw. nach dem Subjekt, falls dieses auf Position 3 steht (Beispiel 5, 7). Stellung der Reflexivpronomen 📖 **s. Seite 92**
Akkusativ- und Dativ-Ergänzung	• Dativ (dunkelblau) steht vor Akkusativ (hellblau) (Beispiel 1, 2, 3, 8). • Ist der Akkusativ ein Personalpronomen, steht er vor dem Dativ (Beispiel 4, 5). • Bei anderen Pronomen (z.B. *einen*) bleibt die Reihenfolge Dativ vor Akkusativ (Beispiel 8).

2 Angaben

Objekte und Angaben	• Angaben können auf Position 1 stehen (Beispiel 2, 5). • Für die Stellung der Angaben im Mittelfeld lassen sich kaum feste Regeln geben. Temporale Angaben (z.B. *manchmal, nie*) stehen häufig nach der Dativ-Ergänzung. (Beispiel 1, 3, 4, 7).
mehrere Angaben	Auch hier lassen sich keine exakten Regeln angeben. Normalerweise gilt: temporal vor kausal/konzessiv/konditional vor modal vor lokal.

	wann? temporal	warum? welche Bedingung? kausal / konzessiv /konditional	wie? modal	wo? wohin? lokal	
Karin will	*heute*	*wegen des schönen Wetters*	*unbedingt*	*ins Freibad*	*gehen.*
Else steht	*in der Woche gegen 7 Uhr*				*auf.*

1 **Im Computerkurs – Formulieren Sie Sätze.**
a) Die Kursleiterin gibt das neue Arbeitsbuch – den Teilnehmern.
Die Kursleiterin gibt den Teilnehmern das neue Arbeitsbuch.
b) Ihr Kollege macht Fotokopien von den Unterlagen – uns.
c) Sie beantwortet alle meine Fragen – mir.
d) Herr Meier bringt die vermisste Diskette – uns.
e) Die Trainerin erklärt die Möglichkeiten des Programms – meiner Kollegin.
f) Wir schenken einen Blumenstrauß – der Kursleiterin.

2 **Ergänzen Sie die Sätze aus Übung 1 im Mittelfeld durch folgende Angaben.**
a) nächste Woche
Die Kursleiterin gibt den Teilnehmern nächste Woche das neue Arbeitsbuch.
b) bis morgen   c) sofort   d) gleich   e) noch einmal   f) am Kursende

3 **Ersetzen Sie das Nomen im Akkusativ durch ein Personalpronomen.**
a) *Die Kursleiterin gibt es den Teilnehmern nächste Woche.*

4 **Fragen und Antworten – Ergänzen Sie die Pronomen.**
a) Könntest du mir mal kurz deinen Kugelschreiber leihen? – Wenn du möchtest,
schenke ich *ihn dir*.
b) Gibst du mir bitte mal das Lineal? – Ich habe .... doch bereits hingelegt.
c) Würden Sie mir ein Mineralwasser bringen? – Ich habe .... schon dort
hingestellt.
d) Würden Sie mir bitte meine Frage beantworten? – Ich habe .... doch
bereits beantwortet.
e) Könntest du mir den Weg zur Universität beschreiben? – Ich habe ....
hier auf diesem Blatt aufgezeichnet.
f) Herr Murr, wo bitte ist das Protokoll von der letzten Sitzung? – Ich habe ....
.... bereits hingelegt.

5 **Frauen wie Elsa – Erweitern Sie die Sätze. Stellen Sie eine**
der Angaben an den Satzanfang. Es gibt mehrere Lösungen.

a) Elsa steht auf. – in der Woche / gegen 7 Uhr
In der Woche steht Elsa gegen 7 Uhr auf. • Gegen 7 Uhr steht Elsa in der
Woche auf.
b) Sie verlässt das Haus. – bei gutem Wetter / um Viertel nach acht
c) Sie fährt mit dem Fahrrad. – bei gutem Wetter / normalerweise
d) Ihre Einkäufe erledigt Elsa. – in einem Einkaufszentrum / nach der Arbeit
e) Sie treibt Sport. – in einem Fitnesscenter für Frauen / zweimal pro Woche
f) Sie macht mit zwei Freundinnen Wassergymnastik. – in einem Kurbad /
am Wochenende
g) Sie sieht sich gerne die neuesten Filme an. – samstagabends / in einem der großen Kinos
in der Stadt
h) Elsa leistet sich ein Abendessen im Restaurant. – mindestens einmal pro Monat / trotz
knapper Kasse

7

NEGATION

nichts – niemand

1 Negation eines Satzes

Die Musiker enttäuschten nicht. *Die Musiker enttäuschten das Publikum nicht.* *Die Musiker enttäuschten das Publikum gestern im Konzert nicht.*	*nicht* steht möglichst weit am Ende
Wir haben uns nicht gefreut. *Er hört einfach nicht auf.* *Er braucht nicht zu arbeiten.*	vor dem zweiten Teil des Verbs
Er spielt nicht Klavier.	vor Akkusativ-Ergänzungen, die eng zum Verb gehören
Er erinnert sich nicht an seine Schulzeit.	vor Präpositional-Ergänzungen
Wir gehen nicht in die Schule.	vor Lokal-Ergänzungen
Wir freuen uns nicht besonders.	vor qualitativen Ergänzungen

2 Negation eines Satzteils

Nicht die Musiker enttäuschten, sondern die Sänger. *Die Musiker haben uns nicht enttäuscht, sondern begeistert.* *Ich habe nicht das heutige Konzert gemeint, sondern das von gestern Abend.*	*nicht* steht vor dem Satzteil, der negiert wird

3 Negation von Artikeln, Pronomen, Adverbien

positiv	negativ	
das/ein	*kein*	*Ich habe kein neues Auto.*
ein(e)s	*kein(e)s*	*Haben wir noch Brot? Nein, wir haben keins mehr.*
alles, etwas	*nichts**	*Mit Brille sehe ich alles, ohne kann ich nichts erkennen.* *Hast du etwas? Nein, ich habe nichts.*
jemand	*niemand,** keiner*	*Niemand versteht mich.* *Keiner liebt mich.*
immer	*nie, niemals*	*Ich werde nie/niemals verstehen, warum du das getan hast.*
überall *irgendwo*	*nirgendwo,* *nirgends*	*Ich habe überall nach meiner Brille gesucht – ich habe sie nirgends/nirgendwo gefunden.*
schon	*noch nicht/nie*	*Hast du schon mal Golf gespielt? Nein, noch nie.*

* s. Seite 54 (Indefinitpronomen)

ÜBUNGEN

1 Wohnungen – Warum ist Wohnung 2 ein besseres Angebot?

	Wohnung 2	Wohnung 1
die Tiefgarage	ja	nein
die Zentralheizung	ja	nein

	Wohnung 2	Wohnung 1
das Bad	ja	nein
das separate WC	ja	nein
die Einbauküche	ja	nein
die Abstellkammer	ja	nein
der Balkon	ja	nein

Sie hat eine Tiefgarage, Wohnung 1 hat keine.

2 Zur Person – Negation mit nicht, kein, keine.

a) Formulieren Sie Fragen und negative Antworten.

	Hannah	Matthias
verheiratet	+	–
Kinder	–	–
berufstätig	+	–
Geld gespart	–	–
schon mal in Polen	–	+
Fremdsprachen	+	–
Freunde in Deutschland	–	+
eine E-Mail-Adresse	+	–

Ist Matthias verheiratet? – Nein, er ist nicht verheiratet.
Hat Hannah Kinder? – Nein, sie hat keine Kinder.

b) Vergleichen Sie die beiden Personen.
Hannah ist verheiratet, aber Matthias noch nicht.
Matthias hat keine Kinder, Hannah hat auch noch keine.

3 Moderne Zeiten – Verneinen Sie diese Fragen höflich. Verwenden Sie nicht, nichts oder kein.

a) Wissen Sie, was ein Gameboy ist?
   Nein, das weiß ich leider nicht.
b) Hast du schon mal etwas von „Pokemon" gehört?
c) Hast du vielleicht eine leere Diskette für mich?
d) Kennen Sie ein Computerprogramm gegen Viren?
e) Kennst du den Zugangscode zu diesem Computer?
f) Braucht man für diese Kreditkarte eine Geheimzahl?
g) Muss man diese Uhr per Hand aufziehen?
h) Verstehen Sie etwas von Aktien?
i) Hast du irgendwo meine Uhr gesehen?

4 Kauflust – Ergänzen Sie die Negationswörter.

Ich konnte noch (a) *nie* an einem Modeladen vorbeigehen, ohne mir etwas zu kaufen.
Dabei spielt es (b) .... Rolle, ob ich viel oder wenig Geld in der Tasche habe.
Es fällt mir in diesem Moment auch (c) .... ein, dass ich bereits hundert
ähnliche Sachen im Schrank hängen habe. Ich habe schon alles versucht, um mir diese
Sucht abzugewöhnen, aber bisher hat mir (d) .... geholfen. Ich finde einfach
(e) .... richtiges Mittel dagegen.

7

IMPERATIV (1): FORMEN

Mach bitte deine Hausaufgaben!

_1_ **Funktion**

Frau Huber verreist für drei Wochen. Sie
erklärt Ihrer Nachbarin, was sie tun soll:

> *Bitte gießen Sie einmal pro Woche die Pflanzen!*
> *Den Goldfischen geben Sie bitte täglich Futter!*
> *Leeren Sie bitte regelmäßig unseren Briefkasten!*

*Leeren **Sie** bitte regelmäßig den Briefkasten!*	Bitte
Stoppt die Gewalt!	Appell
Lasst uns doch zusammen ins Kino gehen.	Vorschlag/Angebot
Sei bitte vorsichtig!	Rat/Empfehlung
Mach jetzt deine Hausaufgaben!	Anordnung
Lass das! Tu das bitte nicht! Schnallen Sie sich immer an!	Ermahnung/Warnung
Verwenden Sie für dieses Rezept fettarme Milch.	Anleitung

_2_ **Formen**

Sie-Form	*Essen Sie weniger Zucker!*	Wie in der 3. Person Plural, aber zuerst das Verb, dann das Pronomen.
	Seien Sie unbesorgt!	Ausnahme: *sein*
Du-Form		Wie die 2. Person Singular, aber ohne Endung und ohne Personalpronomen:
	Iss weniger Zucker!	~~du~~ iss~~t~~ – iss
	Sprich etwas lauter!	~~du~~ sprich~~st~~ – sprich
	Sei ruhig, bitte!	Ausnahme: *sein*
		Verben, die auf *-d, -t, -ig, -m* und *–n* enden, behalten das *-e**:
	Antworte mir bitte!	~~du~~ antworte~~st~~ – antworte
	Öffne bitte das Fenster!	~~du~~ öffne~~st~~ – öffne
		Unregelmäßige Verben immer ohne Umlaut:
	Lauf nach Hause!	~~du~~ l~~äu~~fst – lauf
	Fahr nach Köln!	~~du~~ f~~äh~~r~~st~~ – fahr
Ihr-Form	*Gebt mir eine Chance!*	Wie die 2. Person Plural,
	Seid vorsichtig!	es fehlt nur das Pronomen.

* In älteren Texten gibt es die Endung *-e* auch bei anderen Verben, z.B. *Reiche mir bitte das Salz.*

Geh endlich nach Hause!	Das Ausrufezeichen gibt Aufforderungs- bzw. Befehlssätzen Nachdruck.
Gehen Sie doch einfach nach Hause.	Punkt, wenn ohne Nachdruck gesprochen wird.

1 Stressfreie Reise – Unterstreichen Sie alle Imperative.

> Überprüfen Sie vor einer Reise Ihren Pass und lassen Sie ihn eventuell rechtzeitig verlängern. Wenn Sie in Hauptreisezeiten fliegen wollen: Beeilen Sie sich mit der Buchung ihres Fluges oder Hotels. Ziehen Sie bei einem längeren Flug bequeme Kleidung an. Schließen Sie Ihre Wertsachen im Hotelsafe ein. Rufen Sie Ihre Lieben zu Hause an, wenn Sie am Ziel angekommen sind.

2 Tischmanieren für Deutschlandbesucher – Geben Sie Ratschläge in der Sie-Form.

falten | fassen | halten | schließen | ~~stellen~~ | verdecken | verlassen | verwenden

a) die Ellbogen nicht auf den Tisch
   Stellen Sie die Ellbogen nicht auf den Tisch.
b) die Serviette nicht nach Gebrauch
c) die Gabel in der linken und das Messer in der rechten Hand
d) die Lippen beim Kauen
e) die kleine Gabel für den Kuchen
f) das Weinglas am Stiel
g) die rechte mit der linken Hand, wenn Sie einen Zahnstocher benutzen
h) nicht den Tisch, bevor alle fertig gegessen haben

3 Gesundheits-Tipps – Ergänzen Sie die Verben in der Ihr- und in der Du-Form.

essen | kontrollieren | putzen | sein | spülen | ~~trinken~~ | verwenden

> **MIT ZUCKER SPARSAM UMGEHEN**
> a) *Trinkt / Trink* öfter mal ungesüßten Tee oder Mineralwasser statt Cola oder Limonade!
> b) .... vorsichtig bei klebrigen Süßwaren, insbesondere Bonbons!
> c) .... öfter mal Obst statt Schokolade oder Bonbons!
> d) .... möglichst nach jeder Mahlzeit die Zähne!
> e) .... den Mund mit Wasser aus, wenn Zähneputzen nicht möglich ist!
> f) .... Süßigkeiten nicht als Belohnung!
> g) .... regelmäßig das Körpergewicht!

4 Ratschläge – Formulieren Sie Sätze in der Du-Form.

a) Obst / frisch / essen / täglich
   Iss täglich frisches Obst!
b) Flüssigkeit / Liter / mindestens / täglich / trinken / zwei
c) Sport / treiben / pro / Woche / zweimal
d) acht Stunden / schlafen / täglich
e) achten / beim Einkaufen / auf / gesunde Lebensmittel
f) auf Alkohol / möglichst / verzichten

IMPERATIV (2): ALTERNATIVEN

Gibst du mir mal die Zeitschrift?

Durch den Zusatz des Wortes *bitte* oder die Verwendung des Konjunktivs *(Es wäre schön, wenn du ... könntest.)* wird aus einem Befehl eine freundliche oder höfliche Aufforderung. In erster Linie kommt es aber auf die Betonung an.

Aufforderung

Imperativ	*Räum dein Zimmer auf!*
Konditionalsatz Konjunktiv II	*Es wäre schön, wenn du endlich dein Zimmer aufräumen könntest.*
Frage + Modalverb Konjunktiv II	*Könntest du endlich dein Zimmer aufräumen?*

Bitte

Imperativ	*Reichen Sie mir bitte das Salz.*
Frage + Konjunktiv II + *bitte* + Modalpartikeln	*Könnten Sie mir bitte mal das Salz reichen?*
	Würdest du mir mal die Limonade bringen?
	Gibst du mir bitte mal die Zeitschrift?
	Hätten Sie mal bitte Feuer?
Kurzform	*Das Salz bitte. / Bitte das Salz.*
Aussagesatz	*Ich möchte bitte mal das Salz.*
	Ich brauche mal bitte einen Stift.
Konditionalsatz	*Wenn Sie mir vielleicht noch das Salz reichen könnten.*

Rat und Empfehlung

Imperativ	*Nimm besser Honig statt Zucker!*	
Frage	*Warum nehmen Sie nicht Honig statt Zucker?*	vorsichtig
sollen	*Sie sollten Honig statt Zucker nehmen.*	energisch
Konjunktiv II	*Du solltest Honig statt Zucker nehmen.*	
würde	*Ich würde eher Honig statt Zucker nehmen.*	persönlich
man	*Man nimmt besser Honig statt Zucker.*	unpersönlich

Anleitung

Imperativ	*Geben Sie die Backmischung, Fett, Eier und Wasser in eine Schüssel.*
Infinitiv	*Die Backmischung, Fett, Eier und Wasser in eine Schüssel geben.*

ÜBUNGEN

__1__ **So nerven Sie Ihre Lieben schon am frühen Morgen – Formulieren Sie zuerst Bitten und dann weniger höfliche Aufforderungen.**

a) aufstehen

Würdest du bitte aufstehen? Könntest du bitte mal aufstehen?
Steh endlich auf!

b) sich rasieren　d) sich duschen　f) sich frisieren　h) sich beeilen
c) sich waschen　e) sich anziehen　g) sich kämmen　i) Regenschirm mitnehmen

2　**Wie bediene ich eine Waschmaschine? – Formulieren Sie persönlicher in der Sie-Form.**
(a) Zuerst sortiert man die Wäsche. (b) Dann legt man die Wäsche in die Maschine hinein.
(c) Dann schließt man die Tür. (d) Dann kontrolliert man, ob der Stecker in der Steckdose
steckt. (e) Anschließend dreht man den Wasserhahn auf. (f) Als Nächstes lässt man das
Waschpulver einlaufen. (g) Dann wählt man das gewünschte Programm. (h) Schließlich stellt
man die Temperatur ein und drückt den Start-Knopf.

(a) *Sortieren Sie zuerst die Wäsche.*

3　**Backstudio – Formulieren Sie die Anleitung in der Du-Form.**

1. Teig bereiten	2. Belag herstellen
(a) Backmischung, weiches Fett, Eier und Wasser in eine Rührschüssel geben. (b) Drei Minuten rühren.	(c) Die Äpfel schälen. (d) Drei Äpfel entkernen, in Würfel schneiden und unter den Teig heben. (e) Den Teig in eine Backform füllen. (f) Den vierten Apfel in Scheiben schneiden und auf den Teig legen. (g) Die Form in den Backofen schieben und den Kuchen backen.

(a) *Gib die Backmischung, weiches Fett, Eier und Wasser in eine Rührschüssel.*

4　**Ratschläge zum guten Benehmen – Formulieren Sie Sätze.**
a) der Gastgeberin Blumen mitbringen
　　Sie sollten der Gastgeberin Blumen mitbringen.
　　Man bringt der Gastgeberin Blumen mit.
b) das Papier vor dem Klingeln von dem Blumenstrauß entfernen
c) das Papier in die eigene Tasche stecken
d) die Gastgeber mit Händedruck begrüßen
e) saubere, möglichst gebügelte Sachen und geputzte Schuhe tragen
f) seine Schuhe anbehalten
g) bei offiziellen Einladungen einen Anzug und eine Krawatte tragen

5　**Vater und Sohn als Heimwerker – Formulieren Sie höfliche Bitten in der Form, die jeweils angegeben ist.**

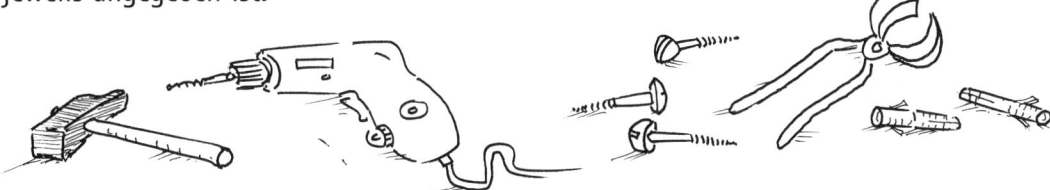

a) mir den Hammer geben (Imperativ + *doch mal bitte)*
　　Gib mir doch mal bitte den Hammer.
b) mir den Werkzeugkasten bringen (Frage + Modalverb Konjunktiv II + *mal)*
c) die Schrauben Nummer 5 suchen (Frage + *mal bitte)*
d) auch die passenden Dübel dazu suchen (Frage + Modalverb Konjunktiv II)
e) in den Keller laufen (Imperativ + *doch mal)*
f) die Bohrmaschine holen (Imperativ + *bitte)*
g) nachsehen, ob zweiter Werkzeugkasten dort sein (Frage + Modalverb Konjunktiv II + *bitte)*

FRAGESATZ

Wann geht der nächste Zug nach Hamburg?

1 **Funktion**

Ist der Zug nach Hamburg schon weg?	sich informieren
Können Sie mir bitte helfen?	bitten

2 **Formen**
   a direkte Fragen

	Frage			Antwort
		Verb		
Entscheidungsfrage		*Hast*	*du ein Lieblingstier?*	*Ja. / Nein.*
= ohne Fragewort		*Hast*	*du kein Lieblingstier?*	*Doch. / Nein.*
Ergänzungsfrage	*Welches Tier*	*magst*	*du am liebsten?*	*Den Delfin.*
= mit Fragewort				

   b indirekte Fragen

	Einleitungssatz	Nebensatz		
		Konnektor		Verb
Entscheidungsfrage	*Kannst du mir sagen,*	*ob*	*du ein Lieblingstier*	*hast?*
= ohne Fragewort				
Ergänzungsfrage	*Sag mir bitte,*	*welches*	*Tier du am liebsten*	*magst.*
= mit Fragewort				

Interpunktion	*Wohin gehst du?*	Fragezeichen **nach direkten,**	
	Sag mir bitte, wohin du gehst.	Punkt **nach indirekten Fragen.**	

ÜBUNGEN

1 **Im Zoo – Ordnen Sie passende Antworten zu. Es sind mehrere Lösungen möglich.**

‹ die Faultiere I die Menschenaffen I doch I ja I nein

a) Hast du noch keine Eintrittskarte? *Doch.*
b) Bist du auch schon so müde wie ich?
c) Hast du keine Lust mehr, noch zu den Elefanten zu gehen?
d) Hättest du Lust, die Ziegen zu füttern?
e) Vielleicht sollten wir uns mal hinsetzen und ein Eis essen.
f) Warst du schon mal im Streichelzoo, wo man die Tiere anfassen darf?
g) Welche Tiere findest du besonders langweilig?
h) Welche Tiere schaust du dir am liebsten an?

2 **Sicherheitsmaßnahmen – Formulieren Sie Fragen.**
a) Doch, ich habe die Fenster fest geschlossen.
   Haben Sie denn die Fenster nicht fest geschlossen?

b) Doch, ich habe auch die Kellertür abgeschlossen.

c) Doch, ich habe den Schlüssel zweimal herumgedreht.

d) Doch, ich habe das Licht abends brennen lassen.

e) Doch, ich habe die Alarmanlage eingeschaltet.

f) Doch, ich habe den Briefkasten vom Nachbarn leeren lassen.

3   **Abendprogramm – Formulieren Sie indirekte Fragesätze mit** ob **oder** wann**.**

a) im Kino   das bestellte Buch schon da

b) bei der Theaterkasse   Kurs schon angefangen

c) im Restaurant   noch ein Tisch frei

d) im Fitness-Studio   noch Karten für diesen neuen Thriller / der Film anfangen

e) in der Bibliothek   geöffnet

f) in der Volkshochschule   Vorstellung zu Ende

a) *Ruf doch bitte im Kino an und frag, ob es noch Karten für diesen neuen Thriller gibt und wann der Film anfängt.*

4   **Um Auskunft bitten – Formulieren Sie indirekte Fragesätze.**

a) Der Bus fährt alle zehn Minuten. (Wie oft?)

    Können Sie mir sagen, wie oft der Bus fährt?

b) Der Taxistand ist da drüben. (Wo?)

c) Die Straße ist wegen Bauarbeiten gesperrt. (Warum?/Weshalb?)

d) Es ist gleich sieben. (Wie?)

e) Die Banken schließen heute um 16 Uhr. (Wann?)

f) Der Fernsehturm ist 150 Meter hoch. (Wie?)

g) In diesem Haus befindet sich das Fremdenverkehrsamt. (Was?)

h) Hier wohnt niemand. Es ist ein Bürogebäude. (Wer?)

5   **Kinobesuch – Formulieren Sie indirekte Fragesätze.**

a) Was gibt es heute Abend im Kino? Kannst du mir sagen, ...

    Kannst du mir sagen, was es heute Abend im Kino gibt?

b) Von wem ist denn dieser Film? Weißt du, ...

c) Und wer spielt mit? Und weißt du auch, ...

d) Was kosten die Karten da eigentlich? Sag mal, ...

e) In welchem Kino läuft der Film? Noch wichtiger ist, ...

f) Wann fängt die Vorstellung an? Weißt du noch, ...

g) Wer geht noch mit? Darf ich fragen, ...

6   **Ehestreit – Ergänzen Sie den Dialog.**

a) Du hättest wirklich etwas früher nach Hause kommen können.   Wieso? Du interessierst dich doch sonst nicht dafür, *wann ich nach Hause komme*. (nach Hause kommen)

b) Und dann dieser Anzug!   Du achtest doch sonst nicht darauf, ... (aussehen)

c) Diese Krawatte ist das Letzte.   Ich ziehe doch nur an, ... (im Schrank finden)

d) Hast du übrigens den Föhn gesehen? Du musst ihn irgendwie verlegt haben.   Wieso ich? Du weißt doch selber nicht, ... (die Sachen liegen).

e) Du sitzt genau vor dem Fernseher.   Ich entscheide selber, ... (sitzen).

f) Warum gehst du nicht einfach ins Bett?   Ich entscheide ebenfalls selber, ... (schlafen gehen).

FRAGEWÖRTER

wer – was – worüber

wer	Wer hat gewonnen?	Person	Nominativ
was	Was sagst du dazu?	Sache	
wen	Wen rufst du an?	Person	Akkusativ
wem	Wem schenkst du diese Blumen?		Dativ
wessen	Wessen Telefonnummer ist das?		Genitiv
wo	Wo bist du geboren?	Ort	
wohin	Wohin fährst du in Urlaub?		
woher	Woher stammt deine Familie?		
wann	Wann musst du gehen?	Zeitpunkt	
wie lange	Wie lange seid ihr schon da?	Dauer	*wie* + Adverb
wie oft	Wie oft besucht ihr den Kurs?	Häufigkeit	
warum	Warum willst du schon gehen?	Grund	
wieso	Wieso gehst du schon wieder zur Bank?		
weshalb	Weshalb gehst du schon wieder zur Bank?		
wie	Wie gefällt dir der Roman?	Qualität	*wie* + Verb
	Wie hoch ist der Eiffelturm?		*wie* + Adjektiv
wie viel	Wie viel Geld hast du noch?	Menge	Nomen im Singular
wie viele	Wie viele Freunde willst du einladen?	Anzahl	Nomen im Plural
welcher, -e, -es	Welches von diesen hier gefällt dir am besten?	Auswahl	
was für ein	Was für ein Auto willst du?	Qualität	

Fragewort bei Verben mit Präposition

Person	über + Akkusativ	Über wen habt ihr euch denn gerade so intensiv unterhalten?
	mit + Dativ	Mit wem hast du dich denn da unterhalten?
Sache	worüber	Worüber habt ihr denn gerade so gelacht?
	womit	Womit bist du gerade beschäftigt?

wo(r) + Präposition: *r* wird eingefügt, wenn die Präposition mit Vokal beginnt, 📖 **s. Seite 56**.

ÜBUNGEN

1 **Viele Fragen – Formulieren Sie Fragen zu den unterstrichenen Wörtern.**

a) Die CD gehört <u>Peter</u>.
   Wem gehört die CD?

b) Es ist <u>etwas</u> passiert.

c) Ich bin <u>über etwas</u> besorgt.

d) Ich habe mir Geld <u>von Helga</u> geliehen.

e) Ich spüre <u>etwas Kaltes</u> auf der Hand.

f) Ich suche <u>Angela</u>.

g) Ich habe <u>meinen Geldbeutel</u> verloren.

h) Wir haben am Wochenende <u>meine Eltern</u> besucht.

i) Das ist <u>Egons</u> Mantel.

2   Steckbrief – Formulieren Sie direkte Fragen.

a) Alter: 15 Jahre - *Wie alt bist du?*
b) Augenfarbe: grünbraun
c) Größe: 1,67 cm
d) Gewicht: 50 kg
e) Schule: Gymnasium, 9. Klasse
f) liebstes Schulfach: Biologie
g) Hobby: Gitarrespielen
h) Lieblingstier: Delfin
i) Lieblingsgericht: Gemüselasagne
j) Mag am liebsten: Natur

3   Schaufensterbummel – Ergänzen Sie die Fragewörter.
- ■ Sieh mal, (a) *wie* gefällt dir die Jacke da?
- ■ (b) .... meinst du, die graue oder die blaue?
- ■ Die blaue.
- ■ Die gefällt mir nicht. Aber (c) .... sagst du zu dem Pullover da hinten?
- ■ (d) .... meinst du, den mit dem Rollkragen oder den daneben?
- ■ Den mit dem Rollkragen meine ich.
- ■ Finde ich gut. Was ich aber viel dringender brauche, ist ein neuer Rock.
- ■ Und an (e) .... denkst du?
- ■ An so einen kurzen, schwarzen, wie sie jetzt modern sind.
- ■ Und (f) .... Schuhe ziehst du heute Abend zur Tanzstunde an?
- ■ Weiß ich noch nicht. Ich weiß auch noch nicht, (g) .... Kleid ich anziehe.

4   Im Kurs – Ergänzen Sie das Fragewort.

an I aus I für I in I mit (2x) I über (3x) I um (2x) I von (2x) I zu

a) *Womit*   beschäftigt sich der Kurs im Moment?
b) .... besteht das Problem?
c) .... dient dieser Apparat?
d) .... diskutieren die Teilnehmer im Unterricht?
e) *Mit wem*   (Person) gehst du heute Abend zur Kursparty?
f) .... hängt die Note im Zeugnis ab?
g) .... schließt du, dass der Kurs schwer ist?
h) .... (Person) hast du denn dieses Briefchen bekommen?
i) .... geht es in dieser Lektion?
j) .... müssen sich die Teilnehmer gewöhnen?
k) .... (Person) interessieren sich alle am meisten?
l) .... ärgert sich der Kursleiter?
m) .... muss sich jeder Teilnehmer selber kümmern?
n) .... (Person) lacht die ganze Klasse?

HAUPTSATZVERBINDENDE KONNEKTOREN

und – oder – aber – denn – sondern

1 Funktion

und	*Er geht gerne aus und amüsiert sich gern.*	Aufzählung*
oder	*Nimmst du schwarz oder rot?*	Alternative
aber	*Peter ist arm, aber glücklich.*	Kontrast
denn	*Eva versteht Peter, denn sie hatte dasselbe Problem.*	Grund
sondern	*Peter will nicht mehr Geld, sondern mehr Freizeit.*	Kontrast, Differenz
	Maria kommt nicht erst morgen, sondern schon heute.	nach Negation

* bedeutungsgleich mit *und* ist *sowie*. Es wird nur bei Satzgliedern verwendet und vermeidet eine Wiederholung von *und* bei mehreren Nomen: *Insekten haben sechs Beine und zwei Paar Flügel sowie ein Paar Fühler.*

2 Satzstrukturen

Hauptsatz	Hauptsatz			
	Konnektor POS 0		Verb POS 2	
Insekten haben sechs Beine (,)	*und*	*(sie)**	*(haben)*	*zwei Paar Flügel.*
Sie leben in der Luft (,)	*oder*	*(sie)**	*(leben)*	*in der Erde.*
Die Arbeiterinnen sind Weibchen,	*aber***	*sie*	*können*	*keine Eier legen.*
Die Feuerameise ist gefährlich,	*denn*	*sie*	*kann*	*schmerzhaft beißen.*
Die Königin arbeitet nicht,	*sondern*	*(sie)*	*legt*	*die Eier.*

* Wenn Verben und Subjekt identisch sind, können sie im zweiten Hauptsatz wegfallen.
  Ausnahme: *denn*

** *aber* kann auch im Satz stehen: *Die Arbeiterinnen sind Weibchen, (sie) legen aber keine Eier.* 📖 **s. Seite 178** (Adversativsatz)

Interpunktion: immer Komma bei *aber, denn, sondern*
                kein Komma bei *oder, sowie*

ÜBUNGEN

1 Kurzmeldung in der Zeitung – Verbinden Sie die Sätze mit *und*.

V. F. Le Front, französischer Lehrer, ist in der niederländischen Presse zum „ehrlichsten Finder des vergangenen Jahres" ausgerufen worden. (a) Der 55-Jährige entdeckte auf einem Parkplatz in Frankreich einen liegen gelassenen Fotoapparat. Er nahm ihn mit. (b) Von einem Autofahrer erfuhr er, dass an der Stelle kurz zuvor eine niederländische Familie gepicknickt hatte. Er entschloss sich sofort, die Familie zu suchen. (c) Le Front brachte den Film in ein Fotolabor. Er ließ ihn entwickeln. (d) Auf den Bildern war eine Frau zu sehen. Es waren zwei Kinder zu sehen. (e) Er schickte die Fotos an die größte niederländische Zeitung. Er bat darum, sie zu veröffentlichen. (f) Am Freitag druckte *De Telegraaf* tatsächlich ein Bild der Frau ab. *De Telegraaf* fragte: „Wem gehört dieses Foto?" (g) Nun hofft Le Front, dass die Frau das Foto sieht. Er hofft, dass sie sich meldet.

(a) *Der 55-Jährige entdeckte auf einem Parkplatz in Frankreich einen liegen gelassenen Fotoapparat und nahm ihn mit.*

2   Insekten – Ergänzen Sie die fehlenden Konnektoren.

Wozu sie gut sind.

Wir alle haben täglich Kontakt mit Insekten: Sie stechen und beißen uns, (a) *und* sie übertragen dabei leider auch zahlreiche teilweise gefährliche Krankheiten. (b) .... sie tun auch viel Gutes, (c) .... sie verarbeiten zum Beispiel tote Tiere und Pflanzen, (d) .... sie dienen vielen anderen Lebewesen als Nahrung. Wir gewinnen aus ihnen Produkte wie Seide, (e) .... wir erforschen Genetik und die Evolution an ihnen.

Was sie fressen.

Insekten sind „Überlebenskünstler", (f) .... sie können sich von allem Möglichen ernähren. Sie fressen nicht nur Pflanzen, Blätter, Wurzeln, (g) .... sie machen sich auch über gelagerte Lebensmittel, Bücher und sogar Haushaltsgegenstände her.

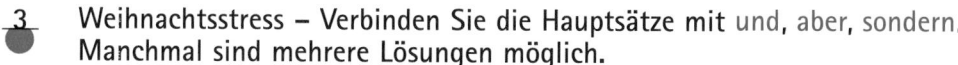

3   Weihnachtsstress – Verbinden Sie die Hauptsätze mit und, aber, sondern. Manchmal sind mehrere Lösungen möglich.

a) Herbert K., 31 Jahre:
Als Lehrer hat man vor Weihnachten Stress: Die Weihnachtsfeier in der Schule muss vorbereitet werden, Konferenzen finden statt.
– Dann soll man auch noch Geschenke kaufen.

Als Lehrer hat man vor Weihnachten Stress: Die Weihnachtsfeier in der Schule muss vorbereitet werden, Konferenzen finden statt, und dann soll man auch noch Geschenke kaufen.

b) Susanne H., 73 Jahre:
Mein Mann kümmert sich nicht um Weihnachten.
– Er geht nur mit dem Hund spazieren.

c) Eva C., 57 Jahre:
Mein Mann macht sich keine Gedanken, was er zu Weihnachten schenkt. Das war schon immer meine Angelegenheit.
– Das wird weiterhin so bleiben.

d) Klaus O., 50 Jahre:
Ich bin wirklich total im Weihnachtsstress. Gott sei Dank weiß ich ungefähr, was ich meiner Frau schenken werde.
– Der Stress bleibt einfach bis zum 24. Dezember.

e) Silke H., 39 Jahre:
Für die Geschenke bin ich zuständig. Die Männer sitzen nur vor dem Fernseher. Sie rühren keinen Finger.
– Sie erwarten, dass zu Weihnachten alles da ist, Christbaum, Geschenke, selbst gebackene Plätzchen.

NEBENSATZ

Weil ich müde bin.

1 Funktion

Nebensätze ergänzen einen Hauptsatz. Sie bilden mit Hauptsätzen komplexe Sätze. Konnektoren stellen die Verbindung zwischen Haupt- und Nebensatz her.

2 Satzstruktur

In Nebensatz steht das konjugierte Verb am Ende. Es bildet mit dem Konnektor, der den Nebensatz einleitet, eine Klammer.

ⓐ Nebensatz nach dem Hauptsatz

Hauptsatz	Nebensatz		
	Konnektor		Verb
Wir machen ein Fest,	*weil*	*Lilli 18*	*wird.*
Ich nehme an,	*dass*	*etwa 20 Gäste kommen*	*werden.*
Ich wollte fragen,	*ob*	*ihr zu dem Fest kommen*	*wollt.*
Es wäre schön,	*wenn*	*ihr kommen*	*könntet.*

ⓑ Nebensatz vor dem Hauptsatz

Nebensatz			Hauptsatz
Konnektor		Verb	
Wenn	*ihr kommen*	*könntet,*	*wäre das schön.*

Interpunktion: Zwischen Haupt- und Nebensatz steht ein Komma.

3 Nebensatz-Konnektoren

während, wohingegen	adversativ	📖 **s. Seite 178**
damit, um ... zu	final	📖 **s. Seite 172**
da, weil	kausal	📖 **s. Seite 168**
wenn, falls, sofern	konditional	📖 **s. Seite 170**
(so) dass	konsekutiv	📖 **s. Seite 174**
obwohl	konzessiv	📖 **s. Seite 176**
indem, (an)statt, dadurch ... dass	modal	📖 **s. Seite 180**
als, wenn, sooft, bevor, ehe, bis, seit(dem), nachdem, sobald	temporal	📖 **s. Seite 162-167**

weitere Nebensätze: Relativsatz 📖 **s. Seite 154-157**, indirekte Frage 📖 **s. Seite 142**, *dass*-Satz 📖 **s. Seite 150**, Infinitivsatz 📖 **s. Seite 152**

1 Was Kinder brauchen. – Kreuzen Sie an: Welche Ergänzung passt?

a) Kinder wünschen sich vor allem Zeit, **da** ...
- ☐ Vater und Mutter oft berufstätig sind.
- ☐ sind Vater und Mutter oft berufstätig.
- ☐ Vater und Mutter sind oft berufstätig.

b) Man muss sich um die Kinder kümmern, **weil** ...
- ☐ brauchen sie ein Vorbild.
- ☐ sie brauchen ein Vorbild.
- ☐ sie ein Vorbild brauchen.

c) Viele Eltern machen sich erst Sorgen um ihre Kinder, **wenn** ...
- ☐ etwas ist schon passiert.
- ☐ ist schon etwas passiert.
- ☐ schon etwas passiert ist.

d) **Bevor** ... sollten Sie mal wieder etwas mit ihrem Kind unternehmen.
- ☐ kaufen Sie ein teures Spielzeug,
- ☐ Sie ein teures Spielzeug kaufen,
- ☐ Sie kaufen ein teures Spielzeug,

2 Analyse – Unterstreichen Sie im Text die Wörter, die einen Nebensatz einleiten, und das konjugierte Verb im Nebensatz.

Jan, 15: **Was wünsche ich mir von den Erwachsenen?**

Hört auf zu glauben, <u>dass</u> Statussymbole alles im Leben <u>sind</u>! Es ärgert mich wahnsinnig, wenn Leute behaupten, es ginge ihnen schlecht, nur weil sie in einer Mietwohnung leben und nur einmal im Jahr in den Urlaub fahren können. Das zeigt doch, dass unsere Gesellschaft übersättigt ist! Die Erwachsenen sollten Konsumterror und Markenverrücktheit nicht als Problem der Jugend sehen. Es ist doch nur peinlich, wenn Erwachsene sich gegenseitig bedauern, weil sie Opel statt Mercedes fahren. Ich finde es schlimm, wenn man sich in Deutschland und fast allen anderen Industrienationen mit solchen Problemen beschäftigt, während in manchen Ländern Tausende von Menschen heimatlos durch die Gegend irren oder bei Katastrophen sterben.

3 Satzpuzzle – Formulieren Sie Sätze.

a) Er spart gerade eisern, – einen BMW – sich kaufen – weil – will – er
Er spart gerade eisern, weil er sich einen BMW kaufen will.

b) sie – als – zum Bahnhof – kam, fuhr der Zug gerade ab.

c) Sie beantwortet ihre E-Mails, Zeit und Lust – haben – wenn sie

d) Sie findet den Kurs langweilig, – obwohl – besucht – sie – ihn regelmäßig

e) Er ist ein völlig neuer Mensch, – seit – eine Freundin – hat – er

f) ich – nach Hause – gehe – bevor, muss ich noch ein oder zwei Dinge erledigen.

4 Franz, der Kunst-Kenner – Formulieren Sie als Haupt- und Nebensatz.

a) Franz interessiert sich für Kunst. Deshalb besucht er alle aktuellen Ausstellungen. (weil)
Franz besucht alle aktuellen Ausstellungen, weil er sich für Kunst interessiert.

b) Er hat eine Ausstellung besucht. Anschließend liest er zu Hause in seinem Katalog wichtige Informationen nach. (nachdem)

c) Er kennt alle wichtigen Bauwerke in seiner Stadt. Trotzdem entdeckt er immer wieder neue Kunstschätze. (obwohl)

d) Er macht Reisen. Vorher kauft er sich einen guten Kunstführer. (bevor)

e) Viele Leute wissen nicht, was sie in ihrer Freizeit tun sollen. Franz dagegen wird es nie langweilig. (während)

DASS-SATZ

Ich hoffe, dass wir uns bald wiedersehen.

1 Funktion

Ich weiß, dass du keine Zeit hast.	Verbergänzung
Dass er gelogen hat, ist ziemlich sicher.	

dass-Sätze stehen häufig vor oder nach:

Verben des Sagens	*In dem Artikel wird berichtet, dass im Zoo ein weißes Tigerbaby geboren wurde.*	*sagen, berichten, herausfinden* u.a.
Verben der persönlichen Haltung	*Ich hoffe, dass ich dich bald wiedersehe.* *Dass er kommt, bezweifle ich.*	*ich denke, meine, finde, bezweifle, hoffe, vermute* u.a.
Verben mit Präpositionen	*Ich erinnere mich daran, dass wir einen Termin ausgemacht hatten.*	*sich erinnern an, denken an, träumen von* u.a.
unpersönlichen Ausdrücken	*Es stimmt, dass wir uns gestritten haben.*	*es ist richtig, es ist wichtig* u.a.

Liste der wichtigsten Verben mit Präpositionen 📖 **s. Seite 203**

2 Satzstrukturen

Hauptsatz	Nebensatz			Hauptsatz
	Konnektor		Verb	
Ich weiß,	*dass*	*du keine Zeit*	*hast.*	
Ich weiß,	*dass*	*du keine Zeit*	*hast,*	*hatte es aber vergessen.*
	Dass	*du so wenig Zeit*	*hast,*	*finde ich wirklich schade.*

Interpunktion: Zwischen Haupt- und Nebensatz steht ein Komma.

3 Alternativen

dass-Satz	Infinitiv + *zu*	Präposition
Ich hoffe, dass ich dich bald wiedersehe.	*Ich hoffe, dich bald wiederzusehen.*	*Ich hoffe auf ein baldiges Wiedersehen.*
Ich habe beschlossen, dass ich bei ihm einziehe.	*Ich habe beschlossen, bei ihm einzuziehen.*	
Er hat mich eingeladen, dass ich bei ihm wohne.	*Er hat mich eingeladen, bei ihm zu wohnen.*	

Infinitiv + *zu:* stilistisch eleganter als der *dass*-Satz. Kann den *dass*-Satz ersetzen, wenn das Subjekt des Nebensatzes im Hauptsatz vorkommt. 📖 **s. Seite 152**

1 Frauen – Geben Sie die unterstrichenen Ergebnisse der Forscher mit dass-Sätzen wieder.

Das haben Frauen Männern voraus

Sie schlafen mehr, essen gesünder und rauchen weniger: Frauen achten einer neuen Studie zufolge mehr auf ihre Gesundheit als Männer. Mehr als 60 Prozent aller Bundesbürgerinnen, die von einem Forscherteam der Uni Landau (Pfalz) befragt wurden, sagten, sie seien ziemlich körperbewusst – das sagten nur 40 Prozent der Männer.

Die Forscher haben herausgefunden, dass Frauen mehr schlafen als Männer, ...

2 Ihre Meinung? – Formulieren Sie dass-Sätze. Es gibt verschiedene Lösungen.
a) Man sollte verheiratet sein, wenn man Kinder in die Welt setzen will.
   Ich denke, dass man verheiratet sein sollte, wenn man Kinder will.
   Ich finde nicht, dass man verheiratet sein sollte, wenn man Kinder will.
b) Hausarbeit ist nichts für einen Mann.
c) Man sollte mit seinem Partner eine Ehe auf Probe versuchen, bevor man sich für die Hochzeit entscheidet.
d) Frauen sollten zuerst einen Beruf haben, bevor sie heiraten.
e) Kinder sind die beste Altersvorsorge.
f) Singles sind glücklicher als Menschen in einer festen Partnerschaft.

3 Diskussion – Sagen Sie Ihre Meinung mit einem dass-Satz.
a) Fremdsprachen sind überflüssig.   • Ich bin nicht dieser Meinung.
b) Latein ist die wichtigste Fremdsprache überhaupt.   • Mich überzeugt das nicht.
c) Es ist gut, wenn man mehrere Fremdsprachen kann.   • Das finde ich auch.
d) In Zukunft werden Fremdsprachen immer wichtiger.   • Ich bin davon überzeugt.

a) *Ich bin nicht der Meinung, dass Fremdsprachen überflüssig sind.*

4 Über andere reden – Formulieren Sie Sätze mit dass.

Stimmt es,	a) Helga hat einen neuen Freund.
Ist es wahr,	b) Theo hat schon wieder beim Pferderennen verloren.
Hast du auch gehört,	c) Iris geht demnächst auf Weltreise.
Das darf doch nicht wahr sein,	d) Tobias will sich scheiden lassen.

a) *Stimmt es, dass Helga einen neuen Freund hat?*

5 Ein neues Produkt – Formulieren Sie mit dass-Sätzen.
a) Herr M. berichtet von der Entwicklung eines neuen Lernprogramms für Deutsch.
   Herr M. berichtet, dass ein neues Lernprogramm für Deutsch entwickelt wurde.
b) Unsere Analyse hat gezeigt: Es gibt eine Marktlücke in diesem Bereich.
c) Wir hoffen, das Programm in wenigen Monaten auf dem Markt platzieren zu können.
d) Unsere Werbung hat das Ziel: Eltern werden aufmerksam auf das Produkt.
e) Sie müssen das Gefühl haben, etwas Gutes für ihre Kinder zu kaufen.

INFINITIV + *ZU*

Ich hoffe zu gewinnen.

1 Funktion

Ich hoffe, dass ich die Prüfung bestehe. *Ich hoffe die Prüfung zu bestehen.*	Ersetzt einen *dass*-Satz, wenn das Subjekt des Nebensatzes im Hauptsatz vorkommt. Wirkt knapper und ökonomischer.

Infinitive + *zu* stehen nach:

Nomen + *haben*	*Angst / Lust / Zeit / den Plan haben*
unpersönlichen Ausdrücken	*es ist wichtig, es ist schwierig*
Partizip + *sein*	*verboten / erlaubt / beabsichtigt sein*
Verben: Erlaubnis	*erlauben, verbieten*
Verben: Anfang/Ende	*anfangen, beginnen, aufhören*
Verben: Absicht	*versuchen, vorhaben, sich vornehmen, beabsichtigen*
Verben: Gefühl	*bedauern, befürchten, hoffen, sich freuen*
anderen	*erinnern, vergessen, bitten, einladen, gefallen*
	sein, haben

haben + Infinitiv + *zu* 📖 **s. Seite 96**, *sein* + Infinitiv + *zu* 📖 **s. Seite 116**

Infinitive + *zu* stehen nicht nach:

Verben des Sagens	*sagen, fragen, antworten, berichten, erzählen, informieren*
Verben der Wahrnehmung	*sehen, hören, riechen, spüren, bemerken, lesen*
Verben des Wissens	*wissen, zweifeln, vermuten, kennen*
anderen	*helfen, lernen*

2 Satzstrukturen

Hauptsatz	Infinitivsatz		
		zu + Infinitiv	
Es ist schön,	*Zeit*	*zu haben.*	
Es ist schön,		*auszuschlafen.*	trennbares Verb
Es ist schön,	*ausschlafen*	*zu können.*	Modalverb
Es ist schön,	*mit dir spazieren*	*zu gehen.*	zwei Verben
Es freut mich,	*dich überzeugt*	*zu haben.*	Perfekt
Ich freue mich darauf,	*von dir verwöhnt*	*zu werden.*	Passiv

Interpunktion: Bei Infinitivgruppen kann man ein Komma setzen, um die Gliederung des Satzes deutlich zu machen bzw. um Missverständnisse auszuschließen. Infinitivgruppen, die durch ein hinweisendes Wort (*es*, Präpositionalpronomen, z.B. *dafür*) angekündigt werden, müssen mit Komma abgegrenzt werden.

3 Alternativen

Infinitiv mit *zu*	Nebensatz	zwei Hauptsätze
Ich habe beschlossen, bei ihm einzuziehen.	*Ich habe beschlossen, dass ich bei ihm einziehe.*	*Ich habe beschlossen: Ich ziehe bei ihm ein.*

1 Martin fühlt sich nicht wohl. – Formulieren Sie Sätze mit dem Infinitiv + zu. Verwenden Sie die Verben versuchen und sich vornehmen.
a) möglichst viel schlafen
Er versucht, möglichst viel zu schlafen.
Er nimmt sich vor, möglichst viel zu schlafen.
b) abnehmen
c) bequemere Kleidung tragen
d) mehr Vitamine zu sich nehmen
e) nicht mehr rauchen
f) weniger fernsehen
g) zweimal pro Woche joggen

2 Reisepläne – Formulieren Sie Sätze mit Infinitiv + zu und dem Verb vorhaben.
a) Fahrt ihr wieder ans Meer? – in die Berge
Wir hatten eigentlich vor, in die Berge zu fahren.
b) Fahrt ihr mit dem Auto? – mit der Bahn
c) Nehmt ihr wieder eine Freundin mit? – allein reisen
d) Packt ihr wieder die Videokamera ein? – zu Hause lassen
e) Nehmt ihr wieder das Boot mit? – vor Ort eins ausleihen

3 Was ist hier verboten? – Formulieren Sie Sätze mit Infinitiv + zu.
a) Fußballspielen auf dem Rasen nicht erlaubt
Es ist verboten, auf dem Rasen Fußball zu spielen.
Es ist nicht erlaubt, ...
b) Rauchen verboten
c) Bitte den Rasen nicht betreten
d) Bitte nicht aus dem Fenster lehnen (+ sich)
e) Kein Durchgang

4 Ihr Rat – Formulieren Sie Vorschläge und Ratschläge.
a) Theo will im Freibad schwimmen, hat aber seine Badehose vergessen. – leihen
Ich rate ihm, / Ich schlage ihm vor, eine Badehose zu leihen.
b) Fünf Minuten vor dem Fußball-Länderspiel geht Helgas Fernseher kaputt. – das Spiel beim Nachbarn ansehen
c) An Marions Rad ist bei einer Tour ein Reifen geplatzt. Sie hat kein Werkzeug dabei. – einen Passanten um Hilfe bitten
d) Gisela bleibt mit ihrem Schuh in einem Gitter hängen. – den Schuh ausziehen
e) Lukas hat den Bus verpasst und kommt zu spät zur Musikstunde. – anrufen und Bescheid sagen

5 Formulieren Sie Infinitivsätze.
a) Ich bedaure, dass ich nicht daran gedacht habe.
Ich bedaure, nicht daran gedacht zu haben.
b) Ich erinnere mich, dass ich Ihnen vor ein paar Wochen geschrieben habe.
c) Ich kann mich nicht erinnern, dass ich Sie schon einmal gesehen habe.
d) Ich glaube, dass ich bald mehr sagen kann.
e) Ich hoffe, dass ich den Auftrag bald fertig habe.

RELATIVSATZ (1)

Der Mann, der niemals lachte.

1 Funktion

Hier sehen wir Bernd. *Bernd spült gerade.* *= Hier sieht man Bernd,* *der gerade spült.*	Definition eines Nomens durch Zusatzinformation. Verbindung von zwei Sätzen

2 Formen

ⓐ Relativpronomen

	maskulin	neutral	feminin	Plural
Nominativ	*der*	*das*	*die*	*die*
Akkusativ	*den*	*das*	*die*	*die*
Dativ	*dem*	*dem*	*der*	*denen*
Genitiv	*dessen*	*dessen*	*deren*	*deren*

welche, welches, welcher, welche als Alternative zu *der, das, die, die* wird nur noch verwendet, um Doppelung *(die, die)* zu vermeiden: *An der Universität Essen wurde eine Flasche für Coca-Cola entwickelt,* *welche* *die Vorteile von Glas und Kunststoff miteinander verbindet.*

ⓑ Satzstrukturen

Der Relativsatz ist ein Nebensatz und steht direkt nach dem Nomen, das er definiert:

Hauptsatz	Relativsatz			Fortsetzung
	Relativ- pronomen		Verb	Hauptsatz
1 *Ich suche einen Wein,*	*der*	*sehr trocken*	*ist.*	
2 *Der Wein,*	*den*	*ich bestellt*	*habe,*	*schmeckt nicht.*
3 *Ich nehme den Wein,*	*von dem*	*ich gerade probiert*	*habe.*	
4 *Der Wein,*	*dessen*	*Name mir nicht*	*einfällt,*	*stammt aus Frankreich.*

1 Das Relativpronomen richtet sich in Genus und Numerus nach dem Nomen, auf das es verweist, z.B. *der Wein.*

2 Im Kasus richtet es sich nach dem Verb des Relativsatzes, z.B. *bestellen* + Akkusativ.

3 Bei Ausdrücken mit Präpositionen *(probieren von* + Dativ) steht die Präposition vor dem Relativpronomen; der Kasus richtet sich nach der Präposition.

4 Das Relativpronomen im Genitiv bezieht sich auf ein Genitivattribut *(der Name des Weins)* oder einen Possessivartikel *(sein Name).* Das folgende Nomen hat keinen Artikel.

Interpunktion: Vor und nach dem Relativsatz steht ein Komma.

3 Alternativen

Relativsatz	Adjektiv / Partizipialkonstruktion
die E-Mail, die abgeschickt wurde	*die abgeschickte E-Mail*
Für die Überstunden, die Sie leisten *müssen, werden Sie bezahlt.*	*Für die zu leistenden Überstunden* *werden Sie bezahlt.*

s. Seite 44 (Partizip als Adjektiv)

1 **Was tun diese Menschen? – Formulieren Sie Relativsätze.**

a) ein Babysitter / Person, auf kleine Kinder aufpassen –
Ein Babysitter ist eine Person, die auf kleine Kinder aufpasst.

b) ein Schulkind / Kind, zur Schule gehen

c) ein Fotograf / jemand, Fotos machen

d) ein Koch / jemand, Essen zubereiten

e) eine Medizinstudentin / eine Frau, Medizin studieren

2 **Der ideale Partner – die ideale Partnerin. Formulieren Sie Sätze.**

Eva sucht einen Partner, a) er schenkt ihr ab und zu Blumen.

Eva sucht einen Partner, der ihr ab und zu Blumen schenkt.

                                  b) er ist treu.

Peter sucht eine Partnerin, c) sie geht mit ihm auf den Fußballplatz.

                                  d) sie hat viel Humor.

Petra sucht einen Partner, e) sie kann sich auf ihn verlassen.

                                  f) sie muss nicht für ihn waschen und bügeln.

Uwe sucht eine Partnerin, g) er vertraut ihr.

                                  h) mit ihr kann er fünf Kinder haben.

3 **Getränke – Ergänzen Sie die Relativpronomen.**

a) Das Bier, *das* eiskalt war, habe ich schon aus dem Kühlschrank geholt.

b) Die Getränke, ... nicht so kühl lagern müssen, stehen auf den Balkon.

c) Die Traube, auf .... sich unser Weinbauer spezialisiert hat, heißt Müller-Thurgau.

d) Leider ist der Wein, ... Sie bestellt haben, im Moment aus.

e) Natürlich war die Milch, mit .... wir den Pudding gekocht haben, fettarm.

4 **Rotkäppchen – Ergänzen Sie die Relativpronomen.**

In Grimms Märchen hat sich der Wolf als Großmutter
verkleidet. Er hat besonders große Ohren, mit
(a) *denen* er gut hören kann, scharfe Augen, mit
(b) .... er gut sehen kann, eine lange Nase,
mit (c) .... er besser riechen kann, große
Hände, mit (d) .... er Rotkäppchen packen
kann, und einen riesigen Mund, mit (e) ....
er Rotkäppchen fressen kann.

5 **Tierisches – Formulieren Sie aus den unterstrichenen Satzteilen Relativsätze.**

a) Diese Schlange hat ein <u>sehr schnell wirkendes</u> Gift.
Diese Schlange hat ein Gift, das sehr schnell wirkt.

b) Eine Maus ist in eine <u>mit Speck präparierte</u> Falle gegangen.

c) In unserem Gelände gibt es <u>frei herumlaufende</u> Pinguine.

d) Der <u>ausgebrochene</u> Eisbär ist wieder eingefangen.

RELATIVSATZ (2)

Das ist der Raum, wo sich alles abspielt.

1 Formen

Relativpronomen

wo	Ich wohne in einer Stadt, *wo* sich die Leute noch persönlich kennen. Ich wohne in einer Stadt, *in der* sich die Leute noch persönlich kennen.	bei Ortsangaben kann *in* + Relativpronomen durch *wo* (= *in* + Dativ) oder *wohin* (= *in* + Akkusativ) ersetzt werden.
wohin woher	Sie zog nach Berlin, *wohin* auch ihre Schwester gegangen war. Ich fahre an einen Ort, *wohin* / = an den es schon viele Künstler gezogen hat.	*wo* und *wohin* / *woher* nach Städte- und Ländernamen und nach *Ort* / *Platz* / *Stelle*
was	So ein Urlaub wäre *etwas, was* mir Spaß machen würde.	nach Indefinitpronomen *etwas, nichts, alles, vieles*
	Das ist *das Beste, was* uns passieren konnte.	nach substantiviertem Superlativ
	Edwina ist (das), *was* man als Karrierefrau bezeichnet.	bezieht sich auf den Inhalt eines ganzen Satzes
wo(r)-*	Er hat den ganzen Abend mit mir verbracht, *worüber* ich mich sehr gefreut habe.	
wer, wen, wem	Wer will, kann bei dem Spiel mitmachen. Wem es hier gefällt, der kann bleiben.	nicht näher bezeichnete Person

* *r* wird eingefügt, wenn die Präposition mit Vokal beginnt; **s. Seite 56** (Präpositionalpronomen).

2 Satzstrukturen
Das Verb steht im Relativsatz am Ende.

Hauptsatz	Relativsatz		
	Konnektor		Verb
Ich habe den Preis gewonnen,	*was*	*mich sehr*	*freut.*

Interpunktion: Vor bzw. nach Relativsätzen steht ein Komma.

ÜBUNGEN

1 Lernprozess – Formulieren Sie Sätze mit alles und was.
a) gemerkt – gesagt – der Lehrer
Hast du dir alles gemerkt, was der Lehrer gesagt hat?
b) verstanden – gelesen – du
c) mitbekommen – erklärt – die Lehrerin
d) gelernt – aufgegeben – die Lehrerin
e) verbessert – falsch gemacht – du
f) notiert – diktiert – der Lehrer

2 Mein neuer Arbeitsplatz – Ergänzen Sie was, wer, wo, wohin.

An meinem Arbeitsplatz gibt es vieles, (a) *was* man kritisieren könnte. Meine Kollegin kommt meistens zu spät, (b) .... mich wahnsinnig ärgert. Frau Liebich geht ständig in die Kantine, (c) .... sie stundenlang mit Kolleginnen über andere redet. Herr Fischer raucht bei der Arbeit eine Zigarette nach der anderen, (d) .... ich bald nicht mehr aushalten kann. Es gibt keinen rauchfreien Raum, (e) .... man sich in der Pause flüchten könnte. Unser Kopierraum ist das Chaotischste, (f) .... man sich vorstellen kann. Die Bus- und Bahnverbindung zu unserem Büro ist nicht besonders gut, (g) .... den Weg zur Arbeit sehr umständlich macht. Leider gibt es in der Nähe keine Geschäfte, (h) .... man nach der Arbeit mal rasch zum Einkaufen gehen könnte. (i) .... ich mir aber vor allem wünsche, ist ein besseres Betriebsklima. (j) .... das alles nicht glauben will, soll mal einen Tag bei uns arbeiten.

3 Wo möchten Sie wohnen? – Formulieren Sie die Sätze in zwei Versionen.

a) in einem Park, (m) – man kann morgens Vögel beobachten
   In einem Park, wo man morgens Vögel beobachten kann.
   In einem Park, in dem man morgens Vögel beobachten kann.
b) in der Nähe eines Waldes (m) – man kann gut spazieren gehen
c) in einem Fischerdorf am Meer (n) – es gibt keine Hotels
d) in einem kleineren Ort (m) – die Leute kennen sich noch mit Namen
e) in einer Gegend (f) – die Menschen sind noch natürlich und freundlich
f) auf einer Insel (f) – keine Autos dürfen fahren
g) nahe bei einem Fitnesscenter (n) – man kann bis spätabends trainieren
h) in einer Kleinstadt (f) – es gibt noch alte Gebäude
i) in einer Stadt (f) – man hat verschiedene Kinos zur Auswahl

4 Schulfreundinnen – Formulieren Sie was-Sätze.

a) Gestern bekam ich Besuch von zwei alten Schulfreundinnen – hat mich sehr gefreut.
   Gestern bekam ich Besuch von zwei alten Schulfreundinnen, was mich sehr gefreut hat.
b) Gabi hat sich überhaupt nicht verändert – hat mich sehr überrascht.
c) Brigitte hat ziemlich viel zugenommen – liegt sicherlich an ihrem Beruf als Köchin.
d) Brigitte hat mir einen riesigen Blumenstrauß mitgebracht – fand ich sehr nett.
e) Gabi hat ihre beiden Töchter zu Hause gelassen – fanden wir alle drei gut.
f) Gabi hat sich von ihrem Mann getrennt – wusste ich noch nicht.
g) Sie kam sehr leicht über diese Trennung hinweg – überraschte mich ein wenig.

5 Sorge um die gesunde Ernährung – Verbinden Sie die Sätze.

a) Viele Menschen kaufen kaum noch Fleisch. Das macht den Fleischproduzenten Sorge.
   Viele Menschen kaufen kaum noch Fleisch, was den Fleischproduzenten Sorge macht.
b) Der Anteil an Vegetariern wächst ständig. Das ist verständlich.
c) Gesunde Lebensmittel haben ihren Preis. Das müssen wir endlich einsehen.
d) Die Verbraucher verlieren das Vertrauen in die Lebensmittel. Das wird zunehmend zum Problem.
e) Tiere in der Landwirtschaft leben nicht mehr natürlich. Darauf machen Tierschützer immer wieder aufmerksam.
f) Viele dieser Tiere haben noch nie eine Wiese gesehen. Das ist schon lange bekannt.
g) Sie werden kreuz und quer durch Europa transportiert. Dagegen protestieren Tierschützer.

AUFZÄHLUNG

und – sowohl ... als auch – nicht nur ... sondern auch – weder ... noch

1 Funktion

und sowie*	*Ich lerne Deutsch und Englisch sowie Französisch.*	positiv
sowohl ... als auch	*Ich lerne sowohl Deutsch als auch Französisch.*	
nicht nur ... sondern auch	*Ich lerne nicht nur Deutsch, sondern ich besuche auch einen Französischkurs.*	
weder ... noch	*Er kann weder Deutsch noch Englisch.*	negativ

* nur für Satzglieder, nicht für Sätze
sowie ist bedeutungsgleich mit *und*. Es vermeidet die Wiederholung von *und*.

2 Satzstruktur

a Satzglieder, Konnektor vor dem Satzglied

	Konnektor 1		Konnektor 2	
Elke lernt	*sowohl*	*Englisch*	*als auch*	*Französisch.*
Ich glaube, dass Elke	*sowohl*	*Englisch*	*als auch*	*Französisch lernt.*
Ihre Lieblingsfächer sind Englisch	*und*	*Mathematik*	*sowie*	*Musik.*

b Hauptsätze, Konnektor auf Position 0

Hauptsatz 1	Hauptsatz 2			
	Konnektor		Verb	
Elke ist eine gute Schülerin(,)	*und*	*(sie)*	*treibt*	*viel Sport.*

   s. auch Seite 146

c Hauptsätze, Konnektor 2 auf Position 0

Hauptsatz 1				Hauptsatz 2			
				Konnektor 2		Verb	
Elke	*lernt*	*nicht nur*	*Englisch,*	*sondern*	*(sie)*	*(lernt)*	*auch Französisch.*

nicht nur steht vor dem negierten Satzglied, Negation   **s. Seite 136**

d Hauptsätze, Konnektor 2 auf Position 1

Hauptsatz 1				Hauptsatz 2			
				Konnektor 2	Verb		
Elke	*lernt*	*weder*	*Englisch*	*noch*	*(lernt)*	*(sie)*	*Französisch.*

weder steht vor dem negierten Satzglied, Negation   **s. Seite 136**

Interpunktion: Zwischen den Hauptsätzen mit *nicht nur ... sondern auch, und* und *weder ... noch* steht ein Komma.

__1__ **Partyvorbereitungen – Ergänzen Sie** und, sowie, sowohl ... als auch, nicht nur ...
sondern auch. **Es gibt manchmal mehrere Lösungen.**
- Wir brauchen (a) *nicht nur* etwas zu trinken, (b) .... es muss (c) ....
etwas zu essen geben.
- Ich schlage vor, wir besorgen Mineralwasser (d) .... Saft (e) ....
ein paar alkoholische Getränke.
- Ja, und bei den nicht alkoholischen Getränken brauchen wir (f) .... kalte
Getränke, (g) .... es sollte (h) .... warme geben, wie zum Beispiel
Kaffee (i) .... Tee.
- Und was ist mit dem Essen?
- Ich schlage vor, (j) .... Brote mit Wurst oder Käse anzubieten, (k) ....
Salate hinzustellen.
- Ich bin für Sachen, die man ohne Besteck essen kann.
- Ja, wenn es geht, (l) .... Salziges, wie Kartoffelchips (m) ....
Erdnüsse, (n) .... etwas Süßes, Kekse (o) .... Schokolade zum Beispiel.

__2__ **Frauen heute – Ergänzen Sie** als auch, nicht nur, noch, sondern auch, sowohl, **weder.**
Manche Frauen leben im Zwiespalt: Sie können sich (a) *weder* für den Beruf
(b) .... für die Familie entscheiden. Es gibt einige positive Beispiele, die zeigen,
dass eine Frau (c) .... eine gute Mutter (d) .... eine kompetente
Mitarbeiterin in der Firma sein kann. Viele Frauen hoffen, dass sie in Zukunft
(e) .... Erfolg im Beruf haben werden, (f) .... ein
befriedigendes Privatleben führen können.

__3__ **Berühmte Persönlichkeiten – Formulieren Sie positive und negative Aufzählungen.**

		+	–
W. A. Mozart F. Schubert		bedeutender Komponist sein in Österreich geboren sein	sehr alt werden
Maria Theresia von Österreich Queen Victoria		Königin sein glücklich verheiratet sein viele Kinder haben ein großes Reich regieren	langweilige Personen
J. W. von Goethe H. Hesse		Dichter sein sich für fremde Kulturen interessieren große Reisen unternehmen	arme Poeten
Aschenputtel Schneewittchen		Märchenfiguren sein eine böse Stiefmutter haben Walt Disney hat einen Film über sie gemacht.	eine glückliche Kindheit haben von ihren Vätern Hilfe erhalten

+ Sowohl Mozart als auch Schubert waren bedeutende Komponisten.
- Weder Mozart noch Schubert sind sehr alt geworden.
+ Queen Victoria war nicht nur glücklich verheiratet, sondern (sie) hatte auch viele Kinder.

ALTERNATIVEN

entweder ... oder – (an)statt – stattdessen

1 Satzstrukturen

ⓐ Hauptsätze, Konnektor 1 auf Position 1 oder 3, Konnektor 2 auf Position 0

Hauptsatz 1				Hauptsatz 2			
POS 1	Verb	POS 3		Konnektor 2		Verb	
Elke	*lernt*	*entweder*	*am Abend (,)*	*oder*	*(sie)*	*(lernt)*	*am Wochenende.*
Entweder	*lernt*	*Elke*	*am Abend (,)*	*oder*	*(sie)*	*(lernt)*	*am Wochenende.*

ⓑ Hauptsatz, Konnektor auf Position 1 oder 3

Hauptsatz	Hauptsatz			
	POS 1	Verb	POS 3	
Sie besucht keinen Kurs.	*Stattdessen*	*lernt*	*sie*	*mit einer Tandempartnerin.*
Sie besucht keinen Kurs.	*Sie*	*lernt*	*stattdessen*	*mit einer Tandempartnerin.*

ⓒ Infinitivsatz

Hauptsatz	Infinitivsatz		
	Konnektor		*zu* + Infinitiv
Sie lernt mit einer Tandempartnerin,	*(an)statt*	*einen Kurs*	*zu besuchen.*

zu steht vor dem Infinitivverb; bei trennbaren Verben: *fernzusehen;* bei Sätzen mit
Modalverb: *fernsehen zu können.*
Auch möglich: *Sie lernt mit einer Tandempartnerin, (an)statt dass sie einen Kurs besucht.*
Der Infinitivsatz ist bei gleichem Subjekt im Haupt- und Nebensatz stilistisch besser.
dass-Satz 📖 **s. Seite 150**

2 Alternativen

Infinitivsatz	Präposition	
Anstatt/Statt spazieren zu gehen, mache ich einen Mittagsschlaf.	*Statt eines Spaziergangs mache ich einen Mittagsschlaf.*	*statt* + Genitiv

ÜBUNGEN

1 Samstagabend – Ergänzen Sie entweder ... oder, (an)statt, stattdessen.

- ■ Was hältst du davon, wenn wir heute Abend essen gehen?
- ■ Warum nicht? Welches Lokal schlägst du vor?
- ■ Also, ich würde (a) *entweder* den „Alten Wirt" vorschlagen (b) .... den „Goldenen Schwan".
- ■ Sind die nicht beide sehr teuer?
- ■ Schon. Aber auf eine billige Pizza habe ich heute keinen Appetit.
- ■ Könnten wir (c) .... ins Restaurant nicht einfach ins Kino gehen?
- ■ Von mir aus.

- Ich würde (d) .... gerne diesen neuen Film mit Richard Gere sehen
  (e) .... diesen neuen französischen Film, der im Cinema gerade läuft.
  Wie heißt der denn noch?
- Keine Ahnung. Ich schlage (f) .... die Rocky Horror Picture Show vor.
- Schon wieder? Na, wenn es sein muss.
- Vor dem Gloria-Palast-Kino bekommen wir aber heute Abend keinen Parkplatz.
- Das könnte sein. Also: (g) .... wir fahren mit öffentlichen
  Verkehrsmitteln, (h) .... wir leisten uns ein Taxi.
- Ist das Taxi denn viel teurer als die U-Bahn?
- Keine Ahnung.
- Ach, irgendwie habe ich weder Lust auf Kino noch auf ein teures Essen im Restaurant.
  Bleiben wir doch (i) .... einfach gemütlich zu Hause.

2 Wie man Geld sparen kann – Formulieren Sie Sätze mit (an)statt.

a) das Buch lieber aus der Bibliothek ausleihen – selber kaufen
   Ich leihe das Buch lieber aus der Bibliothek aus, (an)statt es mir selber zu kaufen.
b) mit dem Fahrrad fahren – den Bus oder das Auto nehmen
c) Skier lieber ausleihen – selber welche kaufen
d) täglich joggen – Mitglied im Fitnessklub werden
e) T-Shirts selber färben oder bemalen – in der Boutique kaufen
f) am Stadtrand wohnen – in der Innenstadt wohnen und hohe Mieten zahlen

3 Lebenswandel – Formulieren Sie Sätze mit stattdessen.

a) aufgehört zu rauchen – Kaugummi kauen
   Ich habe aufgehört zu rauchen. Stattdessen kaue ich Kaugummi.
b) kaum noch Fleisch kaufen – ich öfter Fisch kochen
c) nicht mehr täglich drei Stunden fernsehen – öfter mal Musik hören
d) weniger Überstunden machen – mehr Zeit mit meinen Freunden verbringen
e) weniger Kaffee trinken – eine Kanne Früchtetee pro Tag trinken
f) oft auf ein warmes Mittagessen verzichten – mittags nur ein Sandwich essen

4 Was ich lieber tun würde – Formulieren Sie Sätze mit stattdessen. Mehrere Lösungen sind möglich.

den Film zu Ende sehen | einen Mittagsschlaf machen | mein Buch weiterlesen | mit Eva
zum Baden gehen | noch ein Glas Wein bestellen | meine Lieblingssendung im Radio hören

a) Hausaufgaben machen
   Ich muss meine Hausaufgaben machen.
   Stattdessen würde ich jetzt lieber mein Buch weiterlesen.
   Oder:
   Stattdessen würde ich jetzt lieber mit Eva zum Baden gehen.
b) meinen Aufsatz fertig schreiben
c) schlafen gehen
d) meine E-Mails beantworten
e) nach Hause gehen
f) das Essen machen

TEMPORALSATZ (1): GLEICHZEITIG

als – wenn

1 Funktion

Mehrere Handlungen/Zustände gleichzeitig

Konnektor		Handlung	Zeit
als	*Als ich gestern zur Schule ging, passierte etwas Lustiges.*	einmalig	Vergangenheit
wenn	*Wenn ich wieder nach Köln fahre, besuche ich Tante Helga.*	einmalig	Zukunft
(immer) wenn *(jedes Mal) wenn* *sooft*	*(Immer) wenn ich koche, höre ich dabei Musik.* *(Jedes Mal) wenn Onkel Eduard uns besuchte, brachte er mir etwas mit.* *In Zukunft werde ich (jedes Mal) vorher anrufen, wenn ich dich besuchen möchte.* *Er ist immer gut gelaunt, sooft ich ihn sehe.*	wiederholt	Gegenwart Vergangenheit Zukunft

wenn hat auch konditionale Bedeutung, 📖 **s. Seite 170**

2 Satzstrukturen

Hauptsatz	Nebensatz			Hauptsatz
	Konnektor		Verb	
Gestern passierte etwas Lustiges,	*als* *Als*	*ich zur Schule* *ich gestern zur Schule*	*ging.* *ging,*	*passierte etwas Lustiges.*
Ich esse eine Kleinigkeit,	*wenn* *Wenn*	*ich Hunger* *ich Hunger*	*bekomme.* *bekomme,*	*esse ich eine Kleinigkeit.*

Interpunktion: Vor bzw. nach Nebensätzen steht ein Komma.

3 Alternativen

Nebensatz	Präposition + Nomen	
Als meine Eltern heirateten, waren sie noch sehr jung.	*Bei ihrer Hochzeit waren meine Eltern noch sehr jung.*	*bei* + Dativ
Immer wenn ich koche, höre ich Musik.	*Beim Kochen höre ich immer Musik.*	
Als Elke ein Kind war, lernte sie ihren späteren Mann kennen.	*In ihrer Kindheit lernte Elke ihren späteren Mann kennen.*	*in* + Dativ
Als Max 18 Jahre alt war, machte er den Führerschein.	*Mit 18 Jahren machte Max den Führerschein.*	*mit* + Dativ
Als Max seinen 18. Geburtstag feierte, machte er seinen Führerschein.	*An seinem 18. Geburtstag machte er seinen Führerschein.*	*an* + Dativ

__1__ Biografische Daten einer Lehrerin – Formulieren Sie Sätze mit als.

1976 Abitur (machen)	*Sie war 18 Jahre alt, als sie das Abitur machte.*
1981 Erstes Staatsexamen (machen)	*Sie war 23, ...*
1983 Zweites Staatexamen (machen)	*Sie war 25, ...*
1984 Heirat (heiraten)	*Sie war 26, ...*
1986 erstes Kind (bekommen)	*Sie war 28, ...*
1989 Wiedereinstieg in den Beruf (wiedereinsteigen)	*Sie war 31, ...*

__2__ Problemfälle – Formulieren Sie Fragen und antworten Sie mit erst als und dem Präteritum.
   a) das Ticket – am Check-in-Schalter sein
      Wann hast du das Ticket vermisst? – Erst als ich am Check-in-Schalter war.
   b) den Schlüssel – die Wohnungstür aufschließen wollen
   c) die Brieftasche – den Ausweis rausnehmen wollen
   d) die Kamera – den Film einlegen wollen
   e) die Scheckkarte – an der Kasse sein

__3__ Antworten Sie jetzt mit erst wenn und dem Präsens.
   a) eine Vokabelkartei – die Wörter so nicht merken können
      Wann schaffst du dir endlich eine Vokabelkartei an? – Erst wenn ich mir die Wörter so nicht mehr merken kann.
   b) ein gutes Wörterbuch – in der Mittelstufe sein
   c) einen Computer – mein neues Arbeitszimmer einrichten
   d) ein neues Radio – das alte ganz kaputt sein

__4__ Wenn einer eine Reise tut ... – Formulieren Sie Sätze mit als oder wenn.
   a) Ich kam gestern am Flughafen an. Ich hatte etwas Wichtiges vergessen.
      Als ich gestern am Flughafen ankam, hatte ich etwas Wichtiges vergessen.
   b) Wir kamen gestern am Flughafen an. Die Maschine war schon weg.
   c) Ich kam oft zu früh zum Flughafen. Das Flugzeug hatte Verspätung.
   d) Frau Huber wollte ihren Pass vorzeigen. Sie fand ihn nicht in ihrer Handtasche.
   e) Herr Martens kam in der Maschine zu seinem Platz. Jemand anders saß dort.
   f) Ich war oft verreist. Meine Pflanzen zu Hause sind immer vertrocknet.

__5__ Hermann – Formulieren Sie Sätze mit als.
   a) Bei seiner Geburt wog er nur knapp 1000 Gramm.
      Als Hermann geboren wurde, wog er nur knapp 1000 Gramm.
   b) Bei der Untersuchung im ersten Lebensjahr waren die Ärzte besorgt.
   c) Mit 18 Monaten wog er so viel wie andere Kinder in diesem Alter.
   d) Mit zwei Jahren konnte er bereits ganze Sätze sprechen.
   e) Bei der Einschulung sah man kaum noch Unterschiede zu seinen Mitschülern.

7

TEMPORALSATZ (2): GLEICHZEITIG

während – solange – bis – seit – seitdem

1   Funktion

Mehrere Handlungen, Zustände gleichzeitig

Konnektor		Handlung ...	Zeit
während	*Ich kann keine Musik hören, während ich arbeite.*	... gleichzeitig	Gegenwart Vergangenheit Zukunft
*solange**	*Solange ich noch zur Schule gehe, wohne ich bei meinen Eltern.*	... gleichzeitig	
bis	*Ich warte, bis die Besprechung zu Ende ist.*	... endet im Hauptsatz, wenn sie im Nebensatz beginnt.	
seit	*Seit er keine Sekretärin mehr hat, schreibt er alle Briefe selbst. Seit er den Unfall hatte, ist er vorsichtiger.*	... beginnt in der Vergangenheit, dauert bis in die Gegenwart.	
seitdem	*Seitdem er einen Computer hat, braucht er keine Sekretärin mehr.*		

* *solange* hat auch eine vorzeitige Funktion: *Solange du deine Aufgaben nicht gemacht hast, gehst du nicht zum Fußball!* = Handlung im Nebensatz vor der Handlung im Hauptsatz.

2   Satzstrukturen

Hauptsatz	Nebensatz			Hauptsatz
	Konnektor		Verb	
Er braucht keine Sekretärin mehr,	*seit(dem)*	*er einen Computer*	*hat.*	
	Seit(dem)	*er einen Computer*	*hat,*	*braucht er keine Sekretärin mehr.*

Interpunktion: Vor bzw. nach Nebensätzen steht ein Komma.

3   Alternativen

Nebensatz	Präposition + Nomen	
Seitdem flexible Arbeitszeiten eingeführt wurden, sind die Mitarbeiter zufriedener.	*Seit der Einführung flexibler Arbeitszeiten sind die Mitarbeiter zufriedener.*	*seit* + Dativ
Die Mitarbeiter können kurze private Telefongespräche führen, während sie arbeiten.	*Die Mitarbeiter können während der Arbeitszeit kurze private Telefongespräche führen.*	*während* + Genitiv (auch: Dativ)
Warten Sie bitte, bis die Besprechung zu Ende ist.	*Warten Sie bitte bis zum Ende der Besprechung.*	*bis zu* + Dativ

1 Einbruch – Formulieren Sie Sätze mit während.

a) einkaufen sein *Der Einbrecher kam, während wir einkaufen waren.* b) schlafen c) im Garten arbeiten d) vor dem Fernseher sitzen e) im Kino sein f) das Abendessen machen

2 Vorschriften – Formulieren Sie Sätze mit während.

a) sich anschnallen – das Flugzeug durch ein Gewitter fliegen
   Bitte schnallen Sie sich an, während das Flugzeug durch ein Gewitter fliegt.
b) elektronische Geräte ausschalten – das Flugzeug landen
c) keinen Lärm machen – die Nachbarn Mittagspause machen
d) sich nicht aus dem Fenster lehnen – der Zug fahren
e) nicht sprechen – die Vorstellung laufen
f) nicht stören – der Gast schlafen

3 Ergänzen Sie bis, seit(dem).

Kegelrobben im Wattenmeer

Robben sind (a) *seit* dem Mittelalter an deutschen Küsten weit verbreitet. Doch (b) .... der Mensch den Küstenraum immer stärker besiedelt, haben sich die Robben an wenige sichere Strände zurückgezogen. (c) .... Mitte des 20. Jahrhunderts haben Menschen die Robben gejagt. (d) .... die Jagd verboten wurde, nimmt die Zahl der Robben wieder zu. Eine kleine Kegelrobbenkolonie nahe den Inseln Sylt und Amrum wird (e) .... 1988 beobachtet und betreut.
Die kleinen Robben werden im Frühling oder Herbst geboren. Täglich muss das Baby zwei Kilo zunehmen, (f) .... es genug Körpergewicht erreicht hat. Es dauert etwa eine Woche, (g) .... ein Robbenbaby genug Fett hat, um im kalten Wasser der Nordsee überleben zu können. (h) .... es soweit ist, wird es von seiner Mutter dreimal am Tag mit Muttermilch gestillt.

4 Lebenspläne – Formulieren Sie Sätze mit solange oder bis. Achten Sie auf das Tempus und stellen Sie den Nebensatz auch voran.

a) Niko noch Schüler sein – kann sich kein Auto leisten – muss warten – Geld verdienen
   Solange Niko noch Schüler ist, kann er sich kein Auto leisten. Er muss warten, bis er selber Geld verdient. Oder: Niko kann sich kein Auto leisten, solange er noch Schüler ist.
b) Barbara noch studieren – mit ihrem Studentenausweis viel Geld sparen – den Ausweis behalten – Studium beenden
c) Dennis noch keinen festen Job haben – bei seinen Eltern wohnen
d) Evelyns Kinder zur Schule gehen – die Familie in diesem Stadtteil bleiben – mit dem Umzug warten – Kinder die Schule wechseln
e) Petra in einer Wohngemeinschaft leben – Peter kennenlernen

5 Wirtschaftsentwicklung – Formulieren Sie Nebensätze mit seit, seitdem, bis.

a) Seit dem Abbau der Arbeitslosigkeit sind die Chancen gewachsen.
   Seit(dem) die Arbeitslosigkeit abgebaut wurde, sind die Chancen gewachsen.
b) Bis zum Abschluss der Tarifverhandlungen bleiben die Unternehmer zurückhaltend.
c) Seit dem Anstieg der Inflationsrate sind die Chancen der Unternehmen gesunken.
d) Bis zum Rückgang der Staatsschulden bleiben die Aussichten schlecht.
e) Seit der Einführung der Öko-Steuer ist die Stimmung negativ.
f) Bis zur Reform der Steuergesetze halten sich die Investoren zurück.

TEMPORALSATZ (3): NICHT GLEICHZEITIG

bevor – nachdem – sobald

1 Funktion

Mehrere Handlungen/Sachverhalte nacheinander

Konnektor		Handlung	Tempus
bevor	*Du solltest es dir gut überlegen, bevor du so viel Geld ausgibst.*	Nebensatz nach Hauptsatz	im Haupt- und Nebensatz gleich
ehe	*Ich kontrolliere alle Rechnungen, ehe ich sie bezahle.*		
nachdem	*Er bezahlt Rechnungen erst, nachdem er eine Mahnung bekommen hat.*	Nebensatz vor Hauptsatz	Hauptsatz: Präsens Nebensatz: Perfekt
	Nachdem er alles erledigt hatte, ging er schlafen.		Hauptsatz: Perfekt/ Präteritum
sobald	*Er geht, sobald er aufgegessen hat. Er ging, sobald er aufgegessen hatte.*	Nebensatz vor Hauptsatz; beide folgen sofort aufeinander	Nebensatz: Plusquamperfekt
	Ich rufe dich an, sobald ich fertig bin.		oft gleich im Haupt- und im Nebensatz

2 Satzstrukturen

Hauptsatz	Nebensatz			Hauptsatz
	Konnektor		Verb	
Ich räume noch rasch mein Zimmer auf,	*bevor*	*ich zur Arbeit*	*gehe.*	
	Bevor	*ich zur Arbeit*	*gehe,*	*räume ich noch rasch mein Zimmer auf.*

Interpunktion: Vor bzw. nach Nebensätzen steht ein Komma.

3 Alternativen

Nebensatz	Präposition + Nomen	
Bevor ich zur Arbeit gehe, räume ich rasch auf.	*Vor der Arbeit räume ich rasch auf.*	*vor* + Dativ
Nachdem ich zu Abend gegessen habe, gehe ich oft noch ins Fitnesscenter.	*Nach dem Abendessen gehe ich oft noch ins Fitnesscenter.*	*nach* + Dativ
Sobald ich mit den Hausaufgaben fertig bin, rufe ich eine Freundin an.	*Gleich nach den Hausaufgaben rufe ich eine Freundin an.*	*gleich/sofort nach* + Dativ

1 Was machst du morgens? – Formulieren Sie Sätze mit bevor oder ehe.

a) Ich mache einen Spaziergang mit meinem Hund. – zur Arbeit gehen
Bevor/Ehe ich zur Arbeit gehe, mache ich einen Spaziergang mit meinem Hund.

b) Ich kaufe noch rasch etwas für das Abendessen ein. – den Bus nehmen

c) Ich lese Zeitung. – sich fertig machen

d) Ich gebe den Fischen etwas zu fressen. – aufräumen

e) Ich räume schnell noch auf. – das Haus verlassen

f) Ich jogge im Park. – Müsli essen

2 Ratschläge für Ihre Gesundheit – Formulieren Sie Sätze mit bevor.

Schlaf	a) vor dem Aufstehen Kaffee oder Tee trinken
	b) vor dem Schlafengehen ein Glas Tee trinken
Schlankheit	c) vor dem Essen ein Glas Wasser zu sich nehmen
Fitness	d) vor dem Frühstück Frühsport oder Gymnastik
	e) vor dem Joggen einige Stretching-Übungen

a) *Trinken Sie Kaffee oder Tee, bevor Sie aufstehen.*

3 Alle haben es eilig – Formulieren Sie Sätze mit sobald.

a) abreisen – die Konferenz vorüber sein
Ich reise ab, sobald die Konferenz vorüber ist.

b) hier ausziehen – eine neue Wohnung finden

c) bei Freunden anrufen – die Hausaufgaben machen

d) wir können essen – der Tisch gedeckt sein

e) nach Hause gehen – die Schule aus sein

f) zahlen – die Rechnung geschrieben sein

g) frühstücken – Gymnastik machen

4 Einen Lebenslauf nacherzählen – Formulieren Sie Sätze mit nachdem.

a) das Abitur – Studium für das Lehramt am Gymnasium.
Nachdem sie das Abitur gemacht hatte, studierte sie für das Lehramt am Gymnasium.

b) fünf Jahre Studium – Erstes Staatsexamen ablegen

c) das Staatsexamen – Referendarausbildung an einer Schule beginnen

d) die Referendarausbildung beenden – Zweites Staatsexamen machen

e) die Ausbildung beenden – heiraten

f) zwei Jahre verheiratet – erstes Kind bekommen

5 Wie benutze ich einen Computer? – Ergänzen Sie bevor oder nachdem.

(a) *Bevor* du mit dem Computer arbeiten kannst, musst du den Netzschalter einschalten. (b) .... du den Computer eingeschaltet hast, kannst du das Programm aufrufen, das du verwenden willst. (c) .... du einen Text schreibst, öffnest du eine Datei. (d) .... du deine Datei speicherst, musst du entscheiden, wohin du sie speichern willst, auf Diskette oder Festplatte. (e) Gleich .... du einen Text geschrieben hast, kannst du ihn ausdrucken. (f) .... du das Gerät abschaltest, solltest du Datei und Programm schließen.

KAUSALSATZ

weil – da – denn

1 Funktion

> „*Warum kriechst du eigentlich auf allen Vieren?*"
> „*Weil ich eine Kontaktlinse verloren habe.*"
> *Heinz braucht seine Kontaktlinse, denn ohne sie sieht er sehr schlecht.*

Grund

2 Satzstrukturen

a Hauptsatz, Konnektor auf Position 0

Hauptsatz	Hauptsatz			
	Konnektor		Verb	
Ich lebe allein,	*denn*	*ich*	*habe*	*keine Zeit für eine Familie.*

b Hauptsatz, Konnektor auf Position 3

Hauptsatz	Hauptsatz			
		Verb	Konnektor	
Ich lebe allein.	*Ich*	*habe*	*nämlich*	*keine Zeit für eine Familie.*

📖 **s. Seite 146**

c Nebensatz

Hauptsatz	Nebensatz			Hauptsatz
	Konnektor		Verb	
Ich lebe allein,	*weil*	*ich keine Zeit für eine Familie*	*habe.*	
Ich lebe allein,	*da*	*ich keine Zeit für eine Familie*	*habe.*	
	Weil	*ich keine Zeit für eine Familie*	*habe,*	*lebe ich allein.*
	Da	*ich keine Zeit für eine Familie*	*habe,*	*lebe ich allein.*

Wenn der Nebensatz zuerst steht, ist *da* stilistisch besser als *weil*.

Interpunktion: Vor bzw. nach Nebensätzen steht ein Komma.

Der Nebensatz mit *weil* kann als Antwort ohne Hauptsatz stehen: *Warum bist du nicht gekommen? – Weil ich krank war.*

3 Alternativen

Nebensatz	Präposition	
Ich konnte keine Familie haben, weil ich berufstätig war.	*Wegen meiner Berufstätigkeit konnte ich keine Familie haben.*	*wegen* + Genitiv
	Aufgrund meiner Berufstätigkeit konnte ich keine Familie haben.	*aufgrund* + Genitiv
Er zitterte, weil er Angst hatte.	*Er zitterte vor Angst.*	*vor/aus* + Nomen ohne Artikel
Er hat es getan, weil er diese Frau liebt.	*Er hat es aus Liebe zu dieser Frau getan.*	

__1__ **Warum ich keine Hausaufgabe machen konnte! – Formulieren Sie Sätze mit** weil.
   a) Es war einfach viel zu heiß.
       Weil es einfach viel zu heiß war.
   b) Ich hatte den ganzen Nachmittag Kopfschmerzen.
   c) Ich war erschöpft und bin vor Müdigkeit eingeschlafen.
   d) Mein Füller hat plötzlich nicht mehr funktioniert.
   e) Mein Freund hat meine Schultasche versteckt.
   f) Mein Hund hat das Aufgabenblatt gefressen.

__2__ **Analysieren Sie Struktur und Bedeutung der Sätze.**
   A: Struktur + Bedeutung gleich; B: Struktur gleich, Bedeutung verschieden;
   C: Struktur verschieden, Bedeutung gleich

		A	B	C
a) Hermann kündigt, **weil** er bei seiner Firma zu wenig verdient.	Hermann kündigt, **denn** er verdient bei seiner Firma zu wenig.			✕
b) Hermann kündigt, **weil** er keine Gehaltserhöhung bekommt.	Hermann kündigt, **da** er keine Gehaltserhöhung bekommt.			
c) Hermann kündigt, **weil** er seine Tätigkeit langweilig findet.	**Wegen** seiner langweiligen Tätigkeit kündigt Hermann.			
d) **Weil** er keine Gehaltserhöhung bekommt, kündigt Hermann seinen Job.	**Wenn** er keine Gehaltserhöhung bekommt, kündigt Hermann seinen Job.			

__3__ **In der Schule – Formulieren Sie Sätze mit** da **oder** weil. **Stellen Sie den Nebensatz bei b), d), e) und g) voran.**
   a) Vanessa will endlich Pause machen / schaut sie ständig auf die Uhr.
       Weil Vanessa endlich Pause machen will, schaut sie ständig auf die Uhr.
   b) Doro lernt täglich drei Stunden / sie braucht unbedingt bessere Noten.
   c) Sandra hat nicht mehr so gute Noten / übt sie täglich noch mehr.
   d) Dennis findet seine neue Lehrerin super / sie so wenig Hausaufgaben aufgibt.
   e) Nico ist durch die Prüfung gefallen / er sich nicht konzentrieren kann.
   f) Kims Lieblingsfach ist Latein / sie da was über die alten Römer erfährt.
   g) Den Eltern sind die Schulerfolge sehr wichtig / sie an die Zukunft ihrer Kinder denken.

__4__ **Formulieren Sie die Sätze mit den Präpositionen** wegen **und** aufgrund **um.**
   a) Weil Helga einen schweren Unfall hatte, kann sie jetzt nicht mehr arbeiten.
       Aufgrund/Wegen eines schweren Unfalls kann Helga jetzt nicht mehr arbeiten.
   b) Weil Isabella ein Stipendium erhält, kann sie einen Deutschkurs in Österreich besuchen. (nur *aufgrund*)
   c) Weil Sofia ein hervorragendes Zeugnis hat, kann sie studieren, was sie möchte. (nur *aufgrund*)
   d) Amelie kann nicht Medizin studieren, weil ihre Noten zu schlecht sind.
   e) Tobias hat die Schule verlassen, weil er große Probleme mit einem Lehrer hatte.
   f) Die Schule in unserem Dorf wird geschlossen, weil akuter Schülermangel herrscht.

7

KONDITIONALSATZ

wenn – falls – sofern – sonst

1 Funktion

„Mami wird sauer sein, *wenn* sie das merkt." | Bedingung
„Ja, *falls* sie das merkt! Aber vielleicht merkt
sie es ja nicht."

2 Satzstrukturen

a Nebensatz

Hauptsatz	Nebensatz			Hauptsatz
	Konnektor		Verb	
Wir gehen spazieren,	wenn	du Lust	hast.	
Wir gehen spazieren,	wenn	du Lust	hast,	und essen unterwegs ein Eis.
	Wenn	du Lust	hast,	gehen wir spazieren.

Genauso: *falls, sofern*
wenn kann auch temporale Bedeutung haben, **s. Seite 162**

Interpunktion: Vor bzw. nach Nebensätzen steht ein Komma.

b Hauptsatz, Konnektor auf Position 1 oder 3

Hauptsatz	Hauptsatz			
	POS 1	Verb	POS 3	
Ich brauche deine Hilfe.	Sonst	werde	ich	nicht fertig.
Ich brauche deine Hilfe.	Ich	werde	sonst	nicht fertig.

3 Alternativen

Nebensatz	ohne Konnektor	Präposition *bei* + Dativ	Modalverb (Konjunktiv II)
Wenn es regnet, gehen wir nicht in den Park.	Regnet es, gehen wir nicht in den Park.	Bei Regen gehen wir nicht in den Park.	Sollte es regnen, gehen wir nicht in den Park.

ÜBUNGEN

1 Moderne Bedürfnisse – Formulieren Sie wenn-Sätze.

einen ~~Anrufbeantworter~~ I Kontaktlinsen I ein Modem I ein Handy I einen stärkeren
Computer I einen besseren Wecker I einen Videorekorder

a) Ich will Nachrichten am Telefon aufzeichnen.
Sie brauchen einen Anrufbeantworter, wenn Sie Nachrichten am Telefon aufzeichnen wollen.

b) Mich stört die Brille beim Joggen.

c) Ich will im Internet surfen.
d) Ich will außer Haus Anrufe annehmen.
e) Ich will moderne Computerspiele ausprobieren.
f) Ich komme oft zu spät zur Arbeit.
g) Ich will Fernsehsendungen aufzeichnen.

2 **Formulieren Sie die Sätze aus Übung 1 nun ohne** wen.
a) *Wollen Sie Nachrichten am Telefon aufzeichnen, brauchen Sie einen Anrufbeantworter.*

3 **Armer Moritz! – Formulieren Sie Sätze mit** sonst.
a) Moritz, mach jetzt deine Hausaufgaben. – Du bekommst kein Eis.
   Moritz, mach jetzt deine Hausaufgaben, sonst bekommst du kein Eis.
b) Moritz, räum dein Zimmer auf. – Du darfst nicht schwimmen gehen.
c) Moritz, wasch deine Hände. – Du bekommst kein Abendessen.
d) Moritz, zieh dich warm an. – Du erkältest dich.
e) Moritz, mach nicht so einen Krach. – Die Nachbarn beschweren sich wieder.
f) Moritz, sei nett zu deiner kleinen Schwester. – Ich bin nicht nett zu dir.

4 **Lust, Zeit, Geld – Formulieren Sie Sätze mit** wenn, falls **oder** sofern.

Lust haben   (a) wir gehen heute Abend ins Theater (b) wir gehen in die Picasso-Ausstellung (c) wir sehen uns das neue Kabarettprogramm an.

Zeit haben   (d) ich besuche noch meine Freundin Elke (e) ich lese noch meine E-Mails (f) ich gehe endlich mal richtig gut essen (g) ich räume endlich mal mein Zimmer auf

Geld brauchen   (h) such dir einen Job in einem Lokal (i) leih dir etwas von deinen Eltern (j) hol dir welches an dem Bankautomaten

(a) *Wenn/Falls/Sofern du Lust hast, gehen wir heute Abend ins Theater.*

5 **Was machen Sie, wenn ...? – Formulieren Sie** wenn-**Sätze.**

a) Sie haben eine Reifenpanne.   Ich benutze eine Taschenlampe.
b) Der Strom fällt aus.   Ich fahre mit dem Auto zu einer Tankstelle.
c) Es kommen unerwartet Gäste.   Ich serviere Getränke.
d) Sie treffen auf der Straße einen   Ich verabrede ein Treffen.
   alten Klassenkameraden.   Ich rufe Hilfe.
e) Sie haben nichts zu Hause und die
   Geschäfte in der Nähe sind geschlossen.

a) *Wenn ich eine Reifenpanne habe, rufe ich Hilfe.*

6 **Abhängig vom Wetter – Sagen Sie es anders.**
a) Sollte es regnen, findet das Grillfest nicht statt.
   Wenn es regnet, findet das Grillfest nicht statt. oder:
   Regnet es, findet das Grillfest nicht statt.
b) Sollte es heute noch schneien, können wir morgen Ski fahren.
c) Bei schlechtem Wetter gehen wir ins Museum.
d) Sollte der Pullover nicht warm genug sein, musst du noch einen anziehen.
e) Sollten Sie in der Nacht frieren, benutzen Sie die Decke.

FINALSATZ

damit – um ... zu

<u>1</u> Funktion

*Der Wolf hat Großmutters Nachthemd angezogen,
um Rotkäppchen zu täuschen.*
„Großmutter, was hast du für große Ohren?"
„Damit ich dich besser hören kann." | Absicht,
Ziel

<u>2</u> Satzstrukturen

Hauptsatz	Nebensatz			Hauptsatz
	Konnektor		Verb	
Ich schlafe täglich acht Stunden,	*damit*	*ich ausgeruht*	*bin.*	
	Damit	*ich ausgeruht*	*bin,*	*schlafe ich täglich acht Stunden.*
Ich schlafe täglich acht Stunden,	*um*	*ausgeruht*	*zu sein.*	

um ... zu   eleganter als *damit*; *um ... zu* kann *damit* ersetzen, wenn das Subjekt des
Nebensatzes mit dem Subjekt des Hauptsatzes identisch ist:
<u>*Ich*</u> *mache diese Reise, damit* <u>*ich*</u> *mich erhole.*
⟶ *Ich mache diese Reise, um mich zu erholen.*

zu   steht vor dem Infinitiv-Verb
bei trennbaren Verben zwischen Vorsilbe und Verb: *auszuschlafen,*
zwischen Vollverb und Modalverb: *schlafen zu können.*

Interpunktion: Vor bzw. nach Nebensätzen steht ein Komma.

<u>3</u> Alternativen

Nebensatz	Präposition	
Ich trinke eine Tasse Tee, um mich zu beruhigen.	*Zur Beruhigung trinke ich eine Tasse Tee.*	*zu* + Dativ
Sie tut alles, damit sie Karriere macht.	*Für ihre Karriere tut sie alles.*	*für* + Akkusativ

ÜBUNGEN

<u>1</u> Sparsamkeit – Ergänzen Sie um ... zu.
a) Man glaubt gar nicht, was Leute alles tun. – Geld sparen
   Man glaubt gar nicht, was Leute alles tun, um Geld zu sparen.
b) Mein Nachbar zum Beispiel fährt bei jedem Wetter mit dem Fahrrad ins Büro. – das
   Fahrgeld für den Bus sparen

c) Außerdem kauft er fast nur Sonderangebote. – bloß kein Geld verschwenden

d) Strom sparen – Er dreht nie vor November die elektrische Heizung an, egal wie kalt es draußen ist.

e) Im Büro sammelt er das Papier und verwendet die Rückseiten für Notizen. – nicht so viel Papier verbrauchen

f) Auf der Autobahn fährt er nie schneller als 120 Kilometer. – Benzin sparen

g) weniger Steuern zu zahlen – Neulich hat er geheiratet.

2 Gesundheitstipps – Formulieren Sie Nebensätze.

a) sich vor Zivilisationskrankheiten schützen – nicht mehr als 80 Gramm Fleisch am Tag essen.
  Essen Sie nicht mehr als 80 Gramm Fleisch am Tag, um sich vor Zivilisationskrankheiten zu schützen.
  Um sich vor Zivilisationskrankheiten zu schützen, sollten Sie nicht mehr als 80 Gramm Fleisch am Tag essen.

b) fit bleiben – sich täglich eine Stunde im Freien bewegen

c) ein gesundes Herz behalten – Treppen steigen, statt Lift zu fahren

d) Muskeln aufbauen – regelmäßig ins Fitnessstudio gehen

e) Fett abbauen – so wenig tierisches Fett wie möglich essen

f) Erkältungen vermeiden – im Winter einmal wöchentlich in die Sauna gehen

g) Nerven beruhigen – vor dem Schlafengehen Milch trinken

h) gut schlafen – die richtige Matratze kaufen

3 Was die Menschen alles tun ... – Formulieren Sie Sätze mit um ... zu. Wenn das nicht möglich ist, mit damit.

a) Bewerber: einen guten Job bekommen
  Was Bewerber alles tun, um einen guten Job zu bekommen.

b) Eltern: aus ihren Kindern etwas wird
  Was Eltern alles tun, damit aus ihren Kindern etwas wird.

c) Ärzte: Leben retten

d) Frauen: schön sein

e) Männer: einen muskulösen Körper bekommen

f) Mütter: ihre Kinder genug Schlaf bekommen

g) Regierungen: die Arbeitslosigkeit bekämpfen

h) Schüler: ihre Lehrer ihnen weniger Hausaufgaben aufgeben

4 Richtig lernen – Formulieren Sie Sätze mit um ... zu. Wenn das nicht möglich ist, mit damit.

a) Wir * in der Klasse * oft Gruppenarbeit machen * alle sich möglichst viel am Unterricht beteiligen
  Wir machen in der Klasse oft Gruppenarbeit, damit sich alle möglichst viel am Unterricht beteiligen.

b) Ich * sehen * gerne deutsche Filme im Original * mein Hörverstehen verbessern
  Ich sehe gerne deutsche Filme im Original, um mein Hörverstehen zu verbessern.

c) Manchmal * ich * auswendig lernen * kurze Texte * mir neue Sätze merken

d) Ich * meine Hausaufgaben sorgfältig machen * schneller Fortschritte machen

e) Ich * übersichtlicher schreiben * meine Notizen besser lesen können

f) Ich * täglich zehn neue Wörter lernen * mein Wortschatz rasch wachsen

g) Ich * jeden Tag eine Viertelstunde üben * das Lernen wird nicht zu anstrengend

KONSEKUTIVSATZ

so dass – deshalb – infolgedessen

1 Funktion

> *Heinz will abnehmen. Deshalb isst er zur Zeit nur noch Weintrauben.* | Folge

2 Satzstruktur

ⓐ Nebensatz

Hauptsatz	Nebensatz		Verb
	Konnektor		
Er war so hungrig,	*dass*	*er nur noch ans Essen denken*	*konnte.*
Er hatte solchen/derartigen Hunger,	*dass*	*er nur noch ans Essen denken*	*konnte.*
Er isst nun fünf mal pro Tag,	*sodass*	*er keinen Heißhunger mehr*	*bekommt.*

so bzw. *derartig* stehen vor einem Adjektiv oder Adverb, z.B. *hungrig*,
solch- bzw. *derartig-* stehen vor einem Nomen, z.B. *Hunger*.

Interpunktion: Vor bzw. nach Nebensätzen steht ein Komma.

ⓑ Hauptsatz, Konnektor auf Position 1 oder 3

Hauptsatz	Hauptsatz			
	POS 1	Verb	POS 3	
Heinz fühlt sich nicht wohl.	*Deshalb*	*macht*	*er*	*eine Diät*
Heinz fühlt sich nicht wohl.	*Er*	*macht*	*deshalb*	*eine Diät.*

Genauso: *also, deswegen, daher, darum, folglich, infolgedessen.*

3 Alternativen

Nebensatz	Präposition	
Er hat so viel geraucht, dass seine Gesundheit geschädigt ist.	*Infolge starken Rauchens ist seine Gesundheit geschädigt.* *Seine Gesundheit ist infolge starken Rauchens geschädigt.*	*infolge* + Genitiv
Es sind so viele (Mitarbeiter) erkrankt, dass wir den Termin nicht einhalten können.	*Infolge von Erkrankungen können wir den Termin nicht einhalten.*	*infolge von* + Dativ

ÜBUNGEN

1 Alles fing im Bein an – Formulieren Sie Sätze mit dass.

   a) Hans bekam Schmerzen im Knie (solch-) – er konnte nicht mehr laufen.
   Hans bekam solche Schmerzen im Knie, dass er nicht mehr laufen konnte.

   b) Dann tat ihm plötzlich am rechten Fuß ein Zeh weh (so) – er wollte keinen Schuh mehr anziehen.

c) Schließlich stieß er mit dem Bein hart gegen etwas (so) – es wurde ganz blau.

d) Außerdem bekam er ein Spannungsgefühl in der Brust (derartig) – er konnte nicht mehr richtig durchatmen.

e) Seine Schultern waren verspannt (derartig) – er konnte nicht länger als eine Stunde am Schreibtisch arbeiten.

2 Schule – Verbinden Sie die Hauptsätze. Setzen Sie den Konnektor auf Position 1 oder 3.

a) Die Eltern denken an die Zukunft ihrer Kinder.   Dennis findet sie super.
b) Die neue Lehrerin gibt wenig Hausaufgaben auf.   Er kann sich nicht konzentrieren.
c) Jana braucht unbedingt bessere Noten.   Gute Noten sind ihnen wichtig.
d) Nico hat letzte Nacht nur fünf Stunden geschlafen.   Sie hat nicht mehr so gute Noten.
e) Sandra übt nicht mehr täglich.   Sie lernt täglich drei Stunden.

a) *Die Eltern denken an die Zukunft ihrer Kinder. Darum sind ihnen gute Noten wichtig. / Ihnen sind deshalb gute Noten wichtig.*

3 Ursachen und Folgen – Formulieren Sie Sätze mit infolgedessen.

a) Er hatte einen sehr stressigen Job – war fast nie zu Hause.
   Er hatte einen sehr stressigen Job. Infolgedessen war er fast nie zu Hause.
b) Sie war glücklich – sah über vieles hinweg.
c) Er war unglücklich – hatte oft schlechte Laune.
d) Sie hatte Geldsorgen – fühlte sich oft unter Druck.
e) Er hatte wenig Geld – konnte sich kaum etwas leisten.
f) Sie war kinderlos – stürzte sich voll auf die Arbeit.

4 Verbinden Sie die Sätze mit darum, deshalb, deswegen und, wenn möglich, mit so-dass, so ... dass.

a) Ich muss morgen ausgeschlafen sein – ich gehe früh schlafen.
   Ich muss morgen ausgeschlafen sein, deshalb/darum/deswegen gehe ich früh schlafen.
   Ich gehe früh schlafen, sodass ich morgen ausgeschlafen bin.
   Ich gehe so früh schlafen, dass ich morgen ausgeschlafen bin.
b) Ich brauche etwas frische Luft – ich gehe noch eine halbe Stunde joggen.
c) Ich hatte gestern hohes Fieber – ich konnte nicht in den Kurs kommen.
d) Ich bin etwas schüchtern – ich besuche eine Selbsterfahrungsgruppe.
e) Ich bin heute schlecht gelaunt – ich möchte keinen sehen.
f) Ich habe eine Gehaltserhöhung bekommen – ich kann dich zum Essen einladen.
g) Wir schreiben morgen einen Test – ich muss heute lernen.

5 Radrennen – Formulieren Sie Sätze mit deshalb, deswegen, darum.

a) Infolge eines Sturzes musste ein Fahrer ausscheiden.
   Ein Fahrer stürzte. Deshalb musste er ausscheiden.
b) Infolge eines Radschadens musste einer aus dem Sieger-Team des Vortages aufgeben.
c) Infolge eines Gewitters waren einige Straßen unpassierbar.
d) Infolge eines Unwetters waren die Straßen spiegelglatt.
e) Infolge einer Verletzung konnte der Sieger des letzten Rennens nicht mehr an den Start gehen.

KONZESSIVSATZ

obwohl – trotzdem – dennoch

1 Funktion

Obwohl die Mannschaft ihr Bestes gegeben hat, hat es am Ende nicht zu einem Sieg gereicht.	Widerspruch, Gegensatz

2 Satzstrukturen

a Nebensatz

Hauptsatz	Nebensatz			Hauptsatz
	Konnektor		Verb	
Mein Geld reicht nicht,	*obwohl*	*ich ständig*	*spare.*	
	Obwohl	*ich ständig*	*spare,*	*reicht mein Geld nicht.*

Genauso: *obgleich.*
Interpunktion: Vor bzw. nach Nebensätzen steht ein Komma.

b Hauptsatz, Konnektor auf Position 1 oder 3

Hauptsatz	Hauptsatz			
	POS 1	Verb	POS 3	
Die Mannschaft hat sich total eingesetzt.	*Trotzdem*	*hat*	*es*	*am Ende nicht zu einem Sieg gereicht.*
Die Mannschaft hat sich total eingesetzt.	*Es*	*hat*	*trotzdem*	*am Ende nicht zu einem Sieg gereicht.*

Genauso: *dennoch.*

3 Alternativen

Nebensatz	Präposition	
Es hat nicht zu einem Sieg gereicht, obwohl die Mannschaft sich enorm eingesetzt hat.	*Trotz des enormen Einsatzes der Mannschaft hat es nicht zu einem Sieg gereicht.*	*trotz* + Genitiv

ÜBUNGEN

1 Zum Teufel mit den Gesundheitstipps – Formulieren Sie Sätze mit obwohl.

a) eine Diät machen – sich heute ein zweites Frühstück gönnen
   Obwohl ich eine Diät mache, gönne ich mir heute ein zweites Frühstück.
b) viel Zucker enthalten – ab und zu eine Cola trinken
c) es ist nicht gesund – nicht auf Salz verzichten
d) viel Schokolade essen – nicht dick sein
e) Obst besser sein – zum Fernsehen lieber Kartoffelchips knabbern
f) der viele Rauch mir nicht gut tun – freitagabends in die Kneipe gehen

2 Tante Frieda ist vor kurzem am Magen operiert worden. – Formulieren Sie Sätze mit trotzdem.

a) Der Arzt hat ihr jeden Sport verboten. Sie läuft schon wieder Ski.
   Der Arzt hat ihr jeden Sport verboten. Trotzdem läuft sie schon wieder Ski.
b) Sie darf auf keinen Fall Alkohol trinken. Sie trinkt schon wieder Bier.
c) Sie müsste eigentlich noch ein paar Tage im Bett bleiben. Sie steht schon wieder auf.
d) Sie soll das Rauchen aufgeben. Sie raucht schon wieder.
e) Sie soll fünfmal am Tag Obst essen. Sie isst schon wieder Schweinebraten.

3 Sagen Sie es anders. – Formulieren Sie die Übung 2 mit obwohl/obgleich.

a) *Obwohl/Obgleich der Arzt ihr jeden Sport verboten hat, läuft sie schon wieder Ski.*

4 Fallstudien – Ergänzen Sie obwohl, trotzdem, trotz.

Partnersuche

(a) Obwohl Heiko nicht hässlich ist, findet er keine Partnerin. Er ist auch nicht dumm. (b) .... hat sich noch keine für ihn interessiert. Ich habe ihm geraten, ein Seminar für Singles zu besuchen, (c) .... das einiges kostet. Heiko ist zwar skeptisch, (d) .... wird er sich für das Seminar einschreiben.

Umweltsünder

(e) .... jeder weiß, wie man seinen Abfall reduzieren kann, verhalten sich viele unvernünftig. Mein Nachbar hat nur 5 Minuten zur Arbeit, (f) .... fährt er täglich mit dem Auto. Und (g) .... die Bahn häufig gar nicht teuer ist, fahren viele mit dem Auto in den Urlaub. Und das (h) .... des Risikos, stundenlang im Stau zu stehen.

Berufschancen

Mein Freund Axel hat gerade ein sehr gutes Examen gemacht. (i) .... findet er keine Stelle. (j) .... er neben dem Studium bei verschiedenen Firmen gearbeitet hat, hat er im Moment keine Angebote. (k) .... des großen Mangels in bestimmten Berufen haben viele Hochschulabsolventen große Schwierigkeiten, eine Stelle zu finden.

5 Fußball – Formulieren Sie mit dennoch, trotzdem.

a) Der Spieler ist schon 30 – er ist für einen Profi nicht zu alt.
   Der Spieler ist schon 30, dennoch/trotzdem ist er für einen Profi nicht zu alt.
b) Die Mannschaft besteht vorwiegend aus jungen Spielern – sie ist ein ernst zu nehmender Gegner.
c) Das Foul war nicht eindeutig – der Schiedsrichter gab Elfmeter.
d) Der Club hat das Spiel verloren – er hat noch eine Chance, ins Finale zu kommen.
e) Die Regeln für „Abseits" habe ich schon oft gehört – sie sind mir immer noch nicht klar.
f) Die Stürmer sind sehr stark – sie wurden nie richtig gefährlich.
g) Unsere Abwehr zeigte einige Schwächen – am Ende siegte unsere Mannschaft.

6 Reise mit Hindernissen – Formulieren Sie Sätze mit trotz.

a) lange Anfahrt; unsere gute Laune nicht verloren
   Trotz der langen Anfahrt haben wir unsere gute Laune nicht verloren.
b) geringes Freizeitangebot; uns nicht gelangweilt
c) horrende Preise; unser Budget nicht überschritten
d) kühles Wetter; im Meer gebadet
e) miserables Essen; zugenommen

ADVERSATIVSATZ

aber – doch – sondern – während

1 Funktion

> *Heinz ist Frühaufsteher, seine Frau Lotte dagegen schläft gerne lang.*
> *Er liegt nicht lange im Bett herum, sondern möchte gleich etwas unternehmen.* | Gegensatz

2 Satzstrukturen

a Hauptsatz, Konnektor auf Position 0

Hauptsatz	Hauptsatz			
	Konnektor		Verb	
Elke lernt (zwar) gern,	*aber**	*(sie)*	*(lernt)*	*nicht genug.*
Elke lernt gern.	*Doch*	*sie*	*lernt*	*nicht genug.*
Elke lernt kaum Vokabeln,	*sondern***	*(sie)*	*konzentriert*	*sich auf die Grammatik.*

* *aber* kann auch auf Position 3 stehen.
** *sondern* steht nach einer Negation/Einschränkung im ersten Hauptsatz, 📖 **s. Seite 146**

b Hauptsatz, Konnektor auf Position 1 oder 3

Hauptsatz	Hauptsatz			
	POS 1	Verb	POS 3	
Elke lernt gern.	*Dagegen*	*hat*	*ihr Bruder*	*wenig Spaß am Lernen.*
Elke lernt gern,	*ihr Bruder*	*hat*	*dagegen*	*wenig Spaß am Lernen.*

Genauso: *jedoch, hingegen*

c Nebensatz

Hauptsatz	Nebensatz			Hauptsatz
	Konnektor		Verb	
Er äußert Kritik offen,	*während*	*sie eher kooperativ*	*ist.*	
	Während	*er Kritik offen*	*äußert,*	*ist sie eher kooperativ.*

während kann auch temporale Bedeutung haben, 📖 **s. Seite 162**

Interpunktion: Zwischen Haupt- und Nebensatz steht ein Komma.

3 Alternativen

Nebensatz	Präposition	
Während viele anderer Meinung sind, …	*Entgegen der allgemeinen Meinung …*	*entgegen* + Dativ
Frauen sind kooperativ, während Männer das nicht sind.	*Im Gegensatz zu vielen Männern sind Frauen kooperativ.*	*im Gegensatz zu* + Dativ

1 Widersprüche – Formulieren Sie Sätze mit aber, doch, jedoch, sondern.

a) Max: hat kaum Geld – stört ihn nicht
   Max hat kaum Geld, aber das stört ihn nicht.
   Max hat kaum Geld, doch das stört ihn nicht.
   Max hat kaum Geld, das stört ihn jedoch nicht.
b) Lisa: nicht mehr Geld – mehr Zeit für ihre Kinder
   Lisa wünscht sich nicht mehr Geld, sondern mehr Zeit für ihre Kinder.
c) Richard: lebt allein – kommt mit dem Haushalt gut zurecht
d) Daniel: interessiert sich nicht für Computerspiele – surft lieber im Internet
e) Charlotte: geschieden – sieht ihren Ex-Mann regelmäßig
f) Julius: alleinerziehender Vater – beklagt sich nie
g) Eva: liest nicht so gerne Bücher – lieber Zeitschriften
h) Sandra: viel Zeit – weiß nichts damit anzufangen

2 Eine Wohnung mieten – Verbinden Sie die Sätze mit sondern. Überlegen Sie, welche Wörter aus dem zweiten Satzteil wegfallen können.

a) Bei einer Wohnung sollte man weniger an die Größe denken. Man sollte an die Lage denken.
   Bei einer Wohnung sollte man weniger an die Größe denken, sondern an die Lage.
b) Leute, die eine Wohnung besichtigen, haben oft kein echtes Interesse. Sie wollen nur die Preise vergleichen.
c) Zum Besichtigungstermin war nicht der Vermieter gekommen. Der Mieter, der auszieht, war da.
d) Zu der Besichtigung bin ich nicht allein gegangen. Ich habe eine Freundin mitgenommen.
e) Die Energiekosten zählen nicht zur Miete. Die Energiekosten zählen zu den Nebenkosten.

3 Wohnungssuche – Formulieren Sie Sätze mit aber, doch. Es gibt mehrere Lösungen.

a) die Wohnung liegt nach Norden; nicht dunkel
   Die Wohnung liegt nach Norden, aber/doch sie ist nicht dunkel.
   Die Wohnung liegt nach Norden, ist aber nicht dunkel.
b) die Fenster gehen zur Straße raus; man hört nichts vom Verkehr
c) die Wohnung hat eine gute Lage; Straße ist sehr laut
d) das Haus ist alt; ist total renoviert
e) die Wohnung hat 100 Quadratmeter; wirkt klein und eng
f) die Wohnung hat einen Balkon; ist sehr klein

4 Wohnstile – Ergänzen Sie dagegen, im Gegensatz zu, während.

Mir gefallen alte Häuser. Moderne Wohnblocks finde ich (a) *dagegen* unromantisch. (b) .... dem Geschmack der Mehrheit finde ich Reihenhäuser langweilig. Der Traum vieler Leute ist eine Dachterrasse. Ich (c) .... brauche keine, (d) .... ich nicht auf hohe Zimmerdecken verzichten könnte. Für meinen Freund Uwe (e) .... kann ein Haus nicht modern genug sein, (f) .... er Altbauwohnungen regelrecht hasst.

MODALSATZ

indem – dadurch ... dass – je ... desto – als – wie – ohne dass

1   Funktion

Über Filme informiert man sich am besten, indem man die Kritiken in der Zeitung liest.	Art und Weise
Der Film war so toll, wie ich es mir gedacht habe. *Und die Schauspieler waren viel besser, als ich dachte.*	Vergleich

2   Satzstrukturen

a Nebensatz

Hauptsatz	Nebensatz		
	Konnektor		Verb
Der Film war (genau)so gut,	*wie**	*wir erwartet*	*haben.*
Der Film war (noch) besser,	*als**	*wir erwartet*	*haben.*
Ich merke mir Wörter,	*indem*	*ich sie auf Kärtchen*	*schreibe.*
Ich erweitere meinen Wortschatz dadurch,	*dass*	*ich viel Zeitung*	*lese.***
Ich merke mir Wörter auch,	*ohne dass*	*ich sie ins Vokabelheft*	*schreibe.*

* 📖 **s. auch Seite 38**

** auch möglich: *Dadurch, dass ich viel Zeitung lese, erweitere ich meinen Wortschatz.*

b Nebensatz, zweiteilige Konnektoren

Nebensatz		Hauptsatz	
Konnektor 1		Konnektor 2	
Je	*öfter ich Wörter wiederhole,*	*desto/umso*	*besser merke ich sie mir.*

Zwischen *je* und dem Komparativ bzw. *desto/umso* und dem Komparativ dürfen keine anderen Wörter stehen.

Interpunktion: Vor bzw. nach Nebensätzen steht ein Komma.

c Infinitivsatz

Nebensatz	Infinitivsatz	
		zu + Infinitiv
Ich merke mir Wörter auch,	*ohne sie ins Vokabelheft*	*zu schreiben.*

3   Alternativen

Nebensatz	verkürzter Nebensatz: *wie/als* + Partizip II
Der Film war so gut, wie wir erwartet haben.	*Der Film war so gut wie erwartet.*
Der Film war besser, als wir erwartet haben.	*Der Film war besser als erwartet.*

_1_ Die Prüfung – Verbinden Sie die Sätze mit als oder wie.

a) Die Prüfung war leichter, annehmen
b) Der Lesetext war nicht so lang, befürchten
c) Die Aufgaben waren so schwer, erwarten
d) Die Prüferin war netter, erwarten
e) Die Prüfung dauerte länger, es sich vorstellen
f) Beim Hörverstehen wurde nicht so schnell gesprochen, befürchten
g) Die Zeit verging schneller, glauben
h) Ich war schneller fertig, hoffen

a) *Die Prüfung war leichter, als ich angenommen habe. / ... hatte.*

_2_ Formulieren Sie die Sätze c), d) und f) von Übung 1 in der verkürzten Version.

b) *Der Lesetext war nicht so lang wie befürchtet.*

_3_ Lerntechnik – Formulieren Sie Sätze mit indem oder dadurch ... dass.

a) Wortschatz erweitern – Wörter im Zusammenhang lernen
   Ich erweitere meinen Wortschatz, indem ich Wörter im Zusammenhang lerne.
   Ich erweitere meinen Wortschatz dadurch, dass ich Wörter im Zusammenhang lerne.
b) Wortschatz erweitern – Vokabeln regelmäßig wiederholen
c) Wortschatz erweitern – Vokabeln in ein Heft notieren
d) Grammatikregeln lernen – ein Merkheft anlegen
e) Grammatikregeln lernen – Regeln übersichtlich aufschreiben
f) Lernstoff erarbeiten – Notizen farbig markieren und übersichtlich anordnen
g) Auf eine Prüfung vorbereiten – den Lernstoff zwei- bis dreimal wiederholen

_4_ Weinproduktion – Formulieren Sie Vergleichssätze mit je ... desto/umso.

a) Die Traube bleibt lange am Stock. Der Wein wird süß.
   Je länger die Traube am Stock bleibt, desto/umso süßer
   wird der Wein.
b) Der Wein lagert lange. Er wird wertvoll.
c) Die Ernte ist klein. Der Wein wird teuer.
d) Die produzierte Menge ist gering. Der Preis ist hoch.
e) In Europa wird viel Wein produziert. Die Preise sinken stark.
f) Der Wein ist trocken. Er ist heutzutage bei den Kunden beliebt.

_5_ Ohne Schweiß kein Preis – Formulieren Sie Nebensätze mit ohne dass.

a) Katharina hat den Wettbewerb gewonnen, ohne sich besonders anzustrengen.
   Katharina hat den Wettbewerb gewonnen, ohne dass sie sich besonders angestrengt hat.
b) Peter läuft mit 46 Jahren noch Marathon, ohne täglich zu trainieren.
c) Elfie arbeitet täglich bis zu zwölf Stunden, ohne sich zu beklagen.
d) Karsten muss Überstunden machen, ohne dafür bezahlt zu werden.
e) Erik tut sehr viel für seine Kollegen, ohne ständig darüber zu reden.
f) Luise möchte endlich ein paar Kilo loswerden, aber möglichst ohne hungern zu müssen.
g) Henry fährt am liebsten Fahrrad, ohne den Lenker festzuhalten.

VERBALSTIL – NOMINALSTIL

träumen – der Traum

1 Funktion

Verbalstil	*Der Tierpsychologe Dröscher hat das Verhalten von Affen erforscht.*	Alltags- und Erzählsprache
Nominalstil	*Die Erforschung des Verhaltens von Affen durch den Tierpsychologen Dröscher ...*	Sprache der Wissenschaft, der Technik und der Verwaltung

2 Formen

	verbale Struktur	nominale Struktur	
Verb[1]	*Auch die Affen* träumen.	*die Träume der Affen* *die träumenden Affen*	Nomen[1] Adjektiv[2]
Nominativ	*Auch die Affen träumen.*	*die Träume der Affen*	Genitiv
Akkusativ/Aktiv	*Jemand analysiert das soziale Verhalten.*	*die Analyse des sozialen Verhaltens*	
Nominativ/Passiv	*Das soziale Verhalten wird analysiert.*		
Nomen ohne Artikel	*Affen träumen.*	*die Träume von Affen*	*von* + Dativ
Nominativ + Akkusativ	*Ein Verhaltensforscher untersuchte den Affen-Clan.*	*die Untersuchung des Affen-Clans durch einen Verhaltensforscher*	Genitiv + *durch* + Akkusativ
Verb + Präposition	*Die Affen gewöhnen sich an Stresssituationen.*	*die Gewöhnung der Affen an Stresssituationen*	Nomen + Präposition
Personalpronomen	*Sie küssen sich zur Begrüßung.*	*ihre Küsse zur Begrüßung*	Possessiv- artikel
Adverb	*Sie pflegen gegenseitig ihr Fell.*	*ihre gegenseitige Fellpflege*	Adjektiv
sein + Adjektiv	*Auch die Affen sind traurig.*	*die Traurigkeit der Affen*	Nomen
haben + Nomen	*Die Affen haben Angst.*	*die Angst der Affen*	Nomen
Konnektor[3]	*Wenn es blitzt und donnert.*	*bei Blitz und Donner*	Präposition[3]

Oft werden zwei Nomen zusammengesetzt.	*die Pflege des Fells* *die Analyse des Verhaltens* *die Küsse zur Begrüßung*	*die Fellpflege* *die Verhaltensanalyse* *die Begrüßungsküsse*

[1] s. auch Wortbildung Nomen, 📖 **Seite 20**
[2] s. Partizip als Adjektiv, 📖 **Seite 44**
[3] s. Anhang, 📖 **Seite 212**

ÜBUNGEN

1 Was tun Sie ...? – Formulieren Sie Sätze mit wenn ... dann.

a) ... bei großer Kälte?
   Wenn es sehr kalt ist, dann mache ich ein Feuer im Kamin.
b) ... bei einem plötzlichen Regenschauer?   c) ... bei einem langweiligen Film?

d) ... beim Absturz Ihres Computers?   f) ... bei Müdigkeit?
e) ... bei extremer Hitze?   g) ... im Schlaf?

2 Lernatmosphäre – Nominalisieren Sie die Verben und formulieren Sie dann Sätze.
Ich lerne besonders gut/schlecht,

a) wenn ich etwas esse.   bei ...
   Beim Essen lerne ich besonders gut/schlecht.
b) wenn ich klassische Musik höre.   bei/mit ...
c) wenn ich gut gelaunt bin.   mit ...
d) wenn die Sonne scheint.   bei ...
e) wenn es regnet.   bei ...
f) wenn mich niemand ablenkt.   ohne ...

3 Nominalisieren Sie die Ausdrücke und ergänzen Sie den Text.

SMS*-(a) *sucht*   süchtig sein
Auf Spiel- und Internetsucht folgt jetzt das Laster SMS. Nach einem
(b) .... der dänischen Zeitung *Jyllands-*   berichten
Posten wurde jetzt der erste Fall von mobiler Chat-Sucht bekannt.
Ein 25-Jähriger hat sich kürzlich zur (c) ....   sich behandeln lassen
in eine Spezialklinik begeben, die sich auf Therapie von   nach Spielen süchtig
(d) .... spezialisiert hat. Der junge   sein
Mann hatte sich durch das (e) .... von   etwas versenden
über 200 Nachrichten pro Tag finanziell fast ruiniert.
In Dänemark gibt es 2,6 Millionen registrierte (f) ....   ein Handy besitzen
und 1,1 Millionen (g) ....   das Internet nutzen

* SMS = kurze Nachricht, die mit dem Handy verschickt wird.

4 Ihr erster Anruf mit dem neuen Handy – Ergänzen Sie den Text.

a) Vor dem Einschalten des Handys den Akku laden.

b) Durch Drücken der Taste ***** das Telefon einschalten.

c) Eingabe des PIN-Codes und Drücken auf **OK**.

d) Warten bis zur Anzeige des Namens des Netzbetreibers im Display.

e) Eingabe der Vorwahl und der Telefonnummer.

f) Drücken der Taste **OK**.

g) Den Anruf beenden durch Drücken der Taste **C**.

a) Laden Sie den Akku, bevor *sie das Handy einschalten*.

b) Schalten Sie das Telefon ein, indem ....
....

c) Geben ....
.... und ....
.... auf OK.

d) Warten Sie, bis ....
....
....
....

e) Geben Sie .... und
....

f) Nun müssen Sie ....
....

g) Beenden Sie .... ,
indem Sie ....
....

7

DIE WICHTIGSTEN UNREGELMÄSSIGEN VERBEN

Alphabetische Liste

Die regelmäßigen Formen sind grau gedruckt.

Infinitiv	Präsens	Präteritum	Perfekt	
backen	backt (bäckt)	backte (buk)	hat	gebacken
befehlen	befiehlt	befahl	hat	befohlen
beginnen	beginnt	begann	hat	begonnen
beißen	beißt	biss	hat	gebissen
betrügen	betrügt	betrog	hat	betrogen
bewegen	bewegt	bewog	hat	bewogen[1]
biegen	biegt	bog	hat	gebogen
bieten	bietet	bot	hat	geboten
binden	bindet	band	hat	gebunden
bitten	bittet	bat	hat	gebeten
blasen	bläst	blies	hat	geblasen
bleiben	bleibt	blieb	ist	geblieben
braten	brät	briet	hat	gebraten
brechen	bricht	brach	hat	gebrochen
brennen	brennt	brannte	hat	gebrannt
bringen	bringt	brachte	hat	gebracht
denken	denkt	dachte	hat	gedacht
dürfen	darf	durfte	hat	gedurft
eindringen	dringt ein	drang ein	ist	eingedrungen
empfangen	empfängt	empfing	hat	empfangen
empfehlen	empfiehlt	empfahl	hat	empfohlen
empfinden	empfindet	empfand	hat	empfunden
erlöschen	erlischt	erlosch	ist	erloschen
erschrecken	erschrickt	erschrak	ist	erschrocken
erwägen	erwägt	erwog	hat	erwogen
essen	isst	aß	hat	gegessen
fahren	fährt	fuhr	ist/hat	gefahren[2]
fallen	fällt	fiel	ist	gefallen
fangen	fängt	fing	hat	gefangen
finden	findet	fand	hat	gefunden
fliegen	fliegt	flog	ist/hat	geflogen[2]
fliehen	flieht	floh	ist	geflohen
fließen	fließt	floss	ist	geflossen
fressen	frisst	fraß	hat	gefressen
frieren	friert	fror	ist/hat	gefroren[3]
geben	gibt	gab	hat	gegeben
gehen	geht	ging	ist	gegangen
gelingen	gelingt	gelang	ist	gelungen
gelten	gilt	galt	hat	gegolten
genießen	genießt	genoss	hat	genossen

Infinitiv	Präsens	Präteritum	Perfekt	
geraten	gerät	geriet	ist	geraten
geschehen	geschieht	geschah	ist	geschehen
gewinnen	gewinnt	gewann	hat	gewonnen
gießen	gießt	goss	hat	gegossen
gleichen	gleicht	glich	hat	geglichen
gleiten	gleitet	glitt	ist	geglitten
graben	gräbt	grub	hat	gegraben
greifen	greift	griff	hat	gegriffen
haben	hat	hatte	hat	gehabt
halten	hält	hielt	hat	gehalten
hängen	hängt	hing	hat	gehangen[4]
heben	hebt	hob	hat	gehoben
heißen	heißt	hieß	hat	geheißen
helfen	hilft	half	hat	geholfen
kennen	kennt	kannte	hat	gekannt
klingen	klingt	klang	hat	geklungen
kommen	kommt	kam	ist	gekommen
können	kann	konnte	hat	gekonnt
kriechen	kriecht	kroch	ist	gekrochen
laden	lädt	lud	hat	geladen
lassen	lässt	ließ	hat	gelassen
laufen	läuft	lief	ist	gelaufen[14]
leiden	leidet	litt	hat	gelitten
leihen	leiht	lieh	hat	geliehen
lesen	liest	las	hat	gelesen
liegen	liegt	lag	hat	gelegen
lügen	lügt	log	hat	gelogen
meiden	meidet	mied	hat	gemieden
messen	misst	maß	hat	gemessen
mögen	mag	mochte	hat	gemocht
müssen	muss	musste	hat	gemusst
nehmen	nimmt	nahm	hat	genommen
nennen	nennt	nannte	hat	genannt
pfeifen	pfeift	pfiff	hat	gepfiffen
raten	rät	riet	hat	geraten
reiben	reibt	rieb	hat	gerieben
reißen	reißt	riss	hat	gerissen[5]
reiten	reitet	ritt	ist/hat	geritten[2]
rennen	rennt	rannte	ist	gerannt
riechen	riecht	roch	hat	gerochen
rufen	ruft	rief	hat	gerufen
schaffen	schafft	schuf	hat	geschaffen[6]

DIE WICHTIGSTEN UNREGELMÄSSIGEN VERBEN

Infinitiv	Präsens	Präteritum	Perfekt	
scheinen	scheint	schien	hat	geschienen
schieben	schiebt	schob	hat	geschoben
schießen	schießt	schoss	hat	geschossen
schlafen	schläft	schlief	hat	geschlafen
schlagen	schlägt	schlug	hat	geschlagen
schleichen	schleicht	schlich	ist	geschlichen
schließen	schließt	schloss	hat	geschlossen
schmeißen	schmeißt	schmiss	hat	geschmissen
schmelzen	schmilzt	schmolz	ist/hat	geschmolzen[7]
schneiden	schneidet	schnitt	hat	geschnitten
schreiben	schreibt	schrieb	hat	geschrieben
schreien	schreit	schrie	hat	geschrien
schweigen	schweigt	schwieg	hat	geschwiegen
schwellen	schwillt	schwoll	ist	geschwollen
schwimmen	schwimmt	schwamm	ist	geschwommen[14]
schwören	schwört	schwor	hat	geschworen
sehen	sieht	sah	hat	gesehen
sein	ist	war	ist	gewesen
senden	sendet	sandte (sendete)	hat	gesandt (gesendet)[8]
singen	singt	sang	hat	gesungen
sinken	sinkt	sank	ist	gesunken
sitzen	sitzt	saß	hat	gesessen
sprechen	spricht	sprach	hat	gesprochen
springen	springt	sprang	ist	gesprungen
stechen	sticht	stach	hat	gestochen
stehen	steht	stand	hat	gestanden
stehlen	stiehlt	stahl	hat	gestohlen
steigen	steigt	stieg	ist	gestiegen
sterben	stirbt	starb	ist	gestorben
stinken	stinkt	stank	hat	gestunken
stoßen	stößt	stieß	hat	gestoßen[9]
streichen	streicht	strich	hat	gestrichen
streiten	streitet	stritt	hat	gestritten
tragen	trägt	trug	hat	getragen
treffen	trifft	traf	hat	getroffen
treiben	treibt	trieb	hat	getrieben
treten	tritt	trat	hat	getreten
trinken	trinkt	trank	hat	getrunken
tun	tut	tat	hat	getan
verderben	verdirbt	verdarb	hat	verdorben[10]
vergessen	vergisst	vergaß	hat	vergessen
verlieren	verliert	verlor	hat	verloren
verschwinden	verschwindet	verschwand	ist	verschwunden
verzeihen	verzeiht	verzieh	hat	verziehen

Infinitiv	Präsens	Präteritum	Perfekt	
wachsen	wächst	wuchs	ist	gewachsen[11]
waschen	wäscht	wusch	hat	gewaschen
weichen	weicht	wich	ist	gewichen
weisen	weist	wies	hat	gewiesen
wenden	wendet	wandte (wendete)	hat	gewandt (gewendet)[12]
werben	wirbt	warb	hat	geworben
werden	wird	wurde	ist	geworden
werfen	wirft	warf	hat	geworfen
wiegen	wiegt	wog	hat	gewogen[13]
wissen	weiß	wusste	hat	gewusst
wollen	will	wollte	hat	gewollt
ziehen	zieht	zog	hat	gezogen
zwingen	zwingt	zwang	hat	gezwungen

[1] unregelmäßig: *Motiv/Grund sein für etwas. Die Aussicht auf eine schnelle Karriere hat ihn bewogen, die Firma zu wechseln.* regelmäßig: *von einem Ort zum anderen. Wer sich nie viel bewegt hat, wird auch im Alter keinen Sport mehr treiben.*

[2] ohne Akkusativ: *sein. Katharina ist nach Hamburg gefahren.* mit Akkusativ: *haben. Tom hat den Wagen in die Garage gefahren.* Das Gleiche gilt für alle weiteren Verben mit *sein* oder *haben* im Perfekt.

[3] *Das Wasser ist gefroren.* (= unpersönliches Subjekt) – *Ich habe gefroren.*

[4] unregelmäßig: *Der Mantel hing eben noch in der Garderobe.* regelmäßig: *Er hängte die Küchenuhr über die Tür.*

[5] *Das Seil ist gerissen.* (= unpersönliches Subjekt) – *Ich habe ein Loch in die Hose gerissen.*

[6] unregelmäßig: *Dieses Werk hat Picasso geschaffen.* (= künstlerisches Werk); regelmäßig: *Denis hat seine Arbeit für heute geschafft.* (= normale Arbeit)

[7] *Der Schnee ist geschmolzen.* (= unpersönliches Subjekt) – *An Silvester haben wir immer Blei geschmolzen.*

[8] unregelmäßig: *schicken*; regelmäßig: *im Rundfunk/TV senden. Im Radio haben sie gerade Verkehrsnachrichten gesendet.*

[9] *Ich habe das Glas vom Tisch gestoßen.* – *Ich bin mit dem Kopf an die Wand gestoßen.*

[10] *Das Gemüse ist verdorben.* (= nicht mehr genießbar; unpersönliches Subjekt) – *Er hat das Gemüse verdorben.* (= falsch gekocht.)

[11] unregelmäßig: *größer werden*; regelmäßig: *mit Wachs überziehen*

[12] unregelmäßig: *Sie wussten nicht mehr weiter und haben sich deshalb an einen Experten gewandt.* regelmäßig: *umdrehen. Er hat den Wagen gewendet und ist wieder zurückgefahren.*

[13] unregelmäßig: *messen, wie schwer etwas ist*; regelmäßig: *(z.B. ein Baby) hin und her bewegen*

[14] auch möglich: *Er hat den Marathon in Rekordzeit gelaufen. Er hat die 1000 Meter geschwommen.*

DIE WICHTIGSTEN UNREGELMÄSSIGEN VERBEN

Liste nach Ablauten

Die regelmäßigen Formen sind grau gedruckt.

Infinitiv	Präsens	Präteritum	Perfekt	
		a		**a**
denken	denkt	dachte	hat	gedacht
haben	hat	hatte	hat	gehabt
kennen	kennt	kannte	hat	gekannt
nennen	nennt	nannte	hat	genannt
rennen	rennt	rannte	ist	gerannt
senden	sendet	sandte (sendete)	hat	gesandt (gesendet)[8]
stehen	steht	stand	hat	gestanden
tun	tut	tat	hat	getan
wenden	wendet	wandte (wendete)	hat	gewandt (gewendet)[12]
		a		**e**
bitten	bittet	bat	hat	gebeten
essen	isst	aß	hat	gegessen
fressen	frisst	fraß	hat	gefressen
geben	gibt	gab	hat	gegeben
geschehen	geschieht	geschah	ist	geschehen
lesen	liest	las	hat	gelesen
liegen	liegt	lag	hat	gelegen
messen	misst	maß	hat	gemessen
sehen	sieht	sah	hat	gesehen
sein	ist	war	ist	gewesen
sitzen	sitzt	saß	hat	gesessen
treten	tritt	trat	hat	getreten
vergessen	vergisst	vergaß	hat	vergessen
		a		**o**
befehlen	befiehlt	befahl	hat	befohlen
beginnen	beginnt	begann	hat	begonnen
brechen	bricht	brach	hat	gebrochen
empfehlen	empfiehlt	empfahl	hat	empfohlen
erschrecken	erschrickt	erschrak	ist	erschrocken
gelten	gilt	galt	hat	gegolten
gewinnen	gewinnt	gewann	hat	gewonnen
helfen	hilft	half	hat	geholfen
kommen	kommt	kam	ist	gekommen
nehmen	nimmt	nahm	hat	genommen
schwimmen	schwimmt	schwamm	ist	geschwommen[14]
sprechen	spricht	sprach	hat	gesprochen
stechen	sticht	stach	hat	gestochen
stehlen	stiehlt	stahl	hat	gestohlen
sterben	stirbt	starb	ist	gestorben
treffen	trifft	traf	hat	getroffen
verderben	verdirbt	verdarb	hat	verdorben[10]

Infinitiv	Präsens	Präteritum	Perfekt	
werben	wirbt	warb	hat	geworben
werfen	wirft	warf	hat	geworfen

	a		u	
binden	bindet	band	hat	gebunden
eindringen	dringt ein	drang ein	ist	eingedrungen
empfinden	empfindet	empfand	hat	empfunden
finden	findet	fand	hat	gefunden
gelingen	gelingt	gelang	ist	gelungen
klingen	klingt	klang	hat	geklungen
singen	singt	sang	hat	gesungen
sinken	sinkt	sank	ist	gesunken
springen	springt	sprang	ist	gesprungen
stinken	stinkt	stank	hat	gestunken
trinken	trinkt	trank	hat	getrunken
verschwinden	verschwindet	verschwand	ist	verschwunden
zwingen	zwingt	zwang	hat	gezwungen

	i		a	
blasen	bläst	blies	hat	geblasen
braten	brät	briet	hat	gebraten
empfangen	empfängt	empfing	hat	empfangen
fallen	fällt	fiel	ist	gefallen
fangen	fängt	fing	hat	gefangen
gehen	geht	ging	ist	gegangen
geraten	gerät	geriet	ist	geraten
halten	hält	hielt	hat	gehalten
hängen	hängt	hing	hat	gehangen[4]
lassen	lässt	ließ	hat	gelassen
laufen	läuft	lief	ist	gelaufen[14]
raten	rät	riet	hat	geraten
schlafen	schläft	schlief	hat	geschlafen

	i		ei	
heißen	heißt	hieß	hat	geheißen

	i		i	
beißen	beißt	biss	hat	gebissen
bleiben	bleibt	blieb	ist	geblieben
gleichen	gleicht	glich	hat	geglichen
gleiten	gleitet	glitt	ist	geglitten
greifen	greift	griff	hat	gegriffen
leiden	leidet	litt	hat	gelitten
leihen	leiht	lieh	hat	geliehen
meiden	meidet	mied	hat	gemieden
pfeifen	pfeift	pfiff	hat	gepfiffen
reiben	reibt	rieb	hat	gerieben
reißen	reißt	riss	hat	gerissen[5]
reiten	reitet	ritt	ist/hat	geritten[2]

ANHANG

DIE WICHTIGSTEN UNREGELMÄSSIGEN VERBEN

Infinitiv	Präsens	Präteritum	Perfekt	
scheinen	scheint	schien	hat	geschienen
schleichen	schleicht	schlich	ist	geschlichen
schmeißen	schmeißt	schmiss	hat	geschmissen
schneiden	schneidet	schnitt	hat	geschnitten
schreiben	schreibt	schrieb	hat	geschrieben
schreien	schreit	schrie	hat	geschrien
schweigen	schweigt	schwieg	hat	geschwiegen
steigen	steigt	stieg	ist	gestiegen
streichen	streicht	strich	hat	gestrichen
streiten	streitet	stritt	hat	gestritten
treiben	treibt	trieb	hat	getrieben
verzeihen	verzeiht	verzieh	hat	verziehen
weichen	weicht	wich	ist	gewichen
weisen	weist	wies	hat	gewiesen

		i		o
stoßen	stößt	stieß	hat	gestoßen[9]

		i		u
rufen	ruft	rief	hat	gerufen

		o		o
betrügen	betrügt	betrog	hat	betrogen
bewegen	bewegt	bewog	hat	bewogen[1]
biegen	biegt	bog	hat	gebogen
bieten	bietet	bot	hat	geboten
erlöschen	erlischt	erlosch	ist	erloschen
erwägen	erwägt	erwog	hat	erwogen
fliegen	fliegt	flog	ist/hat	geflogen[2]
fliehen	flieht	floh	ist	geflohen
fließen	fließt	floss	ist	geflossen
frieren	friert	fror	ist/hat	gefroren[3]
genießen	genießt	genoss	hat	genossen
gießen	gießt	goss	hat	gegossen
heben	hebt	hob	hat	gehoben
können	kann	konnte	hat	gekonnt
kriechen	kriecht	kroch	ist	gekrochen
lügen	lügt	log	hat	gelogen
mögen	mag	mochte	hat	gemocht
riechen	riecht	roch	hat	gerochen
schieben	schiebt	schob	hat	geschoben
schießen	schießt	schoss	hat	geschossen
schließen	schließt	schloss	hat	geschlossen
schmelzen	schmilzt	schmolz	ist/hat	geschmolzen[7]
schwellen	schwillt	schwoll	ist	geschwollen
schwören	schwört	schwor	hat	geschworen

Infinitiv	Präsens	Präteritum	Perfekt	
verlieren	verliert	verlor	hat	verloren
wiegen	wiegt	wog	hat	gewogen[13]
ziehen	zieht	zog	hat	gezogen

		u		a
backen	backt (bäckt)	backte (buk)	hat	gebacken
fahren	fährt	fuhr	ist/hat	gefahren[2]
graben	gräbt	grub	hat	gegraben
laden	lädt	lud	hat	geladen
schaffen	schafft	schuf	hat	geschaffen[6]
schlagen	schlägt	schlug	hat	geschlagen
tragen	trägt	trug	hat	getragen
wachsen	wächst	wuchs	ist	gewachsen[11]
waschen	wäscht	wusch	hat	gewaschen

		u		o
werden	wird	wurde	ist	geworden

		u		u
dürfen	darf	durfte	hat	gedurft
müssen	muss	musste	hat	gemusst
wissen	weiß	wusste	hat	gewusst

[1] unregelmäßig: *Motiv/Grund sein für etwas. Die Aussicht auf eine schnelle Karriere hat ihn bewogen die Firma zu wechseln.* regelmäßig: *von einem Ort zum anderen. Wer sich nie viel bewegt hat, wird auch im Alter keinen Sport mehr treiben.*

[2] ohne Akkusativ: *sein. Katharina ist nach Hamburg gefahren.* mit Akkusativ: *haben. Tom hat den Wagen in die Garage gefahren.* Das Gleiche gilt für alle weiteren Verben mit *sein* oder *haben* im Perfekt.

[3] *Das Wasser ist gefroren.* (= unpersönliches Subjekt) – *Ich habe gefroren.*

[4] unregelmäßig: *Der Mantel hing eben noch in der Garderobe.* regelmäßig: *Er hängte die Küchenuhr über die Tür.*

[5] *Das Seil ist gerissen.* (= unpersönliches Subjekt) – *Ich habe ein Loch in die Hose gerissen.*

[6] unregelmäßig: *Dieses Werk hat Picasso geschaffen.* (= künstlerisches Werk); regelmäßig: *Denis hat seine Arbeit für heute geschafft.* (= normale Arbeit)

[7] *Der Schnee ist geschmolzen.* (= unpersönliches Subjekt) – *An Silvester haben wir immer Blei geschmolzen.*

[8] unregelmäßig: *schicken*; regelmäßig: *im Rundfunk/TV senden. Im Radio haben sie gerade Verkehrsnachrichten gesendet.*

[9] *Ich habe das Glas vom Tisch gestoßen.* – *Ich bin mit dem Kopf an die Wand gestoßen.*

[10] *Das Gemüse ist verdorben.* (= nicht mehr genießbar; unpersönliches Subjekt) – *Er hat das Gemüse verdorben.* (= falsch gekocht.)

[11] unregelmäßig: *größer werden*; regelmäßig: *mit Wachs überziehen*

[12] unregelmäßig: *Sie wussten nicht mehr weiter und haben sich deshalb an einen Experten gewandt.* regelmäßig: *umdrehen. Er hat den Wagen gewendet und ist wieder zurückgefahren.*

[13] unregelmäßig: *messen, wie schwer etwas ist*; regelmäßig: *(z.B. ein Baby) hin und her bewegen*

[14] auch möglich: *Er hat den Marathon in Rekordzeit gelaufen. Er hat die 1000 Meter geschwommen.*

KONJUGATION DER MODALVERBEN

dürfen	Präsens	Präteritum	Perfekt	Konjunktiv II
ich	darf	durfte	habe gedurft*	dürfte
du	darfst	durftest	...	dürftest
er/sie/es	darf	durfte		dürfte
wir	dürfen	durften		dürften
ihr	dürft	durftet		dürftet
sie/Sie	dürfen	durften		dürften

können	Präsens	Präteritum	Perfekt	Konjunktiv II
ich	kann	konnte	habe gekonnt*	könnte
du	kannst	konntest	...	könntest
er/sie/es	kann	konnte		könnte
wir	können	konnten		könnten
ihr	könnt	konntet		könntet
sie/Sie	können	konnten		könnten

mögen	Präsens	Präteritum	Perfekt	Konjunktiv II
ich	mag	mochte	habe gemocht*	möchte
du	magst	mochtest	...	möchtest
er/sie/es	mag	mochte		möchte
wir	mögen	mochten		möchten
ihr	mögt	mochtet		möchtet
sie/Sie	mögen	mochten		möchten

müssen	Präsens	Präteritum	Perfekt	Konjunktiv II
ich	muss	musste	habe gemusst*	müsste
du	musst	musstest	...	müsstest
er/sie/es	muss	musste		müsste
wir	müssen	mussten		müssten
ihr	müsst	musstet		müsstet
sie/Sie	müssen	mussten		müssten

sollen	Präsens	Präteritum	Perfekt	Konjunktiv II
ich	soll	sollte	(habe gesollt)**	sollte
du	sollst	solltest	...	solltest
er/sie es	soll	sollte		sollte
wir	sollen	sollten		sollten
ihr	sollt	solltet		solltet
sie/Sie	sollen	sollten		sollten

wollen	Präsens	Präteritum	Perfekt	Konjunktiv II
ich	will	wollte	habe gewollt*	wollte
du	willst	wolltest	...	wolltest
er/sie/es	will	wollte		wollte
wir	wollen	wollten		wollten
ihr	wollt	wolltet		wolltet
sie/Sie	wollen	wollten		wollten

* Zusammen mit einem anderen Verb steht das Modalverb im Perfekt mit *haben* + doppeltem Infinitiv: *Ich habe nicht mehr rauchen dürfen.*

** ohne zusätzliches Verb ungebräuchlich

abbauen AKK	*Die Firma hat 500 Stellen abgebaut.*
abfragen AKK (AKK)	*Kannst du mich (die Vokabeln) abfragen?*
abgewöhnen DAT AKK	*Ich muss ihm sein schlechtes Benehmen abgewöhnen.*
abholen AKK	*Sie holt dich vom Flughafen ab.*
abhören AKK	*Die Polizei hörte das Telefongespräch ab.*
abkaufen DAT AKK	*Ich kaufe dir dein Auto ab.*
abladen AKK	*Er lud den schweren Koffer ab.*
abnehmen (AKK)	*Peter hat (10 Kilo) abgenommen.*
abnehmen DAT AKK	*Zum Glück hat er mir diese Arbeit abgenommen.*
absagen (DAT) (AKK)	*Susan hat (mir) (die Verabredung) abgesagt.*
abschaffen AKK	*Man hat dieses Gesetz 1988 abgeschafft.*
abschlagen DAT AKK	*Ich kann ihm keine Bitte abschlagen.*
abschrecken AKK	*Dieser Pfeifton schreckt Hunde ab.*
abschreiben AKK	*Max schreibt immer die Hausaufgabe ab.*
abtransportieren AKK	*Man hat den Gefangenen abtransportiert.*
abverlangen DAT AKK	*Mein neuer Chef verlangt mir eine Menge ab.*
achten AKK	*Paula achtet ihre Eltern.*
ähneln DAT	*Sie ähnelt ihrem Vater sehr.*
ärgern AKK	*Warum ärgerst du mich immer?*
analysieren AKK	*Der Arzt analysierte die Blutprobe.*
anbieten (DAT) AKK	*Sie bot mir eine Zigarette an.*
androhen (DAT) AKK	*Er drohte (seinem Nachbarn) rechtliche Schritte an.*
anfahren AKK	*Der Autofahrer hat einen Fußgänger angefahren.*
anfangen (AKK)	*Er hat (die Arbeit) schon angefangen.*
anfassen AKK	*Bitte fass diese Katze nicht an!*
abgewöhnen DAT AKK	*Ich habe Peter seine Ungeduld abgewöhnt.*
anklagen AKK (GEN)	*Man hat ihn (des Mordes) angeklagt.*
anlachen AKK	*Sie hat den jungen Mann freundlich angelacht.*
annehmen AKK	*Nimmst du das Angebot an?*
anreden AKK	*Ich rede ihn mit Vornamen an.*
anrufen (AKK)	*Rufst du (mich) heute noch an?*
ansehen AKK	*Er sah die junge Frau nachdenklich an.*
sich ansehen AKK	*Ich habe mir diesen Film schon angesehen.*
antun DAT AKK	*Das kannst du ihm nicht antun.*
antworten (DAT)	*Martin hat (mir) leider nicht geantwortet.*
anvertrauen DAT AKK	*Ich muss dir ein Geheimnis anvertrauen.*
applaudieren (DAT)	*Das Publikum applaudierte (dem Pianisten).*
auffallen DAT	*Mir ist seine neue Frisur noch gar nicht aufgefallen.*
auffordern AKK	*Er hat sie zum Tanzen aufgefordert.*
aufhalten AKK	*Tut mir Leid, meine Tochter hat mich so lange aufgehalten.*
aufmachen AKK	*Neugierig machte er das Päckchen auf.*
aufräumen (AKK)	*Kannst du bitte (dein Zimmer) aufräumen?*
aufschreiben AKK	*Moment, das muss ich aufschreiben.*
aufweisen AKK	*Diese Konstruktion weist zahlreiche Neuerungen auf.*
ausgeben AKK	*Der kleine Max hat sein ganzes Taschengeld ausgegeben.*
ausführen AKK	*Der Soldat hat den Befehl ausgeführt.*
ausfüllen AKK	*Muss ich dieses Formular ausfüllen?*
auslösen AKK	*Der Skifahrer hat eine Lawine ausgelöst.*

KASUSERGÄNZUNGEN

ausmachen AKK	*Hast du das Licht ausgemacht?*
ausweichen (DAT)	*Er ist (meiner Frage) ausgewichen.*
ausziehen (DAT) AKK	*Die Mutter zog (ihrem Sohn) die nassen Schuhe aus.*
beantworten (DAT) AKK	*Sie beantwortete (mir) keine Frage.*
bedürfen GEN	*Der Skandal bedarf einer völligen Aufklärung.*
begegnen DAT	*Mir ist auf der Straße niemand begegnet.*
beibringen DAT AKK	*Der Lehrer brachte den Schülern die Regeln bei.*
beichten (DAT) (AKK)	*Der Gläubige beichtete (dem Pfarrer) (seine Sünden).*
beitreten DAT	*Mit 19 Jahren trat er der Gewerkschaft bei.*
bereiten DAT AKK	*Meine Frau bereitete mir eine große Überraschung.*
berichten (DAT)	*Michael hat (uns) von seiner Reise berichtet.*
beschuldigen AKK (GEN)	*Der Richter beschuldigte den Angeklagten (des Betrugs).*
besorgen (DAT) AKK	*Besorgst du (mir) eine Zeitung?*
bestellen (DAT) AKK	*Der Vater bestellte (den Kindern) ein Eis.*
bevorstehen (DAT)	*Ein unangenehmes Gespräch stand (den Mitarbeitern) bevor.*
beweisen (DAT) AKK	*Der Chemiker bewies (den Kollegen) die Richtigkeit seiner These.*
bewilligen (DAT) AKK	*Der Chef bewilligte (der Assistentin) die Dienstreise.*
bieten (DAT) AKK	*Was für Sozialleistungen bietet (dir) deine Firma?*
borgen DAT AKK	*Borgst du ihm dein Fahrrad?*
braten (DAT) AKK	*Die Mutter hatte (dem Sohn) ein Steak gebraten.*
brauchen AKK	*Wir brauchen ein neues Auto.*
bringen (DAT) AKK	*Tom bringt (uns) noch heute das Geld.*
buchstabieren AKK	*Wie buchstabiert man dieses Wort?*
danken DAT	*Ich danke dir für deine Hilfe.*
darlegen (DAT) AKK	*Der Direktor legt (den Mitarbeitern) die neue Strategie dar.*
darstellen AKK	*Diese Grafik stellt die Entwicklung der letzten Jahre dar.*
dienen (DAT)	*Dieses Gerät dient (den Autofahrern) zur Navigation.*
drohen (DAT)	*Der Nachbar drohte (mir) mit einem Prozess.*
einfallen DAT	*Leider ist uns keine Lösung eingefallen.*
einkaufen (AKK)	*Sie hat schon (alle Sachen) fürs Wochenende eingekauft.*
einladen AKK	*Zum Geburtstag habe ich alle meine Freunde eingeladen.*
einpacken AKK	*Pack die Badehose ein!*
einreden DAT AKK	*Ich redete ihr Schuldgefühle ein.*
einstellen AKK	*Der Elektriker hat den Fernseher falsch eingestellt.*
empfangen AKK	*Die österreichischen Sender kann man bei uns nicht empfangen.*
empfehlen (DAT) AKK	*Hans hat (mir) dieses Hotel empfohlen.*
entfallen DAT	*Mir ist sein Name leider entfallen.*
entfernen AKK	*Diesen Fleck entfernt man mit Benzin.*
entgegenbringen DAT AKK	*Der Polizist brachte uns großes Misstrauen entgegen.*
entgehen DAT	*Meine Frau ist sehr neugierig, ihr entgeht nichts.*
enthalten AKK	*Diese Flasche enthält reinen Alkohol.*
sich enthalten (GEN)	*Drei Parlamentarier enthielten sich (der Stimme).*
entkommen (DAT)	*Der Dieb konnte (der Polizei) entkommen.*
entlassen AKK	*Die Firma entließ 2300 Arbeiter.*
entscheiden (AKK)	*Du musst (das) selbst entscheiden.*
entsprechen DAT	*Das neue Auto entspricht nicht unseren Erwartungen.*
erfinden AKK	*Wer hat das Telefon erfunden?*
ergänzen AKK	*Bitte ergänzen Sie folgende Sätze.*

erhalten AKK	*Wir haben deine Postkarte erhalten.*
erkennen AKK	*Mein alter Lehrer hat mich nicht mehr erkannt.*
erklären (DAT) AKK	*Kannst du (mir) die Spielregeln erklären?*
erlauben (DAT) AKK	*Sie erlaubte (mir) meine freche Bemerkung.*
erledigen AKK	*Eva hat ihre Arbeit schon erledigt.*
ermöglichen (DAT) AKK	*Dieses Instrument ermöglicht (uns) präzises Arbeiten.*
ernähren AKK	*Sie ernährt ihre Kinder zu fett.*
erreichen AKK	*Ich habe mein Ziel erreicht.*
erscheinen DAT	*Dir erscheint diese Aufgabe vielleicht als zu einfach.*
erschweren (DAT) AKK	*Musst du (mir) meinen Job auch noch künstlich erschweren?*
erwähnen AKK	*Sie hat ihre Scheidung von Klaus nur kurz erwähnt.*
erzählen (DAT) AKK	*Soll ich (dir) einen Witz erzählen?*
erziehen AKK	*Meine Schwester hat ihre Kinder schlecht erzogen.*
fassen AKK	*Die Polizei konnte den Einbrecher nicht fassen.*
fehlen (DAT)	*Ein Band fehlt (mir) noch, dann ist die Enzyklopädie komplett.*
finden AKK	*Nach einer Stunde hatte sie den Schlüssel gefunden.*
folgen DAT	*Folgen Sie der schwarzen Limousine!*
fordern AKK	*Früher forderten die Gewerkschaften mehr Lohn.*
fragen (AKK)	*Habt ihr schon (meinen Onkel) gefragt?*
geben DAT AKK	*Er hat uns die Schokolade gegeben.*
geben AKK	*Es gibt keinen Wein in diesem Geschäft.*
gefallen DAT	*Wie gefällt dir mein neuer Haarschnitt?*
gefährden AKK	*Arbeiten gefährdet die Gesundheit!*
gehorchen (DAT)	*Der Hund gehorchte (meiner Mutter) überhaupt nicht.*
gehören DAT	*Wem gehört dieser Mantel?*
gelingen (DAT)	*Das Essen ist (ihr) leider nicht besonders gelungen.*
genügen (DAT)	*Genügt (dir) diese Riesenportion etwa nicht?*
gestehen (DAT) AKK	*Der Ehemann gestand (seiner Frau) die Affäre.*
gewinnen (AKK)	*Er hat (eine Million) im Lotto gewonnen.*
glauben (DAT) AKK	*Ich habe (deinem Bruder) die Geschichte nie geglaubt.*
glauben DAT (AKK)	*Ich habe deinem Bruder (die Geschichte) nie geglaubt.*
glücken (DAT)	*Beim dritten Mal ist (den Forschern) das Experiment geglückt.*
gratulieren (DAT)	*Der Geschäftsführer hat (mir) zu meiner Beförderung gratuliert.*
grüßen (AKK)	*Soll ich (deine Schwester) von dir grüßen?*
hassen AKK	*Meine Freundin hasst meinen Vater.*
heiraten (AKK)	*Er hat (sie) doch nicht geheiratet.*
helfen (DAT)	*Dein Rat hat (mir) sehr geholfen.*
herstellen AKK	*Diese Firma stellt Computer her.*
holen (DAT) AKK	*Holst du (mir) bitte eine Flasche Wein aus dem Keller?*
hören AKK	*Tut mir leid, aber ich höre dich nicht.*
imponieren DAT	*Sein Verhalten gegenüber dem Chef hat allen Kollegen imponiert.*
informieren AKK	*Du darfst nicht vergessen, unsere Freunde zu informieren.*
kaufen (DAT) AKK	*Kaufst du (mir) ein Eis?*
kennen AKK	*Ich kenne diesen Menschen nicht.*
kritisieren AKK	*Petra hat ihren Freund hart kritisiert.*
leihen DAT AKK	*Soll ich dir das Geld leihen?*
lernen AKK	*Möchtest du meinen Bruder näher kennenlernen?*
lieben AKK	*Er liebte sein altes Auto.*
loben AKK	*Der Lehrer lobte seine Schüler viel zu selten.*
liefern (DAT) AKK	*Wann sollen wir (Ihnen) das Gerät liefern?*
machen (DAT) AKK	*Ich habe (dem Chef) meine Bedingungen klargemacht.*

KASUSERGÄNZUNGEN

missfallen DAT	*Das Theaterstück hat den Kritikern missfallen.*
misslingen (DAT)	*Das Fest ist (den Gastgebern) komplett misslungen.*
misstrauen DAT	*Seine Freundin misstraut ihm völlig zu Unrecht.*
missverstehen AKK	*Ich glaube, du hast ihn missverstanden.*
mitteilen (DAT) AKK	*Bitte teil (uns) noch deine genaue Ankunftszeit mit!*
nachlaufen DAT	*Boris läuft jedem hübschen Mädchen nach.*
nachschicken (DAT) AKK	*Würden Sie (mir) die Post nachschicken?*
nachtragen DAT AKK	*Er hat seiner Freundin ihren Flirt mit Ralf lange nachgetragen.*
sich nähern DAT	*Endlich näherten wir uns dem Reiseziel.*
nennen AKK AKK	*Stell dir vor, unser Nachbar nannte mich einen Idioten.*
notieren (DAT) AKK	*Soll ich (dir) die Adresse notieren?*
nützen (DAT)	*Worte allein nützen (mir) nichts.*
opfern (DAT) AKK	*Er opferte (seinem Hobby) seine gesamte Freizeit.*
passen (DAT)	*Nach dem Urlaub hat (ihm) keine Hose mehr gepasst.*
passieren DAT	*Ich hoffe, deinen Freunden ist nichts Schlimmes passiert.*
probieren (AKK)	*Möchtet ihr (den Saft) mal probieren?*
rauben (DAT) AKK	*Drei Jugendliche raubten (der alten Frau) 300 Euro.*
reichen DAT AKK	*Reichst du mir mal die Kartoffeln?*
reichen DAT	*Mir reichen deine dummen Bemerkungen!*
reizen AKK	*Drei Wochen Brasilien, das würde mich schon reizen.*
retten AKK	*Mutig rettete er die kleine Katze vor dem Ertrinken.*
rufen AKK	*Der Vater rief die Kinder zum Essen.*
sagen (DAT) AKK	*Sie sagt (ihrem Mann) nicht immer die Wahrheit.*
schaden DAT	*Mit deinem Benehmen schadest du dir nur selbst.*
schaffen AKK	*Wolfgang schaffte den Job einfach nicht.*
schenken (DAT) AKK	*Sie schenkte (ihrem Sohn) ein Buch.*
schlagen AKK	*Musst du deinen Bruder immer auf den Kopf schlagen?*
schmecken (DAT)	*Deine Suppe hat (uns allen) geschmeckt.*
schulden DAT AKK	*Hans schuldet mir noch eine Menge Geld.*
sehen AKK	*Karin sieht die Unordnung in ihrer Wohnung nicht.*
stören (AKK)	*Die Musik stört (uns) beim Schlafen.*
trauen DAT	*Anna traute diesem Kerl überhaupt nicht.*
treffen AKK	*Weißt du, wen ich heute zufällig beim Einkaufen traf?*
trösten AKK	*Manfred tröstete seine weinende Schwester.*
überholen (AKK)	*Karl überholte (den Fahrradfahrer).*
überraschen AKK	*Sie überraschten das Geburtstagskind mit einer Torte.*
überreden AKK	*Martina überredete den müden Jürgen zu einem Kinobesuch.*
überreichen (DAT) AKK	*Die Kinder überreichten (der Mutter) ein Geschenk.*
übertreffen AKK	*Dieser Erfolg übertraf alle Erwartungen.*
überzeugen AKK	*Dein Vorschlag hat mich überzeugt.*
umbauen (AKK)	*Die Müllers haben (ihr Haus) komplett umgebaut.*
unterbrechen (AKK)	*Entschuldigung, wenn ich (Sie) unterbreche.*
unterliegen (DAT)	*Der FC Bayern unterlag (den Gegnern) mit 1:2.*
unterstützen AKK	*Zum Glück unterstützen mich meine Eltern finanziell.*
verachten AKK	*Er verachtete sie wegen ihrer Boshaftigkeit.*
verbieten (DAT) AKK	*Der Chef hat (seinen Mitarbeitern) private Telefonate verboten.*
verdächtigen AKK (GEN)	*Die Behörden verdächtigten ihn (der Steuerhinterziehung).*
verfolgen AKK	*Die Polizei verfolgt die flüchtigen Bankräuber.*

verlangen AKK	*Die Banken verlangen die sofortige Rückzahlung der Schulden.*
vermeiden AKK	*In seinem neuen Job versuchte er alle Fehler zu vermeiden.*
verraten (DAT) AKK	*Ich verrate (dir) ein großes Geheimnis.*
verteidigen AKK	*Der Anwalt hat seinen Mandanten geschickt verteidigt.*
vertrauen DAT	*Du kannst ihm absolut vertrauen.*
verzeihen DAT (AKK)	*Verzeihst du mir (meine Ungeduld)?*
vorbereiten AKK	*Er bereitete das Abendessen vor.*
vorschlagen (DAT) AKK	*Nicola schlug (ihren Eltern) eine Reise nach Neapel vor.*
vorstellen (DAT) AKK	*Martha stellte (mir) gestern ihre ganze Familie vor.*
vorwerfen DAT AKK	*Franz warf seiner Freundin mangelnde Zärtlichkeit vor.*
wahrnehmen AKK	*Gestern auf der Party hat er mich überhaupt nicht wahrgenommen.*
wehtun DAT	*Der kleine Axel hat seinem Freund beim Spielen wehgetan.*
widersprechen (DAT)	*Du sollst (deiner Mutter) nicht immer widersprechen!*
wiederholen AKK	*Ihr müsst diese Übung wiederholen.*
winken (DAT)	*Die Kinder winkten (mir) zum Abschied.*
wissen AKK	*Wisst ihr den Weg dorthin?*
zeigen (DAT) AKK	*Gerd zeigte (mir) gestern sein neues Haus.*
zuhören (DAT)	*Kannst du (ihm) nicht einmal zuhören, wenn er etwas sagt?*
zulächeln DAT	*Schau mal, wie nett sie dir zulächelt!*
zumachen AKK	*Bitte mach das Fenster zu!*
zureden DAT	*Du musst ihm gut zureden, dann kommt er schon mit.*
zurückzahlen (DAT) AKK	*Ich werde (der Bank) meine Schulden zurückzahlen.*
zusagen (DAT)	*Max kommt auf unser Fest, gerade eben hat er (mir) zugesagt.*
zuschauen (DAT)	*Wir schauten (den Kindern) beim Spielen zu.*
zusenden (DAT) AKK	*Bis wann können Sie (uns) den Katalog zusenden?*
zustimmen (DAT)	*Stimmen Sie (meinem Vorschlag) zu?*
zutrauen DAT AKK	*Er traute seinem Sohn nicht das Geringste zu.*
zuvorkommen DAT	*Ein anderer wollte den Wagen kaufen, doch ich kam ihm zuvor.*
zwingen AKK	*Du kannst ein Kind nicht zwingen, Spinat zu essen.*

Verben mit den Vorsilben *be-* und *zer-* haben fast immer eine Akkusativ-Ergänzung:

betreten AKK	*Sie betraten das Zimmer.*
zerstören AKK	*Die Soldaten zerstörten die Stadt.*

NOMEN-VERB-VERBINDUNGEN

Nomen-Verb-Verbindung	„einfaches" Verb / Bedeutung
einen Vertrag abschließen	unterschreiben
ein Thema anschneiden	über etwas zu sprechen beginnen
die Hoffnung aufgeben	keine Hoffnung mehr haben
einen Beruf ausüben	beruflich machen
einen Irrtum begehen	sich irren
eine Straftat begehen	etwas Illegales tun
eine Enttäuschung bereiten	enttäuschen
Freude bereiten	erfreuen
zum Abschluss bringen	abschließen
zum Ausdruck bringen	ausdrücken
in Bewegung bringen	bewegen
zu Ende bringen	beenden
vor Gericht bringen	verklagen
unter Kontrolle bringen	kontrollieren
in Ordnung bringen	ordnen
in Schwierigkeiten bringen	schwer machen
zur Sprache bringen	ansprechen
zum Stehen bringen	anhalten
in Verlegenheit bringen	verlegen machen
zur Verzweiflung bringen	aufregen
Ärger einbringen	Ärger verursachen
Gewinn einbringen	Gewinn verursachen
eine Pflicht erfüllen	etwas tun, was man tun soll
Protest erheben	protestieren
den/einen Vorwurf erheben	vorwerfen
eine Niederlage erleiden	scheitern
Auskunft erteilen	informieren
zur Last fallen	lästig werden
in Ohnmacht fallen	ohnmächtig werden
zum Opfer fallen	zum Opfer werden
eine Entscheidung fällen	entscheiden
ein Urteil fällen	urteilen
den/einen Beschluss fassen	beschließen
den/einen Entschluss fassen	sich entschließen
Anerkennung finden	anerkannt werden
Anwendung finden	angewendet werden
Beachtung finden	beachtet werden
Gefallen finden an + DAT	gefallen
Interesse finden an + DAT	sich interessieren
eine Lösung finden	lösen können
Unterstützung finden	unterstützt werden
Verständnis finden	verstanden werden
Zustimmung finden	zugestimmt werden
eine Ehe führen	verheiratet sein
zu Ende führen	beenden
ein Gespräch führen	besprechen

einen Kampf führen	kämpfen
eine Antwort geben	beantworten
einen Auftrag geben	beauftragen
in Auftrag geben	herstellen lassen
das Einverständnis geben zu + DAT	einverstanden sein
die Erlaubnis geben	erlauben
eine Garantie geben	garantieren
Gelegenheit geben zu + DAT	ermöglichen
einen Hinweis geben (auf + AKK)	hinweisen
sich Mühe geben (mit + DAT)	sich bemühen
einen Rat geben	raten
den Vorzug geben (vor + DAT)	vorziehen
zu Ende gehen	enden
in Erfüllung gehen	sich erfüllen
vor Gericht gehen	klagen
auf die Nerven gehen	lästig werden
zur Vernunft gelangen	vernünftig werden
in Abhängigkeit geraten (von + DAT)	abhängig werden
in Gefahr geraten	gefährdet sein
in Schwierigkeiten geraten	in eine schwierige Lage kommen
in Vergessenheit geraten	vergessen werden
in Verlegenheit geraten	verlegen werden
in Wut geraten	wütend werden
eine/die Absicht haben	beabsichtigen
eine Ahnung haben	ahnen
Angst haben	sich fürchten
Auswirkungen haben (auf + AKK)	sich auswirken
Einfluss haben	beeinflussen
zur Folge haben	bewirken
Hoffnung haben	hoffen
Interesse haben	sich interessieren
ein Recht haben auf + AKK	berechtigt sein
den Verdacht haben	verdächtigen
Abstand halten	sich entfernt halten
in Ordnung halten	sich kümmern
eine Rede halten	reden
ein Referat halten	referieren
ein Versprechen halten	Versprochenes tun
zum Abschluss kommen	abgeschlossen werden
zur Abstimmung kommen	abgestimmt werden
zum Ausdruck kommen	ausgedrückt werden
zu Bewusstsein kommen	bewusst werden
zur Einsicht kommen	einsehen
zu einer Entscheidung kommen	entscheiden
in Fahrt kommen	schneller werden
in Frage kommen	relevant sein
in Gang kommen	lebendig werden
zu Hilfe kommen	helfen
zu Ohren kommen	hören
zur Ruhe kommen	ruhig werden
zu einem/dem Schluss kommen	schließen

NOMEN-VERB-VERBINDUNGEN

zur Sprache kommen	besprochen werden
zustande kommen	herauskommen
zu Wort kommen	reden können
außer Acht lassen	nicht berücksichtigen
in Ruhe lassen	nicht stören
im Stich lassen	in der Not allein lassen
einen Beitrag leisten (zu + DAT)	beitragen
Gesellschaft leisten	begleiten
Hilfe leisten	helfen
Widerstand leisten (gegen + AKK)	aktiv opponieren
die Aufmerksamkeit lenken auf + AKK	machen, dass andere etwas beachten
zugrunde liegen	der Grund sein
auf der Hand liegen	klar sein
im Sterben liegen	bald sterben
im Streit liegen (mit + DAT)	zerstritten sein
eine Andeutung machen	andeuten
Examen machen	fertig studieren
Gebrauch machen von + DAT	gebrauchen
sich Gedanken machen (über + AKK)	nachdenken
einen/den Vorschlag machen	vorschlagen
einen/den Vorwurf machen	vorwerfen
Abschied nehmen (von + DAT)	sich verabschieden
in Angriff nehmen	etwas Schwieriges beginnen
zum Anlass nehmen	veranlasst werden
Anstoß nehmen an + DAT	sich empören
sich in Acht nehmen	aufpassen
in Anspruch nehmen	beanspruchen
in Betrieb nehmen	eine Anlage starten
Einfluss nehmen (auf + AKK)	beeinflussen
in Empfang nehmen	empfangen
in Kauf nehmen	Nachteiliges akzeptieren
Notiz nehmen von + DAT	beachten
Rücksicht nehmen (auf + AKK)	rücksichtsvoll sein
in Schutz nehmen	vor Kritik schützen
Stellung nehmen (zu + DAT)	sich äußern
Frieden schließen (mit + DAT)	sich wieder verstehen
einen Kompromiss schließen	sich einigen
einen Vertrag schließen (mit + DAT)	einen Vertrag unterschreiben
außer Atem sein	erschöpft sein
der Auffassung sein	meinen
von Bedeutung sein (für + AKK)	bedeutend sein
im Begriff sein	gleich beginnen
zu Besuch sein	besuchen
in Betrieb sein	laufen (Anlage)
im Einsatz sein	eingesetzt sein
am Ende sein	keine Kraft mehr haben
zu Ende sein	vorüber sein
in Gefahr sein	gefährdet sein

in Kraft sein	gelten
in der Lage sein	die Möglichkeit haben
auf dem Laufenden sein	informiert sein
der Meinung sein	meinen
in Ordnung sein	funktionieren
im Recht sein	Recht haben (juristisch)
imstande sein	fähig sein
in Stimmung sein	gelaunt sein
(sich) in Bewegung setzen	bewegen
unter Druck setzen	beanspruchen (Person)
in Gang setzen	starten
in Kenntnis setzen	informieren
außer Kraft setzen	abschaffen
aufs Spiel setzen	riskieren
sich in Verbindung setzen mit + DAT	kontaktieren
Vertrauen setzen in + AKK	vertrauen
sich zur Wehr setzen (gegen + AKK)	sich wehren
sich zum Ziel setzen	anstreben
eine Rolle spielen	relevant sein
vor dem Abschluss stehen	bald abgeschlossen werden
zur Debatte stehen	soll diskutiert werden
unter Druck stehen	beansprucht sein (Person)
infrage stehen	bezweifelt werden
im Gegensatz stehen zu + DAT	entgegengesetzt sein
in Konkurrenz stehen (zu + DAT)	konkurrieren
unter Strafe stehen	bestraft werden
zur Verfügung stehen	kann gebraucht werden
in Verhandlung(en) stehen (mit + DAT)	verhandeln
zum Verkauf stehen	soll verkauft werden
zur Wahl stehen	kann gewählt werden
in Widerspruch stehen zu + DAT	widersprechen
in Zusammenhang stehen (mit + DAT)	zusammenhängen
außer Zweifel stehen	bezweifelt werden
Anforderungen stellen (an + AKK)	erwarten
einen Anspruch stellen (an + AKK)	beanspruchen
einen Antrag stellen	beantragen
in Aussicht stellen	versprechen
eine Bedingung stellen	verlangen
zur Diskussion stellen	ansprechen
eine Forderung stellen	fordern
eine Frage stellen	fragen
infrage stellen	anzweifeln
auf die Probe stellen	testen (Person)
zur Verfügung stellen	zum Gebrauch anbieten
auf Ablehnung stoßen	abgelehnt werden
auf Kritik stoßen	kritisiert werden
eine Absprache treffen (mit + DAT)	absprechen
eine Auswahl treffen	auswählen
eine Entscheidung treffen	entscheiden
Maßnahmen treffen	handeln
eine Vereinbarung treffen (mit + DAT)	vereinbaren

NOMEN-VERB-VERBINDUNGEN

Vorbereitungen treffen	vorbereiten
in Aktion treten	aktiv werden
in Kraft treten	gültig werden
in Streik treten	zu streiken beginnen
Kritik üben (an + DAT)	kritisieren
Anstrengungen unternehmen	sich anstrengen
in Angst versetzen	Angst machen
in Aufregung versetzen	aufregen
in Erstaunen versetzen	erstaunen
eine Ansicht vertreten	meinen
eine Meinung vertreten	meinen
einen Standpunkt vertreten	meinen
eine Überzeugung vertreten	überzeugt sein
in Erwägung ziehen	erwägen
die Konsequenzen ziehen (aus + DAT)	lernen
zur Rechenschaft ziehen	verantwortlich machen
den Schluss ziehen (aus + DAT)	schließen
zur Verantwortung ziehen	verantwortlich machen

Liste nach Präpositionen

Verben mit Präpositionen + Dativ

aus *woher jemand/etwas kommt*
bestehen aus
entstehen aus
übersetzen aus

bei *Person/Institution, bei der man etwas macht*
anrufen bei
arbeiten bei
sich bedanken bei (für)
sich beklagen bei (über)
sich beschweren bei (über)
sich entschuldigen bei (für)
sich erkundigen bei (nach)
sich informieren bei (über)

mit *Partner*
sich einigen mit (auf)
handeln mit
kämpfen mit (um)
schimpfen mit (auf)
spielen mit (um)
sprechen mit (über)
streiten mit (um)
telefonieren mit
sich vertragen mit

Beginn/Ende einer Handlung
anfangen mit
aufhören mit
sich beeilen mit
beginnen mit
warten mit (auf)
zögern mit

nach sich erkundigen nach
fragen nach
riechen nach
schmecken nach
sich sehnen nach
suchen nach

unter *unangenehmer Zustand*
leiden unter

von *Thema*
berichten von
handeln von
sprechen von
träumen von
erwarten von
fordern von
leben von
überzeugen von
verlangen von
abhängen von
sich befreien von
sich erholen von
sich ernähren von

vor *„Gefahr"*
sich ekeln vor
erschrecken vor
fliehen vor
sich fürchten vor
verheimlichen vor
warnen vor

zu *Ziel*
auffordern zu
befördern zu
beglückwünschen zu
bringen zu
sich eignen zu
einladen zu
sich entschließen zu
ernennen zu
erziehen zu
gehören zu
gratulieren zu
passen zu
überreden zu
wählen zu
werden zu

ANHANG

VERBEN MIT PRÄPOSITIONEN

Verben mit Präpositionen + Akkusativ

auf	*„Gefahr"*
	achten auf
	ankommen auf (Es kommt darauf an.)
	antworten auf
	aufpassen auf
	sich konzentrieren auf
	schießen auf
	schimpfen auf
	zielen auf

Bezug auf etwas Zukünftiges
sich einigen auf (mit)
sich freuen auf
hoffen auf
sich vorbereiten auf
warten auf (mit)

für	danken für
	sich bedanken für
	sich eignen für
	sich entscheiden für
	sich entschuldigen für
	sich interessieren für
	kämpfen für
	sorgen für
	stimmen für
	werben für

gegen	sich entscheiden gegen
	kämpfen gegen
	protestieren gegen
	stimmen gegen
	verstoßen gegen
	(sich) verteidigen gegen
	sich wehren gegen

über	*Bezug auf etwas Gegenwärtiges*
	sich ärgern über
	sich aufregen über
	sich beklagen über
	berichten über
	sich beschweren über
	sich freuen über
	herrschen über

sich informieren über
lachen über
nachdenken über
regieren über
siegen über
sprechen über
verfügen über
sich wundern über

um	*Zugriff auf ein Objekt*
	sich ängstigen um
	sich bemühen um
	sich bewerben um
	bitten um
	kämpfen um
	sich kümmern um
	sich sorgen um
	spielen um
	streiten um
	wetten um

Zugriff auf ein Thema
es geht um
es handelt sich um

Verben mit Präpositionen + Akkusativ
oder Dativ

an	*+ Akkusativ: Kontakt*
	sich erinnern an
	denken an
	sich gewöhnen an
	glauben an
	schicken an
	schreiben an

+ Dativ
etwas ändern an
arbeiten an
leiden an
sterben an
teilnehmen an
zweifeln an

in	*+ Akkusativ: Transformation in einen neuen Zustand*		Verben mit Gleichsetzungskasus

in   *+ Akkusativ: Transformation in einen*
      neuen Zustand
      geraten in
      übersetzen in
      sich verlieben in
      sich verwandeln in

      + Dativ
      bestehen in (Das Problem besteht
      darin, dass ...)

Verben mit Gleichsetzungskasus

als   *Feststellung einer Identität*
       + Nominativ
       arbeiten als
       gelten als

       + Akkusativ
       ansehen als
       bezeichnen als

Einige Verben können auch mit verschiedenen Präpositionen verwendet werden:
Herr Mayr arbeitet bei der Firma Consens.
Freiberuflich arbeitet er auch für eine Unternehmensberatung.
Heute muss ich noch an meiner Dissertation arbeiten.

VERBEN MIT PRÄPOSITIONEN

Alphabetische Liste

abhängen von + DAT
achten auf + AKK
etwas ändern an + DAT
anfangen mit + DAT
sich ängstigen um + AKK
ankommen auf + AKK (*Es kommt darauf an.*)
anrufen bei + DAT
ansehen als + AKK
antworten auf + AKK
arbeiten als + NOM
arbeiten an + DAT
arbeiten bei + DAT
sich ärgern über + AKK
auffordern zu + DAT
aufhören mit + DAT
aufpassen auf + AKK
sich aufregen über + AKK
sich bedanken bei + DAT
sich bedanken für + AKK
sich beeilen mit + DAT
befördern zu + DAT
sich befreien von + DAT
beginnen mit + DAT
beglückwünschen zu + DAT
sich beklagen bei + DAT
sich beklagen über + AKK
sich bemühen um + AKK
berichten über + AKK

berichten von + DAT
sich beschweren bei + DAT
sich beschweren über + AKK
bestehen aus + DAT
bestehen in (*Das Problem besteht darin, dass ...*)
sich bewerben um + AKK
bezeichnen als + AKK
bitten um + AKK
bringen zu + DAT
danken für + AKK
denken an + AKK
sich eignen für + AKK
sich eignen zu + DAT
sich einigen auf + AKK
sich einigen mit + DAT
einladen zu + DAT
sich ekeln vor + DAT
sich entscheiden für + AKK
sich entscheiden gegen + AKK
sich entschließen zu + DAT
sich entschuldigen bei + DAT
sich entschuldigen für + AKK
entstehen aus + DAT
sich erholen von + DAT
sich erinnern an + AKK
sich erkundigen bei + DAT
sich erkundigen nach + DAT
sich ernähren von + DAT

VERBEN MIT PRÄPOSITIONEN

ernennen zu + DAT	siegen über + AKK
erschrecken vor + DAT	sorgen für + AKK
erwarten von + DAT	sich sorgen um + AKK
erziehen zu + DAT	spielen mit + DAT
fliehen vor + DAT	spielen um + AKK
fordern von + DAT	sprechen mit + DAT
fragen nach + DAT	sprechen über + AKK
sich freuen auf + AKK	sprechen von + DAT
sich freuen über + AKK	sterben an + DAT
sich fürchten vor + DAT	stimmen für + AKK
gehören zu + DAT	stimmen gegen + AKK
es geht um + AKK	streiten mit + DAT
gelten als + NOM	streiten um + AKK
geraten in + AKK	suchen nach + DAT
sich gewöhnen an + AKK	teilnehmen an + DAT
glauben an + AKK	telefonieren mit + DAT
gratulieren zu + DAT	träumen von + DAT
handeln mit + DAT	überreden zu + DAT
handeln von + DAT	übersetzen aus + DAT
es handelt sich um + AKK	übersetzen in + AKK
herrschen über + AKK	überzeugen von + DAT
sich informieren bei + DAT	unterscheiden zwischen + DAT
sich informieren über + AKK	sich unterscheiden durch + AKK
sich interessieren für + AKK	sich unterscheiden in + DAT
kämpfen für + AKK	verfügen über + AKK
kämpfen gegen + AKK	verheimlichen vor + DAT
kämpfen mit + DAT	verlangen von + DAT
kämpfen um + AKK	sich verlieben in + AKK
sich konzentrieren auf + AKK	verstoßen gegen + AKK
sich kümmern um + AKK	(sich) verteidigen gegen + AKK
lachen über + AKK	sich vertragen mit + DAT
leben von + DAT	sich verwandeln in + AKK
leiden an + DAT	sich vorbereiten auf + AKK
leiden unter + DAT	wählen zu + DAT
nachdenken über + AKK	warnen vor + DAT
passen zu + DAT	warten auf + AKK
protestieren gegen + AKK	warten mit + DAT
regieren über + AKK	sich wehren gegen + AKK
riechen nach + DAT	werben für + AKK
schicken an + AKK	werden zu + DAT
schießen auf + AKK	wetten um + AKK
schimpfen auf + AKK	sich wundern über + AKK
schimpfen mit + DAT	zielen auf + AKK
schimpfen über + AKK	zögern mit + DAT
schmecken nach + DAT	zweifeln an + DAT
schreiben an + AKK	
sich sehnen nach + DAT	

Liste nach Präpositionen

Adjektive mit Präpositionen + Dativ

an	arm/reich	Milch ist reich an Mineralstoffen.
	beteiligt	Angestellte sind manchmal am Gewinn beteiligt.
	interessiert	Lisa ist vor allem an Sicherheit interessiert.
	schuld/unschuldig	Norbert ist schuld daran, dass wir uns verspätet haben.
bei	angesehen	Heiner ist bei seiner neuen Firma sehr angesehen.
	(un)bekannt	Der Schauspieler war bei Jung und Alt bekannt.
	(un)beliebt	Frau May ist bei allen Nachbarn sehr beliebt.
gegenüber[1]	aufgeschlossen	Sie ist neuen Ideen gegenüber immer sehr aufgeschlossen.
	zurückhaltend	Gegenüber Fremden ist Mariechen sehr zurückhaltend.

[1] *gegenüber* kann vor und nach dem Nomen stehen

in	gut	Henry ist gut in Mathe.
	(un)erfahren	Herr Brand ist jung und deshalb noch etwas unerfahren in seinem Beruf.
	nachlässig	Thomas ist im Haushalt schrecklich nachlässig.
	tüchtig	Seine Frau soll in ihrem Beruf sehr tüchtig sein.
mit	befreundet	Wolfgang ist schon seit drei Jahren mit Helene befreundet.
	beschäftigt	Er ist seit zwei Stunden damit beschäftigt, den Wasserhahn zu reparieren.
	einverstanden	Mit euren Urlaubsplänen bin ich einverstanden.
	fertig	Gott sei Dank bin ich mit dieser Arbeit endlich fertig.
	verheiratet	Julia ist seit fünf Jahren mit Moritz verheiratet.
	verwandt	Die Leiterin der Bayreuther Festspiele ist mit Richard Wagner verwandt.
	(un)zufrieden	Hermann ist sehr zufrieden mit seinem neuen Rennrad.
nach	verrückt	Franz ist ganz verrückt nach alten James-Bond-Filmen.
von	(un)abhängig	Max ist schon seit langem nicht mehr von seinen Eltern abhängig.
	begeistert	Der Chef war begeistert von unserer neuen Idee.
	entfernt	Die Insel Rügen ist ungefähr 80 km von Rostock entfernt.
	enttäuscht	Von seinem letzten Roman war ich sehr enttäuscht.
	frei	Unsere Bio-Produkte sind frei von Zusatzstoffen.
	müde	Ich bin von der langen Bergtour richtig müde.
	überzeugt	Alle waren von seiner Unschuld überzeugt.
	voll	Nach dem letzten Urlaub waren wir voll von neuen Eindrücken.
vor	blass	Julia war blass vor Schreck.
	rot/grün	Schau mal, Corinna ist richtig rot vor Wut.
	stumm	Als Bernd den Bären sah, war er vor Angst ganz stumm.

ANHANG

ADJEKTIVE MIT PRÄPOSITIONEN

zu	bereit	Ich habe beste Laune und bin wirklich zu jedem Unsinn bereit.
	entschlossen	Robert sieht so aus, als wäre er zu allem entschlossen.
	(un)fähig	Er ist so wütend, im Moment ist er zu allem fähig.
	(un)freundlich	Vielen Dank, Sie waren sehr freundlich zu mir.
	gut	Oma Braun ist gut zu allen ihren Enkeln.
	nett	Kinder, gleich besucht uns der Hausbesitzer! Seid bitte nett zu ihm!

Adjektive mit Präpositionen + Akkusativ

an	adressiert	Der Brief ist an Sie persönlich adressiert.
	gewöhnt	Claudia ist noch nicht an das hiesige Klima gewöhnt.
auf	ärgerlich	Obelix war sehr ärgerlich auf seinen Freund Asterix.
	angewiesen	Seit zwei Jahren ist Frau Steffens auf fremde Hilfe angewiesen.
	böse	Paulchen ist sehr böse auf seinen Vater.
	eifersüchtig	Agnes war früher unheimlich eifersüchtig auf die Freundin von Peter.
	gespannt	Ich bin sehr gespannt auf deine neue Wohnung.
	neidisch	Herr Moor ist neidisch auf die schönen Rosen seines Nachbarn.
	neugierig	Ich bin neugierig auf sein Gesicht, wenn er dieses Auto sieht.
	stolz	Auf ihr neues Pferd war Annette schrecklich stolz.
	wütend	Du Idiot! Wie kannst du das sagen? Ich bin wirklich wütend auf dich!
für	(un)angenehm	Die Baustelle war sehr unangenehm für die Anwohner.
	bekannt	Max und Moritz sind für ihre dummen Streiche bekannt.
	bezeichnend	Für diesen Maler sind die klaren Farben bezeichnend.
	charakteristisch	Dieses alberne Benehmen ist für sie sehr charakteristisch.
	dankbar	Ich bin dir sehr dankbar für den Tipp.
	entscheidend	Dieser Hinweis war entscheidend für das weitere Vorgehen der Polizei.
	(un)geeignet	Wenn Sie Rückenprobleme haben, ist dieser Stuhl ungeeignet für Sie.
	nützlich	Diese Bestätigung kann sehr nützlich für Sie sein.
	offen	Für solche Verbesserungsvorschläge ist der Chef doch immer offen.
	(un)schädlich	Zu große Hitze ist schädlich für die Pflanzen.
	schmerzlich	Der Verlust ihres Bruders war sehr schmerzlich für Eva.
	verantwortlich	Wir warten jetzt schon 20 Minuten! Wer ist hier für den Service verantwortlich?
	wichtig	Dieser Auftrag ist sehr wichtig für uns.

gegen	(un)empfindlich	*Dieses Medikament macht Sie unempfindlich gegen Schmerzen.*
	immun	*Seit der Impfung ist sie immun gegen Tbc.*
in	unterteilt	*Das Projekt ist in drei Phasen unterteilt.*
	verliebt	*Hast du das schon gewusst? Ulla ist jetzt in Jakob verliebt.*
über	ärgerlich/verärgert	*Über seine Verspätung war ich wirklich ärgerlich/verärgert.*
	beunruhigt	*Die Ärzte sind sehr beunruhigt über seinen Zustand.*
	entsetzt	*Ludwig war entsetzt über das Aussehen seines Vaters.*
	erfreut	*Willkommen! Wir sind sehr erfreut über Ihren Besuch.*
	erstaunt	*Ich bin etwas erstaunt über Ihren letzten Bericht.*
	froh	*Über seinen Besuch war Karin sehr froh.*
	(un)glücklich	*Anna war sehr glücklich über den Brief ihres Freundes.*
	traurig	*Über den Tod seines Großvaters war Lutz sehr traurig.*
	verwundert	*Franz ist so seltsam. Ich bin etwas verwundert über sein Benehmen.*
	wütend	*Karl war sehr wütend darüber, dass er das Essen versalzen hatte.*

Adjektive mit *als* + Gleichsetzungskasus

als	anerkannt	*Anna Wimschneider ist seit langem als Schriftstellerin anerkannt.*
	bekannt	*Ludwig ist bekannt als guter Geschichtenerzähler.*

ADJEKTIVE MIT PRÄPOSITIONEN

Alphabetische Liste

abhängig von + DAT	*Max ist schon seit langem nicht mehr von seinen Eltern abhängig.*
adressiert an + AKK	*Der Brief ist an Sie persönlich adressiert.*
anerkannt als + GLEICHSETZUNGS-KASUS	*Anna Wimschneider ist seit langem als Schriftstellerin anerkannt.*
angenehm für + AKK	*Die Baustelle war nicht sehr angenehm für die Anwohner.*
angesehen bei + DAT	*Heiner ist bei seiner neuen Firma sehr angesehen.*
angewiesen auf + AKK	*Seit zwei Jahren ist Frau Steffens auf fremde Hilfe angewiesen.*
ärgerlich auf + AKK	*Obelix war sehr ärgerlich auf seinen Freund Asterix.*
ärgerlich über + AKK	*Über seine Verspätung war ich wirklich ärgerlich.*
arm an + DAT	*Die meisten europäischen Länder sind arm an Rohstoffen.*
aufgeschlossen gegenüber + DAT	*Sie ist neuen Ideen gegenüber immer sehr aufgeschlossen. / Sie ist gegenüber neuen Ideen ...*
befreundet mit + DAT	*Wolfgang ist schon seit drei Jahren mit Helene befreundet.*
begeistert von + DAT	*Der Chef war begeistert von unserer neuen Idee.*

ADJEKTIVE MIT PRÄPOSITIONEN

bekannt als + GLEICHSETZUNGSKASUS	*Ludwig ist bekannt als guter Geschichtenerzähler.*
bekannt bei + DAT	*Der Schauspieler war bei Jung und Alt bekannt.*
bekannt für + AKK	*Max und Moritz sind für ihre dummen Streiche bekannt.*
beliebt bei + DAT	*Frau May ist bei allen Nachbarn sehr beliebt.*
bereit zu + DAT	*Ich habe beste Laune und bin wirklich zu jedem Unsinn bereit.*
beschäftigt mit + DAT	*Er ist seit zwei Stunden damit beschäftigt, den Wasserhahn zu reparieren.*
beteiligt an + DAT	*Angestellte sind manchmal am Gewinn beteiligt.*
beunruhigt über + AKK	*Die Ärzte sind sehr beunruhigt über seinen Zustand.*
bezeichnend für + AKK	*Für diesen Maler sind die klaren Farben bezeichnend.*
blass vor + DAT	*Julia war blass vor Schreck.*
böse auf + AKK	*Paulchen ist sehr böse auf seinen Vater.*
charakteristisch für + AKK	*Dieses alberne Benehmen ist für sie sehr charakteristisch.*
dankbar für + AKK	*Ich bin dir sehr dankbar für den Tipp.*
eifersüchtig auf + AKK	*Agnes war früher unheimlich eifersüchtig auf die Freundin von Peter.*
einverstanden mit + DAT	*Mit euren Urlaubsplänen bin ich einverstanden.*
empfindlich gegen + AKK	*Durch eine seltene Krankheit ist er sehr empfindlich gegen Hitze.*
entfernt von + DAT	*Die Insel Rügen ist ungefähr 80 km von Rostock entfernt.*
entscheidend für + AKK	*Dieser Hinweis war entscheidend für das weitere Vorgehen der Polizei.*
entschlossen zu + DAT	*Robert sieht so aus, als wäre er zu allem entschlossen.*
entsetzt über + AKK	*Ludwig war entsetzt über das Aussehen seines Vaters.*
enttäuscht von + DAT	*Von seinem letzten Roman war ich sehr enttäuscht.*
erfahren in + DAT	*Herr Gosch ist schon älter und deshalb sehr erfahren in seinem Beruf.*
erfreut über + AKK	*Willkommen! Wir sind sehr erfreut über Ihren Besuch.*
erstaunt über + AKK	*Ich bin etwas erstaunt über Ihren letzten Bericht.*
fähig zu + DAT	*Er ist so wütend, im Moment ist er zu allem fähig.*
fertig mit + DAT	*Gott sei Dank bin ich mit dieser Arbeit endlich fertig.*
frei von + DAT	*Unsere Bio-Produkte sind frei von Zusatzstoffen.*
freundlich zu + DAT	*Vielen Dank, Sie waren sehr freundlich zu mir.*
froh über + AKK	*Über seinen Besuch war Karin sehr froh.*
geeignet für + AKK	*Wenn Sie Rückenprobleme haben, ist dieser Stuhl für Sie nicht geeignet.*
gespannt auf + AKK	*Ich bin sehr gespannt auf deine neue Wohnung.*
gewöhnt an + AKK	*Claudia ist noch nicht an das hiesige Klima gewöhnt.*
glücklich über + AKK	*Anna war sehr glücklich über den Brief ihres Freundes.*
grün vor + DAT	*Schau mal, Nicole ist richtig grün vor Neid.*
gut in + DAT	*Henry ist gut in Mathe.*
gut zu + DAT	*Oma Braun ist gut zu allen ihren Enkeln.*
immun gegen + AKK	*Seit der Impfung ist sie immun gegen TBC.*
interessiert an + DAT	*Lisa ist vor allem an Sicherheit interessiert.*
müde von + DAT	*Ich bin von der langen Bergtour richtig müde.*
nachlässig in + DAT	*Thomas ist im Haushalt schrecklich nachlässig.*

neidisch auf + AKK	*Herr Moor ist neidisch auf die schönen Rosen seines Nachbarn.*
nett zu + DAT	*Kinder, gleich besucht uns der Hausbesitzer! Seid bitte nett zu ihm!*
neugierig auf + AKK	*Ich bin neugierig auf sein Gesicht, wenn er dieses Auto sieht.*
nützlich für + AKK	*Diese Bestätigung kann sehr nützlich für Sie sein.*
offen für + AKK	*Für solche Verbesserungsvorschläge ist der Chef doch immer offen.*
reich an + DAT	*Milch ist reich an Mineralstoffen.*
rot vor + DAT	*Schau mal, Corinna ist richtig rot vor Wut.*
schädlich für + AKK	*Zu große Hitze ist schädlich für die Pflanzen.*
schmerzlich für + AKK	*Der Verlust ihres Bruders war sehr schmerzlich für Eva.*
schuld an + DAT	*Norbert ist schuld an unserer Verspätung.*
stolz auf + AKK	*Auf ihr neues Pferd war Anette schrecklich stolz.*
stumm vor + DAT	*Als Bernd den Bären sah, war er vor Angst ganz stumm.*
traurig über + AKK	*Über den Tod seines Großvaters war Lutz sehr traurig.*
tüchtig in + DAT	*Seine Frau soll in ihrem Beruf sehr tüchtig sein.*
überzeugt von + DAT	*Alle waren von seiner Unschuld überzeugt.*
unabhängig von + DAT	*Max ist schon seit langem von seinen Eltern unabhängig.*
unangenehm für + AKK	*Die Baustelle war sehr unangenehm für die Anwohner.*
unbeliebt bei + DAT	*Herr Schmid ist bei allen Nachbarn sehr unbeliebt.*
unempfindlich gegen + AKK	*Dieses Medikament macht Sie unempfindlich gegen Schmerzen.*
unerfahren in + DAT	*Herr Brand ist jung und deshalb noch etwas unerfahren in seinem Beruf.*
unfreundlich zu + DAT	*In diesen Laden gehe ich nicht mehr. Die waren sehr unfreundlich zu mir.*
ungeeignet für + AKK	*Wenn Sie Rückenprobleme haben, ist dieser Stuhl ungeeignet für Sie.*
unglücklich über + AKK	*Helga und Richard waren sehr unglücklich über das Zeugnis ihrer Tochter.*
unschädlich für + AKK	*Dieses neue Pflanzenschutzmittel ist unschädlich für Insekten.*
unschuldig an + DAT	*Selbstverständlich bin ich unschuldig an diesem Chaos.*
unterteilt in + AKK	*Das Projekt ist in drei Phasen unterteilt.*
unzufrieden mit + DAT	*Mit seinem alten Fahrrad war er schon lange unzufrieden.*
verantwortlich für + AKK	*Wir warten jetzt schon 20 Minuten! Wer ist hier für den Service verantwortlich?*
verärgert über + AKK	*Über seine Verspätung war ich wirklich verärgert.*
verheiratet mit + DAT	*Julia ist seit fünf Jahren mit Moritz verheiratet.*
verliebt in + AKK	*Hast du das schon gewusst? Ulla ist jetzt in Jakob verliebt.*
verrückt nach + DAT	*Franz ist ganz verrückt nach alten James-Bond-Filmen.*
verwandt mit + DAT	*Die Leiterin der Bayreuther Festspiele ist mit Richard Wagner verwandt.*
verwundert über + AKK	*Franz ist so seltsam. Ich bin etwas verwundert über sein Benehmen.*
voll von + DAT	*Nach dem letzten Urlaub waren wir voll von neuen Eindrücken.*

ANHANG

ADJEKTIVE MIT PRÄPOSITIONEN

wichtig für + AKK	*Dieser Auftrag ist sehr wichtig für uns.*
wütend auf + AKK	*Du Idiot! Wie kannst du das sagen? Ich bin wirklich wütend auf dich!*
wütend über + AKK	*Karl war sehr wütend darüber, dass er das Essen versalzen hatte.*
zufrieden mit + DAT	*Hermann ist sehr zufrieden mit seinem neuen Rennrad.*
zurückhaltend gegenüber + DAT	*Gegenüber Fremden ist Mariechen sehr zurückhaltend. / Fremden gegenüber ist Mariechen ...*

KONNEKTOREN – PRÄPOSITIONEN

Bedeutung		Konnektoren		Präposition
		Nebensatz	Hauptsatz	
adversativ	Gegensatz	während wohingegen	dagegen demgegenüber	entgegen + DAT im Gegensatz zu + DAT
alternativ	mehrere Möglichkeiten	(an)statt	stattdessen entweder ... oder	statt + GEN
final	Ziel Zweck	damit um zu (+ Infinitiv)	dafür dazu zu diesem Zweck	zu + DAT für + AKK
kausal	Grund	da weil zumal	daher darum deshalb deswegen nämlich*	aufgrund + GEN wegen + GEN/DAT aus + DAT vor + DAT
konditional	Bedingung	wenn falls sofern wenn ... nicht	sonst / andernfalls	bei + DAT mit + DAT ohne + AKK
konsekutiv	Folge	sodass so, ... dass	infolgedessen folglich also daher darum deshalb deswegen	infolge + GEN infolge von + DAT
konzessiv	Gegensatz Widerspruch	obwohl obgleich obschon	dennoch trotzdem	trotz + GEN ungeachtet + GEN
modal	Art und Weise	indem dadurch, dass je ... desto/umso	auf diese Weise	mithilfe von + DAT mithilfe + GEN durch + AKK

temporal	Zeit, gleichzeitig	als		bei + DAT
				in + DAT
				mit + DAT
				an + DAT
		(immer) wenn		bei jedem
		sooft		
		während	währenddessen	während + GEN/DAT
		solange		
		bis		bis zu + DAT
		seit		seit + DAT
		seitdem		von + DAT ... an
	Zeit, nicht gleichzeitig	bevor/ehe	davor/vorher	vor + DAT
		nachdem	danach	nach + DAT
		sobald	anschließend	gleich nach + DAT

* Steht nur auf Position 3: *Er hat nämlich keine Stelle.*

Seite 9
Genus

1   b) die c) der d) der e) die f) der g) die h) die
    i) die j) der k) die l) die

2   b) die c) der d) die e) die f) die g) der h) der
    i) die j) die k) die l) der m) die n) das o) die
    p) der q) das r) der s) die t) die u) die

3   b) der c) das d) die e) das f) der g) das h) der
    i) der j) der k) die l) der m) die n) der o) der
    p) der q) der r) der

4   der Champagner, Fiat Punto, Freitag, Leser,
    Mai, März, Nebel, Norden, Opel, Spätsommer
    das Abendrot, Blümchen, Hühnchen, Mädchen
    die Fahrt, Frechheit, Hilfe, Kawasaki, Leistung,
    Schönheit, Schwierigkeit, Vorlesung, Wirk-
    lichkeit

Seite 10/11
Plural

1   -e: Berufe, Ergebnisse, Hefte, Jahre
    ⸚e: Bäume, Stühle
    -: Computer, Kalender, Kugelschreiber,
    Ordner, Zettel
    ⸚er: Bücher, Fächer

2   c) en d) s e) nen f) n g) en h) n i) nen j) s
    k) n l) en m) s n) nen o) en

3   (b) Sorgen (c) Wochen (d) Cafés (e) Studenten
    (f) Freundinnen (g) Abende (h) Discos

4   (b) Dias (c) Freunde/Gäste (d) Märkte (e) Strän-
    de (f) Sonnenschirmen (g) Bilder (h) Berge
    (i) Stunden (j) Gäste/Freunde

Seite 13
Kasus

1   b) Nominativ Dativ c) Nominativ Akkusativ
    Nominativ d) Dativ Nominativ Akkusativ
    e) Dativ Nominativ Genitiv

2   b) einen Euro c) eine Flasche d) einen Tag
    e) ein Kilo

3   (b) dem Fitness-Programm (c) den Sportlern
    (d) den Fotos (e) einer Figur (f) meinem
    Vorschlag (g) meinen Freundinnen

4   b) Mein Bruder und ich schenken meiner
    Schwester einen CD-Player. c) Meine Schwester
    kocht ihren Freunden ein Menü. d) Mein Vater
    schenkt seinen Nachbarinnen Blumen. e) Leo
    pflückt seiner Freundin einen Blumenstrauß.

Seite 15
Genitiv

1   b) Hugos Socken c) Toms Bücher d) Annas
    Handtuch

2   (b) seiner Glatze (c) seines ... Bauches (d) der
    Gesundheit (e) eines Diätplans (f) kurzer Zeit

3   b) Ach schau mal, das ist Frau Sturms Katze.
    c) Und der Typ da, das ist der Sohn unseres
    Lateinlehrers. d) ... Sie war schon immer die
    beste Freundin meines Bruders.

4   (b) des Einzelnen (c) des Lesens (d) der Er-
    kenntnisziele (e) der Texte

Seite 17
n-Deklination

1   n-Deklination: der Bauer, der Experte, das
    Herz, der Löwe, der Nachbar, der Name, der
    Produzent, der Russe, der Tourist
    normale Deklination: der Chef, der Direktor,
    die Familie, der Hund, der Informatiker, der
    Ingenieur, die Katze, der Mathematiker, der
    Professor

2   (b) Paragrafen (c) Kommilitonen (d) Gedan-
    ken (e) Bürokraten (f) Studenten (g) Willen

3   b) ... ich werde mit dem Lieferanten telefo-
    nieren. c) ... ich werde mit dem Fotografen
    sprechen. d) ... ich werde Herrn Schäfer so-
    fort anrufen. e) ... ich werde den Praktikanten
    gleich einarbeiten. f) ... ich werde mich mit
    dem Kunden in Verbindung setzen.

Seite 18/19
Adjektiv/Partizip als Nomen

1   b) Deutsche, Deutscher, Deutsche, Deutschen /
    Deutsche c) Verwandte, Verwandter, Verwand-
    te, Verwandten / Verwandte d) Angestellte,
    Angestellter, Angestellte, Angestellten / Ange-
    stellte e) Abgeordnete, Abgeordneter, Abge-
    ordnete, Abgeordneten / Abgeordnete f) Ver-
    liebte, Verliebter, Verliebte, Verliebten / Ver-
    liebte

2 b) ein Angestellter c) ein Reisender d) ein
Betrunkener e) ein Abwesender f) alle An-
wesenden

3 b) Schuldige c) Armen d) Gesunder
e) Schwarzer f) Tote g) Uninteressantes
h) Falsches

4 (b) Folgendes (c) Angenehmes (d) Schwieriges
(e) Unterbewusste (f) Neues (g) Wichtiges
(h) Besseres

Seite 21
Wortbildung

1 b) die Autorin c) die Fabrikantin d) die Hö-
rerin e) die Historikerin f) die Kommissarin
g) die Leserinnen h) die Physikerinnen i) die
Politikerinnen j) die Spezialistinnen k) die
Studentinnen l) die Zuschauerinnen m) die
Redakteurinnen n) die Chefinnen

2 a) das Geldinstitut, der Geldautomat, der Geld-
schein, die Geldanlage b) das Kunstwerk, das
Kunstbuch, der Kunsthändler, die Kunstaus-
stellung, die Kunstgalerie c) die Abendschule,
die Ballettschule, das Schulhaus, die Skischule,
die Grundschule, die Hochschule d) der Groß-
markt, die Großfamilie, die Großmacht, die
Großmutter, die Großstadt e) der Buchladen,
der Blumenladen, der Schreibwarenladen, der
Spielwarenladen f) die Freizeit, die Hochzeit,
die Reisezeit, der Zeitpunkt, die Mahlzeit, die
Schulzeit

3 die Aggression, Emotion, Evolution, Information, Kommunikation, Nation, Variation,
Identität, Kapazität, Solidarität, Demokratie,
Diplomatie, Drogerie, Philosophie, Soziologie,
Theologie
das Argument, Dokument, Instrument, Tes-
tament, Inventar, Glossar
der Egoist/Egoismus, Faschist/Faschismus,
Kapitalist/Kapitalismus, Katholizismus, Kom-
munist/Kommunismus, Protestantismus

4 (b) s (c) s (d) – (e) – (f) s (g) s (h) s (i) s (j) –
(k) – (l) – (m) s (n) es

Seite 23
Bestimmter Artikel

1 (b) den (c) der (d) den (e) des (f) am (g) die
(h) im (i) im (j) ans (k) Der

2 a) den b) das c) das d) das e) die f) der der

3 Die Nomen bezeichnen Dinge, die nur ein-
mall existieren oder die aus dem Kontext
(Taste, Dreieck) oder der Alltagswelt (Telefon)
bekannt sind.

4 (b) am (c) am (d) der (e) Die (f) das (g) der
(h) Der (i) des (j) den

Seite 25
Unbestimmter Artikel

1 b) Ein Zwerg ist ein sehr kleiner Mann mit
Bart und Zipfelmütze. c) Eine Hexe ist eine
hässliche, alte Frau, die zaubern kann und
meistens böse ist. d) Geister sind übernatürliche Wesen ohne Körper. e) Ein Ritter ist ein
Mann aus dem Mittelalter mit Pferd. f) Ein
Drache ist ein gefährliches Tier, das Feuer
spuckt.

2 b) Das ist der Geruch einer Zitrone. Das ist der
Geruch von Zitronen. c) Das ist der Duft einer
Rose. Das ist der Duft von Rosen. d) Das ist der
Ton einer Flöte. Das ist der Ton von Flöten.
e) Das ist der Gesang eines Vogels. Das ist der
Gesang von Vögeln. f) Das ist das Schreien
einer Möwe. Das ist das Schreien von Möwen.
g) Das ist der Schatten einer Wolke. Das ist der
Schatten von Wolken.

3 b) – ... eins c) eine ... keine d) – ... – e) einen
... einer f) eine g) eine ... ein ... eins h) Ein ...
eine ... ein

5 Meine Freundin Christine hat ein Baby bekommen. Deshalb muss ich noch schnell in
ein Geschäft, um ein Geschenk zu kaufen.
Hast du vielleicht eine Idee, was ich Christine
für das Baby schenken könnte? Das Baby ist
ein Junge, ein kleines Auto wäre ganz gut.
Aber dafür ist der Junge jetzt noch ein bisschen zu klein. Vielleicht eine Mütze für den
nächsten Winter. Mal sehen, das Geschenk
darf auch nicht zu teuer sein. Auf jeden Fall
kaufe ich ein Buch mit Jogaübungen für
Christine.

Seite 26/27
Nullartikel

1 Kaffee, Alkohol, Nikotin: Stoff; Einschlaf-
störungen: Plural; Einschlafrituale: Plural;
Kindern: Plural; Hilfe: generelle Bedeutung;
Gute-Nacht-Geschichten: Plural; Erwachsenen: Plural; Professor Hartmann: Eigen-
name

2 (b) der (c) – (d) – (e) – (f) – (g) – (h) die
   (i) – (j) – (k) – (l) – (m) Das (n) –

3 (c) einen (d) Der (e) am (f) dem/einem (g) der
   (h) die (i) den (j) die (k) einem (l) einem
   (m) einer (n) einer/der (o) einer/der (p) – (q) –
   (r) – (s) – (t) – (u) – (v) einer (w) – (x) –

Seite 29
Possessivartikel

1 (b) Ihren (c) mein (d) Ihrem (e) Ihrem (f) Ihr

2 b) sein Wagen c) seine Straße d) ihr ...
   Fitness-Studio

3 (b) meinen (c) ihrer (d) ihre (e) seinen (f) seine
   (g) seinem (h) Meine (i) seiner

4 b) meine c) seine d) ihr(e)s e) ihrer

Seite 30/31
Adjektivdeklination Typ 1

1 b) der bunte c) jener alte d) das herrliche
   e) dieses einmalige f) jedes einzelne g) die
   klare h) die einzige i) diese prima

2 b) das geplante c) die kleinste d) dem alten
   e) diesem kleinen f) der goldenen g) des
   ganzen h) des guten i) der beginnenden

3 b) alle hungrigen c) die hölzernen d) den
   dunklen e) diesen hohen f) den grünen g) der
   hohen h) der verschneiten i) der kürzer wer-
   denden

4 (b) restlichen (c) Schweizer (d) gefülltem
   (e) grünen (f) Wiener (g) gekauften (h) ge-
   spülten (i) traurigen (j) gestrigen (k) nächsten
   (l) ganze (m) letzten (n) arme (o) alte
   (p) dunklen (q) weißen

Seite 32/33
Adjektivdeklination Typ 2

1 einen: mit; kein: ohne; keine: mit; Ihr: ohne;
   seinen: mit; sein: ohne; mein: ohne; deinem:
   mit; Ihre: mit; unser: ohne; unsere: mit; dein:
   ohne; meinen: mit; Ihren: mit

2 b) roter c) französischer d) starker e) ver-
   rostetes f) altes g) dunkles h) scharfes i) leise
   j) gesalzene k) würzige l) frische m) hohe
   n) süße o) lachende p) große

3 (b) exzellenten (c) klassische (d) sportliche
   (e) langes (f) komfortables (g) unvergessliche
   (h) frischem (i) klarer (j) gezieltem (k) eiskal-
   tem (l) kleinen (m) kürzester (n) individueller
   (o) untrainierter (p) trüber

4 (b) e (c) en (d) en (e) en (f) e (g) e (h) e (i) er
   (j) er (k) er (l) e (m) e (n) en (o) e (p) er (q) e

5 b) Ein guter und augenschonender Bildschirm
   darf nicht flimmern. c) Ein professioneller
   Drucker muss hohe Farbqualität bieten.
   d) Zwei kleine Aktiv-Boxen sind auch im
   Kaufpreis enthalten. e) An das Telefon kann
   ein modernes Faxgerät angeschlossen werden.

Seite 34/35
Adjektivdeklination Typ 3

1/2 Ein Kasussignal haben: keinem, deinen,
     keine, einem, meine, seiner, unseres, euren,
     eurer, Ihrem, ihren

3 b) ganzen c) gemieteten d) privaten e) modernes f) altes g) wunderbaren h) engen i) hässliche j) gebrauchte k) neuen l) alten m) weitere n) antiken o) zusätzliche p) ganzen
   q) viele r) nächsten

4 b) teure c) helle d) sonnige e) kleines f) dunklen g) wunderschöne h) altmodische i) gebrauchten j) gemütlichen k) wichtige l) schöner m) gemütlicher n) gebrauchten o) modernes p) großen q) rostigen r) alten s) Mün-
   ch(e)ner

5/6 Alle Leute sind hier allein, denn jeder Gast
     kommuniziert über seinen (a) eigenen Bild-
     schirm gerade mit dem Rest der (b) großen
     (c) weiten Welt. 5 Euro kostet jede Stunde, die
     man am Computer verbringt. An allen (d) ver-
     fügbaren Computern kann man online die
     (e) neuesten Zeitungen lesen, mit (f) anderen
     Leuten „chatten" oder sich zu Hause in (g) an-
     genehme Erinnerung bringen. Jonathan zum
     Beispiel muss gerade eine (h) schwierige Frage
     beantworten, die ihm sein (i) alter Freund Pit
     in Kanada stellt. Pit hat schon allen (j) ge-
     meinsamen Freunden in Kanada erzählt, dass
     Deutschland ein (k) schönes Land ist. Aber
     besonders interessiert ihn, wie die (l) hübsche
     Studentin heißt, von der Jonathan das
     (m) letzte Mal erzählt hat. Jonathan hat schon

zwei (n) kleine Bier getrunken, und jedes
(o) weitere Bier vermehrt seine Tippfehler beim
Plaudern mit Pit. Aber das macht nichts, denn
bei diesem (p) elektronischen Brief kommt es
nicht so sehr auf (q) genaue Rechtschreibung
an. Und Tanja schreibt gerade an ihren
(r) neuen Freund in Berlin. Eine E-Mail für
Verliebte – in diesem Fall ist natürlich jedes
(s) einzelne Wort wichtig.

Seite 36/37
Artikel oder Adjektiv?

1 (b) zahlreiche ... wohnende (c) etlichen modernen (d) viel wertvolle (e) alle älteren
(f) zahlreichen jugendlichen (g) mehrere ein-
deutige (h) etlichen konservativen (i) keine
entspannten (j) alle coolen (k) manche wichtigen

2 b) ... mehr freie Zeit. c) ... mehr bezahlten
Urlaub. d) ... nur wenig künstliches Licht im
Büro. e) ... viel frische Luft. f) ... mehr grüne
Pflanzen.

3 b) Es gibt nur noch wenige freie Plätze.
c) Der Personalchef hat viele neue Informationen. d) Er äußert sich zu allen gestell-
ten Fragen. e) Es gibt allerdings auch etliche
gut hörbare Zwischenrufe. f) Ein junger Mitarbeiter macht einige kritische Bemerkungen.
g) Der Personalchef beantwortet plötzlich
keine weiteren Fragen mehr.

4 b) wenig c) wenig d) wenige e) viel ... mehr
f) einiges g) mehrere h) Solche i) viele
j) mehrere

Seite 39
Komparativ und Superlativ

1 b) härter, am härtesten c) viel, am meisten
d) breiter, am breitesten e) stärker, am stärks-
ten f) gut, besser g) teurer, am teuersten
h) lieb/gern, lieber i) klüger, am klügsten
j) schwächer, am schwächsten

2 b) höchste c) längste d) giftigste e) schwierigste

3 c) Im Urlaub schläft Herbert besser als zu
Hause. d) Zu Hause steht er nicht so spät auf
wie im Urlaub. e) Im Urlaub ist er aktiver als
zu Hause. f) Zu Hause ist es sowieso langwei-
liger als im Urlaub.

4 b) hässlichste – ... er ist einer der hässlichsten
Hunde der Welt. c) hübscheste – ... es ist eine
der hübschesten Städte Deutschlands.

d) beste – ... dort gibt es eines der besten
technischen Museen Europas. e) netteste – ...
er ist einer der nettesten Menschen der Welt.

Seite 40/41
Graduierung durch Adverbien

1 b) Abschwächung c) Abschwächung d) Abschwächung e) Verstärkung f) Verstärkung
g) Verstärkung

2 (b) relativ (c) ungewöhnlich (d) ziemlich
(e) sehr (f) recht (g) besonders (h) vergleichs-
weise

3 (b) zu spät (c) zu früh (d) zu langsam (e) zu
lang(e)/viel (f) zu müde

4 a) supergut b) hochmoderne ... vollautoma-
tisch c) todmüde ... topfit d) stocksteif ...
hochwirksamen

Seite 43
Zahlwörter

3 b) einer c) Achtzigern d) Tausende e) Fünfziger
... Zwanziger ... Zehner

4 a) erste ... zweite b) viertes ... dritten ... zweite ... erster c) hundertsten d) Erstens ... zweitens e) dritt

Seite 44/45
Partizip als Adjektiv

1 Für dieses Rezept benötigen Sie folgende Zutaten: 2 Liter kochendes Wasser, 3 gewürfelte
Kartoffeln, 3 geschälte Karotten, einen Bund
gehackte Petersilie, ein frisch geschlachtetes
Huhn, unsere nicht spritzende Margarine, 4
getrocknete Lorbeerblätter, 1 klein geschnittene Peperoni, eine ungespritzte Zitrone –
und natürlich unsere bewährten aromatisierenden Zusätze.

2 b) das sinkende Angebot, das gesunkene Angebot c) die zunehmende Zahl der offenen
Stellen d) die reduzierten Kosten e) die zu be-
zahlenden Rechnungen, die bezahlten
Rechnungen f) die sich verbessernde wirt-
schaftliche Lage, die verbesserte wirtschaft-
liche Lage

3 c) gebackenes d) streitendes e) Bellende
f) schließende g) geputztes h) vertrocknen-
de/vertrocknete

4 b) auf der verschneiten Straße c) die aus dem
Wrack befreiten Passagiere / die aus dem

Wrack zu befreienden Passagiere d) mit einem nicht funktionierenden Airbag e) mit quietschenden Bremsen f) der sofort alarmierte Krankenwagen g) die nicht zu unterschätzende Unfallgefahr

5   (b) versammelten (c) hergestellte (d) zu öffnende (e) arbeitende (f) gesteuerte (g) laufendem (h) stehendem (i) klatschenden (j) kalkulierten

Seite 47
Wortbildung

1   a) hyperaktiv c) praktikabel d) irreparabel e) uninformiert f) hochinteressant

2   Negation: kostenfrei, Unvergessliche
Verstärkung: himmelhoch, abgrundtief, supergünstigen
-ig: feurig, traurig, witzig
-lich: nächtliche, königlicher, Unvergessliche
-isch: musikalischen, romantischen
andere: neue, aktive, Toller, rasant, Deutsche

3   a) ... ohne Gebühren b) kann sich anpassen, kann lernen c) hat Humor, macht etwas mit Liebe d) ohne Verantwortung, ohne Bargeld e) der Preis ist gerechtfertigt / Preis und Qualität stehen in einem guten Verhältnis, es ist sinnvoll, genauer darüber nachzudenken f) funktioniert ohne weitere Installation, bereit zu helfen g) hat (viel) Erfolg, in großer Zahl

4   b) Der 98er Riesling ist leider nicht mehr lieferbar. c) Dieser Jahrgang ist nicht mehr bezahlbar. d) Der Markenname auf dem Etikett ist schwer lesbar. e) Eine Lieferung frei Haus ist nicht durchführbar / undurchführbar. f) Unser Lieferproblem ist lösbar.

5   b) unkritisch c) unberechtigt d) informell e) unhöflich f) inkompetent g) unübersichtlich h) ununterbrochen i) unordentlich j) irrational k) irrelevant l) unverbindlich m) unverständlich n) unvernünftig

Seite 48/49
Personalpronomen

1   (b) ich (c) mir (d) er (e) mich (f) ich (g) ihm (h) Ich (i) ich (j) ich (k) ihn (l) ich (m) Ich (n) Sie (o) ich (p) ihm (q) mir (r) mir (s) ich

2   (b) Den (c) der (d) den (e) Den (f) den (g) Den (h) die (i) die (j) die (k) Das (l) der (m) der (n) der (o) der (p) den (q) den (r) der

3   b) ... ich bringe ihn dir gleich. c) ... ich erkläre sie dir gleich. d) ... ich zeige es dir gleich. e) ... ich erkläre sie dir gleich.

4   b) mir das c) mir die d) mir den e) mir die f) mir den

5   b) Julia soll es dir suchen! c) Julia soll sie dir geben! d) Julia soll ihn dir reichen! e) Julia soll sie dir bringen! f) Mama soll ihn dir holen!

Seite 51
es

1   b) Diesen Harry-Potter-Band gibt es leider gerade nicht. c) Bei diesem Roman kommt es auf den Schluss an. d) Es hängt von der Vermarktung ab, wie gut sich ein Buch verkauft. e) Bei diesem Atlas handelt es sich um einen Sprachatlas.

2   b) Seit drei Tagen regnet es ununterbrochen, und ihr geht es wirklich schlecht. c) In ihrem Kopf summt es wie in einem Bienenkorb. d) Spät ist es auch schon, sie muss jetzt ins Bett. e) Ihr gefällt es auch nicht, dass Rudolf sich nicht meldet.

3   b) richtig c) falsch d) richtig e) falsch f) falsch g) richtig

4   c) Bei diesem Surfbrett handelt es sich um Sperrgepäck. e) Wenn es neblig ist, ... f) ... Also ich habe es nicht.

5   Sie haben es im Job weit gebracht, und deshalb haben sie es auch den ganzen Tag sehr eilig. Umso wichtiger ist (es), nach der Arbeit abschalten zu können. Denn nur so erholt sich ihr Nervensystem – und Sie brauchen es ja am nächsten Tag wieder in Bestform, denn Sie wollen es in Ihrem Job ja noch weit bringen. Leider gibt es bei uns keinen Knopf zum Ausschalten wie bei einer Maschine. Ihnen kann es körperlich gut gehen, aber wenn es Streit mit der Kollegin gegeben hat, ist klar, dass Sie nicht einfach abschalten können. Finden Sie heraus, wie Sie persönlich am besten entspannen können. Manche Leute

mögen es, in der Hängematte zu träumen. Andere nehmen ein Bad mit Prickel-Kugeln, dann sprudelt es in der Badewanne überall – und für manche gibt's nur eins: eine Viertelstunde mit geschlossenen Augen ausruhen.

Seite 52/53
das

1 b) Vokabeln lernen – das mag ich überhaupt nicht. c) Morgens lange schlafen – das mag ich. d) Gemütlich frühstücken – das finde ich super. e) Die Mathearbeit morgen schreiben müssen – das gefällt mir gar nicht.

2 b) Das hier bist du im Swimmingpool, und das da bin ich im Liegestuhl. c) Das hier ist Peter mit seinem Mountainbike, und das da seid ihr beim Volleyballspielen. d) Das hier ist Frau Bolte mit ihrem schrecklichen Hund, und das da sind meine Freunde auf dem Segelboot. e) Das hier ist der nette Ober, und das da bist du, als du mit ihm geflirtet hast. f) Das hier ist Herr Schmid, der schon ziemlich viel Bier getrunken hat, und das da sind wir alle beim Sommerfest.

3 b) Das schmeckt mir wirklich sehr gut. c) Das gefällt mir einfach nicht. d) Dass du kommst, das finde ich gut. / Das finde ich gut, dass du kommst. e) Am Sonntag mal auszuschlafen, das ist doch normal. / Das ist doch normal, am Sonntag mal auszuschlafen.

4 (b) es (c) es (d) Das (e) es (f) es (g) Das (h) Es (i) Das (j) Das (k) es (l) Das

Seite 54/55
Indefinitpronomen

1 (b) nichts (c) nichts (d) etwas/was (e) etwas/ was (f) nichts

2 (b) niemand(en) (c) niemand (d) jemand (e) jemand(en) (f) niemand (g) niemand (h) jemand

3 (b) man (c) Man (d) man (e) einen (f) man (g) einen (h) man (i) einem (j) man (k) man (l) einem

4 (b) er (c) jemand(en) (d) ihn

5 b) Das kann einen wirklich wahnsinnig machen. Wie soll man da seine Seminararbeit rechtzeitig fertig bekommen? c) Bei der Vorlesung über Reptilien muss man unbedingt mitschreiben. d) Wenn man in der Prüfung nicht weiß, was der Professor über Krokodile

gesagt hat, kann man leicht durchfallen. e) Wenn man doch nur wüsste, was einen in der Zukunft erwartet.

Seite 56/57
Präpositionalpronomen

1 von dem Gewinn: Wovon hat ihm seine Frau erzählt? bei dem Chef der Lottostelle: Bei wem hat er sich erkundigt? über den Gewinn: Worüber freuen sie sich? auf einen gemeinsamen Urlaubsort: Worauf müssen sie sich noch einigen? an wohltätige Organisationen und an seine vier Kinder und sechs Enkel: An wen will er einen großen Teil verteilen?

2 c) Wie bitte? Woran habt ihr euch gewöhnt? d) Was sagst du? In wen hat sich Franz verliebt? e) Wie bitte? Wofür hat er sich interessiert? f) Was sagst du? Woran hat er teilgenommen? g) Wie bitte? An wen denkt er nur noch?

3 b) damit c) darüber d) daran e) darauf

4 (b) geht ... darum (c) riecht ... danach (d) spielt mit ihnen (e) darüber beschwere (f) mit ihm sprechen (g) hört ... auf dich

Seite 58/59
Lokaladverbien (1)

1 b) Oben c) Hier oben d) draußen e) Außen f) da

2 b) nach draußen (raus) c) nach oben (rauf) d) nach unten (runter) e) nach links/rechts f) von draußen

3 (b) nach oben (c) Vorne (d) Rechts (e) links (f) oberen (g) nach unten (h) oben (i) Hinten (j) linken (k) rechten

Seite 61
Lokaladverbien (2)

1 b) raus c) rüber d) runter ... rauf e) rauf f) rein

2 (b) hin- (c) hin- (d) her (e) her- (f) hin-

3 (b) Stell ... hin (c) gehen ... hin (d) bringe ... hin (e) hinfahren (f) Leg ... hin (g) ist ... hergefahren

Seite 62/63
Temporaladverbien und -adjektive

1 b) Wie oft isst du in der Mensa? c) Wann findet ein Kolloquium zur Vorlesung statt? d) Seit wann hast du einen Computer? e) Bis wann musst du eine eigene E-Mail-Adresse haben? f) Wie oft erscheint diese Zeitschrift?

2   (b) morgendliche (c) täglich (d) wöchentliche
(e) Abends (f) abendliche

3   (b) am meisten (c) meistens (d) meistens
(e) meistens (f) am meisten (g) meistens

4   b) vierwöchigen c) monatlich d) einstündige
e) täglich f) zweitägigen g) stündlich

5   Dann habe ich mich umgezogen und habe/bin
eine halbe Stunde gejoggt. Danach habe ich
mich geduscht und mir die Haare gewaschen.
Dann habe ich eine Kleinigkeit gegessen.
Zuletzt habe ich mir die 23-Uhr-Nachrichten
im Fernsehen angeschaut.

Seite 65
Lokale Präpositionen (1)

1   b) bei c) bei / außerhalb von d) Von ... aus
e) entlang f) um g) Bis nach

2   Von Ute. Aus London. Aus der Klinik. Aus
dem Kino. Vom Skifahren. Aus dem Keller.
Von der Arbeit. Vom Gardasee. (Aus dem
Gardasee.) Von seinem Chef. Aus dem
Wasser. Aus dem Bahnhof. / Vom Bahnhof.
Vom Joggen. Von oben. Vom Domplatz. Aus
der U-Bahn. / Von der U-Bahn.

3   (b) bei (c) bei (d) Nach (e) zu (f) zu (g) nach
(h) bei (i) zu (j) bei (k) bei (l) nach (m) zur
(n) nach (o) bei (p) zur (q) bei (r) bei

4   (b) ab (c) durch (d) von ... aus (e) Von ... aus
(f) gegenüber (g) um (h) entlang

Seite 67
Lokale Präpositionen (2)

1   (b) der (c) der (d) dem (e) das (f) der (g) im
(h) die (i) den (j) dem (k) der (l) dem (m) der
(n) der (o) die (p) der

2   b) ... gehen Sie zur Bank. / auf die Bank. c) ...
gehen Sie zur Post. / auf die Post. d) ... gehen
Sie ins Reisebüro. e) ... gehen Sie zum Arzt.
f) ... gehen Sie ins Theater. g) ... gehen Sie
zum Bahnhof.

3   (b) Vor (c) im / in einem (d) im / mit dem
(e) in das / ins (f) im / auf dem (g) auf den
(h) in den (i) in den (j) in den (k) in die

(l) zwischen/neben (den) (m) Im / Auf dem /
Am (n) im (o) in (p) auf der / in der

Seite 68/69
Temporale Präpositionen (1)

1   b) – c) Bis zu d) Während e) Von ... bis
f) Über g) Ab h) Innerhalb i) beim j) –

2   b) Während c) innerhalb d) Außerhalb
e) während f) Innerhalb

3   a) vom ... bis zum b) Ab ... – c) zwischen ...
vom 20. an ... bis zum

4   (b) bis (zum) (c) bis (d) ab (e) beim
(f) während

5   (b) – (c) innerhalb von (d) von ... an (e) –
(f) zwischen (g) bis (h) Beim (i) Bei (j) über
(k) außerhalb der (l) Während der (m) über
(n) Bis

Seite 70/71
Temporale Präpositionen (2)

1   b) – c) Vor d) gegen e) um f) Im g) nach
h) an i) um j) in k) am l) Im m) in n) zu
o) gegen

2   b) in der c) in d) am e) im f) an g) am h) im
i) am j) im l) gegen m) um n) gegen o) um

3   (b) vor (c) Seit (d) vor (e) seit (f) vor (g) seit

4   a) zu der b) in c) Zu d) Zur e) in

5   (b) Nach (c) im (d) aus dem (e) um (f) gegen/–
(g) an (h) –/um (i) gegen (j) Im/Bis (k) an/zu
(l) am (m) zu dem

Seite 73
Präpositionen

1   a) Aus diesem Grund ... Zur Überraschung
seiner Freunde ... mit dem Fahrrad b) Infolge
geringerer Steuereinnahmen ... nach einem
Bericht der „Süddeutschen Zeitung" ... Aufgrund der geplanten Familienförderung ...
Angesichts dieser Belastungen ... zur
Gegenfinanzierung

2   (b) Mithilfe (c) Auf (d) ohne (e) für (f) Trotz
(g) aus (h) In (i) nach (j) Durch ... (k) Mithilfe
(l) für (m) auf

3　(b) trotz des schlechten Wetters (c) Wegen des
　　starken Schneefalls (d) mit dem Zug (e) in
　　einem schrecklichen Zustand (f) Zu seinem
　　großen Ärger (g) Zum Pausemachen (h) Ohne
　　Unterbrechung (i) vor

Seite 75
Modalpartikeln

1　b) Hör doch mal klassische Musik! – Ich höre
　　eigentlich nicht gerne klassische Musik.
　　c) Sprich doch mal mit deiner Chefin! – Ich
　　spreche eigentlich nicht gerne mit meiner
　　Chefin. d) Schau dir doch mal die alten Fotos
　　an! – Ich schaue eigentlich nicht gerne alte
　　Fotos an. e) Treib doch ein bisschen mehr
　　Sport! – Ich treibe eigentlich nicht gerne Sport.

2　(b) denn (c) ja/aber (d) ruhig (e) vielleicht/
　　aber (f) ja (g) denn (h) vielleicht

3　(b) doch (c) eben/einfach (d) denn (e) eben/
　　einfach (f) doch (g) doch

4　(b) denn (c) ja (d) denn (e) denn/eigentlich
　　(f) denn/eigentlich (g) ja (h) denn/eigentlich
　　(i) eigentlich (j) ja (k) denn/eigentlich
　　(l) eigentlich/ja (m) ja (n) ja/eigentlich

Seite 77
Präsens

1　b) Seit wann lernen Sie schon Spanisch?
　　c) Seit wann sind Sie schon Ingenieur? d) Seit
　　wann spielen Sie schon Golf? e) Seit wann
　　arbeiten Sie schon bei BMW? f) Seit wann
　　fahren Sie schon Rallyes?

2　(b) fliegst (c) arbeitest (d) liest (e) hoffe
　　(f) nimmst (g) belästige (h) stiehlt (i) sehe
　　(j) ausgibt (k) fragt (l) bekommt (m) sieht
　　(n) antwortet (o) stehle (p) sammle (q) bricht
　　(r) rätst

3　a) ... gehen wir zum Einkaufen. In einer
　　Woche fahren wir nach Berlin. Kommt ihr
　　mit? b) Im Oktober beginne ich mit meinem
　　Studium. Ich studiere dann Ökonomie in
　　Konstanz am Bodensee. Ich brauche drei Jahre
　　dafür. Danach mache ich ein Aufbaustudium
　　in Harvard. c) In etwa zehn Jahren übernehme
　　ich die Firma meines Vaters. Anschließend
　　gründe ich eine Familie und baue ein Haus. In
　　20 Jahren bekomme ich die Midlife-Crisis.
　　Dann suche ich mir eine Freundin. In 30
　　Jahren bin ich vielleicht bereits Großvater.
　　Und in 40 Jahren höre ich zu arbeiten auf. /
　　auf zu arbeiten.

4　c) Nein, ich bin gerade dabei, mir das
　　Rauchen abzugewöhnen. d) Nein, ich bin
　　gerade am Weggehen. e) Nein, ich bin gerade
　　dabei, mein Auto zu reparieren. f) Nein, ich
　　bin gerade am Fernsehen. g) Nein, ich bin
　　gerade dabei, die Küche zu putzen. h) Nein,
　　ich bin gerade am Kofferpacken.

Seite 79
Perfekt

1　(...)ge...t: ausgemacht, gedacht, abgestellt,
　　weggebracht
　　(...)ge...en: geschrieben, angekommen, ge-
　　stritten, angeboten, umgezogen, eingeladen,
　　geschnitten
　　...t: bekämpft, versucht, misstraut, entdeckt,
　　studiert
　　...en: besprochen, sich entschieden, empfohlen

2　(b) habe (c) hat (d) sind (e) habe (f) haben
　　(g) haben (h) sind (i) habe (j) bin (k) habe
　　(l) sind (m) hat (n) habe (o) haben (p) ist
　　(q) hat (r) hat (s) hat (t) hat (u) Haben (v) ist
　　(w) hat (x) ist

3　b) In einem Monat hat er die schlimmste
　　Krise überstanden. c) Der Arzt hat ihm auch
　　gesagt, dass ... d) Heute ist mein Vater erst-
　　mals eine halbe Stunde gelaufen. Das hat ihn
　　fast umgebracht. e) Danach hat er sich gleich
　　wieder hingelegt und ist eingeschlafen. f) Erst
　　um 12 Uhr ist er aufgestanden und ins Bad
　　gegangen. g) Zum Mittagessen hat er nur
　　Gemüse und etwas gekochtes Fleisch bekom-
　　men. h) Das hat ihm überhaupt nicht gefallen,
　　und vor lauter Ärger ist er fast explodiert.

Seite 80/81
Präteritum

1　b) fingst an c) glaubte d) argumentierten
　　e) rannten f) hattet g) lag h) dachten i) saß
　　j) regnete k) nahm l) wart m) durften n) ant-
　　wortete o) wolltest p) hängte q) zerstörte
　　r) brachten

2　König Johann war ein mächtiger König. In sei-
　　nem Land lebten 30 Millionen Menschen. Aber
　　all seine Macht und sein Reichtum brachten
　　ihm kein Glück. Er fühlte sich einsam, und die
　　Leute an seinem Hof begannen, sich Sorgen zu
　　machen. Doch eines Tages rettete ihn seine
　　Hofköchin Fanni aus seiner Depression. Sie
　　versuchte, durch ständig neue Knödel-Rezepte
　　die Laune des Königs zu verbessern. Jeden
　　Abend bis spät in die Nacht studierte sie des-
　　wegen Kochbücher. Als man dem König eines

LÖSUNGEN

Tages ihre neueste Kreation, einen Spinat-Pilz-Knödel mit 20 cm Durchmesser, brachte, wusste er, dass sein Leben wieder einen Sinn hatte. Obwohl er nach dem Essen des riesigen Knödels kaum noch sitzen konnte, ließ er die Hofköchin kommen. König Johann verliebte sich sofort in sie. „Meine Knödel-Königin" nannte er sie satt lächelnd. Bald darauf machte er ihr einen Heiratsantrag. Sie wollte zuerst nicht, da sie bereits verlobt war, aber als man sie mit lebenslangem Reichtum lockte, stimmte sie zu.

3 Der Zeuge kam gerade aus dem Restaurant, als er sah, wie ein Bagger auf den Parkplatz fuhr. Dabei beschädigte der Bagger mehrere Autos, auch das Auto des Zeugen. Dann hielt der Bagger endlich an. Aus dem Fahrzeug stieg ein junger Mann. Als der Zeuge versuchte, ihn festzuhalten, erzählte der Mann etwas von „persönlichen Problemen". Dann blieb er freiwillig stehen und bat den Zeugen, nichts davon seiner Freundin zu erzählen. Der Mann machte einen sehr verwirrten Eindruck auf den Zeugen. Der Zeuge rief dann über sein Handy die Polizei, die nach etwa 10 Minuten kam.

4 (b) lag (c) drehte (d) berührte (e) wechselte (f) wählte (g) ließ (h) hatte (i) drückten (j) ging

Seite 82/83
Plusquamperfekt

1 (b) hängte Präteritum (c) gereinigt hatte Plusquamperfekt (d) gab Präteritum (e) wusch Präteritum (f) wurden verschoben Präteritum (Passiv) (g) entstand Präteritum (h) habe ... getraut Perfekt (i) gesehen habe Perfekt (j) sagte Präteritum (k) Verletzt wurde Präteritum (Passiv) (l) glaubt Präsens (m) verflüchtigt hatten Plusquamperfekt (n) hatte ... bewahrt Plusquamperfekt (o) wurde ... belohnt Präteritum (Passiv) (p) hatte ... gehört Plusquamperfekt (q) versuchte Präteritum (r) wehrte Präteritum (s) stieß Präteritum (t) erlitt Präteritum (u) macht Präsens (v) hat ... gefasst Perfekt
Außerdem in der Überschrift: explodiert (Präsens), belohnt (Präsens)

2 In Argentinien (a) haben Wissenschaftler einen etwa 150 Millionen Jahre alten Dinosaurier-Friedhof mit versteinerten Knochen entdeckt. „Von einem Dinosaurier (b) ist fast das vollständige Skelett erhalten", (c) berichtete einer der dort tätigen Wissenschaftler. Die Nachrichtenagentur ANA (d) schrieb von einem „Jurassic Parc" in Patagonien. Paläontologen (e) hatten seit langem gehofft, eine Lücke in der Forschung schließen zu können. Argentinien (f) erweist sich immer mehr als einer der wichtigsten Fundorte der Paläontologie: Erst vor einem Jahr (g) waren die Überreste des längsten bekannten Dinosauriers gefunden worden. Der pflanzenfressende Riese (h) kommt auf eine Länge von 48 bis 59 Metern. Bauarbeiter (i) hatten entsprechende Hinweise gegeben. Im Jahr zuvor (j) hatten Forscher in Patagonien bereits Überreste des vermutlich größten fleischfressenden Dinos gefunden. „An der neuen Fundstätte (k) sind auch Versteinerungen von Schildkröten, Flugechsen und sogar einem Säugetier ausgegraben worden", (l) teilte der Wissenschaftler mit.

3 (b) zusammengelebt hatten (c) gerieten (d) geworfen hatte (e) gegangen war (f) wurde (g) erlebt hatte (h) sollte (i) plante (j) hingelegt hatte (k) erklärte (l) gab ... auf

4 b) Nachdem er einen Anruf seiner kranken Mutter erhalten hatte, konnte er nicht ins Kino gehen. c) Nachdem sein Kollege krank geworden war, musste er dessen Arbeit auch noch übernehmen. d) Nachdem er sein Auto von der Reparatur abgeholt hatte, ging es gleich wieder kaputt. e) Nachdem er die Verabredung mit seiner Freundin vergessen hatte, wartete sie umsonst. f) Nachdem es deswegen Streit mit ihr gegeben hatte, ging er zu Freunden Karten spielen.

Seite 85
Futur

1 b) V c) S d) A e) Z f) V

2 b) Ja, ich werde sicher auch ein paar Tipps für den „Neuen Markt" geben. c) Nein, dieses Jahr wird es vermutlich/wahrscheinlich/wohl nicht zu einer Krise kommen. d) Ja, ich werde wahrscheinlich/wohl auch in Aktienfonds investieren.

3   b) Du wirst dein Fahrrad putzen! c) Du wirst jetzt den Hobbyraum aufräumen! d) Du wirst sofort mit dem Hund spazieren gehen! e) Ihr werdet auf der Stelle den Fernseher ausschalten!

4   Das Auto der Zukunft wird kaum noch Umweltprobleme verursachen. Es wird einen Wasserstoff- oder Elektroantrieb haben. Außerdem wird es leiser sein als die Autos von heute. Und es wird viel sicherer sein: Airbags werden die Körper der Passagiere nicht nur von vorne und seitlich, sondern auch von oben und im Fußraum schützen. Es wird dann ein Radar geben, das die Bremse automatisch betätigt.

5   ..., weil ich mich so lange nicht gerührt habe. Du wirst von meiner Trennung von Maria bereits gehört haben. Sie wird unglücklicher sein über unsere Trennung als ich. Aber so, wie ich sie einschätze, wird sie mich in einem Monat schon vergessen haben. Demnächst erzähle ich Dir mehr. Es wird Dich ja interessieren, wie das passiert ist.

Seite 86/87
werden
1   b) P c) F d) K e) V f) V g) F h) P

2   b) wird sie c) werde ich d) er wird e) Sie wird f) er ist ... geworden

3   (b) geworden (c) worden (d) geworden (e) geworden (f) worden (g) geworden (h) worden (i) geworden

4   (b) wird (c) werden (d) wird (e) werden (f) wurde (g) worden (h) wird (i) worden (j) wurden (k) geworden (l) würde

Seite 89
Verbergänzungen
1   D/N, N, A/D, A/G

2   (b) Es gelingt mir heute nichts. (c) Leihst du mir dein Auto? (d) Er kennt mein Problem. (e) Ich danke dir für die Hilfe. (f) Er ist ein fairer Spieler. (g) Du wirst immer fauler. (h) Man überführte mich des Betrugs. (i) Ich glaube dir kein Wort. (j) Er scheint nett zu sein.

3   (b) ihr (c) uns Frauen (d) jedem (e) ihre Meinung (f) ein ewiger Problemfall (g) dieser Frau (h) keinem Menschen (i) ihr (j) einen

Menschen (k) anderen (l) Meinem Freund (m) keinen ruhigen Moment (n) privaten Kontakte (o) seinen alten Freunden (p) einen Gruß (q) ihm (r) mir (s) ihn (t) des Steuerbetrugs

4   b) Ein langjähriger Mitarbeiter der Spionageabwehr BND hat dem Dienst von 1990 bis 1995 dessen eigene geheime Informationen verkauft. c) Als „Nachrichtenquelle" trat ein ehemaliger Kollege auf. d) Der 49-Jährige muss jetzt den ergaunerten Agentenlohn zurückbezahlen. e) Die Aufklärung dauerte Monate und bedurfte der Hilfe polnischer Kollegen. f) Das Duo hatte seine Informationen dem polnischen Geheimdienst angeboten. g) Dieser informierte die Münchner Kollegen. h) So gelang den deutschen Justizbehörden, den guten Geschäften der beiden ein Ende zu bereiten.

Seite 91
Verben mit Präpositionen
1   um: es geht um
bei: helfen bei
über: nachdenken über, sich freuen über
als: gelten als (2 x), empfinden als
an: denken an
mit: sich treffen mit

2   (b) nach (c) über (d) für (e) als (f) über

3   (b) ins (c) von dem (d) davon (e) über (f) über die (g) für ein (h) von (i) von frischem (j) in einen (k) über

Seite 93
Reflexive Verben
1   b) D c) A d) A e) D

2   (b) sich (c) miteinander (d) mir (e) sich (f) dir (g) sich (h) mich (i) dich (j) uns (k) uns (l) sich (m) sich (n) sich

3   b) Überlegen Sie sich manchmal, sich von ihm zu trennen? c) Aber Sie fürchten sich vor dem Alleinsein? d) Dann sollten Sie sich auf jeden Fall unseren Ratgeber „ex" kaufen. Sie finden dort 1000 Tipps, wie Sie sich an ein Leben ohne „sie" oder „ihn" gewöhnen. e) Am besten, Sie besorgen sich das Buch noch heute, um sich auf das Leben von morgen vorzubereiten.

4   b) Dann kämm dir doch die Haare! c) Dann zieh dir doch den Pullover aus! d) Dann wasch dir doch die Hände! e) Dann kauf dir doch das Fahrrad! f) Dann holt euch doch die Tennisschläger rauf!

5   b) Dann kämm sie dir doch! c) Dann zieh ihn dir doch aus! d) Dann wasch sie dir doch! e) Dann kauf es dir doch! f) Dann holt sie euch doch rauf!

Seite 95
Modalverben (1)

1   (b) durftest (c) durfte (d) durftet (e) durften (f) durften

2   b) kannst c) kann/darf d) kannst e) kann/darf f) kann g) können h) darf

3   b) Nach weiteren sechs Monaten konnten wir die ersten Gespräche mit ihm führen. Du konntest in diesem Alter nur schreien. c) Mit vier Jahren durfte/konnte er die Schule besuchen. d) Als Peterchen fünf war, konnte er sich mit euch bereits über Aktien unterhalten. e) In der Schule konnten die Lehrer ihm kaum etwas beibringen. f) Und er war so höflich: Wenn Besuch kam, fragte er sofort: Darf/Dürfte ich Ihnen ein Stück Kuchen anbieten? g) Man konnte/durfte ihn allerdings nicht berühren: Er biss sofort zu.

4   (b) verboten/untersagt (c) fähig (d) erlaubt (e) Recht (f) Möglichkeit (g) untersagen/verbieten

Seite 97
Modalverben (2)

1   b) N c) P d) E e) R f) N

2   (b) soll (c) sollte (d) sollen/müssen (e) Musst (f) sollen/müssen (g) soll (h) müssen (i) soll (j) muss

3   c) Paul braucht sie nur noch zu gießen. d) Ihr braucht sie nur noch auszupacken. e) Eva muss ihn nur noch füttern. f) Wir müssen nicht essen gehen. g) Du brauchst den Kindern keine Geschichte vorzulesen.

4   b) Ich soll das Examen mit Bestnote machen. c) Darum muss ich jeden Tag bis Mitternacht lernen. d) Leider muss ich noch dreißig Bücher durchlesen. e) Mein Vater will, dass ich ab nächstem Jahr in seiner Firma arbeite. / Ich soll ab nächstem Jahr in der Firma meines Vaters arbeiten. f) Dann muss ich Tag für Tag tun, was der „alte Herr" sagt. g) Er will

sich leider erst in 10 Jahren aus der Firmenleitung zurückziehen. h) Ich glaube, ich sollte erst mal ein halbes Jahr verreisen.

Seite 99
Modalverben subjektiv (1)

1   b) 1 c) 2 d) 1 e) 1 f) 2

2   b) will c) soll d) soll e) will f) soll g) soll h) will

3   b) Das Nachrichtenmagazin „Fakten" will als erstes Presseorgan davon erfahren haben. c) Innerhalb der Regierung soll es noch Differenzen über den Zeitpunkt geben. d) Der Wirtschaftsminister soll gegen eine sofortige Erhöhung sein. e) Der Finanzminister will alle Alternativen geprüft haben. f) Die Erhöhung soll nur 1,5 Prozent betragen.

4   Man berichtet, dass er sich seit seinem sechsten Lebensjahr für Pilze interessiert hat. Es heißt, dass er in seiner Jugend ein Einzelgänger gewesen ist. Er behauptete, dass er schon mit 18 Deutschlands Pilzexperte Nr. 1 gewesen ist. Gerüchten zufolge hat er seine spätere Frau Charlotte auf einem internationalen Pilzkongress kennengelernt. Sie versichert, dass sie große Teile ihres Vermögens für die Rettung gefährdeter Pilzarten ausgegeben hat.

Seite 101
Modalverben subjektiv (2)

1   b) 50 % c) 75 % d) 100 % e) 90 %

2   (b) könntest (c) kann (d) können (e) muss (f) müsste

3   Nur er kann dieses Verbrechen begangen haben. Das Motiv dürfte Geldgier gewesen sein. Aber auch Eifersucht könnte eine Rolle gespielt haben. Auch der Chauffeur dürfte beteiligt gewesen sein. Der Fall müsste bald abgeschlossen sein.

4   Die Rettungsmannschaft ist überzeugt, dass sie bei Nebel vom richtigen Weg abgekommen sind. Zu diesem Zeitpunkt war es wahrscheinlich bereits dunkel. Dabei sind möglicherweise einige der Jugendlichen in Panik geraten. / Dabei sind einige der Jugendlichen möglicherweise in Panik geraten. Es hat sich bei ihnen mit

Sicherheit um völlige Anfänger gehandelt. Die Schweizer Behörden: Sie haben bestimmt aus Sparsamkeitsgründen auf einen Bergführer verzichtet.

Seite 103
kennen – wissen – können • mögen – gefallen

1   <u>Weißt</u> Du noch, wer ich bin? Es ist ja schon lange her, dass wir uns in Rom getroffen haben, und ich <u>kenne</u> Dich ja kaum. Deshalb <u>weiß</u> ich nicht, ob es richtig ist, Dir diese E-Mail zu schicken. Aber ich <u>kenne</u> nur wenige Männer, mit denen ich mich gleich so gut unterhalten habe. <u>Kannst</u> Du Dich noch an unser kleines Café erinnern? Ich <u>kann</u> mich genau noch an den Abend erinnern, als wir uns <u>kennen</u>gelernt haben. Vielleicht <u>kannst</u> Du mir ja mal antworten. Ciao! Maria
P.S.: Wie findest Du mein Deutsch? Leider <u>kann</u> ich immer noch nicht so genau zwischen können, kennen und wissen unterscheiden.

2   a) kann ... kenne ... Kennen/Wissen b) wusste ... gewusst ... konnte c) wissen ... Kennen ... gewusst ... gekannt ... konnte

3   (b) mag (c) geschmeckt (d) gefallen (e) habe ... gern (f) mag (g) hat ... gern (h) liebt (i) liebt (j) gefallen (k) möchte

Seite 104/105
legen/liegen • setzen/sitzen

1   Karin stellt den Blumenstrauß auf den Tisch. Max hängt den Mantel in den Schrank. Veronika steckt in großen Schwierigkeiten. Christina legt sich ins Bett. Jürgen setzt sich auf die Gartenbank. Felix hängt wie eine Spinne an der Felswand. Georg sitzt auf dem Barhocker. Karl-Heinz steckt den Brief in die Jackentasche. Erich steht an der Bushaltestelle.

2   Karin stellte den Blumenstrauß auf den Tisch. / Karin hat den Blumenstrauß auf den Tisch gestellt. Max hängte den Mantel in den Schrank. / Max hat den Mantel in den Schrank gehängt. Veronika steckte in großen Schwierigkeiten. / Veronika hat in großen Schwierigkeiten gesteckt. Christina legte sich ins Bett. / Christina hat sich ins Bett gelegt. Jürgen setzte sich auf die Gartenbank. / Jürgen hat sich auf die Gartenbank gesetzt. Felix hing wie eine Spinne an der Felswand. / Felix hat wie eine Spinne an der Felswand gehangen. Georg saß auf dem Barhocker. / Georg hat auf dem Barhocker gesessen. Karl-

Heinz steckte den Brief in die Jackentasche. / Karl-Heinz hat den Brief in die Jackentasche gesteckt. Erich stand an der Bushaltestelle. / Erich hat an der Bushaltestelle gestanden.

3   a) den ... gelegt ... liegen ... die ... aufgesetzt ... steckt ... die ... gesteckt b) setzen ... sitzt ... setze ... die ... sitzt c) die ... gehängt ... hing ... steht ... stell ... den

4   Wo ist denn der Teddy? Der sitzt auf dem Herd. Wo sind denn die Löffel? Die stecken in der Teekanne. Wo ist denn die Hose? Die hängt an der Wand. Wo ist denn der Zucker? Der liegt im Waschbecken. Wo sind denn die Handtücher? Die liegen auf dem Boden. Wo ist denn der Kaffee? Der steht in der Mikrowelle. Wo sind denn die Spaghetti? Die liegen unter dem Tisch / auf dem Boden. Wo sind denn die Pfannen? Die hängen am Fenster. Wo ist denn das Geschirr? Das steht im Kühlschrank. Wo ist denn das Messer? Das liegt auf dem Hocker / auf dem Stuhl. Wo ist denn die Milch? Die steht auf dem / im Regal.

5   Wohin hat er den Teddy getan? Den hat er auf den Herd gesetzt. Wohin hat er die Löffel getan? Die hat er in die Teekanne gesteckt. Wohin hat er die Hose getan? Die hat er an die Wand gehängt. Wohin hat er den Zucker getan? Den hat er ins Waschbecken gelegt. Wohin hat er die Handtücher getan? Die hat er auf den Boden gelegt. Wohin hat er den Kaffee getan? Den hat er in die Mikrowelle gestellt. Wohin hat er die Spaghetti getan? Die hat er unter den Tisch / auf den Boden gelegt. Wohin hat er die Pfannen getan? Die hat er ans Fenster gehängt. Wohin hat er das Geschirr getan? Das hat er in den Kühlschrank gestellt. Wohin hat er das Messer getan? Das hat er auf den Hocker / auf den Stuhl gelegt. Wohin hat er die Milch getan? Die hat er auf das / ins Regal gestellt.

Seite 107
Trennbare Verben

1   h) ~~versorgen~~ k) ~~entsorgen~~

2   b) Bitte mach das Seil / die Schnur los/auf. c) Bitte mach das Fenster auf/zu. d) Bitte mach das Licht im Keller an/aus. e) Bitte mach das Preisschild von der neuen Hose ab/weg. f) Bitte mach den Fleck am Ärmel weg. g) Bitte mach den Videorekorder an/aus. h) Bitte mach die Dose auf/zu.

3   ER: Hast du was dagegen, wenn ich mir diese neue CD mal anhöre. SIE: Nein, hör sie dir ruhig an. – ER: Hast du was dagegen, wenn ich dein Handy mitnehme? SIE: Nein, nimm es ruhig mit. – ER: Hast du was dagegen, wenn ich damit meine Mutter mal kurz anrufe? SIE: Nein, ruf sie ruhig an. – ER: Hast du was dagegen, wenn ich deinen Computer einschalte? SIE: Nein, schalt ihn ruhig ein. – ER: Hast du etwas dagegen, wenn ich deine neuen Rollerblades mal ausprobiere? SIE: Nein, probier sie ruhig aus.

4   Mutter: Kauf bitte Milch ein. Tochter: Aber ich habe doch schon welche eingekauft. – Mutter: Mach bitte mit den Hausaufgaben weiter. Tochter: Aber ich habe sie doch schon fertig gemacht. – Mutter: Hör bitte mit dem Telefonieren auf. Tochter: Aber ich habe doch noch gar nicht / gerade erst angefangen. – Mutter: Trag bitte den Mülleimer raus. Tochter: Aber ich habe ihn doch schon rausgetragen.

5   b) ein c) ab d) weg e) vor f) bei g) auf h) ab i) aus

Seite 108/109
Untrennbare Verben
1   b) Wir führen die Reformen zügig durch. c) Wir freuen uns, dass Sie gestern unser Angebot angenommen haben. d) Wir erweitern unser Angebot baldmöglichst. e) Wir erhöhen die Preise im nächsten Jahr.

2   (b) berichten (c) besucht (d) begrüßt (e) bemerkte/merkte (f) benutzen (g) riet (h) beschloss (i) kämpfte (j) besteht (k) sitzen

3   untrennbar: gewinnen (2x), erkämpfen, erstechen, bekommen, versprechen, besiegen, verlieren, unterstützen
trennbar: herbeischleppen, wegstoßen, durchsetzen, anziehen
Vorsicht: *gewinnen* und *verlieren* haben keine Version ohne Vorsilben *(winnen, lieren)!*

4   ... den Schatz der Nibelungen gewonnen, er hat sich eine Tarnkappe erkämpft, die ihn unsichtbar machen kann, und er hat einen Drachen erstochen und in seinem Blut gebadet. Schließlich ist Siegfried nach Worms gekommen, wo König Gunther regiert hat. Um Gunthers Schwester Kriemhild zur Frau zu bekommen, hat Siegfried dem König versprochen, ihm zu helfen, die schöne, aber übermenschlich starke Brunhild von Island zur Frau zu gewinnen. Gunther musste seine zukünftige Braut im Wettkampf besiegen. Dazu ist ein riesiger Speer von mehreren Männern herbeigeschleppt worden. Riesengroß war auch der Stein, den er wegstoßen musste. Gunther hat den Mut verloren. Er hat gefürchtet, dass er sich gegen Brunhild nicht durchsetzen wird. Siegfried hat Gunther unterstützt. Er hat seine Tarnkappe angezogen und wurde dadurch für die Zuschauer des Wettkampfs unsichtbar.

Seite 111
Passiv
1   b) Die alte Kantine wurde renoviert. c) Die Wände wurden weiß gestrichen. d) Neue Lampen wurden installiert. e) Endlich wurde eine Klimaanlage eingebaut. f) Die Renovierung wurde übrigens von den Mitarbeitern höchstpersönlich durchgeführt.

2   b) Die alte Kantine ist renoviert worden. c) Die Wände sind weiß gestrichen worden. d) Neue Lampen sind installiert worden. e) Endlich ist eine Klimaanlage eingebaut worden. f) Die Renovierung ist übrigens von den Mitarbeitern höchstpersönlich durchgeführt worden.

3   ... über Privates wird nicht gesprochen, und im Team wird auch nicht gearbeitet. Stattdessen wird ständig an die Konkurrenz gedacht. Natürlich wird nicht geraucht, es wird nur selten gelacht und nie gefeiert. ...

4   b) In „Chatrooms" wird geplaudert und geflirtet. c) Hier wirst du von wildfremden Leuten angesprochen. d) Wenn per Internet eingekauft und bezahlt wird, werden die Daten durch ein persönliches Passwort geschützt. / Die Daten werden durch ein persönliches Passwort geschützt, wenn per Internet eingekauft und bezahlt wird. e) Wenn die Kreditkarten-Daten ungesichert eingegeben werden, wird das eigene Konto vielleicht von einem unberechtigten „Einkäufer" missbraucht.

5 Man hat das @-Zeichen für E-Mail-Adressen ausgewählt, weil dieses Zeichen in keiner Sprache dieser Welt benutzt wird. Das Zeichen wird als Trennung zwischen dem Adressaten-Namen und dem Provider-Namen gebraucht. Für das @-Zeichen drückt man meistens die Tasten „Alt Gr" und „Q".

Seite 112/113
Passiv mit Modalverben

1 b) ... wollen das veraltete Heizungssystem modernisieren. c) ... wollen in jeder Wohnung moderne Fenster einbauen. d) ... wollen die alten Bäder erneuern. e) ... wollen den Hinterhof begrünen. f) ... wollen neue Bäume pflanzen. g) ... wollen im ganzen Haus die Mieten erhöhen.

2 b) Ein großer Kinderspielplatz soll angelegt werden. c) Frühlingsblumen sollen gepflanzt werden. d) Im Zentrum soll eine Fußgängerzone eingerichtet werden. e) Mehr Straßen sollen zu Spielstraßen gemacht werden. f) Ein neuer Tunnel soll gebaut werden. g) Mehr Straßenlampen sollen aufgestellt werden.

3 b) Das neue Faxgerät konnte nicht richtig bedient werden. c) ..., der Termin mit dem Unternehmensberater konnte nicht vorbereitet werden. d) ..., deshalb konnten die Unterlagen nicht kopiert werden. e) ..., deshalb konnte der Reparaturservice nicht benachrichtigt werden. f) Die Besprechung mit dem Abteilungsleiter konnte auch nicht geplant werden. g) ..., weshalb die Post nicht rechtzeitig verschickt werden konnte.

4 b) Ein genauer Plan muss gemacht werden. c) Ein Fluchtauto muss organisiert werden. d) Die Nummernschilder müssen unbedingt ausgetauscht werden. e) Ein Bankkonto für Schwarzgeld muss eröffnet werden. f) Pässe und Flugtickets müssen besorgt werden. g) Der Boss muss laufend informiert werden.

5 b) Der Ort sollte beobachtet werden. c) Die Geldübergabe konnte aber nicht verhindert werden. d) ... war kaputt und konnte nicht mehr rechtzeitig repariert werden. e) Der Erpresser muss nun anhand alter Fotos identifiziert werden. f) Der Mann konnte allerdings nicht erkannt werden. g) Der Kaufhauserpresser soll aber ganz sicher beim nächsten Mal gefasst werden.

Seite 114/115
Zustandspassiv

1 Das Mail-Programm wird vom Sender – also von Ihnen – gestartet. Man muss aber nicht online gehen, um die Mail zu schreiben. Ist der elektronische Brief geschrieben, werden die fertigen Nachrichten im Postausgang gespeichert. Erst durch die Verbindung zum Internet und einen Klick auf „senden" kann der elektronische Brief losgeschickt werden. Vom Postausgang Ihres Providers werden die Mails dann zum Posteingang des Mail-Empfängers gesendet. Der Empfänger wird über neue E-Mails nur dann benachrichtigt, wenn eine Verbindung zum Internet besteht. Viele Programme sind so eingerichtet, dass der Posteingang in bestimmten Intervallen überprüft wird. Neue E-Mails können dann automatisch abgerufen werden.

2 *Ist geschrieben:* Zustandspassiv, *werden gespeichert:* Passiv, *kann losgeschickt werden:* Passiv mit Modalverb, *werden gesendet:* Passiv, *wird benachrichtigt:* Passiv, *sind eingerichtet:* Zustandspassiv, *überprüft wird:* Passiv, *können abgerufen werden:* Passiv mit Modalverb

3 b) Das Gerät ist schon angeschlossen. c) Der Strom ist schon eingeschaltet. d) Die CD ist schon eingelegt und gestartet. e) Die Software ist schon installiert. f) Der Internet-Zugang ist schon hergestellt. g) Das Passwort ist schon eingegeben.

4 b) ... die Blumen sind gegossen. c) ... die Wäsche ist aufgehängt. d) ... die Steckdose ist schon repariert. e) ... das Fax ist eingeschaltet. f) ... die Rechnungen sind noch nicht bezahlt.

5 b) Das Geschirr war schon abgewaschen. c) Die Aschenbecher waren schon ausgeleert. d) Das Zimmer war schon gelüftet. e) Der Frühstückstisch war schon gedeckt. f) Der Kaffee war schon gekocht. g) Der Orangensaft war schon eingeschenkt.

Seite 116/117
Passiv-Ersatzformen

1 b) essbare Früchte c) leicht waschbarer Stoff d) unbezahlbare Preise e) brauchbare Idee f) undefinierbare Farbe

2 b) leicht zerbrechliches Material c) unverkäufliches Produkt d) gut verständlicher Text e) unverzeihlicher Fehler f) unverantwortlicher Leichtsinn

3   b) Die Schuhe sind zur Stabilisierung des Fußes fest zu schnüren. c) Die Muskulatur ist vor jedem Lauf aufzuwärmen. d) Bei Verletzungen ist der Fuß mindestens sechs Wochen ruhig zu stellen. e) Der Fuß ist bei Schmerzen zu entlasten.

4   b) noch zu veröffentlichendes Ergebnis c) noch weiter zu bearbeitendes Thema d) auszufüllendes Formular e) abzulegende Prüfung f) nicht zu verschiebender Prüfungstermin g) ernst zu nehmender Vorschlag

5   …, denn sie <u>können</u> direkt <u>beantwortet</u> und dann <u>gelöscht werden</u>. Die Post <u>kann</u> in drei Stapel <u>sortiert werden</u>: Stapel eins für Sachen, die sofort <u>erledigt werden müssen</u>. Stapel zwei für Projekte, die auch später <u>bearbeitet werden können</u>. Stapel drei für Informationen, die Sie irgendwann einmal studieren können. Alles andere <u>sollte</u> gleich <u>weggeworfen werden</u>. Und so <u>kann</u> auch die Urlaubslaune in den Alltag <u>gerettet werden</u>: Gehen Sie die ersten Tage ruhig und entspannt an.

6   Danach sind die E-Mails zu lesen, denn sie lassen sich direkt beantworten und dann löschen. Die Post lässt sich in drei Stapel sortieren: Stapel eins für Sachen, die sofort zu erledigen sind. Stapel zwei für Projekte, die sich auch später bearbeiten lassen. Stapel drei für Informationen, die Sie irgendwann einmal studieren können. Alles andere ist gleich wegzuwerfen. Und so lässt sich auch die Urlaubslaune in den Alltag retten: Gehen Sie die ersten Tage ruhig und entspannt an.

7   b) Ein neues Grafikprogramm lässt sich mühelos installieren. c) Die Soundkarte des Computers lässt sich ersetzen. d) Allerdings lassen sich einige Anfangsprobleme nicht vermeiden. e) Die meisten Schwierigkeiten lassen sich aber schnell überwinden.

Seite 119
Konjunktiv II (1)
1   b) wusste, wüsste c) hatten, hätten d) waren, wären e) blieb, bliebe f) konntet, könntet g) fandest, fändest h) wurde repariert, würde repariert i) sollte, sollte j) hielt, hielte k) wart, wär(e)t l) wollten, wollten m) durfte, dürfte

n) wurden gefangen, würden gefangen o) ging, ginge

2   b) Aber sie hätte gern allein ein Zimmer. c) Aber sie wäre gern bildhübsch. d) Aber sie würde sich gern schminken. e) Aber sie hätte gern ein Mofa. f) Aber sie würde gern mit ihren Freundinnen in Urlaub fahren. g) Aber sie würde gern neben Hans-Peter sitzen. / Aber sie säße gern neben Hans-Peter.

3   b) Wir könnten jetzt Mittagspause machen. c) Ich würde gerne nach Hause fahren. d) Ich wüsste gerne, / Ich würde gerne wissen, wo Peter bleibt. e) Du müsstest schon seit zwei Stunden schlafen. f) Ich würde gerne noch im Bett bleiben. / Ich bliebe gerne noch im Bett. g) Sonst dürftet ihr ausschlafen.

4   b) An ihrer Stelle würde ich mehr / nicht so wenig schlafen. c) An seiner Stelle würde ich weniger / nicht so viel trinken. d) An ihrer Stelle würde ich nicht so oft / weniger (oft) fehlen. e) An ihrer Stelle würde ich mich öfter / nicht so selten um den alten Onkel kümmern. f) An ihrer Stelle würde ich die Kinder früher / nicht so spät ins Bett schicken.

Seite 121
Konjunktiv II (2)
1   b) sie wäre gelaufen c) wir hätten gedacht d) wir hätten gedacht e) es wäre gebaut worden f) du wär(e)st gewesen g) du wär(e)st gewesen h) ihr hättet fernsehen dürfen i) wir wären verletzt worden j) er wäre gewachsen k) sie hätten angeboten l) es wäre passiert m) sie wären gestiegen n) sie hätte gehabt o) sie hätte gehabt p) sie hätte gehabt q) ich hätte lesen müssen

2   b) Nein, aber fast hätten wir es verpasst. c) Ja, aber fast hätten wir nicht landen können. d) Nein, aber fast hätten wir wieder stundenlang warten müssen. e) Nein, aber fast wäre ich (am Strand) bestohlen worden. f) Nein, aber fast wäre sie (im Urlaub wieder von Moskitos) (wieder) gestochen worden.

3   b) Der neue Kollege hätte diesen Fall schon am Mittwoch bearbeiten sollen. c) Meine Assistentin hätte Ihnen alle nötigen Infor-

mationen geben können. d) Sie hätten vor unseren Geschäftspartnern nicht darüber reden dürfen. e) Ihre Mitarbeiter hätten mehr auf die Details achten müssen. f) Man hätte jemand anderen für diesen Job nehmen sollen.

4 (b) hätte ... getan (c) hätte ... bedankt (d) hätte ... gewusst (e) wäre ... gekommen (f) wäre ... gewesen (g) wäre ... gegangen (h) hätten ... gefehlt (i) hättest

Seite 123
Konjunktiv II (3)

1 b) ... wenn Sie sich früher gemeldet hätten. c) ... wenn Sie morgen kommen könnten. d) ... wenn wir zuerst essen gingen? e) ... wenn es nicht so viel geregnet hätte. f) ... wenn er einen Stadtplan hätte.

2 b) Wenn der Dieb nicht in eine fremde Handtasche gegriffen hätte, wäre er nicht von einer Tarantel gebissen worden. c) Wenn Kakerlaken keinen / nicht den „sechsten Sinn" hätten, könnten sie nicht so frühzeitig jeden Menschen erkennen. d) Wenn die Finnin Karoliina S. nicht eines Morgens neben einer Kobra aufgewacht wäre, müsste sie nicht zum Psychotherapeuten gehen. e) Wenn der Gewehrschrank nicht offen gestanden hätte, hätte der Jagdhund nicht mit dem Gewehr gespielt und dabei (nicht) sein Herrchen erschossen.

3 Wenn du weniger Geld ausgegeben hättest, dann hätten wir mehr sparen können. Was heißt denn hier, wenn ich weniger ausgegeben hätte? Das heißt zum Beispiel, wenn du weniger oft zu diesem italienischen Masseur gegangen wärst. Wenn ich einen Körper wie du hätte, würde ich mich schämen. Wenn ich so oft an meinen Körper denken würde wie du, dann könnten wir uns nicht einmal ein Puppenhaus leisten.

4 b) Wenn Ernst Geschmack hätte, hätte er dieses Sakko nicht gekauft. c) Wenn Maria nicht sehr gutmütig wäre, wäre sie längst explodiert. d) Wenn Fritz Geld hätte, hätte er sich längst ein neues Auto gekauft. e) Wenn Ulrich momentan nicht sehr beschäftigt wäre, würde er sich sicher bei mir melden.

Seite 124/125
Konjunktiv II (4)

1 b) Wenn er doch einen besseren Job bekommen würde! c) Wenn doch das Fernsehprogramm nicht immer so langweilig wäre! d) Wenn doch der Wagen etwas schneller fahren würde! e) Wenn wir doch etwas mehr Glück im Lotto hätten! f) Wenn doch das Wetter nicht so schlecht wäre!

2 b) Wenn er nur (im Moment) nicht lauter andere Dinge im Kopf hätte! c) Wenn bloß seine Freunde nicht so einen schlechten Einfluss auf ihn hätten! d) Wenn er nur nicht jeden Tag mit dieser Petra herumlaufen würde! e) Wenn er (bloß) wenigstens das Notwendigste machen würde! f) Wenn er nur nicht bei jedem Gespräch über das Thema total kindisch reagieren würde! g) Wenn er bloß nicht die halbe Nacht fernsehen würde! h) Wenn er nur dieses Schuljahr schaffen würde! i) Wenn er es bloß einmal versuchen würde. j) Wenn er nur so fleißig wäre wie sein Vater in dem Alter!

3 b) Hätte ich doch nur nicht lauter andere Dinge im Kopf gehabt! c) Hätten doch bloß meine Freunde nicht so einen schlechten Einfluss auf mich gehabt! d) Wäre ich doch nur nicht jeden Tag mit dieser Petra herumgelaufen! e) Hätte ich doch bloß wenigstens das Notwendigste gemacht! f) Hätte ich doch nur nicht bei jedem Gespräch über das Thema total kindisch reagiert! g) Hätte ich doch bloß nicht die halbe Nacht ferngesehen! h) Hätte ich doch nur dieses Schuljahr geschafft! i) Hätte ich es doch bloß wenigstens versucht! j) Wäre ich doch nur so fleißig gewesen wie mein Vater in dem Alter!

4 b) Charlotte ist zu vergesslich, um dieses Projekt durchzuführen. / Charlotte ist so vergesslich, dass sie dieses Projekt nicht durchführen kann. c) Herr Meier war zu unzuverlässig, um diesen Job zu übernehmen. / Herr Meier war so unzuverlässig, dass er diesen Job nicht übernehmen konnte. d) Eva ist zu kaputt, um noch in die Disco zu gehen. / Eva ist so kaputt, dass sie nicht noch / mehr in die Disco gehen kann. e) Sibylle war zu verärgert über Karl, um mit ihm noch länger zusammenzuleben. / Sibylle war so verärgert über Karl, dass sie nicht länger mit ihm zusammenleben wollte. f) Frau Schneider ist zu geizig, um sich einen neuen Wintermantel zu kaufen. / Frau Schneider ist so geizig, dass sie sich keinen neuen Wintermantel kauft.

5 b) Die Discos waren zu laut, als dass ich hätte schlafen können. c) Das Meer dort ist

zu warm, als dass es einen erfrischen würde. d) Die Zimmer waren zu klein, als dass man sich hätte setzen können. e) Die Leute dort sind zu unfreundlich, als dass ich sie wiedersehen möchte. f) Die Hitze war zu groß, als dass ich mich erholt hätte. g) Aber der Barkeeper war zu süß, als dass ich ihm hätte widerstehen können.

Seite 127
Konjunktiv II (5)

1 b) ... als ob sie große Schmerzen hätte. c) ... als ob er gleich explodieren würde. d) ... als ob ich seinen Wagen kaputt gemacht hätte. e) ... als ob ich ein Einbrecher wäre. f) ... als ob sie nie wieder aufhören würde.

2 b) ... als hätte sie große Schmerzen. c) ... als würde er gleich explodieren. d) ... als hätte ich seinen Wagen kaputt gemacht. e) ... als wäre ich ein Einbrecher. f) ... als würde sie nie wieder aufhören.

3 b) ... als ob er den sichersten Wagen der Welt hätte. c) ... als würde er hervorragend sehen. d) ... als hätte sie ein unangenehmes Erlebnis gehabt. e) ... als ob sie einsam wäre. f) ... als wäre sie arm. g) ... als ob sie enge Freunde wären. h) ... als ob er ihren Brief nicht bekommen hätte. i) ... als hätte es noch (einen) Sinn, sich mit ihr zu treffen.

4 b) Jeden Morgen beschimpft er mich, als wäre ich ein kleiner Schuljunge. c) Seine Sekretärin benimmt sich, als wäre sie die Königin von England. d) Meine Kollegen reden über mich, als wäre ich ein Idiot. e) Selbst der Hund des Pförtners behandelt mich, als wäre ich Luft. f) Die Dame am Empfang sieht mich an, als wäre ich ein Fremder. g) Die neue Praktikantin spricht mit mir, als wäre sie meine Vorgesetzte.

Seite 129
Indirekte Rede

1 Statt wallendes Haar zu tragen, sei der Mann nun aber völlig kahl. Ein Gericht in Aveiro habe die Schönheitsklinik dazu verurteilt, dem Kläger die 3300 Euro zurückzuzahlen. Außerdem müsse sie ihn für sein „seelisches Leiden" mit weiteren 3000 Euro entschädigen. Man hätte den Mann vorher über die möglichen

Folgen informieren müssen, begründete das Gericht sein Urteil. ... Die Zeremonie sei daraufhin abgebrochen worden, das Bankett habe jedoch stattgefunden, berichteten Zeitungen in der tschechischen Hauptstadt. „Es herrschte eine Stimmung wie auf einer Beerdigung", kommentierte der Bräutigam. Für das überraschende Scheitern wählte er einen originellen Vergleich: Es sei, als ob man Billard spiele, und die Kugel rolle wider Erwarten nicht ins Loch. Nach ihren Gründen habe er seine Ex-Braut nicht gefragt: „Das übersteigt sowieso mein Verständnis", meinte er.

2 (b) finde (c) habe (d) könne (e) sei (f) wolle (g) hätten (h) müssten (i) hätten (j) kämen (k) wisse

3 b) Der Richter fragte den Zeugen, ob er sich noch genau an den Unfall erinnern könne. Der Zeuge erwiderte, dass er noch jedes Detail in Erinnerung habe. / er habe noch jedes Detail in Erinnerung. / Auf die Frage des Richters, ob der Zeuge sich noch genau an den Unfall erinnern könne, erwiderte dieser, dass er noch jedes Detail in Erinnerung habe. / er habe noch jedes Detail in Erinnerung. c) Der Journalist wollte von der Schauspielerin wissen, wie alt sie sei. Die Schauspielerin antwortete, das gehe ihn gar nichts an. / dass ihn das gar nichts angehe. d) In der Krisensitzung betonte der Vorstandsvorsitzende, dass sie wegen der schlechten Auftragslage harte Maßnahmen ergreifen müssten. / sie müssten wegen ... Maßnahmen ergreifen. Sein Assistent fügte hinzu, dass die Großaktionäre schon ungeduldig würden. / die Großaktionäre würden schon ungeduldig.

Seite 130/131
Nomen-Verb-Verbindungen

1 Klaus O., Journalist: „Immer mehr Menschen vertreten die Ansicht, man sollte Abschied nehmen von der Vorstellung, dass man ein Tier haben kann, das andere Menschen in Gefahr bringt. Die Politik sollte endlich die passenden Maßnahmen ergreifen."
Sigmund M., Psychologe: „Ich bin zu der Auffassung gelangt, dass ein Verbot auf überzeugte Kampfhundbesitzer keinen großen Eindruck machen würde. Darüber muss man sich im Klaren sein. Eher sollte man ‚Wieder-

holungstäter' <u>unter</u> psychologische <u>Beobachtung stellen</u>."

Jan R., Kampfhundbesitzer: „Also ich finde ein Verbot total übertrieben. Nach den Unfällen müssen wir Kampfhundbesitzer sicherlich ein paar Einschränkungen <u>in Kauf nehmen</u>. Und man muss natürlich auch <u>die Frage stellen</u>, wer überhaupt qualifiziert ist, solche Tiere zu besitzen."

2 a) Tausende brasilianische Landarbeiter sind in Streik getreten / traten in Streik ... [Vorsicht: Tempus im Übungssatz Präsens, im Lösungssatz Perfekt oder Präteritum!] b) Vertreter der ASEAN-Staaten haben den Beschluss gefasst ... c) Noch ist völlig unklar, ob die EU und die USA in allen strittigen Punkten einen Kompromiss erzielen werden. d) ... ab wann die verschärften Umweltvorschriften in Kraft treten sollen. e) Die russische Regierung trifft Vorbereitungen zur Bergung eines abgestürzten Flugzeugs im Kaukasus. Experten ziehen den Erfolg dieses Plans in Zweifel.

3 ich muss ein Thema ansprechen, das mir sehr unangenehm ist. Ich habe gehört, dass Sie ihre Wohnung seit einiger Zeit untervermieten. Ich muss Ihnen mitteilen, dass ich Ihnen das nie erlaubt habe, und möchte Sie bitten, sich zu diesem Punkt unverzüglich zu äußern. Außerdem werden Sie verdächtigt / verdächtigt man Sie, dass Sie auf ihrem Balkon Marihuana anpflanzen. So etwas wird bestraft! Ein Nachbar hat Ihre letzte Ernte fotografiert. Außerdem wird Ihnen vorgeworfen, dass Sie nach 22 Uhr noch laute Musik hören und die Interessen der übrigen Hausbewohner nicht berücksichtigen. Wir sollten uns über alle Punkte so schnell wie möglich ernsthaft unterhalten.

Seite 132/133
Hauptsatz

1

Position 0	Position 1	Position 2
Und	so	fragen
Aber	es	kann
–	Es	dauert
Denn	Tag für Tag	lassen
–	In unserem Land	muss

2 b) ... In jeder Stunde gibt es in Deutschland ... c) Das ist der Preis für unsere Mobilität. d) Bei einem Zug ist hundertprozentige Sicherheit nicht möglich. e) In einem Auto mit Airbags haben wir auch ... f) Neue

Technik garantiert nicht automatisch ein besseres Leben. g) Denn der Fortschritt bringt auch viele Gefahren. h) Aber wir denken meistens nicht an diese Folgen. i) Und wir wollen auch nichts davon hören.

3 b) Weil mein Fahrrad kaputt ist, wollte ich mit der S-Bahn fahren. c) Gegen zwei Uhr nachmittags stand ich am Bahnsteig. d) Über vierzig Minuten wartete ich auf die S-Bahn. e) Nach einer halben Stunde wurde ich langsam sauer. f) Als die S-Bahn endlich kam, war ich fast eingeschlafen. g) Eine so lange Wartezeit finde ich unzumutbar.

4 ... Ich habe ihn in dem ICE um 17.33 Uhr von München nach Frankfurt liegen lassen und möchte Sie fragen, ob jemand den Mantel bei Ihnen abgegeben hat. Er ist grün und aus Wolle, in der Tasche des Mantels steckte ein roter Schal. Bitte schicken Sie mir den Mantel, wenn das möglich ist, oder lassen Sie mir eine Nachricht zukommen, wenn ich den Mantel selber abholen soll. Selbstverständlich übernehme ich die Kosten für das Porto. ...

Seite 135
Mittelfeld des Satzes

1 b) Ihr Kollege macht uns Fotokopien von den Unterlagen. c) Sie beantwortet mir alle meine Fragen. d) Herr Meier bringt uns die vermisste Diskette. e) Die Trainerin erklärt meiner Kollegin die Möglichkeiten des Programms. f) Wir schenken der Kursleiterin einen Blumenstrauß.

2 b) Ihr Kollege macht uns bis morgen Fotokopien von den Unterlagen. c) Sie beantwortet mir sofort alle meine Fragen. d) Herr Meier bringt uns gleich die vermisste Diskette. e) Die Trainerin erklärt meiner Kollegin noch einmal die Möglichkeiten des Programms. f) Wir schenken der Kursleiterin am Kursende einen Blumenstrauß.

3 b) Ihr Kollege macht sie uns bis morgen. c) Sie beantwortet sie mir sofort. d) Herr Meier bringt sie uns gleich. e) Die Trainerin erklärt sie meiner Kollegin noch einmal. f) Wir schenken ihn der Kursleiterin am Kursende.

4 b) es dir c) es Ihnen d) sie Ihnen e) ihn dir f) es Ihnen

5 b) Bei gutem Wetter verlässt sie um Viertel nach acht das Haus. / Um Viertel nach acht

verlässt sie bei gutem Wetter das Haus. c) Bei gutem Wetter fährt sie normalerweise mit dem Fahrrad. / Normalerweise fährt sie bei gutem Wetter mit dem Fahrrad. d) In einem Einkaufszentrum erledigt Elsa nach der Arbeit ihre Einkäufe. / Nach der Arbeit erledigt Elsa ihre Einkäufe in einem Einkaufszentrum. e) In einem Fitnesscenter für Frauen treibt sie zweimal pro Woche Sport. Zweimal pro Woche treibt sie in einem Fitnesscenter für Frauen Sport. f) In einem Kurbad macht sie am Wochenende mit zwei Freundinnen Wassergymnastik. / Am Wochenende macht sie mit zwei Freundinnen in einem Kurbad Wassergymnastik. g) Samstagabends sieht sie sich gerne in einem der großen Kinos der Stadt die neuesten Filme an. / In einem der großen Kinos der Stadt sieht sie sich samstagabends gerne die neuesten Filme an. h) Mindestens einmal pro Monat leistet sich Elsa trotz knapper Kasse ein Abendessen im Restaurant. / Trotz knapper Kasse leistet Else sich mindestens einmal pro Monat ein Abendessen im Restaurant.

Seite 136/137
Negation

1 Sie hat eine Zentralheizung, Wohnung 1 hat keine. Sie hat ein Bad, Wohnung 1 hat keins. Sie hat ein separates WC, Wohnung 1 hat keins. Sie hat eine Einbau-Küche, Wohnung 1 hat keine. Sie hat eine Abstellkammer, Wohnung 1 hat keine. Sie hat einen Balkon, Wohnung 1 hat keinen.

2 a) Ist Matthias berufstätig? – Nein, er ist nicht berufstätig. Hat Hannah Geld gespart? – Nein, sie hat kein Geld gespart. War Hannah schon mal in Polen? – Nein, sie war noch nicht in Polen. Kann Matthias Fremdsprachen? – Nein, er kann keine Fremdsprachen. Hat Hannah Freunde in Deutschland? – Nein, sie hat keine Freunde in Deutschland. Hat Matthias eine E-Mail-Adresse? – Nein, er hat keine E-Mail-Adresse.
b) Hannah ist berufstätig, Matthias noch nicht. Hannah hat kein Geld gespart, Matthias auch noch nicht. Matthias war schon mal in Polen, aber Hannah noch nicht. Hannah kann Fremdsprachen, aber Matthias kann noch keine. Matthias hat Freunde in Deutschland, Hannah (hat) noch keine.

Hannah hat eine E-Mail-Adresse, aber Matthias hat noch keine.

3 b) Nein, davon habe ich noch nichts gehört. c) Nein, ich habe leider keine. d) Nein, ich kenne keins. e) Nein, den kenne ich nicht. f) Nein, dafür braucht man keine. g) Nein, die muss man nicht aufziehen. h) Nein, davon verstehe ich nichts. i) Nein, ich habe sie nicht gesehen.

4 (b) keine (c) nicht/nie (d) nichts (e) kein

Seite 139
Imperativ (1)

1 <u>Überprüfen Sie</u> vor einer Reise Ihren Pass und <u>lassen Sie</u> ihn eventuell rechtzeitig verlängern. Wenn Sie in Hauptreisezeiten fliegen wollen: <u>Beeilen Sie sich</u> mit der Buchung ihres Fluges oder Hotels. <u>Ziehen Sie</u> bei einem längeren Flug bequeme Kleidung <u>an</u>. <u>Schließen Sie</u> Ihre Wertsachen im Hotelsafe <u>ein</u>. <u>Rufen Sie</u> Ihre Lieben zu Hause <u>an</u>, wenn Sie am Ziel angekommen sind.

2 b) Falten Sie die Serviette nicht nach Gebrauch. c) Halten Sie die Gabel in der linken und das Messer in der rechten Hand. d) Schließen Sie die Lippen beim Kauen. e) Verwenden Sie die kleine Gabel für den Kuchen. f) Fassen Sie das Weinglas am Stiel an. g) Verdecken Sie die rechte mit der linken Hand, wenn Sie einen Zahnstocher benutzen. h) Verlassen Sie nicht den Tisch, bevor alle fertig gegessen haben.

3 b) Seid/Sei c) Esst/Iss d) Putzt/Putz e) Spült/Spül f) Verwendet/Verwende g) Kontrolliert/Kontrollier(e)

4 b) Trink täglich mindestens zwei Liter Flüssigkeit. c) Treib zweimal pro Woche Sport. d) Schlaf acht Stunden täglich. e) Achte beim Einkauf auf gesunde Lebensmittel. f) Verzichte möglichst auf Alkohol.

Seite 140/141
Imperativ (2)

1 b) Würdest du dich bitte rasieren? Könntest du dich bitte mal rasieren? Rasier dich endlich! c) Würdest du dich bitte waschen? Könntest du dich bitte mal waschen? Wasch

dich endlich! d) Würdest du dich bitte duschen? Könntest du dich bitte mal duschen? Dusch dich endlich! e) Würdest du dich bitte anziehen? Könntest du dich bitte mal anziehen? Zieh dich endlich an! f) Würdest du dich bitte frisieren? Könntest du dich bitte mal frisieren? Frisier dich endlich! g) Würdest du dich bitte kämmen? Könntest du dich bitte mal kämmen? Kämm dich endlich!
h) Würdest du dich bitte beeilen? Könntest du dich bitte mal beeilen? Beeil dich endlich!
i) Würdest du bitte den Regenschirm mitnehmen? Könntest du bitte den Regenschirm mitnehmen? Nimm den Regenschirm mit!

2 (b) Legen Sie dann die Wäsche in die Maschine hinein. (c) Schließen Sie dann die Tür. (d) Kontrollieren Sie dann, ob der Stecker ... (e) Drehen Sie anschließend den Wasserhahn auf. (f) Lassen Sie als Nächstes das Waschpulver einlaufen. (g) Wählen Sie dann das gewünschte Programm. (h) Stellen Sie schließlich die Temperatur ein und drücken Sie den Start-Knopf.

3 (b) Rühr drei Minuten. (c) Schäl die Äpfel. (d) Entkerne drei Äpfel, schneid(e) sie in Würfel und heb sie unter den Teig. (e) Füll den Teig in eine Backform. (f) Schneid(e) den vierten Apfel in Scheiben und leg ihn auf den Teig. (g) Schieb die Form in den Backofen und back den Kuchen.

4 b) Sie sollten das Papier vor dem Klingeln von dem Blumenstrauß entfernen. Man entfernt das Papier vor dem Klingeln von dem Blumenstrauß. c) Sie sollten das Papier in die eigene Tasche stecken. Man steckt das Papier in die eigene Tasche. d) Sie sollten die Gastgeber mit Händedruck begrüßen. Man begrüßt die Gastgeber mit Händedruck. e) Sie sollten saubere, möglichst gebügelte Sachen und geputzte Schuhe tragen. Man trägt saubere, möglichst gebügelte Sachen und geputzte Schuhe. f) Sie sollten Ihre Schuhe anbehalten. Man behält seine Schuhe an. g) Sie sollten bei offiziellen Einladungen einen Anzug und eine Krawatte tragen. Man trägt bei offiziellen Einladungen einen Anzug und eine Krawatte.

5 b) Könntest du mir mal den Werkzeugkasten bringen? c) Suchst du mal bitte die Schrauben Nummer 5? d) Könntest du auch die passenden Dübel dazu suchen? e) Lauf doch mal in den Keller. f) Hol bitte die Bohrmaschine.

g) Könntest du bitte nachsehen, ob ein zweiter Werkzeugkasten dort ist?

Seite 142/143
Fragesatz

1 b) Ja./Nein. c) Nein./Doch. d) Ja./Nein. e) Ja./Nein. f) Ja./Nein. g) Die Faultiere./ Die Menschenaffen. h) Die Faultiere./Die Menschenaffen.

2 b) Haben Sie denn die Kellertür nicht abgeschlossen? c) Haben Sie denn den Schlüssel nicht zweimal herumgedreht? d) Haben Sie denn das Licht abends nicht brennen lassen? e) Haben sie denn die Alarmanlage nicht eingeschaltet? f) Haben Sie denn den Briefkasten nicht vom Nachbarn leeren lassen?

3 b) Ruf doch bitte bei der Theaterkasse an und frag, wann die Vorstellung zu Ende ist. c) Ruf doch bitte im Restaurant an und frag, ob noch ein Tisch frei ist. d) Ruf doch bitte im Fitness-Studio an und frag, wann / wie lange es geöffnet ist. e) Ruf doch bitte in der Bibliothek an und frag, ob das bestellte Buch schon da ist. f) Ruf doch bitte in der Volkshochschule an und frag, ob der Kurs schon angefangen hat.

4 b) Können Sie mir sagen, wo der Taxistand ist? c) Können Sie mir sagen, warum/weshalb die Straße gesperrt ist? d) Können Sie mir sagen, wie spät es ist? / wie viel Uhr es ist? e) Können Sie mir sagen, wann die Banken heute schließen? f) Können Sie mir sagen, wie hoch der Fernsehturm ist? g) Können Sie mir sagen, was sich in diesem Haus befindet? h) Können Sie mir sagen, wer hier wohnt?

5 b) ... von wem dieser Film ist? c) ... wer mitspielt? d) ... was kosten da eigentlich die Karten? e) ... in welchem Kino der Film läuft. f) ... wann die Vorstellung anfängt? g) ... wer noch mitgeht?

6 b) ... wie ich aussehe. c) ... was ich im Schrank finde. d) ... wo die Sachen liegen. e) ... wo ich sitze. f) ... wann ich schlafen gehe.

Seite 144/145
Fragewörter

1 b) Was ist passiert? c) Worüber bist du besorgt? d) Von wem hast du dir Geld geliehen? e) Was spürst du auf der Haut? f) Wen suchst du? g) Was hast du verloren? h) Wen habt ihr am Wochenende besucht? i) Wessen Mantel ist das?

2 b) Welche Farbe haben deine Augen? / Welche Augenfarbe hast du? / Wie ist deine Augenfarbe? c) Wie groß bist du? d) Wie schwer bist du? / Wie viel wiegst du? e) In welche Schule und in welche Klasse gehst du? f) Was ist dein liebstes Schulfach? / Welches Schulfach magst du am liebsten? g) Was ist dein Hobby? h) Was ist dein Lieblingstier? / Welches Tier magst du am liebsten? i) Was ist dein Lieblingsgericht? / Welches Gericht magst du am liebsten? / Was isst du am liebsten? j) Was magst du am liebsten?

3 (b) Welche (c) was (d) Welchen (e) was für einen (f) welche / was für (g) welches / was für ein

4 b) Worin c) Wozu d) Worüber f) Wovon g) Woraus h) Von wem i) Worum j) Woran k) Für wen l) Worüber m) Worum n) Über wen

Seite 146/147
Hauptsatzverbindende Konnektoren
1 (b) Von einem Autofahrer erfuhr er, dass an der Stelle kurz zuvor eine niederländische Familie gepicknickt hatte, und entschloss sich sofort, die Familie zu suchen. (c) Le Front brachte den Film in ein Fotolabor und ließ ihn entwickeln. (d) Auf den Bildern waren eine Frau und zwei Kinder zu sehen. (e) Er schickte die Fotos an die größte niederländische Zeitung und bat darum, sie zu veröffentlichen. (f) Am Freitag druckte *De Telegraaf* tatsächlich ein Bild der Frau ab und fragte: „Wem gehört dieses Foto?" (g) Nun hofft Le Front, dass die Frau das Foto sieht und (dass sie) sich meldet.

2 (b) Aber (c) denn (d) und (e) und (f) denn (g) sondern

3 b) Mein Mann kümmert sich nicht um Weihnachten, sondern geht nur mit dem Hund spazieren. c) ... Das war schon immer meine Angelegenheit, und das wird weiterhin so bleiben. d) ... Gott sei Dank weiß ich ungefähr, was ich meiner Frau schenken werde, aber der Stress bleibt einfach bis zum 24. Dezember. e) ... Sie rühren keinen Finger und erwarten, / erwarten aber, dass zu Weihnachten alles da ist, Christbaum, Geschenke, selbst gebackene Plätzchen.

Seite 149
Nebensatz
1 a) Vater und Mütter oft berufstätig sind. [1] b) sie ein Vorbild brauchen. [3] c) schon etwas passiert ist. [3] d) Sie ein teures Spielzeug kaufen, [2]

2 Es ärgert mich wahnsinnig, <u>wenn</u> Leute <u>behaupten</u>, es ginge ihnen schlecht, nur <u>weil</u> sie in einer Mietwohnung <u>leben</u> und nur einmal im Jahr in den Urlaub fahren <u>können</u>. Das zeigt doch, <u>dass</u> unsere Gesellschaft übersättigt <u>ist</u>! Die Erwachsenen sollten Konsumterror und Markenverrücktheit nicht als Problem der Jugend sehen. Es ist doch nur peinlich, <u>wenn</u> Erwachsene sich gegenseitig <u>bedauern</u>, <u>weil</u> sie Opel statt Mercedes <u>fahren</u>. Ich finde es schlimm, <u>wenn</u> man sich in Deutschland und fast allen anderen Industrienationen mit solchen Problemen <u>beschäftigt</u>, <u>während</u> in manchen Ländern Tausende von Menschen heimatlos durch die Gegend <u>irren</u> oder bei Katastrophen <u>sterben</u>.

3 b) Als sie zum Bahnhof kam, ... c) ... wenn sie Zeit und Lust hat. d) ... obwohl sie ihn regelmäßig besucht. e) ... seit er eine Freundin hat. f) Bevor ich nach Hause gehe, ...

4 b) Nachdem er eine Ausstellung besucht hat, liest er zu Hause in seinem Katalog wichtige Informationen nach. c) Obwohl er alle wichtigen Bauwerke in seiner Stadt kennt, entdeckt er immer wieder neue Kunstschätze. d) Bevor er Reisen macht, kauft er sich einen guten Kunstführer. e) Während viele Leute nicht wissen, was sie in ihrer Freizeit tun sollen, wird es Franz nie langweilig.

Seite 151
dass-Satz
1 dass sie gesünder essen und weniger rauchen. ... sagten, dass sie ziemlich körperbewusst seien.

2 (b) Ich denke / finde nicht, dass Hausarbeit nichts für einen Mann ist. (c) Ich finde nicht / denke, dass man mit seinem Partner eine Ehe auf Probe versuchen sollte, bevor man sich für eine Hochzeit entscheidet. (d) Ich finde nicht / denke, dass Frauen zuerst einen Beruf haben sollten, bevor sie heiraten.

(e) Ich denke / finde nicht, dass Kinder die beste Altersvorsorge sind. (f) Ich finde nicht / denke, dass Singles glücklicher sind als Menschen in einer festen Partnerschaft.

3   b) Mich überzeugt nicht, dass Latein die wichtigste Fremdsprache überhaupt ist. c) Ich finde auch, dass es gut ist, wenn man mehrere Fremdsprachen kann. d) Ich bin davon überzeugt, dass in Zukunft Fremdsprachen immer wichtiger werden.

4   b) Ist es wahr, dass Theo schon wieder beim Pferderennen verloren hat? c) Hast du auch gehört, dass Iris demnächst auf Weltreise geht? d) Das darf doch nicht wahr sein, dass Tobias sich scheiden lassen will.

5   b) Unsere Analyse hat gezeigt, dass es eine Marktlücke in diesem Bereich gibt. c) Wir hoffen, dass wir das Programm in wenigen Monaten auf dem Markt platzieren können. d) Unsere Werbung hat das Ziel, dass Eltern auf das Produkt aufmerksam werden. e) Sie müssen das Gefühl haben, dass sie etwas Gutes für ihre Kinder kaufen.

Seite 153
Infinitiv + zu

1   b) Er versucht / nimmt sich vor, abzunehmen. c) Er versucht / nimmt sich vor, bequemere Kleidung zu tragen. d) Er versucht / nimmt sich vor, mehr Vitamine zu sich zu nehmen. e) Er versucht / nimmt sich vor, weniger zu rauchen. f) Er versucht / nimmt sich vor, weniger fernzusehen. g) Er versucht / nimmt sich vor, zweimal pro Woche zu joggen.

2   b) Wir hatten eigentlich vor, mit der Bahn zu fahren. c) Wir hatten eigentlich vor, allein zu reisen. d) Wir hatten eigentlich vor, sie zu Hause zu lassen. e) Wir hatten eigentlich vor, vor Ort eins auszuleihen.

3   b) Es ist verboten / nicht erlaubt, zu rauchen. c) Es ist verboten / nicht erlaubt, den Rasen zu betreten. d) Es ist verboten / nicht erlaubt, sich aus dem Fenster zu lehnen. e) Es ist verboten / nicht erlaubt, hier durchzugehen.

4   b) Ich schlage ihr vor / rate ihr, das Spiel beim Nachbarn anzusehen. c) Ich schlage ihr vor / rate ihr, einen Passanten um Hilfe zu bitten. d) Ich schlage ihr vor / rate ihr, den Schuh auszuziehen. e) Ich schlage ihm vor / rate ihm, anzurufen und Bescheid zu sagen.

5   b) Ich erinnere mich, Ihnen vor ein paar Wochen geschrieben zu haben. c) Ich kann mich nicht erinnern, Sie schon einmal gesehen zu haben. d) Ich glaube, bald mehr sagen zu können. e) Ich hoffe, den Auftrag bald fertig zu haben.

Seite 155
Relativsatz (1)

1   b) Ein Schulkind ist ein Kind, das zur Schule geht. c) Ein Fotograf ist jemand, der Fotos macht. d) Ein Koch ist jemand, der Essen zubereitet. e) Eine Medizinstudentin ist eine Frau, die Medizin studiert.

2   b) ... der treu ist. c) ... die mit ihm auf den Fußballplatz geht. d) ... die viel Humor hat. e) ... auf den sie sich verlassen kann. f) ... für den sie nicht waschen und bügeln muss. g) ... der er vertraut. h) ... mit der er fünf Kinder haben kann.

3   b) die c) die d) den e) der

4   (b) denen (c) der (d) denen (e) dem

5   b) Die Maus ist in eine Falle gegangen, die mit Speck präpariert war. / ... Falle, die mit Speck präpariert war, gegangen. c) In unserem Gelände gibt es Pinguine, die frei herumlaufen. d) Der Eisbär, der ausgebrochen war [Plusquamperfekt], ist wieder eingefangen.

Seite 156/157
Relativsatz (2)

1   b) Hast du alles verstanden, was du gelesen hast? c) Hast du alles mitbekommen, was die Lehrerin erklärt hat? d) Hast du alles gelernt, was die Lehrerin aufgegeben hat? e) Hast du alles verbessert, was du falsch gemacht hast? f) Hast du alles notiert, was der Lehrer diktiert hat?

2   (b) was (c) wo (d) was (e) wohin (f) was (g) was (h) wo/wohin (i) Was (j) Wer

3   b) In der Nähe eines Waldes, wo / in dem man gut spazieren gehen kann. c) In einem Fischerdorf am Meer, wo / in dem es keine Hotels gibt. d) In einem kleineren Ort, wo / in dem sich die Leute noch mit Namen kennen. e) In einer Gegend, wo / in der die Menschen noch natürlich und freundlich sind. f) Auf einer Insel, wo / auf der keine Autos fahren dürfen. g) Nahe bei einem Fitnesscenter, wo / in dem man bis spätabends

trainieren kann. h) In einer Kleinstadt, wo / in der es noch alte Gebäude gibt. i) In einer Stadt, wo / in der man verschiedene Kinos zur Auswahl hat.

4 b) ... verändert, was mich sehr überrascht hat. c) ... zugenommen, was sicherlich an ihrem Beruf als Köchin liegt. d) ... mitgebracht, was ich sehr nett fand. e) ... gelassen, was wir alle drei gut fanden. f) ... getrennt, was ich noch nicht wusste. g) ... hinweg, was mich ein wenig überrachte.

5 b) ... ständig, was verständlich ist. c) ... Preis, was wir endlich einsehen müssen. d) ... Lebensmittel, was zunehmend zum Problem wird. e) ... natürlich, worauf Tierschützer immer wieder aufmerksam machen. f) ... gesehen, was schon lange bekannt ist. g) ... transportiert, wogegen Tierschützer protestieren.

Seite 159
Aufzählung

1 (b) sondern (c) auch (d) und (e) und / sowie (f) nicht nur (g) sondern (h) auch (i) und (j) sowohl / nicht nur (k) als auch / sondern auch (l) sowohl / nicht nur (m) und (n) als auch / sondern auch (o) und

2 (b) noch (c) sowohl (d) als auch (e) nicht nur (f) sondern auch

3 Sowohl Mozart als auch Schubert sind in Österreich geboren.
   Maria Theresia und Queen Victoria waren Königinnen. Sowohl Maria Theresia als auch Victoria waren glücklich verheiratet. Sowohl Maria Theresia als auch Victoria hatten viele Kinder. Nicht nur Maria Theresia, sondern auch Victoria hatte ein großes Reich zu regieren. Weder Victoria noch Maria Theresia waren langweilige Personen.
   Sowohl Goethe als auch Hesse waren Dichter. Sowohl Goethe als auch Hesse haben sich für fremde Kulturen interessiert. Nicht nur Goethe, sondern auch Hesse hat große Reisen unternommen. Beide haben sich sowohl für fremde Kulturen interessiert als auch große Reisen unternommen. Weder Goethe noch Hesse waren arme Poeten.
   Sowohl Aschenputtel als auch Schneewittchen sind Märchenfiguren. Nicht nur

Aschenputtel, sondern auch Schneewittchen hatte eine böse Stiefmutter. Über Aschenputtel und Schneewittchen hat Walt Disney einen Film gemacht. / Walt Disney hat sowohl über Aschenputtel als auch über Schneewittchen einen Film gemacht. Die beiden hatten weder eine glückliche Kindheit noch haben sie Hilfe von ihren Vätern erhalten.

Seite 160/161
Alternativen

1 (b) oder (c) statt (d) entweder (e) oder (f) stattdessen (g) Entweder (h) oder (i) stattdessen

2 b) Ich fahre mit dem Fahrrad, (an)statt den Bus oder das Auto zu nehmen. c) Ich leihe die Skier lieber aus, (an)statt selber welche zu kaufen. d) Ich jogge täglich, (an)statt Mitglied im Fitnessklub zu werden. e) Ich färbe oder bemale T-Shirts selber, (an)statt sie in der Boutique zu kaufen. f) Ich wohne am Stadtrand, (an)statt in der Innenstadt zu wohnen und hohe Mieten zu zahlen.

3 b) Ich kaufe kaum noch Fleisch. Stattdessen koche ich öfter Fisch. c) Ich sehe nicht mehr drei Stunden täglich fern. Stattdessen höre ich öfter mal Musik. d) Ich mache weniger Überstunden. Stattdessen verbringe ich mehr Zeit mit meinen Freunden. e) Ich trinke weniger Kaffee. Stattdessen trinke ich eine Kanne Früchtetee pro Tag. f) Ich verzichte oft auf ein warmes Mittagessen. Stattdessen esse ich mittags nur ein Sandwich.

4 b) Ich muss meinen Aufsatz fertig schreiben. Stattdessen würde ich jetzt lieber den Film zu Ende sehen. c) Ich muss jetzt schlafen gehen. Stattdessen würde ich jetzt lieber mein Buch weiterlesen. d) Ich muss meine E-Mails beantworten. Stattdessen würde ich jetzt lieber einen Mittagsschlaf machen. e) Ich muss nach Hause gehen. Stattdessen würde ich jetzt lieber noch ein Glas Wein bestellen. f) Ich muss das Essen machen. Stattdessen würde ich jetzt lieber meine Lieblingssendung im Radio hören.

Seite 163
Temporalsatz (1)

1 Sie war 23, als sie das Erste Staatsexamen machte. Sie war 25, als sie das Zweite Staats-

examen machte. Sie war 26, als sie heiratete. Sie war 30, als sie das erste Kind bekam. Sie war 33, als sie wieder in den Beruf einstieg / eingestiegen ist.

2   b) Wann hast du den Schlüssel vermisst? Erst als ich die Wohnungstür aufschließen wollte. c) Wann hast du die Brieftasche vermisst? Erst als ich den Ausweis rausnehmen wollte. d) Wann hast du die Kamera vermisst? Erst als ich den Film einlegen wollte. e) Wann hast du die Scheckkarte vermisst? Erst als ich an der Kasse war.

3   b) Wann schaffst du dir endlich ein gutes Wörterbuch an? Erst wenn ich in der Mittelstufe bin. c) Wann schaffst du dir endlich einen Computer an? Erst wenn ich mein neues Arbeitszimmer einrichte. d) Wann schaffst du dir endlich ein neues Radio an? Erst wenn das alte ganz kaputt ist.

4   b) Als wir gestern am Flughafen ankamen, war die Maschine schon weg. c) Immer wenn ich zu früh zum Flughafen kam, hatte das Flugzeug Verspätung. d) Als Frau Huber ihren Pass vorzeigen wollte, fand sie ihn nicht in ihrer Handtasche. e) Als Herr Martens in der Maschine zu seinem Platz kam, saß jemand anderes dort. f) Immer wenn / Wenn ich verreist war, sind meine Pflanzen zu Hause (immer) vertrocknet.

5   b) Als Hermann im ersten Lebensjahr untersucht wurde, waren die Ärzte besorgt. c) Als er 18 Monate alt war, wog er so viel wie andere Kinder in diesem Alter. d) Als er zwei Jahre alt war, konnte er bereits ganze Sätze sprechen. e) Als er eingeschult wurde, / Als er in die Schule kam, sah man kaum noch Unterschiede zu seinen Mitschülern.

Seite 165
Temporalsatz (2)

1   b) Der Einbrecher kam, während wir schliefen. c) ..., während wir im Garten arbeiteten. d) ..., während wir vor dem Fernseher saßen. e) ..., während wir im Kino waren. f) ..., während wir das Abendessen machten.

2   b) Bitte schalten Sie die elektronischen Geräte aus, während das Flugzeug landet. c) Bitte machen Sie keinen Lärm, während die Nachbarn Mittagspause machen. d) Bitte lehnen Sie sich nicht aus dem Fenster, während der Zug fährt. e) Bitte sprechen Sie

nicht, während die Vorstellung läuft. f) Bitte stören Sie nicht, während der Gast schläft.

3   (b) seit/seitdem (c) Bis (d) Seit/Seitdem (e) seit (f) bis (g) bis (h) Bis

4   b) Solange Barbara noch studiert, kann sie mit ihrem Studentenausweis viel Geld sparen. Den Ausweis kann sie behalten, bis sie das Studium beendet hat. c) Solange Dennis noch keinen festen Job hat, wohnt er bei seinen Eltern. d) Solange Evelyns Kinder zur Schule gehen, bleibt die Familie in diesem Stadtteil. Mit dem Umzug wartet sie, bis die Kinder die Schule wechseln. e) Petra lebte in einer Wohngemeinschaft, bis sie Peter kennenlernte.

5   b) Bis die Tarifverhandlungen abgeschlossen sind, bleiben die Unternehmer zurückhaltend. c) Seit(dem) die Inflationsrate angestiegen ist, sind die Chancen der Unternehmen gesunken. d) Bis die Staatsschulden zurückgegangen sind / zurückgehen, bleiben die Aussichten schlecht. e) Seit(dem) die Öko-Steuer eingeführt ist/wurde, ist die Stimmung negativ. f) Bis die Steuergesetze reformiert sind, halten sich die Investoren zurück.

Seite 167
Temporalsatz (3)

1   b) Bevor/Ehe ich den Bus nehme, kaufe ich noch rasch etwas für das Abendessen ein. c) Bevor/Ehe ich mich fertig mache, lese ich die Zeitung. d) Bevor/Ehe ich aufräume, gebe ich den Fischen noch etwas zu fressen. e) Bevor/Ehe ich das Haus verlasse, räume ich noch schnell auf. f) Bevor/Ehe ich Müsli esse, jogge ich im Park.

2   b) Trinken Sie ein Glas Tee, bevor Sie schlafen gehen. c) Nehmen Sie ein Glas Wasser zu sich, bevor Sie essen. d) Machen Sie Frühsport oder Gymnastik, bevor Sie frühstücken. e) Machen Sie einige Stretching-Übungen, bevor Sie joggen.

3   b) Ich ziehe hier aus, sobald ich eine neue Wohnung gefunden habe. c) Ich rufe bei Freunden an, sobald ich die Hausaufgaben gemacht habe. d) Wir können essen, sobald der Tisch gedeckt ist. e) Wir gehen nach Hause, sobald die Schule aus ist. f) Wir zahlen, sobald die Rechnung geschrieben ist. g) Wir frühstücken, sobald wir Gymnastik gemacht haben.

4   b) Nachdem Sie fünf Jahre studiert hatte, legte sie das Erste Staatsexamen ab. c) Nachdem Sie das Staatsexamen gemacht hatte, begann sie die Referendarausbildung an einer Schule. d) Nachdem sie die Referendarausbildung beendet hatte, machte sie das Zweite Staatsexamen. e) Nachdem sie die Ausbildung beendet hatte, heiratete sie. f) Nachdem sie zwei Jahre verheiratet war, bekam sie das erste Kind.

5   (b) Nachdem (c) Bevor (d) Bevor (e) nachdem (f) Bevor

Seite 169
Kausalsatz

1   b) Weil ich den ganzen Nachmittag Kopfschmerzen hatte. c) Weil ich erschöpft war und vor Müdigkeit eingeschlafen bin. d) Weil mein Füller plötzlich nicht mehr funktioniert hat. e) Weil mein Freund meine Schultasche versteckt hat. f) Weil mein Hund das Aufgabenblatt gefressen hat.

2   b) A c) C d) B

3   b) Weil/Da Doro unbedingt bessere Noten braucht, lernt sie täglich drei Stunden.
c) Sandra übt täglich noch mehr, weil/da sie nicht mehr so gute Noten hat. d) Weil/Da Dennis neue Lehrerin so wenig Hausaufgaben aufgibt, findet er sie super. e) Weil/Da Nico sich nicht konzentrieren kann, ist er durch die Prüfung gefallen. f) Latein ist Kims Lieblingsfach, weil/da sie da etwas über die alten Römer erfährt. g) Weil/Da die Eltern an die Zukunft ihrer Kinder denken, sind ihnen Schulerfolge sehr wichtig.

4   b) Aufgrund eines Stipendiums kann Isabella einen Deutschkurs in Österreich besuchen.
c) Aufgrund eines hervorragenden Zeugnisses kann Sofia studieren, was sie möchte. d) Wegen/Aufgrund ihrer schlechten Noten kann Amelie nicht Medizin studieren.
e) Wegen/Aufgrund großer Probleme mit einem Lehrer hat Tobias die Schule verlassen. f) Wegen/Aufgrund akuten Schülermangels wird die Schule in unserem Dorf geschlossen.

Seite 170/171
Konditionalsatz

1   b) Sie brauchen Kontaktlinsen, wenn Sie die Brille beim Joggen stört. c) Sie brauchen ein Modem, wenn Sie im Internet surfen wollen. d) Sie brauchen ein Handy, wenn Sie außer Haus Anrufe annehmen wollen. e) Sie brauchen einen stärkeren Computer, wenn Sie moderne Computerspiele ausprobieren wollen. f) Sie brauchen einen besseren Wecker, wenn Sie pünktlich zur Arbeit kommen wollen. g) Sie brauchen einen Videorekorder, wenn Sie Fernsehsendungen aufzeichnen wollen.

2   b) Stört Sie die Brille beim Joggen, brauchen Sie Kontaktlinsen. c) Wollen Sie im Internet surfen, brauchen Sie ein Modem. d) Wollen Sie außer Haus Anrufe annehmen, brauchen Sie ein Handy. e) Wollen Sie moderne Computerspiele ausprobieren, brauchen Sie einen stärkeren Computer. f) Wollen Sie pünktlich zur Arbeit kommen, brauchen Sie einen besseren Wecker. g) Wollen Sie Fernsehsendungen aufzeichnen, brauchen Sie einen Videorekorder.

3   b) ... auf, sonst darfst du nicht schwimmen gehen. c) ... Hände, sonst bekommst du kein Abendessen. d) ... an, sonst erkältest du dich. e) ... Krach, sonst beschweren sich die Nachbarn wieder. f) ... Schwester, sonst bin ich nicht nett zu dir.

4   (b) Wenn/Falls/Sofern du Lust hast, gehen wir in die Picasso-Ausstellung. (c) Wenn/Falls/Sofern du Lust hast, sehen wir uns das neue Kabarettprogramm an. (d) Wenn/Falls/Sofern ich Zeit habe, besuche ich noch meine Freundin Elke. (e) Wenn/Falls/Sofern ich Zeit habe, lese ich noch meine E-Mails. (f) Wenn/Falls/Sofern ich Zeit habe, gehe ich endlich mal richtig gut essen. (g) Wenn/Falls/Sofern ich Zeit habe, räume ich endlich mal mein Zimmer auf. (h) Wenn/Falls/Sofern du Geld brauchst, such dir einen Job in einem Lokal. (i) Wenn/Falls/Sofern du Geld brauchst, leih dir etwas von deinen Eltern. (j) Wenn/ Falls/ Sofern du Geld brauchst, hol dir welches an dem Bankautomaten.

5   b) Wenn der Strom ausfällt, benutze ich eine Taschenlampe. c) Wenn unerwartet Gäste

kommen, serviere ich Getränke. d) Wenn ich auf der Straße einen alten Klassenkameraden treffe, verabrede ich ein Treffen. e) Wenn ich nichts zu Hause habe und die Geschäfte in der Nähe geschlossen sind, fahre ich mit dem Auto zu einer Tankstelle.

6   b) Wenn es heute noch schneit, ... / Schneit es heute noch, ... c) Wenn das Wetter schlecht ist, gehen ... / Ist das Wetter schlecht, gehen ... / Sollte das Wetter schlecht sein, gehen ... d) Wenn der Pullover nicht warm genug ist, ... / Ist der Pullover nicht warm genug, ... e) Wenn Sie in der Nacht frieren, ... / Frieren Sie in der Nacht, ...

Seite 172/173
Finalsatz

1   b) ... Büro, um das Fahrgeld für den Bus zu sparen. c) ... Sonderangebote, um bloß kein Geld zu verschwenden. d) Um Strom zu sparen, dreht er nie ... e) ... Notizen, um nicht so viel Papier zu verbrauchen. f) ... 120 Kilometer, um Benzin zu sparen. g) Um weniger Steuern zu zahlen, hat er neulich geheiratet.

2   b) Bewegen Sie sich täglich eine Stunde im Freien, um fit zu bleiben. / Um fit zu bleiben, sollten Sie sich täglich eine Stunde im Freien bewegen. c) Steigen Sie Treppen, statt Lift zu fahren, um ein gesundes Herz zu behalten. / Um ein gesundes Herz zu behalten, sollten Sie Treppen steigen, statt Lift zu fahren. d) Gehen Sie regelmäßig ins Fitnessstudio, um Muskeln aufzubauen. / Um Muskeln aufzubauen, sollten Sie regelmäßig ins Fitnessstudio gehen. e) Essen Sie so wenig tierisches Fett wie möglich, um Fett abzubauen. / Um Fett abzubauen, sollten Sie so wenig tierisches Fett wie möglich essen. f) Gehen Sie im Winter einmal wöchentlich in die Sauna, um Erkältungen zu vermeiden. / Um Erkältungen zu vermeiden, sollten Sie im Winter einmal wöchentlich in die Sauna gehen. g) Trinken Sie vor dem Schlafengehen Milch, um die Nerven zu beruhigen. / Um die Nerven zu beruhigen, sollten Sie vor dem Schlafengehen Milch trinken. h) Kaufen Sie die richtige Matratze, um gut zu schlafen. / Um gut zu schlafen, sollten Sie die richtige Matratze kaufen.

3   c) Was Ärzte alles tun, um Leben zu retten. d) Was Frauen alles tun, um schön zu sein. e) Was Männer alles tun, um einen muskulösen Körper zu bekommen. f) Was Mütter alles

tun, damit ihre Kinder genug Schlaf bekommen. g) Was Regierungen alles tun, um die Arbeitslosigkeit zu bekämpfen. h) Was Schüler alles tun, damit ihnen die Lehrer weniger Hausaufgaben aufgeben.

4   c) Manchmal lerne ich kurze Texte auswendig, um mir neue Sätze zu merken. d) Ich mache meine Hausaufgaben sorgfältig, um schneller Fortschritte zu machen. e) Ich schreibe übersichtlicher, um meine Notizen besser lesen zu können. f) Ich lerne täglich zehn neue Wörter, damit mein Wortschatz rasch wächst. g) Ich übe jeden Tag eine Viertelstunde, damit das Lernen nicht zu anstrengend wird.

Seite 174/175
Konsekutivsatz

1   b) ... ein Zeh so weh, dass er keinen Schuh mehr anziehen wollte. c) ... Bein so hart gegen etwas, dass es ganz blau wurde. d) ... ein derartiges Spannungsgefühl in der Brust, dass er nicht mehr richtig durchatmen konnte. e) ... waren derartig verspannt, dass er nicht länger als eine Stunde am Schreibtisch arbeiten konnte.

2   b) Die neue Lehrerin gibt wenig Hausaufgaben auf. Deswegen findet Dennis sie super. / Dennis findet sie deswegen super. c) Jana braucht unbedingt bessere Noten. Darum lernt sie täglich drei Stunden. / Sie lernt darum drei Stunden täglich. e) Nico hat letzte Nacht nur fünf Stunden geschlafen. Deshalb kann er sich nicht konzentrieren. / Er kann sich deshalb nicht konzentrieren. f) Sandra übt nicht mehr täglich. Folglich hat sie nicht mehr so gute Noten. / Sie hat folglich nicht mehr so gute Noten.
(jeweils möglich: deswegen/deshalb/darum/folglich)

3   b) Sie war glücklich. Infolgedessen sah sie über vieles hinweg. c) Er war unglücklich. Infolgedessen hatte er oft schlechte Laune. d) Sie hatte Geldsorgen. Infolgedessen fühlte sie sich oft unter Druck. e) Er hatte wenig Geld. Infolgedessen konnte er sich kaum etwas leisten. f) Sie war kinderlos. Infolgedessen stürzte sie sich voll auf die Arbeit.

4   b) Ich brauche etwas frische Luft, darum/deshalb/deswegen gehe ich noch eine halbe Stunde joggen. c) Ich hatte gestern hohes Fieber, darum/deshalb/deswegen konnte ich nicht in den

Kurs kommen. Ich hatte gestern hohes Fieber, sodass ich nicht in den Kurs kommen konnte. Ich hatte gestern so hohes Fieber, dass ich nicht in den Kurs kommen konnte. d) Ich bin etwas schüchtern, darum/deshalb/deswegen besuche ich eine Selbsterfahrungsgruppe. Ich bin etwas schüchtern, sodass ich eine Selbsterfahrungsgruppe besuche. Ich bin so schüchtern, dass ich eine Selbsterfahrungsgruppe besuche. e) Ich bin heute schlecht gelaunt, darum/deshalb/deswegen möchte ich keinen sehen. Ich bin heute schlecht gelaunt, sodass ich keinen sehen möchte. Ich bin heute so schlecht gelaunt, dass ich keinen sehen möchte. f) Ich habe eine Gehaltserhöhung bekommen, darum/deshalb/deswegen kann ich dich zum Essen einladen. Ich habe eine Gehaltserhöhung bekommen, sodass ich dich zum Essen einladen kann. g) Wir schreiben morgen einen Test, darum/deshalb/deswegen muss ich heute lernen. Wir schreiben morgen einen Test, sodass ich heute lernen muss.

5   b) Einer aus dem Sieger-Team des Vortages hatte einen Radschaden. Deshalb/Deswegen/Darum musste er aufgeben. c) Es gab ein Gewitter. Deshalb/Deswegen/Darum waren einige Straßen unpassierbar. d) Es gab ein Unwetter. Deshalb/Deswegen/Darum waren die Straßen spiegelglatt. e) Der Sieger des letzten Rennens hatte eine Verletzung / war verletzt. Deshalb/Deswegen/Darum konnte er nicht mehr an den Start gehen.

Seite 176/177
Konzessivsatz

1   b) Obwohl sie viel Zucker enthält, trinke ich ab und zu eine Cola. c) Obwohl es nicht gesund ist, verzichte ich nicht auf Salz. d) Obwohl ich viel Schokolade esse, bin ich nicht dick. e) Obwohl Obst besser ist, knabbere ich zum Fernsehen lieber Kartoffelchips. f) Obwohl der viele Rauch mir nicht guttut, gehe ich freitagabends in die Kneipe.

2   b) ... Trotzdem trinkt sie schon wieder Bier.
c) ... Trotzdem steht sie schon wieder auf.
d) ... Trotzdem raucht sie schon wieder.
e) ... Trotzdem isst sie schon wieder Schweinebraten.

3   b) Obwohl/Obgleich sie auf keinen Fall Alkohol trinken darf, trinkt sie schon wieder Bier. c) Obwohl/Obgleich sie eigentlich noch ein paar Tage im Bett bleiben müsste, steht sie schon wieder auf. d) Obwohl/Obgleich sie das Rauchen aufgeben soll, raucht sie schon wieder. e) Obwohl/Obgleich sie fünfmal am Tag Obst essen soll, isst sie schon wieder Schweinebraten.

4   (b) Trotzdem (c) obwohl (d) trotzdem (e) Obwohl (f) trotzdem (g) obwohl (h) trotz (i) Trotzdem (j) Obwohl (k) Trotz

5   b) ... Spielern, dennoch/trotzdem ist sie ein ernst zu nehmender Gegner. c) ... eindeutig, dennoch/trotzdem gab der Schiedsrichter Elfmeter. d) ... verloren, dennoch/trotzdem hat er noch eine Chance, ins Finale zu kommen. e) ... gehört, dennoch/trotzdem sind sie mir immer noch nicht klar. f) ... stark, dennoch/trotzdem wurden sie nie richtig gefährlich. g) ... Schwächen, dennoch/trotzdem siegte am Ende unsere Mannschaft.

6   b) Trotz des geringen Freizeitangebots haben wir uns nicht gelangweilt. c) Trotz der horrenden Preise haben wir unser Budget nicht überschritten. d) Trotz des kühlen Wetters haben wir im Meer gebadet. e) Trotz des miserablen Essens habe ich zugenommen.

Seite 179
Adversativsatz

1   c) Richard lebt allein, aber/doch er kommt mit dem Haushalt gut zurecht. / er kommt jedoch mit dem Haushalt gut zurecht. d) Daniel interessiert sich nicht für Computerspiele, sondern surft lieber im Internet. e) Charlotte ist geschieden, aber/doch sie sieht ihren Ex-Mann regelmäßig. / sie sieht ihren Ex-Mann jedoch regelmäßig. f) Julius ist alleinerziehender Vater, aber/doch er beklagt sich nie. / er beklagt sich jedoch nie. g) Eva liest nicht so gerne Bücher, sondern lieber Zeitschriften. h) Sandra hat viel Zeit, aber/doch sie weiß nichts damit anzufangen. / sie weiß jedoch nichts damit anzufangen.

2   b) Leute, die eine Wohnung besichtigen, haben oft kein echtes Interesse, sondern wollen nur die Preise vergleichen. c) Zum Besichtigungs-

termin war nicht der Vermieter gekommen, sondern der Mieter, der auszieht(, war da).
d) Zu der Besichtigung bin ich nicht allein gegangen, sondern habe eine Freundin mitgenommen. e) Die Energiekosten zählen nicht zur Miete, sondern zu den Nebenkosten.

3 b) Die Fenster gehen zur Straße raus, aber/doch man hört nichts vom Verkehr. / man hört aber nichts vom Verkehr. c) Die Wohnung hat eine gute Lage, aber/doch die Straße ist sehr laut. / die Straße ist aber sehr laut. d) Das Haus ist alt, aber/doch total renoviert. / ist aber total renoviert. e) Die Wohnung hat 100 Quadratmeter, aber/doch sie wirkt sehr klein und eng / wirkt aber sehr klein.
f) Die Wohnung hat einen Balkon, aber/doch sie ist sehr klein. / ist aber sehr klein.

4 (b) Im Gegensatz zu (c) dagegen (d) während (e) dagegen (f) während

Seite 181
Modalsatz

1 b) Der Lesetext war nicht so lang, wie ich befürchtet habe/hatte. c) Die Aufgaben waren so schwer, wie ich erwartet habe/hatte. d) Die Prüferin war netter, als ich erwartet habe/hatte. e) Die Prüfung dauerte länger, als ich es mir vorgestellt habe/hatte. f) Beim Hörverstehen wurde nicht so schnell gesprochen, wie ich befürchtet habe/hatte. g) Die Zeit verging schneller, als ich geglaubt habe/hatte. h) Ich war schneller fertig, als ich gehofft habe/hatte.

2 c) Die Aufgaben waren so schwer wie erwartet. d) Die Prüferin war netter als erwartet. f) Beim Hörverstehen wurde nicht so schnell gesprochen wie befürchtet.

3 b) Ich erweitere meinen Wortschatz, indem / dadurch, dass ich die Vokabeln regelmäßig wiederhole. c) Ich erweitere meinen Wortschatz, indem / dadurch, dass ich die Vokabeln in ein Heft notiere. d) Ich lerne Grammatikregeln, indem / dadurch, dass ich ein Merkheft anlege. e) Ich lerne Grammatikregeln, indem / dadurch, dass ich die Regeln übersichtlich aufschreibe. f) Ich erarbeite den Lernstoff, indem ich Notizen farbig markiere und übersichtlich anordne. / Ich erarbeite den Lernstoff dadurch, dass ich Notizen ... g) Ich bereite mich auf eine Prüfung vor, indem ich den Lernstoff zwei- bis dreimal wiederhole. / Ich bereite mich auf eine Prüfung dadurch vor, dass ich den Lernstoff ...

4 b) Je länger der Wein lagert, desto/umso wertvoller wird er. c) Je kleiner die Ernte ist, desto/umso teurer wird der Wein. d) Je geringer die produzierte Menge ist, desto/umso höher ist der Preis. e) Je mehr Wein in Europa produziert wird, desto/umso stärker sinken die Preise. f) Je trockener der Wein ist, desto/umso beliebter ist er heutzutage bei den Kunden.

5 b) ...ohne dass er täglich trainiert. c) ... ohne dass sie sich beklagt. d) ... ohne dass er dafür bezahlt wird. e) ... ohne dass er ständig darüber redet. f) ... aber möglichst ohne dass sie hungern muss. g) ... ohne dass er den Lenker festhält.

Seite 182/183
Verbalstil – Nominalstil

1 Beispiele: b) Wenn es plötzlich einen Regenschauer gibt, hole ich meinen Schirm raus. c) Wenn der Film langweilig ist, schlafe ich ein bisschen. d) Wenn mein Computer abstürzt, schimpfe ich auf den Hersteller der Software. e) Wenn es extrem heiß ist, esse ich noch mehr Eis als sonst. f) Wenn ich müde bin, gehe ich ins Bett. g) Wenn ich schlafe, arbeite ich im Traum weiter.

2 b) Beim Hören klassischer Musik ... / Mit klassischer Musik lerne ich ... c) Mit guter Laune ... d) Bei Sonnenschein ... e) Bei Regen ... f) Ohne Ablenkung ...

3 (b) Bericht (c) Behandlung (d) (nach Spielen) Süchtigen (e) Versenden (f) Handy-Besitzer / Besitzer eines Handys (g) Internet-Nutzer

4 b) Schalten sie das Telefon ein, indem Sie die Taste ✳ drücken. c) Geben Sie den PIN-Code ein und drücken Sie auf OK .
d) Warten Sie, bis der Name des Netzbetreibers im Display angezeigt wird. e) Geben Sie die Vorwahl und die Telefonnummer ein.
f) Nun müssen Sie die Taste OK drücken.
g) Beenden Sie den Anruf, indem Sie die Taste C drücken.

Die Einträge im Register sind so aufgebaut: Zunächst das Wort / der Begriff in alphabetischer Reihenfolge, danach die Seitenzahlen der Fundstellen: Ableitung   20; 46. Bei drei oder mehr Fundstellen steht vor der Seitenzahl, in welchem Kontext der Begriff dort steht. Wenn das Stichwort und die Überschrift der Seite identisch sind, ist die Seitenzahl **fett** gedruckt.

Wörter, Silben etc. aus den Beispielen und Listen sind *kursiv* gedruckt, grammatische Begriffe und Begriffe aus den Erklärungen gerade.

ANHANG